The World in the Long Twentieth Century

THE WORLD IN THE LONG TWENTIETH CENTURY

An Interpretive History

Edward Ross Dickinson

UNIVERSITY OF CALIFORNIA PRESS

University of California Press, one of the most distinguished university presses in the United States, enriches lives around the world
by advancing scholarship in the humanities, social sciences, and
natural sciences. Its activities are supported by the UC Press Foundation and by philanthropic contributions from individuals and
institutions. For more information, visit www.ucpress.edu.

University of California Press
Oakland, California

Library of Congress Cataloging-in-Publication Data
Names: Dickinson, Edward Ross, author.
Title: The world in the long twentieth century : an interpretive
    history / Edward Ross Dickinson.
Description: Oakland, California : University of California
    Press, [2017] | Includes bibliographical references and index. |
    Identifiers: LCCN 2017022061 (print) | LCCN 2017024015 (ebook) |
    ISBN 9780520960961 () | ISBN 978-0-520-28554-5 (cloth: alk.
    paper) | ISBN 9780520285552 (pbk. : alk. paper)
Subjects: LCSH: History, Modern—20th century—Chronology. |
    History, Modern—21st century. | World politics—20th century. |
    World politics—21st century. | Globalization—Social aspects. |
    Civilization—20th century.
Classification: LCC D421 (ebook) | LCC D421 .D53 2017 (print) |
    DDC 909.82—dc23

Manufactured in the United States of America

25 24 23 22 21 20

10 9 8 7 6 5 4 3 2

This book is dedicated to the memory of my father
William Richard Dickinson
1931–2015
geologist, scholar, and good, keen, steady man.

Contents

Introduction   1

1. The Biological Transformation of Modern Times   9
   Population Explosion, 1800–2000   9
   Expansion into Challenging Biomes, 1800–2000   20
   A Century of Mass Migrations, 1840–1940   30

2. Foundations of the Modern Global Economy   38
   The Global Development Project, 1850–1930   38
   Scientific-Technical Revolution, 1850–1900   47
   Technological Change, Efficiency, and Growth, 1850–1930   59

3. Reorganizing the Global Economy   63
   Global Commodity Extraction, 1870–1914   63
   Free Trade and Emancipation, 1840–1890   77
   "Free" Trade and Imperialism, 1840–1920   84

4. Localization and Globalization   98
   Race, Ethnicity, and Nationalism, 1830–1940   98
   Cultural Globalization: Religious Innovation, 1800–1920   109
   Cultural Globalization: Peace and Dance, 1890–1930   116

5. The Great Explosion   129
   The Global Revolutionary Moment, 1890–1923   129
   War for World Domination: Phase I, 1914–1923   140
   The Problem of the Peasant in the 1920s and 1930s   150

6. New World (Dis)Order   163
   War for World Domination: Phase II, 1935–1950   163
   Decolonization and Cold War, 1945–1990   178

7. High Modernity   199
   The Great Acceleration, 1950–1975   199
   The Welfare State, 1950–1975   225
   Development, 1950–1980   229

8. Revolt and Refusal   236
   Counterglobalization, 1960–1980   236
   The Great Deceleration? 1975–1990   248
   The Ecological Moment, 1960–1990   252

9. Transformative Modernity   263
   Real Development, 1975–2000   263
   The New Right, 1968–2000   280
   The Gender Revolution, 1950–2000   289

10. Democracy and Capitalism Triumphant?   298
   The Global Triumph of Democracy after 1980   298
   "Financialization"   308
   The End of the World?   320
   The End of the "Natural" World   326
   The End of the Twentieth Century   330

Notes   335
Select Bibliography   353
Illustration Credits   369
Index   373

Introduction

This book lays out a framework for understanding world history in the past century and a half. What were the factors, the largest-scale trends and patterns, that determined the fates of nations, economies, cultures, and individuals across the whole globe? This book seeks to understand the particular histories of regions, nations, states, and individual lives as playing out within this global framework. As the subtitle suggests, the book is an interpretive essay on world history between the middle of the nineteenth century and the present. It creates a coherent model of the causes and effects of decisive long-term transformations on a global scale. It identifies the fundamental forces and developments that have shaped world history—particularly relationships between and among societies across the whole planet—since the mid-nineteenth century. And it describes how the dynamics of the interactions between those forces and developments have driven world-scale events. The question it seeks to answer, then, is: Within the framework of a coherent set of broad and interrelated determining forces and developments, how and why did major world events unfold through the twentieth century?

The framework of global history laid out in this book is fairly simple in its basic outlines. It is also quite dramatic. In the past century and a half, human societies have passed through a massive transformation, unique in the history of the last five or six millennia. That transformation has been almost unbelievably rapid and has affected virtually the entire world. There have of course been distinctive developments and trends in the various parts of the world—regions (such as Europe, Latin America, and South Asia) and countries have experienced particular, often very different histories. And obviously there have been distinctive histories at the local level as well. But those particular histories have played out within a broader radical transformation of the system of interactions among human societies, and between human societies and their natural environment, on the planet as a whole. And they have been profoundly affected by that context of interactions. Human history in the long twentieth century has been the history of the unprecedented transformation of the natural world by human activity; and it has also been, as never before, a shared and interwoven history.

In some cases societies have been entangled with one another by political power—by conquest, occupation, hegemony. In other cases, economic exchange has woven them together, through the rapid growth of trade and the ways in which the economies of different parts of the world have reacted to the challenges and opportunities trade has posed. In other cases still, they have been interwoven by the exchange of ideas—Marxism, for example, or nonviolence. In most cases, they have been woven together by all these factors, at least to varying degrees.

Human societies have passed through a radical transformation for the past 150 years because they have been so interwoven. The two processes drive each other—transformation drives interconnection, and interconnection drives transformation—and for that reason, this process has also been intensifying and accelerating for 150 years.

What is more, the relationship between humans and their natural environment has become global, in the sense that particular environments have been transformed in the past century not only by the development of local human communities but by that of communities far away—often on the other side of the globe. The human impact on the natural environment has become ubiquitous, and very rapidly so. To give just one measure, a hundred years ago the world was still relatively full of dangerous beasts—lions, tigers, bears, wolves, elephants. Almost all those populations have been virtually eradicated since 1900, almost everywhere in the world, often in part by people who have traveled halfway round the world to kill them. Another example: over the course of the long twentieth century, it has become increasingly clear that human action in any one region can have a profound and extremely dangerous impact on the chemistry of the entire planet's atmosphere. In the past quarter century, such ramifications have precipitated two potential crises for the whole planetary biosphere: ozone depletion and global warming.

The transformation that has yielded such outcomes in the human and natural worlds has been so large, so comprehensive, and has affected so many different aspects of human history, that it is hard to give it a more specific name than "the modern age" or "modernity." It has affected human biology—population, fertility, mortality, life expectancy, health. It has affected the natural environment—biodiversity, biomes, species distribution. It has revolutionized the world economy. It has altered human culture. This book offers a way to untangle these processes, to lay out the connections between and among them.

The perspective presented here is that starting in the middle decades of the nineteenth century, technological changes have continuously and increasingly transformed the relationship between the human species, on the one hand, and the environment and resources of our planet, on the other. All of world history in this period has fundamentally been driven by this development. That is not to say that other factors have had no effect. Ideas; political structures; calculations of national prestige or of strategic military positioning; legal, religious, and cultural traditions and standards; wars and their sometimes unpredictable outcomes; economic booms and busts and the policy responses to them; and the decisions of individual historical actors have all shaped the specific ways in which this fundamental transformation has played out. The technological revolution of the past century and a half has not transformed the whole world in automatic, predictable, or uniform ways, but rather in ways determined by the specific characteristics of particular historical situations, in particular places and times. One way to think of that causal relationship is this: the mere fact of technological change does not tell us how particular people will decide to employ technologies in particular historical circumstances. Those decisions are the product of (among other things) specific situations, needs, organizational capacities, political structures, and beliefs. Nevertheless, these complex forces and factors have all operated within the broader framework of the underlying profound, unprecedented, and explosive transformation of the relationship between humanity and its planet in the modern era, and between human societies living in different parts of the planet, brought about by a unique period of innovation and advance in science and technology.[1]

That transformation has been unprecedented in its speed and in its scope—in the number of different sciences and technologies involved, and in the rapid translation of scientific advance into technological innovation and, in turn, technological innovation into economic, social, and cultural transformation. Vaclav Smil, author of a recent history of science and technology from 1867 to 1914, has called this development an "unprecedented saltation" (leap), an "extraordinary concatenation of a large number of scientific and technical advances" of fundamental character. The impact of those advances was "almost instantaneous" in historical terms, with major discoveries and then technical, scientific, and engineering refinements proceeding at a "frenzied pace." He concludes that "such a profound and abrupt discontinuity with such lasting consequences has no equivalent in history."[2]

Arguably, this book is not just about one particular period of history, chosen from among many others. It offers an interpretation—an understanding—of the most extraordinary period of human history.

This is not to say that the developments treated in this book came out of nowhere. They grew organically out of developments in earlier periods. The great imperial states that dominated the first half of the long twentieth century grew out of early-modern empires constructed between the sixteenth and late eighteenth centuries, including, among others, the Muscovite-Russian conquest of what is now southern Russia and Central Asia; the Portuguese and Spanish empires in South and Central America; the Mughal Empire in northern India; the French empire in North America; the Ottoman Empire in Anatolia, the Middle East, and North Africa; the Qing Empire in East and Central Asia; and the British and Dutch colonial empires in South, Southeast, and East Asia. The global economy built in the late nineteenth century was an extension of patterns of exchange at least as old as those empires. The modern period of population growth dates to the middle of the eighteenth century (though it accelerated significantly in the nineteenth). The construction of the global pattern of commodity extraction (discussed in chapter 3) reaches back at least to the 1830s, and arguably well back into the seventeenth century when, for example, commercial sugar production began in the Caribbean Basin and that of tobacco started in North America. The global culture of the early twentieth century was prefigured by cultural exchanges reaching back at least to the seventeenth and eighteenth centuries—including the impact of missionary Christianity in Japan and China and the reception of Chinese culture in Europe in the eighteenth century.[3]

And yet, in the course of the nineteenth century, all these exchanges reached a new, critical mass, a quantitative threshold that constituted a qualitative change. The unprecedented mass migrations of the nineteenth century, the rapid expansion of world commerce, the intensity and rapidity of imperial conquests after about 1870, the articulation of a global transportation and communications network of incomparable density and speed, the sudden and massive surge in the global production of food and manufactures, the acceleration of population growth, the global circulation of people and ideas involved in every sort of economic, religious, political, intellectual, and even touristic enterprise—all these quantitative changes added up in each case to a fundamental rupture, a saltation. Taken together, they have fundamentally changed the relationship between humanity and its planetary home. We are now in a new kind of relationship with the planet. The technological transformation has so intensified our exploitation of the resources of this planet that we are now in uncharted territory.

This, in simple terms, then, is the framework laid out in this book: technological transformation, global interaction, and the massively escalating exploitation of the natural environment. The book's chronological frame fits its content. The period from the mid-nineteenth century to the beginning of the twenty-first is the period in which human societies were reshaped, in an often chaotic process but in coherent ways, by these large-scale forces. This is the "twentieth century" defined not arbitrarily as a period of one hundred years, but substantively, as a period in which an identifiable and fundamentally coherent transformation reshaped the human world. It is a "long century"—roughly 150 years, though its origins can be traced back another hundred before that, and some of its forms will no doubt survive another hundred from now. But this central period, from about the 1860s to perhaps the 2010s, was the period in which the world was reshaped, and knit together, by an identifiable complex of technologies.

What dynamics have those forces set up? What has the "story" of the past 150 years been, driven by those deeper forces? This book lays out that story in three overlapping chronological steps.

The first step, "expansion," began as early as the eighteenth century, but took off in the second half of the nineteenth century. In this period a massive array of basic technological innovations and scientific advances were achieved that created the twentieth-century world. Those innovations had roots reaching far back in time—to Asian technological advances in the fifteenth and sixteenth centuries and to European ones in the seventeenth century; and certainly the process of innovation continued to accelerate after 1900. But a cluster of innovations of fundamental practical importance occurred from the 1850s through the 1890s, and most scientific and technical developments since then have to a large extent refined those basic advances. Historians often refer to this period (from the late eighteenth to the late nineteenth century) as the Industrial Revolution. The transformation affected far more than just industry, but the term is a useful shorthand. As this process gained momentum, people all over the world used those basic scientific and technical advances to create a massive boom in world population, in the world economy, and—in the case of the more powerful states—in colonial expansion, drawing almost every human society around the whole planet into one highly interconnected global society. The balance of demographic and economic power in the world shifted rapidly as populations and economies in some regions burgeoned as never before, while others remained far less dynamic. And these developments had a profound impact on how people thought about human societies, about states, and about themselves. New forms of communication, new intensities of cross-cultural contact, and a radical shift in the balance of military power between different regions and societies all encouraged or forced people to rethink basic political, social, and religious categories and systems.

In the second step, "explosion," human societies struggled more and more intensely over who would run the new, modern world they had created. Between the 1890s and 1950 virtually the entire world exploded in a series of massive, immensely destructive revolutions and wars that determined, more or less, who would be in charge of this new world, and the societies it comprised, for decades to come. Ideas about race, class, nationality, empire, and religion that had developed as a consequence of the new interconnections and contacts built up in the previous half-century played key roles in bringing about those wars and revolutions. In concrete terms, two problems in particular were central to most of those explosions: those of food and energy—or, put another way, the problem of oil and of peasants. Solving these two problems appeared to many people in this period to hold the key both to societal dynamism and well-being and to power.

The third step, "acceleration," began as the questions posed in the period of explosive upheaval were gradually settled, after about 1950. In the relatively stable global political context created by the mid-century wars, all the processes of technological, economic, biological, and cultural change that had reshaped the world in the first phase (and had continued to do so in the second) became more intense, pervasive, and powerful. It is useful to see this as a process of *maturation*: the new, modern society that emerged and then assumed some sort of order by 1950 was now becoming fully developed and universal. It is also useful, however, to see this step as a process of *radicalization,* in which the transformative potentials of that modern world society increasingly take hold and run amok. Or perhaps we could call it a *deepening*—a period in which trends already present before 1950 took deeper and deeper hold on more and more societies. Some sociologists and social theorists have called it postmodernity; others have called it late modernity; still others have called it high modernity. I have chosen to call its more recent stages *transformative modernity,* because by the 1980s and 1990s those processes of change had effectively resolved (at least temporarily) the questions of food and energy and were creating a fundamentally new ordering of global society, different in some crucial ways from that of the long twentieth century. All these terms are useful shorthand for the process analyzed in the final third of the book.

Focusing as it does on the broadest developments, this book does not seek to recount in detail the great "events" of the long twentieth century—the two World Wars and the Cold War, say; or the great revolutions (Mexican, Russian, Chinese); or the details of colonial expansion. Rather, it seeks common patterns—for example, in what ways were the great revolutions similar? It identifies broad causes—for example, why were there two World Wars in the middle of the long twentieth century? And it looks for connections, for example, between the explosive growth of the British industrial economy and the Argentine agricultural economy in the nineteenth century, between colonial genocide and the simultaneous creation of the global market for food and minerals, between the politics of the Cold War and the emergence of the "Asian Tiger" economies in the 1960s, between "financialization" and the collapse of dictatorships around the world in the 1980s and 1990s.

To capture these broad patterns, this book frequently relies on statistical data, which can often give us a revealing bird's-eye view of the development of particular societies or of the whole world (for example, world trade). There are of course risks involved in this approach, because statistics are often not very accurate. To give one example, even today economists debate the relative purchasing power of citizens of the United States and of the People's Republic of China. Do Americans have four times as much purchasing power as Chinese? Eleven times? It depends on how one calculates the cost of living, how accurately the Chinese government measures economic activity (probably not very) and what assumptions we make in the absence of accurate numbers, how one defines the value of various goods (different sorts of motor-driven vehicles, for example), how one compares standards of living (is chicken the same as beef economically?), and so on. Reaching back further in time, the numbers become increasingly speculative. This book relies extensively, for example, on two sets of statistics—the Maddison Project's figures on per capita incomes and population, and the many statistical series published in the collection *International Historical Statistics*. Both are explicit in characterizing much of their data as estimates, not "facts."[4]

Even estimated figures can reveal important global patterns, however, on two conditions: (1) that the same methodology is used to generate estimates across wide geographies; and (2) that we focus on broad trends. We don't know, for example, whether Americans have four times as much or eleven times as much purchasing power as Chinese—different databases give us different estimates. But we do know that the available data sets are broadly in agreement that Chinese purchasing power has been rising rapidly compared to American for two or three decades now. For the purposes of this book, that generalization is sufficient and useful. Exactly who has exactly how much money is not the issue; the issue is that the world as a whole is clearly caught up in a massive, accelerating, increasingly pervasive process of economic and technological change. Exactly how much more money exactly which people have today is less important than the fact that every available measure we have indicates that this process of change has reached a new velocity and power in the past twenty or thirty years, creating a new and distinctive phase or stage in global development—that of post, high, late, or transformative modernity.

Whatever we want to call it, and by whatever statistical series we measure it, that process clearly now resembles a freight train that is growing longer and heavier and moving faster and faster. The endpoint of this dynamic is unsettling. The human species is now in a strange, nerve-wracking position. We know that we are probably beginning to approach the limits of the planet's capacity to support modern humanity's development, and that biological systems around the world are beginning to crack under the strain of human impact. We are also doing more and more of the things that are making them crack, and it increasingly appears that we cannot stop doing them. We are intervening more and more aggressively in more and more biological systems—by using pesticides and fertilizers, digging groundwater wells, building dams and roads, cutting trees, farming land, releasing complex bioactive molecules into the water and air, and burning fossil fuels. Those interventions are driven by the insatiable hunger of billions of people not only for "consumer goods" (automobiles, ovens, televisions, clothes) but also for food, decent housing, good health and for knowledge. It is abundantly clear that we will neither satiate nor even reduce that hunger. There appears therefore to be a finite chance that we will kill ourselves if we do not find more effective ways than we have so far developed to manage or mitigate our impact on our planet.

We also know that we have been, for more than a century, a very clever species and that we have solved problems that seemed insoluble, even some that seemed to threaten the end of civilization as we know it. One example is food. Shortly after the mid-twentieth century, it seemed to some impossible that the world would be able to feed the number of people that would inevitably be born by the year 2000. But that problem was solved through an astonishing revolution in agricultural technology and methods. Another, more recent example is fossil fuels. At the turn of the twenty-first century, it seemed likely that humanity was going to start to run out of oil within a very few decades. But in the first ten years of the century, geologists and petrochemical engineers figured out how to produce so much oil and gas from "unconventional" sources (the deep oceans, tar sands, oil shale) that we can be fairly sure that we will not run out for at least a century, and very possibly several centuries.

Ironically, of course, those solutions have created more radical problems. The earth's population has about doubled in the half century since predictions of mass starvation and population collapse sparked a major public controversy; and the scale of our impact on the planetary ecology has well more than doubled. New technologies have given us virtually unlimited supplies of hydrocarbon fuels that are the cause of what may become the greatest threat to the biosphere since the last major asteroid strike—global warming.

But the point is this: the historical experience of solving problems on this scale suggests that we might be smart enough, and creative enough, to innovate our way out of our accelerating drive toward planetary ecological collapse. We don't know. But we do know that the livelihoods of millions, if not tens of millions, of individuals almost certainly hangs in the balance. Possibly our existence as a civilization does as well. Indeed, it is just conceivable that our collective life as a species does too.

It doesn't get more dramatic than that. This book explains how we got here.

The Biological Transformation of Modern Times

POPULATION EXPLOSION, 1800–2000

Any educated person today has seen a graph of estimated world population since the year 1 BCE (chart 1.1). Nothing illustrates more efficiently the uniqueness of the period since the middle of the nineteenth century. From the point of view of the human species as a biological phenomenon, the past 150 years have been unprecedented and revolutionary. World population probably doubled between 1000 and 1500; it roughly doubled again in the three hundred years to 1800; doubled in the following hundred years; doubled in about the next seventy years; and doubled in the thirty years leading to the beginning of our century. World population in 2000 was almost four times what it had been in 1900, and more than six times what it had been in 1800.[1]

In those few cases in which historical demographers can make an educated guess as to populations even before the year 1 BCE, we can construct an even more remarkable story. Up until 1600 the population of Egypt was subject to massive fluctuations for close to 6,000 years, due to plagues, wars and the famines they caused, and dislocations of the regional trade network and the economic crises they produced; in 1600 it may have been roughly similar in size to what it was 3,400 years earlier. Since then, however, it has risen steadily and rapidly and is now about thirty-five times that size.[2] The population of the basin of Mexico followed a similar pattern: in the middle of the seventeenth century it may have been about what it was in 300 BCE; by the middle of the 1980s it was two hundred times as large.[3]

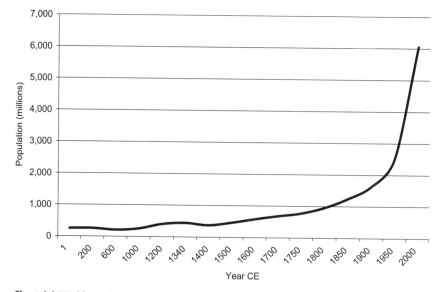

Chart 1.1 World Population, 1–2000 CE.

Growth in population has been unevenly distributed, with different regions growing at different rates in different periods (charts 1.2 and 1.3). In global terms the story of world population can be divided into two halves. In the period starting around 1700 until about 1915, Europeans multiplied very quickly and poured millions of immigrants into North and South America. Then, after 1900, population growth in Africa and Asia outstripped that in the Euro-American world. Between 1850 and 1900 the population of Europe and the Americas grew almost four times as fast as that of Asia and Africa; between 1950 and 2000 the population of Asia and African grew more than twice as fast as that of Europe and the Americas. As a result, the proportion of world population living in Europe and the Americas surged from about 20 percent in 1700 to 36.5 percent in 1900, and it has since fallen rapidly, to 27 percent.

Three processes explain this pattern, starting fairly weakly before about 1750 and becoming stronger at an accelerating pace since then. Together, these processes have created what historians usually call the demographic transition of modern times: from high fertility and high mortality to low fertility and low mortality.

First, beginning as early as the seventeenth century, important advances in agricultural technology and practices helped to improve human nutrition in key population centers around the world. Those advances included new crop rotation systems, which helped to avoid the rapid depletion of soil nutrients; the greater use of animals as a source of labor and fertilizer; new crops, including not only those adopted from the New World (such as the potato and maize/

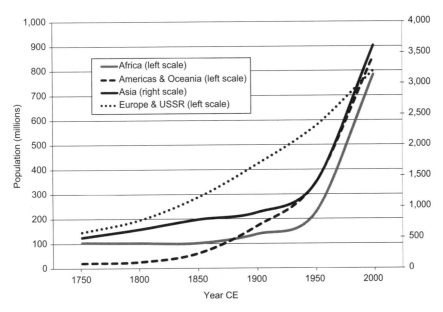

Chart 1.2 Comparative Regional Population Growth.

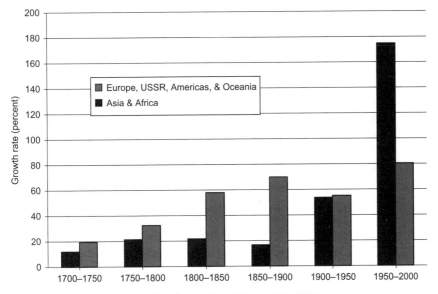

Chart 1.3 Comparative Regional Population Growth Rates, 1700–2000.

corn) but also new varieties bred for greater productivity; the improvement of domestic animal breeds and their broader distribution around the world; improved drainage and water control techniques that helped expand arable land; and new implements that improved the efficiency of cultivation. In parts of Western Europe, for example, agricultural surpluses above the requirements of producers themselves may have doubled in the course of the eighteenth century, from a quarter to a half of total production. Similar, if less dramatic, improvements helped to support China's rapidly expanding population as well—in fact, some of the implements important in Europe may have been borrowed from China in the course of the seventeenth century. In both parts of the world, improved famine control through state intervention helped to smooth population fluctuations and avoid severe setbacks in growth.[4]

Second, at least as important were extraordinary advances in the prevention of disease. Until the mid-nineteenth century, progress in this respect was slow because it was not yet known what caused contagious diseases. With the emergence of germ theory and then the identification of particular microbes as the specific cause of a growing number of diseases late in the century and into the early twentieth century, preventive health measures took an enormous leap forward. Beginning in the 1850s, for example, major cities around the world began to build sewage systems, leading to sharp reductions in deaths from cholera, dysentery, typhus, and other diseases spread by excrement. Cities also began to build filtration plants to purify water supply. After 1910, chlorination of water further reduced bacterial load in municipal water supplies. In the 1930s, cities began building sewage treatment plants to cut off infection at the source.

All of these advances have helped to eliminate epidemic outbreaks, particularly of intestinal diseases such as cholera, especially in urban centers, where high population density had made them particularly lethal. But more important for overall population growth, they have helped to reduce the background level of infant mortality, because infants are especially vulnerable to such infections. Chart 1.4 shows infant mortality plotted against the percentage of the population served by a sewage system, in fifty-five nations in the 1980s. The message is stark: under the right conditions, simply providing sewerage can reduce infant mortality by 90 to 99 percent. Pasteurization to prevent gastrointestinal diseases from bad milk or other drinks was developed by Louis Pasteur in France in 1862; since then it has spread rapidly throughout the world and has been critical in reducing infant mortality. Finally, while antiseptics have been part of folk medicine traditions around the globe for centuries, if not millennia, more effective chemical antiseptics were developed in the 1840s and 1850s, and especially by Joseph Lister in 1867. While their most spectacular successes came in the area of surgery, they also helped to radically reduce maternal and infant mortality at childbirth.[5]

The deployment of such methods has been uneven and is by no means completed. As of 1980, half the world's population had no wastewater treatment.[6]

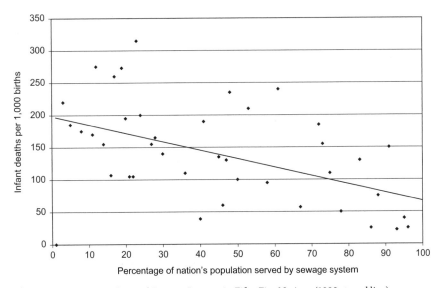

Chart 1.4 Infant Mortality and Sewage Systems in Fifty-Five Nations (1980s trend line).

For the most part, clean water was secured first in Europe and North America, then progressively in other parts of the world. For that reason, the decline of disease mortality, and the consequent acceleration of population growth, has been uneven and slow. Nevertheless, over time, infant mortality rates around the world have converged (chart 1.5).

While hygienic techniques were the most critical factors affecting population in the middle decades of the nineteenth century, other forms of prevention and prophylaxis were also important. A crucial preventive measure was the use of quinine to inhibit malarial infection, the single biggest killer in tropical regions. Quinine is found in the bark of the South American cinchona tree, which Europeans "discovered" in use among the Quechua people in Peru in the seventeenth century. Gradually, methods of purification and use were perfected, and by the last third of the nineteenth century quinine was being systematically cultivated and widely used. Even more important was the discovery in the late 1890s that mosquitos are the specific disease vector of malaria; thereafter swamp drainage and other mosquito-control techniques in some regions helped to control malaria and other mosquito-borne diseases. Similar successes were scored against yellow fever and a handful of other major killers in tropical and subtropical environments.[7] Of still broader significance was vaccination, which had been practiced in basic form in India and China for several centuries, was transmitted via the Ottoman Empire to Europe in the early eighteenth century, and was eventually perfected in the 1880s in France and

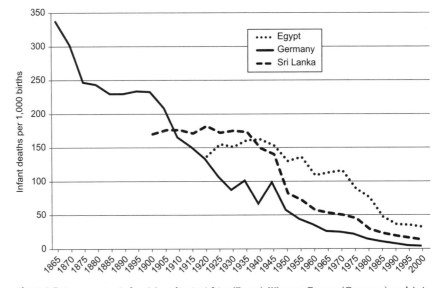

Chart 1.5 Comparative Infant Mortality in Africa (Egypt), Western Europe (Germany), and Asia (Sri Lanka), 1865–2000.

Germany. The germ theory of disease triumphed in the late 1870s in European medicine, and from the 1880s the specific microbes that cause individual diseases began to be identified. Immunization through inoculation began to bring some key diseases under control.

While these preventive measures were decisive in the first century of population expansion, from the mid-twentieth century, modern scientific medicine began to develop effective therapies for many of the greatest microbial killers. The decisive instance was the development of antibiotics—with the first sulfa drugs developed in the early 1930s (in Germany) and penicillin in the early 1940s (in Britain). Both were brought into widespread use after 1945. These drugs were particularly important in reducing both childhood and adult mortality caused by endemic diseases such as pneumonia and tuberculosis, which were major killers well into the mid-twentieth century.[8]

The chronology of the widespread adoption of all these methods and drugs was the same as that for water purification—first Europe and North America and spreading from there to the rest of the world. The global pattern in the decline of overall mortality is therefore the same as in the case of infant mortality (chart 1.6). Mortality began to fall in Europe in the 1870s, and in Asia, Latin America, and Africa between 1910 and 1930, and is converging now around the whole planet on a very low level. To give just one example, in 1910 mortality in Mexico was 33.5 per 1,000 inhabitants, while that in the United Kingdom was only 13.5—a gap of 20 per 1,000. By 1990 the level in Mexico was

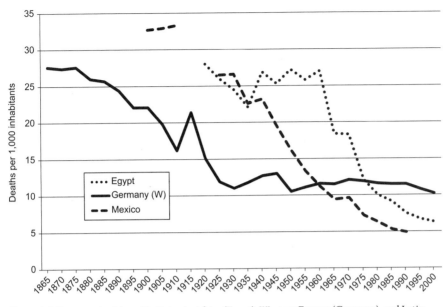

Chart 1.6 Comparative Mortality Rates in Africa (Egypt), Western Europe (Germany), and Latin America (Mexico).

4.9; in the United Kingdom, 11.1. (The higher rate in developed countries today is explained by the greater average age of people in those countries.)

The pattern in the development of life expectancy is the same, as one would expect (chart 1.7). Everywhere in the developed world, life expectancy is converging on the upper seventies. People in Western Europe, the United States, Canada, and a few other places still live much longer than most people anywhere else. In the case of Africa, in fact, the gap has actually grown. For most of the world, though, that gap is now closing rapidly. The gap between Western Europe and India rose from eighteen to thirty-five years between 1820 and 1950, but it has now closed again to eighteen years. The gap between China and Western Europe has narrowed from twenty-four years in 1900 to seven years today.

The second part of the demographic transition, the decline in fertility, is somewhat harder to explain. Historically, fertility decline appears to be roughly correlated to economic growth, and particularly to the growth of industry. This has led some historians to argue that the rising demand for more skilled and often more sustained labor in industrial jobs has put a premium on investment in human capital—in other words, in the health and education of children, rather than in sheer numbers. The correlation between the spread of compulsory public education and declining fertility indicates that this has not always been a purely individual decision, but rather a political and societal one as well.

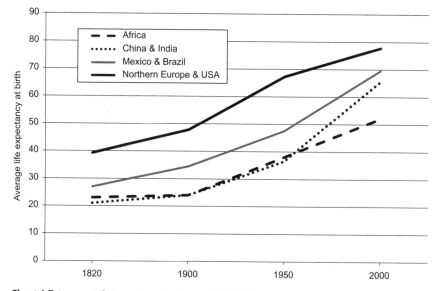

Chart 1.7 Average Life Expectancy by Region, 1820–2000.

The spread and extension of schooling—and of child labor laws—raise the net cost of children, since children cannot work and attend school at the same time. Rising opportunities for paid labor for women (for example in textile factories, an important early industrial sector whose labor force was disproportionately female) form another likely factor. Longer life expectancy, better health, more opportunities to put aside money in savings, and early social insurance programs (including health, disability, and retirement programs) may have helped make children less essential to familial strategies of "income smoothing" over the life span. Growing urbanization and participation in the money economy may also play a role, in part by reducing the value to the family of children's unpaid labor (for example, in tending animals or weeding crops).[9] In the initial stages of fertility decline, methods of contraception were fairly rudimentary; but over time the development and improvement of condoms, diaphragms, and ultimately, technologies like the contraceptive pill probably played an important role as well.

Whereas all these factors are primarily economic or technological, other historians stress political, cultural, and even psychological factors. Most basically, one historian has argued that "control over death promoted the emergence of rational attitudes," spurred the decline of traditional fatalism, and facilitated the birth of the idea of progress. Greater confidence that they were not going to die might encourage people to make long-term investments, for example, or to limit their fertility in order to maximize their ability to seize on new economic opportunities.[10] The growth of public schooling was not just an economic strategy; it was also a tool of political nation-building (as by teaching a national language to children who spoke regional dialects, or by teaching them patriotic stories about their country's greatness). Rising literacy helped to spread knowledge about contraception; another historian has even suggested that "fertility was talked down," though perhaps "written down" would be as accurate.[11] Early European studies emphasized the role of important cultural and social changes reflected in or created by the late eighteenth-century "Atlantic revolutions" (particularly in what became the United States and in France) and the subsequent rise of political liberalism and cultural individualism. The disruption of social structures by political upheavals and by economic change may have encouraged people to believe that they could achieve upward social mobility—and to adopt fertility restriction as one strategy for doing so. As one early theorist put it, "Democratic civilization lowers fertility."[12]

Whatever the causes, a crucial feature of the demographic transition was that in most societies mortality fell first, followed after a delay of up to a century by a decline in fertility. In fact, in many societies the decline in mortality was actually accompanied at first by a rise in fertility. The reasons for that coincidence are complex. Customs and expectations regarding the number of children a family needs to secure the desired size probably take at least a generation to catch up to falling infant and child mortality. It takes time for contraceptive knowledge to spread. In many societies it has taken at least a generation for important moral, religious, and cultural taboos against interfering with fertility to erode. Again, falling mortality was usually accompanied by economic (particularly industrial) growth and an increase in per capita income, which may have meant that more families felt they could afford more children. Better nutrition due to rising incomes probably brought higher biological fertility too. Finally, effective means of contraception were for many decades relatively expensive; it took time to build the affluence that allowed the mass of the population access to them. In contrast, the techniques that reduce mortality are relatively cheap and uncontroversial and are often introduced by political bodies (usually cities). They have consequently been deployed relatively rapidly across the whole world.

The lag between the drop in mortality and that in fertility explains why Europe flooded the world with immigrants between about 1800 and 1914: mortality was falling precipitously, but fertility was not—yet. Then, between the 1880s and the 1920s, fertility in Europe began to drop as well, first in France, the United Kingdom, and Germany, and a decade or two later in Southern and Southeastern Europe. The same pattern holds for Japan, the United States, and Australia: by the third or fourth decade of the twentieth century, fertility rates around the developed world were falling quite quickly. Today, natural population increase—fertility minus mortality—is close to or below zero throughout the developed world.

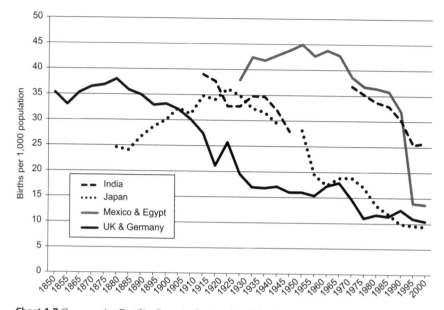

Chart 1.8 Comparative Fertility Rates in the Developed (Germany, UK average) and Developing (Egypt, India, Mexico, Japan average) World, 1850–2000.

Starting early in the twentieth century and at an accelerating pace since 1950, less developed countries have adopted modern public health and medical practices and technologies. The same pattern has been repeated in these countries, with mortality dropping first, followed later by fertility (chart 1.8). The result has been massive population growth in much of the less developed world—similar to the rate of population growth in the developed world some decades earlier, but outstripping it because the maturing of basic preventive technologies and economies of scale have made it relatively cheaper to achieve lower mortality rates than it was fifty or one hundred years ago.

Some comparisons of demographic development in various countries reveal how extreme the resulting patterns have become. The gap between fertility and mortality—the rate of population growth—in Mexico and Egypt from the 1960s through the 1980s, for example, was roughly twice what it had been in the United Kingdom a century earlier (chart 1.9). In the 1890s the German population was growing ten times as fast as the Mexican population, because fertility rates in the two countries were quite similar but mortality rates were radically different; but by 1990 Germany had zero population growth, while Mexico was at about 3 percent annually. In 1870 Germany had a population four times that of Mexico; by 1985, the two populations were roughly the same size. The same sort of comparison can be made between many richer and poorer countries. Japan, for example, had a population in 1875 three and a

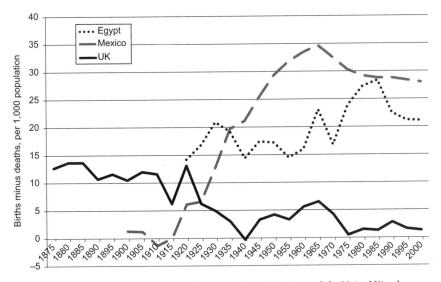

Chart 1.9 Comparative Population Growth Rates in Egypt, Mexico, and the United Kingdom, 1875–2000.

half times that of Brazil; by 1980 Brazil's population was slightly larger than Japan's.

Most of Europe, North America, and Japan passed through this demographic transition between the late nineteenth and the late twentieth century; by the early twenty-first century natural (nonimmigration) population growth was near or below zero in those regions. Most of the rest of the world passed through a similar transition beginning in the early or mid-twentieth century. By the 1990s fertility in the less developed world was falling precipitously—a development discussed in chapter 9.

This broad pattern of demographic development—two waves of rapid population expansion, in different periods, in two "halves" of the world—amply demonstrates the importance of technological change in shaping the broad pattern of world history over the past 150 years. The development and deployment of scientific knowledge of disease, of effective preventive measures, and finally of effective therapies have been fundamental to this expansion. Again, this has not been the only factor involved—advances in agriculture and increases in per capita income have also played a role (though technological change has been a crucial factor in driving those developments, too); so too have changes in income distribution, laws governing inheritance, and policies regarding such matters as the relative value of public health and the availability of contraceptives. The precise timing of demographic transitions has varied from place to place even within particular regions, for historical reasons that are evidently quite complex. While the British and German populations boomed through most of the nineteenth century, for example, that of France was almost stagnant. Nevertheless, the development of world population has been made possible to great extent by technologies as simple as sewers. The overall result has been dramatic.

EXPANSION INTO CHALLENGING BIOMES, 1800–2000

> The Great Spirit made us, the Indians, and gave us this land we live in. He gave us the buffalo, the antelope, and the deer for food and clothing. We moved in our hunting grounds from the Minnesota to the Platte and from the Mississippi to the great mountains. No one put bounds about us. We were as free as the winds. . . . Then the white man came and took our lands from us. . . . Now where the buffalo ranged there are wires on posts that mark the land where the white man labors and sweats to get food from the earth; and in the place of the buffalo there are cattle that must be cared for to keep them alive; and where the Lakota could ride as he wished from the rising to the setting of the sun for days and days on his own lands, now he must go on roads made by the white man.[13]
>
> Chief Red Cloud of the Lakota Sioux, 1903

A second process drove world population growth after about 1800: migration. Over the course of the past two centuries, in a series of overlapping waves or phases, humans have settled in high density a range of natural environments that posed challenges which until 1800 had permitted only very low concentrations of population. We might call them biomes, or particular regimes of climate and vegetation.

The first of these waves settled the world's dry grasslands. These include a vast range of more or less similar environments, which have different names in different regions—such as the steppe of southern Russia and Central Asia, the Great Plains of the American Midwest and prairies of Canada, the pampas in Argentina, the dry plains of southeastern Australia, the plains and grasslands of Algeria, the high veldt of South Africa, the cold and dry plains of Inner Mongolia and Manchuria, the Central Valley of California, the Punjab in northern India, and the cold grasslands on the island of Hokkaido in northern Japan.

All of these areas were inhabited in 1800 by relatively thin populations using relatively low-impact technologies—like Red Cloud's Native American people, the Lakota Sioux. Some were primarily nomadic or seminomadic hunter-gatherers, such as the Great Plains tribes. Others were primarily pastoralists—animal raisers rather than crop growers—who practiced transhumance, moving their animals from one area to another and then back, as seasonal rainfall dictated. Beginning in the late eighteenth and early nineteenth century, the development of a whole range of new technologies made it possible to settle these areas in much greater density, by making settled pastoralism and agriculture feasible. The result was a series of massive waves of settlement that flowed out from the older centers of population into the dry grasslands—and over-whelmed their established populations.

The first region to be affected was southern Russia where farmers from the old forested and hilly core of central Russia, as well as from similar regions in Germany, Poland, and Southeastern Europe, flooded onto the steppe from the late eighteenth century on. That wave of settlement continued for a hundred years and more, moving farther and farther east and south and into ever drier plains, until it hit its limit in the 1950s under Soviet rule. Slightly later, from the 1810s, a similar movement brought massive settlement to the pampas of Argentina, first as pasture and then as cropland.[14] In the 1830s and 1840s, a wave of settlement by the Boers—Dutch and French settlers who had moved to the Cape Province as early as the seventeenth century—moved up into the veldt of Natal, the Transvaal, and the Orange River country, in what is now the Republic of South Africa. In the United States, the wave of European settle-ment that had filled the Ohio and Mississippi valleys and the flatlands along the north and west shore of the Caribbean (for example, in Alabama, Louisi-ana, and East Texas) was succeeded in the middle of the century by a new wave that flooded into the dry Great Plains—present Iowa, Kansas, Oklahoma, Nebraska, and West Texas. This movement was encouraged by the Homestead Act of 1862, which made land available to settlers at cheap prices. The same process was repeated about a decade later on the cold prairie of central Canada, encouraged by the Dominion Lands Act of 1872, similar to the US Homestead Act.[15] Systematic encouragement of settlement by the Japanese government, also from the 1870s, helped to create a similar wave of settlement on the north-ernmost Japanese island of Hokkaido, whose Japanese population was 60,000 in 1860 and 2.4 million in 1920.[16] Siberia, the Kazakh steppe, Manchuria, and Inner Mongolia became home to millions of Russians and Chinese, particu-larly after the 1890s. In the Punjab, in northeastern India, arid grassland gave way to crops as irrigation was expanded from the late 1880s.[17]

In many cases these movements of people were encouraged by government policy. The Homestead Act, the Dominion Lands Act, similar legislation for Hokkaido, special privileges granted to German and Russian settlers in southern Russia, and official recruitment or assisted immigration into Argentina and Bra-zil (in which governments in the receiving countries paid for or subsidized the cost of the ocean journey to their shores) all played important roles.[18] In South Africa the so-called Great Trek of the Boers up from the Cape Province into the Transvaal and the Orange River area was driven in part by their desire to escape British suzerainty—partly because the British outlawed slavery in 1833.[19]

Even more important, in many cases the indigenous inhabitants of these grasslands were killed, expelled, or relocated by major military campaigns launched by the states that now claimed their lands. In other cases more or less informal militias of settlers attacked indigenous populations themselves. The expansion of dense settlement and large populations into challenging biomes was not an automatic process. The people already living in those biomes had to be forced to give up their land through a massive and deliberate application of coercive and not infrequently genocidal violence.

The Russian state, for example, defeated and absorbed the Cossacks of the southern steppe over a period of some 150 years from the early eighteenth century, with many becoming part of a special military class or caste in service to the same state that had crushed their political independence. The Boers collided with the Zulus in Natal, to the east of the Cape Province, at the end of the 1820s, defeating them in bitter warfare before moving up into the high veldt of the interior in the 1840s. The indigenous population in Australia was subjected to genocidal violence from the 1820s on; that of California from the 1850s (not counting the earlier history of Spanish mission settlement). In the Great Plains, the Sioux were defeated and expropriated after a series of wars: the Dakota War in 1862, Red Cloud's War in 1866–1868, and the Great Sioux War in 1876–1877, with George Armstrong Custer's defeat at the Little Bighorn forming part of the final chapter of that process. The Argentine government launched a major campaign of pacification, expropriation, and extermination against the inhabitants of the southern pampas in 1879, seizing and then selling some 20 million hectares (close to 47 million acres) of land in Patagonia by 1882. At the same time, the Russian state was busy expropriating nomads and pastoralists across the dry steppes of Russian Central Asia, transferring land ownership to a wave of peasant settlers. And Hokkaido's native Ainu population, expropriated and forced to give up many traditional hunting and fishing practices, dropped from almost 67,000 in 1871 to below 18,000 in 1901.[20]

In short, the appropriation of the world's grasslands by settled farmers was often an extraordinarily violent process. One critical reason was that as domestic livestock replaced the game on which indigenous communities depended, they were forced to raid farmers' herds. Farmers and governments often responded with disproportionate violence. In 1851, for example, the governor of California argued for a "war of extermination" against indigenous people in that state, "until the Indian race becomes extinct." From the end of the 1840s through the 1870s in California, settler militias launched murderous raids on "Indian" villages in response to theft of cattle, killing men, women, and children and enslaving survivors. In one instance in 1859, a raid in retaliation for the killing of one horse claimed the lives of 240 members of the Yuki people in Northern California. Later that year, after the U.S. Army refused to participate in exterminating the Yuki, the state governor paid a private paramilitary group to carry out that action. Survivors were confined to a reservation where, between 1873 and 1910, four-fifths of them died. Such episodes were neither new nor unique to North America. While the violence of the 1850s and 1860s was more concentrated, it was a continuation of patterns established as early as the 1630s; and there were similar genocidal campaigns in, for example, Australia, South Africa, and Patagonia.[21]

People were not the only victims of such exterminatory campaigns. Large predators in particular were no less in the way of the settlement of the world's grasslands than were the indigenous human communities. As indigenous game was replaced by domesticated cattle, predators too were forced to raid famers' herds. They too were targeted for deliberate extermination by settlers and governments using guns, traps, and poison. In South Africa, for example, the introduction of bounties on predators in the Cape Colony in 1889 raised the number of jackals killed from 1,512 in that year to 60,863 ten years later, baboons from 1,394 to 21,321, and leopards from 22 to 569. In Japan in the 1870s, American advisers familiar with the necessary techniques were invited to help exterminate the Hokkaido wolf in order to make room for ranching.[22] From the early twentieth century until the late 1930s state and federal authorities in the United States waged a veritable war against predators across the American West, using bounties, poison, and trained government hunters to attempt to wipe out bears, wolves, mountain lions, bobcats, and coyotes.[23]

In the early stages of settlement, useful animals suffered even greater massacres, as hunters, trappers, and settlers trapped, shot, and poisoned game for fur, leather, fats and oils, or meat. Of perhaps 30 million bison that lived on the plains and prairies of North America before the arrival of guns and railroads, about a thousand were left by 1900. Far from being horrified, most contemporary nonindigenous observers were delighted, since the slaughter both cleared the way for more commercially valuable cattle and deprived the Native peoples of the plains of their livelihood's key source. As one government spokesman remarked in 1893, "We were never able to control the savages until their supply of meat was cut off. We have had no trouble worth speaking of since 1883."[24] The population of North American passenger pigeons may have been 5 billion as late as the 1860s; by 1914 it was zero.[25] Similar population collapses occurred around the world, particularly in grassland and prairie regions.[26]

While there were economic reasons for these campaigns, especially in the early stages a kind of mindless joy in killing appears to have played an important role as well. A good example is Samuel White Baker, an Englishman whose family wealth was founded in part on a sugar estate on Mauritius, an island colony in the Indian Ocean. Born in 1821, Baker moved to Mauritius in 1845 to run the family plantation business there; but he found it boring because there was very little to kill. In 1846 he moved to Ceylon (now Sri Lanka), attracted by the idea of killing elephants. He proceeded to do that with great energy: on one hunt he killed thirty-one elephants in five days; on another he killed fourteen in one day. For the next five decades he traveled the world, killing things. He shot bears, deer, boars, wolves, partridges, and ducks in Turkey and Hungary; tigers and antelope in India; hippopotamuses, wild asses, pigeons, hares, rhinoceroses, and antelope in the Sudan; elks, grizzly bears, and bison in the Rocky Mountains; elks and boars in Scotland; foxes and deer in England; and snipe, ducks, partridges, rabbits, and larks on Cyprus. Along the way he established a cattle farm in Sri Lanka; bought and married a Hungarian slave woman in Ottoman Romania; helped conquer the South Sudan for Egypt; wrote several books about the animals he shot; and became hunting buddies with Maharajah Duleep Singh, whom the British had exiled to Scotland after conquering his kingdom in the Punjab in 1849 and who was a splendid chap who once shot 769 partridges in one day. Toward the end of his life Baker became a conservationist, "aware," as his biographer wrote, "that the slaughter had to stop while there was some game left."[27]

By the early twentieth century this kind of violence prompted some to question the fundamental assumption that both people and nature had the purpose only of serving the accumulation of wealth and power. An early example was the German scientist Ludwig Klages, who wrote in 1913 that the previous century had shown that the whole principle of "'progress' is the lust for power and nothing else," that it was a "sick destructive joke" and had yielded "horrendous results." Human beings had somehow convinced themselves that "every increase in mankind's power entails an equivalent increase in mankind's *value*," encouraging a blind faith in a completely utilitarian and fundamentally violent approach both to the natural world and to people. As "soon as the man of 'progress' arrives on the scene," he lamented, "he announces his masterful presence by spreading death. . . . An unparalleled orgy of destruction has seized mankind," a frenzied "lust for murder." The "final goal of 'progress' is nothing less than the destruction of life"—of forests, animals, and even mankind's own cultural diversity and spiritual wealth. The only hope for the world was a reawakening of the "knowledge of the world-weaving power of all-embracing love"—including love for nature.[28]

Fifty years later, many would come to see critiques like Klages's as prophetic. Around 1900, however, ideas like his were far less influential than more moderate critiques, which held that the world was indeed a resource for "civilized" humanity but that it had to be managed better. As early as the 1860s and 1870s, scientists and governments in various parts of the world were beginning to argue that natural resources had to be husbanded carefully to ensure they were not simply destroyed outright. This idea gave rise to the idea of conservation and of scientific resource management—what one historian called the "Gospel of Efficiency" in the use of resources. Forestry experts from Germany to colonial India and Australia argued for better management of forests; California established a Board of Fish Commissioners in 1870 to preserve the state's extraordinarily rich fisheries; nature preserves and national parks were created starting in the 1870s in the United States, Australia, Europe, and elsewhere; societies for the protection of wildlife were formed as well, such as the Society for the Preservation of the Fauna of the Empire and the Royal Society for the Protection of Birds in Britain in 1903 and 1904, respectively.[29] The aim of most of this regulatory activity was economic: to determine and then produce a "maximum sustainable yield" of a given resource, ensuring its long-term

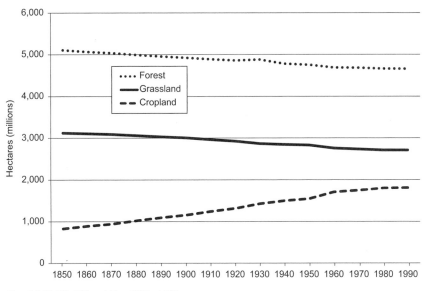

Chart 1.10 World Land Use, 1850–1990.

contribution to human welfare and national wealth. Some conservationists did emphasize not only efficiency and the elimination of wasteful practices but also aesthetic and spiritual values—for example, opportunities for recreation—or preserving broad access, rather than short-term profit for particular individuals or companies. But the emphasis was usually on the usefulness of nature to humans—and specifically to "civilized" humans.[30]

In short, the idea of conservation was a critique not of violence in general, but only of wasteful violence. Most saw the expansion of settled agriculture across the world's grasslands, for example, as evidence of the unparalleled progress and success of humanity in their time. And many argued that the extermination of so-called "primitive" peoples and of "noxious" animals was both desirable and inevitable. The disappearance of peoples and species might inspire a certain melancholy, but it was the price paid for the transformation of the dangerous, sterile, empty wilderness into a prosperous garden and habitation of civilization.[31]

In fact, with indigenous populations cleared off the land, in each case settlers introduced a radical change in the pattern of land use. This process was in fact so gigantic that we can represent it statistically, in square miles (or, rather, hectares) of land cover. Above all, there was a rapid decline in open grasslands and a corresponding rise in land devoted to cropland and pasturage (chart 1.10).[32] The world's forests as a proportion of land cover fell fairly steadily, too. In contrast, world cropland almost doubled between 1850 and 1950.[33]

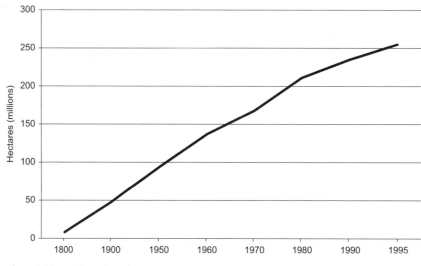

Chart 1.11 World Lands under Irrigation, 1800–1995.

What made the world's grasslands an attractive target for settlement was the development of new agricultural technologies that turned them into highly productive farming and herding lands. Critical advances were made in irrigation, which permitted the use for crops and animals of lands with quite low rainfall, or rainfall with a radical seasonal distribution (a good example is the Central Valley of California). An early innovation was the modern windmill, which could draw water from aquifers up to thirty feet below the surface. By the 1930s, gasoline- and natural gas–powered pumps could draw water from much deeper, and a second surge occurred in irrigation.[34] Steel and then plastic tubing also played a key role, as did concrete, which made canals more efficient and cheaper. Overall, the amount of irrigated land in the world has skyrocketed over the past 150 years, as more and more dry plains areas have been brought into cultivation (chart 1.11).

In most of these dry grasslands, however, heavier plows with iron and steel plowshares were also critical, because older, lighter plows were not strong enough to permit plowing of dense sod. Eventually, in the mid-twentieth century, the use of tractors would permit a further massive expansion of cultivation in grasslands—leading to a second surge in conversion of grassland to cropland (chart 1.12).[35] Barbed wire, which helped control herds on the vast grazing lands needed to support animals on dry pasturage, was also critical— with the key patents taken out in Ohio and Illinois in 1867 and 1874, respectively. Argentina, for example, imported 5.5 million kilograms of barbed wire in 1876, 13.5 million in 1880, and 40 million in 1889—a development that was,

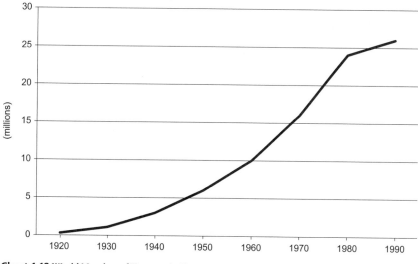

Chart 1.12 World Number of Tractors in Use, 1920–1990.

obviously, part of the effort to bring into production all the land seized by military force after 1879.[36]

The key technologies that permitted all of these transformations, however, were actually not agricultural, but transportation technologies—above all, the railroad, and to a lesser extent the steamship. Railroads began to be laid in earnest in the 1840s, and expanded extremely rapidly thereafter for a hundred years (chart 1.13). Railways and steamships were critical because the settlement of the world's grasslands was driven in large part by the demand for food generated by rapid population growth in the old "core" areas of human settlement—Europe, the Eastern Seaboard of North America, China, and India. The world's grasslands could feed the old "core" populations only if the food could be moved from farms, often in deep continental interiors, to markets, often across oceans. This was a massive transportation challenge, which the railway solved. Moving bulk goods by rail is far cheaper than moving them by road—or at least it was until the invention of internal combustion engines. As for ocean transport, steamships helped to make that cheaper and more efficient, particularly in the 1860s and 1870s, when technical improvements reduced their fuel consumption by a factor of up to five. And the creation of the Suez Canal in 1869 and the Panama Canal in 1914 reduced global freight route distances and travel times. Freight costs between North America and Britain, for example, dropped by about 70 percent between 1840 and 1910. The Suez Canal cut the distance of ocean travel from Britain to India by half. The world's shipping tonnage rose from some 4 million tons in 1800 to about 47 million in 1913; and

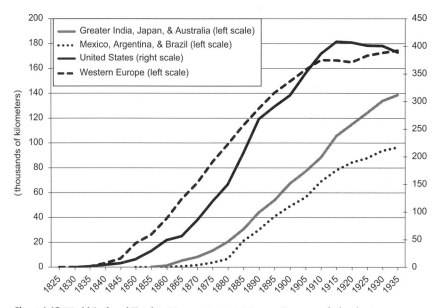

Chart 1.13 World Railroad Track in Use, 1825–1935. Western Europe includes the France, Germany, Italy, Spain, and the United Kingdom.

total shipping grew even more, because steam- or diesel-driven ships moved considerably faster than sailing ships and so carried more freight annually per ton of capacity.[37] Finally, by the 1870s and 1880s, the development of effective refrigeration permitted the movement not only of grain but also of meat and dairy products across great distances on land and by sea. By the 1920s, to give just one example, 80 percent of the meat consumed in London was imported, most of it from Argentina.[38]

As important as the settlement of the world's grasslands was, however, this was not the only "challenging biome" that saw massive human settlement. A second kind of environment, settled slightly later, consisted of mountainous and high-plateau regions, such as those found in Tibet, Peru, Ethiopia, Turkey or Anatolia, and the Colorado Plateau. A third, settled intensively in the last two decades of the nineteenth century and the first decades of the twentieth, was arid steppe and semidesert regions, such as parts of Mongolia, the Sahel in North Africa, dry Central Asia, and the dry and desert West of the United States (Utah, Colorado, West Texas, New Mexico, and the Imperial Valley in California).

Ultimately much more important, however, was the settlement of tropical biomes—first a number of important river delta floodplains, and then of low-land tropical rainforests. The former process took off a good four to six decades after the movement onto the world's grasslands was launched, in the 1870s and

1880s. Those decades saw massive settlement and development of major river deltas, particularly in South and Southeast Asia—the Irrawaddy in Burma (Myanmar), the Chao Phraya in Thailand, the Ganges and Brahmaputra in India, and the Mekong in Viet Nam. But something similar took place in other, temperate (nontropical) areas as well—for example, in the delta of the San Joaquin River in California starting in 1874. These deltas came to play an important role in the world economy as rice-exporting regions by the 1890s and 1900s.[39] A bit later, after the turn of the century, the great rainforest regions began to see similar rapid development—for example, in Brazil, Indonesia, and Nigeria.

No less than in grasslands, arid, and mountain regions, technological developments played a crucial role in the settlement of the tropics (and of temperate river deltas). Railways were critical, enabling producers to get their goods to market. Equally important was flood control, which turned swamp and flood basin in the great river deltas into rich rice-growing land. But less obvious technologies were also important. Quinine, for example, was important for tropical development since those same flood basins that were so fertile for rice growing were also outstanding producers of mosquitoes, and hence of malaria. The development of those river deltas, therefore, had to await the development of giant quinine plantations in colonial Asia and the industrial production of purified quinine. Until the 1880s, 95 percent of world quinine supply came from South America and was collected in the wild; thereafter the Dutch and British established plantations in Sri Lanka, India, and Indonesia, and by the 1920s Indonesia produced 90 percent of a tremendously expanded world output.[40] Another example is the chainsaw, first produced in 1917, after the development of efficient small internal combustion engines. The chainsaw allowed people to cut down trees up to one hundred times faster than they could with handsaws and axes, permitting rapid land clearance in heavily forested areas. This was crucial for the opening up of tropical rainforest regions for agriculture or pastoralism. Fertilizers, too, were particularly important in cleared-rainforest areas, where soils were often poor.[41]

The history of world population distribution reflects this phased conquest of different environments (chart 1.14). The aggregate population of the old core areas of human population in China and Europe—largely mixed grassland and forested hills—is still larger than that of all other regions; but the population of other kinds of terrains has surged much faster, particularly since 1900. We can trace this pattern in the case of individual regions, as well. In South America, for example, the population of Argentina (with a geography dominated by grasslands) at first grew much faster than Brazil (mostly tropical), up until about 1940; but then, in the second half of the century, the population of Brazil grew faster than that of Argentina. In India, the relatively dry United Provinces (now Uttar Pradesh) grew faster in the early twentieth century that did the lowland delta of Bengal and Bangladesh; but after about 1930 the tropical lowland delta population grew faster.

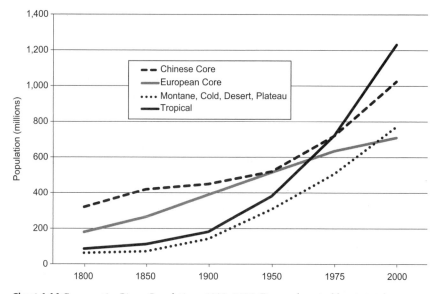

Chart 1.14 Comparative Biome Populations, 1800–2000. Figures do not add up to total world population, because many countries cannot usefully be classified as fitting into only one biome.

Since 1850, then, the center of gravity of the human population has steadily shifted from the old centers of human population toward more challenging biomes, which have been substantially re-engineered to support high population densities. People made wet areas drier and dry areas wetter; they eliminated certain fauna and replaced them with others; and they cleared masses of old vegetation to make way for new. Last but not least, they displaced or killed entire communities of people who, over periods of centuries and even millennia, had maintained a rough equilibrium with those biomes.

A CENTURY OF MASS MIGRATIONS, 1840–1940

The history of early Russia is the history of a country which is colonizing itself. Because of this there was a constant powerful movement of population across enormous spaces. . . . The settler does not remain long [in any one place]: as soon as he is constrained to work harder, he goes off to settle new areas . . . land property has no value, for the important factor is population. To people the land as quickly as possible, to summon people from all over to new regions, to lure them with all sorts of privileges; to set off for new and better regions, regions more peaceful and tranquil, with more favorable conditions . . . all these are the principal questions of a country colonizing itself.[42]

Sergei Solov'ev, *Istoriia Rossii* (History of Russia)

Re-engineering entire biomes and turning them into rich food-producing regions required a lot of people. Where did all those people come from? For one thing, there was rapid natural increase in some of the newly settled environments—cheap land and abundant natural resources meant high fertility, relatively good nutrition, and low mortality. But, particularly in the early period of expansion, the much stronger cause of population gain was mass migrations of people from the old core zones of human settlement. These mass migrations are an extraordinary feature of the past two centuries of human history, a period in which tens of millions of people have moved from their country, continent, or even hemisphere of birth to new ones.

All told, in the century from the 1840s to the 1940s, on the order of 150 million people moved, permanently or temporarily, great distances from the old core regions of human population to areas previously less densely inhabited. Since the world population in 1800 was probably just under a billion, this is a huge proportion of the people who lived over the next century. Certainly in absolute terms this was the largest migration in human history.

We return to the topic of migration in chapter 9, as there was a second wave of migration after World War II, one that flowed mostly in the other direction, from Asia, Africa, and Latin America to North America and Europe (as well as the Middle East). That second wave, obviously, was powered mainly by an overall shift in global demographic patterns. But it was also quite different in structure and origins from the first wave, in the previous century.

In the first wave of mass migration, from the mid-nineteenth to the mid-twentieth century, almost 75 million people migrated from Europe, 50 to 55 million from China, and 30 to 35 million from India (chart 1.15). About 60 million left Europe for the Americas; about 50 million left from China, Korea, Japan, and Russia for Siberia, Mongolia, and Manchuria; about 50 million left from India and South China for Southeast Asia. Africa, which had been a major source of migrants in the eighteenth century due to the slave trade, saw a smaller number move in the nineteenth century—about 3 million people. Internal migrations were on the same scale, though harder to count: some 75 million Europeans, up to 40 million Chinese, and 35 million Americans moved significant distances within those regions.[43]

This first period of mass migration has a clear chronological structure. The forced migration of Africans was confined almost exclusively to the first half of the nineteenth century, because slavery in the Americas was abolished in the middle of the century. Later in the century, the direction of population flow was even reversed in the case of Africa, with about 3 million French and Italians moving to North Africa, and roughly a million Europeans, Chinese, Indians, and Middle Easterners to South and East Africa.

In contrast, Europeans began to migrate to the Americas in large numbers just about at the time slavery was beginning its decline, starting with some 1.8 million Irish people emigrating during the great potato famine between 1845

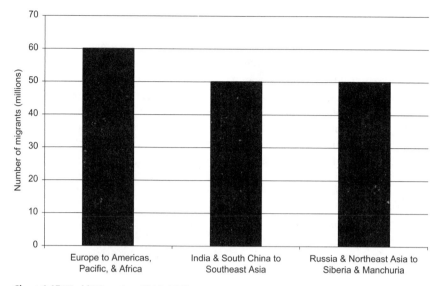

Chart 1.15 World Migration, 1846–1940.

and 1855. Thereafter, the number of European emigrants rose annually from the 1870s. At the peak of this migration in 1913, a whopping 2.1 million people crossed the Atlantic—close to one half of 1 percent of the entire European population, in one year.[44] Different groups left at different times. Britain, Scandinavia, and Central Europe saw massive emigration from the middle of the nineteenth century right through the 1910s, but then it slowed down. Southern and Eastern Europe had moderate migration rates up until the 1890s, then accelerating rates right up until World War I. In the decade between 1906 and 1915, over half a million Italians left the country every year.[45] Of almost 75 million European migrants, about 70 percent went to the United States and Canada. More than 15 percent (13 million) were Russians who went to Siberia and Central Asia; over 10 percent went to Latin America; under 10 percent went to Australia, New Zealand, and South Africa.[46]

European migration slowed drastically after World War I; in contrast, emigration from Russia, China, and India continued to grow after 1914. Over the whole period, about 15 million Chinese went to Southeast Asia and Indonesia, and another 4 million to the Philippines, Australia, New Zealand, California, Hawai'i, and Latin America. About 30 million Chinese moved to Mongolia, Manchuria, and Siberia. Some 30 million Indians emigrated during this century and a half, as well—most of them not very far, with about 15 million going to Burma (now Myanmar) and 8 million to Ceylon (now Sri Lanka). But 4 to 5 million went as far as Malaysia; and 1 to 2 million went to Africa, the Pacific islands (including Australia and New Zealand), and even Latin America.[47] Over a million Japanese emigrated between 1885 and 1925, about a third of them to Hawai'i and the United States, another third to Korea and Siberia, and smaller numbers to China, Brazil, and Peru.[48]

There was one very profound difference between European and Asian migration patterns. Of the European emigrants 30 to 40 percent actually returned to their countries of origin over the course of these 150 years. Fewer returned earlier on; more after 1900; and the rate of return varied greatly by destination region. Only about 10 percent returned from Australia, about a third from North America, and about half from Latin America. In contrast, however, about 70 percent of Chinese emigrants and probably an even higher proportion of Indian emigrants ultimately went home. For this reason, some historians have come to refer to two patterns of population movement: emigration, which was most common in Europe; and sojourning, most common in Asia.[49]

There were two primary reasons for this difference. Particularly in North America and Australia disease and genocidal violence almost eliminated the people who had previously occupied the land, so that many European settlers acquired landed property and built lasting communities of people from the same countries or even villages of origin. Many of these people in fact came with the intention of staying, and 30 to 40 percent were women. Something similar happened in Siberia. In contrast, most Chinese and Indian immigrants went to countries with reasonably dense populations, did not acquire land, and in fact never expected to stay. Only 10 to 15 percent were women; people did not migrate as families, expecting to settle down. Many young men were sent by their extended families to take advantage of particular labor opportunities, earn some cash, and bring it back to add to the family wealth. Some Indian and Chinese migrants—perhaps 10 percent in each case—were indentured laborers. They signed work contracts for a limited number of years and often worked in isolated plantations, mines, and construction gangs in conditions often approaching those of slavery—complete with barrackslike housing, poor food and medical care, and even corporal punishment for infractions of work rules or for breach of contract.[50]

Again, as in the case of European migrants, this pattern varied from one place to another, depending on opportunities and conditions. Of the 2.6 million Indians who went to Burma between 1852 and 1887, for example, three-quarters returned home; of the 150,000 who went to South Africa before 1911, only half came back.[51]

A different mechanism operated in Latin America. There, the particular political, social, and economic conditions prevailing in many areas (such as Argentina and Brazil) resulted in the concentration of land ownership in the hands of wealthy elites who had settled well before the great wave of immigration got under way in the 1880s. A higher proportion of later immigrants came to work on farms and plantations to save some money and return to make better lives in Europe. Where there were greater opportunities to become wealthier than they had been in their home country, people tended to stay—hence the high rate of retention in Australia and the United States. Latin American standards of living, at least for the mass of the populace, were not significantly better than in poorer parts of Europe, such as Spain and southern Italy. Incomes being more equal, other incentives (such as family ties or access to locally controlled resources) created higher rates of return. This is a mechanism that may have played a role in high rates of return in Asia, as well, since the gap in standards of living between China and India on the one hand and Southeast Asia on the other was also small.

A third mechanism encouraged high rates of return, specifically among Chinese migrants: racism. On the one hand, between the late nineteenth and the early decades of the twentieth centuries, a number of societies passed exclusionary legislation that made it extremely difficult for Chinese immigrants to stay and become citizens. After some decades of using rising entry fees to limit Chinese immigration, the United States passed an outright ban (the Chinese Exclusion Act) in 1882 (the Japanese and other Asians were excluded in 1924); Australia followed suit in 1901, as did Canada in 1923.[52] On the other hand, a number of countries attempted as a matter of public policy to attract European settlers. For example, they sent out recruiting missions to inform potential immigrants of opportunities in Argentina, Brazil, California, Australia, and Canada; some established subsidies for the cost of passage, particularly for people possessing skills their economies needed; and some established labor agencies to connect immigrants with jobs.

There is a specific reason for this contrast: in the course of the nineteenth century, racism became a powerful ideology having a greater and greater impact on public policy. This topic is discussed in chapter 4.

The result of all these trends by 1950 was that whereas the descendants of European immigrants to the Americas and the Pacific numbered 250 to 300 million, those of Indian and Chinese immigrants to Southeast Asia and the Pacific numbered only 15 or 16 million.[53] This pattern decisively shaped twentieth-century political history in that it changed the global balance of power profoundly. When the modern world exploded in world war between 1914 and 1945, those societies that had established relatively densely populated and economically dynamic offshoots had a decisive strategic advantage. Most of those offshoot societies were politically independent by then, but they had close cultural, economic, political, military, and often personal ties to the countries of their origin.

The societies dominated by the descendants of emigrants from Britain—the United States, Canada, Australia, New Zealand, and South Africa—form the prime example. They constituted a globe-spanning community of heritage that could muster overwhelming economic power by the middle of the twentieth century because they controlled the resources of two entire continents (North America and Australia), the richest part of a third (South Africa), and until

1947 most of the Indian subcontinent as well.[54] Other states were aware of the potential advantages of establishing such empires of settlement. German strategic thinkers and racialist national chauvinists at the turn of the twentieth century, for example, deplored the fact that in contrast to Britain, Germany had during the previous century "lost" millions of emigrants (above all to the United States).

Yet, while people of British descent wielded great political, social, and economic power in North America, Australia, New Zealand, and South Africa, these were true immigrant societies, with populations of highly diverse origins. One critical reason for this fact was that global migration patterns reflected the need to match the skills of people—migrants—to the requirements of settlement. In most cases matching skills to resources mattered more than ethnicity in determining who went where.

A striking example of this pattern is that of the migration of ethnic German inhabitants of the southern plains of the Russian Empire. These "Volga Germans" originated with seven thousand families that migrated in the 1760s from central and southern Germany to the steppe, or grasslands, in southern Russia on the Volga River. They came in response to a shortage of land in Germany and to Russian government incentives for settlement on this land. Those incentives included free land, taken from the native inhabitants, and exemption from military service.[55] By the 1870s and 1880s, however, these ethnic German subjects faced the revocation of their privileges and growing pressure from the central government's "Russification" campaign, which sought to create a more culturally, linguistically, and even religiously homogenous population. In response, about 150,000 of them left the Russian Empire. The question was, Where to go? Volga German communities sent scouts out to various parts of the New World to find likely homes. The places they liked best, not surprisingly, were rather like the southern Russian steppe: the pampas; the cold northern Great Plains, in Kansas and Nebraska; and the Canadian prairie still farther north—all environments that matched their skills and knowledge relatively well.

Volga Germans settled in all three places. And they brought with them not only the grassland farming skills they had developed in Russia but even some of the same varieties of grain they had grown there—notably hard red winter wheat, or "Turkey" wheat. Large-scale wheat farming was just beginning to be seriously established in all three areas in the 1860s; and these migrants brought important resources to the project of developing these regions, and shaped them in lasting ways. By the 1920s, about 80 percent of the wheat grown in Kansas and Nebraska was descended from the Russian variety the emigrants had brought with them; and that variety was more common in the United States than any other, accounting for about 30 percent of all wheat grown in the country.[56] But the Volga Germans were an important presence also in Argentina; in fact, there were even contacts between the US and Argentine groups. One Volga German went first to Argentina, but couldn't stand the fact that, as he put it, "everything seemed upside down" there. The sun stood north in the sky during the day, and the cold wind came from the south. So he moved to Saskatchewan, in Canada, where things felt homier.[57]

The point of this example is that, to a remarkable extent, nineteenth-century mass migration made the settlement of the world's grasslands one integrated global process—one in which the same knowledge sets, technologies, and organisms (crops and animals), and in some cases even the same individuals, were involved, on a global scale. Another example is provided by Mennonite Germans from further south and west in the Russian Empire. Often called Black Sea Germans, they settled in the same grassland areas (though they preferred slightly warmer parts of those regions). A third group consisted of the Ukrainians who settled in large numbers in southern Saskatchewan between the 1880s and 1890s.

There was a similar global redistribution of people with expertise in pastoralism—raising sheep and cows. Many Argentines today have Irish or Basque family names, for example, because they are descended from Irish and Basque shepherds recruited during Argentina's wool boom in the middle decades of the nineteenth century. Many Basque place- and family names can be found in in eastern California and Nevada for the same reason. And some of the wealthiest landowning families in Argentina have English last names because they are descended from British stockbreeders who brought their knowledge of scientific animal husbandry, and their animals, with them in the later nineteenth century.

Fishing offers yet another example. Portugal experienced rapidly rising emigration through the entire period before World War I, reaching almost 1 percent per year just before the war. About 85 percent of these emigrants went to Brazil; but Portuguese fisherman settled on coastlines in almost every part of the world, including Northern California, Australia and New Zealand, Hawai'i, and New England.[58]

California was a striking microcosm of the process by which immigrants were sorted by region and skill. Hawai'ian sailors and laborers played an important role in the early history of post-Mexican California. Welsh and Chinese coal miners and Cornish tin miners worked in the goldfields of California in the 1850s. Italian and Portuguese fishermen settled all along the Northern California coast. Dairy farmers of northern Italian origin are still a major factor in Marin and Sonoma Counties. Northern Italian and Italian-Swiss winegrowers established powerful dynasties in the Central Valley—including the Mondavi and Gallo families, whose names are known worldwide. Japanese horticultural workers, who learned their skills in a land-poor, intensive-agriculture economy, played a critical role in the settlement of the Santa Clara Valley and the Central Valley in the late nineteenth century. Chinese workers accustomed to highly cooperative heavy-labor techniques built the western end of the first transcontinental railway; soon after it was completed in 1869, they turned to building the elaborate water-control system that made the delta of the Sacramento River an agricultural powerhouse. They were well prepared for that work, since most of them came from the Pearl River Delta in Guangdong Province, where a similar system had been built.[59]

California was typical in this respect. There are similar ethnic Italian, Greek, and Portuguese fishing and wine-making populations all over the Pacific and Atlantic—in Hawai'i, Australia, New Zealand, Peru, Chile, Argentina, and New England. Welsh and Chinese miners worked in the goldfields not only of California but also of Australia and New Zealand in the mid-nineteenth century. Japanese horticulturalists were critical in shaping the Hawai'ian economy and played a role in Latin America as well; by 1933, for example, Japanese farmers produced three-quarters of the tea, over half the silk, and almost half the cotton grown in Brazil. German, Polish, and Czech coal miners—alongside those from Wales, Cornwall, and the North of England—played important roles in building the US coal-mining industry in, for example, Pennsylvania and West Virginia. Indian indentured laborers were brought to Fiji, Surinam, East Africa, South Africa, and Australia in the 1870s and 1880s to develop the sugar industry in those areas, based on skills they brought with them. All these people moved to places similar to their homes and continued working in the trades in which they were skilled.[60]

It was not simply luck that matched people and skills to environments and resources on a global scale. This was a pattern deliberately fostered. Specific opportunities drove mass migration, but mass migration was also a product of deliberate recruitment in which those who owned or controlled particular economic resources sought to attract the people who could exploit them effectively. This was not merely a blind movement of masses of people—an unplanned, random, individual process. People went where they knew their skills were needed; and governments, corporations, nongovernmental agencies, and individual entrepreneurs made deliberate, self-conscious efforts to create a global economy, and a global distribution of people and skills, that could effectively exploit the resources of the entire planet.

Chapter 2 turns to that project.

Foundations of the Modern Global Economy

THE GLOBAL DEVELOPMENT PROJECT, 1850–1930

There was not, of course, a central planning body in the nineteenth century that undertook to exploit the resources and economic potential of the entire planet. But individual governments, private companies and other organizations, and entrepreneurs did deliberately and consciously set out to just do that in particular regions, countries, or industries. One important example was immigration recruitment and assistance—finding potential immigrants with particular skills and helping to bring them to one's country. Another, mentioned in chapter 1, was generous land distribution schemes—the US Homestead Act of 1860, the Canadian Dominion Lands Act of 1872, and similar schemes in New Zealand, South Africa, Siberia, Australia, and Japan.

In places where differentials in technological, demographic, economic, and military power were particularly great, the dispossession, displacement, or murder of the resident population was a central part of this redistribution policy. A concentrated period of violent expropriation occurred just at the moment the global development project intensified in the third quarter of the nineteenth century. The inhabitants of the Great Plains, the Argentine pampas, the Central Valley of California, and the southeastern plains of Australia were all pushed aside or killed in a great wave of land wars between the 1850s and the 1880s.

Major international collaborative research efforts also played a key role in enabling the settlement and exploitation of new biomes. The cases of beef, wool, and wheat on the world's temperate and cold grasslands were early and striking examples. In Argentina from the 1860s on, both the government and the private farmers' organization Sociedad Rural de Argentina (founded in 1866) deliberately brought in expertise from abroad to help in the development of the Argentine plains. The president of the Sociedad Rural studied agriculture in France and brought in sheep from Germany to improve the quantity and quality of Argentine wool. In 1881 the government of Buenos Aires province sent two major landowners on a two-year study trip to Australia, the United States, and England to investigate best agricultural practices in those economies. In 1883 the government established the first major agricultural school in Argentina. All of these measures contributed to massive growth in the Argentine export economy, with an annual growth rate of around 7 percent for the economy as a whole.[1]

The United States government and agricultural societies undertook similar efforts. Acutely aware that Russia was the largest wheat exporter in the world, the US Department of Agriculture (USDA)—established, not coincidentally, in 1862—sent missions to the Russian Empire in the 1880s and 1890s to select wheat varieties suited to the climate of the Great Plains. The Russians, on the other hand, were aware that the United States had the most technologically advanced agriculture in the world, and they sent missions to the Great Plains to get ideas about how to farm similar regions in the Russian empire.[2] The Japanese government, confronted with the task of developing its cold northern frontier on the island of Hokkaido, sent its vice-minister of colonization to the United States in 1870 to study US agricultural policy particularly on the Great Plains. A second mission in 1871–73 assessed American legal, financial, military, economic, educational, and governmental methods. In 1870 the Japanese government hired a prominent USDA commissioner, Horace Capron, as special advisor to the colonial administration in Hokkaido; he was there for four years and introduced farming methods, equipment, crops, and cattle; established experimental farms; and laid out the city plan for Sapporo. After he left, the government hired William Smith Clark, president of the Massachusetts Agricultural College (now the University of Massachusetts at Amherst, established in 1863) to help build the Sapporo Agricultural College (now Hokkaido University).[3]

A transnational mobilization of expertise thus guided the development of new frontiers of settlement across the world. An interlocking, international web of government initiatives, ideas, institutions, and even individuals worked to develop the world's grasslands. As we will see, this effort lasted more than a century, between the 1870s and the 1970s, and with some variations right into the twenty-first century.

In some cases, transnational institutions were set up to encourage and facilitate cooperation and transfer of expertise. In 1878, for example, the first International Congress of Agriculture was held in Paris; a second was held in Budapest in 1885; by 1905 a permanent International Institute of Agriculture was

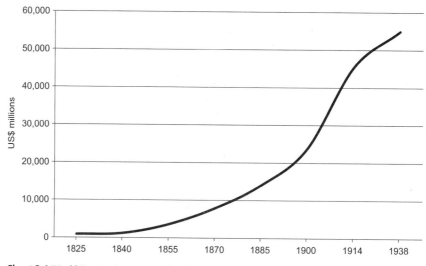

Chart 2.1 World Foreign Investment Stock, 1825–1938.

established in Rome as an intergovernmental clearinghouse for agricultural information. Most European nations, most of the South American states, and Australia, Russia, Japan, Egypt, and Persia were members.[4] Somewhat later, charitable institutions such as the Rockefeller Foundation (established in 1913) played a crucial role in world agricultural development, as well.

In addition to people and expertise, economic development of the new territories of settlement required one other factor: money. The massive mobilization of foreign investment in this period is one further illustration of the global scope of this development project. Europe, in particular, poured money into the newly developing areas throughout the nineteenth century. The total amount of capital invested internationally rose almost geometrically from the early decades of the nineteenth century until World War I (chart 2.1). By 1914 the greatest share of this money, some 40 percent, had gone to develop the Americas; the second-largest share, to colonial regions in Africa, the Middle East, and Asia; only the third-largest share went to investments in Europe, the industrial core of the world economy in 1900 (chart 2.2). In other words, the pattern over the nineteenth century was that massive amounts of money poured out of Europe and into the developing regions and nations, particularly in those challenging biomes then attracting tens of millions of new migrants and settlers.

The great engine of this development was Britain, the banking and financial core of the world economy at this time (chart 2.3)—with six of the world's ten largest banks (measured by deposits) in 1913.[5] In 1830, 67 percent of British foreign investment was in Europe; by 1914 the proportion had fallen to only

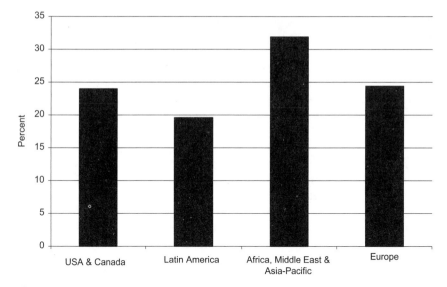

Chart 2.2 World Foreign Direct Investment Share by Receiving Region, 1914.

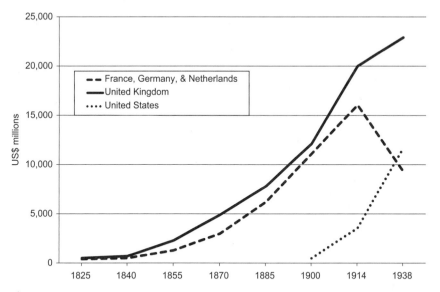

Chart 2.3 Outward Foreign Direct Investment Stocks by Origin, 1825–1938.

5 percent. In contrast, 58 percent of French investment—the second-largest share of all European foreign investment in 1914—was still in Europe (though that figure was down from 71 percent seventy-five years earlier).[6] The avalanche of British foreign investment capital in this period is astonishing in scale. By 1910, 7.4 percent of British gross domestic product (GDP, a measure of a society's total production) was invested overseas each year, and accumulated total British foreign investment amounted to 53 percent of GDP. By contrast, total accumulated foreign investment for the United States in 1914 was only 6.8 percent of GDP, and it rose to 9 percent in 1994.[7] Not coincidentally, Britain was also far and away the greatest imperial power in this period. But British money was critical in developing many areas that were not part of its colonial empire, as well. Almost a quarter of all British foreign investment before 1914 went to the United States, two-thirds of it into railways. British money made up about one-third of all investment in manufacturing in the United States.[8] In 1892 two-thirds of all telegraph lines in the world had been built by the British (another quarter by American and French firms); as late as 1908 the British still owned half of all cables (the French and Americans together, more than one-third).[9] The point here is that the story of the late-nineteenth-century world economy, viewed from a global perspective, is to a significant extent one of British banks funding the settlement of the temperate grasslands and (somewhat later) tropical rice-growing deltas of our planet. And Britain continued to play this role right up until World War II. American money started to rival British in the 1920s; but by 1938 American capital still accounted for only 21 percent of all foreign investment globally, and British for 42 percent.[10]

Yet a key characteristic of the development project is precisely that it was global; therefore, it is often difficult to assign a particular initiative, source of capital, or individual human player to any one nationality. A good example is the mining engineer, financier, philanthropist, and later US president Herbert Hoover. Hoover was born in Iowa in 1874; was educated in geology at Stanford University in California; worked as a geologist in Nevada and California; and soon after graduation got a job with a leading British mining firm with offices in Johannesburg, South Africa; Tianjin (Tientsin), China; Kalgoorlie, Australia; Auckland, New Zealand; and Tarkwa, Gold Coast; as well as London. The firm sent him to Western Australia in 1897 to assess, acquire, and manage gold mines—the most successful being the Sons of Gwalia mine, first worked by immigrant Welsh miners (Gwalia being the Welsh name for Wales). Among other accomplishments, Hoover eliminated both administrative waste and inefficient labor rules (such as no Sunday work) and imported Italian miners, who were more tractable than the resident English, Irish, and Welsh labor force, which had a longer tradition of labor organization. Successful in Australia, Hoover was transferred in 1899 to China and oversaw a massive mining concession in the northern provinces of Chihli (now Hebei) and Jehol, where the local viceroy was attempting to build industrial and economic capacity in order to strengthen China in the face of Japanese and Russian expansion. Surviving the Boxer Rebellion, Hoover left China with a considerable fortune in 1902.

By 1908 Hoover was able to go into business for himself, now primarily not as a mine manager or geologist, but as a financier based in what was then the financial capital of the world, London—though he still traveled the world assessing potential mining investments. Over the following six years he investigated, invested in, or helped develop enterprises in Nicaragua, Korea, Newfoundland, Siberia, California, Alaska, Peru, Japan, Madagascar, Romania, Russia, Argentina, Cornwall, Brazil, and Mexico; he was involved in the production of gold, zinc, copper, tin, iron, silver, lead, and oil. In his most successful single operation, in Burma (now Myanmar), he assessed the site, arranged the financing, and organized the corporate structure; saw to the building of the mine, a smelter, a railway to transport ore and metal, and a mile-and-a-half-long drainage tunnel; imported labor from China, India, and Indochina (now Viet Nam, Cambodia, and Laos) and managers from the United States and Britain; and made the greater part of his enormous personal fortune. A rather judgmental fellow, Hoover remarked once while still a student, "If a man has not made a million dollars by the time he is forty, he is not worth much." By 1914 (when he turned forty) he had done that many times over, and turned increasingly to the philanthropic and political interests that eventually landed him in the White House.

Clearly, Hoover was a man accustomed to getting what he wanted, and he didn't tolerate opposition. After his experiences during the Boxer Rebellion (during which his house, along with those of other foreigners, was shelled by the mutinous Chinese army), he concluded that the only way to negotiate with an "Asiatic" was "with a gun in your hand, and let him know that you will use it." In his memoirs he would later observe that he thrived on "the sheer joy" of "creating productive enterprises," while "correcting the perversities and incompetence of men" (his employees). Others characterized him as "uncouth," "a grunter," and "blunt, almost to the point of utter tactlessness," and as someone who created "a certain atmosphere of aggressiveness" wherever he went. But he was also hardworking and tenacious, "radiated leadership," displayed remarkable personal generosity, and became an extremely effective organizer of international relief efforts for those suffering from the devastation of World War I. On the strength of his business acumen and his philanthropic service, he was elected president of the United States in 1928. In short, he got the job done. He had just about the ideal character one probably needed to participate fully in the development of the planet's mineral wealth.[11]

In Hoover's own view, getting the job done meant participating in and helping to propel the extraordinarily broad and vibrant creative ferment in global society around the turn of the century. That creative ferment included scientific, technological, and engineering advances; the building of globe-spanning business enterprises; the revision of labor and social arrangements; and—not least in Hoover's personal experience—the generation of enormous wealth. But as his somewhat autocratic instincts suggest, those processes were also often coercive, and in fact frequently violent. By 1900 the extreme genocidal violence of the first three quarters of the century was mostly past; but endemic violent coercion and resistance—and a striking degree of mayhem—were still an important part of the development project, as different groups struggled to shape new industries, new social roles, and new productive processes in their own interests.

Further down the hierarchy of authority, wealth, and power in Hoover's own mining industry, for example, coercion and violence were very much in evidence in many places. The life of the miner and radical labor organizer William "Big Bill" Haywood is illustrative. Born in Salt Lake City in the United States five years before Hoover, Haywood was still in his teens and working mines in Nevada and Idaho when he got to know a member of the Molly Maguires, a clandestine Irish immigrant organization. This miner had seen twenty of his comrades hanged for murders they may not have committed during a violent period of labor conflict in the coal mines of Pennsylvania in the late 1870s. Haywood saw federal soldiers called in to arrest more than a thousand striking miners and confine them for months in prison camps—on two separate occasions. He saw martial law declared or local militias called out multiple times; saw miners "deported" from towns or counties at gunpoint; saw multiple armed confrontations between miners and hired thugs or hastily recruited police deputies. The first hundred pages of Haywood's memoirs record the deaths of some two dozen men in low-level labor conflict in the 1890s. His experience was hardly unique: violence continued to be endemic in mining towns in Pennsylvania through the 1890s; in the "Lattimer Massacre" in 1897, for example, nineteen striking miners were shot dead by police while trying to shut down a mine. In an extraordinary struggle between miners and militias organized by mine owners in the coal fields of Colorado in 1913 and 1914, as many as one hundred men were killed. And there were certainly still echoes in Haywood's experience of the much more widespread and deadly violence of earlier decades. In Nevada, for example, Haywood met both a white participant in a massacre of Paiute men, women, and children and one of the Paiute survivors of that massacre.[12] In none of this violence was the United States extraordinary: similar fatal confrontations erupted between laborers and owners (of mines, ranches, plantations, railways, and other enterprises) in many other parts of the world, including South Africa, Australia, and Chile. Indeed, Haywood was one of the founders (in 1905) of a movement designed to combat the exploitation of workers everywhere—the Industrial Workers of the World, or "Wobblies."

The IWW was a small part of a broader international movement opposed to labor exploitation—the socialist movement. Socialist thought was diverse and often bitterly divided, ranging from utopian visions of harmonious small communes, through violent or pacifist anarchism opposed to any form of government, to syndicalist programs for economic management by autonomous trade union organizations, and on to advocacy of centralized state ownership and control of what Marxists called the means of production (factories, transporta-

tion infrastructure, land, and so on). The most powerful organizations it created were trade unions that sought to improve conditions of labor and wage
rates, and political parties that sought to champion the needs of working people through political action. Starting primarily in Western Europe around
mid-century, socialism in its various forms spread throughout the world in the
later nineteenth century. Particularly in Europe, it created some of the largest
organizations ever seen, with membership figures in the hundreds of thousands and even low millions. The most influential socialist tradition, generally
called social democracy, drew on the thinking of the German socialists Karl
Marx and Friedrich Engels; the utopian and syndicalist branches were influenced particularly by French thinkers such as Joseph Fourier and Georges
Sorel; and anarchism was influenced more by Russian thinkers such as Mikhail
Bakunin and Peter Kropotkin. By the 1920s, communism, influenced above all
by the Russian revolutionary Vladimir Lenin, rivaled the influence of social
democracy (and the two movements were often violently opposed). But in 1900
advocates of all these varieties of socialism were to be found in many societies
around the world—some of them European immigrants, others not.[13]

This expansion in labor organizing and socialist thinking was driven in part
by the extraordinarily harsh conditions workers faced in the early period of
industrialization. Even in the relatively wealthy United States, for example,
steelworkers labored on average more than sixty-six hours per week, and workers in the canning industry seventy-seven hours. Conditions were so brutal
that industrial workers changed jobs on average once every three years, and in
some industries every year. Yet most industrial workers earned little more than
enough to feed, clothe, and house their families—and very often went hungry
or homeless if they lost their jobs. They often lived in atrociously crowded and
unhealthy neighborhoods and communities where medical, educational, consumer, and even religious services were direly insufficient. Conditions were
similar all over the industrial world—and they were frequently defended by
governments sympathetic to employers and hostile to any form of organized
resistance from working people. During a period of intense unrest among railroad workers in the United States in the summer of 1877, for example, the
police, state militias, and federal troops killed more than one hundred strikers.
But those less able or willing to assert their rights and interests suffered worse.
Mortality among Chinese workers building the first transcontinental railway
in the United States in the 1860s was around 10 percent—1,200 men. At least
5,000 and perhaps as many as 22,000 workers died in the first attempt to build
a Panama canal, in the 1880s (a project that became feasible only once malaria
was understood and could be brought under control, after 1897).[14] Conditions
in colonial Africa and Asia were no better, and often worse.

But before the 1890s and 1900s socialists—like critics of the environmental
impact of human population expansion, such as Ludwig Klages—faced an
uphill struggle in convincing others to consider the costs of the global

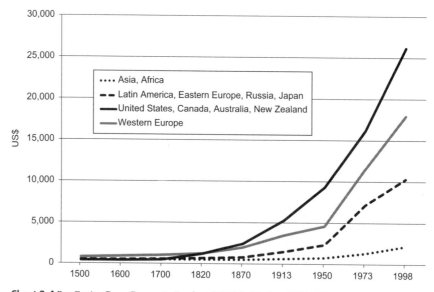

Chart 2.4 Per Capita Gross Domestic Product (GDP) by Region, 1500–1998.

development project. One reason was that for many people around the world it was a massive economic success. World gross domestic product (GDP) per capita, after rising very slowly for three centuries, started to rise quickly in the early nineteenth century, and then passed into a period of sustained, rapid growth for the next 150 years. These benefits were distributed quite unevenly, however. In the period before World War II, growth of per capita GDP was most rapid in the Anglo-American and Antipodean world—Canada, Australia, New Zealand, and the United States; next came Western Europe; then Latin America, Eastern Europe, and Japan. The wealth of most societies in Africa and Asia grew far more slowly (chart 2.4).There were also radical differences, moreover, *within* regions: by 1950 Argentina's per capita GDP was twice that for Latin America as a whole; South Africa's was three times that for Africa as a whole; Japan's, four times that for all of Asia.

Whatever the inequalities within regions, however, a large number of politically independent societies around the world experienced unprecedented economic growth starting at just about the same time—from the 1870s onward. That included not only Western Europe and the United States but also Japan, Argentina, Australia, and Canada and to a somewhat lesser extent Eastern Europe and Russia. In contrast, most nonindependent regions did not experience similar growth. But even Asia and Africa saw some gain in per capita incomes, which they had scarcely seen in the previous three centuries.

This was a remarkable achievement particularly in light of the previous historical relationship between population and economy. In earlier centuries,

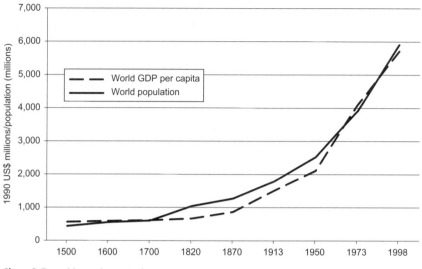

Chart 2.5 World Population and Gross Domestic Product, 1500–2000.

rapid population growth had very often resulted in disaster as population out-stripped resources—particularly food production. Thomas Malthus, famously, formulated this pattern as a general rule of human society in his *Essay on Population* in 1798. At any time before then, he would probably have been right; but within decades of the theory's publication, it became obsolete (chart 2.5). Since the 1870s, explosive population growth has been accompanied by explosive growth in GDP per capita.

Why?

SCIENTIFIC-TECHNICAL REVOLUTION, 1850–1900

The past fifty years represents an epoch of invention and progress unique in the history of the world. It is something more than a merely normal growth of natural development. It has been a gigantic tidal wave of human ingenuity and resource, so stupendous in its magnitude, so beneficent in its results, that the mind is strained and embarrassed in its efforts to expand to a full appreciation of it. Indeed, the period seems a grand climax of discovery, rather than an increment of growth. It has been a splendid, brilliant campaign of brains and energy, rising to the highest achievement. . . . The old word of creation is that God breathed into the clay the breath of life. In the new world of invention mind has breathed into matter, and a new and expanding creation unfolds itself. . . . [B]usy man, . . . seeing with the eye of science the possibilities of matter, . . . has touched it with the divine breath of thought and made a new world.[15]

Edward Byrn, 1896

Starting in the late eighteenth century, human society entered into a sustained, rapid, and massive technological revolution that has transformed human economies and societies fundamentally.[16] The initial innovations appear to have been adopted by Europeans from China, India, and the Middle East in the fourteenth, fifteenth, and sixteenth centuries—these would include the printing press, gunpowder, and modern mathematics. Those innovations helped to power what we call the early Scientific Revolution, in the sixteenth and seventeenth centuries. During that period, relatively slow but important advances in basic science, math, scientific instrumentation, and scientific method laid the foundations for more rapid development in the eighteenth century. By 1800, European science was still not particularly impressive by modern standards. The chemist Joseph Black remarked early in the nineteenth century: "Chemistry is not yet a science. We are very far from a knowledge of first principles."[17] Still, the foundations were laid, and from the late 1820s through the 1860s there were a whole series of scientific breakthroughs that in turn opened the gates to massive innovation, and further progress. These included (to give just a few examples) the discovery of electrical induction in the 1820s; the formulation of the first and second laws of thermodynamics in the 1850s and 1860s; a better understanding of the atomic structure of organic molecules in the 1860s; and the formulation of the periodic table by the Russian scientist Dmitri Mendeleyev in 1869.

Prior to these developments, in the middle and late eighteenth century, important advances in technology and production, though slow, laid important economic foundations. In agriculture, basic advances were made in technique such as improved crop rotation, expanded use of fertilizer (including guano imported from the South Atlantic and Pacific), improved irrigation and drainage techniques, improved stock-breeding, and accelerating enclosure and consolidation of farmland. In transportation there was a surge road and canal building from the mid-eighteenth century. In energy technology, waterwheels and windmills were increasingly deployed from the early eighteenth century. In warfare, moderately effective firearm weaponry began to dominate battlefields from the late seventeenth. The late eighteenth century marked the beginning of what historians call the Industrial Revolution—the development of some basic machinery in the cotton cloth industry, the development of the first effective steam engines, and by 1825 the first railroads and steamships. Statistics on the consumption of such raw materials as cotton and coal reveal the extremely rapid development of these basic industries from the middle of the nineteenth century onward (chart 2.6). Another measure of this leap is the number of scientific journals, which rose roughly by a factor of ten each half century after 1750.[18]

By the late 1860s, this whole concatenation of scientific and technological developments appears to have reached critical mass. From 1867 to 1914 a primarily European and American explosion in scientific and technological innovation occurred.

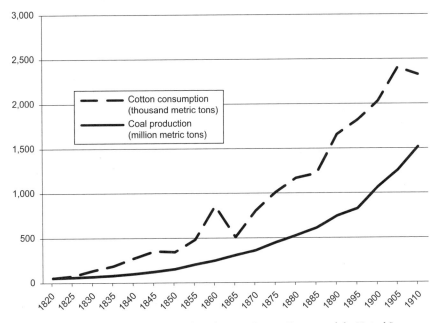

Chart 2.6 Cotton Consumption and Coal Production, Western Europe and the United States, 1820–1910.

Perhaps the easiest way to get a sense of how massive and rapid this process was is to look at the number of patents issued in the world's leading innovative societies (chart 2.7). The explosion of innovation these figures reveal has formed the basis of the world economy's growth ever since the middle decades of the nineteenth century. Many historians refer to this epoch as the Second Industrial Revolution; it created a substantially different new world.

Why did this happen? We don't know. Most fundamentally, human knowledge appears to have a kind of internal logic or dynamic: one discovery builds on another; one invention leads to another; growing knowledge and wealth open the door for further study, discovery, and innovation; and the whole process gathers momentum. Some historians have suggested that the principle of human freedom and human rights has been the critical driver of the process since the mid-nineteenth century. The idea of intellectual freedom that was developed in the Renaissance by humanists and consolidated in the seventeenth century helped free the human imagination and the European and, eventually, global community of scientists from dogma, and permitted limitless exploration. At the same time, the idea of individual property rights, and the gradual process of securing them legally (for example, through patent law), changed the nature of incentives for innovation, allowing individuals to profit from the fruits of their own scientific and technical creativity. Other historians

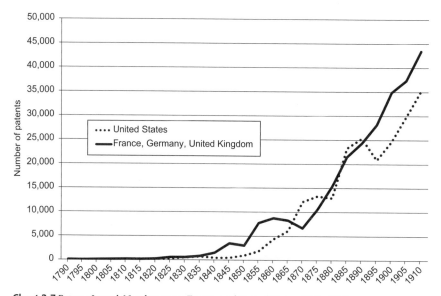

Chart 2.7 Patents Issued, Northwestern Europe and United States, 1790–1910.

have pointed to the development of the European university, a profoundly important institution for the advancement of knowledge. Still other historians have suggested that it was actually the discovery of the rest of the world—from the Crusades in the eleventh century, through the discoveries in Africa, the Americas, and Asia in the fifteenth and sixteenth centuries, to the exploration of the Pacific world in the seventeenth and eighteenth centuries—that broke European minds loose from inherited restrictions by calling religious, social, and scientific orthodoxy into question, opening the way for critical thinking and scientific development. Europeans also used military and administrative means to extract value from other parts of the world—from the sugar colonies in the West Indies, where slaves were ruthlessly exploited to generate massive financial rewards for European investors, and from Britain's expanding empire in India, and Holland's in Indonesia, where peasants were exploited and markets manipulated to generate similar returns. That money may have been crucial in helping to generate innovation in Europe.

Probably each of these factors played a role, but we cannot really know which were most important, at which times. We can, however, identify some shorter-term causes or dynamics that led specifically to the sudden acceleration and diffusion of scientific and technical development from the middle of the nineteenth century onward.

One is that particular innovations led to economic bottlenecks, which then forced further innovation. The best example is the cotton cloth industry, in which the invention and refinement of the spinning jenny created a massive bottleneck by the 1820s—more cotton thread could be produced than people using hand looms could weave into cloth. That led in the 1830s to the development of the power loom and factories, which demanded greater amounts of power, which led to refinements in steam engines. The bottleneck also created an export boom for Great Britain and high demand for cotton from growing regions including India, Egypt, and the US South, which led to further advances in shipbuilding and expansion of rail networks to bring that cotton to ports, which generated new demand for iron and coal, and so on. This domino effect is fundamental to the expansion of technology and industry in the period.

A second crucial factor was the shift in the 1880s and 1890s from individual inventors to large research laboratories as the sites where major advances took place. As the science underlying practical technologies became more complex, even smart and motivated individuals found themselves unable to keep pace with research organizations. Organized labs with long-term research agendas quickly became the chief source of innovation. Some of the great "individual" inventors, such as Thomas Edison and Alexander Graham Bell, actually built their reputations by hiring growing numbers of contract scientists to work in their labs. Edison's labs were in New Jersey; Luther Burbank developed agricultural experiment stations in and around Santa Rosa, California. Other research labs were built by major corporations: German General Electric, Siemens, Bayer, Hoechst, and BASF formed in the 1870s; the Kodak labs in 1895; (American) General Electric in 1900; and Dupont in 1902. By 1940, two thousand firms in the United States—the world leader—had research and development labs, employing seventy thousand people. That number included two thousand scientists at AT&T's Bell Labs, the largest research operation in the world.[19]

Universities played a key role as well. Across the European world, public university systems mushroomed from the 1870s onward. The United States and Germany became the leading industrial-technical economies in the world in this period, in part by following two distinctly different institution-building strategies. In Germany, both government and private industry pushed the curriculum toward the sciences, with major industrial firms pouring money into partnerships with local and state governments that built a whole new system of polytechnical universities. In the United States, the Morrill Acts of 1862 and 1890 granted federally owned land to the states for the express purpose of selling or developing it to fund higher education; on that basis, the United States built the greatest system of public higher education in the world. One result was that while in 1880 there were 7,000 engineers in the United States, by 1950 there were 226,000—thirteen times as many engineers per capita as fifty years earlier.[20] But other countries, particularly in Europe and its colonial offshoots, also made major investments in higher education in the later nineteenth century. The result was a rapid increase in the number of university students as a proportion of national populations (chart 2.8).

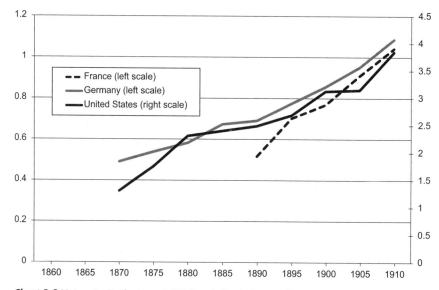

Chart 2.8 University Students per 1,000 Population in France, Germany, and the United States, 1860–1910.

Such forces and policies generated a staggering number of new products, technologies, and companies between 1860 and 1914. The long list of industrial processes, fundamental inventions, and increasingly sophisticated consumer products range from open-hearth steelmaking (1866), the sulfite pulp paper process, and the typewriter (1867), through the steam turbine (1884), motion picture film (1893), and air-conditioning (1902), to the safety razor (1904), vacuum cleaner (1905), and tungsten-filament lightbulb (1913).[21] Listing them all would be unmanageable. How can we organize our understanding of the underlying process that led to all these inventions?

One way is to distinguish between fundamental or basic inventions and subsequent refinements.[22] The basic inventions generated multiple possible applications, which were then developed and refined over following years or decades in smaller steps. The internal combustion engine, for example, was developed in the 1880s by Germans, and then over the following three decades spawned new products such as the motorcycle, automobile, and airplane, and refinements like the diesel motor, which spawned further products like more powerful trucks and locomotives. Other examples include the linotype machine (for setting type in the industrialized printing process), which was invented in 1884 and then refined steadily over the following century. By the middle of the twentieth century, fifteen hundred individual patents applied to advanced linotype machines.[23] One could think of this as an expansionary

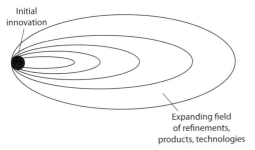

Figure 2.1 Expansion of Innovation.

process: basic scientific and technical innovations generate an expanding field of further refinements (figure 2.1).

Alternatively, one could think of technical innovation as a cascading process: basic innovations lead to a proliferation of more specific, less fundamental discoveries, technologies, and products, each of which is then refined by further innovations, and so on, with many such later refinements building on multiple chains of innovations in an increasingly dense interlocking web (figure 2.2). In many cases, moreover, innovations in one area created bottlenecks in another, leading to further basic innovations and sparking a second cascade (figure 2.3). In the area of transportation technology, for example, the European rail network had grown quite extensively by the 1870s (map 2.1), integrating all major and even medium-sized provincial centers of production and consumption into national and international markets. But at that point it became clear that the railroads would soon reach the limit of their capacity to link smaller centers. The problem then was how to link producers and consumers in small, county-level centers to international and national markets. The answer was the internal combustion engine, developed in the mid-1880s.

In still other cases, basic innovations in one area opened up new possibilities in others, which then generated new basic innovations, in a kind of stair-step process. The development of cheap high-quality steel between 1856–57 (the invention of the Bessemer and Kelly blast furnaces in Britain and the United States) and 1861 (the invention of the open-hearth system at the German firm Siemens) made many other products and processes possible. Steel has a tensile strength up to ten times that of iron; it can withstand impacts up to six times as powerful; it retains its integrity at temperatures twice as high. With steel, suddenly inventors had a material that could be used to build the internal combustion engine, turbines in hydroelectric dams, modern weapons, and the modern bicycle, to name but a few achievements.[24]

Such processes lead to the development of discrete complexes of technologies, each derived from a basic innovation or discovery. This too is a useful way to think about the overall process of scientific-technical revolution. An early example would be steam power: the development of the steam engine powered

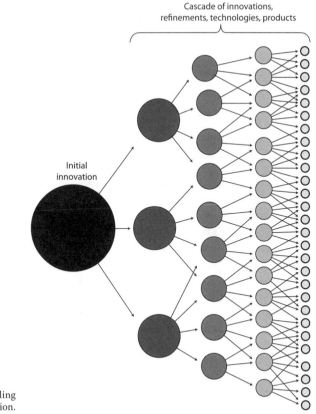

Initial
innovation

Cascade of innovations,
refinements, technologies, products

Figure 2.2 Cascading
Innovation.

the development of the coal industry, drove massive gains in productivity as
steam-powered machines were introduced in factories, and sparked a transportation revolution in the form of the railroad and steamship. Another such
complex, half a century later, derived from early developments in electricity,
which drove the development of the chemicals industry, enabled advances in
metallurgy, generated thousands of new consumer products, and underlay the
growth of the hydroelectric power industry—with five hundred installations
by 1900, most of them in Europe and North America.[25] A third such complex—
built around petroleum—included the internal combustion engine, automobiles, airplanes, artificial fibers, and eventually plastics (particularly polyvinyl
chloride [PVC], polyethylene, and polystyrene, all developed in the 1930s).[26]

    We may conceive of the scientific-technical revolution as a succession of
energy regimes, too. The premodern energy regime, in which muscle power
and heat from wood-burning fire provided the vast majority of energy, gave
way at the end of the eighteenth century to the era of coal; coal gave way to oil

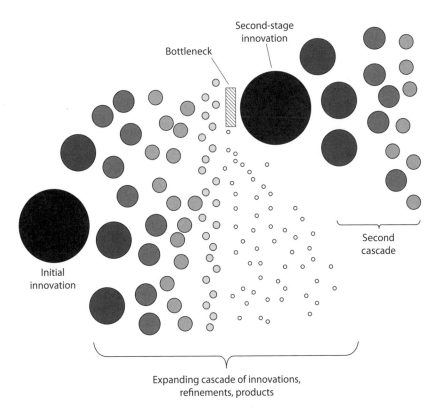

Figure 2.3 Cascade–Bottleneck–Cascade.

and gas roughly a century later; they gave way in turn to electricity. In each case, obviously, the new energy source was added to, rather than replacing, older forms—so that coal is still the largest single source of energy in the world, but now electricity generated in nuclear plants also plays an important role in the world (chart 2.9).

Alternatively, we can see these energy regimes as distinctive technological eras. The late 1820s to the 1870s was the age of coal, iron, and steam; the 1860s to about 1905 was the age of electricity, steel, and organic chemistry; and 1905 to the end of the 1970s was the age of oil, the internal combustion engine, and mass production. In most cases, again, these "eras" are cumulative; complexes of technologies joined, rather than replacing, one another. In fact, the cumulative quality of technological change in part explains its enormous impact. As one layer of new technologies and products was combined with the next, social and economic processes were revolutionized and technology penetrated ever more deeply and broadly, particularly in the societies of the North Atlantic region that formed the epicenter of technological innovation.

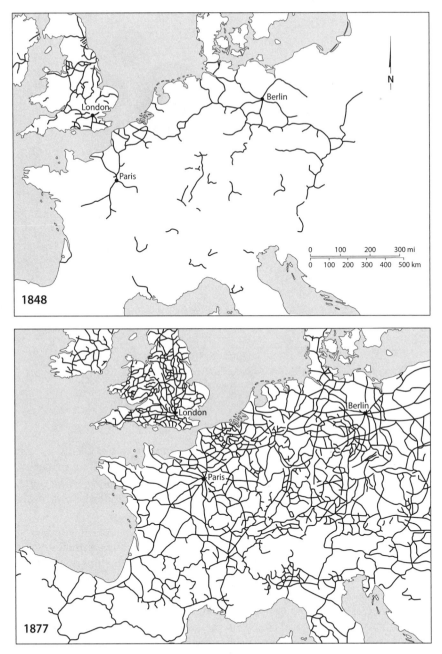

Map 2.1 European Rail Network, 1849 and 1877.

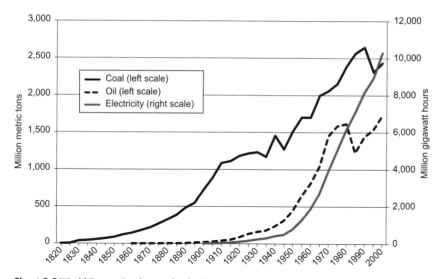

Chart 2.9 World Energy Production by the Top Ten Producers, 1820–2000.

There is one final way we may look at this great shift: Early in the second half of the nineteenth century an interlocking, related, progressive set of scientific and technical breakthroughs created a fundamentally different civilization than any that had ever existed before, bringing about a single, massive rupture, break, or leap in the history of humanity so that nothing has been the same since. The ongoing scientific-technical revolution that gained way (even if its origins lay considerably earlier) in that period has reshaped the whole world ever since, with widening geographic impact and deepening economic and social impact.

From this kind of long-term, global or bird's-eye perspective of the past 150 or 200 years, differentiating between the various complexes of technologies or eras of innovation is a relatively minor issue. So is the fact that the process took hold first in Western Europe and North America and then spread, with greater or lesser rapidity, to most of the rest of the globe. These details of timing and place help us to understand many of the particular ways in which nineteenth- and twentieth-century world history unfolded; but from the perspective of the ultimate outcome by the year 2000 or so, the simple fact of the rupture or break itself is what matters.

Energy production is a good indicator. For the past 200 years, especially since 1900, the amount of energy produced per human on the planet has grown inexorably. To judge by aggregate production of oil, coal, and electricity, the world used 3 times as much energy per capita in 1900 as it had in 1800, and 12.5 times as much energy per capita in 2000 as it did in 1900—37.5 times as much in 2000 as in 1800. There were six times as many people on the planet in 2000 as two centuries earlier, so that overall energy consumption for the human species was up by a factor of 225. And because machines have become progressively more efficient, the effective use of energy per individual human—the real impact of rising energy consumption—is far greater. A diesel engine today, for example, is about 35 times as efficient as a steam engine of 1750; a modern metal-halide lightbulb is 1,600 times more efficient than an eighteenth-century animal-fat candle.[27]

The increasing power of prime movers—the machinery used to drive other machines—is another good indicator. In 1500 most power in the world economy came from people, who can generate 50 to 90 watts of power. By 1700 in some parts of the world, the use of animals (horses or oxen, for example) was much more widespread; they can generate between 400 and 800 watts—a rise of one order of magnitude in one hundred years. By 1750 waterwheels had been added in many parts of the world; they could generate about 4,000 watts. By 1780 early steam engines could produce 20,000 watts. By 1900 the first steam turbine reached a million watts. The first 5 million–watt turbine was built less than a decade later, and the first 25 million watt turbine in 1912.[28]

The development of the major corporations that shape the world economy has been no less striking. Of the ten largest multinational corporations in existence in the year 2000, only two were formed after 1914.[29] In fact, one critical feature of the growth of the international economy in the period before World War I was the creation of a large number of transnational corporations, with operations in multiple countries and even on multiple continents. The French movie company Pathé, for example, had outlets in forty cities worldwide. Thirty British banks operated more than one thousand branches on six continents; three of them attracted one-third of all deposits in Brazil. And this pattern continued to expand into the 1920s. By 1930, International Telephone and Telegraph operated telephone systems in Spain and seven Latin American countries and did business in Romania, Turkey, and China, while Ford Motor Company had assembly plants in nineteen countries outside the United States.[30]

Among the most important of these transnational firms were the integrated oil giants, corporations of tremendous strategic importance for the world economy and, by the first decade of the twentieth century, for the global balance of power as well. Standard Oil (1870), Royal Dutch Shell (1890; merger in 1903), Unocal (1890), Gulf Oil (1900), Texaco (1902), and Anglo-Persian Oil (now British Petroleum or BP, 1908) operated almost from their beginnings on a global scale. The oil fields in the south of the Russian Empire were developed largely by French companies and investment (and those of Swedish immigrants to the Russian Empire, the Nobels); the oil resources of Romania, by American, German, and French companies; those of Indonesia, by British and Dutch companies; those of Persia (today Iran), primarily by British firms; and those of Mexico and Venezuela, by British and American.[31]

In short, the institutions that were founded to exploit the technological innovations of the late nineteenth century established themselves as among the dominant institutions of human social life, and maintained that position for more than a hundred years. The twentieth century is, among other things, the century that these corporations shaped.

TECHNOLOGICAL CHANGE, EFFICIENCY, AND GROWTH, 1850–1930

> Why should things cease at man? Why should not this rising curve rise yet more steeply and swiftly? . . . [W]e are entering upon a progress that will go on, with an ever-widening and ever more confident stride, forever. . . . [W]e can foresee growing knowledge, growing order, and presently a deliberate improvement of the blood and character of the race. . . . [A] day will come, . . . when beings, beings who are now latent in our thoughts and hidden in our loins, shall stand upon this earth as one stands upon a footstool, and shall laugh and reach out their hands amid the stars.[32]
>
> H. G. Wells (1913)

A distinctive feature of the new civilization created by this scientific, technological, and economic revolution was (and continues to be) the extraordinary speed with which new technologies have been developed, adopted, and spread. In previous centuries technologies spread slowly, taking decades or centuries to move from one region or country to another. The printing press, for example, likely originated in China probably in the eleventh or twelfth century, and arrived in Europe in the fifteenth. Even in the late eighteenth and early nineteenth centuries the techniques, machinery, and expertise required for early industrial development spread quite slowly through Europe. Great Britain had a tremendous advantage in cotton cloth, coal, and iron production for some decades, from about 1800 until 1860 or 1870. In the late nineteenth and early twentieth centuries, by contrast, key innovations often moved across the North Atlantic world and beyond in a matter of a few years. The first electric locomotive, for example, was built by the German engineering firm Siemens in 1879; in the United States the first electric streetcar system was built just nine years later in Richmond, Virginia. By 1902, 99 percent of horse-drawn urban mass transit in the United States had been eliminated. London introduced the first of its famous motorized double-decker buses in 1904, and by 1911 horse-drawn buses were gone, eliminating the need for 25,000 horses.[33]

Looking more closely at the development of particular technologies, we can discern a pattern of ever faster adoption and growth. In the case of energy technologies, for example, oil and gas production ramped up after 1880 much faster than coal production had after 1850; and electricity production ramped up faster still after 1900. And note, too, the compressed time to innovation—it took five or six decades to go from coal to oil, but only two decades to go from oil to electricity. Steel production in Europe ramped up much faster in the 1870s through the 1890s than iron production had in the late eighteenth and early nineteenth centuries. It took a century, from 1790 to 1890, for the major producers in Western Europe to reach 15 million tons of iron production annually; it took only thirty-five years for them to go from near zero to 15 million tons of steel, by about 1900. The same dynamic appeared in the United States a bit later, but moved even faster. It took that country eighty years get to 5 million tons of annual iron production, and only twenty to reach 5 million tons of steel. Heinrich Hertz discovered electromagnetic waves in 1886, Guglielmo Marconi invented wireless telegraphy in 1896, and the first transatlantic message was sent in 1901—just fifteen years after the initial scientific breakthrough. We have become accustomed to this pace of change—we are still in the midst of it, and it seems normal. But in the late nineteenth century, such a rapid race forward was unprecedented. As the acute observer of technological innovation Edward Byrn put it in the journal *Scientific American* in 1896, this was "the most remarkable period of activity and development in the history of the world."[34]

The reason for this rapidity in the innovation, adoption, and dissemination of technology is simple: the efficiency gains that could be made were gigantic. Moving from horse-drawn transport to trucks, for example, saved 60 percent of the cost of commercial haulage and mass transit. A delivery truck could cover six times as much area as a horse cart, and required one-seventh of the garage space. In the United Kingdom, between 1861 and 1881, 110,000 manual farm laborers were replaced by 8,000 workers making or using agricultural machinery (tractors, threshers, binders, and the like), for a savings in labor costs of 93 percent. The development of the autoclave to sterilize food for canning in 1874 increased the speed of canning by a factor of thirty and radically improved the average quality and reliability of preserved foods, revolutionizing the food-processing industry. The blast furnace method of producing steel was invented in 1856 by Henry Bessemer; after Siemens developed the open-hearth system five years later, efficiency rose by 70 percent. The death rate due to typhus in Pittsburgh plummeted by 75 percent within three years of the introduction of chlorination in 1907.[35] In the United States as a whole, typhus-related deaths fell by a factor of ten between 1908 and 1940. This disease, a scourge of human society for centuries, was effectively gone within less than a generation.[36]

The impact of the technological revolution on labor productivity and on overall social efficiency, in other words, was revolutionary. These were not the incremental gains of gradually maturing technologies; these were transformative advances derived from completely new technologies. They developed, were adopted, and spread so quickly because the payoff was huge.

By the 1890s, technological advances not only generated enormous productivity gains and returns on investment but also created a qualitatively new kind of economy. The fundamentals of the economic revolution were driven by basic production techniques and new materials, but by the 1890s, advances in technology, in the productivity of labor assisted by machinery, and hence in GDP per capita were generating a new economic structure in Western Europe and North America. This was the consumer economy, in which economic growth was driven as much by mass consumer demand as by demand for capital goods—as much by the production of household appliances, for example, as by demand for locomotives or power plants.

The number of basic consumer products invented in this period is astonishing, including automobiles, refrigerators, typewriters, vacuum cleaners, bicycles, lightbulbs, ballpoint pens, and antiperspirant. A remarkable number of familiar brand names date from this period as well. In the United States alone, the Hoover vacuum-cleaner (1907), Kellogg's Corn Flakes (1896), Coca-Cola (1886), Quaker Oats (1884), Aunt Jemima pancake mix (1889), and Hershey's chocolate (1894) became household names. In tandem with these, the modern cash register was developed as well (1883).[37]

Twenty or thirty years after the emergence of this new economic pattern, mass demand for consumer goods generated a further profound innovation in production techniques: mass production using assembly-line methods. Again, the efficiency gains were tremendous. In the first major deployment of assembly-line techniques, the Ford Motor Company cut assembly time for an automobile chassis from twelve hours and thirty minutes in October 1913 to two hours and forty minutes in December, yielding a labor cost savings of 80 percent. The massive gain in productivity allowed Ford to double wages while cutting the workday from nine to eight hours. It also allowed a rapid expansion in production. In 1909 Ford produced a hundred cars per day; in 1914, it was producing a thousand. Production of this large, expensive consumer durable had exploded by an order of magnitude in just five years. And it continued to grow: by 1929, Ford produced over 5 million automobiles in one year. Similar developments were occurring all across the industrial economy; total industrial production in the United States almost doubled in the 1920s alone. That rate of growth could be sustained in part because higher wages generated demand; as Ford remarked, "Our own sales depend in a measure on the wages we pay. If we can distribute high wages, then that money is going to be spent and it will serve to make storekeepers and distributors and manufacturers and workers in other lines more prosperous and their prosperity will be reflected in our sales."[38]

That pattern—rising productivity, expanded production, consumer demand driven by rapidly rising per capita incomes—was a central feature of economic growth in the twentieth century. It marked birth of the affluent consumer society. These techniques took some time to spread across industries and across economies; and much of the history of the world economy in the past century is the story of how and when that happened.

An appreciation for the suddenness and intensity of this historical rupture, then, is clearly essential to understanding global history in the past century. Equally important, however, is the process's finer geographic structure. In our time, for example, China and India are catching up in GDP per capita, but are still far less wealthy, per capita, than the North Atlantic region, Japan, or Australia. And it was of enormous short-term historical importance in the twentieth century that the scientific-technical revolution took hold first primarily in Western Europe and North America, and that the societies of that region—we can call it the North Atlantic world—were the first it transformed.

The whole process of industrial transformation began in Great Britain; spread first to the United States and parts of Northwest Europe (Belgium, the Netherlands, northern France); and then, by the early twentieth century, moved south and east through Europe—with Russia and Italy, for example, seeing significant industrial development by 1900, and isolated parts of Spain and the Balkans by 1910. This process made the North Atlantic the core of a new, restructured world economy. A long history preceded this transformation, in which European economic, military, and political penetration of other parts of the world occurred, reaching back to the sixteenth century and becoming particularly significant in the eighteenth. What happened in the course of the late nineteenth and early twentieth centuries, however, was the establishment of a new pattern of global economic exchange, characterized by a new level of integration, a massive expansion of trade in basic resources, and the rapid proliferation of truly globe-spanning enterprises.

There is one simple reason for this emergence. The North Atlantic world, where the industrial and technological revolution was taking place, had adequate supplies of some of the resources that the new technologies required—particularly coal and iron, which were mined in great quantities in Britain, Germany, Poland, France, Belgium, Russia, and the eastern United States (Pennsylvania, Alabama, Kentucky, Ohio). But many of the key materials required by modern industries were not available in these places in adequate quantities. This included cotton; nonferrous metals such as copper (for electrical wiring), tin (for canning food), tungsten (for lightbulbs), and aluminum (for airplanes); rubber for tires and oil for fuel (available in great quantities in the Americas, but not in Europe). Phosphates for use as fertilizer were abundant in North America but not in Europe; the same was true of gold. Not least, the revolution also required food. As industrial technology advanced, the North Atlantic economies reoriented toward industrial production, and their populations grew rapidly. Increasingly they sought to feed all those industrial workers by importing food from elsewhere. Consumer demand in the wealthier industrialized societies also included tropical products, such as coffee, tea, cane sugar, and bananas.

As a result, the development of the European industrial economy was interdependent with the development of a global economy geared to supplying those resources. In fact, increasingly global commerce was reoriented toward extracting primary products and commodities from outside the North Atlantic and shipping them there in return for manufactured goods.

That reorganization is the topic of the following chapter.

Reorganizing the Global Economy

GLOBAL COMMODITY EXTRACTION, 1870–1914

> Finance capital is interested not only in the already discovered sources of raw materials but also in potential sources, because present-day technical development is extremely rapid, and land which is useless today may be improved tomorrow if new methods are devised . . . and if large amounts of capital are invested. This also applies to prospecting for minerals, to new methods of processing up and utilizing raw materials, etc. etc. Hence, the inevitable striving of finance capital to enlarge its spheres of influence and even its actual territory.[1]
>
> V. I. Lenin, 1917

The transformation of the economies of the North Atlantic region created a global economic revolution, as industrial producers there reached into many other parts of the world to secure materials crucial to industrial development, while producers of raw materials and food in those regions linked up with buyers in the North Atlantic. Not only did the industrial economies have a burgeoning appetite for such materials, but their rising relative wealth and technological sophistication also gave them the means to satisfy those appetites. They had the economic power to reshape the world economy in such a way as to sustain their unprecedented growth. Increasingly, economies outside the North Atlantic were restructured to enable what we might call *commodity extraction*—trade in raw materials from exporters outside the epicenter of world industrial development in the North Atlantic, in return for finished goods from that region.

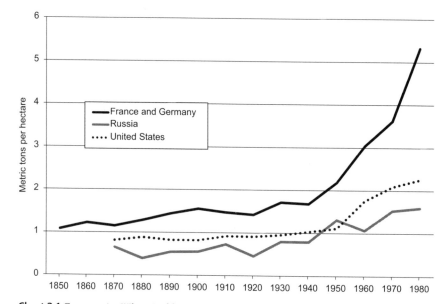

Chart 3.1 Comparative Wheat Yields, 1850–1980.

Food was a critical component of this exchange. Europe's population was growing rapidly; largely because of European immigration, North America was experiencing even faster population growth. But an increasing proportion of that growth was going into cities. In Europe the total population grew by about 70 percent between 1850 and 1910, but the number of people in cities with over 10,000 inhabitants more than quadrupled; there were four times as many people in the United States in 1910 as in 1850, but twelve and a half times as many living in cities with over 100,000 inhabitants. A growing proportion of the labor force was producing not food, but other things.

The productivity specifically of agriculture, however, was not (yet) rising substantially. The production of food per acre would start to rise steeply after World War II; but before 1940 it rose only gradually (chart 3.1). Northwestern Europe in particular, therefore, began to import large amounts of food from other parts of the world. This was particularly true of Great Britain, the most industrialized and urbanized European nation. Some of that food came from Russia and Eastern Europe, but a growing proportion came from outside Europe. The United States was a big exporter of food to Europe in the nineteenth century; but by 1900 its own rapid urbanization meant that it was consuming most of the food it produced, and there was little surplus for export. So food came to Europe from elsewhere—namely, from the newly settled grasslands around the world. Particularly important were Argentina, Canada,

Australia and New Zealand, and Siberia. Somewhat later, the great rice-producing regions in the Asia-Pacific zone began to play a significant role as well. Thus the United States was the greatest world exporter of meat before 1900, but thereafter Argentina, Uruguay, Australia, and New Zealand stepped in to meet European demand (chart 3.2). The pattern of grain exports was similar: before 1885 the United States was the greatest exporter of wheat in the world; thereafter the world grain market was increasingly dominated by wheat and rice from South America, Asia, and Australia (chart 3.3).

The economic opportunity represented by the growth of the world market for food was a critical reason for the conquest and settlement of the world's grasslands and rice deltas after the middle of the nineteenth century. Some of the key food-exporting economies in the Americas and the Asia-Pacific region saw explosive export-led economic growth after mid-1880s. Argentina's economy, for example, grew by about 7 percent per year in the 1880s; between 1890 and 1910 the country's population doubled, but the value of its exports almost quintupled.[2] Many regional economies became highly export-oriented. In Latin America, exports amounted to 18 percent of gross national product in 1900—almost half again as high as in Britain (13 percent) and almost three times as high as in the United States (6.7 percent).[3] In 1909–14, Argentina and Canada together produced 26.8 percent of the world's wheat exports. Russia produced roughly another 25 percent. Butter exports from Siberia—in refrigerated trains—rose by a factor of seven in just fifteen years, between 1897 and 1912.[4] The net result: by the turn of the twentieth century an integrated global agricultural economy had begun to form, centered on the cities of Northwestern Europe and North America as consumers and the new regions of intensive settlement—grasslands and rice deltas—as producers.

Overall, wheat was a much larger share of the world grain market than rice (or other grains, such as rye), but rice played a particularly important role in the broader development of the world economy. Most rice exports flowed to one or another of the major centers of world population; about 80 percent of rice exported from Burma went to Europe, for example, and a large proportion of rice from Southeast Asia went to China. But some of those exports from the new rice delta regions went to feed workers in plantations and mines in the colonial economies of the region itself—for example, tea plantations in Ceylon (Sri Lanka), coffee plantations in Viet Nam and Indonesia, and rubber plantations and tin mines on the Malay Peninsula. By 1900 these areas imported 50 to 70 percent of their food.[5] Some rice went as far as Africa and even the Caribbean. The development of the rice deltas was crucial, therefore, in supporting the extraction of other commodities globally. An interesting example is groundnuts or peanuts, produced in West Africa and used in part for food but mostly as a source of lubricants in the form of peanut oil, which played an important role in industry before the boom in petroleum. Peanut

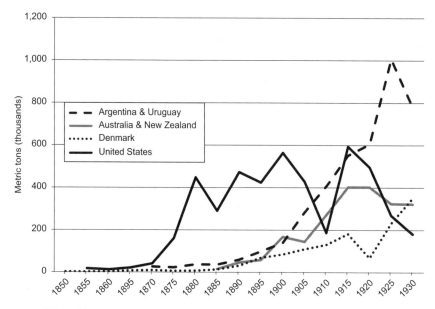

Chart 3.2 World Meat Exports, 1850–1930.

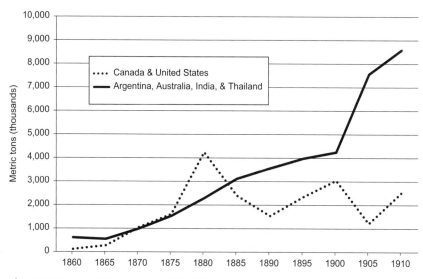

Chart 3.3 Wheat and Rice Exports, 1860–1910.

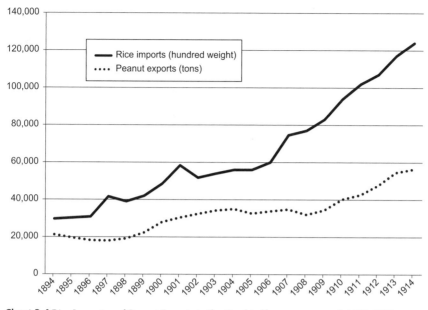

Chart 3.4 Rice Imports and Peanut Exports in the Gambia (five-year averages), 1894–1914.

exports from the Gambia, in West Africa, tracked reasonably well with rice imports into that region up until World War I (chart 3.4). Producers in the Gambia, that is, imported rice in order to feed workers growing peanuts for export to Europe. This was just one case that illustrates a growing pattern of specialization in the emerging global economy from the mid-nineteenth century onward, dependent on the expansion of food production in challenging biomes.

With sufficient labor, capital, and food supplied by the new world economy, expansion in the production of selected raw materials and commodities could be spectacular. Gold, for example, not only had considerable monetary value but also played a key role in underpinning the growth of world trade in the later nineteenth century, when the major currencies were pegged to its value. Initial significant gold discoveries were made in Australia and California in the 1850s; but from the beginning of the 1890s heavy mining investments rapidly ramped up production above all in South Africa, where the newly discovered goldfields of the Boer republics in the interior were conquered by the British Empire in a bloody war between 1899 and 1902. Thereafter, British investment quickly expanded South African production (chart 3.5). Or take sugar, which was important in the global food industry (chart 3.6). In 1900 Europe produced, from beets, about two-thirds of all sugar in the world.[6] But sugarcane from tropical regions was an important secondary source. After it

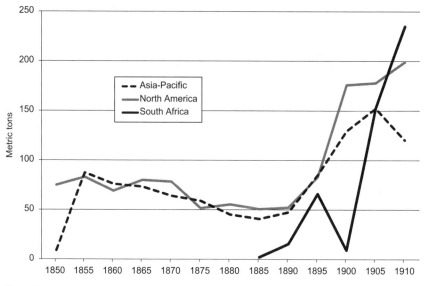

Chart 3.5 World Gold Production, 1850–1910.

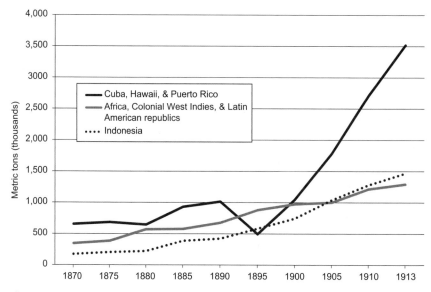

Chart 3.6 World Sugar Production, 1870–1913.

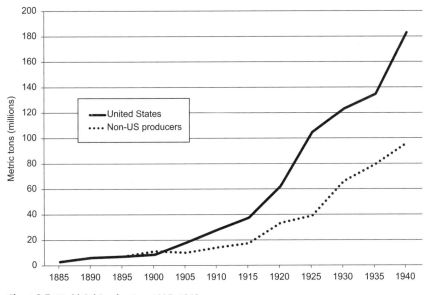

Chart 3.7 World Oil Production, 1885–1940.

conquered key sugarcane-growing areas in the 1890s, the United States made substantial investments in the sugar industry and massively expanded total world production.

But it was not always conquest that led to the expansion of commodity extraction. In the case of oil, the Russian Empire and the United States produced roughly equal (and very small) amounts of oil until 1900; thereafter the United States—at first Pennsylvania, but soon Ohio, Indiana, Oklahoma, Texas, and California—consistently produced about two-thirds of world oil supplies, with Latin America, Russia and Romania, and European colonies in the Asia-Pacific region (before the 1950s, primarily Indonesia) each producing between a fifth and a tenth as much as the United States (chart 3.7). Paper products present a similar picture (chart 3.8). Industrial societies use enormous amounts of paper—for print publications, packaging, record keeping, newspapers, and so on. Newspaper circulation in Japan in 1905 was 1.63 million copies, but by 1931 it was ten million; in Russia in 1913 it was 3.3 million, but by 1940 in was 38.4 million.[7] All that paper requires a lot of trees, which were increasingly scarce in Europe. Scandinavia, long the primary source of paper for the European market, continued to expand production rapidly. But after World War I, Canada flooded the world market, putting itself on the way to becoming the largest exporter of paper products by 1950. Countless other commodities around the globe followed the same pattern: a sudden jump in output starting at some point between 1870 and 1910.

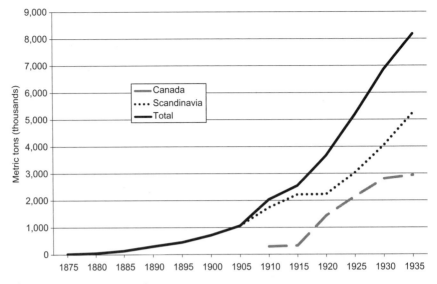

Chart 3.8 Paper and Wood-Pulp Exports, 1875–1935.

The years between about 1870 and World War I, then, constitute a distinctive period in the history of the world economy—when the economies of the North Atlantic (and later of Japan) and many non-European areas became mutually dependent in a new way and to a new degree. Histories of Western Europe and North America in this period often focus on the economic and social revolution created by industrialization; but that revolution depended on economic links to new areas of settlement and development all around the globe—and it sparked complementary economic and social transformations in those regions.

In this early phase of the international division of labor, the narrow targeting of investment and the resulting local specialization of production were often so intense that a single country, colony, or region emerged as the dominant global supplier of one or another of these commodities. At the beginning of the twentieth century, three-quarters of the world's vanadium, for example, used in producing specialty steel for industrial purposes, came from Peru (the rest from Spain and the United States). Chromium came above all from New Caledonia (though also from Russia and Rhodesia). Tungsten, the basis of the lightbulb industry after 1913, came mainly from Burma (though also from the western United States and Portugal). Tin, used in making cans, among other goods, came from Malaysia and Indonesia. Nickel came from Canada.[8] Nor was this true only of mineral resources. Brazilian coffee production almost quadrupled between the 1880s and the 1910s, and Brazil alone produced almost three-quarters of the world's supply by 1901; even in 1930, it still produced almost two-thirds.[9]

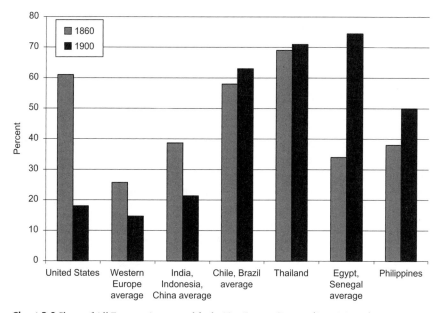

Chart 3.9 Share of All Exports Accounted for by Top Export Commodity, 1860 and 1900.

One consequence of this concentration was the rising dependence of many economies on one export commodity—and of some states, as well, on the revenues from exports of that single commodity. The opposite pattern prevailed in Western Europe and the United States, where single commodities (such as cotton in the United States) made up a declining proportion of the total value of exports. Overall, in the North Atlantic core around 1900, the single largest export in any given economy typically accounted for between 6 and 18 percent of total exports, and usually a declining share; and individual countries tended to have many, and a rising number of, trading partners. A similar pattern emerged in some extremely large, diverse countries or colonies outside Europe—China, India, and Indonesia all diversified exports over time. But smaller countries or colonies often saw heavy and increasing export dependence on a single product. This was true even in Brazil, Egypt, the Philippines, Algeria, and Thailand (chart 3.9). In Egypt cotton made up 78 percent of exports; in Manchuria soy products (used for food, fertilizer, soap, and industrial and cooking oils) accounted for 81 percent; in Nigeria palm oil for over three-quarters. Sugar and tobacco accounted for 93 percent of Cuban exports in 1914; in 1910 coffee and rubber accounted for 72 percent of Brazil's export total.[10] In broader aggregate, in 1913 just the top ten export commodities from non-European countries accounted for 56 percent of all non-European exports.[11] This pattern prevailed well into the twentieth century. In 1928, one product still accounted for more than half of all exports in ten countries in Latin America. And in that year, almost 70 percent of all Latin American trade was conducted with only four countries (the United States, Britain, France, and Germany).[12]

For the global economy as a whole, the improved efficiencies generated by such specialization were enormously beneficial. As later chapters show, those benefits were unevenly distributed, since export-based colonial economies generated profits largely for companies based in the industrial societies of the North Atlantic and Japan, and for the local elites who owned the land, plantations, or mines that drove exports.[13] But the last decades of the nineteenth century saw a remarkable take-off in world trade. Global shipping, in tons of carrying capacity, rose by a factor of almost twelve—from about 4 million tons in 1800 to 47 million in 1913.[14] In some respects the world economy was more integrated in 1913 than it would be in the 1970s. Exports as a proportion of GDP reached a peak for Europe and the United States in 1913, then fell until the 1950s, and did not exceed the 1913 level until the 1970s. For most of Asia and Latin America the peak came in 1929, with recovery again only in the 1970s.[15] Between 1800 and 1914 aggregate world output grew by about 7 percent per decade, but world trade grew by about 33 percent per decade.[16]

Not surprisingly, in terms of sheer value, Europe dominated world trade. That dominance was partly an illusion generated by political geography: European countries are quite small, and goods did not have to travel far to cross international borders. Consequently, a sizable proportion of goods moving internationally within Europe traveled no farther than much domestic trade did in, say, the Russian Empire, China, Brazil, or the United States. Despite this proviso, however, the North Atlantic region's supremacy in the world trade was clear right up to 1913 (chart 3.10). Also not surprisingly, aggregate world trade was dominated by trade in primary products, or raw materials, because many of the industrializing economies exported substantial quantities of not only manufactures but also raw materials—such as coal from Britain and the United States and grain from Russia. Primary products accounted for just over 60 percent of the total in aggregate value throughout this period.[17]

Again, corporations based in the industrializing world actually controlled a large proportion of exports from other regions—either because by controlling trade or through actual ownership of the mines or plantations and direct management of production. By the 1920s foreign companies controlled more than 50 percent of exports from Cuba, Chile, Peru, Venezuela, Iran, Malaysia, and Indonesia. Two French and one British company together controlled two-thirds to three-quarters of all exports from West Africa. Operations run by the giant Anglo-Dutch conglomerate Unilever controlled 80 percent of Nigeria's external trade.[18] Two North American companies—Anaconda and Kennecott—dominated Chilean copper mining, and foreign-owned companies produced about 60 percent of Peru's exports. By 1928 American companies produced three-quarters

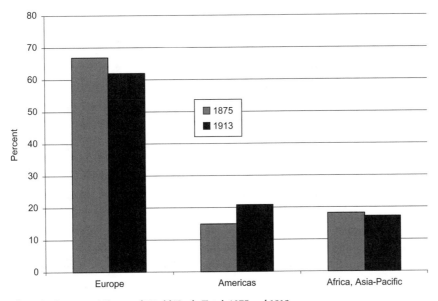

Chart 3.10 Regional Shares of World Trade Total, 1875 and 1913.

of Cuba's sugar, which accounted for most of the country's exports.[19] In this way, the disproportionate concentration of industrial and financial resources in the North Atlantic gave entities based in this region the power to extract commodities from the rest of the world. The dominance of Europe and, later, the United States and Japan as sources of direct investment explains this pattern (see chart 2.3). Corporations there collectively invested huge amounts of money in other parts of the world in order to develop their resources for profit.

Multinational banking and trading companies based in the industrial societies also built the financial infrastructure that enabled such investments, extending banking services to much of the rest of the world. By 1928, British multinational banks operated more than 2,250 branches in Latin America, Africa, Asia, and the Pacific; the Yokohama Specie Bank had forty branches abroad; US-based Citibank had one hundred branches abroad, two-thirds of them in Latin America.[20]

Statistics on exports of manufactured goods, therefore, give a clearer picture of the world balance of economic power. Here Europe was clearly dominant in the early twentieth century (chart 3.11), though its primacy was slowly eroding as North American and Japanese industrial exports grew. The trade relationship between India and Britain is emblematic of the overall pattern of world trade: in 1913, manufactured goods accounted for 79 percent of the value of Indian imports, while 77 percent of the country's exports were food and raw materials.[21]

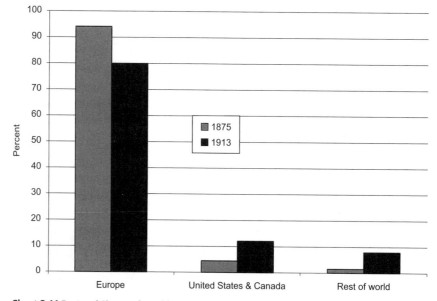

Chart 3.11 Regional Shares of World Trade in Manufactured Goods, 1875 and 1913.

Finally, North American and European companies also usually built the transportation and communications infrastructure that provided the broad foundation for business and economic development. International Telephone and Telegraph (USA) and the Great Northern Telegraph Company (Denmark) were critical in building communications networks in Latin America, for example.[22] The railway network in Argentina (map 3.1) was built out after 1880 primarily with British capital, in part to facilitate the export of food, again largely to Britain. The Argentine meatpacking industry too, which froze meat for export in refrigerated ships, was largely foreign-owned—initially by British, later by American, investors. This pattern was fairly typical for Latin America, where British capital played a key role. For the continent as a whole, British investments rose almost ninefold between 1870 and 1913; by the latter date, they accounted for about two-thirds of all foreign capital invested in Latin America; and in Argentina, where British involvement was particularly heavy, over one-third of all fixed investment (in factories, railroads, and other assets) was owned by foreigners. Whereas Mexico had 750 miles of rails in 1880, it had 12,000 by 1900, almost all of the increase financed by foreign investors. As a result, exports ballooned by a factor of nine between 1877 and 1910.[23] But a similar pattern held in the Russian Empire, in much of Central Europe, in Canada, and to a large extent even in the United States. British capital was particularly important in building the transportation infrastructure

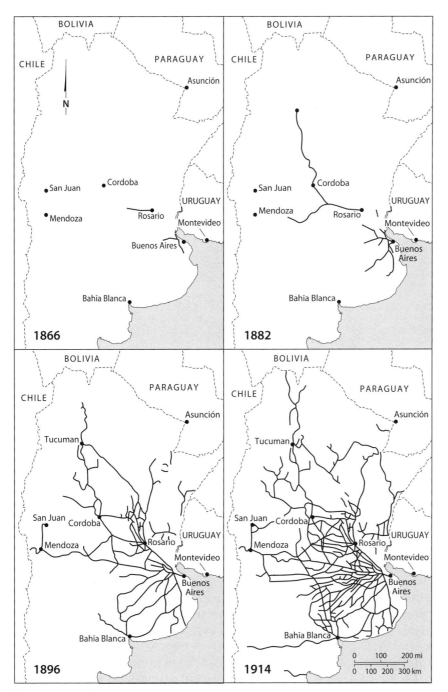

Map 3.1 Argentine Rail Network, 1866, 1882, 1896, and 1914.

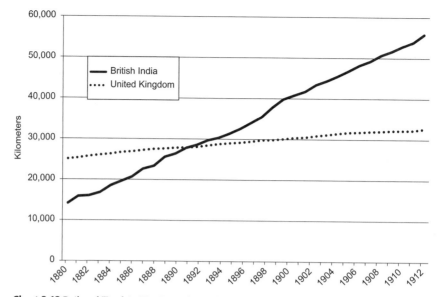

Chart 3.12 Railroad Track in Use, United Kingdom and British India, 1880–1912.

in North America, Australia, and India. For industry in the United Kingdom, investment in colonial or other non-European areas became an important economic opportunity toward the end of the nineteenth century, since the rail network in the home country was more or less complete by the 1880s, while in the colonies it was still expanding apace (chart 3.12). The same was true of Holland and its colony in the East Indies (what later became Indonesia).

Development of the global communications network followed the same pattern. Intercontinental communications, obviously, were critical to the growth of international business and multinational corporations. The first transoceanic telegraph cable was laid across the North Atlantic in 1858. In 1870 Britain completed a telegraph line to its crucial colony in India (extended to Australia in 1872). A transpacific telegraph cable was not completed until 1902. The first transcontinental telephone line was built in 1915, across the United States. Before World War II world telephone systems remained confined almost exclusively to the North Atlantic; indeed, the technology was so rudimentary, and costs so high, that as late as 1927 there were only some fifty telephone conversations per day between New York and Los Angeles.[24] Nevertheless, telegraph and telephone systems did gradually weave an ever denser web of communications around the world. But that web was by far densest in the North Atlantic, and virtually all of it was built and owned by companies based in the same region.

Clearly, then, the economic relationships that emerged as this global commodity economy was built up were quite lopsided. Corporations and capital based in the North Atlantic and Japan formed the dominant elements; the pattern of trade was highly asymmetrical; and in important cases, such as India and Indonesia, producers in the North Atlantic region had the advantage that their own national governments exercised political control over the regions that produced the commodities they bought. Where this was not the case, and where local authorities or businesspeople did not want to cooperate in the development of the global economy, the industrial societies often had the financial and military power to force them to do so. Increasingly in the late nineteenth century, they did so. The global economic order built around commodity extraction was, therefore, often enforced at the point of a gun—through gunboat diplomacy, trade wars, or imperial conquest. This imbalance of power is addressed later in this chapter.

Paradoxically, however, the expansion of world commodity extraction after the middle of the nineteenth century was also sufficiently dynamic to rupture important structures of economic exploitation that, in many parts of the world, had been central to the eighteenth-century economic order. In particular, it turned out that personal servitude was usually not optimally compatible with the new order of commodity extraction. The early stages of the nineteenth-century world economy's development, therefore, saw a large part of the world engulfed by a veritable wave of liberty.

FREE TRADE AND EMANCIPATION, 1840–1890

> The Chilean Government may be assured that a liberal commercial policy will produce the same result in Chile as in England, that is, the increase of government income and the increase of the comforts and morality of the people.[25]
>
> British Foreign Office, 1853

> Chile can be industrial, for it has the capital, arms and activity; but . . . [t]here is strong foreign capital represented in the importation of manufactures. This capital is and will always be disposed to place as many obstacles as it can before the establishment of industry in the country. . . . Protectionism should be the mother's milk of all infant arts or industries . . . because without it any nascent progress is exposed from the beginning to the ferocious and well-combined attack of the foreign imports represented by free trade.[26]
>
> *El Mercurio*, May 4, 1868

Two, apparently opposed trends increasingly roiled the international scene in the last third of the nineteenth century. On the one hand, starting as early as the 1840s, the societies of the North Atlantic region applied direct force to impose unequal economic relationships on societies outside that region, which were falling ever further behind in both financial and military capacity. On the other hand, a wave of emancipation of unfree labor spread throughout the Atlantic world. This linkage—imperialism and emancipation—poses something of a conundrum. We usually think of unfree labor and imperialism as connected, complementary forms of coercion. Historically, they had been linked. An important part of the modern history of serfdom was the expansion of the Prussian, Muscovite Russian, and Austrian Empires in Eastern and East-Central Europe. And the first wave of colonial expansion in the Americas was built at least in part on the enslavement of indigenous American populations and of Africans. Yet the third quarter of the nineteenth century saw both the rise of what historians have called the New Imperialism and an enormous wave of formal emancipations.

Emancipation was a long, slow process.[27] Between the last quarter of the eighteenth century and the first quarter of the nineteenth, slavery was abolished in a large number of societies around the Atlantic world—in Britain in 1777, in most of what soon became the northern United States in the 1770s and 1780s, and in most of the new South and Central American republics after independence in the 1820s. At the same time, serfdom was abolished in Prussia in 1807 and in some western parts of the Russian Empire (what are now the Baltic states) in the 1810s. In 1838 Britain outlawed slavery in its colonies (with a five-year transition period of "apprenticeship"), and France did the same in 1848. The slave trade (as distinct from slavery) was abolished by Britain and the United States in 1807–8 and then, through the first half of the century, by a large number of local measures and international treaties, in most of the rest of the world, ending with Brazil in 1850, the Ottoman Empire in 1857, and Cuba in 1862.[28]

By 1850, however, the greatest centers of unfree labor still had not abolished human bondage. They included Russia, the southern states of the United States, Cuba, and Brazil. Russia emancipated its serfs in 1861; in the United States, slavery was abolished in 1865; Cuba abolished slavery in 1886; and Brazil finally did so 1888.

These emancipations were world historical events. In Russia, emancipation in 1861 freed perhaps 30 million serfs; in the United States in 1865, it freed just short of 4 million slaves, about one-third of the South's population. In Cuba and Brazil the process was more gradual—in 1870–71 the two nations passed laws that freed the children of slave mothers when they reached age twenty-one; the slave population in both countries was already falling before that—in Cuba from 436,000 in 1841, to 370,000 in 1861, to 200,000 in 1877, with only 53,000 slaves remaining when emancipation was finally completed. The pattern was similar in Brazil—2.5 million in 1851, 1.5 million in 1872, and even fewer by 1888.[29] Still, viewed in longer-term perspective, even in Brazil and Cuba the end of slavery was an extraordinary and rapid social revolution. In 1850 one could still describe these societies as built on slavery; by 1890 slavery was gone.

Why?

One reason is that in many cases slavery was held to be incompatible with the ideas of the Enlightenment and the spirit of the Atlantic revolutions of the late eighteenth and early nineteenth century, which were built on those ideas. The ideals of liberty, equality, and fraternity, as well as the liberal faith in material and cultural progress through the release of individual initiative and creativity, underpinned by the recognition of universal rights, were powerful modern ideas in the nineteenth-century world; and many of the champions of those ideals argued that slavery simply did not fit. Thus France abolished slavery in 1794, during the radical phase of the French Revolution; reintroduced it in 1802, under the dictatorship of Emperor Napoleon Bonaparte; and then abolished it again in 1848, during another liberal revolution. Most of Latin America abolished slavery in the course of its struggle for independence against Spain in the 1820s. In many cases the resistance or flight of slaves themselves was an important part of the liberation process, and helped lend credence to the belief that the desire for freedom was universal. The most striking case was that of Haiti, where the greatest slave rebellion in modern times smashed French colonial rule in a drawn-out, destructive, but ultimately successful republican revolution in the 1790s and early 1800s. There were serious, albeit failed, revolts in Jamaica and the US South in the 1830s, and low-level violence and conflict were endemic in servile societies—including the Russian countryside. The fear of insurrection persisted for decades, and the danger of such an upheaval was one argument used by abolitionists.[30]

Yet ideas alone were not sufficient. Although some of the Enlightenment's champions abhorred slavery, many others had no problem reconciling the two. After all, in the United States many leaders of the former southern colonies had managed to take a leading intellectual and practical part in the American Revolution while continuing to own slaves. As for the danger of insurrection, in some cases it merely encouraged the development of more draconian and pervasive disciplinary systems. In fact, slavery was thriving in the American South at mid-century—between 1810 and 1860, the number of slaves in the southern states more than tripled, from 1.1 million to just short of 4 million.[31]

A second cause was religious. The middle decades of the nineteenth century saw a major wave of religious innovation (examined in chapter 4). In the United States this movement is often called the Second Great Awakening; but it was a global phenomenon. A number of radical Protestant sects in this period argued that slavery was incompatible with the Gospel and with the dignity of man, created in the image of God. The moral and religious intensity of the anti-slavery message was one important reason for its political power; the US Civil War, for example, was for many in the northern states, at its roots, a crusade against an institution they considered immoral and even sacrilegious.

Here too, however, ideas did not suffice, for many white Christians in the United States, for example, found religious sanction for slavery in the Bible. And emancipation in Russia and in Latin America involved very little of this religious intensity. So this too is an important factor in bringing about emancipation, but not a sufficient one.

Another crucial factor was the changing structure of the world economy. For one thing, both slavery and serfdom were, in their origins, responses to a shortage of labor—or rather, an imbalance between plentiful available land and a relatively sparse population. In Russia and Eastern Europe, serfdom survived its origins in the Middle Ages because population density was low and land-owners had the opportunity to expand production to feed the growing cities of Western Europe. In the Americas, the ravages of disease, and the disruptions caused by conquest and colonization, brought about the demographic collapse of indigenous populations starting in the sixteenth century, and thereafter tropical diseases continued to decimate populations in some of the most economically important areas—particularly the sugar-producing islands of the Caribbean. The demographic revolution discussed in chapter 1 compensated for these problems. By the second half of the nineteenth century, Russia's population was growing at a healthy rate—indeed Russia would face a massive famine by the 1890s. In the Americas, mass migration from Europe meant a rapid reduction in the need to force people to come there to work—they were coming voluntarily, by the tens of millions. As one historian of Brazil has observed, by the mid-1880s many slaveholders in that country—harassed by abolitionists in the cities, facing increasing difficulty in recovering runaway slaves, and with the state subsidizing mass immigration from Europe—concluded that "the institution had become unworkable, troublesome, and more expensive than hiring immigrants."[32]

Serfdom in Russia took a similar trajectory. Russian peasant serfs farmed the land for mostly absentee landlords, and did so inefficiently. They had little or no training, and lacked the education to pick up the latest advances in technology and technique. They had very little capital, because their landlords took as much as they could get in rents while showing little interest in investing in land they did not directly farm themselves. Peasant land was managed collectively by the village community, thereby stifling entrepreneurial effort. And there was little incentive for serfs themselves to improve their methods, since they did not own the land—any investment they made in their farmland would be the property of their landlords. By the first third of the nineteenth century, as the potential of economic development and technological advance became apparent, the Russian czar and leading figures in his government concluded that the system was outdated and had to go; and the proportion of the population in serfdom was in any case already falling, from over 50 percent in 1800 to under 40 percent by 1858. A growing proportion of those serfs were no longer engaged directly in labor service to their landlords; they paid rents or fees instead.[33]

The United States was the exception: the South was prospering on the basis of slave-powered export-driven commodity extraction—the production of cotton, shipped to the growing textile industry in the northern states and in Britain. Driven by steadily increasing demand, slave agriculture in the South was making steady productivity gains—by developing improved strains of crops, by opening new land to the west (for example, in Texas), and perhaps also through the application of escalating coercion.[34] In the United States, however, slavery was crushed by an invasion from the northern states, where rapid industrialization was attracting tens of millions of immigrants. Those growing industries needed tariff protection from British industry, which was better established and larger. Southern producers, in contrast, benefited from free trade—they were export-dependent. The US Civil War originated in part in a struggle, reaching back to the 1830s, over tariffs. This was hardly the sole cause of the Civil War; moral and religious convictions also played a crucial role. But it was part of the long-term emergence of incompatible social and economic systems in North and South. At the same time, southern slaveowners frightened by the possibility of slave rebellion were concerned to maintain absolute stability in their own social and intellectual environment; and they were increasingly hostile to the spread of ideas associated with the commercial, industrial, and political development of the North. The tensions between the nation's two sections became critical with the conquest and intensifying settlement of the West— including the annexation of Texas, California, and the desert and mountain West (1845–48) and the early settlement of the Great Plains (particularly Kansas and Nebraska, which became states in 1854). The Civil War was fought at least in part over the question of how this expanding continental empire would be integrated into the new Atlantic world economy: as a stability-conscious commodity-extraction dependency on the periphery of the North Atlantic economy, or as a part of that economy's dynamic industrial-commercial core.[35]

A further important economic factor was that by the mid-nineteenth century even economies based on commodity extraction and exports required an increasing degree of flexibility in their labor force. In an ever more dynamic world economy, it was difficult to predict what commodities would be the crucial ones. Export-based economies had to be ready to shift from one commodity to another quickly as the needs of the market changed, often in response to sudden technological advances. In the 1820s, for example, silver mined at Potosí in Peru accounted for 80 percent of Argentina's exports. By 1850, livestock-based exports accounted for 80 percent. Over half of those exports were hides for leather; the rest was dried meat, most of which went to the slave plantations of Brazil and Cuba. The gradual decline of slavery in Brazil and Cuba ate into those exports; but that loss was compensated for by the growth of Britain's textile industry, which created a growing demand for wool. In 1820, there were 4 million sheep in Argentina; in 1850, 14 million; in 1865, 40 million, with wool accounting for 45 percent of Argentina's exports. Then in the 1880s, cotton cloth became more prevalent in the global economy, and the supply of cheap cotton from India, Egypt, and the US southern states ramped up. The Argentine economy shifted gears again, and grain farming expanded. At the same time, improvements in refrigeration revitalized the meat industry, as high-quality meat could now be shipped in refrigerated steamships to markets in Europe.[36] Similar patterns arose in many places around the world—for example in Brazil, where demand generated by new industries and expanding consumer demand created consecutive booms in the production of various commodities (sugar, coffee, cotton, rubber), requiring extremely rapid expansion or reallocation of the labor force.

A free labor force was a major advantage in this economic environment because it allowed greater flexibility. Immigrant countries such as Brazil and Argentina could import the skills they needed—first Irish and Spanish shepherds, then Russian wheat farmers and British stock raisers. Most African slaves had to be trained, and natural population increase could not meet these sudden shifts in labor demand. It was also more difficult—and thus more expensive—to move slaves from one region and industry to another. In Brazil in the 1870s and 1880s priority shifted from sugar production in the North to coffee production in the South. But southern coffee farmers wanted to buy only young male slaves of working age; so northern sugar farmers were stuck with a population consisting increasingly of women, old people, and children—on the whole a less productive labor force.[37] One solution was to free them in order to escape the cost of feeding and housing them.

In fact, modern transportation technologies made possible extraordinary degrees of flexibility in the global deployment of labor. In a number of economies in the Atlantic region by the 1890s, labor could be imported to meet seasonal demand for construction or agricultural work, and could be sent home or to other labor markets in the off-season. Italian farm and construction laborers, for example, could work during the summer and fall in Italy or southern Germany or on the East Coast of the United States; work in the southern summer and fall in Argentina or Brazil; and then return northward again for the summer and fall. This new transatlantic labor market was created by faster and cheaper steamship transportation, which radically reduced times in transit between these hemispheric labor markets. In the middle of the nineteenth century, it took six weeks to cross the Atlantic on a sailing ship; fifty years later, steamships took one week.[38]

There is, of course, something disappointing here—namely, that one of the decisive factors behind this great wave of liberty was economic. Yet, actually, the pattern precisely fit liberalism, one of the two dominant ideological traditions of the period (the other being conservatism) and the intellectual trigger of the late-eighteenth-century Atlantic revolutions. The theory of liberalism was that the advance of knowledge, the growth of commerce, the development of the human spirit, and the progress of freedom all would go hand in hand, creating a world more moral, more godly, more enlightened, and freer—as well as wealthier. Looking back from 1890, this seemed exactly the story of the nineteenth century. Liberals had no problem with the idea that liberty made good economic sense. In the United States, what the great Civil War historian Eric Foner called the ideology of "Free Soil, Free Labor, Free Men" was based precisely on that convergence of moral right and economic benefit.[39] In fact, it would be a mistake to distinguish between economic and moral arguments against slavery, because its opponents argued that the institution was both morally corrupting and economically stifling—the one because of the other.[40]

As it turned out, however, many of those freed by the great emancipations did not find much success in the new economy. The Russian peasant economy only very slowly escaped from the inefficiency of serfdom, in part because the emancipation law required the peasants to pay compensation to their former masters, and in part because farming was mostly still under the control of village communities and absentee landlords, rather than individual farmers. In the American South after the Civil War, most white southern landholders retained their property and were able to use the sharecropping system, debt peonage, vagrancy laws, laws that made failure to pay debts a criminal offense often punishable by a term of convict labor, discriminatory race-based laws, and outright violence (most famously by the Ku Klux Klan) to create a system that in many cases was "little more than a concealed and modernized form of slavery," as one historian has put it. Ex-slaves in Cuba and Brazil struggled with similar obstacles. There, various mechanisms of property rights and credit arrangements were used to create new forms of de facto bound labor. In fact, the expansion of sharecropping, plantation agriculture, and agricultural credit systems conducive to debt peonage appears to have significantly expanded the geographical scope of these diverse forms of technically free but practically coerced labor.[41]

In other areas of the world employers replaced much outright slavery with a system of labor migration that amounted in some ways to *temporary* slavery: contract labor. Particularly for Indian, Chinese, and Pacific Islands workers recruited to work in mines and on plantations in Southeast Asia, Latin America, South Africa, and the Pacific, labor conditions, pay, and the terms of labor contracts were extraordinarily poor. These were often very poor people with few or no resources with which to defend themselves, working in remote areas far from their homes, and citizens of governments that had little clout or of lands that (in the case of India) were colonies and so could not defend their rights effectively. They were recruited for periods of three to five years or longer and paid at set wages; they often lived in barracks or dormitories, sometimes under guard; they could, according to work rules imposed by their contracts, be fined heavily or even beaten for infractions of labor discipline; and they often had no alternative but to shop at company stores where prices were grossly inflated. One historian of Chinese immigration has referred to this system as "paraslavery."[42]

The advantage for employers, on the other hand, was that these workers had no local connections or alternative forms of employment and, once they had served the terms of their contract, they could usually be returned to their country of origin. Particularly in Southeast Asia and South Africa, where local populations were already fairly dense, this was ideal: contract laborers were used to extract a particular commodity—often doing tasks that local people, who might have a small farm or business of their own and who had relatives who could help them fight poor working conditions, were not interested in doing—then they were shipped back home. Far from the dominant form of migrant labor in these regions, it accounted for only about 10 percent of the total. But it was a crucial labor supply for some important forms of commodity extraction and for railroad building.[43]

In the southern United States this form of contract labor was rare; but debt peonage in the context of sharecropping was common. Under this system, people could be legally forced to "work off" debts incurred for seed and equipment. Here, too, conditions often approximated slavery. Once in such a position, it was extremely difficult for people to get out, so debt peonage became a kind of "free market" servitude. A similar system was widely used in Latin America, particularly where plantations produced for export. To a considerable extent, then, the promise of expanding liberty was illusory.

Much more shocking, for liberals, moreover, was the fact that despite the apparent onward march of liberty within societies, the international order in the last third of the nineteenth century was not characterized solely by the peaceful expansion of commerce. Instead, conquest, coercion, and violence quite frequently played an important role in the organization of the new world economy. In some colonial regions—particularly West Africa, where there was a long tradition of slavery—various forms of coerced labor were widely used. These included the so-called corvée, or labor service, and taxes that could be paid in either money or labor. Such systems were commonly used by colonial governments to build roads, railways, levees, and other public works.[44] Here too the treatment of workers was often brutal—in part because colonial authorities faced little accountability for their actions. In other cases, colonial regimes required payment of taxes in kind. The most radical example was in the Congo Free State, a personal colony of the king of Belgium, where quotas for the delivery of rubber to the colonial administration were established and enforced with ferocious brutality—as by burning villages, cutting off the hands or ears of workers, beatings, and mass "resettlement." As many as 5 million Congolese may have lost their lives in thirty-two years under this regime. Ironically, in some cases, particularly in Africa, colonial expansion was rhetorically justified by European aggressors as a means of bringing civilization and freedom to "backward" peoples who, for example, still practiced slavery.[45]

How did societies committed by both inclination and interest to liberty get themselves into the position of imposing this kind of violent exploitation?

"FREE" TRADE AND IMPERIALISM, 1840–1920

Our largest trade must henceforth be with Asia. The Pacific is our ocean. . . . China is our natural customer. . . . The Philippines give us a base at the door of all the East. . . . The Power that rules the Pacific . . . rules the world. . . . A lasting peace can only be established by overwhelming forces in ceaseless action until universal and absolutely final defeat is inflicted on the enemy.... [We must] establish the supremacy of the American republic over the Pacific and throughout the world until the end of time.... Mr. President, this question is deeper than any question of party politics; deeper than any question of the isolated policy of our country even; deeper even than any question of constitutional power. It is elemental. It is racial. God has not been preparing the English-speaking and Teutonic peoples for a thousand years for nothing but vain and idle self-contemplation and self-admiration. No! He has made us the master organizers of the world.... And of all our race He has marked the American people as His chosen nation to finally lead in the regeneration of the world. This is the divine mission of America, and it holds for us all the profit, all the glory, all the happiness possible to man.[46]

Senator Albert Beveridge, 1900

The gangrene of colonial rowdyism is infecting us, and the habit of repressing liberty in weak nations is endangering our own.[47]

Wilfred Scawen Blunt, 1896

In the first three quarters of the nineteenth century the growing appetite of the North Atlantic economy for raw materials and food, and its growing need for markets in which to sell the products of its growing industries, meant that it increasingly depended on commerce and was fueled by it. Not surprisingly, the North Atlantic societies and states took a whole range of steps to facilitate the expansion of global trade.

To begin with, the North Atlantic powers developed key technologies in transportation and communications. More efficient steamships, for instance, drastically lowered the cost of shipping goods around the world. The average cost of seaborne shipping for British producers, for example, surged during the period of imperial wars in the second half of the eighteenth century, but then plummeted by almost three-quarters by 1900 (chart 3.13). The completion of the Suez Canal in 1869 drastically slashed shipping costs to and from Asia. The Panama Canal, completed in 1914, was similarly important, as was the building out of the world rail network (chart 3.14). The global railway network continued to expand rapidly right up until World War I, again, partly because as the European network reached maturity, European firms and investors devoted growing resources to building the transportation infrastructure around the globe. The same pattern held in communications, in which intergovernmental organizational efforts helped by standardizing practices and charges—the formation of the International Telegraph Union in 1865 is an example, as is that of the Universal Postal Union in 1874. The size of the latter indicates the progress of global communications: it was formed by a meeting of representatives from twenty-one, mostly European nations (plus the United States, Egypt, and the Ottoman Empire) in 1874; it had more than fifty member states by 1888 (including British India, nineteen Latin American nations, Liberia, and Japan), more than seventy in 1914 (including China), and eighty-seven in 1929.[48]

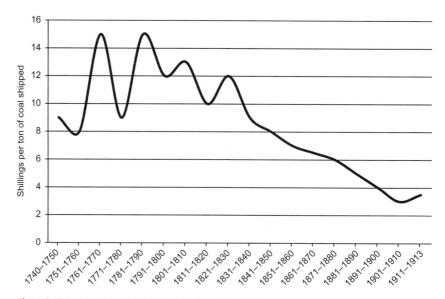

Chart 3.13 Freight Costs for British Shipping, 1740–1913.

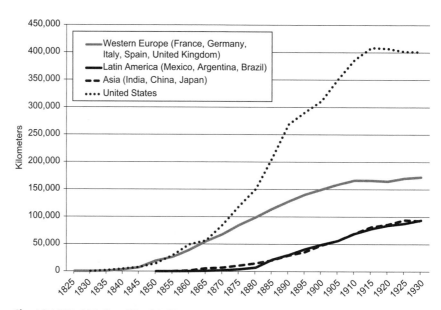

Chart 3.14 World Railroad Track in Use, 1825–1930.

A second important initiative was the signing of a large number of trade treaties that lowered duties on imports and in some cases even established customs unions or free trade zones. A free trade zone was created in northern Germany in 1837, the Zollverein (which simply means "customs union"). Most of what became the German national state (the German Empire) in 1870 joined by the early 1860s. In fact, to some extent the political unification movements that created modern Germany (1862–71) and Italy (1860–71) can be seen as part of this drive to develop larger, more open markets. In both cases, businessmen were an important part of the coalition of social forces that fueled nationalist movements, because they wanted to dismantle restrictions on trade across larger geographies in Central and Southern Europe. Equally emblematic (though less effective) was the Cobden-Chevalier Treaty of 1860 between Britain and France, which established the principle of "most favored nation" trade relations—that is, an agreement that the two countries will not impose higher duties on each other's goods than on any other country. This was a way of automatically updating trade treaties, with the expectation that trade would thereby be progressively liberalized. The Cobden-Chevalier Treaty was followed over the next fifteen years by some fifty other treaties, primarily but not only within Europe. The net result was that import duties within Europe fell on average by more than half.[49] In the 1870s and 1880s tariff levels in Europe rose again, as countries other than Britain began to industrialize and to protect their fledgling industries with import duties. The United States had successfully pioneered this strategy earlier, in the first decades of the nineteenth century, and that nation remained quite protectionist until World War II. Some Latin American countries, too, moved toward greater protection of domestic industry in the 1880s (after having signed treaties early in the century that opened their economies to European manufactured goods and helped to demolish industrial development on that continent). But the average world level of tariffs actually remained relatively stable from the late 1880s to World War I. In the context of rapidly falling transport costs, the net effect was a major decline in financial barriers to international trade.[50]

A third factor promoting global trade was the adoption of the gold standard, which pegged national currencies to a particular weight of gold. This was intended to help foster trade by stabilizing exchange rates; in the pre-computer era, that helped to limit uncertainty regarding prices and thus to reduce business risk. The United States more or less adopted the gold standard already in 1834, Britain in 1844, Germany in 1876, and most of Europe by the early 1880s.[51]

Outside the North Atlantic region, meanwhile, although trade treaties were important here too, European economic influence was in many cases secured primarily by investment and the development of trading and financial networks. Latin America was increasingly integrated tightly with the North Atlantic economy on a largely noncoercive basis (except internally, for example, through debt peonage), both by trade and by investment. Local economic elites were eager to seize the opportunities represented by North Atlantic markets and capital. By seeking out markets and credit and building the regional transportation infrastructure that linked their enterprises to the global market, they met halfway their counterparts in the North Atlantic, who themselves sought out commodities and investment opportunities. The development of the Argentine agricultural economy is illustrative: entrepreneurial landowners in Argentina sought in Europe the expertise, labor, and money they needed to seize the opportunities generated by complementary economic developments there. In the first half of the nineteenth century, such ambitions resulted in numerous low-tariff treaties with European states, particularly Britain.[52] Some countries achieved remarkable economic success with this strategy: Argentina, Canada, Australia, and New Zealand were among the wealthiest societies on earth in the late nineteenth century, largely on the strength of exports of food and raw materials.

The integration of Asia and the Middle East into the global economy was often more complicated. In some cases local initiative integrated economies into the world market in a pattern similar to that in much of the Atlantic world. Russian administrators in Central Asia, for example, found that local merchants were often eager to take advantage of the access to European markets that Russian conquest afforded. In the decades around 1900 more Indians settled in European-controlled eastern and southern Africa than did Europeans, and far more Chinese and Indians in what is now Malaysia. Merchants of both ethnicities used imperial relationships and connections to build globe-spanning commercial enterprises. While European firms dominated exports of rice from Southeast Asia to Europe, Chinese firms dominated exports to East Asia, and Indian firms controlled exports to India. Chinese businessmen commanded two-thirds of tin mining and one-third of rubber processing in Malaya, and 80 percent of rice processing in Indochina (what is now Viet Nam).[53] Conquest and empire, in other words, often created new opportunities for the enterprising.

Yet, in much of Asia, "free" trade was imposed by administrative fiat or even by military force, against the interests of local producers of finished goods. In the case of India and Indonesia, Holland and Britain had already established major colonial holdings in the eighteenth and early nineteenth centuries, and they steadily expanded the territory they controlled right into the 1900s through conquests, annexations, and treaties establishing European suzerainty. Both countries dictated almost free access to these giant markets for their own producers, often with disastrous results for local industry.[54] In fact, Great Britain's commitment to free trade was in part financed by its enforced trade surplus with British-ruled India. That surplus helped offset a trade deficit with Continental Europe and the United States; it thereby allowed British import demand to help fuel economic development around the whole North Atlantic.[55]

In contrast, the major independent states and empires of Asia often carefully controlled European economic penetration in order to preserve the existing structure of economic and social power. But here too, through the mid-nineteenth century the North Atlantic states made major political and military efforts to enforce "free" trade. In some cases, they won commercial concessions by taking sides in regional conflicts; in others, through judicious use of financial power and expertise.

In the Ottoman Empire, for example, Britain supported the central government in its efforts to retain control over its far-flung empire, including Egypt, where the reforming governor Muhammad Ali was seeking to create a more autonomous Egyptian state. In return, Britain required liberalized trade (under a treaty of 1838) and the abolition of government commercial monopolies—again with negative consequences for local industry. Most of British support came in the form of loans, and the Ottoman state fell deeper and deeper into debt; by 1874 about 60 percent of its budget went to interest payments. The Ottoman state was bankrupt by the late 1870s, and in 1881 French and British bankers assumed effective control of the central government's finances and trade policy. This financial dependence only deepened in subsequent decades; indeed in 1914 one British diplomat told the prime minister that the Ottoman Empire's "independence is a vanishing quantity before the advances of the French financiers." The Ottoman state never regained control of tariff policy; it took the nationalist revolutionary war after World War I and the creation of modern Turkey to accomplish that, in 1928.[56] This arrangement was not unique. Under Russian pressure, for example, Iran limited its import taxes to 5 percent of value; it too did not regain control of trade policy until 1928.[57] Nor were such treaties unique to this region, though they were often more draconian than in other parts of the world. Britain used its power as a creditor to induce the Brazilian government, for example, to accept a 15 percent maximum on import taxes.[58]

In other cases, direct military intervention forced local rulers to liberalize trade. The classic case is that of the so-called Opium Wars against the Chinese imperial regime. A system established under the Qing imperial government allowed European merchants to trade only at the port of Canton (Guangzhou) (and to have permanent residences only at Macau); movement of foreigners within China was restricted, and there were no permanent diplomatic or consular services. In 1839 Britain went to war to force the Qing government to allow greater opportunities for trade—in fact, specifically to allow trade in opium. The growing market for Chinese goods (particularly tea) in Britain and India had created a trade imbalance for Britain; opium exports from British India to China were the solution. Opium was at the time big business: by 1860 it accounted for 8.8 percent of the total value of global exports from non-European countries—the third largest share, after sugar at 14 percent and coffee at 10 percent, and ahead of cotton at 6.6 percent.[59] But the Chinese government, horrified by the economic and social consequences of widespread opium use, sought to restrict imports. The British attacked, won a string of victories, and forced the Chinese government to accept a more open trading regime. Tariffs were capped, a large indemnity was levied, the British annexed Hong Kong, and five ports were opened alongside Guangzhou (the so-called Treaty Ports, which were administered under European rather than Chinese law). The Chinese government, however, continued to try to limit opium imports; and in 1856 there was a Second Opium War, in which the French, Russians, and Americans joined the British in attacking China. Twenty thousand European troops marched on Beijing, burned the Imperial Palace, and crushed the Qing army. In the wake of the European victory, eleven more ports were opened, movement within China for foreigners was freed up, permanent embassies were established in Beijing, and the opium trade was legalized. Britain also annexed Kowloon, and Russia annexed Vladivostok, thereby gaining a year-round port on the Pacific Ocean.[60] From 1863 until 1929 Europeans ran the Chinese customs service and made sure tariffs on imports were minimal.

In Japan, a similar system of trade and contact restrictions was in place until 1853, when the Americans used steam-powered gunboats to force the government to "open" Japan to foreign goods and travelers. Perhaps cognizant of the Chinese example, the Japanese government did not attempt to get greater control of the trade relationship, and thus escaped the disastrous consequences of warfare with the West. In fact, the Japanese state and economy were powerful enough that by the end of the nineteenth century Japan was emerging as a powerful rival to the industrial and imperialist societies of the North Atlantic. Thailand too avoided war by opening its economy to imports through a series of treaties culminating in 1855.[61]

In other regions, by the last quarter of the nineteenth century, European economic, financial, and cultural penetration had reached such a degree that in some places intervention became necessary to protect important economic or strategic interests. One important variant was intervention to force countries that had borrowed money to repay loans on time, or at least to pay the interest. In some cases, so-called gunboat diplomacy was used to enforce such payment. In 1902 and 1903, for example, Britain, Germany, and Italy established a collective naval blockade of Venezuelan ports in order to force the Venezuelan government to pay interest on foreign loans and to offer compensation to European nationals for property losses they had suffered in the course of a bitter civil war in that country. Such actions were not at all uncommon; by one historian's count, Britain resorted to gunboat diplomacy seventy-five times during the nineteenth century.[62]

In other cases, outright military occupation was the preferred solution. At the end of the 1870s the Ottoman system of rule in Egypt was threatened by a nationalist revolt led by the military officer Ahmed Urabi. That revolt was sparked in particular by preferential treatment of foreigners (some eighty thousand of them); by the growing concentration of wealth in the hands of landowners producing cotton for export; by a failed war of imperial expansion in

Ethiopia; and by French and British control of Egyptian state finances. As noted above, Egypt had fallen deep into debt over the previous decades, and—as in Istanbul—financial administration had been passed to British and French bankers. Local nationalists resented this important loss of sovereignty. Their revolt seemed to threaten major British interests. Egyptian nationalists, it was feared, might use control of the Suez Canal to impose high transit fees (some three-quarters of shipping through the canal was British), or a nationalist government might default on the massive Egyptian debt to European countries (some of which derived from the cost of building the canal). So in 1882 Britain invaded and occupied the country.[63] The French had taken over Tunisia under similar circumstances the previous year.[64] By the early twentieth century the United States was adopting similar methods: it occupied Cuba for half of the twenty years between 1898 (the year the Spanish-American War began) and 1917, Haiti for the twenty years between 1915 and 1934, and Nicaragua for the twenty years between 1912 and 1933, all in large part to secure business interests. In 1903 it supported independence for Panama (then part of Colombia) in order to secure its direct control of the Panama Canal Zone.[65]

Finally, in regions where smaller-scale, less effective political and social organization prevailed, the problem of regulating burgeoning economic relationships was even more difficult. Here the issue was not so much that organized governments were restricting or regulating trade as that transportation systems were poorly developed, commercial law and legal systems rudimentary, and financial institutions limited or non-existent, and that no political entity was capable of building the kind of infrastructure on which more extensive trade depended. At the same time, local economies were often primarily subsistence-based, which made the development and exploitation of resources difficult. It often proved quite hard, for example, to persuade people to work long hours, for poor pay, at dangerous jobs, when they had the option of staying home and growing their own food. Thus, for example, migrant workers from all over southern Africa worked under contract in gold mines in South Africa from the 1880s, and were sometimes prevented from leaving their jobs and going home by armed guards posted around their dormitories and at mine heads.[66]

As demand for commodities grew, such difficulties often contributed to decisions to take direct political control—to establish colonial rule. This was one critical background factor in the sudden expansion of European empires, particularly in Africa—the "Scramble for Africa"—and in Southeast Asia in the 1880s and 1890s. Again, this new phase of colonial expansion is often referred to as the New Imperialism to distinguish it from earlier phases of conquest. In this period, military aggression and conquest frequently served important economic aims. That is not to say that economic gain was the only cause of European expansion: considerations of prestige, domestic politics, or perceived strategic requirements for the defense of existing colonies, or even simply the actions of local military commanders, also played a role in various cases.[67] But

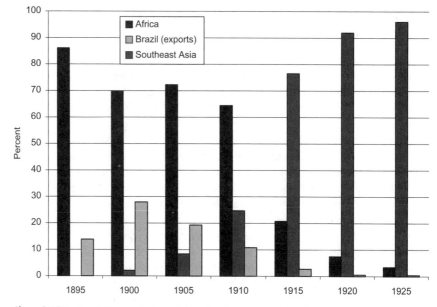

Chart 3.15 Regional Shares of World Rubber Production, 1895–1925.

specific economic goals, often defined by recent technological and economic developments, frequently played a crucial role as well. France, for example, had begun to conquer parts of Viet Nam at the end of the 1850s, and completed that process in 1885, largely for the purpose of establishing coffee, tea, tobacco, and rubber plantations. It established a "protectorate" over Tunisia in 1881, extending its control of North African mineral resources eastward from Algeria. Great Britain gradually took over what is now Malaysia in the 1880s and 1890s, in part to produce rubber and tin (chart 3.15). Both commodities were increasingly important for European industries, rubber for making bicycle and automobile tires, tin for canning food, among other goods.[68] Above all, the European powers sought to gain control of Africa's vast resources—difficult to develop for environmental reasons and given Africa's lack of transportation infrastructure, but potentially of enormous economic and strategic importance. The British seizure of Egypt in 1882, South Africa in a major war in 1899–1902, and much of inland West Africa (above all, Nigeria) in the 1890s; German expansion in what is now Mozambique and Namibia; Italian expansion in what is now Eritrea and Somalia, and later in Libya; and the French conquest of much of North Africa (Tunisia, Morocco, Senegal) were all motivated largely by this kind of calculation.[69]

In a number of cases, particularly in the 1890s, however, imperial expansion came at the expense of relatively large and well-organized states; and here too it was usually motivated at least in part by important economic stakes. Two such instances were the British conquest of the Boer Republics in southern Africa in 1899–1902, followed by massive expansion of gold mining there; and the conquest of Hawai'i, Puerto Rico, Cuba, and the Philippines by the United States in 1898, followed by massive expansion of sugar production. Japan, similarly, attacked its relatively well organized neighbors in the mid-1890s, taking direct control of Taiwan in 1895 and of Korea by 1905—in both cases in large part to build a richer resource base for its expanding industrial economy, as well as for room to settle its soaring population.

Despite all this commercial and colonial activity, the degree of overall dependence of the industrializing economies on markets and sources of raw materials in the less developed world was moderate. Economic historian Paul Bairoch has calculated that between 1800 and 1938 only 17 percent of developed-world exports went to the "Third World" (less developed regions). The proportion for manufactures was somewhat higher, between a quarter and a third in the early twentieth century. The developed world produced its own fuels until the middle of the twentieth century; it produced almost all its own iron; it imported 11 percent of its lead, 20 percent of its fertilizer (mostly phosphates), 21 percent of its copper, and 22 percent of its fibers (cotton, jute). But for some critical resources, the North Atlantic economies were entirely dependent on producers outside that region. Fertilizer, for example, came in the mid-nineteenth century primarily from giant guano (bird poop) deposits in the Pacific (Peru, Chile, Nauru) and South Atlantic (Patagonia, South Africa) and from phosphate deposits in North Africa and North America. The North Atlantic also got 86 percent of its tin and all its rubber from abroad (Brazil, Malaysia, Africa).[70] And the growth of more technologically sophisticated industries requiring rarer raw materials (oil, rubber, copper, aluminum) made imports from the less developed world increasingly important. Securing reliable access to supplies of such goods, or the land on which to produce them, was an important motivation for various forms of colonial expansion.

A further key to understanding this period of colonial conquest and commercial wars is, however, the declining cost of such military action. By the 1880s, advances in weapons technology in the industrial nations were making military victory over the armies of less technologically and industrially advanced societies relatively cheap. The rate of fire for standard infantry small-arms weapons in European armies rose from three bullets per minute in the 1800s, to ten in the 1860s, to sixty per minute for repeating rifles in the 1880s. In 1884 the first effective machine-gun was developed, firing eleven bullets per second. The effective range of infantry small arms rose from one hundred yards in the 1800s, to four hundred yards in the 1850s, to one thousand yards by the 1880s. Rates of fire and range for artillery weapons increased in proportion, and their destructive power was multiplied even more dramatically by the development of high-explosive shells. By the final decades of the nineteenth century, societies that did not have access to modern weapons were completely outgunned.

Where this technological imbalance did not exist, colonial wars could be very costly. It took the French a quarter century and 85,000 deaths to conquer Algeria between 1830 and 1857, because the Algerians were armed with weapons about as effective as those the French soldiers had. In a quarter century of fighting in Aceh, in northern Sumatra, 37,000 Dutch soldiers died before a combination of scorched-earth tactics and repeating rifles enabled the Dutch to conquer the region in the late 1890s. Ethiopia gained access to modern weapons in the 1890s, and defeated the Italian invasion of 1896. In the Second Boer War of 1899–1902 the tiny Boer Republics were able to secure modern weapons, not least because they had gold, and they were able to fight on for three years against the world's mightiest military power, inflicting 17,000 British casualties.

In contrast, the armies of states that could not afford or access these weapons were simply massacred. In 1897, an army of 32 Europeans and 507 Africans defeated the 31,000-man army of the Emirate of Sokoto, in what is now northern Nigeria. At the Battle of Omdurman in the Sudan in 1898, 25,000 invading British and Egyptian soldiers defeated the 40,000-strong army of the theocratic state established two decades earlier by a prophetic religious leader (Muhammad Ahmad, the Mahdi), killing 11,000 men and losing fewer than 100 of their own troops.[71] In fact, the balance of military power was sometimes so lopsided that local European commanders could simply take it upon themselves to launch campaigns of conquest, more or less independently of explicit instructions to do so. A French commander, for example, undertook a number of important conquests in 1882–83 around Hanoi, in the north of Viet Nam, in contravention of his orders. "Since the government . . . was foolish enough to send me 500 men," he remarked, "I set out to accomplish on my own what it lacked the nerve to make me do."[72]

Whatever the reasons, all told, between the late 1870s and 1914 the European powers, Japan, and the United States more than doubled the colonial population under their rule, from about 275 million to about 570 million. They almost doubled the land area they controlled.[73] Almost all of Africa, most of the Pacific, most of Southeast Asia, and parts of East Asia (including what are now Taiwan and Korea) were conquered.

The great majority of the soldiers involved in these wars on the imperialist side were local men hired by the imperial nations. In fact, in 1913 about 70 percent of all soldiers in the colonial empires of the world were local people— including 30 percent of soldiers in American forces, at the one extreme, and 98 percent in Belgian forces, at the other. In this sense, as one historian has put it, most colonies "conquered themselves."[74] British India was an extraordinary case: it supported an army, two-thirds Indian in makeup, that Britain used in the 1880s and 1890s to conquer the Sudan, Egypt, South Africa, Burma, much of the Persian Gulf region, and ultimately what is now Iraq, Kuwait, and Bahrain during World War I (a war in which 850,000 Indian troops served abroad and 62,000 lost their lives). To a remarkable extent, Indian soldiers conquered an empire for Britain.[75]

The same was true of colonial administration: the colonized governed themselves under the direction of a small top tier of colonial administrators. Thus in 1900 Dutch Indonesia, with a population of 35 million, was ruled by 250 European and 1,500 local civil servants who supervised a mixed array of local principalities. The British ruled India with a senior civil service of 1,250, supervising (by 1931) up to a million Indian civil servants and state employees.[76] This system worked in part because, in societies where large regional states had not existed before European conquerors arrived, loyalties were more often local than regional or "national"; but the wealthier industrializing societies also had the financial power to make military service and colonial administration lucrative opportunities for locals.

That is not to say that the new colonial regimes were beneficial to the majority of people they governed. The opening of colonial markets to imports from the industrializing imperialist economies often crippled local industry, and hence hindered long-term economic development. Imperial regimes preferred to negotiate with weaker local authorities, which meant breaking up larger political units and conquered states into smaller tribal entities. Over the long term that policy eroded the political integration of African societies, in particular. Further, in many cases both tribes and chiefs' "traditional" powers over them were at least partly invented by the colonial administrators for their own convenience. In the long run, this often weakened the legitimacy even of local political authority in colonial societies. Imperial governments were also determined to make the colonies pay for themselves. Often the day-to-day administration and development of colonies were simply delegated to private companies as a "concession" of rights to the resources of particular areas, in return for a share of the profits for the government. Before World War I, for example, forty-one private companies held concessionary rights to some 70 percent of the French colonies in West Africa. Motivated purely by profit and not subjected to close scrutiny, this system often resulted in selective investment in infrastructure (for example, rail lines running directly from mines or plantations to the coast, ignoring the needs of the local population) and in underfunded, arbitrary, ramshackle administrative structures. And where local economies and societies were less developed and productive, extraordinarily brutal methods were sometimes deployed to extract value and profits. In a shocking example, private administration of the Congo Free State cost millions of Africans their lives. But what one historian has called an "economy of pillage" was common elsewhere as well.[77]

The goal of administering colonial societies as cheaply as possible also meant that colonial governments invested very little in human capital—in education or health care, for example. At the end of forty years of British colonial rule in East Africa, about 2,000 students were graduating from the equivalent of high school each year—out of a population of some 24 million. Across Africa, 3 to 4 percent of young people were given a high school education, and overall literacy was about 10 percent. When the Congo became independent in 1960, there were fewer than twenty Congolese university graduates in the country, and not even one Congolese army officer.[78]

It should be pointed out, that this "New Imperialism" in Africa and Southeast Asia was escalating almost simultaneously with the great burst of genocidal land wars in settler colonies in the world's great grasslands. Argentina launched the final conquest of Patagonia in 1879; the United States finalized its conquest of the trans-Mississippi West in a whole series of "Indian wars" in the 1870s and 1880s.[79] The great movement of mass migration across the Atlantic also accelerated during this very same period, in the 1870s and 1880s up until World War I. So too did the building-out of the worldwide transportation and communications network. Colonial conquest was just one aspect of a much broader process of global economic development—one that, as we have seen, often entailed coercion, violence, and exploitation.

The historian Mike Davis has argued, moreover, that the most horrific consequence of the often fundamentally lopsided power relations within the emerging global economy was a series of terrible famines in multiple parts of the world in the 1870s and again in the 1890s. The number of fatalities from these famines is uncertain, but estimates of the totals range from 30 to 60 million. India and China suffered most; but Russia, Viet Nam, Java, Korea, Brazil, Algeria, Morocco, Persia (now Iran), and southern and southwestern Africa also saw major famines. These disasters were caused most immediately by a series of severe droughts; but the impact of climatic conditions was exacerbated by a concatenation of economic circumstances, above all the emergence of a global market in agricultural produce. In some areas the demand for nonfood crops (such as cotton, coffee, palm oil, tea, indigo, rubber) from wealthier societies ate into the amount of land devoted to food production; in others the greater purchasing power of consumers in industrializing nations meant that food might be exported from poorer societies even under famine conditions. The commercialization of the market for food also created incentives to hoard food when prices started to rise. Some colonial administrations deliberately structured tax systems and land tenure to maximize revenue generation and exports, rather than food security. In India, taxation drained away resources needed to maintain local irrigation systems critical to the food supply in low-rain years (even as the colonial state invested heavily in larger irrigation projects for export agriculture). At the same time, taxes and rents payable only in cash forced farmers into the global export economy to serve the needs of British industry and consumers, and the gold standard placed India, where silver was the metal traditionally used for currency, at a growing fiscal disadvantage. But in China the dislocations created by the Opium Wars, the Taiping and other revolts, and the predominance of the gold standard in the emerging global economy had a similar effect. In many areas economic reliance on single commodities also made whole regional economies vulnerable to sudden shifts in global production—as when investments in land or transportation, adoption of new technologies, or political and military action opened up new sources of cheaper supply. Where the food market was thoroughly commercialized, the results could be catastrophic. Major ecological stresses—a change in the course of the Yellow River in 1855, or a failure of monsoon rains due to the El Niño weather pattern—could turn these new vulnerabilities into a complex downward spiral of impoverishment, instability, low investment, and hunger.[80]

All of the processes explored in this chapter—mass migration, free trade, the building-out of the world communications and transportation infrastructure, imposed trade treaties, colonial and continental conquests, the growth of multinational corporations, and national unification in Italy, Germany, and the United States (the last between 1860 and 1865)—were part of one essentially unitary global effort: the attempt to reorganize the world economy around exchange between, on one hand, a new industrial, technological, financial, and political core region in the North Atlantic and Japan and, on the other, producers of primary goods and raw materials in much of the rest of the world. That attempt was not completely successful, as subsequent chapters will show. But it certainly was one central feature of world history in the period between the 1830s and 1913.

We have so far examined primarily the political economy of this process. But it also had significant intellectual and cultural origins, implications, and impacts, as well. One of these was directly connected to national unification, genocidal land seizure, and imperial expansion: the development of new languages of identity and difference, new ways to identify people who were "them" or "us." Paradoxically, a second was the emergence of an increasingly global culture in which ideas, institutions, and people circulated more and more rapidly and broadly on a planetary scale.

Chapter 4 turns to these two processes.

Localization and Globalization

RACE, ETHNICITY, AND NATIONALISM, 1830–1940

> I contend that we are the finest race in the world and that the more of the world we inhabit the better it is for the human race.... It is our duty to seize every opportunity of acquiring more territory and we should keep this one idea steadily before our eyes that more territory simply means more of the Anglo-Saxon race more of the best the most human, most honorable race the world possesses.[1]

Cecil Rhodes, 1877

> The carefully nurtured yet noxious plant of national egoism is shedding its seeds all over the world.[2]

Rabindranath Tagore, 1938

By the late nineteenth century the transformation of the world under the impact of the accelerating scientific-technological revolution was having major intellectual and cultural consequences. This chapter is devoted to some of them. Chapter 5 then turns to the "Great Explosion" of the early twentieth century—the massive wave of revolutions and wars between about 1905 and 1945. That wave of wars and revolutions grew out of the economic-political transformation of the period from 1867 to 1905, but it also grew out of the cultural globalization of this period. In no case is that clearer than in that of ideas about race, ethnicity, and nationalism—a complex of closely interrelated ideas that, in various forms and mixtures, grew increasingly important in world history, arguably until the middle decades of the twentieth century.

There are of course important differences between these three ideas, and they are discussed later in this chapter. But equally clearly, they are all ideas about sameness and difference—about who is considered "we" or "us," and how those who are not "us" differ from "us." Historians often refer to these ideas as discourses, languages, or vocabularies of identity.[3] In the nineteenth century all three ideas were substantially new. Before the late eighteenth or early nineteenth century, most people identified themselves in much narrower or much broader terms than these. Most people in most of the world identified locally—as members of a village, city, or regional community or of a clan, tribe, province, or linguistic group. So people thought of themselves not as "Germans," for example, but as "Bavarians" or as citizens of Munich. People thought of themselves not as "Africans" or as "Nigerians," but as "Yoruba" or as citizens of the city of Ifé. Many people, however, also identified themselves primarily by their religion—not French or Spanish, but Catholic or simply Christian; not Nigerian or Malian, but Muslim.

In contrast, in most societies a small number of people of high social status thought of themselves primarily in terms of their caste, and as related to people of similar caste from a broad geographic area. The European nobility, for example, thought of themselves as essentially different from everyone else in Europe, and they intermarried across political boundaries, shared the pleasures of international centers of recreation and education such as spas and universities, and not infrequently served multiple imperial governments (though usually consecutively, not simultaneously). Something similar was true of elites in India and in China, and across the Muslim world in the Middle East and into South and Southeast Asia and East Africa. What is more, wealthy and educated people all over the world—people who, for example, could read and particularly those who could read the great learned languages of the world such as Latin, Arabic, Persian, or Chinese—thought of themselves as "civilized" people and therefore having something fundamental in common.

During the late eighteenth and increasingly into the middle of the nineteenth century, these older forms of identification were gradually supplemented by race, ethnicity, and nationalism. They were certainly not obliterated; in fact, as the following section of this chapter underlines, religious identities continued to be important, and old and new conceptions of identity often became (as one recent study puts it) "entwined."[4] But increasingly, ideas about race, ethnicity, and nationality became a crucial part of how people thought of themselves and others, and therefore also a crucial political force. Chapter 3 touches on the formation of the German and Italian national states, in the 1860s and 1870s, as part of the history of free trade; but the creation of those nations was also the result of a growing wave of nationalist sentiment. That kind of thinking was underpinned by a discovery, in the early nineteenth century, of folklore—the beliefs, practices, and habits that seemed to define people as belonging to a particular cultural community.

The Grimm brothers, authors of a collection of German folktales, offer a good example. In 1837 Jacob Grimm and his brother were dismissed from their university professorships because they supported political liberalism and nationalism; during the wave of liberal revolutions across Europe in 1848 Jacob was elected to the new German National Assembly. After the defeat of that revolution, the Grimms worked to standardize German as a national language by writing a German dictionary—a common project in the period, during which many national languages were effectively invented by nationalist intellectuals.[5]

As the Grimm brothers' political activism suggests, the creation of the idea of nationality, in particular, was a political project, as well as a cultural one. In fact, the rise of nationalism can be seen as in part a response to a broad crisis and consolidation of state structures in many parts of the world, lasting two or three decades from the 1840s. During this time states and societies struggled to deal with the accelerating consequences of the development of the global economy and global cultural exchanges—in some cases violently, in others less so, but in almost every case ultimately by building larger, more interventionist, more centralized, more effective administrative structures and at least attempting to drive forward some degree of modern industrial and commercial development. Such were the aims of the liberal constitutionalist revolutions that swept Europe in 1848 and the 1870s. The US Civil War was part of, and encouraged, the radical expansion of the American state. The regime of Porfirio Díaz in Mexico, which ruled for most of thirty-five years after 1876, centralized the Mexican state and sought to develop the Mexican economy by opening it to foreign capital. In the Great Mutiny in India in 1857, poor Indians and some local elites rose against British domination and perceived threats to indigenous religious communities and practice; that uprising led the British government to take over the administration of much of India (until then in the hands of the private East India Company).[6] The Taiping Rebellion in China (and lesser rebellions in southwest and northwest China in the same period) was one inspiration for subsequent attempts by some of the Qing elite at "self-strengthening" through the adoption of modern industrial and military technology and organization. The Meiji Restoration in Japan in 1868 established a more centralized and effective national government in response to the European challenge, and pushed forward the development of Japanese commerce and infrastructure, laying the foundations for Japan's industrial and imperial expansion after 1890. In the Middle East the Tanzimat reforms in the Ottoman Empire attempted (with less success) a similar transformation starting in 1839.[7]

In many of these cases, more effective states made strenuous efforts to foster a sense of national identity. They used the schools to teach national languages and national histories; formally adopted national anthems and flags; used national armies to forge shared faith in national greatness; pushed forward the building of railways and telegraph systems as a means of tying the nation together economically, culturally, and socially; and required people to use the national language, rather than their own "dialects," in their day-to-day dealings with the authorities, such as teachers, commanding officers, judges, and postal and telegraph officials. In the Ottoman Empire, for example, decades of administrative and economic consolidation after 1839 put in place the whole gamut of administrative, financial, and legal measures common across the globe in this period—including the creation of a national tax service; post offices; new national codes of criminal, civil, and commercial law; a national census; a flag and anthem; national ministries of education and of health; railway and telegraph services; public universities; a central bank and national banknotes; a stock exchange; and legal equality for members of religious minorities. Those measures culminated in the creation of a new constitution in 1876.[8]

Nationalism was important, moreover, even where such efforts failed. As discussed in chapter 3, the British occupation of Egypt in 1882 was sparked in part by an important nationalist or autonomist movement among educated Egyptians who felt that Egypt was a distinct historical and cultural entity that should have political autonomy.[9] Similar nationalist movements were at work all over the world in this period—in Poland, for example, where nationalists rebelled (unsuccessfully) against Russian imperial rule in the 1830s and again in the 1860s; and in Hungary, where nationalists in 1867 won limited autonomy from the (German-speaking) Habsburg government in Vienna under a new "dual" monarchy.

Even within already stable state structures, the idea of nationality was central also to the expansion of parliamentary government and the extension of suffrage (the right to vote) in this period, which again were global phenomena encompassing the North Atlantic, all of Latin America, Japan, Australia and New Zealand, and (less successfully) the Ottoman Empire. Representative government was expanded to give the vote and full rights of political participation to more and more citizens of states, based on the idea that everyone within the nation was "the same" in some essential way, because all shared a "national" identity and interests. Thus, Britain passed important extensions of the suffrage in 1832, 1867, and 1885; Brazil became a republic in 1889; Germany and France adopted universal adult male suffrage in 1871, and Austria in 1907; Italy and Argentina adopted adult male suffrage in 1912; and Japan adopted a limited parliamentary constitution in 1889 and adult male suffrage by 1925. In 1893 women even gained the vote in New Zealand, the first national state to adopt women's suffrage; here, the idea of national identity trumped even gender identity, a very old form of identity politics indeed. Over the following fifty years, the right to political participation would be extended to the female half of the human species in a growing number of countries—in Finland in 1906, Norway in 1913, Russia in 1917, Germany and Austria in 1918, the United

States in 1920, Britain in 1918 (partial) and 1928 (full), Spain and Brazil in 1932, France in 1944, Argentina in 1947, and Mexico in 1953.[10]

But the idea of nationality could also motivate repression of people whom the state and those who identified with it regarded as not fitting in to the nation. Often such groups were defined as "ethnic" minorities. An example is the Volga Germans, discussed in chapter 1; they began to leave the Russian Empire in the 1870s because the czarist state launched a "Russification" program designed to force minorities to assimilate fully with the majority population by, for example, requiring them to speak Russian. But the German Empire launched a similar campaign of "Germanization" in the Polish- and French-speaking areas it ruled. In North America, Australia, and New Zealand enormous coercive force was brought to bear on recently defeated indigenous communities, in an attempt to force them to conform to the standards of the new majority cultures in these settler societies—as by enforcing individual land ownership, Western forms of dress, the pattern of gender and family roles prevalent in British society, and use of the English language. But Irish, Polish, Italian, and Hungarian immigrants were also the target of a determined campaign of "Americanization" in the United States.

The idea of race, too, was increasingly influential in precisely the same period. This concept too had its origins in the late eighteenth and early nineteenth century, when European theorists began to posit the existence of distinct "races" or kinds of humans. One of the most influential texts was *An Essay on the Inequality of the Human Races*, published by the Frenchman Arthur de Gobineau in 1855. Gobineau argued that the white "Aryan" race was the only author of all human civilization, the only creative race of human beings. Other civilizations, in Egypt or India or China, were simply the creation of Aryan migrants; he even thought that the ruling classes of the Aztec and Inca empires were Scandinavians. An influential later restatement of such ideas was Houston Stuart Chamberlain's *Foundations of the Nineteenth Century*, published in 1899. Chamberlain too saw Aryans as the creators of everything; he died in 1927, shortly after joining the Nazi Party and assuring Adolf Hitler that he had been born to save the Aryan race from degeneration.[11]

Racial ideas, too, were important in many parts of the world as a foundation for political action. The United States, Australia, and Canada adopted a policy of Chinese exclusion, for instance. Remarkably, in Brazil, from the 1860s onward, pro-immigration activists argued that the nation had to be "whitened" by recruiting free Europeans, particularly of the English or German "race," to replace the allegedly racially inferior slaves of African descent.[12] The US southern states effected a wave of disenfranchisement of African Americans in the 1880s and 1890s. A generation after emancipation, white southern politicians decided that African Americans were incapable of self-government and therefore could not be allowed to vote. Having deprived African Americans of a political voice, they then imposed a more thoroughgoing system of racial segregation and discrimination as well. A growing series of racial laws in South Africa a decade or two later, including disenfranchisement of nonwhite South Africans, was another important instance. Race was often used as a boundary marker for nationality and for political rights, particularly in settler societies. Those defined as racially superior were regarded as all fundamentally "the same" and equal, so political and social rights were extended to them; those defined as inferior were denied such rights. Finally, racism was often used to justify imperialist expansion and conquest—either by arguing that subject peoples were constitutionally incapable of self-government and effective use of resources, or that the colonial power would "civilize" them and prepare them for—one day in the distant future—self-rule and prosperity.[13]

Why did these new vocabularies of difference arise and spread when they did? While it is difficult to reduce broad intellectual patterns like these merely to the effect of external causes, it is clear that in a number of important respects, ideas about race, ethnicity, and nationalism were the product of the period's broader economic and social transformations.

First, the development of communications and transportation technology during the nineteenth century created much larger economic, social, and cultural units than had existed before. They created more integrated regional economies and societies in which people traded goods, took part in the regional labor market, and exchanged ideas—in newspapers or magazines or novels, for example. They also generated new opportunities to create larger markets—opportunities many businesspeople were eager to see realized and secured within a more unified political nation. All these developments widened people's horizons, encouraging them to identify with other people within the larger, integrated economic, social, and cultural circuits. The same changes also tended to break down broader and looser loyalties based on caste or status, as integrative forces became more powerful at the regional ("national") level.

Second, new patterns of interaction also helped to foster a sense of difference, not just of sameness. Chinese nationalism, for example, was in part a project of missionary-educated and overseas Chinese. The nationalist leader Sun Zhongshan (known in the West as Sun Yat Sen), who lived off and on for seven years with his elder brother in Hawai'i (before its annexation by the United States), studied medicine for five years in (British) Hong Kong, and converted to Christianity, first founded his Chinese nationalist revolutionary movement back in Hawai'i; expanded it to Hong Kong, Japan, and Taiwan (then part of the Japanese Empire); and garnered support from overseas Chinese in the United States, Japan, Hawai'i, London, and even South Africa.[14] In this he was not untypical: many of the architects of ideas about race, ethnicity, and nationalism were people whose lives were shaped by the global exchanges and interactions created by the new global economy and by imperial states. Their contact with people outside their own societies gave them a stronger sense of their own distinctiveness. The Peruvian nationalist and socialist José Carlos

Mariátegui, for example, "discovered" his country—where, as he put it, he had lived in ignorance of its essential nature, "almost like a stranger," throughout his youth—only when he moved to Rome at the age of twenty-five.[15] The great Cuban nationalist leader José Martí lived in New York from 1881 to 1895.[16] And it is not coincidental that some nationalist movements outside the North Atlantic region—notably the Urabi rebellion in Egypt in 1879 and the Indian National Congress in 1885—arose in the critical last third of the nineteenth century, simultaneously with and often in the context of the "New Imperialism" and the growing integration of the world economy.

Third, in many cases particular states or movements quite self-consciously cultivated these ideas. Language is perhaps the most striking example. Most people in most of the world until the nineteenth century spoke either a universal language of learning (Latin, Arabic, Persian, Mandarin) or a "dialect," a language with relatively few speakers and confined to a particular region. States worked hard in the nineteenth and early twentieth centuries to eradicate these regional "dialects" or languages spoken by "ethnic" minorities, and to impose uniform national languages. The English educational official, philosopher, and novelist Matthew Arnold, for example, praised the British government's campaign to eradicate the Welsh, Cornish, and Irish languages as an instance of what he called "swallowing up provincial nationalities,"[17] which he saw as a worthy project. States and professors everywhere also used the academic discipline of history to build patriotism, by praising the past glories of their particular "nations." But, obviously, racial theory was also in part an ideological justification for colonial empire or for systematic discrimination against minority populations. Indeed, various "pan-movements" attempted to create ideological foundations even for states that did not yet exist. The pan-Germans sought to build a massively expanded German empire in Central and Eastern Europe and the Low Countries and even cultivated the loyalty of German emigrants in, for example, Texas and Brazil. Pan-Slavs dreamed of a Russian-Slavic empire stretching into Southeastern Europe (and to the Pacific). Pan-Islamic thinkers sought a revived caliphate under the auspices of the Ottoman Empire, reaching from the Atlantic in North Africa to the Pacific in the Indonesian and Philippine archipelagoes. Anglo-Saxonists dreamed of a world ruled by people of British descent. Pan-Africanists imagined various forms of transatlantic unity for all Africans.[18]

It was primarily within the context of such efforts that the idea of "ethnicity" took shape. Effectively, "ethnicity" was usually a way of referring to targeted minority religious, linguistic, or racial groups within a particular political framework. Often what one meant by "ethnicity" was a group of people who were in some way distinct, but whom one hoped to either eliminate or assimilate. Again, many European immigrant populations in the Americas were classified as ethnic minorities—Poles, Hungarians, Lebanese, Germans, Italians. The Volga Germans, similarly, were an "ethnic" population in the Russian

Empire. An important "ethnic" group within Europe was the Jews, especially true in the Russian Empire, where Jewish settlement was concentrated in its southern and western parts (the "Pale"). From the 1880s and until 1917, the czarist government fomented popular violence—pogroms—against its Jewish citizens, whom it regarded as unacceptably different.

This last case illustrates the important point that religious difference often overlapped with, or was defined as, racial or national difference. European Jews were of course a religious community; but they were increasingly conceived of in ethnic or even racial terms by those who disliked their presence—with the former variant often implying that they must be assimilated, and the latter variant often implying that they could not be. And persecution helped to give rise among European Jews to a new form of nationalism—Zionism, the idea of creating a Jewish nation. Jews began to emigrate from Europe to Palestine in the early nineteenth century; their numbers significantly increased in the wake of pogroms in Russia in 1881–82 and 1903 and of a serious famine that struck the Russian Empire in 1891–92. After the Dreyfus Affair in France, in which anti-Semites tried to frame a Jewish army officer as a spy, Theodor Herzl published his influential pamphlet *The Jewish State* in 1896, the first World Zionist Congress was held in Basel in 1897, and systematic immigration began. By the 1930s, as anti-Semitic legislation ramped up in Poland, Germany, and other parts of East-Central Europe, tens of thousands of European Jews were flooding into Palestine. Still more came after World War II and the Holocaust.[19]

The boundaries between racial, ethnic, and national categories were often fluid. In the United States in the nineteenth century, many people who thought themselves Anglo-Saxons regarded "ethnic" minorities such as the Celts (Irish), Slavs (Russians, Poles, and others), Latins (Italians, Portuguese), and Jews as inferior, and discriminated against them, though for the most part they did not try to exclude them permanently from the political nation. But many Anglo-Americans did support depriving African Americans, Chinese, Native Americans, and Mexicans—none of whom were of European origin—of full rights of citizenship. Across the South and Southwest, they did so in the 1880s and 1890s in a wave of political disenfranchisement. By the 1920s, distinctions between people of European origin were giving way to the idea that there was one "Caucasian" or white "race" that included all European "ethnic" populations (though it took another three or four decades to establish that European Jews were "white").[20] In Europe, most racial theorists made a clear racial distinction between Europeans and non-Europeans. But they also described multiple "races" within Europe—Celtic, Germanic, Slavic, Latin, Mediterranean, Alpine—and they often established a hierarchy among these groups. Even in the 1920s, for example, the popular German race theorist Hans F. K. Günther busily propagated the notion that all the truly heroic figures of world history—from Apollo to George Washington—were racially "Nordic" (figure 4.1). In contrast, people whom he considered enemies of freedom and progress—for example, Ignatius Loyola, founder of the Jesuit order—were "Near Eastern," and hence Semites. As evidence Günther pointed primarily to their noses (figure 4.2). Others argued that "racial" or "ethnic" groups could be distinguished from one another in kind and quality by the shapes of their skulls. Long-skulled groups were allegedly superior to wide-skulled groups—a criterion that Günther too used. Madison Grant peddled similar ideas in the United States, where he feared that "inferior" round-headed stock from Eastern and Southern Europe would overwhelm the long-headed Aryan master race. Such ideas led to the revival in 1915 of the Ku Klux Klan, a terrorist political organization devoted to preserving the power of Northern European Protestants, and to passage of progressively more restrictive immigration laws in 1921, 1924, and 1929. Those laws imposed maximum quotas for immigrants of particular nationalities based on their share of the U.S. population first in 1910 and then in 1890, and excluded Japanese immigrants completely.[21]

Günther and Grant illustrate one of the key developments in racial thought in this period: an increasingly explicit appeal to science—to systems of classification based on measurement, to the biological sciences, and even to models of evolution. Such theories were part of a transition away from an earlier-nineteenth-century cultural language of race, in which it was argued that under the benevolent rule of Europeans, "inferior" races would over time become fully civilized. In the later-nineteenth-century language of "scientific" racism, races were increasingly considered to have immutable, unchangeable characteristics that would prevent them from ever improving and would instead consign them to fading away. That theory could make high death rates among Native Americans, the Maori in New Zealand, and aboriginal Australians seem natural, normal, and even desirable.

To make things even more complex, in some cases racial thought could be turned on its head; as anti-colonial nationalism began to grow more influential in the early twentieth century, this table-turning became more common. José Vasconcelos, for example, was an influential Mexican nationalist who supported the Mexican Revolution of 1910 and played an important role in founding or directing a whole range of national cultural institutions in Mexico, including the National Autonomous University of Mexico, the Ministry of Education, and the National Library. Vasconcelos argued that Latin America was becoming the home of what he called the Cosmic Race, formed by the mixing of all five global races—Iberian, Amerindian, African, white, and Asian. The creation of this mixed race, he believed, would bring about a new era in human history. Vasconcelos published these ideas in 1925, but they had clear roots reaching back to the late nineteenth century when Latin Americans, no less than Europeans, were discovering the folklore and folk culture of their societies. Vasconcelos was a middle-class intellectual, a lawyer for American interests early in his career (though a bitter critic of the United States later), a Catholic interested in Buddhism and Hinduism, and a person convinced that

FIG. 309.—JAMES MONROE
(1758–1831), President

FIG. 310.—THOMAS JEFFERSON
(1743–1826), President

FIG. 311.—R. W. EMERSON
(1803–82), Poet and philosopher

FIG. 312.—ANDREW JACKSON
(1767–1845), President

FIG. 313.—NATHANIEL HAWTHORNE
(1804–64), Writer

FIG. 314.—LONGFELLOW
(1807–82), Poet

Figure 4.1 "Nordic" Americans, according to race theorist Hans F. K. Günther.

FIG. 188.—ETRUSCAN WOMAN
OF NORDIC RACE
Painting from grave at Corneto

Figure 4.2 Hans F. K. Guenther's "Middle Eastern" Ignatius Loyola.

the Spanish conquest had been a good thing. But other Latin American *indigenistas* (indigenists) went further, denouncing the conquest as a disaster and praising the special national qualities derived from Latin America's pre-Columbian heritage.[22] José Mariátegui, for example, celebrated indigenous Peruvian culture as the "foundation of our nationality . . . without the Indian, Peruvianness is not possible."[23]

Similar intellectual movements arose elsewhere. In China and Japan the confrontation with European racial ideas encouraged some nationalists to develop their own theories about the racial unity of their societies. Some included in their imagined racial nations regions they sought to retain or incorporate, such as Tibet or Korea; in China some revolutionaries excluded the "foreign" Manchu dynasty; in Japan some argued for the essential unity of all Asians, in opposition to Western imperialism.[24] Some Ottoman subjects in the Middle East argued that Islam was preeminently a product of Arab culture and that the Turkish Ottoman sultans should relinquish their claim to be the caliph, the leader of all Muslims.[25] The *négritude* movement emerged in the African diaspora in the 1920s and 1930s: in the Caribbean, the poet and theorist of anti-colonialism Aimé Césaire, among others, led the movement; among Africans in Paris, Leopold Senghor was prominent and went on to become the first president of Senegal. Similar ideas were an important part of the pan-African movement launched by the West Indian Marcus Garvey in the United States. These figures argued that Africans had a particular racial character that gave them unique gifts of patience, endurance, insight, and creativity. As Senghor saw it, Africans had a capacity for "intuitive reasoning" and "the joy of life," an antidote to "the anguished reason of Europe."[26]

Or consider the ideas of Luther Standing Bear, a Lakota Sioux who was sent to a boarding school in Pennsylvania in 1879, became a member of Buffalo Bill's Wild West show (which toured the world re-enacting scenes from the "Indian" wars and life on the Great Plains) in the 1890s, went to Hollywood as a film actor, and wrote four books about his people between 1928 and 1934. Standing Bear was proud of having "remained a hostile, even a savage, . . . incurable." He argued that nothing was wrong with the Sioux or any other Native American group and only "tyranny, stupidity, and lack of vision" among white people had "brought about the situation now alluded to as the 'Indian Problem.'" White people, he held, were "troubled with primitive fears" because they did not yet belong to America; the Euro-American "is still a foreigner and an alien." And, "if it be the part of civilization to maim, rob, and thwart, then what is progress?" In contrast, "in the Indian the spirit of the land is still vested. . . . [T]he man who sat on the ground in his tipi meditating on life and its meaning, accepting the kinship of all creatures, and acknowledging unity with the universe of things was infusing into his being the true essence of civilization." White Americans were spiritually ill, alienated from their land, hence obsessed with mere dominance. "But America can be revived, rejuvenated, by recognizing a native school of thought. The Indian can save America."[27]

An equally striking instance of non-Europeans using European racial theories was the First Universal Races Congress, held in London in 1911. The 2,100 participants from around the globe accepted the importance of cultural differences. But they called for global understanding and cooperation so that all humanity could draw on the distinctive gifts and talents of all "races" or cultures, for the collective good of humanity as a whole.[28]

CULTURAL GLOBALIZATION: RELIGIOUS INNOVATION, 1800–1920

> The time has come for widespread recognition of the radical changes in religious beliefs throughout the modern world. . . . Science and economic change have disrupted the old beliefs. Religions the world over are under the necessity of coming to terms with new conditions created by a vastly increased knowledge and experience. . . . Such a vital, fearless, and frank religion . . . is a major necessity of the present.[29]
>
> Humanist Manifesto, 1933

The First Universal Races Congress, however, was yet another example of the way in which the language of race, ethnicity, and nationalism could overlap with the language of religion; for its roots lay in the Society for Ethical Culture, founded by Felix Adler in 1877 in New York City as a vehicle for preaching a religious message of human unity and mutual tolerance. Such overlaps were common. In the Russian Empire, the late-nineteenth-century "Russification" program included efforts to convert members of ethnic and religious minorities to Russian Orthodox Christianity; it also included official encouragement of attacks on Jews, a religious community rather than a "racial" one. Both instances reflect the sense among at least some Russians that Russian Orthodoxy was a defining element of "Russian-ness" as a nationality or ethnicity.[30] In the Ottoman Empire the Armenian minority was identified as both an ethnic and a religious (Christian) group, and persecuted on both bases.[31] In the Qing Empire in China during this period, Muslims in the recently conquered far west came to be regarded as, and increasingly to regard themselves as, an "ethnic" group.[32] At the same time, some Chinese intellectuals and officials came to regard Confucianism as central to Chinese culture and identity, one of the aspects that made Chinese people distinct and different from, for example, the Europeans who were selling them opium and taking over their port cities. In Japan, Shintoism played a similar role—directly patronized by the state as a way of building national unity. In Germany a German-speaking Catholic member of the national parliament argued in 1906 that the campaign of "Germanization" in the part of Poland occupied by the German Empire was actually a campaign of "Protestantization."[33] And European advocates of imperialist expansion often regarded Christianity as the religion of white people, as "civilized" religion.

Yet the relationships among race, ethnicity, nationalism, and religion were not simple or straightforward. Many religions explicitly rejected racism as theologically untenable, arguing that all members of a particular religion were equal in moral and spiritual terms. One conservative Christian activist in Munich in 1907 denounced those imperialist Germans who sought to "spread civilization by the firing-squad," holding that "the black race is originally neither physically nor morally a lower or less worthy one. . . . [We] hold the African to be . . . a human being, with every attribute of the human species."[34] And many missionaries, including some in the US West and in South Africa, were horrified by the genocidal violence and cultural insensitivity of their own societies toward indigenous groups.

Religious ideas and movements also often cut directly across political currents, fostering resistance and rebellion against national states or ethnic majorities. Perhaps the most striking example is that of the Taiping Rebellion in China, a revolt against the Chinese imperial state led by the prophet Hong Xiuquan, who in 1843 realized that he was the brother of Jesus Christ. The quasi-state the Taiping movement created persisted for more than two decades, with its peak lasting from 1852 to 1864, and with some 20 million losing their lives in the civil war its emergence sparked. In Mexico the so-called Caste War in the Yucatán, lasting from the late 1840s until 1901, was inspired in part by religious innovation and in part by a new (or revived) sense of Maya ethnic identity. In New Zealand, British encroachment sparked both the King movement, which aimed to create a sovereign indigenous monarchy, and the Hauhau movement, which combined elements of Christian and indigenous Maori tradition.[35]

How do we make sense of the diversity of movements like these, and of the complex relationship between them and the languages of race, ethnicity, and nation?

Fundamentally, we can discern three simultaneous, contradictory, but often mutually reinforcing patterns in global religious life in the period between 1850 and World War I. First, there was a growing commitment to religious orthodoxy, or uniformity. Second, there was a rapid proliferation of religious heterodoxy, or variety. And third, there was a growing commitment to religious universalism. All three of these processes were directly related to one another and were also directly related to broader technological, political, and economic developments.

First, then, a whole range of major religions around the world in this period saw important movements of popular revival, renewal, or purification in which reformers sought to standardize and systematize doctrine and practice across large geographies, and often also to purge elements that they believed had been imported from indigenous practice or from other religions. As global transportation, communications, and commercial networks became denser, people increasingly knew what their co-religionists in other countries and regions believed and did. The urge to "correct" them, to ensure uniformity, was in part a response to this growing knowledge.

Revival or renewal movements often went hand in hand with a greater degree of popularity and mass participation and with efforts to bring a deeper, more authentic, more demanding conception of the faith to more people. One important influence in this respect was the growing emphasis on pilgrimage within some of the major religions—for example, journeys to Mecca or Karbala or Homs within Islam, and to Santiago de Compostela or Lourdes or Guadalupe in Catholicism. The development of the rail and steamship transportation network played a critical role here. By the 1850s, British and Dutch steamship lines brought Muslim pilgrims from India and Indonesia to Mecca and Medina; by the turn of the century, Muslim pilgrims from Russia and Central Asia could take the train to Odessa, on the Black Sea, and then a steamship to Mecca.[36] British-built rail lines carried Hindu pilgrims to Benares, and Buddhists to Bodh Gaya. And European rail lines brought a growing wave of pilgrims to the small southern French town of Lourdes after the Virgin Mary first appeared in a vision to a farm girl there in 1858.[37]

Improved transportation also made travel easier for people desiring to study in the great religious institutions of the world, bringing them into direct contact with the centers of religious learning and doctrine, including the Vatican in Rome and the al-Azhar mosque in Egypt. Some of those people then returned to their home countries, bringing with them what they saw as a "purer" teaching. A typical case was James Emmanuel Kwegyir Aggrey, who was born in Ghana in 1875, went to a local missionary school, studied at the college of the African Methodist Episcopal Zion Church in North Carolina, and went on to Columbia University before returning to be an educational administrator in Ghana.[38]

But the same developments also made it easier for religious teachers to move outward from the centers of religious life to the geographical peripheries of their communities of faith. The great missionary organizations of North Atlantic Christianity followed this path, as did the Sufi orders, which helped spread religious commitment in the Muslim world. The latter was a long tradition in Islam, reaching back, for example, to Usman Dan Fodio, founder of the Emirate of Sokoto in northern Nigeria in the early nineteenth century; but another, later example is Mohammed 'Abdulle Hassan, a Sufi teacher who studied in Mecca in the late 1880s and then resisted British and Ethiopian imperial power in Somalia from 1900 until the early 1920s.[39]

The advance of printing technology and the growing global flood of words on paper also favored orthodoxy, as increasing numbers of people learned their religious ideas from authoritative texts rather than from individual and sometimes idiosyncratic teachers.[40] Nonsacred publications could help draw religious communities together, as well; examples include the *Osservatore Romano*, founded in 1861 as the semi-official newspaper of the Papacy in Rome, and the *Christian Science Journal* in the United States, which started publishing in 1885.[41]

Some renewal and purification movements overlapped with anti-imperialist sentiment. Buddhism, for example, experienced a major revival in the 1880s and 1890s, partly under the influence of the Sri Lankan teacher Anagarika Dharmapala. Dharmapala also played an influential part in Sri Lankan nationalism, because he regarded Sri Lankans as the historical guardians of Buddhism. He sought to propagate a "purified" Buddhist doctrine and practice, free (as he told an audience in New York in 1893) "from theology, priestcraft, rituals, ceremonies, dogmas, heavens, hells and other theological shibboleths." He is sometimes referred to as the father of "Buddhist modernism," or even "Protestant Buddhism," by those who see parallels with sixteenth-century Protestants' efforts to "purify" Christian doctrine of the historical accretions (ideas, practices, institutions) of a millennium and a half.[42]

In the Islamic world a number of figures active particularly in Egypt led a movement of Islamic modernism that similarly combined anti-imperialism, rationalism, and the goal of purifying the faith. The most famous and influential of these leaders was Muhammad Abduh, who had experience as a student and traveler abroad (in France) and championed both pan-Islamism and a moderate and modernizing approach to religious and political questions, including that of Egyptian independence after the British occupied the country in 1882. A very different case is Muhammad Ahmad, a Sudanese Sufi religious teacher who in 1881 proclaimed himself the Mahdi, or renewer of Islam—

rejecting, among other things, Egyptian expansion into the Sudan and the outlawing of the slave trade. He led a revolt against Egyptian, and then British, rule that took Khartoum in 1885 and established a strict theocratic state that ruled the Sudan until it was destroyed by the British in 1898.[43]

Within Hinduism, an important revival took inspiration from the teaching of Ramakrishna, an influential leader of the middle of the nineteenth century; his wisdom was carried on by, among others, Vivekananda, founder of the Vedanta Society in 1894. This movement too played an important role in fostering Indian nationalism and anti-colonialism, and also developed a small but influential international following (among other places, in California).[44]

Most of the developments that encouraged the growth of religious orthodoxy—in particular, greater ease of transport and communication—also posed a challenge to it, since they brought new ideas and people who subscribed to them to many parts of the world. Religions major and minor responded to that threat by making clearer to their members what their doctrines were, spreading authorized versions of their sacred texts, and expanding their formal educational functions. The Roman Catholic Church, for example, held a world-encompassing General Council in Rome in 1869–70—the First Vatican Council—in order to define the church's teachings more clearly. Among other things, it declared that the pope was able to make infallible, binding pronouncements on matters of faith, clearly a move to make Catholic practice and belief more uniform. The global Anglican Church, too, held a regular series of conferences at Lambeth Palace in London from 1867 onward, with representatives attending from all over the world.[45]

Not all such efforts were successful, and this fact helps explain the second common form of religious creativity in this period: growing heterodoxy, indeed the emergence of a whole range of new religions and of religious conflicts.

In some cases a dynamic relationship formed between orthodoxy and heterodoxy, for "purification" sometimes led to the creation of new churches and faiths. The Brahmo Samaj, for instance, contributed to the rise of Indian nationalism in the nineteenth century. Starting in the 1800s, Ram Mohan Roy and others argued that the Hindu religion had been corrupted over the centuries by the worship of saints, deities, and avatars, whereas originally it had been a monotheistic religion. Critics saw this line of thinking as an importation of Christian or Islamic ideas into Hindu religion, and by 1860 this movement, originally conceived as an orthodox revivalist movement, constituted itself instead as a new religion.[46] Later, in the early twentieth century in Los Angeles, California, modern Pentecostalism (1906) and modern Christian fundamentalism (1907) emerged, both efforts to "return" Christian belief and practice to simplified forms incompatible with theological liberalism. Both gave rise to a whole galaxy of new Christian sects.[47] Even more fundamentally, one recent study has suggested that late-nineteenth-century scholars particularly in Europe invented the whole idea of religion itself, in the sense that they posited the existence of a limited number of originally doctrinally pure "world religions" (Buddhism, Islam, Christianity, Hinduism, Judaism, and so on) of which people's multifarious and varied interpretations and divergent practices are merely "corruptions." In that sense, orthodox reform and unification movements within ancient and diversified religious communities could be seen as a distinctive modern form of heterodoxy.[48]

But the religious ferment of this period gave direct rise to entirely new faiths, as well—and to new religious conflicts. An extraordinary example of this phenomenon was the Taiping Rebellion. In another example, the Baha'i faith started in Iran in 1844, and after it spread through the Middle East, its adherents were subject to repeated bouts of serious persecution. Mormonism, founded as a late offshoot of the Second Great Awakening in the United States in 1830, was a similar case. The Mormon community was driven by popular and state violence from the Northeast to Ohio in 1831, then on to Missouri in 1838, Illinois in 1839, and finally Nebraska, before the Latter-day Saints settled in Utah in 1847. In 1857 the US Army occupied Utah, and Mormons continued to be persecuted until 1890, when the church finally abandoned polygamy (illegal under US law).[49] Some fled to Mexico, which was more tolerant, where they applied in the high, dry Mexican plateau farming techniques they had perfected in the similar climate of Utah and Colorado.

While imperialism helped to fuel some religious purification movements, in other cases it encouraged heterodoxy and the formation of new churches and religions. Sub-Saharan Africa was a major field of European and North American missionary activity, but Christian sects independent of European or American missionary activity also proliferated there starting in the 1880s. They included the Native Baptist Church in Nigeria (1888), which by 1914 had more members in Africa than the American Southern Baptist churches. By 1946 there were as many as thirteen hundred such independent sects in Africa.[50]

A number of religious movements arose, furthermore, specifically in the context of mounting discrimination against ethnic or racial minorities. An early example was the African Methodist Episcopal Church, founded by free African Americans in Philadelphia in 1816. Modern Reform Judaism emerged in Germany in the early nineteenth century, established its first seminary in Hamburg in 1870, and ultimately became highly influential in the United States, with its center in Cincinnati. Conservative Judaism emerged in turn as a middle path between what some Jews saw as the doctrinal laxity of reformed Jews and the rigidity of Orthodox Jews.[51]

A less important, but revealing further source of religious diversity came from attempts to combine spirituality with scientific study. Spiritualism was founded by the Fox Sisters in Hydesville, New York, in 1848, after they made contact with the spirit of a dead woman. Christian Science was founded in the 1870s by Mary Baker Eddy, primarily on the basis of two books, *Science and Health* in 1875 and *Key to the Scriptures* in 1883. The New Thought movement had roots reaching back to the 1830s, but was formalized (to some extent) at a series of conferences beginning in San Francisco in 1894 and ending in Boston in 1899. Through these meetings, the movement declared itself to be a "broad, tolerant, optimistic, constructive" faith committed to "the philosophy of practical idealism" and "conscious oneness with God," with "no hampering creed, no personal dogmas, no forms or ceremonials." Many of its devotees believed in using mental power to heal physical disease; many, too, believed in The Secret, or the power of "thought vibrations" to shape material reality. Not coincidentally, a number of New Thought leaders had a deep interest in Indian spiritual traditions: William Walker Atkinson, whose 1906 book, *Thought Vibration; Or, the Law of Attraction in the Thought World,* was an important text for the movement, was also a teacher of yoga.[52]

Finally, both orthodoxy and heterodoxy also operated in close relationship with the third trend: religious universalism, the search for a least common denominator in moral and spiritual thought that could unite all of humanity. Not surprisingly, particularly in a world ever more integrated by transportation and communications technologies and by such political structures as globe-spanning empires, a growing number of people began to develop religious ideas intended not to make distinctions between groups, but to build unity among all human beings.

Emblematic of this pattern was the Society for Ethical Culture, founded in 1877 by Felix Adler, a German reform Jewish immigrant to New York. The society taught that people of all faiths should be united in a creed of pragmatic humanitarianism: however one might define or worship God, as a practical matter, what counts is ethical action. Adler was a professor of ethics at Columbia University and one of the founders of the American Civil Liberties Union and the National Urban League—organizations that sought, among other things, to defend the rights and encourage the integration of both ethnic and religious minorities in the American republic. Adler's argument was that religion was a matter of private belief about which people would inevitably differ, but that people of all faiths could agree on the vital importance to human societies of a basic code of social ethics. The religion of the future would therefore put "its greatest stress not on the believing but in the acting out, . . . discard the narrow spirit of exclusion," and seek the "common ground" of ethical principles that would permit "diversity in the creed, unanimity in the deed." Adler's transatlantic involvements (he studied in Heidelberg) helped spread the message internationally, and in 1893 the International Ethical Union was formed; by 1900 it had chapters in the United States, Germany, Britain, Austria, France, Japan, Switzerland, Italy, and New Zealand.[53]

In another case, the Sufi Order in the West, or Universal Sufism, was founded in London in 1914 by the Indian teacher Inayat Khan, a musician and spiritual leader with important ties to the arts in Europe. It holds that there is one moral code valid for all people, and it is based on self-denial, reciprocity, and love.[54]

Even more striking was the Theosophical Society, founded in New York in 1875 by the Russian immigrant and world traveler Helena Blavatsky, who formulated its ideas most explicitly in *The Secret Doctrine* in 1888. Blavatsky and her associates developed an extraordinarily eclectic brew of ideas, complete with astral travel, psychic powers, and hidden spiritual Masters secreted away (except for occasional materializations elsewhere) in a Tibetan valley. But the central aim of the society itself was "to form the nucleus of a Universal Brotherhood of Humanity, without distinction of race, creed, sex, caste, or color."[55] A number of Theosophists traveled to Tibet and to Sri Lanka, where they became for a while close associates of Anagarika Dharmapala. In 1909 one of Blavatsky's associates discovered a young Indian boy, Jiddu Krishnamurti, to be the "vehicle" of the World Teacher whom they thought was coming to instruct all of humanity in how to live well. The Theosophist leadership essentially kidnapped Krishnamurti and took him to Britain in 1911 for spiritual training. He settled in Ojai, California, in 1922, attracted an audience of sixteen thousand to the Hollywood Bowl for his first appearance as the embodiment of the World Teacher, and traveled the world extensively. He broke with Theosophy in 1929, but remained an important spiritual leader not only in California but in Europe and India as well.[56]

This universalist tendency in nineteenth-century religion was perhaps most obvious in the Parliament of the World's Religions, held in tandem with the 1893 World's Columbian Exposition in Chicago. Here 194 speakers representing forty-five religions introduced their faiths and discussed various aspects of religious life and thought. Three-quarters were from various Christian sects; but Buddhism, Judaism, Hinduism, Jainism, Islam, and others were also represented. A high point was Vivekananda's speech on religious toleration, calling on the audience to recognize that all religions were valid paths to God and to holiness, and holding up the diversity and coexistence of India's religious communities as a model for the world. Here nationalism, orthodoxy, and universalism came together in one speech—one of a number of similar pronouncements at the same meeting.[57]

CULTURAL GLOBALIZATION: PEACE AND DANCE, 1890–1930

> Does . . . moral progress increase in the same proportion as material progress? . . . Jesus, Mohamed, Buddha, . . . Ramakrishna were men who exercised an immense influence. . . . The world is richer for their having lived in it. And they were all men who deliberately embraced poverty as their lot. . . . I have heard many of our countrymen say that we will gain American wealth but avoid its method. . . . [I]f we are not careful, we shall introduce all the vices that she has been prey to, owing to the disease of materialism.[58]
>
> Mohandas Gandhi, 1916

The Parliament of the World's Religions, and the enthusiasm with which the mass press in the West reported on the speeches of Vivekananda, Dharmapala (who also attended), and others, was an important instance of cultural globalization. But that trend extended well beyond the sphere of religion, into the arts, philosophy, politics, and the sciences. This section explores just two examples to illustrate how such processes shaped the lives of individuals—and also how complex the role of one person could be in shaping those broader processes of cultural globalization. One example is a universally familiar figure of great political importance. The other is today a little-known figure who played an important role in modern art, specifically in the development of modern dance.

Mohandas Karamchand Gandhi was born in 1869 in central western India, the son of a high official in a small princely state—one of many small states that were under British suzerainty. To follow in his father's footsteps and enter state service, he needed to earn a degree in law, and because India was a British colony, the best place to study Indian law at the time was England. In 1888, he went to London to study at the University College of London.

Gandhi was not particularly religious, but his mother was a member of the Jain faith, and therefore a vegetarian, and so was he. The British Vegetarian Society had formed in 1847, but by the late 1880s a new clientele for vegetarian cuisine could be found among people attracted to various Indian religions, including Theosophists. Through meeting them in vegetarian restaurants, Gandhi started to become more interested in religion.[59] Nevertheless, he carried on with the plan to follow his father's example, finished his law studies, and in 1893 accepted employment with an Indian businessman in South Africa. He spent most of the following twenty-three years in South Africa (with several trips to India interspersed).

These two decades in South Africa were essential to his intellectual development in three ways. First, living in South Africa encouraged Gandhi to think of himself as a member of a particular ethnicity or nationality, as an "Indian." Nationalism was of growing importance in India itself and the Indian National Congress, the leading nationalist organization, had been formed in 1885. But probably most Indians still thought of themselves either as members of a particular regional or "ethnic" group (for example, Gujarati, in Gandhi's case; or Bengali; or Tamil), as a citizen of a particular state (whether princely or under direct British rule), or as a member of a particular religion. In South Africa, however, all these people were classified simply as Indians.

Second, Indians in South Africa faced intense and mounting racial discrimination. In the 1890s and 1900s, South Africa was moving gradually toward what would later be called *apartheid*—a race-based social, economic, and political system in which nonwhites faced enormous discrimination. In 1910 the three separate British colonies in South Africa would be amalgamated into the semiautonomous Union of South Africa, and the two Boer republics would impose race-based voting restrictions and progressively more restrictive legislation regarding political participation, social relations, work, access to the professions, freedom of movement, and property ownership. In a precursor to that development, the state that Gandhi was living in (Transvaal) adopted the Black Act in 1906. It required that all "Asiatics" (meaning Indians, Arabs, Lebanese, Turks, and others) register with the police, be fingerprinted, and undergo medical examination to find identifying marks—suggesting that they were all somehow suspects. In the face of such legislation and of personal experiences with discrimination, Gandhi gradually came to identify racism itself as an evil. And since racism was the ideological foundation for imperialism, he came increasingly to question that too. Ironically, during the Boer War Gandhi had recruited more than one thousand Indians to serve as medical orderlies and stretcher-bearers for the British forces, because he was aware that for the Indian population Boer independence was the worse option. To then face the kind of legislation exemplified by the Black Act, under nominal British rule, was a slap in the face for him, and an indication of just how pervasive racism was in European societies and governments.

Third, through the 1890s and 1900s Gandhi came to develop a coherent philosophy and a political strategy of active nonviolent resistance, which he called satyagraha. The technique was used in a partially successful campaign of civil disobedience against the Black Act. Satyagraha was constructed out of a whole range of important influences, which Gandhi wove into a whole that had broad international appeal. The first was Jainism, a religion for which respect for all living things and nonviolence are a central doctrine. Second, during his studies in Britain Gandhi had been influenced by the Society for Ethical Culture, and in particular by William Mackinder Salter's *Ethical Religion,* published in 1889. He found related ideas in Henry David Thoreau's 1847 essay, *On Civil Disobedience,* and in John Ruskin's *Unto This Last,* an influential reflection on the possibilities for a nonviolent social order first published in 1882, which Gandhi translated into his own language (Gujarati) in 1908. Third was the African American educator Booker T. Washington, founder of the Tuskegee Institute, whose ethos of self-help and belief in the ennobling character of work attracted Gandhi. Finally there was Leo Tolstoy, a Russian novelist and theorist of pacifism whose 1893 book, *The Kingdom of God Is Within You,* was a major influence on the global pacifist movement. In 1907 a leading Indian nationalist had written to Tolstoy asking for his advice on how to get the British out of India without using violence, and Tolstoy's response was published in 1908 as *A Letter to a Hindu.* It argued in favor of passive resistance employed in a spirit of love. Gandhi corresponded with Tolstoy for two years before the latter's death in 1910, and translated this pamphlet too into Gujarati in 1909. In 1910, in preparation for a campaign of civil disobedience against racial legislation in the new South African Union, Gandhi set up what was effectively a training camp for satyagraha outside Johannesburg, which he called Tolstoy Farm.

In 1914, Gandhi returned to India to take up the cause of Indian nationalism. His work with both Hindu and Muslim Indians in South Africa helped to win him the confidence not only of the Indian National Congress, which was dominated by

Hindus, but also of Muslims; and he became a spokesman for the All-Indian Muslim Conference, which was part of a global movement to secure Islamic holy places in the Middle East that had been conquered by Britain from the Ottoman Empire in World War I. In 1921 he became head of the Indian National Congress and for the following thirteen years was a key figure in the nationalist movement. He resigned in 1934 because he did not share the socialist convictions of most of the Congress, and was in any case so popular that he feared he was becoming a distraction from the nationalist cause. But ultimately he played a crucial role in the negotiations that led to Indian independence in 1947.

Thereafter, the concept of satyagraha spread to other parts of the world. In the United States there had been increasing contact and sympathy between those struggling for African American civil rights and the Indian independence movement since the visits of Vivekananda and Dharmapala in the 1890s and 1900s. In the 1920s such direct contacts between the two movements intensified. By the late 1930s a number of influential African American leaders traveled to India to meet Gandhi and other Indian nationalists, and satyagraha became an important influence in the nascent American Civil Rights Movement. In 1939 a student of Gandhi who had immigrated to the United States, Krishnalal Shridharani, published in English a book titled *War without Violence,* which became a key text for the Congress of Racial Equality (CORE), a crucial early civil rights organization founded by students at the University of Chicago in 1942. Among those interested in Gandhi's ideas and strategy was Martin Luther King Jr. In his 1958 book about the Montgomery Bus Boycott of 1955, a key episode in the struggle for civil rights, King wrote: "Prior to reading Gandhi I had about concluded that the ethics of Jesus were only effective in individual relationship[s]. . . . [W]hen racial groups and nations were in conflict, a more realistic approach seemed necessary. But after reading Gandhi, I saw how utterly mistaken I was."[60] The Student Nonviolent Coordinating Committee (SNCC), formed in 1960, was also profoundly influenced by the idea of satyagraha.

There were other influences on the Civil Rights Movement. William Mackinder Salter, for example, whose 1889 book influenced Gandhi, was also one of the cofounders of the National Association for the Advancement of Colored People (NAACP); his teacher Felix Adler was a cofounder of the American Civil Liberties Union and the National Urban League. All these organizations played an important role in the triumph of the Civil Rights Movement. But certainly it is also true that the United States owes that triumph in part to Gandhi.

In South Africa nonviolence was much less successful. The African National Congress, formed in 1912, counted Gandhi as one of its inspirations, and held to a nonviolent strategy until 1960; but then it felt forced by the violence of government repression (in particular the Sharpeville Massacre, in which sixty-nine demonstrators were shot dead) to adopt armed struggle. Despite a limited campaign of guerilla war in the late 1970s and 1980s, however, ultimately the apartheid regime was overthrown primarily by nonviolent means. The movement to overthrow the dictatorship of Ferdinand Marcos in the Philippines in 1986 explicitly adopted Gandhian methods. And Gandhian thought also influenced the nonviolent overthrow of Communist regimes in Eastern Europe.[61]

Why did Gandhi's ideas achieve this global reach? The obvious explanation is that those ideas were from their inception global in their origins and affinities. Satyagraha spoke to people in multiple cultural contexts at least partly in a language with which they were familiar and that had powerful resonances for them.

A second telling example of cultural globalization is derived from a quite different sphere of life: not politics, but the arts. As the consumer economy grew and established itself in the late nineteenth and early twentieth centuries, entertainment became one of its benefits—at first, in the 1880s and 1890s, in the societies of the North Atlantic, but increasingly elsewhere around the globe as well. The most striking example of course was the movies, which grew from virtually nothing at the end of the 1890s to become one of the most widespread forms of popular entertainment on the planet. The film industry was from the outset fully international and was dominated in the early years by French and American companies. Pathé, the greatest French filmmaker, had forty-one offices internationally by 1914, and it dominated the market in Asia. In 1913, only 12 percent of films shown in Germany were made in Germany, whereas 31 percent were American-made, and 27 percent Italian. American films became so popular in Latin America that some moral reformers feared they were undermining US influence, because—as one activist in the global temperance (anti-alcohol) movement put it in 1925—so many movies seemed to present "lawlessness, crime, theft, murder, highway robbery, broken homes, . . . and free love as typical of American life."[62]

The whole motion picture industry was a product of technological innovation—the development of the movie camera, advances in chemistry that underlay the development of modern film, the electric railway and streetcar (which brought people to the entertainment districts sprouting up in central-city areas around the world). But it depended too on the spread of urbanization to concentrate populations and hence audiences, on the growth of the cash economy and rise in living standards; and on the spread of electric power provision.

Spectator sports, too, thrived for many of the same reasons—especially because of the global reach of communication and transportation networks and the popular press, and the development of the urban infrastructure to support mass spectatorship. Airplane, automobile, and bicycle races, which drew crowds in the tens of thousands in the 1910s and 1920s, were also directly created by technological advances. But few sports had a more impressive advent than football (soccer, to Americans). Invented in Britain, it was spread around the world by British expatriates from the 1880s onward. By the 1920s soccer was a global sport, flourishing first in port cities exposed to global cultural currents. FIFA (Fédération Internationale de Football Association), the international governing body of the sport, was formed in 1904 by representatives from seven European nations; by 1914 seven more European countries, along with Argentina, Chile, South Africa, and the United States joined; in the 1920s nine more European nations, fourteen Latin American nations, Canada, Turkey, and Egypt all joined. The first World Cup tournament was held in Uruguay in 1930.[63]

Another important form of entertainment that flourished partly as a result of the transportation revolution was the variety theater. Variety theaters were low-brow or middle-brow alternatives to "high culture" theater; they offered light entertainment based on a mix of short acts or "numbers"—songs, short films, strong-man and acrobatic acts, stand-up comedy, trained animal acts, and dance numbers. Many offered "exotic" acts drawn from faraway places around the world—Turkish strong men, Russian dancing bears, Cambodian, Javanese, or Indian dance troupes, and so on.

Modern dance emerged in the context of such innovations—with film and variety theater playing direct roles in generating its popularity. At its inception around 1900, modern dance was primarily offered by individual performers, who could easily slot into a "variety" program. Isadora Duncan, from San Francisco, is the best-known example; she became a dance star and celebrity in Europe in 1902–3.[64] But there was a small army of such performers. Among them, perhaps the second–most prominent was Ruth Dennis, who performed under the stage name St. Denis. Her career well illustrates the complexities of the globalization process.[65]

St. Denis was born in New Jersey, the daughter of an American mother and an English immigrant father—a product, in other words, of the great wave of British migration to North America in the late nineteenth century. In her childhood she studied a movement system developed by the Frenchman Francois Delsarte that was used as a form of performance and also to train young middle-class women in graceful comportment. She went into variety theater and performed for some years in dance productions, primarily in New York, put on by David Belasco, a child of Portuguese-English immigrants (to San Francisco). In 1904 she went into business on her own, performing dances based on the theme of "Oriental" mysticism. About a year later she encountered some Indian musicians and dancers at one of the amusement parks at Coney Island, in New York, and was inspired to develop specifically "Indian" dances. She achieved enormous success in Europe performing these supposedly Indian dances (figures 4.3–4.5).

St. Denis was capitalizing on a popular craze for everything "Oriental" that swept Europe and North America from about the mid-1880s onward. That wave of enthusiasm itself was a reflection of the cultural influence of imperialism and of the reception of Asian culture—not least, for example, at the Parliament of the World's Religions in 1893. The way had been paved for St. Denis's

Figure 4.3 Ruth St. Denis as an "Indian" Dancer.

career by various dancers and dance troupes brought to Europe and North America from colonial dependencies or independent states recently "opened" by European free-trade policy—including, among others, Sada Yacco, a Japanese performer who made a huge splash at the 1900 World's Fair in Paris, and Cambodian dancers brought to Europe in the wake of France's conquests in Southeast Asia. Other European and American dancers did much the same. For example, "Mata Hari," a Dutch woman, married a Dutch colonial official and lived for a time in Java before returning to Europe as an "Oriental" dancer; Regina Woody from New Jersey performed as "Nila Devi"; and Olive Craddock, an Anglo-Indian woman, danced in Europe under the name "Roshanara."

St. Denis was unusual, however, in that in 1911 she returned to the United States, opened the Denishawn Dance School, and ultimately established herself as perhaps the single-greatest influence on American modern dance. In 1926 she took her dance company to India, where members gave more than a hun-

Figure 4.4 Ruth St. Denis as an "Egyptian" Dancer.

dred performances, often to rave reviews. The great nationalist, poet, educator, and advocate for the revival of Indian dance traditions Rabindranath Tagore even urged her to stay in India and teach dance at the arts center and university he founded.[66] St. Denis's visit, along with those of other performers such as the Russian ballerina Anna Pavlova and the Californian Maud Allan, helped to inspire the rediscovery of Indian dance forms—among others, by leading members of the Theosophical Society.[67] Their performances appear to have helped to establish Indian dance traditions as a respectable form of entertainment for the emerging urban nationalist middle class in India—whereas they had previously been regarded as primarily a form of lower-class entertainment. That was effectively a slap in the face to racist ideology, which would have held that Indian dance was inferior to European forms of the art. St. Denis's timing was exquisite, for this was precisely the period when the Indian National Congress was developing a mass base and starting genuinely to threaten British rule.

The flow of ideas hardly flowed in one direction, however. Rabindranath Tagore's private secretary, the English gentleman Leonard Elmhirst, was inspired by Tagore's initiatives in India to found his own experimental school and arts community at Dartington Hall in Devonshire, England, in the mid-1920s. Dartington became a major center of dance innovation in Europe.[68] Before that, the Japanese dancers Michio Ito, who moved to Germany in 1911

Figure 4.5 Ruth St. Denis as an "Spanish" Dancer.

and then on to London, New York, and Los Angeles, had a significant influence on British modernist drama and on dance in the United States.[69]

Modern dance in fact appears to have played this kind of universalizing role on a global scale—helping to generate a global cultural community in which aesthetic codes were not ranked in a hierarchy, but celebrated as part of the variety of human experience. To cite another example, Tórtola Valencia achieved prominence as a modern dancer in England and Spain before World War I, then went on to tour extensively in Latin America during the war and the 1920s. Valencia was a hero of "Latinism" in Spain—the idea that the peoples of Southern Europe shared important cultural and racial characteristics and should band together to counterbalance the influence of the "Germanic" nations—Britain, Germany, and the United States (the last of which had defeated Spain and taken its colonies in 1898).[70] But in Latin America she became a hero of the "indigenist" movement, or *indigenismo,* by developing performances that she claimed were based on American traditions—for example, an "Inca War Dance" that was a big hit in Chile and Peru.[71] Or consider Inayat Khan, an Indian musician and spiritual teacher who was hired by both Ruth St. Denis (in the United States) and Mata Hari (in France) to accompany their dance performances. A few years later, in 1914, he would found Universal Sufism, bringing Islamic mystical and ethical traditions to the West.

Both Gandhian nonviolence and modern dance exemplify an important characteristic of global culture in the early twentieth century. By the 1920s the underlying political and economic transformations of the nineteenth and early twentieth centuries—mass migration, imperialism, growing economic integration, revolutions in transportation and communication—were creating a new degree and kind of global cultural integration. Increasingly, major developments in intellectual life and the arts could not be said to derive from origins lying in any one of the great historic centers of human population and culture, and then to be transferred from there to other societies. Instead they were hybrid phenomena, which had their origins in global cultural networks. From their inception they built on influences from multiple different cultural centers, and they appealed to people across these various centers for that reason.

Gandhi and St. Denis "worked" loose, noninstitutional intellectual and cultural networks. In the fifty years (roughly) before and after 1900, however, an increasingly dense network of transnational organizations and institutions also emerged. In fact, by the years just after 1900, new terms came into circulation to describe the emergence of these institutions: they were expressions of *internationalism,* of the creation of an increasingly international "civil society" of intergovernmental organizations (IGOs) or international nongovernmental organizations (INGOs).[72] Many of these international organizations responded to threats created by the economic, political, and social changes transforming world society from the last third of the nineteenth century. An early example was the creation in 1839 of a number of sanitary offices within the Ottoman Empire (in Constantinople [Istanbul], Tangiers, Alexandria) and in Tehran with international staff in order to meet the threat of the spread of contagious diseases (particularly cholera and the plague) among the pilgrims who traveled to Mecca and then returned home each year. The work of those agencies was guided by international sanitary conferences that met regularly from 1851 on and formed part of a growing network of international organizations devoted to controlling contagious diseases. By 1907 the International Office of Public Hygiene was established in Paris to exchange epidemiological information among national and international health and hygiene agencies. International Veterinary Congresses began meeting in 1863, again primarily to control the spread of animal diseases within the rapidly internationalizing world of animal husbandry.[73] By 1900 horrendous accident rates and other risks of industrial employment, as well as the growing challenge of the socialist working-class movements, moved governments and social work experts and economists, particularly in Europe, to form the International Union for Workers' Protection, with headquarters in Switzerland. It aimed to reduce the social costs (including class tensions) of rapid industrial development by promoting best practices in worker safety—for example, through an international agreement in 1906 to ban the use of white phosphorous in match factories.[74] The horrors of imperialism and war could spark action as well: the Red Cross, formed in 1863; the Geneva Convention of 1864; the burgeoning international peace movement of the early twentieth century and two international peace conferences in The Hague in 1899 and 1907 (and the formation of the Permanent Court of International Justice); and the Congo Reform Association, an international alliance of journalists, activists, philanthropists, and politicians who exposed abuses in the Congo Free State.[75]

A number of international conferences and intergovernmental conventions in the late nineteenth century sought to solve a different problem: protecting rights to intellectual property, a critical precondition for the international mobilization of technology and investment for development. Conferences in Paris in 1883 and Bern in 1886 resulted in international agreement on basic practices, with oversight by the United International Bureau for the Protection of Intellectual Property (1893).[76]

In other cases, organizations were formed, rather, to seize or realize the new opportunities that economic, technological, and political change offered. Both the Universal Postal Union and the International Telegraph Union aimed to maximize the global potential of new communication and transportation technologies. The International Bureau of Weights and Measurements was set up in Switzerland in 1875 to help smooth world trade and collaborative scientific research. The International Agricultural Institute (see chapter 3) would fall in this category too. Scientific societies formed a crucial part of the web of international organizations, helping to generate international scientific communities that could exchange ideas, prevent the duplication of effort, establish shared vocabularies, and share data (for example, in publications). Many first took the form of regular conferences, rather than permanent organizations. The first International Geological Congress, for example, met in 1878, whereas the International Union of Geological Sciences was not formed until 1961. By the late 1930s there were some fifty such organizations.[77] Engineering societies were another important case. The International Congresses of Electricians started in 1881 and gave rise in 1906 to the International Electrotechnical Commission. Such organizations fostered international economic activity by facilitating technology transfer and adoption and by establishing universal engineering standards for such things as the pitch of screw threads, the sensitivity of photographic film, and (eventually) the thickness of credit cards.[78]

Although needs generated by an increasingly globalizing scientific, technological, and business environment played the largest role in motivating the formation of international organizations, they were by no means the only kinds of organizations important in this period. Recreational culture was also being internationalized. The International Olympic Committee, created in 1894, is a good example, and FIFA (1904) is mentioned earlier in this chapter, but fifteen other international sports organizations were created before 1914. The twenty or thirty years around 1900 saw the emergence of a growing number of international women's organizations that sought to use international networks of communication, transportation, and expertise to gain leverage for women's rights. The total of twenty-two organizations included the World Woman's Christian Temperance Union (1876), the International Council of Women (1888), the International Woman Suffrage Alliance (1904), the Young Women's Christian Association (1894), the General Federation of Women's Clubs (1890), the International Socialist Women's Secretariat (1909). The Inter-Parliamentary Union (1889) sought to coordinate the policies among members of national parliaments (at first only French and British)—a means of exchanging policy expertise, but also of trying to contain the national executive's ability to set the context of international relations.[79] The First (1864) and Second (1889) Socialist Internationals pursued similar goals, offering national political parties access to broader expertise and world public opinion and making an end-run around capitalist foreign policy.

Again, the number of such organizations expanded at an accelerating rate (albeit with a pause during the First World War): whereas by 1874 there had been only some thirty-seven INGOs, by 1900 there were two hundred; by 1930 there were eight hundred. In 1907 the density of INGOs particularly in the North Atlantic was sufficient that the Union of International Associations was formed to keep track of them all.[80]

In the articulation of this web of international associations and agreements, then, we can see a piecemeal, uncoordinated, but nevertheless self-conscious effort to contain potentially disruptive tendencies and build on the constructive effects of growing interconnectedness. Their creation was in that sense a part of the global development project—tailored not to developing particular resources, but to managing the broader global processes it set in motion.

While the web was rapidly becoming more intricate, however, in the early twentieth century it was still extremely uneven and tenuous—concentrated in the North Atlantic, with a few strands reaching to Egypt, Japan, Turkey, Australia, South Africa, and Latin America. In fact, cultural globalization had a far greater impact on societies around the world than did organized "internationalism." Among other things, it played an important part in laying the intellectual and cultural foundations for the Great Explosion of modern societies in the period between about 1905 and 1945—a period of massive revolutionary and military upheavals. We can see that explosion in part as the working out, at the political level, of the implications of this growing cultural integration of the globe.

Chapter 5 turns to that topic.

The Great Explosion

CHAPTER

5

THE GLOBAL REVOLUTIONARY MOMENT, 1890–1923

[W]e give notice: that [regarding] the fields, timber, and water which the land-lords . . . or bosses have usurped, the [villages] or citizens who have titles . . . to those properties will immediately enter into possession of that real estate of which they have been despoiled by the bad faith of our oppressors. . . . In virtue of the fact that the immense majority of Mexican [villages] and citizens are . . . suffering the horrors of poverty without being able to improve their social condition in any way or to dedicate themselves to industry or agriculture, because lands, timber and water are monopolized in a few hands, for this cause there will be expropriated one third of those monopolies . . . with prior indemnification. . . . The landlords . . . or bosses who oppose the present plan directly or indirectly, their goods will be nationalized.[1]

Emiliano Zapata, *Plan de Ayala*, 1911

By about 1905, the developments discussed in the foregoing chapters reached a critical mass in many places around the world. Economic changes driven by the growth of the global economy generated severe tensions and conflicts within many societies around the world. As the anthropologist Eric Wolf argued in 1969, in many countries peasants in particular—family or subsistence farmers owning relatively small amounts of land—faced difficulties in adjusting to the growth of the world trade in food and other agricultural products, to the influx into rural economies of foreign and domestically generated investment capital, and to changes in the organization of labor. The resulting "Peasant Question" led to a long series of "peasant wars of the twentieth century," reaching from the Mexican, Russian, and Chinese revolutions in the 1910s to those in Viet Nam, Algeria, and Cuba in the 1950s and 1960s.[2] Equally critical in many societies were the rise of industrial labor, the problem of workers' economic rights, and the question of how to integrate industrial laborers (who were often attracted to socialism) into political structures in which capitalists had increasing influence. The rise of commercial, entrepreneurial, and professional middle classes under the impact of economic change created similar issues in societies where aristocrats and monarchs retained great political and institutional power. Moreover, while some in those new middle classes were eager to collaborate with foreign capital, others resented its power in their societies. For those states that had maintained their independence, the fear of being economically and militarily outclassed or even conquered by the expanding imperialist powers mounted as well, sparking intense debates and conflicts over what economic, social, and political measures might be required to face down those formidable rivals.

The years between 1905 and about 1923 saw the sudden detonation of a wave of revolutions driven by these tensions and conflicts. In the middle of that wave the First World War broke out, eventually sparking a whole new set of revolutions. The Great War, as it was known, was the product of the imperial rivalries and the global struggle for control of resources and markets that had characterized the nineteenth century, as well as an outgrowth of the political forces and conflicts generated by the spreading influence of nationalism and ethnicity. It was unprecedented in its scope and destructiveness, both because decades of imperialism had drawn large parts of the world into the orbit of the North Atlantic societies that were the primary contending parties in it, and because industrial development and advances in armaments technology transformed warfare. The second wave of revolutions that the war helped spawn gave rise to new forms of political organization that rested on the new ideas regarding class, race, and nationality. Those political systems made extensive use of new communications technologies and pursued modernizing economic, social, cultural, and educational agendas. All these conflicts unfolded virtually simultaneously in the space of about two decades; by the 1930s, they had created a distinctly new world order. From the beginning of that decade, however, that order was plunged into disarray, and ultimately into an even bigger and more destructive conflict, the Second World War. That war was brought about both by a profound crisis of the new global economy and by a deepening ideological confrontation between movements and states committed to different ways of organizing the modern world.

In short, between about 1905 and 1945 all the economic, political, and cultural developments discussed in the foregoing chapters came together in a gigantic and profoundly unfortunate concatenation of conflicts. One result was the violent death of between 100 and 200 million human beings. Another was the destruction of the old and the creation of a new order of international relations.

The first and archetypal revolution of this period was the Russian Revolution, which started in 1905, was stamped out by the czarist regime by 1907, and then, ten years later, reignited and ultimately led to the creation of the world's first communist state—the Union of Soviet Socialist Republics (USSR). The revolution grew out of a range of the developments discussed in earlier chapters. One was a rapid growth in population that created a shortage of land and deepening desperation among the Russian peasantry. The peasants had been emancipated from serfdom in 1861; but Russian agriculture remained technologically backward and poorly organized, and peasants were deeply resentful of the fact that only a few had gained ownership of the land they continued to work, while the rest were tenants, many for absentee landlords. Over subsequent decades the success of some peasants as small agricultural entrepreneurs allowed them to expand their landholdings, reducing others to dependency as tenants or sharecroppers; but that widening gap generated intense resentments within peasant communities, as well.

A second destabilizing process was the growth of industry, which created a new class of factory workers in Russia's major cities. A high proportion of those workers felt exploited and abused by their employers. Trade unions were illegal in the Russian Empire, and in the context of rapid population growth and a glut of labor, Russian employers could pay very low wages. Many Russian workers were attracted to socialism, which promised to give them more of the fruits of their own labor. Often they were also concentrated in and around large modern factories owned by foreigners or funded by foreign capital—a situation that both facilitated political organizing and fed the sense of alienation from the rich as (literally or metaphorically) "outsiders" in Russian society.

The international spread of the idea of the nation and of parliamentary government was a third important factor. By 1900, a large proportion of the Russian social and political elite were increasingly committed to the idea that parliamentary government and active citizenship were the only effective ways to organize a modern society and state, and they became impatient with the authoritarianism of the czarist regime.

The spark that ultimately set off the revolution was generated by mass migration, settlement, and imperial war. In 1904 Russia went to war with Japan over control of Manchuria, a region of rapid settlement and intensive commodity extraction (mining and soybean farming). The war turned out to be too much for the still relatively economically backward country to manage. It led to severe dislocations of the financial system and food distribution, food riots, and mass protest marches; radical socialist workers set up local revolutionary governments; peasants occupied lands and killed their landlords; a new Constitutional Democratic Party demanded constitutional reform; and the Russian Empire descended into civil war.

The imperial government won that struggle by making peace with Japan and calling the army back home to crush the political radicals, and by promising parliamentary and legal reforms. It did introduce a number of reforms, but by the time World War I broke out, the social, economic, and governmental problems that had underlain the first revolutionary outbreak in 1905 had not been solved. As a result, the imperial regime's governing capacity was once again overwhelmed by the demands of war, and a crisis emerged almost identical to the earlier one. World War I, however, was a much larger war, and was much harder for the Russian government to extract itself from; and this time, the radicals were able to win the civil war that ensued. What followed—the creation of the Bolshevik dictatorship under the great theorist of communism and leader of the Bolshevik party Vladimir Lenin, and then under Joseph Stalin—is discussed in greater depth in the following chapter. In brief, the collapse of the Russian imperial state was followed by a massive and extremely destructive multiparty civil war, in which socialists, communists, anarchists, liberals, peasant autonomists, conservative monarchists, and multiple foreign powers (Poland, France, Britain, the United States, Japan) struggled for control of the country. The ultimate outcome was the victory of the Bolshevik or Communist Party—which then established a one-party state that set out to abolish or demolish what survived of the imperial social order, including the institutions of the monarchist state, the middle classes, the aristocracy, religious communities, the family, and the nineteenth-century order of gender relations. All these were to be replaced by a new, socialist order that, directed by the party, would drive forward the economic and industrial economy of Russia and challenge the capitalist powers' organization of the world economy.[3]

The initial upheaval in Russia in 1905 was followed by constitutionalist rebellions in Iran (then called Persia) in 1906 and the Ottoman Empire (centered on what is now Turkey) in 1908, in which some segments of local social and political elites—particularly businessmen, administrators, students, and army officers—forced the Ottoman sultan and the shah of Iran to introduce or expand parliamentary government. As in Russia, these groups were convinced that modern societies could be governed effectively only by parliamentary systems. In both cases, furthermore, nationalist sentiment reinforced this view, since parliamentary government was in theory representative of the nation, not of a ruler. As the idea of a Turkish or Persian national identity took hold among people whose business interests or institutional duties were broadening their horizons, they began to see the old monarchies as an obstacle to modernization and national power.

In Iran and Turkey, many of these people were in fact convinced that only such an effective modern government could preserve them from financial dependence on and exploitation (or even conquest) by imperialist powers such as Russia, Britain, and France. Indeed, the British and the Russians had been eyeing Persia (Iran) greedily for more than a decade, particularly because it was clear by the 1890s that the potential for major oil discoveries was high there—a potential duly realized in 1908. In both Iran and Turkey, people who had studied abroad or had been forced into exile played a critical role. Many of the Ottoman radicals—whose organization took the name Committee of Union and Progress (CUP), though they are often called the Young Turks—studied in Paris at the end of the nineteenth century, and they were initially headquartered there.

Outcomes varied. In the Ottoman Empire, the CUP launched a military insurrection in 1908 that forced the reactivation of the constitution of 1876, obliged the sultan to abdicate in 1909, and gradually consolidated power within the Ottoman state after a series of military coups and countercoups culminating in 1913. In the process CUP adherents gradually abandoned their liberal principles ("Liberty, Fraternity, Equality and Justice") in favor of authoritarian rule—including regular use of martial law, rigged elections, the arrest of political opponents on trumped-up charges, a ban on strikes in the public sector, restrictions on freedom of the press, and a political culture that urged people to adopt mottoes such as "I close my eyes / I do my duty." National chauvinism and exclusionary and expansionist racial ideas (pan-Turkism) played an increasing role as well. In the context of the Ottoman defeat in World War I (on the losing side with Germany and Austria) and occupation by the Allies, the Young Turks launched a national war of liberation in 1919 and created the modern, secular Turkish Republic under the leadership of Kemal Atatürk. Among other things, that republic abolished the caliphate; closed down the Sufi orders; separated Islamic and civil law and adopted law codes based on Swiss, Italian, and German models; secularized the schools; introduced the Western calendar and a version of the Latin alphabet; granted rights to women (including the vote, in 1934) and discouraged the veil; quadrupled school enrollments and expanded coeducation in the schools; and established one-party rule by the Republican People's Party, which lasted until 1945.[4]

In Iran, businessmen and religious authorities were initially allied against the shah's dependency on foreign loans and monopolistic commercial concessions to foreign companies (for example, in oil, fishing, and tobacco). They secured promulgation of a parliamentary constitution at the end of 1906. But the coalition that had achieved this largely peaceful revolution soon broke down as more conservative religious leaders became alienated by the liberal constitutionalists' projects for educational and judicial reform, as well as a constitutional guarantee of legal and political equality for Iran's religious minorities. The country fell into disarray, with regional warlords and tribes effectively in control of much of the country and successive interventions by the Russians, the British, and the Persian army. In 1925 the commander of the army, Mohammad Reza Pahlavi, finally reimposed central control and founded a new dynasty. His regime, like that of Atatürk in Turkey, introduced numerous nationalist, modernizing, and secularizing measures, including introducing new secular codes of commercial, criminal, and civil law; stripping the clergy of most of their legal functions as judges and notaries; introducing secular education (including in girls' schools); rapidly developing the transportation infrastructure; and forbidding the wearing of the veil in any public place, while requiring that men wear hats.[5]

In the meantime, Mexico too exploded into a bitter, complex revolution and civil war, which raged off and on from 1910 to 1929. After an attempted French imperialist conquest in the 1860s, Mexico had been ruled for a quarter century by Porfirio Díaz. Using massive voter fraud, press censorship, and imprisonment or exile of opponents to get himself reelected over and over again, Díaz drove forward the country's economic development by repressing the labor movement, the press, and political dissent, and by passing laws encouraging the transfer of land ownership from the state and indigenous "Indian" peasant communities to wealthier groups such as the owners of Mexico's large estates and ranches (*haciendas*) and North American and European investors, with the aim of creating more efficient commercial agricultural enterprises. By 1910 the rail network encompassed thirty times as many miles as in 1876 (with 80 percent of the capital coming from the United States); the mining industry had expanded by a factor of ten (with some three-quarters of it owned by US firms); agricultural exports had grown by a factor of five and overall foreign trade almost by a factor of ten. Mexico had a thriving commodity extraction sector producing for export, including both minerals and agricultural products such as meat, leather, sugar, cotton, and sisal (a natural fiber used for baling twine by mechanical reapers, introduced in North America starting in 1878).[6]

The social consequences of all this change, however, were extreme. One-fifth of the country's entire land area—some 40 million acres—had been transferred from the state or Indian communities to large *haciendas* or substantial independent farms (*ranchos*). Some eight hundred extended and intermarried families owned up to nine-tenths of the cultivable land in the country, concentrated in giant *haciendas* where semifeudal conditions prevailed. Particularly on sisal and sugar plantations in the south, debt peonage became widespread and workers lived in deepening semislavery. Only 3 percent of Mexicans owned any land; some 90 percent of the rural population had no direct access to land at all, either as owners or as members of a village with communal land rights. Foreigners owned a quarter of the country's land. The production of food had stagnated, population growth was rapid, and prices for basic foodstuffs rose, but the incomes of the poor did not. Productivity gains in the economy as a whole just barely exceeded population growth, in part because of the deepening poverty of domestic consumers and the availability of cheap—or desperate—labor. Much of Mexico's ruling elite, mostly of European heritage, saw all of these developments as part of a natural process, since they regarded the indigenous "Indian" (*indio*) majority as racially inferior.[7]

Just as in Russia, however, discontent mounted among the land-hungry peasantry, the growing rural middle class, and the expanding, poorly paid industrial working class—which, here too, was often concentrated in large factories and mines, many of them foreign-owned, and not allowed to form trade unions to negotiate for better pay or conditions. A growing number of Mexicans were also increasingly committed to *indigenismo* and therefore rejected the domination of their society either by its own ethnic European elite or by foreign investors. But many in the elite itself were convinced that Díaz and his friends were hoarding all the benefits of economic development—high office, lucrative business deals, bribes, and access to land. In the context of a financial crisis starting in 1907, some of these people revolted and forced him out of office.[8]

One of their leaders initially was Francisco Madero, who like many other revolutionaries around the world in this period, had studied abroad, in Paris and at the University of California. Madero was a vegetarian, teetotalist, ascetic devotee of Spiritualism who was directed by the spirits he contacted to become "a soldier of liberty and progress" and "carry out a great mission on earth" in the service of the heavenly father.[9] His triumph in 1911—when Díaz was driven into exile—and his assassination in 1913 precipitated an extraordinary explosion of violence, with one military coup or assassination following another and mass mobilization of workers in the center of the country, cowboys in the north led by Pancho Villa, and *indio* peasants in the south led by Emiliano Zapata. By the end of the revolution, up to one in eight Mexicans died of violence or hunger.[10]

By about 1915, nationalists had defeated the more radical social revolutionaries and were gradually consolidating their hold on the government—winning support, among other things, by abolishing debt peonage and redistributing 17 million acres of land seized from their opponents to reconstituted peasant communities, the *ejidos*, or collective farms. Zapata and Villa were assassinated, and the government fought (and then negotiated an end to) a low-level civil war in the late 1920s against Catholic conservatives who objected to laws that seized Church property, secularized education, and subjected priests to draconian social restrictions—for example, prohibiting them from wearing their robes outside church. Ultimately the new regime reorganized itself as the Institutional Revolutionary Party (PRI) and consolidated its power as a one-party state, which ruled the country until 2000. Among other things, it nationalized the petroleum industry (in 1938) and distributed some 85 million acres of land to landless peasants and *ejidos* between 1934 and 1964.[11]

In China, the Qing dynasty, which many nationalists regarded as an ethnically foreign, Manchu regime, was overthrown in 1911, at least in part by people who fit the familiar cast of characters. The Chinese Republican movement was dominated by businessmen, administrators, students, and military men who believed that the outdated institutional structure of the Chinese Empire could not effectively govern a modernizing society. A number of them had studied in Japan, and looked with admiration to the Japanese constitution of 1889, which seemed to have created a highly effective modern political structure. They saw the defeat of China in the Sino-Japanese War of 1894–95 and the disaster of the Boxer Uprising, when an army of Japanese, British, French, and US soldiers once again took Beijing, as signs that China had to either modernize or face the prospect of being carved up by various imperial powers. The Japanese annexation of Korea in 1910 seemed to suggest that this danger was imminent. Meanwhile a class of agricultural entrepreneurs was growing in the countryside and was resentful both of the political stranglehold of the established ruling official–gentry class and its declining economic and international effectiveness. In China's coastal cities, in particular, workers struggled to assert their interests in new work settings, while business interests chafed at foreign influence—as evident in the fact that the "treaty ports" established after the Opium Wars were administered under European, not Chinese, law.

The revolutionary movement drew on all these potentials, and was accordingly internally divided. Nationalist intellectuals, despite their limited influence inside China, did initially succeed in putting their ideological stamp on a revolt that arose out of broad social causes. But the new Chinese Republic immediately fell under the power of its early military ally Yuan Shikai—the commander of the Qing army who brokered the abdication of the emperor, took over from Sun Zhongshan as provisional president of the new republic, and then drove Sun and his nationalists into exile in 1913 and declared himself emperor in 1915. When he died in 1916, the Republic disintegrated into a multisided civil war between rapidly shifting coalitions of regional warlords. The nationalists reconstituted themselves as a new political party structured along highly disciplined and centralized lines—the Guomindang (Kuomintang, in the Wade-Giles system of transliteration, or KMT). The KMT received assistance in money, arms, and political and military training from the new Bolshevik regime in Russia, and for some years cooperated with the Chinese Communist Party (CCP), formed in 1921. But after the death of Sun Zhongshan in 1925, leadership of the KMT fell to his brother-in-law Chiang Kai Shek (Jiang Jieshi), a vehement anticommunist with ties to Shanghai's business community. Jiang consolidated his position in the late 1920s, first by defeating the warlords in 1926 and then by turning on the Communists, massacring perhaps 20,000 of them in 1927.

Despite repeated military campaigns, however, the KMT regime failed to completely eliminate the Communist movement and its People's Liberation Army. Eventually coming under the leadership of Mao Zedong (Mao Tse-tung), who was both the party's most capable military commander and its chief ideologist, the CCP entrenched itself in remote rural northern China by the mid-1930s and in the process transformed itself from a Leninist workers' party into a Maoist peasants' party. At the same time, China came under attack from Japan, which seized mineral-rich Manchuria in 1931 and in 1937 launched a full-scale invasion of China. Over the following twelve years, the country sank into a chaotic three-way war between the KMT, the CCP, and Japan—a conflict that by 1941 was rolled into a titanic struggle for the control of the entire Asia-Pacific region.[12]

Each the foregoing cases had its unique features: in each, distinct histories, institutional structures, economic conditions and social structures, and strategic positions created a different situation and different possibilities. Yet there are striking similarities between them as well. In every case, one of the main sparks for revolution was a split within the social and political elite—some of whom remained committed to the existing political, social, and economic regime, while others favored institutional modernization. In every case, the agenda of institutional modernization was driven particularly by ideas of national or ethnic identity and of representative government, on the one hand, and on the other by the fear that in a world of expanding empires those states that did not modernize would eventually be eaten up. In every case, key leaders were people who had important international experience. In every case, the revolt of discontented elites ran parallel to a broader revolt of ordinary people struggling to deal with the growing day-to-day pressures of the international economy. This revolt included both industrial workers caught up in the development of the modern industrial-commercial economy and poor farmers—peasants—caught up in the creation of the modern global food economy.[13] And in every case, the ultimate outcome was a modernized and modernizing form of dictatorship, mostly one-party rule by a modern mass political movement. In every case, that regime waged a bitter struggle against religious authorities and institutions as it sought to drive forward social change. And many of those dictatorships survived until the second great wave of revolutionary upheavals of the twentieth century, which began with the Iranian Revolution in 1979 and ended with the collapse of the PRI regime in Mexico in 2000.

In almost every one of these revolutions, furthermore, socialism played a central role. Kemal Atatürk had a crucial supporter in the Soviet regime in Russia, which was fighting against Allied invasion and occupation at precisely the same time. The Mexican regime of the PRI adopted important elements of socialist economic strategy. Socialism was central to the Chinese Republican movement, and ultimately it was the Communist Party of China, rather than the KMT, that emerged victorious from the struggle that started in 1911. Why?

For one thing, the rise of socialism after the middle of the nineteenth century was part of a broader pattern of resistance to the capitalist reorganization of global society. Working people used socialism as a form of resistance against the organization of industrial and commercial capitalism and its reorganization of many societies as a result of the nineteenth-century scientific-technological-economic transformations. In fact, most socialists were also anti-imperialist, regarding imperial adventures as predatory capitalist expansion, funded by taxes paid by working people but benefiting primarily the capitalists. In short, the world socialist movement was partly a response to the violent and coercive aspects of the global development project discussed in chapters 1 and 2. Nineteenth-century socialism also belonged, however, to the broader pattern of religious innovation, for it promised the creation of a pacific, harmonious, and virtuous kingdom of God on earth, albeit defined in purely secular terms as a reign of universal peace and justice in the socialist state of the future. Finally, we may see socialism as a fifth vocabulary of difference—besides race, ethnic, national, and religious difference, there is also class difference. As societies became more mobilized, educated, and information-rich, people in different social groups increasingly identified their particular role and place in society in contradistinction to the roles and places of other social groups—just as they learned more about people in other societies. And in the eyes of most socialists, working people were different from and better than people who did not work.

It is equally useful to think of socialism as yet another universalist alternative to the languages of difference. Socialists usually argued, for example, that established religions were at best a private matter, and at worst were effectively a plot to reconcile working people to their oppression. As the greatest theorist of socialism, Karl Marx, put it, religion was "the opium of the people"—something that helped merely to dull the pain of poverty and exploitation and to teach humility and self-abnegation, not to actually change people's situation. In any case it should be politically irrelevant. Socialists usually argued that the national state, too, was just a convenient tool for the ruling class—in Marx's words, "a committee for managing the common affairs of the whole bourgeoisie," the capitalist ruling class.[14] The government was useful for suppressing worker discontent and protest, maintaining a system of laws stacked against the interests of working people, and waging commercial conflicts with the ruling classes of other societies. So-called racial or ethnic differences, too, were merely one more tool the ruling class could use to divide and dominate working people.

In contrast, socialism taught that everyone is fundamentally the same. All working people share one fundamental experience of life, one fundamental set of values, one set of concrete social, political, and economic interests. And everyone should work. For this reason, socialism was organized at an international level—in the first International Workingmen's Association, formed in London in 1864 (with its first meeting in Geneva in 1866). That organization split between socialists and anarchists in 1876, but the Second International was formed in 1889 and lasted until 1916. The socialist movement around the world had one slogan—"Workers of the World, Unite!"—and an anthem, the "Internationale." The national socialist political parties and labor unions were officially committed to "internationalism"; that is, they were opposed to the division of humanity into competing and conflicting political entities.

By the 1890s, in many North Atlantic societies the socialist movement made an important organizational and political breakthrough. As industrialization advanced, incomes rose, literacy became increasingly common, and the density of interaction and communication particularly within urban society grew, working people were increasingly able to organize in trade unions and in socialist political parties to pursue a more equitable distribution of the economic rewards from technological change and from the construction of the world economy. By the 1900s, socialist trade union movements in industrialized countries were building memberships in the hundreds of thousands and even the millions, and receiving up to one-third of all votes in national elections (in Germany). Early social legislation (for example, worker compensation, factory safety, industrial arbitration, social insurance, and public health laws), the expansion of public services particularly in cities, and some success in securing workers' rights, shorter working hours, and higher wages gave the socialist movement both a growing sense of optimism and growing appeal around the world. While the largest socialist unions and parties were in Western Europe, socialist ideas and activism spread around the globe—perhaps not least because they offered a vision of a world order characterized not by conquest and exploitation, but by peace and cooperation.

Not surprisingly in this context, many leading figures in socialist movements led extraordinarily mobile lives, embodying in their biographies the globalization of culture and of politics in this period. Emblematic of this phenomenon is the Vietnamese communist leader Ho Chi Minh.[15] Ho was born in 1890 in the northern part of Viet Nam, at that time a French colony. At the age of twenty-one he went to the United States, and for the next seven or eight years moved back and forth between New York, Boston, and London, working at various jobs mostly in restaurants. From 1919 to 1923 he lived in France, where he took part in the formation of the French Communist Party. In 1923 he was in Moscow, where he worked for the Comintern, the international organization of Communist Parties, founded in 1921. From 1924 to 1927 he lived in southern China, and took part in radical politics there. Between 1928 and 1933 he lived in various places in Asia, including Thailand and Hong Kong, still as an operative of the Comintern. In 1933 he returned to Europe—first to Italy, then back to Moscow. In 1938 he moved back to China and took part in the Chinese Communist movement for the following three years. Finally in 1941 he returned to Viet Nam—thirty years after leaving—to take part in the guerilla war against the Japanese occupiers, then against the returning French colonial army, and then against the armies of the Republic of Viet Nam (South Viet Nam) and the United States. Ho, in short, spent upward of three decades as a participant in the global labor market and in a global revolutionary movement. By the time he emerged as the leader of the communist underground in his country of origin, he had friends and supporters all over the world.

Ho was an extreme case, but a large number of socialists and communists had considerable international experience. In fact, many experienced international solidarity not as an ideal or a theory, but as a lived reality, moving from place to place around the world where other socialists and communists welcomed and supported them. In that sense, we might draw a parallel with the emergence of *hybrid* cultural forms. Such forms had global origins, rather than originating in one place and then spreading to other places; many socialists and communists lived as citizens of a global socialist world, rather than of a particular national state.

In fact, socialism had important connections with cultural globalization, for many artistic "modernists"—champions of aesthetic innovations in painting, theater, or music that emerged in the late nineteenth and early twentieth centuries—were attracted to socialism as an antidote to what they saw as the predatory and destructive characteristics of the new, global capitalist order. The famous American dancer Isadora Duncan, for example, initially saw the Soviet Union as a beacon of the future, and went there in 1921 to set up a school of modern dance that, she hoped, would bring the joy and freedom of modern dance to the masses. The popular science-fiction novelist H. G. Wells was also a socialist and wrote an intensely optimistic, even euphoric essay on the "discovery of the future" (excerpted at the beginning of the third section of chapter 2).

Many socialists shared Wells's and Duncan's sense of optimism about the future, their sense that their movement had history on its side, not only because it aimed to express the political interests of the rapidly growing industrial working class, but also precisely because it was internationalist. As the world was being knit together ever more tightly by communications and transportation technologies, by global trade, by empires, by giant corporations, the socialist movement swam with that tide. True, the language of race, ethnicity, and nationalism or of religious difference might defend regional chauvinisms for a time; but the future seemed to belong to those who imagined a global society.

WAR FOR WORLD DOMINATION: PHASE I, 1914–1923

> I have been wounded in the head but hope to get better soon. My fate now is very lucky [in] that I am alive while all my brethren have been killed. . . . Such a scene has been enacted as when the leaves fall off a tree and not a space is left bare on the ground, so here the earth is covered with dead men and there is no place to put one's foot. . . . The whole ground was covered with blood. . . . [I]f I get killed it does not matter, when so many of my brethren have been slain it would not matter about me. . . . [N]o men are being left, some hundreds of thousands, nay millions; the whole world is being finished.[16]
>
> Rifleman Amar Singh Rawat to a friend in India, March 1915

Despite these international socialist connections, the "global revolutionary moment" did not initially create a more unified world. Instead, a decade after it began, a war erupted in Europe that grew so huge that it soon came to be known as the Great War in Britain and the World War elsewhere. The latter term is something of a misnomer, since the overwhelming share of the fighting took place in Europe. The Middle East saw a consequential military campaign in which British forces sought first to protect the Suez Canal connection to India and their control of oil fields in Persia, and then to dismantle and absorb most of the Ottoman Empire. There were also minor campaigns in East Africa and small battles and the occupation of some German colonies in the Pacific. And the European powers recruited or allied with hundreds of thousands of non-Europeans to fight in Europe and the Middle East—including some 1.2 million Indian soldiers, a million Africans, and several million men from Canada, the United States, Australia, and New Zealand.[17] But in Europe the war was an all-consuming and overwhelming catastrophe, one that transformed the continent's political structures, economies, and social orders. Between 1914 and 1918 all the remarkable technological and industrial achievements of the preceding decades were turned to the task of killing people: factory production, machine building, aviation, internal combustion engines, organic and inorganic chemistry, research and development. Those achievements imparted a new intensity and efficiency to destruction, just as they had to production. Britain lost many more men in the opening phases of the six-month Battle of the Somme in 1916 as in the entire fifteen years of the Napoleonic Wars. In that battle 150,000 British soldiers were killed, 100,000 were permanently incapacitated, and another 170,000 suffered lesser wounds.[18] Other combatant nations suffered similar losses in major battles at Verdun, Tannenberg, Caporetto, and many others. During more than four years of fighting, 8.5 million European men were killed in battle—an average of 5,592 men per day. As many as 6.5 million civilians also died, primarily of diseases related to hunger; 21 million European men were wounded, with 7 million of them permanently incapacitated.[19]

The economic consequences were equally devastating. Food production in Europe was cut by half during the war. By the end of the war, Europe had only half as many pigs as at its beginning. Cows, which give milk as well as meat, fared better: Europe had only 20 percent fewer in 1918 than in 1914. By 1918 the global food situation was so dire that hunger and malnutrition reduced human resistance to a terrible influenza pandemic, which took the lives of somewhere between 18 and 100 million people on five continents (estimates vary wildly).[20] Inflation caused by governments printing money to cover the costs of war and recovery erased the wealth of millions of Europeans. Thousands of ships were sunk, whole towns shattered by artillery fire; massive amounts of money were borrowed and spent on weapons, assets were sold, investment capital redirected and lost. As a result, net European investment abroad actually shrank between 1914 and 1938; and despite the rapid growth of investment from Holland, Japan, and the United States in particular, the world total increased during this twenty-five-year period by only one-half of 1 percent—a stunning reversal after the tremendous growth of world foreign direct investment in the previous half century (chart 5.1). France lost half of its total overseas investments, as its debtors defaulted on loans and foreign currencies inflated away to nothing—as was the case in Russia and Germany. Germany lost almost four-fifths of its prewar overseas investments. Europe overall was a net creditor to the United States in 1914; by 1920 it was a net debtor,

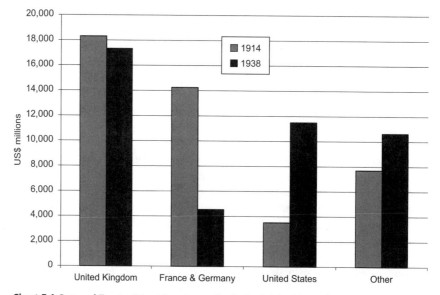

Chart 5.1 Outward Foreign Direct Investment Stocks by Origin, 1914 and 1938.

having borrowed from the United States to fund the war effort and then borrowed still more to rebuild. The total of foreign investment in Europe fell by almost two-fifths between 1914 and 1938; foreign investment in Africa, most of which was ruled by European colonial powers, fell by one-fifth (chart 5.2).

The world financial system recovered only very sluggishly from this economic chaos. It limped along through the 1920s, propped up by the strength of US-based banks; then, when those banks stumbled in the stock market crash of 1929, it collapsed. That financial cataclysm led to the Great Depression and a downward spiral into another war, one that was even more murderous in Europe, killing some 50 million people. But this second world war, unlike the first, was equally deadly in Asia, where, as early as 1937, the Japanese government and military launched a massive program of conquest in China and Southeast Asia and were not defeated until eight years later.

In short, between 1914 and 1945 almost the whole of Europe and Asia exploded in war, starvation, pestilence, and destruction. In 1947, when US secretary of state Henry Stimson was asked why America had decided to use the atomic bomb two years earlier, he answered, "The face of war is the face of death."[21] That was a suitable epitaph for the entire era of war between 1914 and 1945.

Why did the world descend into thirty years of intensifying warfare? Why on earth would political leaders in 1914 think that it was a good idea to turn the

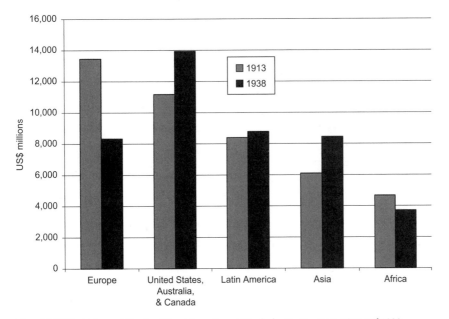

Chart 5.2 World Inward Foreign Direct Investment Stocks by Destination, 1914 and 1938.

power of the late-nineteenth and early-twentieth-century innovations to the task of mass organized killing and conquest?

The answer is that many leaders of powerful nations, undergoing rapid industrial and economic development and inspired by ideas about their own unique glory and mission, were striving to gain control of natural resources and populations on a continental and global scale, so that they could literally dominate the globe—militarily, politically, and economically. They sought to do that for two reasons. First, it seemed possible that they could achieve their aim, and thereby become wealthy, accumulate enormous prestige, and solve most if not all their internal problems (such as the threat of socialist revolution). Second, they feared that if they did not try to reach this goal, someone else would and they would suffer the consequences. Both ideas seemed plausible at the time because, in 1914, the world seemed in flux, creating a world climate full of possibility and danger.

One reason for this perception was that a number of massive imperial states appeared to be accumulating extraordinary power. The prime example was Great Britain. Britain had scored enormous imperial conquests in Africa since the beginning of the 1880s, including the two richest, most populated regions on that continent—Egypt and South Africa. That was on top of a gigantic empire it had already controlled in the early nineteenth century. By 1914 Britain ruled a quarter of the world's entire population. It was starting to develop the resources of at least some of that empire at an enormous rate—building railroads, mines, and farms in India, South Africa, Canada, Australia, and New Zealand, thereby opening up resources to the global economy on a continental scale. And the further ambitions of some of its leaders were extraordinary. Lord George Curzon, viceroy of India, remarked in 1898 that he and other British statesmen were playing a great "game for dominion of the world," and Queen Victoria too spoke of a contest for "supremacy in the world."[22]

But in the same period, the Russian Empire stretched from Warsaw to Vladivostok on the Pacific Ocean, with a population fast approaching 200 million. It poured 10 million settlers into Siberia and 4 million into Central Asia in the thirty years prior to World War I, and more were arriving by the month, building up agriculture, mining, commerce, and industry. Russia's economy was growing at close to 10 percent per year; its railways handled six times as much freight in 1913 as they had in 1883. It had plans to raise its peacetime army from 1.4 million to 2.2 million men—three times as large as the German army, the next largest in Europe.[23]

The United States economy, however, was growing just as fast, building on the recently completed conquest of a continent rich in natural resources, and its population was much richer on a per capita basis. The United States was the dominant world producer of oil, steel, and automobiles; it was the best-educated society on earth; and it was also the most innovative, producing, with a population one-third that of Europe, three-quarters as many patents each year as Europe did. It was the wealthiest large society on the planet. At the turn of the century it had conquered a sizable empire in the Caribbean and the Pacific.

Japan, too, had a rapidly growing industrial economy and was revolutionizing power relations in Asia. Having adopted parliamentary government in 1889, it had increasingly efficient and powerful state machinery. It conquered Taiwan and various other territories by defeating China in 1894–95, defeated the Russian Empire on land and at sea in 1905, annexed Korea in 1910, and was expanding into Manchuria. It was developing the resources of these territories rapidly and creating a language of racialized imperial nationalism in some ways similar to that common in European societies.[24]

Germany was experiencing remarkable growth, as well. Between the 1870s and the 1910s it had vaulted past Britain to become the largest industrial economy in Europe, and the second in the world after the United States. Germans invented the lightbulb, the internal combustion engine, organic chemistry, the open-hearth blast furnace, and the electric railway. Germany was the world leader in basic science—even the Americans copied their university system from Germany. Germany had acquired a relatively small, but nevertheless impressive overseas empire that included colonies in what are now Namibia and Tanzania in the 1880s, a protectorate over the province of Shandong in China in the 1890s, and a potentially important naval base in Western Samoa in 1900. The Germans openly discussed their ambition to create a huge empire in central Africa by absorbing the Belgian Congo and Portuguese Angola and Mozambique. By 1914 Germany was also in discussions with the Austrian Empire about the possibility of creating a customs union in East-Central Europe—Mitteleuropa (Middle Europe), a giant free-trade zone that would have overwhelming economic power in the Balkans, indeed in Europe as a whole, and potentially in the Middle East as well. Some saw control of iron and coal resources in Belgium and eastern France as essential to the industrial power of this German superstate (and in fact the German government sought to annex these regions during World War I).[25]

Even France, which was experiencing relatively slow industrial and demographic growth, had conquered most of Northwest Africa and Viet Nam. It was a world leader in a number of cutting-edge industries—among them, film, automobiles, and aviation. And it was an international center of both banking and education, extending its financial and cultural influence into not only Africa but also the Middle East.

Even in areas left unconquered by these rapidly growing societies, their economic power often gave them formidable leverage. British money, for example, largely funded the infrastructure that opened Latin American resources to the global economy. French loans were modernizing the Ottoman Empire and helped build the trans-Siberian railway, reaching from European Russia to the Pacific, and the Russian oil industry around Baku.

By 1900, all these developments had created a situation of enormous fluidity. As the head of Germany's navy, Alfred von Tirpitz, remarked in 1899, the geostrategic situation of the time was unstable; the constellation of global power politics could change "entirely . . . within a short period."[26] This meant that powerful imperial states faced extraordinary opportunities.

By the same token, however, each of these states also feared the others. Some in the German government were terrified by Russia's development into a gigantic, continent-spanning empire right on their eastern border, with an apparently limitless appetite for expansion. Britain feared that Germany's industrial development would give it the power to carve out a major colonial empire outside Europe, further stoking its rapidly growing economic strength. The French were even more worried, given that Germany was right on their border and had absorbed part of France as a result of the war between the two countries in 1870. As Tirpitz saw it, the planet was increasingly dominated by the four "world empires," Russia, England, the United States, and Germany; but if Germany could not gain access to resources and markets similar in size to those available to the others, it was doomed to become a second-class power, like France, Spain, and Italy.[27] Strategic thinkers in other states harbored similar fears.

In the United States many were more optimistic. Naval planners there saw themselves engaged in a struggle for "industrial and commercial supremacy in the world," but were confident of eventual victory because America was the "richest and most advanced nation" and "the greatest producer on earth." One group of officers at the US Naval War College even argued in 1909 that America would ultimately "control the world." The popular novelist F. Scott Fitzgerald agreed, noting in 1921 that "we will be the Romans of the next generation, as the English are now." But many Americans were fearful that other countries might try to block their rise. By 1910, in fact, US naval planners were particularly concerned about the possibility of war with Germany or Japan, or both—two aspiring industrial powers facing (it seemed at the time) enormous demographic pressure and hence a need for settlement colonies, in the Pacific, the Caribbean, or even South America. Russia too seemed to threaten America's mission to dominate Asia and the Pacific.[28]

The onset of a wave of revolutionary upheavals after 1905 further heightened the perception that the world was in flux, creating new opportunities and threats. By 1910 a number of important, once-powerful imperial states seemed to be disintegrating under the impact of social and economic change. The Chinese Empire appeared on the verge of chaos, and by 1916 had slipped into the hands of competing coalitions of warlords. In 1912 Russia forced China to concede autonomy for Mongolia—clearly a reflection of growing Russian influence in China's borderlands. Half a world away, after 1910 the chaos generated by the Mexican Revolution opened the possibility of similar moves by the United States—or perhaps other outsiders, such as Germany. In Iran, the revolution of 1906 led to a weak military dictatorship, and by 1907 the Russians and British signed an agreement dividing the country into two "spheres of influence," north and south. Within Europe, by 1912 the Austrian Empire seemed endangered, as growing nationalist movements among its many ethnic minorities—Serbs, Croats, Hungarians, Ruthenes, Germans—threatened its unity. The Russians were eyeing Galicia, now southern Poland, as a territory to add to their own Polish dominion.

But most important, by that time the Ottoman Empire seemed on its last legs. It had been unable to keep pace with the growing economic power of Western Europe, or to keep down the growing nationalist movements in its Balkan empire. Modernizing administrative, economic, and military reforms during the Tanzimat period only partially succeeded. Greece became independent in the 1820s; Serbia de facto independent in the 1830s. In 1877–78 the Russians defeated the Ottoman army in the Balkans, leading to de facto independence for Bulgaria and Rumania as well, while Britain took Cyprus, and Austria "occupied" Bosnia (with formal annexation in 1908). In 1882 Britain occupied Egypt. In 1908 the Young Turk revolt imposed a constitutional regime on the Ottoman emperor, suggesting that the central government was no longer able to sustain itself even at the heart of the empire. Sensing that the time had come to carve up the Ottoman lands, in 1911 Italy invaded and annexed Tripoli, in North Africa, and a number of islands in the Aegean Sea. In 1912 the Ottoman army was crushed in the Balkans by an alliance of Serbia, Montenegro, Bulgaria, and Greece.

This crisis of the Ottoman state was the most important single cause of World War I. In fact, the war arguably began in 1911 with the Italian invasion of the Ottoman territories in North Africa (now Libya), escalated in 1912 and 1913 with the outbreak of the Balkan Wars in Ottoman Southeastern Europe, and then became general in 1914 as the Hapsburg (Austrian) Empire attempted to deal with the growing power of the smaller states that profited from those wars (particularly Serbia). And it lasted, arguably, until 1923, when the Treaty of Lausanne established the borders of the new Turkish national state.[29]

The question of who would profit, in what ways, from the disintegration of the Ottoman Empire was important for two main reasons. First, most exports from the southern part of the Russian Empire passed down the Dardanelles and Bosporus straits and through Istanbul. With the settlement and development of the great grain-growing plains of southern Russia and the Ukraine over the two or three generations before 1910, this had become increasingly important for the economic well-being of the entire empire. Russia was driving forward its industrial and agricultural development in order to overcome the weaknesses that had become apparent in the revolutionary upheaval of 1905. That development depended on access to the world's markets. Half of Russian trade passed through the Bosporus, including 75 percent of the country's grain exports.[30] In 1912, in response to the Italian attack, the Ottomans closed trade through the Bosporus, cutting total Russian trade by a third (not fully half, because some of it could be diverted to other routes). The Young Turk government meanwhile began to build a modern military by, among other efforts, contracting with British, American, and French firms to build modern warships for its navy and by bringing in German military advisors to reshape its army. Late in 1913 a German officer, General Liman von Sanders, was even put in charge of the Ottoman units controlling the Bosporus.[31] In fact, the German imperial regime was hoping to form a lasting alliance with the Ottomans as a way of projecting its influence in the Middle East. As another step in that direction, German companies were laying a railway line from Berlin to Baghdad in an attempt to build commercial and economic relations with the Ottoman territories in what are now Iraq, Syria, and Lebanon. All of these moves terrified the Russian government, which feared a Great Power rival sitting on its commercial windpipe through the Bosporus. And time to prevent that seemed to be running out.

The second reason for the importance of the crisis in the Ottoman Empire was that the German regime wanted access to the Middle East as a way out of what it saw as its own military and economic "encirclement" by the other imperial powers. German planners feared that Germany was in danger of being outclassed militarily and excluded from key world markets by rival continental or colonial empires (the United States, Russia, Britain). Gaining access to the Middle East as a market for manufactured goods and a source of raw materials seemed critical to preventing such a dire future.

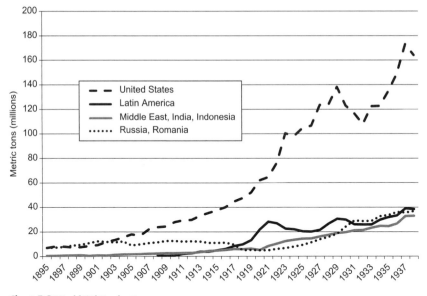

Chart 5.3 World Oil Production.

The key raw material in question was oil. British oilmen had discovered fields in Persia in 1908 and had signed long-term concession agreements to extract the oil; the Russians had begun production in the Caucasus region still earlier; and German geologists had found oil in what is now Iraq. By 1910 it was clear that oil was abundant in the Middle East, and it was no less obvious that oil was going to be a critical resource in the twentieth century—perhaps *the* critical resource. For one thing, as a fuel it allowed ships to go faster and farther than coal did, and the British navy had started to switch from coal to oil already in 1912. Oil was a more efficient fuel for other purposes as well, including electricity generation. And gasoline, derived from oil, was clearly the fuel of the future for aircraft and for automobiles. World War I would show that the internal combustion engine—in trucks, tanks, and airplanes—was going to be the decisive instrument of warfare in the twentieth century.

The problem was that the United States produced about two-thirds of the world's oil, which gave it a key advantage in crucial modern industries. What is more, the next-largest producer was Latin America—which was increasingly under US economic, diplomatic, and military dominance (chart 5.3). Between them, North and South America produced over 80 percent of the world's oil. That control of world oil supplies, among other factors, had allowed the United States to become globally dominant in automobile manufactures and in civil aviation even before World War I (chart 5.4). Americans drove and flew far more than people in Western Europe, the only other part of the world that had a sig-

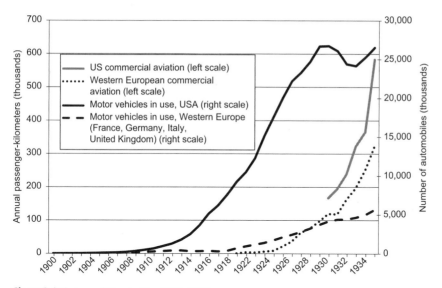

Chart 5.4 Planes and Cars in Use, 1900–1935.

nificant number of cars on its roads or airplanes in its skies. The growth of civilian aviation in the United States was explosive: in 1929 there were some 162,000 passenger flights; just ten years later there were over 1.7 million.[32] Finally, by the 1910s and particularly by the 1920s it was also clear that mechanization was the key to raising agricultural productivity, thereby eliminating the greatest obstacle in most countries to rapid economic growth. Machinery had revolutionized the industrial economies of the North Atlantic since 1850; by 1920, it was clear that tractors would play a crucial role in doing the same for agriculture.

To remain economically and militarily competitive with the United States, then, other countries had to secure sources of oil. Russia's Caucasus region produced significant amounts of oil, as did Romania. India and Indonesia, under British and Dutch control, were also producers. But by 1910 it was clear that the Middle East had unprecedented reserves—especially in Persia (now Iran) and Mesopotamia (now Kuwait and Iraq, but then part of the Ottoman Empire). In the final years before World War I, France, Britain, Russia, and Germany jockeyed furiously for control over or access to these new sources of oil. As part of the plan to build the Berlin-to-Baghdad railway, German firms secured rights to drill for oil under a swath of land extending twenty kilometers (twelve miles) on either side of the planned route.[33] More broadly, German plans for the economic penetration of the Middle East seemed to threaten British access to the region's oil. Concerned for its strategic interests, in 1914 the British government bought a controlling interest (51 percent) in Anglo-Persian Oil (the region's sole production company) and made oil security a lynchpin of its foreign policy. Complex financial negotiations led to the so-called Foreign Office Agreement in 1914, according to which British, French, and German banks and oil companies agreed to exploit the oil resources of the Ottoman Empire collaboratively. But by that time the strategic calculations of the nations involved had already led Europe to the brink of general war.[34]

Ultimately, then, the great war of 1914–1945 was fought over two closely related issues: the industrial economy, and the agricultural economy—or, to put it another way, oil and peasants.

THE PROBLEM OF THE PEASANT IN THE 1920S AND 1930S

The main targets of attack by the peasants are the local tyrants, the evil gentry and the lawless landlords, but in passing they also hit out against patriarchal ideas and institutions, against the corrupt officials in the cities and against bad practices and customs in the rural areas. . . . The peasants are clear-sighted, . . . keep clear accounts, and very seldom has the punishment exceeded the crime. . . . [But] a revolution is not a dinner party; . . . a revolution is an insurrection, an act of violence.[35]

Mao Zedong, 1927

World War I resolved few of the major issues that had caused it. Instead, the war added a new layer of economic and ideological issues, making the international situation all the more tense through the 1920s.

The struggle for global power continued after 1918. The German Empire collapsed and was replaced by a democratic republic, but the German economy remained Europe's greatest industrial dynamo, with a massive hunger for resources and for access to markets. Many in the German business and political elite remained convinced that Germany would lose out to competitors—Russia or the United States in particular—unless it built an empire in Europe. The National Socialist regime in Germany set about doing that when it invaded Poland in September 1939. Italy had been on the winning side in World War I, and had originally been promised various territories, for example, in what became Yugoslavia; but it was not able to secure control of them during the peacemaking process (largely because the Hapsburg Empire had collapsed and been replaced by half a dozen independent republics). Many in the Italian elite believed that their country's future depended on joining the ranks of global imperial powers. In 1936 Italy would lead Europe's slide toward the Second World War by launching an invasion of the independent kingdom of Ethiopia. Japan had managed to pocket Germany's Pacific colonies, but it had a rapidly expanding industrial economy and, despite the seizure of Korea in 1910, a shortage of the necessary natural resources. Over the following two decades, Japan would steadily press forward with a program of expansion on the Asian mainland. In 1937 it would launch the Second World War in Asia by invading China.

None of these wars of aggression came as a great surprise. Already in 1930, for example, one academic in Ohio argued that "the only way to avoid war" was to simply give Japan and Italy land and resources in Asia and North Africa; and that in the case of Germany "the way out is probably more difficult, but if only a tithe of the cost of the next war . . . were devoted to finding a way to avoid it, . . . much could be done to ease the present strains." The author was not very hopeful that any of these preventive measures would be carried out; the implication clearly was that war with Germany, Italy, and Japan was coming.[36]

Russia was a special case. The Russian Empire dissolved into revolution and a gigantic, chaotic civil war beginning in 1917, and over the next five years some 12 to 13 million people lost their lives to violence, hunger, or disease, while another 1 to 2 million fled the country. In the midst of this great calamity the United States, Japan, Britain, and France all sent armies to help defeat the Bolsheviks; the new Polish republic invaded as well. By 1922 the Bolsheviks had beaten all of these enemies and established the Soviet Union. But the USSR was committed to actively exporting revolution to the whole world—the more so as the capitalist powers had proven their deadly hostility to socialism by intervening to prevent its creation.[37] The new state formed the center of a rapidly expanding international web of communist revolutionaries, movements, and parties, which took organizational form in 1921 as the Comintern, mentioned earlier. The new Bolshevik Russian "empire" now had potential communist allies in many societies all over the world. And the Soviet Union was highly successful in building its economic and military power in the 1920s and 1930s—a phenomenon discussed later in this chapter.

The tensions generated by imperial rivalries, then, were not resolved by World War I. Neither were those created by the growth of ideas about race, ethnicity, and nationalism. The United States under President Woodrow Wilson had partially succeeded in its attempt to impose the principle of democratic national self-determination in the peace settlement—a principle Wilson believed would make another great war impossible, since most people the world over desired peace. But in practice, particularly in Europe, this principle created as many problems as it resolved. In Eastern and Central Europe the collapse of the Ottoman, German, Austrian, and Russian empires created a zone of small national states, with a total population of 60 million; but linguistic groups were greatly mixed in the region, and some 25 million of those people lived as "minorities" in states dominated by other linguistic groups.[38]

Outside Europe, national self-determination created other problems. In the later stages of the war, the Ottoman Empire committed one of the first great genocides of the twentieth century against the Armenian minority in eastern Anatolia, many among which were suspected of sympathy with Turkey's enemies—including Russia, just across the border from the region in which most Ottoman Armenians lived. As many as 1.8 million Armenians died in the course of massacres and a brutal mass deportation by forced marches from the border region. The collapse of the Ottoman Empire and a desperate war of national liberation in what is now Turkey generated some 1.7 million refugees, as ethnic Greeks and Turks were expelled from the respective national territories, and caused perhaps another half-million fatalities among Armenians, Greeks, and other minorities. Meanwhile Britain conquered Iraq, Jordan, and Palestine, while France acquired Syria and Lebanon. Under the terms of the peace, these regions were not colonies, however, but "mandates," officially being prepared for full independence. Egypt gained nominal independence in 1922, but was still under British occupation. In 1917 the British also promised a national homeland to Zionists in Palestine (partly as a reward for the help that Jewish volunteers had provided in overthrowing Ottoman rule). But the local Muslim and Christian populations saw the arrival of a growing number of Jewish settlers—mostly from Europe—as tantamount to the creation of a settlement colony in a land already well populated. Saudi Arabia gained its independence because Arab nationalists there had joined the British (who used mostly Indian troops in this theater) in conquering the Ottoman provinces in the Middle East, but it was a relatively weak state—poor, small in population, based on an essentially tribal society. The question was thus open as to who might ultimately dominate this oil-rich region.[39]

That issue was all the more volatile because oil was rapidly becoming more important in the global economy. Global economic growth slowed suddenly in the 1920s, as a result of the economic disaster brought on by the war. But the key modern industries of the 1920s—for example, automobiles, aviation, and electric power generation—were actually booming. Most of them depended on cheap and abundant oil.

The 1920s also added new problems to those of empire and nationality. The crucial one, discussed in chapter 6, was that the war gave rise to three new ideologies, radicalized versions of older ideas about class, race, ethnicity, and nation: communism, fascism, and liberal democracy. Communism sought to use brute force to transform capitalist society immediately into the socialist order that Karl Marx and the Social Democrats who adopted his theory of social and economic development had argued would arise naturally, in a process of economic and social development that might last decades or even centuries. Fascism sought to impose national unity, order, and expansion; in its National Socialist variant in Germany, it developed a radical racist program to "cleanse" the nation of ethnic "impurities" and pursue a program of deliberate territorial expansion, murdering racial "enemies" and replacing them with its own people. Liberal democracy aimed to build a political and institutional framework in which the goals of liberalism—self-reliance, self-betterment, affluence, political participation—would be extended to the entire population (hence, the "democracy" part of the name). All three sought to mobilize and politicize the broad mass of the population to achieve these ends. Through the 1920s and early 1930s, these three ideological systems remained in a state of incipient war, each rejecting the other two as fundamentally wrong, illegitimate, immoral, and incompatible with human dignity—and as irrevocably bent on aggression.[40]

Of almost equal importance, however, was the new fragility of the financial system of the North Atlantic economies in the aftermath of the war. Britain, France, and Russia had borrowed massively from the United States to defeat the Central Powers, and after the war they borrowed still more to rebuild. They imposed a nearly crippling burden of reparations payments on the new German republic in order to lighten the burden of paying interest on that debt. This was a further source of potential political instability, since many Germans regarded the reparations as an unjustified and illegitimate punitive measure. It also created a new degree of fragility in the North Atlantic financial system, because Germany had to borrow money from American banks in order to pay reparations and also run an effective government, one that could at least try to win the support of its citizens by maintaining and expanding essential services. This worked relatively well as long as the US banking system was healthy. But when US banks faced a financial crisis after the stock market crash of October 1929, the system rapidly unraveled, plunging the world into a deep financial crisis, which soon led to the Great Depression and threw international relations into turmoil. It was this crisis, specifically, that set the context for World War II.

Underlying all these postwar problems was a more fundamental one, a metaproblem of global development that was coming to a head after 1920: the problem of the peasant. As we have seen, the conflicts generated by the peasantry's difficult adjustment to the emergence of the integrated world market had been a decisive factor in many of the revolutionary upheavals of the decade before World War I. In the late 1920s the initiative shifted from peasants struggling to reshape states and societies in their own interest to states trying to reshape peasantries. In the 1930s, nations increasingly perceived the question of who would control the land and manage the agricultural economy as a matter of their life and death. New technologies were creating the potential for a revolution in agricultural productivity similar to that experienced in industry during the previous half century. Those societies that managed to make that transformative leap in the rural economy would have a tremendous advantage over those that did not. They would be able to mobilize the capital and labor resources necessary to achieve rapid industrial growth. And peasants, who still dominated agriculture in most of the world, seemed to stand in the way. By the 1930s, policy makers in some countries began to impose radical programs to get them out of the way.

The peasantry posed a problem in the eyes of many political leaders for three reasons. First, culturally and politically, most peasants all over the world passively (and sometimes even actively) resisted participation in the creation and life of nations. Many peasants, relatively isolated from world cultural currents that were strongest in cities, retained identities and loyalties that were primarily local or regional, and often also religious. Few spoke the national language, retaining instead their own local or regional dialects. Most were illiterate and had limited awareness of events outside their region or village. Many were not well connected to transportation and communication networks, and it was difficult for state agencies and their officials to reach them. For people who wanted to build new states and political systems around national identities, this was a problem. These were people whose lives did not make them very interested in nationality, or very accessible to national administrative and cultural institutions.

Second, for the most part, peasants were economically conservative and were not strongly oriented to markets. They focused primarily on subsistence and security, rather than on commercial opportunity and expansion, often tailoring their methods above all to achieving a reliable and diverse food supply, rather than maximum production or profit. Production for markets came second or even third (after fulfilling community or religious roles and obligations, for example). In some areas peasants were able or obliged (as by the requirement to pay a flat cash tax per person or per family) to specialize more and sold cash crops—for example, in the rice-producing deltas in South and Southeast Asia and in the peanut- and cocoa-farming regions of West Africa.[41] In some areas large landholders dominated agriculture, producing for the world market, while most peasants had at most a garden plot. Such was the case in much of Latin America. Some peasants rented extra land, often under sharecropping systems, or worked as agricultural laborers to expand their incomes. But whatever the particular local mix, peasants around the world were quite poor and rarely had the capital to rapidly improve their land (through irrigation or fencing, say) or livestock (for example, by importing superior breeds). And some were skeptical of borrowing money to make improvements, since they might well lose their land if that strategy failed to pay off.

Third, it was difficult for the state to extract revenue from peasant economies. Again, it was often simply physically difficult or time-consuming for tax collectors to reach peasant communities. Large numbers of smallholdings, relative self-sufficiency, barter and communal exchange systems, and often relatively loose connections to the cash economy made it difficult to assess the production, income, or value of family farms. Peasant cultivators often favored fragmented and scattered landholding patterns, and many peasant communities held some resources in common, with shared use rights rather than clear individual tenure. Both were methods of spreading risk, but they made it hard to assess individual incomes. As the historian James C. Scott has put it, peasant agriculture was not very "legible" or "visible" to states interested in gathering revenue.[42]

The Italian author Carlo Levi captured this situation vividly in his account of the years he spent in a small village in southern Italy in the mid-1930s. Levi

Figure 5.1 Russian Peasants, circa 1910.

had gotten into political trouble with the new Fascist regime, and was forced to live in a small village in the south in order to keep him out of circulation. He wrote a book about the experience, *Christ Stopped at Eboli*. Eboli was the town up the road from the village where he was forced to live, and people used this phrase to express their sense that the village was truly a world apart, past the edge of civilization. "None of the pioneers of Western civilization," Levi wrote, "brought here his sense of the passage of time, his deification of the state, or that ceaseless activity which feeds upon itself. No one has come to this land except as an enemy, a conqueror, or a visitor devoid of understanding." There was "an abyss between the State and the peasant" that no worshipper of the state—whether liberal, fascist, or communist—could bridge.[43]

Since the eighteenth century, in some regions of the world, highly productive agricultural systems had developed based on higher capital inputs and larger farms. This was the case, for example, in those grassland regions that formed one of the foundations of the world food market—the pampas of Argentina, the Canadian prairies, the American Great Plains, and Australia. To some extent it was true also in the rice-producing deltas, where peasant farming methods assisted by large-scale flood-control projects could produce substantial surpluses for export. In other areas, the creation of a plantation economy raised productivity for particular commodities—or enabled colonial or national states to extract greater value from their production.

Figure 5.2 Irish Peasant House in Killarney, circa 1900.

Figure 5.3 Modern Farm Implements Used in the United States.

Figure 5.4 Old and New Agricultural Technology, United States, circa 1910.

In the 1920s, however, the urgency of the peasant question grew. One important factor was that the revolutionary elites who were building powerful national states found it difficult to get peasants to participate in national life. In many areas, the basic structures of rural society persisted unchanged, and peasants still had to defer to local large landholders and oligarchs, who were usually more committed to the old order and of course to retaining their own power. In China, Sun Zhongshan complained that the mass of the Chinese people simply weren't interested in his national revolution. "Much as they desired to be the guide of the people," he wrote, the revolutionaries "proceeded without followers." While they succeeded in overthrowing the imperial government, they could not change the actual practices of government in their society. As he put it, it proved impossible to "abolish old corrupt practices" or break up the "age-long customs of autocracy."[44] In Mexico, too, the victorious revolutionary government fought a low-level civil war in the late 1920s against conservative Catholics who rejected its attempts to create a public political culture based on the idea of nationality and socialism rather than on Catholicism, which the revolutionaries regarded as politically conservative, internationalist, and authoritarian.

A second factor was that by the 1920s it was clear that the economic, political, and military power of modern societies was now founded on industry. The outcome of World War I in Europe proved this beyond doubt. The less industrialized states—the Russian, Ottoman, and Hapsburg Empires—all collapsed and were partitioned. The German Empire, which was highly industrialized, was defeated and collapsed, but retained 90 percent of its territory and population. Italy, which was not highly industrialized, was on the winning side, but made almost no territorial gains in the peacemaking process.

Industrial development rested to a large extent on two pillars: abundant capital and cheap labor. That meant that boosting agricultural productivity per worker or extracting revenue from the agricultural economy, or both, were essential to any economic policy favoring industrial development. The development of the more successfully commercialized agricultural economies of the world made this clear. The United States, in particular, had the highest level of per capita income in the world, and it was also the most advanced agricultural economy on earth. By 1930 a million tractors were in use in agriculture in the United States—four-fifths of the world total. People laboring on farms in the United States fell from half of the national labor force in 1880 to less than one-quarter in the 1930s, even as food production grew. That change reflected millions of workers pouring into the industrial economy. It also drew agriculture ever more firmly into the commercial, money-based economy, generating demand and revenue. In that sense, paradoxically, the United States owed its industrial dominance to the effectiveness of its agricultural producers. The same pattern held in Germany. Here, too, the share of the labor force devoted to food production shrank from two-fifths to one-fourth between 1900 and 1930, while food production rose. By comparison, societies in which agriculture was dominated by peasant producers were far more stable. In Mexico—where land reform and redistribution after the revolution and the creation of the *ejidos* helped to stabilize peasant communities—the farm labor force was three-fifths of the national labor force in both years; in India it stayed at 70 percent (chart 5.5).[45] This was why the problem of the peasantry was critical to the many governments of the 1920s that feared, or hoped, there would be another war. To win that war, they would need industrial muscle. To create that muscle, they needed to transform the rural economy.

The Communist Party regime in Russia was among the first and most radical to attack this "peasant problem." The Bolsheviks prevailed in the civil war of 1917–22, not least because they officially approved and confirmed a massive peasant rebellion that seized the land both of better-off peasants and of aristocratic landholders (as well as that of the state and the Russian Orthodox Church) and transferred it to the control of the land-hungry peasantry. While this sweeping land redistribution helped to win the war, however, it was not a way to solve the problem of the peasantry. Peasant farms did not have the capital to raise productivity rapidly and form the foundation for industrial development. Yet the Bolshevik leadership was absolutely determined to build Soviet industry, because they were convinced that the capitalists were coming for them. In early 1931, in fact, the Soviet dictator, Joseph Stalin, told a conference

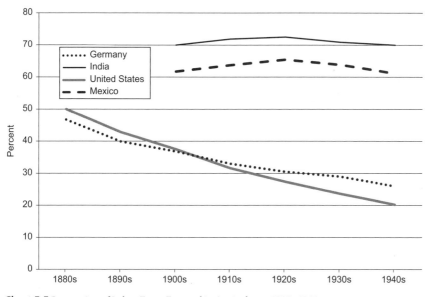

Chart 5.5 Proportion of Labor Force Engaged in Agriculture, 1880–1949.

of Soviet industrial managers: "Those who fall behind get beaten. . . . We are fifty or one hundred years behind the advanced countries. We must make good this distance in ten years. Either we do it, or we shall go under."[46] Starting at the end of the 1920s, under the USSR's first Five-Year Plan (1928–32) for economic development, Stalin turned on the peasants and applied massive coercion to collectivize the land. The 25 million family farms that made up the Russian rural economy were abolished and replaced with 250,000 collective farms.[47]

Two facts motivated this undertaking. One was that bigger farms could leverage efficiencies of scale to generate greater efficiency—particularly in the use of tractors. A large collective farm could both afford and fully utilize a modern tractor in ways one family farm could not. The other fact was that control of the land allowed the Soviet regime to squeeze value out of the farming sector and devote it to a massive crash industrialization program. It accomplished that through, for example, price controls, rationing, and production quotas. Those farmers who objected were labeled "kulaks" (wealthy peasants) and hence class enemies, and were arrested and deported to Siberia, or their villages were shot up with machine guns, or the army and Communist Party activists recruited among urban workers confiscated all the food they could find and left people to starve. In short, as one historian has put it, the Soviet regime launched a "de facto . . . war on the peasant way of life." The result was a disaster. Peasants fled to the cities, hoarded food, killed half their farm animals, and burned their barns. Two to three million were deported to labor camps, mostly in Siberia or Central Asia. Food production fell drastically, creating a famine that killed some 5 million people. As one Communist Party worker put it, "A ruthless struggle is going on between the peasantry and our regime. . . . It's a struggle to the death." The peasants lost; probably somewhere between 7 and 10 million of them died (perhaps as many as 20 million).[48] After 1935, peasants were allowed to maintain small plots of land for private use. But Soviet agriculture never recovered and remained relatively unproductive right down to the collapse of the USSR.

Yet, in the short and medium term, the Soviet regime was able to extract enough value from the agricultural sector to launch a vast industrialization program. By 1940 the Soviet Union produced ten times more electricity than it had in 1928, seven times as much coal, and more than four times as much steel.[49] On the eve of World War II, the USSR had almost tripled its industrial labor force and turned itself into the third-largest industrial power in the world. It had raised the male literacy rate from 40 percent to 94 percent, created millions of new technical and managerial jobs, and quadrupled the total print run of newspapers in the country. It had also adopted mass violence, police terror, mass deportations, and slave labor as everyday tools of government, and had cut real wages by one-half.[50]

Communists, however, were not the only ones who pursued industrial power by expropriating, exploiting, and killing peasants; nor were solutions to the "problem" of the peasants couched only in the language of class. Adolf Hitler's National Socialist regime in Germany had even more sweeping plans, based on the language of race. The Nazi regime murdered some 6 million Jews in Europe as part of a program based on the conviction that the Jews sought to destroy the "Aryan" German "race"—a bizarre and particularly vicious, paranoid variant of thinking about race and nation. But the Nazis also planned to kill tens of millions of Poles and Russians, clearing these "Slavic" peasant populations out of Poland and the Ukraine, and replacing them with far fewer German farmers. The ultimate aim was to create a racially pure German empire stretching from northeastern France to the Black Sea coast in southern Ukraine, and from Norway to the Alps. It would have a population of 150 million, a flourishing market-oriented agricultural base in the east, and an unrivalled industrial heartland in the west. This empire, the Nazis calculated, was what was needed to stand up to the United States, with its giant continental empire.

To Nazi planners, Eastern Europe seemed crammed with too many small, underproductive peasant farms. Nazi estimates of how many of these peasants were surplus to the requirements of a more efficient agricultural system ranged from 31 million to 45 million; they were to be supplanted by some 10 million German farmers. This replacement would create a region of larger, more efficient farms. In the process, tens of millions of people would die. One Nazi plan for Ukraine, for example, claimed that this great grain-growing region would become "a California of Europe," "one of the loveliest gardens of the world." The transformation would take twenty years and would require the labor of 14 million Slavic slave laborers, for whom the annual mortality rate would be 10 percent. The Nazis made a good start on this program in Poland, where in 1939–40 up to a million Poles were expelled from the western part of the country (which was annexed to Germany) and replaced with 200,000 German settlers. Ultimately, between 1939 and 1945, the Nazis killed 3 million Jewish Poles and 2 million non-Jewish Poles, or almost 20 percent of the entire population. Farther east, they killed upward of 20 million Slavic and Jewish citizens of the Soviet Union, as well.[51]

Other authoritarian regimes adopted similar, though far less murderous, policies. The Portuguese administration of Mozambique, for example, forced African farmers to produce cotton for export beginning in the late 1930s. By the early 1940s well over half a million farmers were subject to a regime of compulsory cotton farming, enforced where necessary by whipping or imprisonment.[52]

The contrast between life in totalitarian or colonial regimes and the affluent and democratic United States could hardly be starker. There never had been much of a peasantry in the United States, in the sense of a class of smallholding subsistence farmers. Most of the country was seized from the Native American inhabitants and settled rapidly in the course of the nineteenth century, there was a low labor-to-land ratio, and government policy favored the creation of larger farms. The Homestead Act of 1862, for example, granted homesteaders 160 acres, a substantial farm by the standards of the time. The same was true of most other settler colonies, including those in Argentina, Canada, Australia, and New Zealand—all places where massive land confiscation from indigenous populations, enforced at gunpoint in the last third of the nineteenth century, had supported the creation of large farms. Larger farms were often more efficient and technologically advanced, because they could generate enough capital to invest in raising productivity by using tractors, fertilizer, irrigation pipes, and other technology. In the United States most early homesteaders, faced with the difficulty of farming arid grasslands, failed and sold out to bigger operations. Organized private citizens (or their paid enforcers) not infrequently used low-level violence to sabotage the emergence of an autonomous peasantry. In North America after the US-Mexican War of 1846–48 and the American Civil War, such violence played a role in limiting the emergence in different parts of the country of economically autonomous white, African American, Native American, and Hispanic small farmers or peasants.[53]

From the 1920s on, average farm sizes in the United States rose, as farmers with larger holdings took advantage of new technologies to raise their productivity and outcompete smaller farms. Average farm size in the United States was more or less stable between 1880 and 1920, then rose by half to 1950 (and tripled by 1975).[54] In other words, market forces brought about a consolidation of farm holdings in the United States just at the moment when some other societies were trying to accomplish something similar through violent state action.

Fortunately for the United States, at least in the boom years of the 1920s and then again during World War II, farmers who lost out in this process often had the option of moving to employment in industry. The net result was rising overall wealth.

In societies where peasant farmers did not have alternative employment, and where farm size was not growing, population growth could create grim prospects. From the 1890s to the 1970s, for example, the average size of farms in Java fell by almost two-thirds.[55] Economists call this process "involution": a combination of rising population, shrinking farms, and in many cases stagnant or falling agricultural productivity per capita, stemming from the growth of farming on less productive land due to population pressure. This was the pattern—the trap—that many policy makers around the world in the 1920s feared. That fear was one of the key forces that launched the extraordinary violence of collectivization, ethnic cleansing, and World War II in the 1930s.

In the 1930s, however, a second urgent problem swirled in the minds of modernizers around the world—one closely related to the problem of the peasant. This was the problem of access to oil. Among other things, oil was essential to the operation of modern agriculture and to the distribution of food, as the fuel for tractors, trucks, and ships. That made oil crucial to states' broader ambitions for economic power on the world stage. But oil was also the key to modern, mechanized warfare—to military power.

The question of who would control the world's oil supplies was, therefore, a potent factor in the drift toward World War II. Chapter 6 examines that war and the role that both these problems—peasants and oil—played in shaping it.

New World (Dis)Order

WAR FOR WORLD DOMINATION: PHASE II, 1935–1950

> The entire Japanese people should . . . petition for a manifestation of the imperial prerogative establishing "a national opinion in which no dissenting voice is heard." . . . Truly, our seven hundred million brothers in China and India have no path to independence other than that offered by our guidance and protection. And for our Japan, whose population has doubled within the past fifty years, great areas adequate to support a population of at least two hundred and forty or fifty millions will be absolutely necessary a hundred years from now. . . . [L]et her lift the virtuous banner of an Asian league and take the leadership in a world federation which must come.[1]
>
> Kita Ikki, 1920

World War II was in part the outcome of radical attempts to solve the global economic and political problem of the peasantry. Among other goals, Nazi Germany launched its campaign of genocidal war in Eastern Europe in part to reorganize that region as a more efficient agricultural zone. The Japanese Empire had similar plans for China when it launched its invasion in 1937. In fact, in Korea and in Manchuria it was already engaged in an active program of settlement and of consolidation in the agricultural sector, raising efficiency in order to fuel industrial expansion. That effort accelerated significantly in the early 1930s, especially in Korea, where the Japanese colonial authorities used both compulsion and positive incentives to achieve significant gains in productivity per hectare of crop land planted in rice (for export to Japan). Ultimately the aim was to create an extensive and efficient agricultural basis for industrial expansion, allowing Japan to build the economic and military muscle it would need to face up to the Soviet Union, the United States, and Great Britain.[2] Not coincidentally, the contrast with India

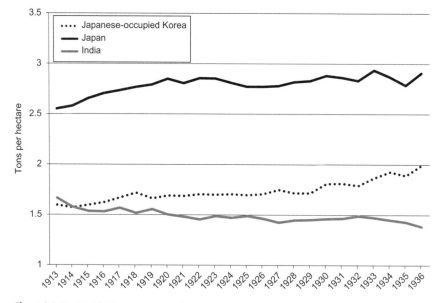

Chart 6.1 Rice Yields (five-year average) in Japan, Korea, and India, 1913–1936.

and Indonesia is striking: in those places a process of agricultural involution was under way, and productivity was actually falling in the 1930s (chart 6.1).

By the 1920s both gains in agricultural productivity and the expansion of the modern industrial sector, however, depended on a single key resource: oil. With respect to oil Japan, Germany, and Italy were in a precarious position. They had rising energy requirements, but almost no oil of their own. Japan imported 90 percent of its fossil fuels, 80 percent of that from the United States. Italy imported virtually all of its oil. Germany had large supplies of coal and was therefore in a far better strategic position; and it developed a successful synthetic oil program that produced liquid fuel from coal. But in the 1930s it still imported two-thirds of the oil it needed—chiefly from the Soviet Union.[3]

The position of the other powers was completely different. The United States produced two-thirds of the world's oil by the 1920s and exported one-third of all oil consumed elsewhere in the world.[4] And American companies were moving rapidly to gain control of oil production in Mexico and Venezuela as well, which together were the second-largest source of oil. The Soviet Union was a major producer from its fields around Baku in the Caucasus region. The British controlled the lion's share of oil production in Persia and in what had been the Ottoman Empire (having confiscated Germany's quarter share under the collective oil agreement worked out in 1914). British, Anglo-Dutch, and American oil companies were also important in the Dutch East Indies (what would become Indonesia), where there were also significant oil reserves.[5]

Oil was increasingly critical as a fuel not only for industry and civilian vehicles but was also for military forces. Whereas outcomes in World War I had turned more on railways than on the internal combustion engine, by 1917 it was abundantly clear that tanks, airplanes, trucks, jeeps, motorcycles, ships, and submarines powered by oil and gasoline would play a decisive role in later-twentieth-century warfare. An important aim of British strategy in the war had been to defend its Persian oil production facilities against the Ottoman Empire and to frustrate German attempts to gain control of Romanian and Russian oil. By contrast, oil from the Americas guaranteed that Germany's opponents would be able to deploy the new methods of mechanized warfare. Less than two weeks after the end of the war, Lord George Curzon, a key figure in British imperial administration and the wartime government, remarked at a meeting of the Inter-Allied Petroleum Conference (which had coordinated wartime fuel supplies) that the "Allied cause had floated to victory upon a wave of oil." That oil came primarily from the United States, but British oil production in Persia had also increased by a factor of more than ten between 1914 and 1918.[6]

What we have come to call combined arms and the mechanization of warfare would also be deciding factors in World War II (figures 6.1 to 6.3). This was fully understood before the war started; indeed, Germany, Japan, and Italy launched the war in part in a desperate attempt to secure oil for their economies and armed forces.[7] The Japanese army occupied the Chinese provinces of Manchuria in 1931 and Jehol in 1933 partly to help secure the Japanese food supply and mineral resources; but from 1937 onward, with the full-scale invasion of China, the United States tightened economic sanctions on Japan, which progressively limited its access to key raw materials, particularly oil. As one high Japanese official put it, by mid-1941 "the whole problem facing Japan had been reduced to a very simple factor, and that was oil."[8] Largely because of that problem, the Japanese army turned aside from China and toward Southeast Asia and the nearest substantial source of oil at the time, what is now Indonesia—though the Japanese army also needed the aluminum and rubber produced in what is now Malaysia (map 6.1).[9] In August 1941, in response to the Japanese occupation of Viet Nam, the United States, Holland, and Britain imposed a full oil embargo on Japan. At that point Japan's leadership had stockpiled about a year's supply of oil, and had to choose either to back down or to take Indonesia. They chose the latter option. The first step, though, was to try to wipe out the American fleet stationed at Pearl Harbor.

That idea emanated from two sources. One was the military calculation that Japan had to disable American offensive naval capacity in order to buy time to put together a stable system for securing strategic resources from the newly occupied areas in China and Southeast Asia. The other was the sense, at least

Figure 6.1 German Tank Riders, Russia, 1940.

Figure 6.2 B-24s of the 15th US Air Force Bombing Ploesti, Romania, 1943.

among some Japanese military officers, that they were embarking on a war for world domination and that the United States was ultimately their opponent in that struggle.

One military officer and philosopher of history who advocated the latter approach was Ishiwara Kanji. Ishiwara constructed a theory of the geopolitical future based on an odd mixture of his military training and experience as an officer in Manchuria and China, Nichiren Buddhism (a thirteenth-century

Figure 6.3 Tokyo after Firebombing, March 1945.

Japanese offshoot), and what he had learned about the West during three years in Germany after World War I. He reasoned that world history was proceeding inevitably toward a grand apocalyptic conflict between Asian civilization—the "way of righteousness" based on justice, harmony and sacrifice through service—and the purely selfish Western civilization based on simple force, the "way of dominance." Japan embodied the former, the United States the latter. Some fifty years after World War I, he predicted, the technology of aerial bombardment would have advanced far enough to allow the contending powers to annihilate whole cities using bombs of unprecedented power, carried by aircraft that could fly anywhere on earth without landing. In the meantime, Japan had to prepare for its role in the "salvation of the world" from the tyranny of the West by securing control of the immense natural and human resources of Asia. And that could be achieved only through protracted war against the United States, which would do whatever it could to block Japan's divine civilizing mission.[10]

Ishiwara Kanji's ideas were idiosyncratic and certainly did not provide a blueprint for Japan's military planning. But they constituted one among a

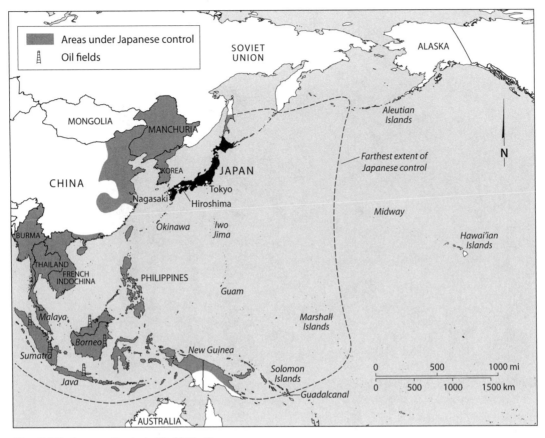

Map 6.1 The Japanese Empire in World War II.

number of similar theories that combined racial-nationalist, religious, and geostrategic ideas into a toxic brew that—not coincidentally—echoed Western ideas about the "Yellow Peril" common since the beginning of Japan's imperial expansion in Asia. It was a fairly common assumption in the 1930s that a great war for world domination was coming, that it would be a war between racial representatives of rival "civilizations," and that it would be decided by control of natural resources.

Unfortunately for the Japanese military, estimates of Japan's ability to weld Asia together as an economic and military unit turned out to be grossly over-optimistic. Perhaps the most decisive factor in the defeat of Japan was the success of American submarine warfare, which almost completely choked off the shipment of oil from occupied Indonesia to the industrial core of the Japanese Empire. By the latter stages of the war, some 95 percent of the Japanese merchant marine had been sunk or disabled, over half of it by US submarines.[11] The Japanese military-industrial base, never remotely as strong as that of the United States, was gradually isolated, starved of fuel, and crushed. Ultimately the United States ended the war by dropping two atomic bombs, developed at enormous expense under the secret Manhattan Project, on Hiroshima and Nagasaki; but by that time the outcome had not been seriously in doubt for at least two years.

Oil was also critical in the European theater. The Italian invasion of Ethiopia in October 1935 was partly motivated by the belief that it would yield rich mineral resources, including possibly oil. That turned out to be a false assumption. But the ambition of Italian dictator Benito Mussolini was to re-create a Fascist version of the Roman Empire reaching from the Strait of Gibraltar to the Strait of Hormuz and including the oil fields of the Middle East.[12] This is one reason the Italian war effort focused on North Africa. The Italians, and later their allies the Nazis (who sent a small expeditionary force to North Africa), pushed east from Libya to cut off the British route to Asia through the Suez Canal, and to take the oil fields of Iraq, Kuwait, and Persia (Iran). Germany produced enough synthetic oil to fuel its army in the short term. But in the long term it would need much more oil to face down the United States. The Nazi regime briefly supported an anti-colonial revolt against the British in Iraq in a bid to secure supplies of oil, but that was quickly crushed. Once the first stage of the Blitzkrieg, or "lightning war," against the Soviet Union failed, therefore, the German army turned south, away from Moscow and toward the oil fields around Baku in the Caucasus region. The Allies had understood the strategic weakness created by Germany's lack of oil from the outset, and after the short-lived Hitler-Stalin Pact of 1939 (which divided up Poland between Germany and the Soviet Union), the British even considered bombing the Russian oil fields around Baku to deny oil to the Nazis. In the end, of course, the Soviet Union was forced into an alliance with the West by Hitler's attack, but the Nazis' push south was ultimately an important factor in their defeat. Not only did the Wehrmacht (the German army) fail to take the oil fields, but they became badly overextended in the attempt and were defeated (map 6.2).[13] By late 1944, Allied bombing had reduced German synthetic oil production by about 90 percent, the Soviet Army conquered the Romanian oil fields around Ploesti, and the Nazi army and air force faced drastic fuel shortages, diminishing their ability to fight effectively as a modern military force. In contrast, the Nazis' own effort of using submarines to cut off the flow of weapons, food, and oil from the United States across the Atlantic to Great Britain came close to success by the spring of 1943, but was ultimately defeated by Allied innovations in anti-submarine aviation and convoying.[14]

More broadly, sheer industrial power ultimately determined the outcome of the conflict. The Blitzkrieg launched by the Nazi armies in June 1941 did come very close to forcing the Soviet Union to surrender in the autumn of that year,

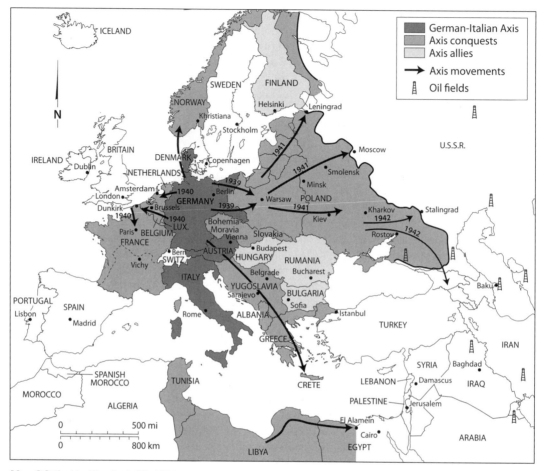

Map 6.2 The Nazi Empire in World War II.

and the Nazi submarine fleet came close to choking off Great Britain's resistance as well. Once those campaigns failed, however, the result was never really in doubt. The Allies massively outproduced the Axis in every category of military materiel and overwhelmed their armies. Over the course of the war the major Allied combatants (the United States, the Soviet Union, and the United Kingdom) produced three times as many combat aircraft and tanks as the major Axis combatants (Germany, Japan, and Italy); and they put almost half again as many men in uniform. In the war's decisive year, 1942, the Allies produced almost seven times as many tanks as the Axis did, five times as many machine guns, and twelve times as many artillery pieces (charts 6.2 and 6.3).[15]

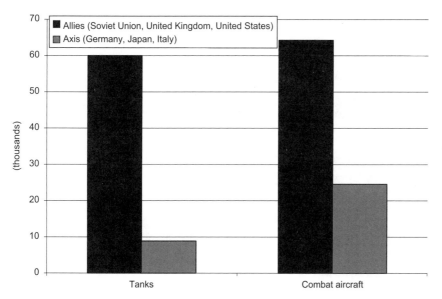

Chart 6.2 Tank and Aircraft Production, 1942.

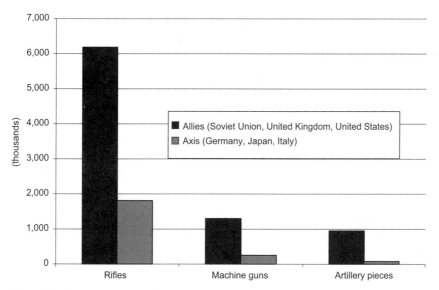

Chart 6.3 Infantry Weapons Production, 1942.

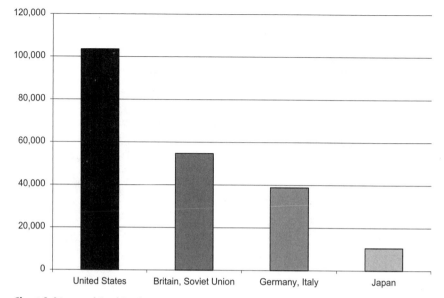

Chart 6.4 Iron and Steel Production, 1940.

That overwhelming superiority in military production was founded on a long-established superiority in production of key raw materials—for example, iron and steel and, again, oil (chart 6.4). The United States, Britain, and the Soviet Union together had a combined industrial capacity some three times that of the Axis in 1940.

To make the Axis cause even more precarious, by 1940 the United States was also the most technologically advanced society in the world, and Britain, while lagging to some degree, was still a technological and scientific behemoth by world standards. The Allies were also able to mobilize a higher proportion of their already superior resources than the Axis because defending themselves against obviously murderous aggressors gave them greater moral authority and popular legitimacy—and these gave them the confidence to devote a higher proportion of national resources to the war effort (and less to civilian con-sumption) than the Axis governments believed they could. Even on a purely military level, the Nazi armies in particular were increasingly constrained by Hitler's megalomaniac confidence in his own (flawed) military intuition, as was the Japanese military by its commitment to ideological principles of self-sacrifice, aggression, and racial superiority. Both yielded increasingly self-defeating decisions. The Western Allies' more collective and sober deci-sion-making processes proved superior.[16]

For the Axis, then, the war was essentially a desperate gamble. Long-term trends pointed to these regimes losing the ability to compete, militarily and potentially economically, with the United States, the British Empire, or the Soviet Union. Their ideologies made that prospect unacceptable. And so the German, Italian, and Japanese leadership at the war's outset hoped to win quickly and decisively enough on the battlefield or on the seas to knock out their opponents before they could bring their vastly superior economic power to bear, and overwhelm them. They staked their existence on their ability to shift the momentum of the process of global economic and demographic change in their own favor by quick, overwhelming military action—to prevent, as Adolf Hitler put it, the "threatened global hegemony of the North American continent" and Soviet Eurasia.[17] Yet, clearly, the long-term trends that (to them) made this gamble seem necessary also made it unlikely to succeed.

The Axis leadership's belief at the time that it was nevertheless justified was in part a legacy of imperialism and racism. Ideas of national and racial superiority encouraged these leaders to think that their people could beat the apparent odds because they were better than their enemies—smarter, more courageous, more organizationally capable, more honorable, stronger of will and body. Many in the Axis countries also believed they had nothing to lose. If their gamble failed, they would be dominated by other states and inferior "races"; but of course that would also be—as they saw it—the certain outcome if they did not even try.

The Great Depression of the 1930s made this last calculation much more urgent even than it had seemed in 1914. One of the Depression's important consequences was a rapid disintegration of the global economy. In the five or six decades before World War I the global economy had seen increasing integration through rising total trade—rising not only in absolute value but as a proportion of world GDP as well. From the outset of the Great Depression this trend radically reversed and trade fell as a proportion of global GDP. By 1938, it was below the level of 1870 (chart 6.5). One reason was that a number of states and colonies in the less developed world—India, China, Turkey, and Iran, among others—gained control of their tariff rates in the late 1920s and promptly raised them.[18] More important, with the onset of the Great Depression many countries imposed higher tariffs in order to protect local producers (and jobs) from overseas competition. The average global tariff rate—taxes on imported goods as a proportion of their total value—almost doubled by 1935 (chart 6.6).

The Smoot-Hawley Tariff, for example, enacted by the US Congress in June 1930, raised tariffs to their highest levels in a century. Other countries responded in kind. In most countries where manufactured goods were the key export commodities, exports plummeted—by almost 70 percent between 1929 and 1934 in Germany, by 60 percent in the United States, and by almost half in Britain. And demand for manufactures fell, not only because of tariff policy but also because of a collapse in demand and prices for primary products exported from less developed countries. The price of Brazilian coffee and Argentine

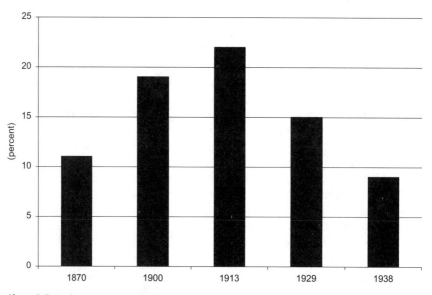

Chart 6.5 Trade as a Percentage of World GDP, 1870–1938.

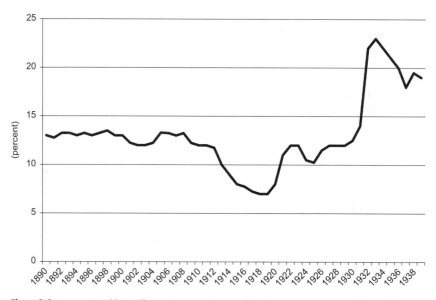

Chart 6.6 Average World Tariff Rate (taxes on imported goods as a proportion of their total value), 1890–1938.

frozen beef fell by more than half, that of Ceylonese tea by over 60 percent, that of Malaysian rubber by over 80 percent. As export revenues fell, debt defaults mounted, import quotas were adopted, and currency controls were imposed.[19] The world economy and global trade started to recover by the late 1930s, only to be disrupted again by the war. It was not until the 1950s that exports as a proportion of world GDP returned to levels comparable to those of 1913 or 1929.

For the United States or the Soviet Union, which as massive continental empires had never depended greatly on exports, this decline in trade was a serious, but manageable problem. Britain and France, too, worked to compensate by constructing systems of preferential exchange within their global empires.[20] But for countries more dependent on exports and imports, the new tariff regime was a disaster. Germany was heavily export-dependent: in 1929, exports earned almost 13 percent of German GDP, as compared to 3.6 percent for the United States and 1.6 percent for the Soviet Union. Britain and the Netherlands depended even more on exports than Germany; but again, Britain, France, and Holland had huge colonial empires, and could focus on developing economic ties with those dependent societies. Germany and Italy did not; the Japanese Empire was expanding, but was still far outclassed by those of its main rivals.[21]

Imperial expansion for the purpose of gaining direct control of resources and markets was, therefore, one obvious answer to the problem of the deliberalization of global trade. China and Russia, which along with the United States were the largest countries on earth in population, land area, and resources, were the obvious places to grasp control of both. That was where the German and Japanese regimes struck.

But World War II was more than a war for economic power. The origins and course of the war also reflected strong ideological elements. These ideological considerations, derived from the languages of race, ethnicity, and nation, profoundly shaped how the key leadership groups in the three Axis regimes understood the geopolitical situation. The National Socialist leaders of Germany were convinced that both communism and capitalist democracy, as egalitarian ideologies, were products of a Jewish plot to sabotage what Hitler called the "aristocratic principle of nature," according to which Aryans (Germans at their head), as the "superior" racial group on the earth, would otherwise inevitably triumph.[22] The Fascist leadership in Italy was convinced that the Italian nation was destined to restore the glory of the Roman Empire. The most prominent Japanese military leaders believed that Japan had a divinely ordained racial mission to dominate Asia. For each, therefore, gaining control of the resources with which to pursue the nation's rightful destiny was a preordained, ideologically defined imperative.

By the mid-1930s the fears, policies, and ambitions of these dictatorial regimes may have seemed plausible to their populaces, in part because there were so many dictatorships in the world by then. The totalitarian regimes were far more aggressive than other, merely authoritarian governments, not only in international relations but also internally. The Nazi, Fascist, and Soviet states intervened far more directly and effectively in economic and social life, in the Soviet case managing almost the entire economy through bureaucratic state agencies. The three states created incomparably large nongovernmental organizations, with memberships in the millions, the better to control almost every area of social life, from the workplace to the arts and from family life to schools, religion, and recreation. They imposed a much more pervasive and far more murderous system of repression and terror than authoritarian and military regimes in the rest of the world. But by the mid-1930s, in all these respects, they appeared to be merely at the extreme end of a spectrum of similar regimes. Less radical despotic governments, too, sought to govern through *corporatist* arrangements in which different functional groups in society (business, the professions, labor, women, young people, and others) were represented and directed by mass organizations, authoritarian in structure, that answered primarily to the state. They deployed police and security forces freely to suppress dissent, impose "order" and "discipline," and silence potential opposition. They frequently used state power to guide the economy, for example, by imposing stringent wage, price, and financial controls.

In fact, what is striking about the 1930s from a global perspective is the prevalence of dictatorship—regardless of local particularities. Between the late nineteenth century and World War I, representative government seemed to be on the march everywhere across the globe, partly as a consequence of the rise of nationalism and the global expansion of its economic and social foundations. By the 1930s, the opposite seemed true: the global revolutionary moment, the war, and the Depression created a world full of dictators. As the Indian nationalist leader Jawaharlal Nehru put it in 1933, "The nineteenth century was the century of democracy"; by the early twentieth, it seemed that "democracy and parliaments are . . . losing ground everywhere."[23]

China was an extraordinary case. There, by the mid-1920s Sun Zhongshan had developed a program for addressing what he saw as the political problem of the peasantry: military dictatorship, which would take on the pedagogical mission of teaching the peasantry to think nationally and preparing them for democracy. After his death Jiang Jieshi attempted to implement this program. But by the early 1930s he was mired in a civil war with the Chinese Communist Party, whose leader, Mao Zedong, in a sense stood Sun's calculation on its head by aiming to generate a revolution from below, not from above. Under Mao the CCP sought to destroy what Sun had called the "age-old customs of autocracy"—the corruption and exploitiveness of the elite, and the peasant culture of deference and passivity—by mobilizing poorer peasants to smash the inherited rural order through, among other measures, carrying out widespread violence against those identified as belonging to the social elite. By 1937 both would-be dictators were embroiled in a three-way war against each other and Japan. The relatively liberal constitutional regime established in Japan after 1889 entered into crisis in the late 1920s, with voices both inside and outside the military calling for a new imperial mission. Anti-liberal forces launched a wave of political assassinations (including three prime ministers and a dozen cabinet ministers, as well as journalists, parliamentarians, and trade-union leaders) intended to intimidate and undermine the government. By the mid-1930s it was replaced by what was effectively a military dictatorship bent on expansion—starting with China in 1937. This three-way war was not finally resolved until the Communists triumphed in China in 1949.[24]

Latin America largely escaped the scourge of war, but not dictatorship. In Mexico, the great social revolution that began in 1910 resulted by the late 1920s in the creation of a one-party (PRI) state. In Brazil, intense political ferment and conflict arose in the 1920s between centralists and federalists; between socialist workers, right-wing radicals, and the oligarchy that dominated the state; and between big landowners and poor peasants. This turmoil ended in the early 1930s with the creation of the Estado Novo, or New State, a dictatorship, backed by the military, under President Getulio Vargas. During the early 1930s, dictatorships emerged as well in Argentina, Chile, Peru, Guatemala, El Salvador, and Honduras.

Europe too was plagued with a growing number of dictators. In Spain, a brutal civil war between 1936 and 1938 brought the fascist dictator Francisco Franco to power; Portugal had its own fascist dictatorship; in Poland Marshal Józef Piłsudski established what was effectively a military dictatorship already in 1926; Hungary was ruled by a conservative military regime from 1919; Austrian democracy collapsed in the mid-1930s; and Turkey, as discussed in chapter 5, was a one-party state under Kemal Atatürk.

Economic hard times played a large role in this development. By the middle of the 1930s, desperate people all over the globe were willing to support extreme and coercive measures to address their economic woes—especially unemployment, which even in 1935 was still 15 or 20 percent in many parts of the world.[25] But ideology played an important role as well, not least in shaping perceptions of the economic crisis, both domestic and global. In the Soviet Union the Communist Party pursued an economic and social transformation, and a foreign policy, dictated by Leninist ideology. Leninism held that capitalism could survive only in a growing economy; that ultimately a capitalist economy could continue growing only by penetrating and exploiting other societies; and that therefore capitalism was necessarily both imperialist and doomed to collapse when it reached the limits of global expansion. With the onset of the Depression, that crisis seemed to have arrived. To the Soviet leadership, fascism looked like a desperate attempt to preserve capitalism from its own internally generated collapse. For the Nazis, on the other hand, the Depression seemed the most outrageous and perhaps the final instance of the manipulation of the global financial economy by the parasitic Jewish financiers whom Hitler and his colleagues imagined as out to destroy the Aryan race. As for communism, that too was just a Jewish plot—the other half of a world conspiracy reaching from Moscow to New York.

In contrast, many defenders of liberal democracy saw both communism and fascism as variants of the same phenomenon—tyranny. Both denied the essential humanity of people, treating them as mere objects rather than as bearers of inalienable rights. Both ideologies held that the individual was completely subordinate to the state and had no right to exist except in service to the state. As Mussolini put it in 1932, "The Fascist conception of life . . . accepts the individual only insofar as his interests coincide with those of the State."[26] As the British novelist E. M. Forster wrote in an essay in 1939, the "Great Men" who dominated totalitarian and authoritarian regimes all had in common the denial of human individuality and human dignity, they all crushed human creativity and decency, and they all therefore "produce a desert of uniformity around them and often a pool of blood too."[27]

Surprisingly, the defeat of the fascist regimes did not reduce the role of Great Men or tyrants in world politics after 1945. In fact, over the following three decades there was a further proliferation of dictators around the globe. An important reason for that growth was that although the war destroyed the most important fascist dictatorships, the astonishing survival and triumph of the USSR gave new power to communist ones. As a result, after 1945 two ideological, economic, and social systems faced each other in a global "cold" war—one that lasted almost half a century, profoundly affecting the domestic politics of many societies and shaping international relations.

DECOLONIZATION AND COLD WAR, 1945–1990

Toward colonial areas and backward or dependent peoples, Soviet policy . . . will be directed toward weakening the power and influence and contacts of advanced Western nations. . . . Efforts will be made in such countries to disrupt national self-confidence, to hamstring measures of national defense, to increase social and industrial unrest, to stimulate all forms of disunity. . . . Here poor will be set against rich, black against white, young against old, newcomers against established residents, etc. . . . Communists will, as a rule, work toward destruction of all forms of personal independence, economic, political or moral.[28]

George Kennan, US ambassador to the Soviet Union, February 22, 1946

Reflecting the imperialistic tendency of American monopoly capitalism, US foreign policy has been characterized in the postwar period by a desire for world domination. This is the real meaning of repeated statements . . . that the US has a right to world leadership. All the forces of American diplomacy, the Army, Navy, and Air Force, industry, and science have been place at the service of this policy. With this objective in mind broad plans for expansion have been developed, to be realized both diplomatically and through the creation of a system of naval and air bases far from the US, an arms race, and the creation of newer and newer weapons.[29]

N. Novikov, Soviet ambassador to the United States, September 27, 1946

The Second World War can be seen as a convergence of two broader conflicts. One was the struggle for global dominance among multiple imperial powers. The other was a struggle between regimes committed to radically divergent and mutually incompatible ideologies—fascism, communism, and liberal democracy. While the war did not resolve this great ideological-political conflict, it did simplify it significantly by eliminating one of those regime forms as a contender for global dominance—fascism and racist totalitarianism—and by ending the more or less equal competition between the imperial powers. Britain and France remained important colonial powers, but the world now was clearly dominated economically and militarily by the Soviet Union and the United States. Almost every country in the world faced enormous economic and ideological pressure to align itself with one or the other of these "superpowers." For the following fifty years, these two states and their subordinate allies and client-states fought the Cold War. But it remained a cold war, not a shooting war; the two superpowers maintained a certain equilibrium of power, and thereby avoided sliding into a third global conflict.

Central to this equilibrium was the dissolution of the colonial empires that had dominated the globe in the nineteenth and early twentieth centuries. Neither the United States nor the Soviet Union established a colonial empire based on the nineteenth-century model. Instead, each functioned as a *hegemon*—an overwhelmingly powerful patron using a combination of financial, economic, military, and cultural tools (diplomacy, propaganda, expertise, technical know-how) to dominate or to assist a large group of other societies. The range of forms this domination and assistance took was quite large—from direct military intervention and occupation to bilateral and multilateral trade and political treaties undertaken by the less powerful societies in relative freedom. But whatever the methods, for each of the superpowers the aim was to create an integrated economic, political, and military *bloc* centered on the hegemon. Other states and societies were not powerful enough to do that, or even to act as fully independent players in international relations. But in a sense they did not need to, because in constructing giant integrated, regional economic blocs, the two superpowers essentially guaranteed their allies and clients access to raw materials and markets. Thus, the superpowers eliminated the multistate imperial rivalries of the pre-1945 period, not only by using brute military power but also by building world economic systems that gave other societies reason to accept their dominance.

The confrontation between the superpowers was stabilized, as well, by the emergence of a new international institutional framework. Most important, both powers were entangled with the United Nations, established immediately after World War II (at a conference in San Francisco in 1945) as a mechanism for keeping order in a world of independent nations, rather than of empires. The UN built on the precedent of the League of Nations, which had been established in 1919 to pursue the same ends, but had not done so effectively—in part because the United States did not join. World War II convinced even the United States and, initially, fifty other countries that a more influential body was essential. Since the UN membership consisted of sovereign nations, its options for actually enforcing any of its declarations, resolutions, conventions, or other agreements were extremely limited—it had effectively no legal powers and no political or military instruments. It was also difficult to generate consensus in such a large assembly—51 nations initially, 132 by 1971, and 192 by 2010. Nevertheless, the United Nations was increasingly important as an influential stage from which to influence world public opinion, and particularly as an agenda-setting institution in which experts in a plethora of fields (including health, education, development, the arts, electoral machinery and practices, women's social and economic roles, and human rights) could collectively establish the global importance of particular issues and problems, in relative autonomy from any one national government. The UN was also important as a permanent nexus for discussion, negotiation, and collaboration between states. And it was a crucial source of information, which like the League of Nations, it published in abundance and steadily increasing quality.[30]

The UN's success in establishing itself in these functions derived partly from its role in bundling, or aggregating the voices of a whole range of intergovernmental organizations formed before and after 1945; for example, the International Office of Public Hygiene, which in 1948 emerged as the UN-affiliated World Health Organization (WHO); the Food and Agriculture Organization (FAO, 1945); and the International Labor Organization (ILO, 1919). The UN established a raft of its own agencies as well—among the most important the UN Educational, Scientific, and Cultural Organization (UNESCO). It was also remarkably successful in bringing together international nongovernmental organizations, a steadily growing number of which were given special consultative status as organizations on which the UN's Economic and Social Council (ECOSOC) would draw for expertise and analysis.[31] This was important in part because the rate at which such INGOs were formed accelerated after 1945. There were some 800 INGOs in 1930, but 2,000 by 1960 and 4,000 by 1980—in fields ranging from the sciences, medicine and technology, through sports and tourism, to education, religion, and the professions.[32] In 1948 only 45 INGOs had consultative status with the ECOSOC; by 2013 close to 4,000 did, ranging from the International Chamber of Commerce and Consumers International to the International Planned Parenthood Federation and the World Fellowship of Buddhists.[33]

The United Nations exercised a considerable amount of soft power through expertise, education, negotiations, and deliberations within and among these agencies and organizations. It also formed an important balancing point in the new world order. Both the Soviet Union and the United States (along with China, France, and Britain) had permanent seats in the UN's executive body, the fifteen-member Security Council, and could veto any UN action other than debate, discussion, and the passing of resolutions in the General Assembly (which included all member nations). But the two superpowers also faced incentives to retain sympathy and support in the General Assembly—which could influence public relations and shape global patterns of political cooperation and economic and cultural influence. The UN therefore acted as a brake on superpower action.

A third element of Cold War stability stemmed from the ongoing revolution in military technology. The development of nuclear weapons and of machines for delivering them—intercontinental bombers and ballistic missiles—created a military standoff. From the late 1940s onward, both superpowers built up massive arsenals of nuclear weapons (chart 6.7). Each side calculated that the threat of nuclear annihilation would deter any attempt by the other side to tip the balance in its favor by conventional military action—say, an invasion of Western Europe by the Soviets and their allies in the communist Warsaw Pact, or of Eastern Europe by the alliance of Western nations dominated by the United States, the North Atlantic Treaty Organization (NATO). But the incentive to build nuclear weapons was also economic, because bombers and missiles are cheaper than soldiers. Maintaining large conventional forces was a terrible economic burden, generating inflationary pressure and skewing economies toward less productive military investments. Partly by relying on nuclear weapons, the United States held military expenditure essentially steady, in inflation-adjusted dollars, for most of the thirty years from the mid-1950s until the early 1980s (with exceptions during the Korean and Viet Nam Wars). Since the US economy was growing rapidly during those decades, that meant that military expenditures as a proportion of GDP fell steadily for more than two decades, gradually easing the burden of defense on the national economy.[34] The Soviet Union adopted a similar policy in 1961, under Nikita Khrushchev, as it became increasingly clear that the Communist economies would have to spend more on consumer goods in order to maintain the loyalty of their citizens and their economic competitiveness.

By the 1970s, the two powers had created a system of "mutual assured destruction" (MAD) and a rough balance of conventional forces in Europe, the key potential flashpoint of the Cold War. The result was a forty-year stalemate.

Given this standoff, the United States and the Soviet Union competed for control of resources and for influence over populations around the globe through various forms of soft power or economic and cultural influence, and through covert and low-level intervention—including financial skullduggery; spying; orchestrated propaganda, campaigns of disinformation, and the manufacture of scandals; support by turns for dissenting and for dominant political parties; financial, technical, or military aid to insurgent groups, antigovernment terrorists, or pro-government death squads; and military coups and assassinations. This long, low-level war by covert means, by proxy, and by soft-power tactics was focused particularly on regions and countries where key

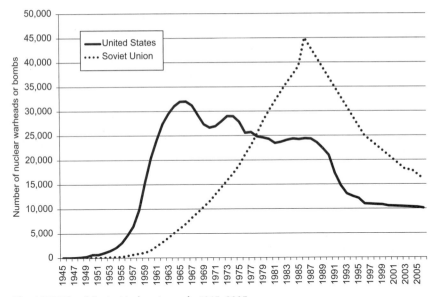

Chart 6.7 US and Soviet Nuclear Arsenals, 1945–2005.

strategic raw materials were concentrated, and on regions of strategic military or commercial importance.[35]

Much of this Cold War activity was carried out from military bases that the United States established around the globe in the 1940s and 1950s, and that the Soviet Union built in the 1940s in Eastern Europe and then in the 1970s in various key locations in Africa and Asia. After rapidly reducing the number of bases it operated from its wartime high, in the early 1950s the United States rapidly built back up again. By the late 1960s the nation had almost as many overseas military stations as it had at the height of World War II (chart 6.8). It took the Soviet Union another ten years to establish a network of bases outside Eastern Europe, but by the 1970s it too was operating a rival (though far less extensive) network of such overseas stations.[36] Neither superpower aimed to exercise direct imperial rule over the territories in which these bases were located. Rather, they made these military bases—usually held on long-term leases—the foundation for their global strategic military, diplomatic, and cultural presence and power.

In fact, one of the most important consequences of the Cold War was that during the height of its intensity, between the late 1940s and the late 1960s, virtually all the old colonial empires unraveled and were replaced by independent nation-states. Between 1947 and 1949 the large nations of South and Southeast Asia became independent—including Korea in 1945, the Philippines in 1946, India in 1947, and Indonesia in 1949. The communist movement in Viet Nam

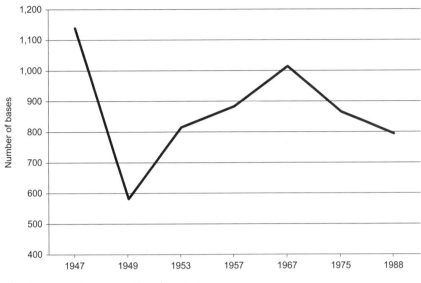

Chart 6.8 US Military Bases Abroad, 1947–1988.

declared independence in 1945 and achieved functional independence at least in the North in 1954. In contrast, independence in most of Africa and the Pacific was delayed until the late 1950s and early 1960s. After a slow start in the 1950s, many African and Pacific colonies were reorganized as independent states in a rush in 1960. That wave was followed by a steady trickle of new nations formed through the mid-1970s when the Portuguese empire in Africa was finally dissolved.[37]

This process generated a great deal of violence—in many cases, even where independence itself was achieved peacefully. British India, for example, became independent through a process of peaceful negotiation, pushed forward by mass civil disobedience; but it then passed through a bitter civil conflict and partition into two states—Hindu-majority India and Muslim-majority Pakistan. Up to 3 million civilians were killed by mass violence, and up to 18 million became refugees. In the Philippines, independence came peacefully, but the new regime fought a long drawn-out guerrilla war against communist insurgents. Korea achieved independence without violence, but then descended into a brutal civil and international war in 1950–53 that killed up to 10 percent of the population and left two states, north and south, where there had been one. In Indonesia there was a brief but intense revolutionary war fought against the Dutch. In Viet Nam a bitter civil and international war dragged on until 1975, fueled by the direct intervention of the United States in support of an anti-communist regime in the south after the French departure in 1954. China was not formally a colony, but it had to fight a titanic and enormously destructive war against Japanese imperialism from 1937 to 1945. Once the Japanese Empire was defeated, the Nationalist or KMT army and the Communist PLA (People's Liberation Army) turned on each other and fought a short but massive civil war. By 1949 the KMT had been ejected from the mainland, retreating to create the Republic of China on Taiwan. The People's Republic of China consolidated its hold on the rest of the country. Most of Africa became independent by peaceful means; but Algeria, Angola, and Mozambique witnessed long, bitter, destructive revolutionary wars of independence, followed by equally bitter civil wars. Nigeria won independence peacefully, but then passed through a terrible civil war between 1967 and 1970 in which up to a million people lost their lives. In the Congo, Belgium hastily granted independence in the face of intense protests, but the country—left virtually without administrative personnel or institutions—dissolved into a civil war that ended with the establishment of a military dictatorship. South Africa slid ever deeper into a racist nightmare, complete with laws against interracial marriage and sex, internal passports, forced removal to impoverished black "homelands" on marginal lands (an echo of "partition" in other ex-colonies), separate educational and employment systems, detention without trial for political prisoners, and violent resistance that slowly mounted throughout the 1960s and 1970s. The transition to independence was relatively peaceful in the Middle East in the short term, but between 1945 and 1949 a confused terrorist struggle and civil war ensued in Palestine, ultimately creating the state of Israel and displacing around a million Palestinian Arab refugees. Further wars erupted in the region in 1956, 1967, 1973, and 1982—not counting chronic low-level violence and terrorism in between.[38]

Not surprisingly, the reasons for this broad but varied process of decolonization also varied from case to case. Whereas racism had been the explicit or implicit ideological basis for colonial rule, it was intensively questioned as early as the 1920s and 1930s, for example, in the *négritude* movement and *indigenismo* by Indian nationalists. But the disaster of Nazi racism and mass murder finally bankrupted it.[39] World opinion largely rejected racism as both ethically heinous and scientifically indefensible. In fact in 1950 the United Nations issued an authoritative statement on race, holding: "The scientific material available to us at present does not justify the conclusion that inherited genetic differences are a major factor in producing the differences between the cultures and cultural achievements of different peoples or groups."[40]

Over the preceding three decades, moreover, the colonial empires had undermined themselves. To gain access to the resources of their colonial dependencies, they had to make at least some investment in transportation, communications, and administrative infrastructure in the societies they governed. After World War I, the imperial regimes were aware, more than ever before, of their colonies' economic and military value, and in many cases intervened more intrusively in their economies and accelerated development.

Greater investment and higher administrative demands (and budgets) fostered the growth of local elites in colonial societies, including both businesspeople and a small, educated administrative class.

In India, to take a textbook example, ethnic Indians made up 12 percent of the Indian Civil Service in 1919, but just under 50 percent by 1939. The Tata Iron and Steel Company—founded in 1911, the beneficiary of wartime demand from the government of India, and now a major global corporation—is only the most remarkable illustration of the rise of a native Indian business class. The Federation of Indian Chambers of Commerce was formed in 1927.[41] The pattern was similar in Nigeria, which exported sixty times as much tin in the second half of the 1920s as it had in the first five years of the century, more than fifty times as much cotton, twenty times as many peanuts, fifteen times as much cocoa. There were six times as many primary school students in Nigeria in 1937 as there had been in 1912; the number of secondary school students rose from fewer than 100 to almost 5,000. There were five times as many civil servants and clerks in the capital, Lagos, in 1921 as in 1901.[42]

What is more, colonial administrative personnel were often educated in Europe or North America—including 34 out of 107 new heads of government in Africa and Southeast Asia between 1958 and 1973.[43] These leaders' broad horizons embraced an understanding of how the economic relationship worked between their own colonial society and that of the imperial power. They often formed global intellectual and political connections and networks, for example, with colonial subjects from other regions governed by the same imperial power. As had been the case during the period of revolutionary upheavals before and during World War I, these were precisely the people most likely to develop a nationalist program for their own society—and to be attracted to socialist or communist visions of liberation and progress.

In many colonial areas, furthermore, imperial administrators had mobilized local resources for war partly by promising colonized peoples a greater degree of self-government after victory was achieved. In India, for example, in 1917 the British administration promised "the gradual development of self-governing institutions" as a reward for the mobilization of 1.4 million Indians to support Britain's war effort. After the war such promises were forgotten or only very grudgingly kept—for instance, in the rather halfhearted Government of India Act of 1935. Holland established a legislative council for Indonesia in 1916, but then incorporated that colony into the Dutch kingdom in 1922. Betrayals like these generated profound resentment, even among colonial elites who were not committed to complete independence.[44]

In some cases, too, the religious renewal movements of the early twentieth century provided important intellectual and institutional support for nationalism. In Indonesia, Muslim reform associations emerged in 1912 and 1926, a communist party was formed in 1920 (and attempted a revolution in 1926–27), and nationalists inspired in part by Theosophy's promise of universal equality and a synthesis of Eastern and Western values brought the colony to such a state of incipient rebellion that by the late 1930s the colonial administration banned all meetings of more than four people. In Egypt the Muslim Brotherhood, formed in 1928, played an important role in mobilizing the broader populace for independence.

For all these reasons, the 1920s and 1930s saw rising anti-colonial activism. In French Indochina, the colonial regime resorted to vicious repression to keep the lid on, ordering seven hundred summary executions in 1930 alone.[45] British India was also in turmoil, facing a widespread, peaceful noncooperation movement; in 1932 a massive crackdown resulted in some forty thousand arrests over three months, but did not bring the opposition under control.[46]

World War II intensified resistance, in part by demolishing the myth of imperial superiority. In the critical cases of Indonesia, the Philippines, and Viet Nam, the Japanese conquest and occupation dismantled colonial rule, leaving either collaborators (as in Indonesia) or resistance movements (as in Viet Nam) to step in as new national governments when the Japanese were kicked out. As Singapore's prime minister Lee Kuan Yew put it in 1965, he belonged to "the generation of young men who went through the Second World War and the Japanese occupation and emerged determined that no one—neither the Japanese nor the British—had the right to push and kick us around."[47] The hardships imposed on colonial societies by mobilization, particularly for World War II, also strained loyalties that were already fraying. The most grotesque case was that of India, where the colonial government's efforts to squeeze resources out of the colony to support Britain's war effort contributed to a terrible famine in which as many as 3.8 million people died in 1943–44.[48] Nigeria offers a less extreme example: the British colonial rulers there allowed imports only from the British Empire and fixed prices of Nigerian exports at below-market levels; Britain's recruitment of thousands of young men to fight overseas created a labor shortage that drove up wages and prices. By 1945 Nigerian labor unions—particularly that of civil servants—launched a general strike to force the government to improve conditions.[49]

By the late 1950s the writing was clearly on the wall: nationalism was on the march throughout the colonial world. At the end of that decade, in many cases, notably in Africa, the colonial rulers simply decamped. A remarkable case is the French departure from sub-Saharan Africa. Its resources having been depleted by World War II, France nevertheless deployed half a million troops to Algeria, yet ultimately failed to put down the revolt in its colony. At this point, the French government under Charles de Gaulle concluded that it could no longer hang on to its empire in the rest of Africa. France had already given up trying to control Morocco and Tunisia in 1956 in order to concentrate on Algeria, where there was a substantial French settler population to be defended. In 1960 de Gaulle's government negotiated independence with the rest of its colonies in Africa, creating fourteen new nations in one year. France abandoned Algeria two years later. Great Britain's exit from West Africa was just as rapid, for similar reasons. Bogged down in a counterinsurgency campaign in Kenya in defense of a sizable white settler population, the British negotiated independence with multiple nationalist movements between 1957 and 1960.[50] The Belgians, as one historian puts it, "effectively fled" the Congo in 1960 in the face of mounting unrest. Portugal hung on to its colonies in Mozambique and Angola for another fifteen years, but only at the cost of a decade of—ultimately failed—counterinsurgency warfare.[51]

The Cold War too eroded the colonial order. The United States and the Soviet Union, both products of revolutionary upheavals, were committed to democracy and self-determination, though their ideologies defined those principles differently. But each also controlled an entire continent with enormous natural resources, and their need for access to global resources was therefore less urgent than it was for smaller states. In any case each also had overwhelming economic power, which could be used to secure indirect access to or control of resources. It was in their interest to negotiate that access directly with smaller, local producers, rather than with more powerful imperial regimes in Western Europe or Japan. And neither power had any interest in brooking competition for world power, for example, in the form of a massive British Empire in Asia or a massive French Empire in Africa.

Egypt presents an interesting case. Formally independent after 1936, with its own constitutional monarch, the country remained essentially a client state of Britain. In 1952 a secret organization within the military, the Free Officers Movement, overthrew the monarchy and established a nominal republic, with Gamal Abdel Nasser soon emerging as de facto dictator. Threatened with the nationalization of the Suez Canal, the British, French, and Israelis invaded Egypt in late 1956 and defeated the Egyptian army. But at that point the United States and the Soviet Union intervened and forced the invading forces to pull back from overthrowing Nasser.[52] The two superpowers, at radical odds with each other, cooperated to block this venture. It was not in the interest of either to have the British and French in control of the Suez Canal, rather than the Egyptians. Though in competition with each other, they were in agreement that the Middle East—and indeed the world—should be their field of influence and competition. Britain, France, and other regional powers like Israel should not compete with them for dominance. The superpowers intervened in other cases as well. The West African state of Guinea achieved independence from Britain in 1958, in part thanks to Soviet economic aid. In Indonesia, in 1949 the United States threatened to cut off aid to the Netherlands under the Marshall Plan (the United States' massive program of economic assistance for the rebuilding of Western Europe, started in 1947) unless it gave up its attempt to reconquer its former colony.[53]

Both the US and the Soviet anti-imperialist positions were oddly self-contradictory. The United States in 1950 was, after all, a racial state—the social organization of most of the South, and of much of the urban North, was built around the idea of race, enforced by powerfully entrenched legal codes and customs. Racist attitudes toward colonial independence movements were common in the United States; at the very least, US diplomats feared that any sudden collapse of the colonial empires of its allies France and Britain would create "immature" new nations, susceptible to Soviet influence.[54] And the Soviet Union was de facto in occupation of Eastern-Central Europe, including Poland, Hungary, Czechoslovakia, Bulgaria, Romania, and the eastern third of Germany, as well as the Baltic States (Estonia, Latvia, and Lithuania), which it had absorbed as confederated republics. In fact in 1956 the Soviet Army invaded Hungary to suppress a reformist communist government in the process of abandoning its dictatorship and leaving the Warsaw Pact (the military alliance of communist states). At first glance, it may seem odd that these two superstates opposed empire. But it was important to both of them to keep the rest of the world open to their own forms of economic and cultural power, and clearly, the old empires stood in the way of their exercise of this hegemony.

Both superpowers had constructed the institutional framework for such hegemony in the closing phase of World War II. On the capitalist side, a first step was taken when a group of seven hundred delegates from the governments of forty-four Allied nations signed the Bretton Woods agreement (named after the New Hampshire resort where they met) in 1944, essentially pegging their currencies to the US dollar and creating the International Monetary Fund (IMF) and the International Bank for Reconstruction and Development (now the World Bank) to maintain currency stability. In 1947, they then signed the General Agreement on Tariffs and Trade (GATT), and met regularly thereafter to negotiate a progressive decrease in tariffs in order to create an ever freer global trade environment among the capitalist economies. At the same time, the United States used its financial muscle to rebuild the Western European economies through the Marshall Plan, which granted a quarter-trillion dollars, in today's value, to Western European nations to help them dig out from the rubble of World War II—in return for accepting relatively open trade policies and excluding communist parties from governing coalitions. And the United States also tied the noncommunist world together in a whole series of military alliances—NATO in 1949, the Organization of American States in 1948, the Southeast Asia Treaty Organization (SEATO) in 1954, and the Central Treaty Organization (CENTO) in 1955.[55] The Soviet Union responded by forming an economic alliance called the Council for Mutual Economic Assistance (CMEA), created in 1949. This structure was never as successful as that built in the West, but it did at least aim to accomplish an analogous economic integration across Eastern-Central Europe. On the military side, the USSR created the Warsaw Pact in 1955. It is worth noting, too, that both alliances were held together economically in part by oil: the United States controlled the lion's share of crude production in the Middle East, while by 1964 the Soviet Union built a 2,500-mile pipeline from its oil fields around Baku into Eastern-Central Europe.[56] Obviously, for each superpower, plentiful oil supplies were an important means of pacifying its own bloc by preventing the fears of energy starvation that had helped motivate the Axis powers in World War II. Under US and Soviet control, oil became an important glue for international relations, not its dynamite.

Where threats to the core areas of these alliances arose, the superpowers did not hesitate to take direct military action. The Soviet Army intervened three times to stifle reform movements in Eastern Europe: in East Germany in 1953, in Hungary in 1956, and in Czechoslovakia in 1968. The United States intervened, to cite but one example, in Guatemala in 1953, when a coup guided by the US Central Intelligence Agency overthrew the president, who was bent on land reform and purchased arms from the Soviets. In 1965 it invaded the Dominican Republic to block a left-wing revolution.

At their margins these two blocs, or systems of alliances, were relatively fluid, and competition and conflict between them took a range of forms. Varying interests and opportunities could create quite complex and contradictory policies in different regions. In Viet Nam the United States was drawn into supporting the French attempt to maintain colonial rule because of its commitment to anti-communism, while the North Vietnamese regime was able to use tensions between China and the Soviet Union to maximize foreign support.[57] In Korea, the United States and the communist powers fought an extended war (partly by proxy, partly by fielding their own troops) in the early 1950s.

More common than these substantial conflicts were smaller, covert or proxy interventions in areas with critical strategic resources, commodities crucial to modern industrial development, or key strategic opportunities. The Allies occupied Iran in 1941 in order to secure Iranian oil and a land route to Russia for supplies from the West; in 1945, the country regained functional independence. The Anglo-Iranian Oil Company had a virtual monopoly on the industry and made tremendous profits (sharing only 16 percent of them with the Iranian government, until 1951, when the parliament passed a law nationalizing the oil industry. What was more, the new government under Mohammed Mossadeq was partially supported by the pro-communist Tudeh Party, and it seemed possible that a left-leaning Iranian government would turn for technical assistance to the Soviets, whose own oil industry gave them expertise similar to that of the Western oil giants. By the summer of 1953 the British and American spy agencies helped Shah Reza Pahlavi to oust the elected government. Iran's oil fields were not formally reprivatized, and the shah's government now got half of all oil revenues, but foreign companies continued to be the de facto producers of Iran's oil.[58] Iran became a strategic partner for the West, alongside Saudi Arabia, Kuwait, Qatar, and the United Arab Emirates. In response, the Soviets developed a close alliance with Iran's neighbors, Iraq and Syria, where Baathist "Arab Socialist" regimes were in power. For two decades, the Soviet Union maintained a close relationship with Egypt as well, sending funding and expertise to Gamal Nasser for massive economic development projects. Needless to say, these alliances were important to the superpowers because the Middle East was rapidly becoming the key source of oil for the world economy.

Another significant conflict zone was central and southern Africa. An upheaval arose in the early 1960s in Zaire, where upon independence in 1960 the first elected prime minister, Patrice Lumumba, spoke publicly about nationalizing the country's natural resources. With Zaire embroiled in a chaotic transition to independence, the mineral-rich Katanga province seceded—with the support of the Belgians, who did not want to lose out economically despite abandoning colonial rule. Lumumba thereupon sought Soviet aid to suppress that move. After a number of Belgian and CIA plots to assassinate Lumumba failed, he was deposed by a military coup, arrested, taken to Katanga, and killed. The army chief of staff, Colonel Mobutu Sese Seko, established a dictatorship that would last until 1997—and that even the US ambassador, in 1963, admitted was "obscurantist, arbitrary, primitive, totalitarian, willful, and irresponsible." But Zaire was a major producer of a number of strategically important minerals. Among others, it supplied two-thirds of the world's industrial diamonds, it was the sixth-largest world producer of copper, and it was a major producer of uranium. Control over such strategic materials was, as one American diplomat had put it in 1947, "an absolute requirement of the very life of our nation" and could not be surrendered to the communists.[59]

A third illustrative case was an even murkier upheaval in Indonesia in 1965. There the nationalist leader Sukarno had been one of the key figures in the Non-Aligned Movement of nations seeking to avoid being drawn into the Cold War. Among other measures, in 1955 he held an important initial meeting of nonaligned states, the Bandung Conference. Establishing what he called "Guided Democracy," Sukarno developed a semitotalitarian political and economic system complete with personality cult and a bizarre language of acronyms and slogans, giant infrastructure projects, crony capitalism, and economic mismanagement leading to massive inflation. The push to expand the new nation and keep the army happy led to minor military conflicts with the Dutch in the western part of Papua New Guinea (PNG) and with the British in Borneo in the late 1950s and early 1960s. By the mid-1960s Sukarno was pursuing an alliance with the Indonesian Communist Party (the largest political party in the country) and buying military equipment from the Soviet Union; western security forces (particularly the CIA) were cultivating right-wing military officers as a possible political alternative. In 1965 Suharto, who had commanded Indonesian forces in the PNG campaign, led a military coup. He then launched a campaign against the Communists during which the army and private militias massacred somewhere between half a million and a million Communists, leftists, and ethnic Chinese. In the chaos, Suharto set up a "New Order" based on military rule, pervasive propaganda, more vague neologisms

and acronyms, and more cronyism and corruption. Probably not coincidentally, within five years of the coup his government signed agreements with
international oil companies that doubled production.[60]

In all these cases (and many others), a complex interplay was at work
between local nationalist forces and the Cold War rivalry of the superpowers.
Nationalists in the former colonial regions were attracted to socialism because
they saw it as the alternative to the export-dominated, commodity-extraction
economic regime established by the imperial states in the late nineteenth century. The same was true in many societies that had long been politically independent but were in an essentially dependent or quasi-colonial economic relationship with the imperial and industrial nations—for example, in Latin
America. Many nationalist leaders thought that state intervention to develop
domestic industrial capacity was the only way to escape from the lopsided relationships, inherited from the late nineteenth century, in which their societies
exchanged a limited range of raw materials for a wide range of manufactured
goods. Some called on the Soviet Union for money, economic and engineering
expertise, and weapons. Their opponents, of course, often called on the United
States for support in achieving the same outcome by a different economic strategy: instead of "import substitution" (expanding local industrial capacity to
build a high-value-added economy), the nation would pursue export-led
growth, in which commodity extraction generated capital that could be
invested in industrial growth.

While the superpowers focused on global strategy and access to resources,
then, in many of these cases local elites sought the aid of either Soviet or Western governments specifically for the project of transforming peasants into
small farmers or proletarians. Cold War politics, in other words, was in no
small part a continuation and expansion of interwar efforts to solve the "problem" of the peasant.

Perhaps the most extraordinary instance of this pattern was that of the People's Republic of China. After winning the civil war against the Nationalist
forces in 1949 (with the two superpowers lending support to each side), the
Communist regime set about consolidating its control of the country, among
other efforts by gradually pushing forward the collectivization of agriculture.
That process was accelerated in 1958, with increasing coercion applied. The
result—as it had been in the Soviet Union a generation earlier—was catastrophic: a state-generated famine that took the lives of somewhere between 16
and 36 million people (depending on the method of counting) between 1958
and 1962.[61] As in the USSR, however, collectivization did give the Communist
regime uncontested control of the rural society and its resources, enabling the
state to extract value from the agricultural economy in order to build the
industrial economy.

Other regimes across the postcolonial world pursued this ultimate aim,
though not by such drastic means. When Patrice Lumumba departed for a visit

to the United States in the summer of 1960, he promised to come back with "technicians, with teachers, with engineers"; speaking to the press in New York, he emphasized the need "for developing the country, for industrialization. . . . If in America, if everywhere in the world, people know how to manufacture medicines, to manufacture cars, why shouldn't the Congolese also be capable of creating new things in their country in five or six years?" His country, he knew, could live from "their fields, their crops, their fruit," but the future was industrial.[62]

In some instances the superpowers responded to pleas for assistance from would-be clients only reluctantly, essentially drawn in colonial nationalists' by the independent initiatives. In Angola, Mozambique, and Ethiopia in the mid-1970s, the Soviet government was actually not much interested in supporting revolutionary regimes, and was acutely aware of its own constrained resources and limited ability to project power so far afield. But the Soviets were "dragged into Africa," as the director of the Soviet intelligence agency, the KGB, later put it, by considerations of prestige and a desire to maintain what appeared to be strategic momentum in the confrontation with the United States.[63] For the United States, involvement in Africa resulted partly from the fear that the Soviets would be able to deny the West key strategic resources—cobalt from Zaire, platinum and vanadium from South Africa, chromium from South Africa and Rhodesia, and so on. As one historian has put it, by the mid-1970s there was "growing concern that Africa had become the West's Achilles heel."[64] But the case of US involvement in the anti-colonial revolution and then civil war in Viet Nam is another, different example. There the United States slid reluctantly into a major military conflict in support of an anti-communist regime, not out of any particular immediate strategic or economic interest but to stop the first "domino" from falling in favor of Communists in the whole region.[65] And in the context of Cold War competition for allies and clients, the United States supported some military dictatorships simply because, as a State Department report in 1959 put it, "our refusal to deal with a military or authoritarian regime . . . could lead almost necessarily to the establishment of that regime's friendly relations with the Soviet Bloc."[66]

In a sense, then, those contests of the Cold War involving competitive economic and military assistance, covert action, and dictators were waged as collaborative efforts between the superpowers and political "entrepreneurs" in other societies, with the latter often taking the initiative. This observation suggests an obvious parallel with the building of the global economy—and in some cases, of colonial empires—in the late nineteenth century as a collaborative effort between capitalists in Europe and North America and economic entrepreneurs in Asia, Latin America, and Africa. We can perhaps see it this way: the competitive imperial project of building a global economy around commodity extraction produced gunboat diplomacy and colonial wars of conquest; the competing projects of building "developed" global capitalist or socialist economies produced proxy wars, insurgencies, and coups.

Not every nation in the world was aligned on one or the other side in the Cold War, however. The Non-Aligned Movement was quite influential even at the height of the Cold War. Based on five principles of peaceful coexistence developed in 1954 by Jawaharlal Nehru, prime minister of India from 1948 to 1964, it tried to steer a middle course between socialism and capitalism and to speak for the interests of the major nations that emerged from the decolonization process. After an important initial meeting in Bandung, Indonesia, in 1955 (mentioned earlier), it was formally constituted at a meeting of representatives of twenty-five nations in Belgrade, Yugoslavia, in 1961. At a second meeting, in 1964, it denounced "economic pressure and domination, interference, racial discrimination, subversion, intervention and the threat of force" as "neo-colonialist devices against which the newly independent nations have to defend themselves" collectively. This was an analysis Nehru had developed as early as 1933, when—writing from a British colonial prison—he had argued that the United States in particular was creating a "new kind of empire, the modern type of empire. It is invisible and economic, and exploits and dominates without any obvious outward signs. . . . In this way imperialism has perfected itself in the course of time."[67]

Nehru and many other Indian nationalists believed socialism was the only viable path to genuine economic independence and development; but they were also committed to federalism and democracy as the only viable political forms for an enormous and diverse country. Politically they were remarkably successful, with the Indian National Congress party in power almost continuously from 1948 until 1992. The more typical pattern, however, was sympathy to socialism and arm's-length relations with the Soviet Union, combined with homegrown military dictatorship. In Egypt, for example, Gamal Nasser nationalized the financial, industrial, and export sectors and established a centrally controlled command economy featuring five-year plans and ambitious development projects centered on radical land reform and extensive electrification and irrigation enabled by the Aswan High Dam, completed in 1970 with Soviet assistance. But he also repressed both the Egyptian Communist Party and the Muslim Brotherhood, the latter formed in 1928 as a bulwark for popular religious opposition to colonial rule and European cultural penetration.[68]

As the last point suggests, while the colonial empires faded during the 1950s and 1960s, the period saw little significant erosion of the prevalence of dictatorship established before World War II. In fact, right into the 1980s the world was even more packed with dictators than it had been in 1930. This was a bit ironic. In the late nineteenth and early twentieth centuries the cause of nationalism and the cause of parliamentary government and individual rights had been closely associated. The concept of citizenship was central to the idea of the nation, a polity in which all citizens are equal in their rights because they are all essentially the same, in that they are all members of an ethnic, linguistic, cultural, historical, and political unity. The nation was built on the idea of universal rights and active political participation. After World War II, a strange situation developed in which the idea of nationalism triumphed over empire, yet dictatorship was virtually the norm. By 1980, there were only some three-dozen democratic regimes in the world, out of about 120 independent nations. In the mid-1970s dictators ruled in Brazil, Argentina, and Chile, to name only the largest states in South America. In the Caribbean region, Cuba, Haiti, and the Dominican Republic all had dictators; so did Panama, Guatemala, and El Salvador; Mexico was ruled by a one-party state under the PRI. The Philippines had the de facto dictator Ferdinand Marcos, Indonesia had Suharto, Taiwan was under martial law from 1949 until 1987, and South Korea was governed by a succession of authoritarian strongmen from 1948 to 1988. Communist dictatorships ruled in North Korea, Viet Nam, Cambodia, and Laos; Turkey, Iran, and Pakistan had what were effectively military dictatorships; Syria, Iraq, and Egypt were one-party states; and Saudi Arabia was a monarchy. Most of Africa was ruled by dictators or one-party states of one kind or another, whether military or "African Socialist" or Marxist. Greece, Spain, and Portugal all suffered under military-fascist dictatorships until the mid-1970s.

The lopsided development of the world economy and the political legacies of imperialism earlier in the twentieth century were important reasons for this pattern. Economic development in many colonies had been sufficient to foster nationalist sentiment among a small elite, but not had laid little of the economic, social, or institutional foundation on which that elite could build a stable and coherent nation. In Africa, in particular, parsimonious and exploitative colonial governments left behind minimal transportation, communications, or administrative infrastructure. Patterns of economic activity tied business enterprise to the old colonial power, rather than generating internal economic cohesion. Literacy rates were no higher than 30 percent, and because most citizens had little shared political life or opportunity to participate in national (or even local) civic organizations, they lacked a strong sense of national cultural belonging. Almost everywhere in Africa the administrative borders imposed by imperialists had little or nothing to do with the linguistic, cultural, social, historical, or economic realities of the areas they arbitrarily divided up. The only thing holding most of these societies together was the state or the army, and few countervailing forces had the power to prevent those institutions from imposing tyrannical government. But fission and reorganization were often an even less attractive option—as post-partition wars in India, Palestine, Korea, Ireland, and other parts of the world demonstrated.

But the Cold War played a major role, as well. The superpowers did not simply install dictators who looked after their interests; again, in many cases the initiative came from the other direction, as strongmen in the former colonial world sought the patronage of one or the other superpower to buttress their own rule. The reasons for this pattern were twofold. On the one hand, almost every society on earth was subject to the competition between the two super-powers for influence. The United States and the Soviet Union had their eco-nomic, cultural, and espionage fingers in every pie around the world. And almost every country, therefore, had to fear that its political system would be subverted by agents of whichever superpower it was not interested in being aligned with—or by agents of both if the country was determined to remain nonaligned. And those agents had overwhelming financial, organizational, military, and cultural power behind them. They could assassinate, manipulate, propagandize, bribe, supply or deny information or weapons, train, fund, recruit, negotiate loans and trade agreements with open or secret concessions, and so on—certainly not without constraints or always with success, but with relatively few constraints and usually with at least some effect.

On the other hand, the rivalry between the superpowers was a golden opportunity for would-be autocrats to gain access to resources from outside their own societies in order to secure power within them. By promising to be a loyal client, and posing as the last line of defense against people who would be clients of the other side, they could gain critical military, financial, and intelli-gence support. What is more, during the world wars a number of countries around the world had expanded industrial production, in order both to sell to belligerent nations focusing their own economies on armaments production and to make local substitutes for imports no longer arriving from those bellig-erent nations. In some of those countries, that policy had led to rapid growth in the local labor movement; and in the context of the global communist appeal to the industrial working class, labor's newfound strength created new and intense conflicts within many of these societies. Local business communities often perceived the growing labor movement (which in many cases was at least partially attracted to the communist alternative) as a serious threat; but the export-led commodity-extraction economies put in place in much of the world in the late nineteenth and early twentieth centuries did not generate large or notably self-confident local middle classes—since so much business was in the hands of foreign investors, and so much profit was exported to those investors' countries. In much of Latin America, in particular, the business middle class therefore could see military rule as an alternative preferable to open demo-cratic elections. What was more, the military had long been as attractive an avenue of upward social mobility as business. Local social elites and middle classes, therefore, often forged and maintained close social and political ties to the officer corps. That too created opportunities for ambitious oligarchs to expand their power at the expense of democratic institutions and procedures.

In contrast, labor and agrarian movements in economies centered on com-modity extraction by foreign corporations could claim to serve not only their own class interests but also the national interest by opposing what often looked like the vampiric exploitation of national resources by offshore corporations and their local business allies. Yet almost nowhere did these movements have the organizational muscle to impose economic nationalist policies through the democratic process. For that, some relied themselves on the military. In Peru, a military dictatorship undertook extensive agrarian reform and nationalization of industries in the late 1960s and early 1970s. The Cuban Revolution of 1959 created a dictatorial one-party state dominated by one man, Fidel Castro, that lasted forty-seven years. In Viet Nam the long struggle for independence against the French, and then for national unification against the South Vietnamese and Americans, extensively militarized the Communist Party. By the time of its victory in 1975, it was essentially a full-blown bureaucratic-military dictatorship. A similar fate befell Zimbabwe (formerly Rhodesia), where a long guerilla war finally put the nominal socialist Robert Mugabe in power in 1980, only to give rise to a disastrously corrupt military-populist regime.[69]

More typically the military was used to crush nascent leftist labor politics. In Brazil in the early 1960s, President João Goulart attempted a whole range of economic reforms, including the creation of a national electric power company, limitations on profits that foreign companies could take out of the country, tax and land reforms, and the nationalization of the country's oil industry, as well as legalization of the its communist party. Goulart was overthrown by a military coup in 1964. In Argentina the populist nationalist Juan Peron, with a strong base of support in trade unions, nationalized the country's central bank, railways, ports, and leading newspaper in the late 1940s and early 1950s, then was exiled by a military coup in 1955; thereafter coups and elections succeeded one another in rapid succession until 1976, when a more stable military regime took over. Both countries were plagued by horrific low-level violence (involving terrorist attacks, "disappearances," and widespread torture) between the military and leftist opponents for over a decade in the late 1960s and early 1970s. A CIA-backed coup against a socialist government in Chile in 1973 created a similarly miserable situation there.[70]

An important and deplorable consequence of all this conflict between military dictatorships and their domestic opponents was a massive expansion of armies and of the arms trade. Some of that expansion was due to superpower exports to their industrialized allies. But the Third World carried a disproportionate share of the cost of this trade, because weapons were an important category of manufactured goods that the underdeveloped world bought from the developed world. Between 1960 and 1980 world arms exports more than doubled; but Third World arms imports more than quintupled (chart 6.9). By 1984 the poorer nations of the (so-called) Third World spent as large a proportion of their national incomes on arms as the developed nations did—a luxury they could afford far less in economic terms.[71] Some of those arms were used to keep the armies of autocratic regimes happy and loyal; others were used to wage wars intended to justify autocratic power; still others were used to wage wars to prove their buyer's value to their superpower patron.

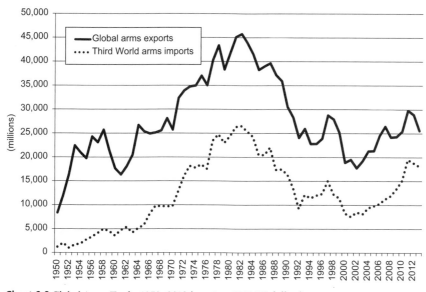

Chart 6.9 Global Arms Trade, 1950–2013 (constant 1990 US dollars).

The relationship between the Cold War and postcolonial nationalism (and dictatorship) was thus dynamic, a two-way street. The Cold War significantly shaped postcolonial states both by posing a permanent threat to the stability of new states and by creating attractive alternatives to a purely domestic political strategy. And postcolonial nationalists helped propel the Cold War by appealing to one or the other of the superpowers and thus helping to draw them further into global competition and confrontation with each other. One result was to sustain a world full of guns and dictatorships.

In some cases the consequences of Cold War competition and conflict, the prevalence of dictatorships, and the abundance of guns were catastrophic for civilian populations. In Guatemala after the 1953 coup, the new military regime waged a three-decade genocidal war against indigenous communities that sought to control their own land and resources. In Indonesia, up to a million civilians were slaughtered following the 1965 coup. In the late 1970s Cambodia, destabilized by the consequences of the Viet Nam War, descended into a genocidal tyranny, in which some 1.6 million people—one-fifth of the population—lost their lives. One exhaustive list compiled shortly after the end of the Cold War identified thirty-four instances of mass murder between 1959 and the end of the Cold War, with the total number of victims probably well in excess of 10 million.[72]

By the 1960s a double irony was clear: One thing that did *not* explain the prevalence of dictatorships was the persistence of the problems that had made them so common in the 1920s. In fact, by the early 1960s at the latest, the global economic situation was clearly being transformed. The legacies of the Depression and the interwar disintegration of the global economy were being erased by a tidal wave of growth in production and trade.

That tidal wave is addressed in chapter 7.

High Modernity

THE GREAT ACCELERATION, 1950–1975

> Man throughout recorded history has struggled . . . to cope with material scarcity. Today, . . . the great challenge in the United States—and soon in Western Europe—is to cope with a threatened over-abundance of the staples and amenities and frills of life. . . . Prodigality is the spirit of the era. Historians, I suspect, may allude to this as the Throwaway Age. . . . [W]astefulness has become part of the American way of life. . . . Today, the average citizen of the United States is consuming twice as much in the way of goods as the average citizen in the years just before the Second World War.[1]

> Vance Packard, *The Waste Makers* (1960)

In 1948 or 1949 anyone would have been justified in being pessimistic about the prospects for human development in the coming two, three, or four decades. The period of revolutions, wars, and upheavals stretching from the first Russian Revolution in 1905 to the victory of the Communist Party in the Chinese Revolution in 1949 had killed tens of millions of people. World War I and the subsequent revolutions in the Russian and Ottoman Empires had killed probably close to 40 million (counting the toll during collectivization in the Soviet Union in the 1930s). World War II and the Chinese Revolution and civil war had killed probably somewhere between 70 and 80 million between 1939 and 1949—probably 52 or 53 million in Europe, and likely not fewer than 20 to 30 million across Asia.[2] Further tens of millions were made refugees in each case.[3] World War I had been followed by twenty years of global financial and economic troubles; there was no reason not to think that it would take even

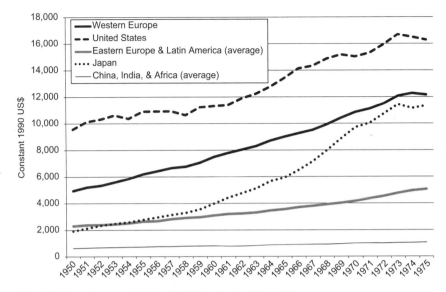

Chart 7.1 Gross Domestic Product (GDP) Per Capita, 1950–1975.

longer to recover from World War II, which had been much worse and had affected much more of the world.

But that is not what happened. Instead, the world economy after 1950 saw a return to the pattern of growth familiar before the "explosion" of the years of war and revolution: rapid growth, particularly in the industrial economies of the North Atlantic and in Japan (chart 7.1).

In fact, between the 1950s and the 1970s, both Western Europe and Japan rapidly closed the income gap with North America, the wealthiest large region on earth (chart 7.2). In 1950 Western Europe's gross domestic product (GDP) per capita was half that of the United States; by 1975 it was three-quarters. Japan's was only 20 percent of the United States' in 1950, but 70 percent by 1975. In contrast, Latin America, the Middle East, and Eastern Europe gained only slightly on the US standard of living, and Africa and mainland Asia and South Asia not at all. In fact in much of Asia and Africa the gap in living standards actually widened. Whereas in 1913 the average citizen of India had an income one-eighth that of the average US American and one-fifth that of the average German, by 1973 the average Indian's income was one-twentieth that of the average American and one-fourteenth that of the average German. Per capita income in China lagged even more radically—one-tenth that of the United States in 1913, one-twentieth in 1973.[4]

One reason for this difference was that the industrial economies did not just pick up where they had left off in 1913. Between 1875 and 1913 the North

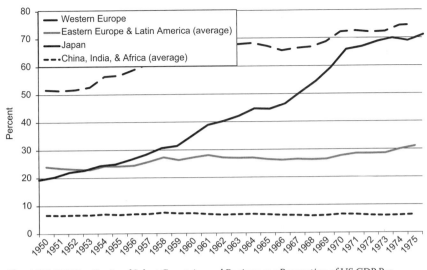

Chart 7.2 GDP Per Capita of Select Countries and Regions as a Proportion of US GDP Per Capita, 1950–1975.

Atlantic economy and that of Japan had grown at a healthy pace, and average incomes had risen with moderate rapidity; after 1950 that pace accelerated substantially (chart 7.3). In Western and Southern Europe, economic growth between 1950 and 1973 was faster than in any previous period in modern history; per capita income in the United States grew almost as much in the twenty-three years between 1950 and 1973 as it had in the thirty-seven years between 1913 and 1950 (chart 7.4). Astonishingly, the rise of per capita income in Japan dwarfed that in the North Atlantic: while the average West European earned 2.7 times as much in 1973 as in 1950, the average Japanese earned 6 times as much. In Europe, this period was often called the "golden age," the years of the "economic miracle," or in French the "thirty glorious years." If those terms are appropriate, then it is not clear what to call this period in Japan.

Given this extraordinary growth in the world's industrial economies, it makes sense to refer to the quarter century from 1950 to 1973 as the Great Acceleration.[5] The processes of economic and technological development that had been transforming primarily the North Atlantic region and Japan since the middle of the nineteenth century suddenly stepped up its pace substantially. But it is important to remember that even after that, from 1973 to 1996, growth in the industrial economies was still quite healthy. It was slightly lower than in the first great industrial boom, from 1890–1913, in North America, but significantly faster in Europe and Japan.

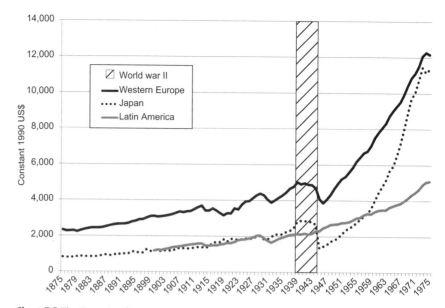

Chart 7.3 The Great Acceleration: Per Capita Income before and after WWII.

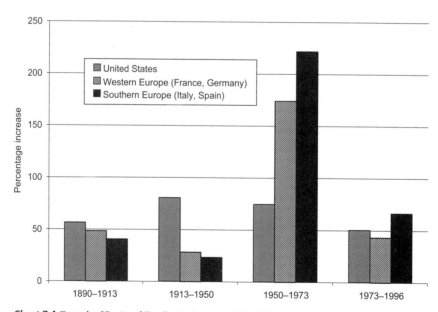

Chart 7.4 Growth of Regional Per Capita Income, 1913–1996.

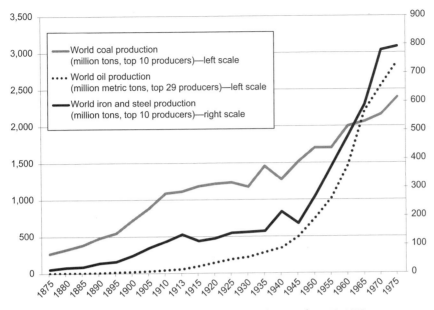

Chart 7.5 Growth in the Production of Industrial Fuels and Materials, 1875–1975.

The production of key industrial commodities reflects that acceleration. World coal production tripled between 1950 and 2000; steel production quadrupled; oil production grew geometrically up to 1913; then there was a slight pause in the period of revolutions, wars, economic chaos, and mass murder, after which production grew on an even steeper geometric curve after 1950 (chart 7.5).

The production of key consumer goods exhibited a similar pattern. The automobile is a good example (chart 7.6), but one could choose anything—telephones, radios, televisions, washing machines, refrigerators: production of all these goods soared in the 1950s and 1960s.

Growth at this pace and on this scale transformed the lives of millions. The family of George W. Romney is illustrative. Romney was born in Mexico in 1907 into a family of American Mormon farmers who until the 1940s seemed to live under a curse. His great grandparents converted to Mormonism in England in 1839 and immigrated to the United States to start a new life in 1841, in time to be driven out of Illinois by the anti-Mormon mob and flee the country to start over in Utah, then part of Mexico. But the United States conquered Utah in 1848 and began enforcing its anti-polygamy laws against polygamous Mormons. In 1885 George Romney's grandfather fled again to north-central Mexico, with his three wives, to start over in a more tolerant country—applying the dry-plateau farming methods learned in Utah. The family built a relatively prosperous

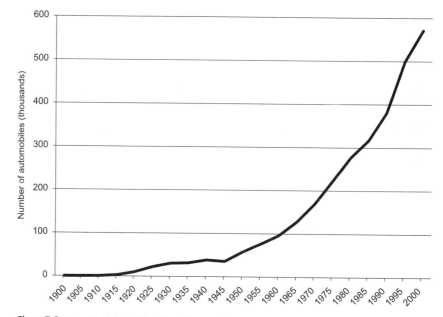

Chart 7.6 Motor Vehicles in Use, Top Nineteen Countries, 1900–2000.

life in one of the colonies of foreigners granted land by the government of Porfirio Díaz as part of its development strategy. But in 1911 most of the community fled the violence of the Mexican Revolution and returned to the United
States. Romney's father (who had only one wife, and hence was now legal under
US law and under the new doctrine his church declared in 1890) started over
again as a potato farmer in Idaho, after a four-year pause in Los Angeles. The
farm went bust; so did a construction business started after that; and by 1921
the family was broke again, back in Salt Lake City, eighty years after leaving
England. George Romney went to Britain as a Mormon missionary in 1926, then
followed his fiancé's family to Washington, DC, in 1929, where he got a job as a
staff aide to a senator from Massachusetts. He and a brother opened a dairy bar
in Virginia; it failed as the Depression set in.

But at that point contacts Romney had made as a legislative aide landed him
a job with the giant aluminum firm Alcoa (Aluminum Company of America),
his talents as an administrator and organizer began to pay off, and he began to
build a solid career as a lobbyist for industry. By 1939 he was hired as a lobbyist
and administrator for the American Automobile Manufacturers' Association;
he played an important role in coordinating industrial production for the
American war effort in World War II; and in 1948 he was hired by a small
American automobile and refrigerator manufacturer. In 1954 that company

merged with another small company to create the American Motor Company (AMC), and Romney became its chief executive officer (CEO). By 1958 he had achieved a remarkable corporate turnaround—based largely on the development of the relatively small, efficient Rambler car model that AMC offered as an alternative to the gas-guzzling "dinosaurs" (as he called them) being built by the larger automobile companies. AMC sold 217,000 cars in 1958 and 485,000 in 1960. Romney made a public name for himself as a vehement champion of "free labor, free management, and free capital in cooperation with free government" and as a critic of big unions, big government, and big corporations (such as the Big Three automobile companies that dominated his industry). In 1961 he made a profit-sharing deal with the United Auto Workers union in which management won greater flexibility and control in return for a share of the profits for workers. And in 1962, 1964, and 1966 he was elected governor of Michigan, largely on the strength of his credentials as a skilled and impartial administrator. He supported the Civil Rights Movement, sought the Republican presidential nomination (unsuccessfully), became Secretary of Housing and Urban Development under President Richard Nixon, and devoted most of the last twenty years of his life to philanthropic activity.

Romney does not appear to have been a genius. One labor union representative (who had no particular reason to like him) characterized him as lacking "real depth or understanding." But he was hardworking, his intentions were impeccable, he got along with people, and he was a gifted manager. He was also smart enough to put himself in the right place at the right time to benefit from the almost unbelievable economic boom of the postwar years. In 1930 every fifth American had a car; in 1950 every third American; in 1970 there was more than one automobile for every two inhabitants of the United States—men, women, and children. As Romney put it in 1955 (in the patronizing gendered language of the day), "Cars nineteen feet long and weighing two tons are used to run a hundred-and-eighteen pound housewife three blocks to the drugstore for a two-ounce package of bobby pins and lipstick."[6] It didn't make sense; but people could afford it.

What explains this extraordinary economic growth? In part this was simply a resumption of the pre-1913 expansion. In fact, an important element in the growth of the European economies (east and west) and Japan's extraordinary economic boom was simply the pent-up demand and the technological backlog that had developed during the years of war and recession between 1914 and 1945. In many cases the return of peace and economic stability gave producers the chance to meet demand for products that had been developed before the wars; in others, the wars had accelerated the maturation of technologies and products (aviation, for example); in others cases, new consumer products could be rapidly and relatively easily developed on the basis of technologies that had already matured before the war, but had not yet been effectively commercialized. An example is the crucial plastics industry and the myriad consumer and industrial products that fueled its growth. Most of the basic forms of plastics were developed in the 1930s, but the plastics industry exploded only after World War II. By 1976, world consumption of plastics, by volume, was greater than world consumption of steel, copper, and aluminum.[7]

The outcome of the war created ideal conditions for this catch-up effect. The major capitalist economies in particular benefited from the stable framework created by the Bretton-Woods agreement and the General Agreement on Tariffs and Trade (GATT), and the strategic stalemate between the United States and the Soviet Union at least guaranteed a degree of predictability. Most of industrial capitalist countries also benefited from the United States' military protection, which allowed them to keep their own military spending much lower—and which was one reason the economies of Western Europe and Japan grew more rapidly than that of the United States. In any case, under these conditions the key drivers of industrial-economic development that had been in play before 1913 once again came into effect.

The most important of these, of course, was innovation. As measured by resident patent applications, the North Atlantic world suffered a grievous decline in commercial innovation as a result of World War II; but by the early 1970s it had recovered to near its historically high rate of the late 1920s (chart 7.7). Japan, in contrast, suddenly became the most commercially innovative society on earth in the 1970s. Not surprisingly, the rate of GDP growth in the two regions roughly correlates with the level of commercial innovation in each. (In contrast, there were relatively few patent applications from other regions: under 4,000 in Brazil in 1970, for example, which was less than one-eighth as many as in Germany; less than 2,000 in Argentina; 805 in Mexico; 89 in Turkey; almost none in Africa outside South Africa.)

Patent applications usually come from educated people, and a second critical driver of growth in the 1950s and 1960s was heavy investment in higher education, as indicated by the number of students enrolled in colleges and universities (chart 7.8). Again, Japan is the striking case: heavy investment in minds in the 1950s paid off in innovation and growth in the 1960s and 1970s. But Western Europe too began to build rapidly in the 1960s on its high historical education levels. Though not exactly a form of innovation, technology transfers played an important role in the economic performance of some societies, as well, increasingly as the result of formalized, commercial transactions. The extreme case was Japan: between 1951 and 1984, Japanese companies spent $17 billion on over 42,000 technology-transfer agreements with overseas entities.[8] And patent applications are not the only important outcome of this kind of investment. It takes educated people simply to run a wealthy modern economy, whether or not they are also developing new products, processes, or ideas.[9] In any case, globally the total number of university students followed much the same pattern as the production of basic industrial goods and con-

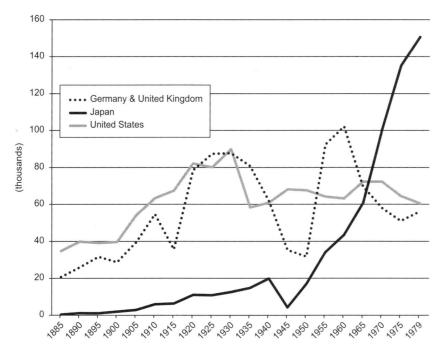

Chart 7.7 Patents Filed Annually, Top Four Countries, 1885–1979.

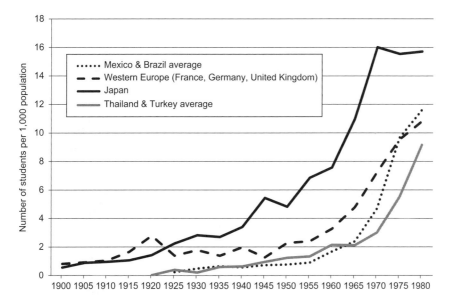

Chart 7.8 University Students, 1900–1980.

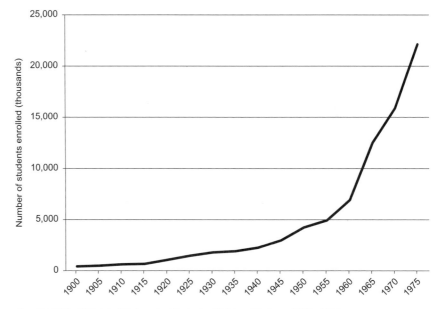

Chart 7.9 World Total of University Students, Eighteen Nations, 1900–1975

sumer durables (chart 7.9). Humanity as a whole made a huge investment in know-how throughout the twentieth century, but the pace of investment in knowledge accelerated remarkably from the mid-1950s to the mid-1960s.

A third driver of growth in the 1950s and 1960s was free(er) trade. Among the important innovations of the period were advances in transportation and communications, which brought on a further rapid drop in the costs of commerce (chart 7.10). Larger ships, more efficient motors, better designs, and more automation cut the cost of shipping freight by sea by three-quarters in the fifty years between 1930 and 1980. The use of container shipping from the 1970s contributed significantly to lowering freight costs. But air freight costs dropped even more—by more than 80 percent between 1930 and 1980. And telephone communications costs virtually evaporated.[10]

Just as important as these technical advances, however, was a profound shift in global trade policy. Average global tariff rates, having risen drastically during the Depression, were after 1950 significantly lower than they had been before 1913 (chart 7.11). The GATT agreements (starting in 1947), and to a lesser extent the economic integration of the Soviet bloc under the Council for Mutual Economic Assistance (CMEA), resulted in an average world tariff level in the 1950s and 1960s significantly lower than before World War I—and that level then fell even further in the 1970s. As a result, in the industrial world by 1973, trade as a proportion of GDP had more than recovered to the level of

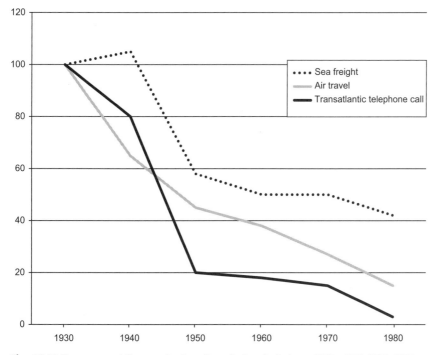

Chart 7.10 Transport and Communications Costs (indexed relative to 1930 = 100), 1930–1980. Average ocean freight charges and port charges per short ton of import and export cargo; average air transport revenue per passenger mile; cost of a three-minute telephone call from New York to London.

1913, after having declined in the 1930s. The process required a full generation—in part because the Cold War erected new barriers to trade between communist and noncommunist economies, and in part because many former colonies adopted restrictive import policies and tariffs in order to foster domestic industry. But already by the mid-1970s the world economy as a whole was more integrated than ever before, and momentum for further expansion of trade was building rapidly.[11] A particularly important instance was the growing economic integration of Western Europe after the formation of the European Economic Community in 1957 under the Treaty of Rome, which by the 1990s turned most of Europe into an enormous free trade zone and currency union (and a loosely integrated political unit, the European Union).

A fourth factor was the continued, but now also accelerating rise in the number of multinational business enterprises. By 1914 there were some 3,000 multinational corporations in the world; by 1970 there were some 6,000; but by 1988 there were 18,500 and by 2000 63,000.[12] The new global capitalist and communist financial and trading infrastructures clearly facilitated that

Chart 7.11 Average World Tariff Level, 1865–1998 (import duties as a share of total import values, thirty-five countries).

development by creating more stable and predictable business conditions across much of the globe. But technology was probably at least as important. The development of computers made the management of enormous and highly dispersed business enterprises a far less daunting task from the 1960s onward; the building out of the global telephone network made communications within organizations far easier and denser; and increasingly rapid and less expensive intercontinental air travel in jet aircraft gave organizations unprecedented flexibility in moving critical personnel on a global scale.

Multinational corporations involved in commodity extraction since the early twentieth century did suffer from nationalizations by socialist or economic nationalist governments. As discussed earlier, the all-important oil industry was nationalized in the Soviet Union in 1917, Mexico in 1937, Iran in 1951, and Brazil in 1964. A dent was also made in international holdings of mining and manufacturing facilities and plantations. The overall pattern, however, was an expansion of multinational corporations, partly because financial, manufacturing, and service companies expanded rapidly. The American fast-food restaurant chain McDonald's, for example, opened its first foreign franchise in 1967 and had 2,500 franchises in fifty countries by 1990. The German chemicals firm Hoechst had 117 plants in forty-five countries by the mid-1990s.[13] Business consulting and service firms exercised steadily growing influence on business practices from the 1960s onward; by the end of the twentieth century, the consulting firm McKinsey had more employees overseas than at home in the United States, and the Chicago law firm Baker and McKenzie had offices in thirty-five countries. International banking hardly registered in the United States in the 1960s, but by the mid-1980s US banks had 860 branches overseas, accounting for 20 percent of all their assets. Many giant multinational commodities firms, such as Unilever in the United Kingdom and Cargill in the United States, maintained or expanded their dominance in trade. By 1980 just three multinational companies accounted for over 60 percent of world trade in bananas, for example.[14]

One result of this expansion was the emergence of corporations whose revenues rivaled or exceeded those of most nations. By 1976 the largest ten corporations in the world each earned more in sales revenues than the tax revenues of all but forty-two nations; Exxon (oil) and General Motors (motor vehicles) each earned more in worldwide sales than all but twenty-five nations' tax revenues.[15]

This growth had important cultural implications. By the end of the century major global companies based in non-English-speaking countries, faced with the internal communications challenge of a multinational managerial labor force, were adopting English as their corporate languages. Such corporations include the German media conglomerate Bertelsmann, the Swedish-Swiss engineering firm Asea Brown Boveri, and the German engineering company Siemens.[16] This is perhaps a superficial measure of internationality; by another measure, the proportion of foreign members on corporate boards of directors, "multinational" corporations are still less than truly global. But it underscores the broader point that multinational corporations played a crucial role in the Great Acceleration by building an ever denser and more globe-spanning institutional, financial, and information network from the 1960s forward. And increasingly, English served as the lingua franca for the entire world's business and science. By 1995 almost 600,000 foreign students were studying in the United States, Great Britain, and Australia (as against 140,000 in France, 116,000 in Germany, and 83,000 in Russia). By the early 2000s, two-thirds of all professional scientists in the world spoke English.[17]

Another crucial factor in the Great Acceleration was cheap oil. Here the decisive supply source was the Middle East. Whereas the region had provided a relatively small portion of the global oil stock before World War II, it expanded production rapidly from the late 1940s as a result of agreements between the region's governments and consortia of European and American oil companies (on terms highly advantageous to the latter). The Soviet Union also ramped up production, and new discoveries in Mexico, the North Sea, and Africa added still more to the deluge. New technologies boosted this expansion, particularly in seismographic imaging, drilling at greater depth, and by the 1970s, deepwater offshore drilling. Despite efforts by some governments to keep prices up (for example in the United States, which imposed quotas on oil imports between 1959 and 1973) and by the oil companies to limit production, the price of oil glided slowly downward for more than twenty years, from the late 1940s until 1971. For the industrial economies this was a definite boon. In 1949 coal supplied two-thirds of the world's energy; by 1971 oil and natural gas provided two-thirds. In some cases the shift was even more dramatic: in Japan, oil accounted for 7 percent of the country's energy supply in 1950, and 70 percent in 1970; and the key supplier was no longer the United States but the Middle East—which also supplied two-thirds of Western Europe's oil.[18]

Cheap and plentiful energy, in short, was a critical component in the explosive industrial growth of the 1950s and 1960s. But it was merely part, and an important driver, of a broader pattern. Overall, prices for basic commodities such as food, metals, and fibers fell slowly in the immediate postwar decades. One reason was that fertilizers derived from fossil fuel boosted food production; plastics derived from fossil fuels competed with metals for many applications; and artificial fibers derived from fossil fuels competed with cotton and wool. These factors in turn help explain why Asian and African per capita incomes fell further and further behind those in the developed industrial world: the commodities that African and Asian countries exported often competed with products derived from cheap oil and gas.[19]

Rapid industrial growth brought about an important shift in the composition of world trade. Whereas before 1914 food and raw materials consistently made up about two-thirds of global trade, now, quite suddenly by the early 1970s, that proportion was reversed: manufactured goods made up almost two-thirds of world trade in 1973 (chart 7.12). That inversion occurred largely because the industrial sectors of different countries were increasingly specialized, and therefore traded increasingly with one another. Italy, for example, was by far the leading producer in Europe of refrigerators, making almost as many as the United States.[20] Germany became the largest producer of automobiles in Europe. The efficiency gains enabled by that kind of specialization also help to explain the rapid growth of productivity in this period.

The glaring exception to the decline of primary products (food and raw materials) as a share of world trade was fuel—above all oil. Fuel's proportion of the value of all exports from nonindustrial to industrial economies rose from one-fifth in 1950 to two-thirds by 1980 (chart 7.13). This ballooning occurred not because exports of other raw materials declined, but because the growth of world trade in oil simply dwarfed the growth of other extractive industries.

One of the more significant new features of the global economy after 1950, however, was that agricultural yields, after rising slowly from the middle of the nineteenth century until 1913, finally rose quickly in the 1950s and 1960s (chart 7.14). Crop yields per acre in Europe grew more than twice as fast between 1950 and 1975 as ever before. The same pattern held in Japan, where rice yields soared (chart 7.15). This revolution in productivity was accomplished primarily by massive application of fertilizer and pesticides; in fact

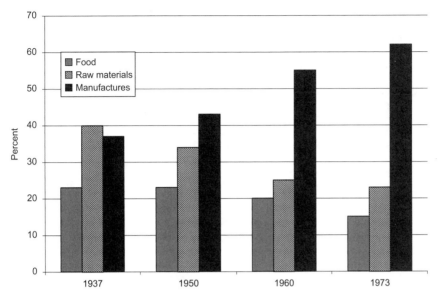

Chart 7.12 Composition of World Trade, 1937–1973.

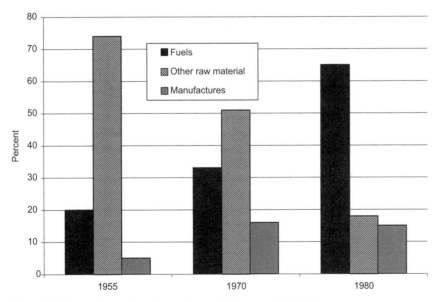

Chart 7.13 Composition of Developing Countries' Exports, 1955–1980.

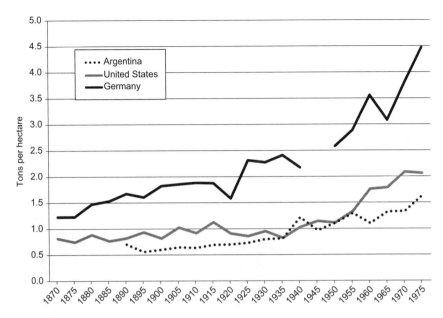

Chart 7.14 Wheat Yields, 1870–1975

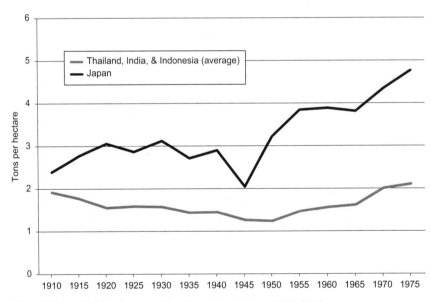

Chart 7.15 Rice Yields in Japan and Southeast Asian Nations, 1910–1975.

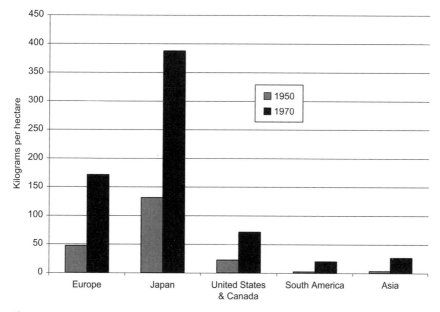

Chart 7.16 Fertilizer Used, 1950 and 1970.

average yield of grain per acre (or hectare) of land strongly correlated with average application of fertilizer (in kilograms or pounds per acre or hectare). US farmers were less aggressive in their use of artificial fertilizers (first developed in 1909 and marketed from the 1920s) and achieved smaller gains in productivity per acre than European farmers. Latin America used even less, and made still smaller gains.[21] Japanese farmers drenched their fields in fertilizer and made rapid gains, while farmers in most other Asian countries used far less fertilizer and made smaller gains (chart 7.16). Another major contributor to the agricultural boom, one that increased the productivity of labor more than of land, was the increased mechanization of agriculture. The number of tractors in use in agriculture around the world rose precipitously, so that by 1980 there were almost ten times as many in use in the world as there had been in 1930—and outside the United States, almost one hundred times as many (chart 7.17). (The apparent decline in North and Central America was due to the consolidation of farms in the United States, which allowed the use of fewer but bigger farm machines.) Of course, rising totals of irrigated acres around the world also contributed to productivity (see chart 1.11). Advances in animal science yielded unprecedented growth in meat and dairy production, too. In 1900 dairy cows in the United States produced an average of 3,600 pounds of milk annually; by 1950 the average had risen to only 5,300 pounds, but over the following twenty-five years it doubled to 10,500 pounds; nineteen years later, in

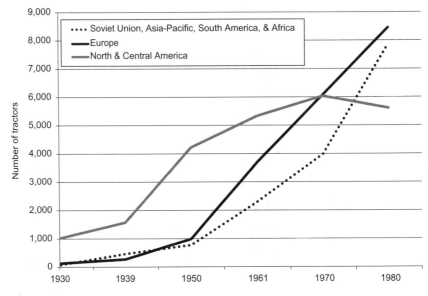

Chart 7.17 Tractors in Use, 1930–1980.

1994, it was 16,100 pounds.[22] Perhaps paradoxically, capital-intensive agriculture was fostered in many countries by increasingly aggressive protectionism. The most extreme case was Western Europe, where governments imposed minimum prices, import quotas, tariffs, and other mechanisms to keep prices up. In this sense, agriculture was a great exception to the growth of free trade in this period, and a reflection of the relative power of the developed economies vis-à-vis the rest of the world.[23]

Japan and the North Atlantic benefited most from these developments, because they were the richest areas in the world and could best afford to apply the new technologies to agriculture. Those advantages brought about a profound shift in world trade in agricultural products. By the 1960s most of the North Atlantic was virtually self-sufficient in food and, in fact, was increasingly exporting specialty foods such as cheese, wine, and meat. Denmark, for example, suddenly replaced Argentina as the biggest source of meat for Europe, and the United States started to export rising quantities again in the 1960s (chart 7.18). Even more striking, the United States and Canada suddenly flooded the world with wheat after 1950. In contrast, Argentina, Australia, and South and Southeast Asia only maintained the level of exports achieved by 1940 (chart 7.19). It was not that they were producing less food. Rather, booming population growth in India and Burma (Myanmar) meant those countries virtually ceased exporting food; for the same reason, Indochina (Viet Nam) and Thailand exported less than they had in the 1920s. The net result of these

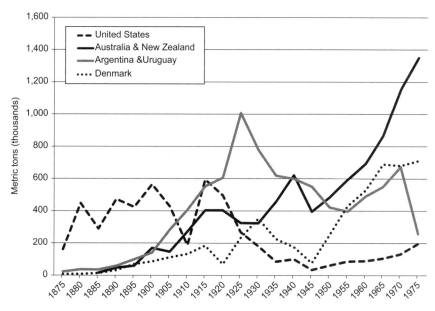

Chart 7.18 Meat Exports, 1875–1975.

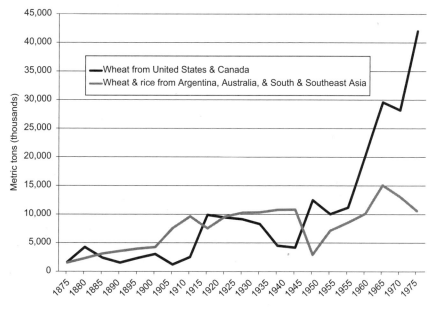

Chart 7.19 Grain Exports, 1875–1975.

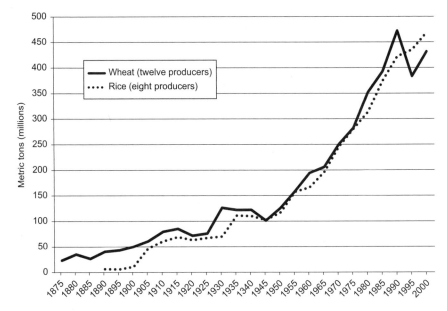

Chart 7.20 Wheat and Rice Production, 1875–2000.

various trends in agricultural commodities was that global grain production followed a more radical version of the pattern that global industrial production showed: healthy, though only moderate, growth up to 1913; a pause for thirty years during the Explosion; and then, after 1950, a striking acceleration (chart 7.20).

The Great Acceleration featured one strange characteristic, however: the greatest growth in population usually did not occur where economies made the greatest gains. As discussed in chapter 1, population growth between 1950 and 2000 was most rapid in Asia and Africa; the Americas came next, with Latin America leading; and population growth in Europe actually slowed compared to the half century 1900–1950.

The relationship between population growth rates and growth in per capita incomes is complex. Under some circumstances, rapid population growth encourages rising wealth: an expanding labor force may allow the exploitation of previously untapped resources; rising demand for goods and services or rising resource constraints, or both, may encourage innovation; longer life expectancy and improved health may raise the individual's economic contribution over his or her lifetime; population growth may produce rising economies of scale; or a country's or industry's competitive advantages may mean that production can be profitably expanded as population grows.[24] Some nineteenth-century settler colonies, including the United States, Argentina, and Australia, are examples. Under other circumstances—such as limited

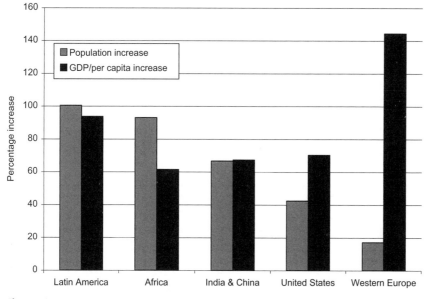

Chart 7.21 Population Growth and Growth of GDP Per Capita, 1950–1973

resources, limited land, lack of capital to fund innovation, relatively uncompetitive industries—rapid population growth can suppress the rise of per capita incomes. Some of the less developed world appears to have fallen into this latter pattern in the generation born after 1950. Economic performance across most of the world was quite vigorous in this period; but in some countries high fertility ate up some or even most of the gain, so that per capita incomes rose only slowly (chart 7.21). One could argue, in fact, that the most impressive economic performer was really Latin America, which experienced extremely rapid population increase, but a rate of growth in income per capita second only to that achieved in Western Europe and Japan. And Western Europeans look almost like cheaters: they gained massively in per capita income in part simply by not having children. The case of Japan is a warning against applying this model too generally: the Japanese population rose twice as fast as in Western Europe, but per capita income rose much faster than in Europe. But in other cases, population growth may well have been an important constraint on economic performance. The extreme cases were China and India. These were two of the poorest countries in the world, and both were experiencing rates of population growth for which the term *explosive* is inadequate; *thermonuclear* might be more appropriate (chart 7.22).

A number of trends explain this radical divergence in demographic patterns—a divergence that was, in historical terms, a reversal of the pattern that

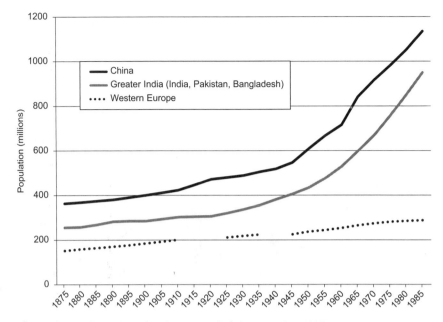

Chart 7.22 Population Growth in Poor versus Rich Regions, 1875–1985.

had prevailed from 1800 to 1950, when the North Atlantic population burgeoned. One such development was simply technological advance. Fertility in the industrialized countries actually did rise briefly in the 1950s and 1960s—a phenomenon often referred to as the baby boom. But then it plummeted again, quite drastically, from the middle of the 1960s—in Europe by about 44 percent, in Japan by a little more. One reason was the refinement of existing contraceptive technologies and the advent of new ones. Condom sales rose rapidly in the 1960s, and finer synthetic rubber, spermicides, and lubricants improved their reliability. The diaphragm saw similar improvements, as did intrauterine devices (IUDs); surgical techniques of sterilization improved as well. The birth control pill was introduced in 1960 and became widely available in Western Europe and Japan in the late 1960s and early 1970s. Many of these methods were not cheap, and some required the intervention, assistance, or advice of a medical doctor. Knowledge about them was difficult to spread among populations with low literacy rates. Contraception was therefore usually much less widespread in poorer societies having less medical provision and less educated populations.[25]

Differential rates of secularization may have played a role as well. Western Europe in particular passed through a rapid phase of secularization in the late 1960s and 1970s, one important consequence of which was a sudden liberalization of cultural codes regarding sexuality, including laws regarding the advertising and sale of contraceptive devices. Comparing France and Ireland presents an illustrative test case. France experienced the wave of secularization and liberalization in extreme form, so that by 1980, 60 percent of French people said they never went to church. Fertility in France fell by one-third between 1950 and 1980. Ireland did not experience that wave of secularization, and in 1980 fertility was slightly higher than in 1950. Large parts of the less affluent world were more like Ireland in this respect than like France, and that is one reason their fertility levels remained high. The correlation certainly does not hold up in every case: West Germans in the 1980s, for example, reported higher rates of religious belief than the French, but had a significantly lower fertility level. Despite such variations, however, there appears to be a broad correlation between high rates of religious belief and practice and high fertility.[26]

It would be too simplistic, however, to conclude that poor countries sabotaged themselves during the decades of the Great Acceleration by having too many children. There is some truth to that argument; in fact, when and where fertility rates dropped, as they did in many places around the world after 1980, per capita income did start to rise steeply. But other factors, as well, clearly helped to limit gains in per capita income. Although Asia and Africa had escaped direct colonial rule, they often remained in an unfavorable economic relationship with the industrial societies. In many cases they inherited or subsequently negotiated unfavorable institutional arrangements, such as ownership of resources by foreign corporations and long-term concessions to foreign corporations to exploit those resources. Particularly in Africa, many newly independent governments retained, as one of their revenue sources, marketing boards that paid farmers stable but low prices for their export products; this was supposed to even out price fluctuations for producers, but many cash-strapped governments yielded to the temptation to keep prices lower than the market average.[27]

In fact, the sudden spike in oil prices in the 1970s and 1980s—often referred to as the oil "crisis"—was arguably the most important single instance of economic "decolonization" after World War II, an epic political and organizational struggle in which independent oil-producing nations sought to free themselves from the quasi-colonial economic relationships of the late nineteenth and early twentieth centuries. In the late 1940s and 1950s, the newly independent oil-producing nations had managed, through a combination of tax legislation and negotiation with Western oil companies, to impose a fifty-fifty division of oil profits between themselves and the companies. This had corrected a situation in which the producing companies had often received a quarter or less of the profits, and in some cases received less revenue from their oil production than the United States (for example) received in taxes from its oil companies. Government oil revenues in Saudi Arabia tripled; in Venezuela they rose by a factor of six. In the early 1970s the process then entered a second phase. In 1960 oil-producing nations had formed an economic association, the Organization of

Petroleum Exporting Nations (OPEC). For a decade OPEC was relatively ineffective, but by the beginning of the 1970s, world oil consumption began to catch up with production capacity, and collective action began to be more effective. The United States, in particular, ran out of excess capacity and began to import a growing amount of oil; and Japan relied on imported oil for four-fifths of its total energy consumption (so that oil made up half of all its imports by value—with coal and natural gas another 14 percent).[28] At the same time, by the 1970s many oil-producing nations had at their disposal a substantial pool of their own nationals who had the education and technical expertise needed to run the production, refining, and distribution of oil. Nationalization therefore became a plausible threat. In the early 1970s, a growing number of states either used that threat to renegotiate their relationship with the oil companies, or actually nationalized—as Algeria did in 1971, Iraq in 1972, Libya in 1973, Saudi Arabia in a series of steps between 1974 and 1980, Kuwait in 1975, and Venezuela in 1976. With full control of their own oil reserves, and in many cases the ability to bring them to market, these states could now drive oil pricing. In 1973, only 8 percent of oil exports were directly marketed by the producer nations, the rest by multinational oil companies. Just six years later, the proportion had risen to 42 percent. As one Gulf Oil Company executive put it in 1975, "For the Kuwaitis, it was the overthrow of the colonial power"—fourteen years after formal political independence in 1961. From that point, the producer nations could use oil as a tool of a genuinely independent economic and foreign policy. The result was a sudden spike in energy costs on the global market—and in per capita incomes in the Middle East.[29]

One telling aspect of this process is that representatives of some oil-producing nations were able to outmaneuver the major oil companies not only because the changing balance of supply and demand gave them the upper hand, or because the US government wished to avoid alienating nationalist forces in these nations, but also because they were often simply better informed and more sophisticated than their counterparts. The story of Ahmed Zaki Yamani, minister of oil in Saudi Arabia from 1962 to 1986, is revealing. Yamani's father, Hassan, was an Islamic scholar in Mecca and for a time grand mufti (the leading religious authority) in Indonesia and Malaysia. His son Ahmed completed his undergraduate studies in Cairo, then earned law degrees at New York University and Harvard. As a government minister he adopted a remarkably long-term approach, helping to establish what would become the Saudi national oil company in 1962 and, to staff it, a university for petroleum engineers in 1964, and completing the process of nationalization in 1980. Another case is the Venezuelan Juan Pablo Perez Alfonzo, one of the key intellectual fathers of OPEC. Alfonzo studied medicine at Johns Hopkins University in Baltimore and law at the Central University of Venezuela; he spent time as a law professor in Caracas, in prison in his home country, and then, during a military dictatorship in Venezuela, in exile in the United States and Mexico. Returning home in 1958, he served as minister of mines and hydrocarbons and played a crucial role in establishing OPEC. Among other contributions, he brought Arabic translations of Venezuelan oil laws and regulations to a key meeting in Cairo in 1960. The oil companies were represented by smart and well-educated men, but few of them had Perez Alfonso's breadth of experience and perspective.[30]

This "decolonization" of oil resources offers an example of a beneficial shift in the global balance of economic power starting in the 1970s. In fact, of 575 nationalizations of assets of foreign companies between 1960 and 1985, two-thirds were carried out in just seven years, between 1970 and 1976. Besides oil, targets included mining companies, banks, and plantation land. This transfer was just one aspect of a broader attempt to restructure economic relations between the old industrial and commercial core of the international economy (the United States, Europe, and Japan) and the "Third World"; other methods included multilateral trade agreements and bilateral development aid relationships. The results were mixed. Nationalization did not often succeed as an economic strategy: 43 percent of nationalizations were imposed in Africa, which remained the poorest continent in the world, while only 10 percent were undertaken in Asia, where, as the following chapter shows, a number of countries did achieve notably high growth rates in the 1960s and 1970s.[31] An attempt within the United Nations to create a broad agreement on what the organization called the New International Economic Order failed. But some agreements did have beneficial effects. The Lomé Convention of 1975 between the European Economic Community and forty-six states in Africa, the Caribbean, and the Pacific, for example, included development aid, trade preferences, and price stabilization mechanisms.[32] Perhaps most important of all, through the 1970s and accelerating in the 1980s, the centers of innovation began to move out of the old core countries to mainland Asia, as investments in education and expertise made in the 1960s and 1970s began to pay off. We return to this subject in chapter 8.

For now, two points are worth noting. First, rapid population growth may explain some of the lag in per capita incomes in the less developed world during the Great Acceleration in the 1950s and 1960s, but certainly not all of it. The political and organizational legacies of imperialism and of the lopsided power relations typical of the early-twentieth-century world economy were important as well. Second, however, as those legacies lost their power, the less developed world would be able to make rapid economic gains. The so-called oil crisis suggested that potential more clearly than any other incident.

What is more, the role of fertility in suppressing gains in per capita income also had a positive implication. Particularly if its economic growth was strong, if a country could get its fertility down, it would not be difficult to match the rates of growth in per capita income that the developed world was achieving.

Latin America, for example, doubled its population between 1950 and 1980, while Western Europe increased its population by only 20 percent. If during those thirty years Latin America had had population growth similar to that in Europe, it could have substantially closed the gap in per capita incomes with Europe.

But could Latin America have achieved the same growth in GDP while expanding its population much more slowly? Again, the relationship between population growth and rising wealth is historically variable, but there are some indications that in Mexico, for example, in the 1950s and 1960s it may well have been negative. First, fewer children means a higher proportion of working adults in the population (including women freed from child rearing), and thus higher per capita economic productivity. In Europe in the early 1970s, working adults made up 43.3 percent of the population; in Mexico they made up only 26.3 percent (in Brazil the percentage was 32.1, in Argentina 37.3). Further, the Mexican economy struggled to employ the country's exploding population: in 1976, 40 percent of adult Mexicans were either unemployed or underemployed.[33] Between 1950 and 1973 many Latin American countries achieved solid annual gains in worker productivity; if they could also have kept population growth down, they might have started to close the gap between per capita incomes there and those in Europe, the United States, and Japan.

For reasons discussed in chapter 8, between 1973 and 1998 productivity growth in Europe slowed, but in Latin America it collapsed—to one-half of 1 percent in Mexico and around 1 percent in Argentina and Brazil. This helped to delay convergence of per capita incomes for another generation.[34] Nevertheless, what both the example of the oil-producing nations and the problem of high fertility suggest is that by 1980 the world was on the verge of an economic revolution much greater than the Great Acceleration of 1950–75. By 1980, almost the entire world was potentially within one generation of practically wiping out the economic head start that the North Atlantic and Japan had gained in the entire 1850–1975 period. For economic planners and policy makers in the 1950s and 1960s, the potential for even more massive and truly global economic growth seemed clear. And they set out to try to make it happen. After the mid-1950s, in fact, they embarked on a global social engineering project: they would use the state to mobilize and organize capital, institutions, and expertise in order to maximize gains in wealth, health, and welfare—first and foremost in the industrialized world, but ultimately around the whole globe.

We may refer to this as the project of "High Modernity." It was underpinned by the belief that the development of the industrial world since the middle of the nineteenth century had demonstrated how societies become wealthy, healthy, creative, stable—in short, "modern," and that we can use the state to make that transformation happen elsewhere as well, to "modernize" the whole world.

THE WELFARE STATE, 1950–1975

> We . . . consider it Our duty to reaffirm that the remuneration of work is not something that can be left to the laws of the marketplace; nor should it be a decision left to the will of the more powerful. It must be determined in accordance with justice and equity; which means that workers must be paid a wage which allows them to live a truly human life and to fulfill their family obligations in a worthy manner. . . . Economic progress must be accompanied by a corresponding social progress, so that all classes of citizens can participate in the increased productivity. The utmost vigilance and effort is needed to ensure that social inequalities, so far from increasing, are reduced to a minimum.[35]
>
> Pope John XXIII, 1961

One important facet of the project of High Modernity was the major global investment in innovation witnessed in the 1950s and 1960s. That investment in people's minds and talents was an essential element in building what came to be called the welfare state in the wealthy, industrial societies of the North Atlantic, Japan, and Australia and New Zealand. There was never a unitary welfare state agenda or program; instead lawmakers and reformers in each country chose a distinct mix from a range of policy options in pursuit of a shared set of goals. Some welfare states focused more on planning, while others concentrated more on state ownership of infrastructure; some adopted needs-testing, while others provided more universal benefits; some relied more on regulation of markets, while others "freed" their citizens from the demands and constraints of the market economy; some created incentives for corporations to take care of their workers, while others relied more on direct state intervention—and so forth. The more liberal-democratic welfare states sought to maximize the societal space for individual responsibility and entrepreneurial spirit. The more Social Democratic welfare states sought to build societies founded on the idea of solidarity. In most of Western Europe the welfare state was built primarily by Christian Democrats who believed in individualism and markets, but also thought that societies had a duty to make sure that selfishness and materialism were sufficiently constrained that they did not compromise economic and societal efficiency—and to ensure that the Christian principle of the essential dignity of man could be concretely realized in social life broadly.[36] Nevertheless, the term *welfare state* is useful, in part because all the welfare states actually shared four fundamental goals.

The first was to stabilize their societies, to foster social integration and inclusion, to reduce social discontent and rule out social upheavals, and thereby to reduce the attractiveness of radical alternatives—whether left or right—to the existing system. Obviously, the disaster of fascism and communism in the 1930s and 1940s was crucial in focusing minds on that goal. The second was to minimize the kinds of social and economic inefficiencies that the unpredictable risks of free markets can create. That meant above all reducing poverty and its social and economic costs (ill health, ignorance, low productivity, poor labor allocation, and so on); but it also meant providing a stable economic environment in order to encourage productive investment in growth and the future. The third goal was to maximize creativity—to encourage innovation, whether in the realm of technology, business, culture, the arts, or social organization. That meant providing a level of economic security and even affluence that would encourage risk taking. It also meant giving people the means to be creative—including the knowledge and skills acquired through education, as well as public health programs, adequate nutrition for children, and improved housing stock. And fourth, the welfare state aimed to create a society in which the fundamental dignity of every human being was not only recognized in principle but also anchored practically in the institutions and procedures that shape social life—the state, the courts, local government, public schools, businesses, the family, and so on. A campaign poster used by US president Harry Truman in 1948 summed up the program pithily: running on a platform that included an expansion of social insurance, higher funding for education, a higher minimum wage, public housing projects, a national medical insurance program, and civil rights legislation for minorities, he urged voters to "Keep America Human with Truman."[37]

This fourth goal was the most important, because it was the precondition for the other three. The people who built the welfare states after World War II were shaped largely by the negative experience of totalitarianism. Both fascism and communism treated people as mere things, resources with which the state could do whatever it wished. And both doctrines had generated catastrophe—mass murder, starvation, war. Totalitarian states had also been inept at innovation. Most emblematically, it was the United States and Britain that had built the atomic bomb; neither Japan nor Germany had even had a coherent program for developing such a weapon, and the Soviet Union had to catch up after the United States and Britain proved it could be done.

The belief of the welfare state's founders was that a viable modern society had to be built on the principle of human dignity. Only on that foundation could the full potential of the technological and economic revolutions and the social transformation of modern times be realized, while preventing the grotesque and horrifying failures of totalitarianism. Only a society's commitment to human dignity would release the full potential of all its citizens, thereby ensuring innovation, stability, peace, and prosperity. The state's foundation and ultimate aim must be the dignity of all humans and the elevation of human culture, of "civilization," as the collective expression of our spiritual and creative capacities. US president Lyndon B. Johnson's "Great Society" speech of May 22, 1964, announcing his intention to pursue something like the welfare state strategy already maturing in Western Europe, is a telling statement of this principle. Again and again in that speech, Johnson emphasized that policy had to center not just on wealth or power, but on the "quality" of "civilization," not just "quantity" or "products" or "soulless wealth" or "the needs of the body and the demands of commerce but the desire for beauty and the hunger for community," and the creation of a society in which the "meaning of our lives matches the marvelous products of our labor."[38]

The heart and soul of this conception of human dignity was the idea of freedom. The dignity of human beings, the builders of the welfare state held, rests in their autonomy, the fact that each is a reasoning, thinking, morally responsible person—not an object to be manipulated by others. The human being is sovereign over her- or himself; only a society that recognizes and realizes that can thrive. The central aim of the welfare state, therefore, was to secure the substantive freedom of every citizen—not just the formal freedom of abstract legal rights, but substantive freedom, freedom in actual practice. As President Johnson put it, "It is not enough just to open the gates of opportunity. All our citizens must have the ability to walk through those gates."[39] Only substantive freedom would make it possible for people to fully develop their potential—to their own benefit, but also to the benefit of their whole society.

Ensuring substantive freedom required giving everyone who had the ability to learn the opportunity to do so by expanding access to quality public education at all levels. It meant ensuring that people had adequate nutrition and health care and were protected against workplace accidents and environmental threats to their health, so that they had the physical capacity to make the most of their innate abilities. It meant expanding social insurance so that people did not lose the ability to contribute fully to society because of sickness, injury, or loss of employment. It also meant ensuring that particular groups of citizens were not trapped in poverty. In a racially divided society, achieving greater equality could mean imposing it: in 1957 the United States sent 1,000 soldiers to Little Rock, Arkansas, to enforce integration of its schools; five years later it took 16,000 soldiers to integrate the University of Mississippi. And it is no coincidence that Lyndon Johnson tackled the problem of race relations in the United States at the same time he launched the Great Society—through the Civil Rights Act of 1964, the Voting Rights Act of 1965, the Fair Housing Act of 1968, the introduction of affirmative action in 1965, and other measures.[40]

Such actions were examples of a broader pattern: the use of the state to address historical inequalities and patterns of privilege and discrimination that prevented people from participating fully in their nation's life. European welfare states were less focused on ethnic groups than on, for example, regional development in poor areas such as the south of Italy or the north of England. Johnson's policy instrument of choice, typical of the more liberal approach the United States adopted in most fields of public policy, was the dismantling of legal forms of discrimination and prejudicial practices; other governments sought to do the same thing through planning, regional investment incentives, or infrastructure projects such as construction of highways, railroads, and hydroelectric plants. Particularly in Europe—less so in Japan, Canada, or the United States—the welfare state thus aimed to create a "mixed" economy, or a guided market economy, in which the state sought to create incentives for business to pursue strategies that also served broader social purposes. The United States frequently pursued much the same aim through legislation to encourage private litigation—giving people legal instruments they could use to pursue equal opportunity. But the goal was the same.

The architects of the welfare state also argued, however, that substantive freedom depends on social stability. The period of Explosion in the first half of the century had made it abundantly clear that instability, upheaval, revolution, war, and economic depression make it difficult, if not impossible, for societies to innovate and prosper. The welfare states sought to prevent such disruptions. One strategy many adopted was the elaboration of laws governing labor relations that would help reduce industrial strife—strikes and lockouts in conflicts over wages and working conditions. Those conflicts harmed overall economic efficiency, of course, but ultimately they also helped to foster an adversarial relationship between capital and labor that could lead to catastrophe—to revolutionary upheavals on the part of workers, or to dictatorships that aimed to prevent revolutionary upheavals.

Another primary aim for the welfare state was to stabilize the family, which was understood to be the foundation of social stability and of the development of the individual, particularly in childhood. Lyndon Johnson's greatest speech on civil rights, "To Fulfill These Rights" (June 4, 1965), for example, directly addressed this strategy, calling for public policy that supported the family, "the cornerstone of our society." Commitment to family was even stronger in most of the West European welfare states. Christian Democracy was founded on Catholic social teaching, which insisted that the family was the heart and soul of a free society and that the power of the state should be used to defend it and its social and spiritual functions from harmful influences. These principles had been laid out progressively in three influential papal encyclicals: *Rerum Novarum* (1891), *Quadragesimo Anno* (1931), and *Mater et Magistra* (1960).

As these dates make clear, the welfare state as it was erected after 1945 had roots that reached far into the past: in some places, particularly Great Britain and Scandinavia, Social Democrats played a major role in building welfare states based on an ideological tradition dating to the late nineteenth century. The growth of state expenditures as a proportion of GDP was also a long-term trend that began well before 1945. Across Western Europe, typically 5 to 10 percent of GDP was taken in taxes before World War I; between the wars the proportion jumped to 20 to 25 percent; in the 1950s and 1960s it rose again to between 30 and 40 percent.[41]

The welfare state thus had deep historical roots, but what was different after 1945 was that across the political spectrum in the noncommunist world there was virtual consensus on the fundamental aims and instruments of the welfare state. Western European Social Democrats, horrified by what Stalinist communism had done to socialism, abandoned the idea of state ownership in favor of the "guided" capitalism of the welfare state. In Britain, for example, the socialist theorist C. A. R. Crosland remarked in 1956 that "modified capitalism plus welfare state works perfectly well" in creating a "prosperous and generally tolerable society," and that therefore socialists had no reason to worry about the fact that it wasn't socialism, since it was already achieving their substantive aims: "a distribution of rewards, status, and privileges egalitarian enough to minimise social resentment, to secure justice between individuals, and to equalise opportunities."[42] And the conservative Tory Party's One Nation Group actually agreed that "security . . . is a spring-board for vigour and family devotion" and that "social services enlarge the scope of the freedom of the individual."[43] The two sides quibbled over more minor issues of technique—for example, whether there should be means-testing and whether benefits should be equal or differential, funded by general taxes or by targeted contributions. On the fundamentals there was broad agreement.

That consensus held together, in part because of the direct connections between the welfare state agenda and the Cold War. The ideal of freedom central to the concept of the welfare state was explicitly advanced as a contrast to totalitarian communism. The welfare state's proponents intended it to show people exactly what Crosland argued: that it could achieve the aims of socialism; therefore, working people had no need to resort to communist dictatorship. At the same time, the welfare state's strategy in domestic politics was essentially the same as the West's economic strategy in the Cold War internationally. The goal was to create the necessary stability and security within which nations—or individuals—could have the freedom to develop their particular resources and talents, to their own individual material benefit but also to the collective benefit of everyone else. It is therefore not surprising that the key architects of the welfare state in Western Europe were also the key architects of West European economic integration. The 1957 Treaty of Rome, in particular, played a critical role in generating the West European economic "miracle."

DEVELOPMENT, 1950–1980

We are filled with an overwhelming sadness when We contemplate the sorry spectacle of millions of workers in many lands and entire continents condemned through the inadequacy of their wages to live with their families in utterly sub-human conditions. This is probably due to the fact that the process of industrialization in these countries is only in its initial stages, or is still not sufficiently developed. . . . Again, some countries use primitive methods of agriculture, with the result that, for all their abundance of natural resources, they are not able to produce enough food to feed their population; whereas other countries, using modern methods of agriculture, produce a surplus of food. . . . It is therefore obvious that the solidarity of the human race and Christian brotherhood demand the elimination as far as possible of these discrepancies.[44]

Pope John XXIII, 1961

One of the more extraordinary features of High Modernity was that by the 1960s, policy makers in the North Atlantic societies explicitly advocated applying the same strategy that underlay their domestic policies to the rest of the world. This notion was common across the political spectrum. Pope John XXIII argued for such an approach in *Mater et Magistra* in 1961; but the British socialist theorist C. A. R. Crosland, too, held in 1956 that since what he called "primary poverty" (actual want and the stifling of human potential) was on the verge of being eradicated in Western Europe: "The most obvious fulfillment of socialist ideals lies in altering not the structure of society in our own country, but the balance of wealth and privilege between advanced and backward countries."[45] Domestically, the welfare state sought to eliminate pockets of poverty, say, in isolated rural areas or in blighted inner cities. But from the late 1950s and early 1960s its champions also argued that their governments should work toward much the same achievement on a global scale—to maximize security, substantive freedom, creativity, and wealth *for the whole human species.* This gave rise to the idea of *development* and to the flourishing of "development aid," pursued by international agreements and organizations whose aim was to encourage the evolution of the economies of the whole world in the direction of the affluent, guided free-market, industrial capitalist consumer welfare-state economies of the North Atlantic and Japan.

Again, the connection to the Cold War was obvious—a great deal of development aid from the Western countries was intended specifically to prevent the governments of poorer nations from seeking the aid of the Communist bloc led by the Soviet Union, or to prevent those countries' people from turning to communist revolution in a desperate attempt to escape poverty. And one model for development aid to the rest of the world was the Marshall Plan of the late 1940s and early 1950s. Under that program, the United States had helped to rebuild the economies of Western Europe through massive financial grants and cheap loans, in order to prevent the spread of communism and to build a better-integrated capitalist world economy. That effort had been an enormous success, both economically and politically.

Yet it was not only Cold War fears and hatreds that inspired development aid, but also an almost euphoric sense that the whole world was on the verge of a breakthrough to universal prosperity. In other words, aside from a profound sense of the dangers posed by the spread of communism to poor countries or the capitalist world's tightening hold on those nations, there was also a profound sense, on both sides, of the opportunity to create a just and affluent world—not just a few affluent societies or regions in a world of relative poverty.

This sense of possibility gathered momentum through the 1950s as the economies of Japan, the North Atlantic, and the Soviet bloc boomed. Already in the early 1950s, various agencies were operating development programs, but an important turning point came later in that decade when a whole range of aid agencies were established and amounts of development aid ramped up. The

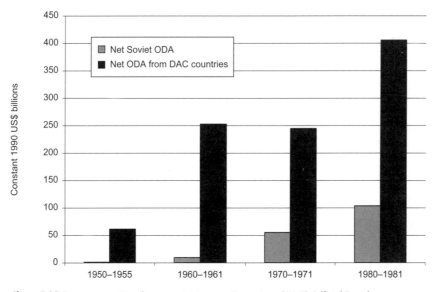

Chart 7.23 Soviet versus Development Assistance Committee (DAC) Official Development Assistance (ODA), 1950–1981.

most important of these in the short run was the Organization for Economic Cooperation and Development. The OECD was founded in 1961 as an organization committed to democratic government and free market economics; its thirty-four member states included much of Western Europe, the United States, Japan, Australia, and Canada. Alongside programs to encourage economic integration among wealthier economies, the OECD also formed the Development Assistance Committee (DAC), which targeted aid from wealthier countries to "developing" (that is, poorer) countries.[46] Other important agencies included the World Bank's International Development Association (1960), the European Economic Community's foreign development aid agency (1957), the Inter-American Development Bank (1959), the French Development Agency (1961), the United States Agency for International Development (USAID, 1961), the Asian Development Bank (1965), and the Canadian International Development Agency (1968). The Soviet Union too began distributing development aid in 1955, particularly through assistance to massive hydroelectric projects like the Aswan High Dam in Egypt. Here the Soviets intended to pursue Cold War aims by demonstrating the superior benefits of socialist economics, as well as to build a stronger global socialist economy to rival the capitalist opponent.[47] All these agencies funneled a growing amount of aid to poorer countries around the world. They stumbled badly in the early 1970s when faced with the first oil shock, but by the late 1970s, total aid was growing faster than ever (chart 7.23).

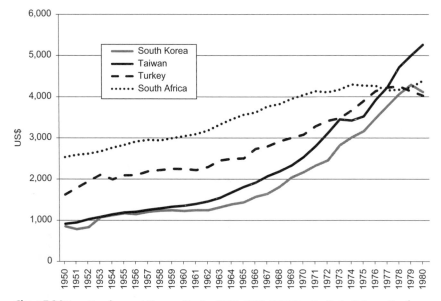

Chart 7.24 Four Development Success Stories, 1950–1980: GDP Per Capita in Taiwan, South Korea, South Africa, and Turkey.

Major infrastructural projects—roads, rails, factories, mines, dams, power plants, and other major installations—were a central focus of development aid in this first period. By providing local producers with greater access to markets and affordable power and fuel supplies, improved infrastructure would lay the foundation for the kind of rapidly growing industrial economy that had made European and North American societies rich. The whole world would be remade in the image either of the capitalist societies of the North Atlantic or the communist ones of Eastern Europe, and would thus be "modernized"—industrial, urban, democratic (by one definition or another), stable, educated, and affluent.

As it happened, over the twenty years from the mid-1950s to the mid-1970s, this expectation proved to be only partially justified. Societies that had relatively secure property rights, social equality, transparent governments, and higher levels of social capital and economic infrastructure (organizations such as trade unions, chambers of commerce, financial institutions, and institutions of higher education) could achieve substantial economic gains this way. Countries regarded as strategically important in the Cold War also got far more development aid (and other forms of support—for example, preferential trade policies) and were able to make more substantial investments in growth. Taiwan, South Korea, Turkey, and South Africa were favored this way early on; and we could include Japan too (chart 7.24). The Soviet Union had less presence on the global stage, but its client states in Eastern Europe also saw tremendous rates of growth in the 1950s and 1960s.

Many poor societies, however, struggled against high degrees of social stratification and against oligarchic elites who stubbornly defended their privileges; low levels of education and a shortage of technical skills; heavy dependence on exports for which prices could be volatile, sabotaging effective fiscal planning; high levels of corruption in the absence of a robust civil society that could keep tabs on government; and intense government instability, caused among other factors by the superpowers' Cold War machinations. Many of these nations were unable to capitalize on aid to generate rising prosperity. Development aid there often merely assisted the familiar forms of commodity extraction by major foreign corporations, much as in the colonial period. Big infrastructure projects helped to draw investments by major corporations, but they often brought in most of their skilled technical and managerial labor, hired unskilled local labor at low wages, and fed low-value raw materials into the industrial economies of other countries—with the profits going primarily to foreign corporations. Sizable amounts of money targeted for development also disappeared into the pockets of dictators and the small elites around them; and foreign companies also freely disbursed bribes in order to assure that they would secure advantageous contracts and concessions.[48]

A further problem was that much of the aid distributed in this period was "tied"; that is, a condition of the grant was that it be used to buy goods and services from companies in the country granting the aid. As late as 1981, only 44 percent of development aid was not tied.[49] This was one way to make giving away money acceptable at home, but it also meant that the countries receiving the grants did not actually operate in a free market, and so could not buy goods and services at the best prices.

As a result, development aid in many cases was not particularly successful. Nigeria, for example, became the world's ninth-largest oil producer between 1959 and the late 1980s, but it managed only a 34 percent rise in per-capita GDP between 1959 and 1980. After that, as oil prices fell from the peak reached between 1973 and 1982, GDP per capita flatlined at a level just marginally above that of 1965 (chart 7.25). In less than fifty years the Nigerian population had almost tripled, which helped to frustrate the effort to raise per capita wealth. Another drag on per capita wealth was that over half of all investment in Nigeria came from foreign private sources, the lion's share of it going into the oil industry. Massive amounts of oil money generated both corruption and inflation. The military government was in no position to correct this development, as it was maintained in power by an expensive standing army of 200,000 men and garnered four-fifths of its revenue from oil. Agriculture languished, and Nigeria had to import growing amounts of food. Thus, building the infrastructure that allowed commodity extraction and linking it to the world economy did not lead to a long-term rise in the standard of living. In fact, whereas from the early 1960s to the early 1980s GDP per capita rose and fell directly in proportion to oil production, after that the relationship loosened, and higher oil production only slightly affected GDP per capita.[50]

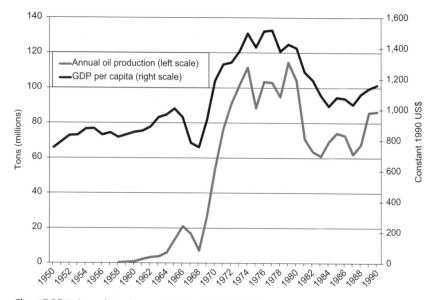

Chart 7.25 Failure of Development in Nigeria, 1950–1980.

As early as the late 1950s, critics argued that such "failures" of development aid were not failures at all, but instances of assistance doing exactly what it was intended to do: developing the rest of the world as a source of cheap labor and cheap raw materials for the old imperialist powers. It wasn't really development aid; it was "neocolonialism," the "development of underdevelopment," or the "development of dependence" (as critics variously called it)—simply a new mechanism for ensuring the successful extraction of resources and profits from the poorer, nonindustrialized world for the benefit of the richer, industrialized world.[51] This was the interpretation of the Organization for Solidarity with the Peoples of Asia, Africa, and Latin America, or the "Tri-Continental," organized by socialist countries in 1957 as an alternative and rival to the concept of development. The Tri-Continental advocated not development, but revolution—not the integration of poor countries into the global capitalist economy, but escape from it and integration into the socialist world economy. Only when the underlying exploitive economic relationships created by capitalism were demolished, the organization argued, could real development proceed. And since capitalism was now clearly global, the movement to destroy it had to be global as well.

In fact, by the late 1960s this critique of development was only one part of a broader critique of High Modernity, the idea that wonderful things would happen if technological innovation, material wealth, expertise, and organizational capacity could be expanded, accelerated, universalized. By the end of the 1960s many people around the world began to conclude not only that the development strategies adopted earlier in the decade did not work (or worked mainly to exploit and oppress), but also that successful development might not be a good idea at all. The culture of High Modernity, they argued, was bankrupt; it was time for a counterculture.

Chapter 8 looks at that counterculture.

Revolt and Refusal

COUNTERGLOBALIZATION, 1960–1980

> Our enemy is white Western imperialist society. . . . [O]ur destinies are intertwined. . . . We are moving to control our African-American communities as you are moving to wrest control of your countries, of the entire Latin continent, from the hands of foreign imperialist powers. . . . We know very well that what happens in Vietnam affects our struggle here and what we do affects the struggle in Vietnam. . . . Our people are a colony within the United States, and you are colonies outside the United States.[1]

Stokely Carmichael, 1967

Critics of development could point to a simple fact that seemed to reveal the fraud on which claims about international development aid were based: that such assistance came overwhelmingly from former imperialist nations. These included the United States, the dominant organizing power in the global capitalist economy, and France and Britain, two of the greatest of the old imperial powers. These three countries accounted for 90 percent of non-Soviet development aid in the 1950s, and still 62 percent at the beginning of the 1970s. By the 1970s Japan too—yet another of the great imperialist powers before and during World War II—played an important role. By the beginning of the 1970s, these four countries accounted for three-quarters of development aid from the capitalist world.[2] The other major source of aid was the Soviet Union, to some extent the heir to the traditions and ambitions of the Russian Empire. Development aid, the critics argued, was the new form of imperialist exploitation, employed by the same old imperialist powers.

What is more, in the context of Cold War covert action, critics could point to a large number of dictatorships around the world that these very same powers supported. Under the old colonial system, the imperial powers had ruled with dictatorial force in order to extract valuable commodities from poorer countries while keeping them poor. Under the new, neocolonial system, the imperial powers used bribery, mercenaries, espionage, patronage of military and "security" establishments, and economic blackmail to install dictators, who accomplished the same thing. In a number of cases a direct connection could be drawn between the overthrow of relatively democratic governments in favor of dictatorships and the extraction of particular raw materials. In Iran in 1953 and in Indonesia in 1965, it was oil; in Zaire in 1960 and in Chile in 1973 it was copper and other minerals.

There was a certain truth to this argument. The US State Department argued, for example, in 1959 that "authoritarianism is required to lead backward societies through" the development process by establishing stability, political cooperation with the West, and an orderly environment for economic growth—including, of course, protection for Western investments. And many development theorists and advocates were at heart elitist experts, skeptical of what they denigrated as "populist" politics even in affluent and well-educated societies.[3] But the point is not that the criticism was valid, but that by the late 1960s this kind of argument was quite plausible to a growing number of people around the world.

By the late 1970s, moreover, there was another aspect to the picture that seemed to confirm the critics' view: one important consequence of the development program and the Cold War was ballooning debt. Through the 1960s, less than 60 percent of development aid was in the form of grants, while upward of 40 percent was in the form of loans.[4] But many governments also took on large nonaid loans from governments and private banks in North America and Western Europe. In part this was a way to deliver services to populations that might otherwise be more inclined to resent the political repression and economic cronyism imposed by dictatorships. Argentina, for example, tripled its debt between 1978 and 1983, partly because the regime there lacked popular legitimacy and sought to "buy" support. Poland took the same approach, for the same reason.[5] But particularly in Latin America, incurring more debt was also a successful strategy for funding economic development. And creditors were eager to lend large amounts of money both because by the mid-1970s they were awash in "petro-dollars" deposited by oil producers after the spike in oil prices, and because they assumed that securing market share for the future was more important than conservative risk assessment. As one historian put it, the lenders wanted to secure their share of future growth potential, "regardless of credit-worthiness."[6] The result was an explosion of government debt—about a twelvefold increase in the debt of Latin American, African, and Eastern European countries from 1970 to 1983.[7]

The theory was that economic growth would enable the countries to pay off loans later. But by the late 1970s a rising number of poor countries were facing growing debt burdens without generating the kind of economic dynamism supposed to make it easy to repay the loans. In fact, global development efforts tended to drive down prices for many raw materials exports. Too many producers were entering the market, and some governments in developing nations continued to encourage expanding exports (by means of subsidies or tax policies), even at ruinously low prices, in order to earn hard currency with which to pay off loans. Development in such cases might lead to expanding production, but not rising incomes. And in the meantime the United States and Western Europe addressed mounting inflation (brought on in part by rising energy prices) in the 1970s by raising interest rates. By the early 1980s some two-thirds of loans to developing countries had variable interest rates; the interest rate hikes meant suddenly expanding interest burdens for those borrowers. In 1982, for example, Latin America as a whole paid two and a half times as much in interest on its foreign debt as it had in 1979; in Mexico, it was three times as much.[8] To make things worse, higher interest rates in the developed nations also made investing there—in bonds, for instance—extremely attractive to investors in the developing world, leading to a massive flight of capital. The fifteen most indebted countries in the world, for example, borrowed $115 billion between 1979 and 1983, but during those same years investors in those countries poured $93.7 billion into capital markets in the wealthier lender countries.[9] These problems were only made worse by some important underlying changes in developed economies: a drop in demand due to the economic slowdown caused by the oil crisis; the increasing use of synthetic substitutes, such as plastics, for some imported raw materials; and the rapid rise in agricultural productivity, which reduced demand for food imports.[10]

As early as 1970 a new category of aid was becoming increasingly important: financial assistance to help countries pay interest on the financial assistance that they had already received. Such loans made up less than 4 percent of development aid in 1973, but by 2005 the figure was almost 25 percent.[11] Nevertheless, in the early 1980s many debtor nations lurched into financial and economic crisis. Poland suspended interest payments in 1981, and Mexico and Argentina did so in 1982; at that point the United States and international organizations such as the International Monetary Fund and the World Bank stepped in to bail out a number of major debtors, imposing "structural adjustment programs" and austerity plans in return for assistance in preventing financial meltdown. The position of many African nations was particularly awful. Nigeria adopted a structural adjustment program developed by the IMF in 1986; over the following eight years its external debt more than doubled. Whereas total African debt to foreign lenders was $81.7 billion in 1984, by 1989 it had skyrocketed to $256.9 billion—roughly equivalent to the entire continent's GDP.[12]

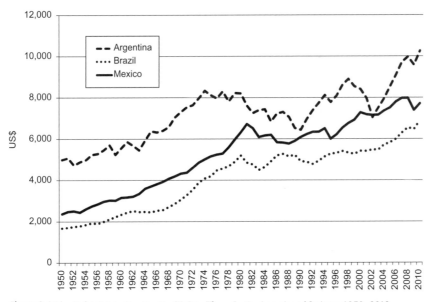

Chart 8.1 The Debt Crisis: Per Capita GDP in Three Latin American Nations, 1950–2010.

The burden of dealing with this mountain of debt made investment capital painfully scarce, with the result that productivity virtually stagnated in many poorer countries for at least a decade. In Latin America productivity per hour worked had risen by 3.3 percent per year from 1950 to 1973; between 1973 and 1992 it the rate of growth in productivity plummeted to 0.3 percent per year. In the fifteen most indebted countries in the world, per capita GDP grew in only four years between 1982 and 1993 and shrank in the other eight years. The cumulative loss was so great that in many places—including most of Latin America—it took until the late 1990s just to return to the per capita income levels of the early 1980s (chart 8.1). As one historian put it, the "costs of holding together the global financial system were . . . borne by the debtor countries and were extremely high."[13]

To critics of development, all of these trends looked suspicious. The whole project of development, it seemed, had ended up landing poorer countries in a position of debt peonage to banks in the wealthy, industrialized countries—a convenient outcome for the financial wizards in North America and Western Europe.

Partly as a consequence, the whole international system of development aid passed through a profound crisis and reorientation in the 1980s. Aid was increasingly redirected from major infrastructure projects to what came to be called human development—investments in education, health, and fertility control and in making capital available to small producers rather than major corporations. The goal was to enable local people to take advantage of improvements in market access and infrastructure. In the 1970s, about a third of aid had gone to economic infrastructure and industrial projects, and a fourth to social services; by the 2000s, those proportions were reversed. At the same time, a growing proportion now came in the form of outright grants—by 1996 over 80 percent—instead of loans. And while in 1981, 56 percent of aid was still "tied" (that is, it could be used only for purchases of goods or services from the granting nation), by 1997 the proportion dropped to only 12.4 percent. Finally, a growing proportion of aid came from countries other than the old imperial powers—by the 1980s, almost half.[14] Strikingly, at that point development aid appeared to begin to work more effectively. Chapter 9 returns to this subject.

For our purposes here, the point is that by the late 1970s and early 1980s the whole development project was discredited in the eyes of a large number of people, particularly in some of the countries that had received the largest amounts of aid. That fact had important consequences.

One was that the Soviet Union was able to expand its role and influence in the nondeveloped world. Soviet development aid rose in the early 1970s, while Western aid declined slightly (see chart 7.23). Soviet aid spending was fueled in part by the giant financial windfall that the Soviet Union, as a major oil exporter, got from the sudden spike in oil prices after 1973. In some ways Soviet development aid was similar to Western aid, as in the preference for large industrial and infrastructure projects. But the conditions for Soviet aid were in some cases quite different. The Soviets commonly accepted repayment of loans in kind—that is, in products or in cheaper prices for products from industrial projects, or even in cheap contract labor. Obviously, this had the advantage of preventing direct financial debt from piling up.[15]

Partly because of this "aid offensive" during the 1970s, the Soviet Union was also able to score some impressive victories in the war of covert or indirect action. By 1975 the Soviets' client state North Viet Nam had successfully conquered the South. The Vietnamese regime subsequently conquered Cambodia and defeated a Chinese invasion from the north. In southern Africa, Marxist regimes allied with the Soviet Union took power in both Angola and Mozambique in 1975—though both then had to fight twenty-seven years of civil war against Western-backed opposition. In Rhodesia (now Zimbabwe) by 1980, a Marxist regime won the country's first democratic election. In the northeast, the Soviets had a close relationship with the Marxist government of Somalia between 1969 and 1977; and in Ethiopia a Marxist regime took over in a coup d'état in 1974.[16] Across the Red Sea, the Soviet Union built an alliance with South Yemen. As a result of these successes, the Soviet Union was able for the first time to expand its strategic military presence on a global scale. Up until then, the Soviets had had a powerful military presence in Eastern Europe and Central Asia, but no equivalent to the network of US military bases around the world. By the late 1970s they had naval and air bases in Yemen, Angola,

Mozambique, and Viet Nam. The Soviet Union lost an important ally in Egypt in 1976, but shifted its naval operations in the Mediterranean to Syria. And it began building up a fleet that could project Soviet power into the Mediterranean Sea and the Pacific and Indian Oceans, as well as expanding its conventional forces in Europe. In 1979, it invaded Afghanistan—a move that proved to be a ghastly strategic mistake, but at the time, looked like a further expansion of Soviet power.

A second important consequence, however, was the formation of what we might call a *counterglobalization movement*—a complex of ideas, people, and organizations that criticized and opposed the global development project and offered in its place a program of global revolution against capitalism. The most emblematic figure in this counterglobalist movement was Ernesto "Che" Guevara, who played an important part in the Cuban Revolution and in the formation and thinking of the Tricontinental. Guevara argued that "Third World" insurgents could defeat capitalism by fighting it from the edges in, so to speak—not through a revolution in the capitalist heartland in the North Atlantic, but by confronting it with endless struggle around the globe, drawing the capitalist powers into expensive conflicts and denying them cheap access to markets and strategic resources.[17] This was sometimes referred to as a Third World strategy of global revolution. Its advocates argued that development was extending the tentacles of capitalist domination throughout the globe, and that what was needed instead was global revolution. This Third Worldist strategy could draw inspiration from the actions and ideas of Ho Chi Minh, who not only was leading the North Vietnamese regime in its war with France and then the United States, but had argued as early as the mid-1920s that "today the poison and life energy of the capitalist snake is concentrated more in the colonies than in the mother countries" and that therefore "the fate of the world proletariat, and especially the fate of the proletarian class in aggressive countries that have invaded colonies, is closely tied to the fate of the oppressed peoples of the colonies."[18]

This idea of revolution from the edges was highly influential among the so-called New Left in the developed nations—people who argued that from a global perspective the welfare state rested on the exploitation of the resources and cheap labor of poor nations. They hoped to help overthrow it not through a revolution at home—clearly impossible given its economic and social success—but by supporting revolutionary struggles in the Third World. In the late 1960s, protests against persistent structural inequalities in the United States (which Great Society programs were easing but not resolving), including major race riots Los Angeles, Detroit, Washington, Cincinnati, and other major cities, encouraged some to see themselves as part of a global struggle against race and class privilege. During the 1960s and 1970s, people who took this view built up important international networks—exchanging ideas, offering each other moral and financial support, and forming personal and organizational relationships.

Figure 8.1 Antiwar Demonstration at the Pentagon, 1967.

Che Guevara offers an interesting example of this phenomenon.[19] Born into a well-to-do Argentine family, Guevara was radicalized as a student and by experiences during an extended trip through Latin America. He moved to Guatemala in 1953, where a leftist regime was embarked on a radical land reform program. That regime was soon overthrown by a CIA-backed coup, and Guevara moved to Mexico; but while in Guatemala he had met Fidel Castro, and in 1956 he joined Castro in a guerilla war against the American-backed regime in Cuba. He became Castro's second-in-command during and after the revolution, but then, in 1965, he disappeared and went secretly to Zaire to fight a guerilla war against the regime that had overthrown Patrice Lumumba in 1960. When that failed, he went to Bolivia to try to start a guerilla war similar to that waged in Cuba. There he was captured and executed, becoming a martyr figure for the New Left globally.

Clearly, Guevara saw himself as a revolutionary on a world stage; for him, since capitalism was globally integrated, it really didn't matter where he fought. In fact, it appears that one reason Guevara left Cuba in 1965 was that Castro had formed an important military and economic alliance with the Soviet Union, and Guevara considered the Soviets both too bureaucratic and too willing to coexist with capitalism. His concept was that there should be relentless, unceasing confrontation between the global revolutionary movement and capitalism, no matter what the cost. The caution he saw in the Soviet global strategy seemed to him too much like compromise.

This skepticism concerning the Soviet Union was widespread among people attracted to the New Left. Another emblematic case is that of the German student radical Rudi Dutschke, who fled East Germany and became a leader of the radical student movement in West Germany. Much the same perspective was common among radicals in the United States, where the radicalized Black Power and Chicano movements frequently drew direct parallels and connections between their own struggles and those of "Third World" revolutionaries. For many of these activists, the Soviets and the West were one and the same thing—rich white people exploiting the global nonwhite poor. Three examples illustrate this highly internationalist, cosmopolitan character of counterglobalization in the 1960s.

One is Stokely Carmichael.[20] Carmichael was born in the Caribbean nation of Trinidad and Tobago in 1941 and moved to New York with his parents in 1952. He was apparently a bit of a hooligan, but was highly intelligent and went to Howard University in 1960. He became involved with the Student Nonviolent Coordinating Committee (SNCC) and the Congress of Racial Equality (CORE), took part in the Freedom Rides that helped to break up the discriminatory "Jim Crow" system of segregation in the American South, was arrested dozens of times, and by 1966 was elected SNCC chairman. By that time, however, he and others were drifting away from Gandhian nonviolent direct action, and Carmichael was heavily influenced by the writings of Frantz Fanon. Fanon, another Caribbean, had served in the Free French army in World War II, then moved to Algeria in 1953, where he supported the nationalist revolution against French colonial rule. In 1961 he published *The Wretched of the Earth*, which argued that violence was the most appropriate response to colonialism, because colonialism was itself inherently violent. In 1967 Carmichael stepped down as chairman of the SNCC; traveled to Viet Nam, Cuba, China, and Guinea in West Africa (where a socialist government was in power); published *Black Power*, and joined the Black Panther Party, which identified African American communities as "internal colonies" within the United States and favored a separatist approach rather than the nonviolent, assimilationist approach of the Civil Rights Movement. When Che Guevara was killed,

Carmichael remarked: "The death of Che Guevara places a responsibility on all revolutionaries of the World to redouble their decision to fight on to the final defeat of imperialism. . . . That is why—in essence—Che Guevara is not dead. His ideas are with us."[21] Along the way, Carmichael met and married the South African singer Miriam Makeba. By 1967, under mounting pressure from FBI surveillance and alienated from the Black Panthers by their willingness to cooperate with white activists, he left the United States and visited a multitude of countries in Europe, Africa, and Asia, including Cuba, China, North Viet Nam, Algeria, and Egypt. Ultimately he settled in Guinea, where he lived for the following three decades.

Miriam Makeba is a second example.[22] Born in Johannesburg in 1932, by the mid-1950s Makeba had achieved great success in South Africa as a jazz singer. In 1959 she appeared in an anti-apartheid film made by an American filmmaker that won a prize at the Venice film festival that year, making her internationally famous. She went to Venice to receive the award, appeared on the *Steve Allen Show*, met the American singer and political activist Harry Belafonte, and obtained a visa to perform in the United States. When she tried to return to her own country of South Africa in 1960, the government refused her entry. She settled in the United States, and in 1963 she testified at the United Nations against apartheid; in retaliation the South African government revoked her citizenship.

Makeba went on to achieve massive international success by popularizing Zulu and Xhosa musical traditions. When she married Stokely Carmichael in 1968, her recording contracts and tours in the United States were canceled because the US government considered Carmichael a dangerous radical; and one reason the American security apparatus was committed to supporting the South African regime at this time was that communists played important roles in the African National Congress. But Makeba's international fame was such that she was relatively unaffected. She became Guinea's ambassador to the United Nations; sang at the famous George Foreman–Muhammad Ali boxing match in Zaire in 1974 (the so-called "rumble in the jungle"); outlived the boycott against her in the United States; recorded the massive international hit album *Graceland* with the American singer Paul Simon in 1986; campaigned for the release of Nelson Mandela, who had helped found the military arm of the African National Congress in 1961 and spent twenty-seven years in prison after his arrest on sedition charges in 1962; and returned to South Africa on a French passport in 1990, thirty years after she left, at the invitation of Mandela—who would shortly be elected president of South Africa.

A third and rather different example is another African musician, Fela Ransome (later Anikulapo) Kuti.[23] Kuti's mother was a prominent nationalist, socialist, and feminist leader in Nigeria; his father was president of Nigeria's first national teacher's union. In 1958 Fela, as most called him, moved to London to study music. He returned to Nigeria in 1961 and achieved moderate success playing highlife, a popular musical style. In the late 1960s, in Ghana, he encountered the influence of American soul music, including that of the "God-father of Soul," James Brown. In 1969 he went to the United States, fell in love with a member of the Black Panther Party, and was "Africanized" by the ideas of the Black Power movement. While living in Los Angeles, he began to develop a new musical style, heavily influenced by soul and funk but building on African percussion traditions. He returned to Nigeria, started a commune in Lagos called the Kalakuta Republic, married twenty-seven women, smoked copious amounts of marijuana, and became enormously popular as a musician and political commentator on Nigeria's manifold problems—particularly its neocolonial economy, its government corruption, and the army, which ruled Nigeria for most of the three decades after 1975.

When, in 1970, James Brown came to Nigeria, his band went to hear Fela perform at the latter's headquarters. Bootsy Collins, Brown's bassist, remembered the occasion: "Even before I got into James Brown's band, the James Brown band was number one to me. But once I got there and saw Fela and them, then I had second thoughts about it. . . . [W]hen I heard these cats, it was like another dimension . . . a deeper feel to me . . . it was like, 'Man, this is IT. We gotta try to be like this!'"[24] Fela's music also influenced Paul McCartney in Britain, Gilberto Gil in Brazil, and Brian Eno in the United States. Meanwhile, in 1975, the Nigerian army took power in a coup; in 1976 Fela recorded the song "Zombie," poking fun at soldiers; and in 1977 the army burned down his commune, beat him and threw him in jail, and threw his mother out a window, causing injuries that ultimately took her life. When Fela was released from jail, he recorded the song "Sorrow Tears and Blood," referring to what army rule meant for the people of Nigeria.[25] For the following nineteen years he was in and out of trouble with the government, particularly the army, while becoming gigantically popular worldwide. When he died in 1997, one million people gathered for his funeral.

The cultural globalization that Carmichael, Makeba, and Kuti exemplified was nothing new. By the late 1960s and 1970s, however, the broader trend of cultural globalization appeared to involve an important subtrend: the spread of a radical dissenting counterglobalization that rejected the power of the capitalist West, and often of both the superpowers; that called for the liberation of the world not by, but from the gigantic corporations that were the vehicles of development; that appeared to be tied together by a dense network of international connections; and that increasingly succeeded at using the global corporate media (such as the music industry) to spread its message.

While Fela Kuti and Miriam Makeba offer illuminating individual examples of the globalization of a critical counterculture, other institutional forms of resistance to the development project and the global economic relations on which it rested were also becoming important in the 1970s. The Non-Aligned Movement was one; another was the Group of 77, a loose alliance consisting largely of newly independent states (with, by 2009, 191 members) that sought to form a counterbalance to the power of the major developed capitalist nations.[26] Both groups leaned toward the Left and often acted in alliance with Soviet bloc nations. As more former colonial societies won independence, the political climate in the United Nations became increasingly hostile particularly to the United States, which was widely perceived as the great imperialist power of the age—due to its economic power and strategic alliances, its global network of military bases, and its role in various wars, revolutions, and coups, and because of its support for South Africa and Israel, both increasingly treated as pariah states by the growing anti-racist majority. In 1960 the United States voted against the majority in the UN General Assembly in two cases; in 1970 in seventeen cases; in 1980 in forty-five instances.[27]

Perhaps equally important in the long term was the global human rights movement that emerged in the 1970s. By the middle of the twentieth century the idea of human rights had a long history—one that included the global campaign against slavery in the late eighteenth and early nineteenth centuries, attempts to protect the rights of religious minorities (particularly Christians) in the Ottoman Empire in the later nineteenth century, and the international campaign against abuses in the Congo Free State at the beginning of the twentieth century. But the idea of human rights gathered momentum at mid-century. In the wake of the massive abuses perpetrated by totalitarian regimes, the United Nations adopted the Universal Declaration of Human Rights in 1948.[28] As part of the drive toward decolonization in the 1940s and 1950s, anti-colonial independence movements launched a vehement critique of colonial administrations' abuse of their subjects. Both sides in the Cold War attempted to make use of the idea of universal human rights, denouncing abuses whether of capitalist imperialists or of ruthless dictatorial communist bureaucrats.

By the early 1960s, however, it was clear that neither the United Nations nor the superpowers would be the key advocates for human rights. Most governments (which appointed their nation's representative to the United Nations) aimed to secure individual civil, political, and legal rights through national constitutions; the legal foundation for universal human rights, as opposed to citizens' rights, was less clear. The problem of enforcement was a knotty one, as it implied a contradiction of the principle of national sovereignty, the autonomous ability to make and enforce policies and decisions internally with no external interference. To many governments the idea of human rights looked suspiciously like a tool that more powerful states could use to intervene in the internal affairs of weaker states. And the credibility of the superpowers in matters pertaining to human rights was drastically compromised by their support for dictatorial regimes around the world, many of which committed egregious abuses of their own citizens' human rights. The United Nations did adopt a number of agreements on rights—such as the International Covenant on Civil and Political Rights of 1966. But these were agreements between sovereign states on the rights their citizens should have, and they were effectively unenforceable and in fact were regularly contravened.

Human rights discourse, therefore, came to be dominated during the 1970s and 1980s not by states but by nongovernmental organizations. These included Amnesty International, formed in 1961 and claiming 700,000 members in 150 countries by the 1980s; the Mothers of the Plaza de Mayo, formed in 1977 to protest the "disappearance" of 20,000 to 30,000 leftists under the military dictatorship that took power in Argentina in 1976; and the various "Watch" committees established in the wake of the Helsinki Accords of 1975, an agreement in which the contending powers in the Cold War effectively recognized the borders established by force in Eastern Europe at the end of World War II while guaranteeing human rights for their citizens. These committees included Helsinki Watch (1978), Americas Watch (1981), Asia Watch (1985), Africa Watch (1988), Middle East Watch (1989), and as an umbrella organization Human Rights Watch (1988). There was also an expanding universe of local and regional human rights groups in many parts of the world, organizations that came to rely not on international law, but on the expanding international public opinion embodied in and influenced by the print, broadcast, and ultimately electronic media. Their central method was to "name and shame" those who abused human rights, to organize protests, and eventually to organize boycotts or "divestment" (or "disinvestment") campaigns, which brought public and shareholder pressure to bear on companies doing business with abusive regimes.[29]

The divestment strategy played an important role in bringing down South Africa's apartheid regime, but that was an almost unique success. By the 1990s the global human rights campaign appeared, for all its high media profile, to have accomplished remarkably little. Nevertheless, it was by then an important part of global political and cultural life. And it was more often critical of governments than supportive of them—including even governments that formally guaranteed individual rights in their constitutions. In that sense, the human rights movement was an important element of the broader pattern of counter-globalization in the 1970s.

The pattern of transnational organization characteristic of the global human rights campaign was repeated in other policy arenas during this period as well. The environmental movement is discussed below. The peace and anti-nuclear movements flourished during the 1970s but dated back to the foundation of the Campaign for Nuclear Disarmament in Britain in 1957 and Friends of the Earth in 1969. These movements helped to create the grounding in public opinion for the Partial Test Ban Treaty (between the United States, Britain, and the Soviet Union) in 1963 and the later Strategic Arms Limitations Talks (1972 and 1979), and spawned a welter of NGOs that in some countries—for example, the United States and West Germany—brought the expansion of the nuclear power industry to a virtual halt by the end of the 1980s. The frustrations of those involved in the peace, human rights, ecological, and anti-nuclear movements helped to fuel the citizens' movements that brought about the collapse of Eastern European communism at the end of the 1980s, though in the short term they could get very little leverage in changing policy. In fact, an important incident in the lead-up to the Soviet collapse was a meltdown at a nuclear power plant at Chernobyl, Ukraine, in 1986, which killed thousands of citizens and displaced more than three hundred thousand.[30] In the West these anti-nuclear and other movements were less heavily policed and more openly hostile to politics as usual, and had greater impact on public policy.

By the mid-1970s, then, both contenders in the Cold War—the capitalist, democratic West and the Soviet-dominated, communist East—were faced with a protean moral challenge from the expanding world of NGOs and the enormous explosion of the popular media. But there was worse to come, for by the end of the 1970s, it appeared that both capitalist and communist economic systems were—quite suddenly—failing to deliver the prosperity they promised. Not surprisingly, one key reason was the sudden transformation in the global political economy of oil.

THE GREAT DECELERATION? 1975–1990

In the 1940s and 1950s massive oil fields were discovered in the Middle East and Africa, and oil from those fields sustained the Great Acceleration by feeding cheap energy into the industrial economies of Japan and the North Atlantic (chart 8.2). As a result, world oil prices fell gradually but significantly from the early 1920s to the early 1970s (chart 8.3). But the whole industrial world's dependence on oil by 1970 offered the new oil-exporting nations the opportunity to take the industrial economies' thirst for oil to the bank. As discussed in chapter 7, they did just that. Having made substantial investments in engineering expertise, the oil-exporting nations had the ability; an important added trigger in the Middle East was the escalating conflict between Israel and its Arab neighbors, culminating in two wars in 1967 and 1973, in both of which Israel received important support from the West. In 1973 the oil-producing Arab nations used an oil embargo as a stick to punish the United States, in particular, for its support of Israel in those wars. Then, in 1979, the upheaval and turmoil of the Iranian Revolution cut oil production there drastically, and a US ban on imports of Iranian oil created further chaos in the global oil market. The result was a sudden spike in oil prices.

As a consequence economic growth in the North Atlantic and Japan slowed drastically. The US economy grew only two-thirds as fast between 1973 and 1996 as between 1950 and 1973; those of Europe only a third or a quarter as fast; in Japan growth was only about an eighth or a tenth as fast (see chart 7.4). Inflation mounted as well, rising in Western Europe from about 3 percent in the 1960s to 12 percent in the late 1970s. And unemployment rates surged

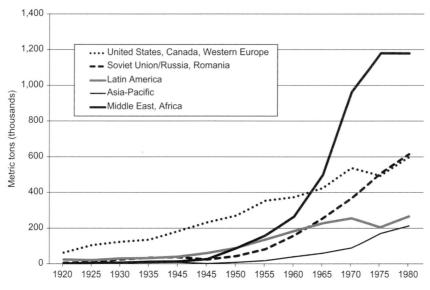

Chart 8.2 World Oil Production by Region, 1920–1980.

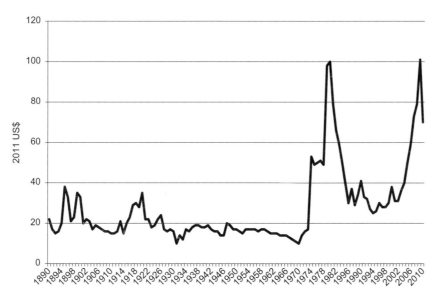

Chart 8.3 Crude Oil Price per Barrel, 1890–2010.

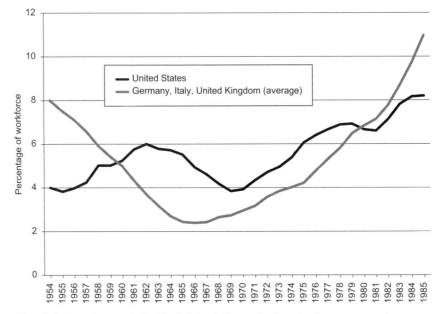

Chart 8.4 Unemployment in the North Atlantic Economies (running five-year average), 1954–1985.

(chart 8.4). Increased joblessness in turn caused the cost of unemployment benefits to skyrocket, creating a serious fiscal problem. By 1977 or 1978, Italy, Britain, and Spain had to take out loans from the International Monetary Fund in order to pay their debts, largely as a result of short-term fiscal crises stemming from the oil shock and inflation.[31] As pointed out in chapter 7, in historical terms, growth in per capita GNP in Western Europe, the United States, Japan, and other industrial countries was quite healthy in the 1970s; but the economic "miracle" of the 1950s and 1960s was clearly over.

If the situation in Western Europe was difficult, that in Eastern Europe was much worse. By the late 1960s it was becoming clear to economists in the Soviet bloc that the command economy there, in which government departments ran virtually all of industry and most of agriculture—was not flexible or innovative enough to keep pace with technological and product development in the West. In fact growth slowed steadily in the communist world (chart 8.5).[32] By the mid-1970s, standards of living in Eastern Europe were visibly slipping compared to those in the West (chart 8.6). Between 1973 and 1988 GDP per capita rose twice as fast in Western Europe as in Eastern Europe. And that was despite the economic windfall that higher oil prices gave the Soviet Union.

In short, just at the moment when many people around the world were questioning whether either of the two economic systems could really deliver global

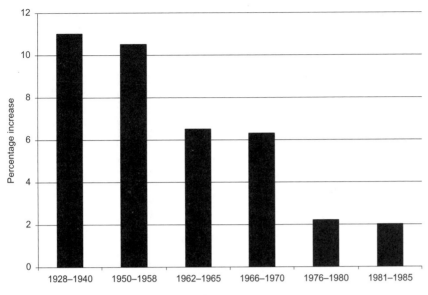

Chart 8.5 Annual Growth in Soviet Industrial Output, 1928–1985.

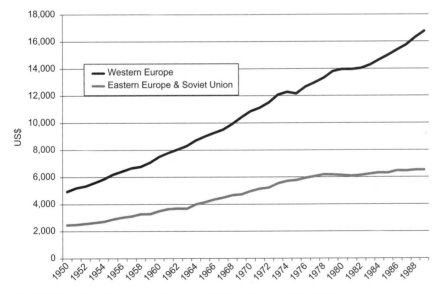

Chart 8.6 Per Capita Incomes in Eastern and Western Europe, 1950–1988.

"development," both of them were faltering at home as well. Faltering, but not yet failing. The economies of the capitalist industrial world in particular did not shrink in this period; they just "decelerated" to a more historically normal pace. And while the communist economies faced profound, fundamental problems in the 1970s, they were not yet actually disintegrating. In the context of the history of technological advance and economic growth since the last third of the nineteenth century, however, this deceleration in itself seemed to many people a failure. In the century from 1873 to 1973, rapid growth had come to seem the norm for modern economies and societies—an underlying pattern disrupted only by the Explosion of 1905–45. After 1973, suddenly, and without the "excuse" of war or revolution, the global economy deviated from that norm. The project of High Modernity appeared to have broken a wheel.

THE ECOLOGICAL MOMENT, 1960–1990

(1) The flourishing of human and non-human life on Earth has intrinsic value. The value of non-human life forms is independent of the usefulness these may have for narrow human purposes. (2) Richness and diversity of life forms are values in themselves and contribute to the flourishing of human and non-human life on Earth. (3) Humans have no right to reduce this richness and diversity except to satisfy vital needs. (4) Present human interference with the non-human world is excessive and the situation is rapidly worsening. (5) The flourishing of human life and cultures is compatible with a substantial decrease of the human population. The flourishing of non-human life requires such a decrease.[33]

Arne Naess and George Sessions, 1984

It is ironic that at the very moment when the global economy was faltering, a growing number of people around the world began to question whether the whole industrial, technological, growth-centered model—whether in its capitalist or socialist version—that had revolutionized human life in the century since 1873 was actually a good thing. Many of these people began to argue that the whole idea was outlandish in principle and a catastrophe in practice. Humanity inhabits a finite world—one planet, with finite space and finite resources. Endless growth is therefore impossible. By the late 1960s and early 1970s it appeared that humanity was going to run out of room and resources in the foreseeable future. This was the "ecological moment"—an intense period of thinking and activism when a new perspective on the relationship between humanity and its planetary home emerged.

As chapter 2 discussed, warnings about the potential consequences of over-exploitation of natural resources were almost as old as the global development project itself; such jeremiads were in part a reaction to unrestrained "bonanza" exploitation of newly expropriated resources, of the kind that, for example, almost eliminated the American bison. But after mid-century, the number of such instances grew. California's sardine fishery started around 1900, peaked in the 1930s, and collapsed in the 1940s—a story repeated over and over again in the world's fisheries since. As humanity expanded into the tropics, numerous jungle-dwelling species were decimated—including tigers, rhinoceroses, orangutans, chimpanzees, gorillas, and giant pandas, to name just a few among the mammals that were killed or whose habitats were destroyed or disrupted. A signal case in the twentieth century's second half was the near disappearance of whales. Whales had been hunted down and slaughtered in a series of technologically enabled waves since the early nineteenth century. By the 1980s whales—harmless, intelligent, magnificent—became an iconic and politically significant instance of the broader massacre of large animal populations. By then the world population of blue whales had fallen some 95 percent, that of humpback whales by about 97 percent, and that of many other whale species by 90 percent or more.[34]

The environmental concerns of the 1960s and 1970s, however, had a new character, for two reasons. First, as lethal as hunting, trapping, and poisoning were, over the long term farming and logging turned out to be far more lethal. By the 1970s the leveling of entire ecosystems was coming into focus as of greater concern even than the decimation of particular species of flora and fauna. The virtual destruction of Brazil's Atlantic coastal rain forest is an iconic case; the redwood forest of California would be another; the destruction of the forests of Southeast Asia has been alarmingly rapid as well. In the 150 years between 1700 and 1850, world forest cover shrank by about 4 percent; trees were cut at an accelerating rate after that, until in just the thirty years from 1950 to 1980 world forest cover declined by 6.2 percent. One recent history refers to the half century from 1945 to 1995 as the "Great Onslaught" on the world's forests.[35] Wetlands and the creatures that lived in them were even more severely affected as marshes and swamps were drained for settlement or for agriculture. By the end of the twentieth century, 132 of the 170 species of mammals that had lived in the wetlands around the Aral Sea in Soviet Central Asia, for example, were gone—along with 80 percent of the sea's water, which had been diverted to agriculture. In the Everglades of Florida, 90 percent of wading birds disappeared as the great swamp was drained for housing or sugarcane plantations.[36] Such developments helped spur the growth of ecology as a scientific field: in the United States, for example, there were six times as many ecological scientists in 1970 as there had been in 1945.[37]

A second reason for heightened concern about the environment, however, was that by 1965 pollution, the poisoning of the environment with toxic chemicals, was having a direct negative impact on humans. Early industrial and urban development was extraordinarily dirty—spewing coal smoke, toxic chemicals, and sewage into the air and landscape and in some cases creating horrifying filth and even major public health disasters. In 1909 a combination of fog and smog in Glasgow, Scotland, killed 1,063 people. In December 1952 London suffered a catastrophic smog event, resulting in 4,000 to 12,000 fatalities over three months. These "crises" were exceptional, but by the 1960s lower levels of air and water pollution had been major killers in large industrial cities for decades. Air pollution, for example, was conducive to pulmonary diseases, and tuberculosis and pneumonia had long been among the main causes of mortality in early industrial cities. By the late twentieth century, while some cities were cleaning up their soot and coal smoke problems, air pollution as a whole was becoming ever more intense. World emissions of sulfur dioxide increased by a factor of seventy-five between 1850 and 2000, and emissions of nitrogen oxides by a factor of twenty-seven between 1900 and 2000. Acid rain began to have severe consequences for forests, lakes, and rivers in many areas, including Eastern Europe and southern Canada. The cumulative cost to human beings and the environment outweighed even the worst individual industrial disasters, though they reached a crescendo in the late twentieth. A chemical leak in 1984 in Bhopal, India, for example, took the lives of 20,000 people and severely injured 120,000 more, many of whom lost their sight.[38]

Nor was air pollution the only threat. Already by 1948 so much nitrogen was leaching into the Rhine River in Germany from fertilized fields that algae blooms became dense enough to interfere with shipping. Industrial pollutants raised the salt content of the river's water by a factor of six compared to 1880, making it unsuitable for flower cultivation downstream in Holland. Pesticides wiped out insect life in the river, and fish starved, so that by the time it reached Holland, the river was lifeless. By the 1980s fish in the Rhine had levels of toxic chemicals in them four hundred times what was considered safe to eat. And it seemed frighteningly possible that not only rivers but even the vast oceans might be killed by pollution. By 1973 the United States dumped 6 million tons (or 12 billion pounds) of industrial waste into the sea each year. Even worse, the United States produced 9 million tons of hazardous waste each year in 1970, but by 2000 that figure had risen to 400 million tons.[39] In the late 1960s and early 1970s the oil industry's potential to create serious ocean pollution from spills became clear as well. A major oil spill occurred in Britain when the tanker *Torrey Canyon* ran aground in 1967, and another issued from an offshore drilling rig near Santa Barbara, California, in 1969. In Japan heavy metals dumped into the sea near the towns of Minamata and Niigata so poisoned fish that people who ate them sickened or even died; some of their children suffered catastrophic birth defects.[40]

While these problems were concentrated in the industrial societies of the North Atlantic and in Japan, by the 1960s "megacities" were emerging around the globe that produced unprecedentedly gigantic pollution plumes. Mexico City had 350,000 inhabitants in 1900, 1.8 million in 1940, and 14 million in 1980. It had 100,000 cars in 1950, but 2 million by 1980. In 1988, air pollution levels in the city exceed the World Health Organization's safety limits on 312 days.[41] Calcutta had a million people in 1900, but 10 million by 1980. Los Angeles had 1.4 million in 1930, and 7.5 million by 1980.[42] In 1950 just two cities in the world had

Figure 8.2 Zinc Mill, Donora, Pennsylvania, ca. 1920.

Figure 8.3 London Smog, 1950s.

populations exceeding 10 million, New York and Tokyo; by 1975 they had been joined by Mexico City, São Paolo, and Shanghai; by 2000 there were twenty cities with populations over 10 million.[43] Cities of this size created tremendous pollution problems; not even counting industrial pollution, they poured tons and tons of pollutants into the air and water from cars and sewage alone.

What was more, as Rachel Carson pointed out in her smash best seller, *Silent Spring*, the rising use of pesticides—deliberately spraying toxic chemicals on the landscape—was having serious effects up the food chain, particularly on birds that ate the bugs that ate pesticides. Worse, because insects developed resistance to pesticides in seven to ten years, in the long term the whole exercise of killing bugs with chemicals might prove pointless. In the meantime, however, the biological effects of pesticides could have catastrophic effects on bird populations (some species of which, ironically, were important in keeping down insect populations)—hence the reference in Carson's title to a spring without birdsong. An iconic example was California's brown pelican, driven to the brink of extinction because the pesticide DDT caused female birds to produce weakened eggshells that were crushed in the nest.[44]

Under these circumstances earlier radical critiques of the violence inherent in "progress" became increasingly persuasive. By the middle of the twentieth century this defense of nature could be stated in soberer, scientific terms, as the discipline of ecology explored connections and interdependence within natural communities or interacting complexes of species (including between humans and their environment), and articulated the growing conviction that humankind's welfare depended on the continued health of complex biological systems. As awareness of the complexity of ecological relationships grew, a growing chorus argued that this deepening understanding of the natural world must entail an important shift in consciousness. In 1949 the American scientist and naturalist Aldo Leopold argued that if mankind were to survive, we must develop a sense of ethical obligation to the whole natural world, of the "land community" or "biotic team" of which humanity itself is only one part. The key to developing such an ecological ethic was "simply this: quit thinking about decent land-use as solely an economic problem." Decisions about mankind's relationship to nature must be based on a consideration of "what is ethically and aesthetically right, as well as what is economically expedient. A thing is right when it tends to preserve the integrity, stability, and beauty of the biotic community. It is wrong when it tends otherwise." Natural environments have a "sustained carrying capacity" (that is, a population maximum) for all forms of life, including humans, that is determined by a complex web of relations between land, plants, and animals. Where that complex web of relations was disturbed by humans, carrying capacity could be degraded. Doing more violence to nature, therefore, could ultimately endanger human survival. Leopold's essay on this "land ethic," as he called it, received little attention when he wrote it in 1948; but by the late 1960s *A Sand County Almanac* was a mass-market best seller.[45]

The fear of overpopulation was central to Leopold's thinking. In this, he was building on a long-established tradition. Already in the 1900s some observers in the North Atlantic were disturbed by the decline of fertility rates in their own nations as compared to steady and high fertility rates in other parts of the world. By 1900 some Europeans and North Americans noted that there were already 400 million Chinese and they were multiplying rapidly. This so-called Yellow Peril would, the racist argument went, conquer the global labor market—or perhaps be conquered by the Japanese and organized as a massive empire, a powerful contender against the North Atlantic empires for global domination. US president Theodore Roosevelt told the National Conference of Mothers in Washington, D.C., in 1905 that Anglo-Saxons were committing "race suicide" by limiting their fertility while the "lower" races did not. The American race theorist Lothrop Stoddard made the same argument in *The Rising Tide of Color against White World Supremacy*, published in 1920. Yet in light of the fact that Europeans had so recently flooded the world with immigrants, some non-Europeans expressed the opposite fear. Sun Zhongshan warned his compatriots in 1924 that if the demographic trends of the previous two hundred years continued for another century, there would be two and a half times as many citizens of the United States as of China. And at an international conference on birth control and family planning in 1925, one Indian speaker warned of the "white peril" threatening the rest of the world.[46] More generally, in the context of imperial rivalries before and during the Explosion of 1914–45, many feared that rapid population growth in some countries might lead to war, as those countries sought land and resources at the expense of their neighbors.

After the end of World War II, concerns about population converged with the project of development. Population growth, many experts feared, would eat up any gains in productivity and exhaust natural resources, sabotaging economic development. At worst, population growth might even so far outstrip food production that mass famine would ensue. The first head of UNESCO, Julian Huxley, remarked in 1947, for example, that stopping rapid population growth was "necessary if man's blind reproductive urges are not to wreck his ideals and his plans for material and spiritual betterment."[47] In 1948 the director of the United Nations' Food and Agriculture Organization warned, "If we cannot solve the problem [of rapid population growth] in this century, then we are headed for the greatest catastrophe in history."[48] And in the late 1940s and early 1950s a raft of books were published warning that population growth was the problem of the near-term future—books such as *Our Plundered Planet*, *The Road to Survival*, and *The Limits of the Earth.* And concern only deepened as population growth ramped up in the 1950s. The International Conference on Population and Resources was held in 1948; that was followed by UN Conferences on Population in 1954, 1965, and 1974. From the early 1950s on, private efforts to spread contraceptive knowledge expanded rapidly.[49] By the late 1960s support for birth control ("family planning") was becoming an important part of development aid: between 1965 and 1969, for example, US development aid for family planning programs rose from $2.1 million to $131.7 million.[50]

Socialists were generally less concerned about population growth, believing that technology would overcome any resource constraints. But by the late 1960s even Communist China was growing concerned over its dizzying increase in population, and in 1979 China imposed a draconian one-child policy on urban families. A number of states in India, too, embarked on coercive fertility-control programs in the mid-1970s, including, among other measures, incentive payments for sterilization, denial of food rations to poor families with more than three children, pay reductions for teachers who refused sterilization, and hiring preferences for those who had been sterilized.[51]

In fact, development increasingly seemed a race against time. As standards of living rose, fertility was expected to fall—at least according to the historical pattern Europe had followed. But would development proceed fast enough, and would fertility respond quickly enough, to prevent catastrophe? As it became apparent that development was not going to be so easy, the fear grew that hunger would win the race. At the same time, as the Cold War escalated, fear grew, particularly in the West, that rapid population growth and deepening poverty would increase the appeal of communism. As one family planning organization put it in 1960, many of the world's countries were afflicted with "geometric population increase which devours their resources and beggars and embitters their peoples. With the Communists capitalizing on this situation, we in the industrialized West are threatened with loss of raw materials essential to our way of life—and in fact vital to our defense."[52]

Yet the problem clearly transcended the Cold War, and governments in the developing world were urgently concerned as well. In 1963, at a conference on Asian population growth in India, planners from around Asia concluded that their countries had to seek western aid in controlling population growth through contraception. By 1968 the United Nations declared contraception and family planning an integral part of "health care" and a human right. Also that year, Paul Ehrlich, a professor at Stanford University, published *The Population Bomb*, which suggested that population growth might prove as big a disaster as nuclear war. It predicted that within a decade, hundreds of millions of people would be starving. A huge hit, the book sold 2 million copies by 1974.[53]

Fears that the globe would be overrun by fast-breeding poor people were only part of the emerging ecological perspective on humanity's relationship to the planet. Many residents of the world's wealthy countries were concerned about population growth there, too. In the United States, for example, federal government support for domestic family planning rose rapidly in the late 1960s—from $8.6 million in 1965 to $56.3 million in 1969. Paul Ehrlich pointed out that each affluent consumer in the wealthy countries, in using far more energy and resources and created far more pollution, contributed a much heavier burden on the world environment than each individual in poorer countries.

Americans in particular, he wrote in 1969, were "consumers and polluters par excellence, and the average American baby puts more strain on the life support systems of our planet than two dozen Indian or Latin American children."[54] The problem was not just more people; it was more people, each consuming more resources.

Around 1900, humanity's technological and economic advance had seemed to many people (such as H. G. Wells and Edward Byrn) to be godlike. Seventy years later, some began to argue that endless growth was impossible and could lead only to ultimate collapse. A growing number of critics began to use an altogether different metaphor: humanity's demographic and economic growth was like a cancer. It was out of control and in danger of killing everything. In 1969 UN secretary general U Thant expressed the growing sense of the fragility of the planetary environment in rather shocking terms: humanity had perhaps ten years to solve the problems of pollution, population, development, and peace; after that, "I very much fear that the problems . . . will have reached such staggering proportions that they will be beyond our capacity to control."[55]

One image helped to bring this concern home to millions of people: the photograph of planet Earth from space, delivered by the US space program. That image underscored both how beautiful Earth is and how small; and the drama, expense, and danger of the Apollo program of manned exploration of the moon underlined, for many people, how difficult it is to get off the planet, let alone reaching another or actually living there. As one commentator wrote in 1974, "We found in space nothing but the awareness that we are dependent on Earth, unique in its beauty and plenty, and from which there is no escape." The emergence of a growing consensus on the need to take action to preserve the environment was symbolized by the first UN Conference on the Human Environment, held in Sweden in 1972. By the early 1970s, books decrying humanity's hubris and its incipient self-destruction through greed and carelessness on a planetary scale were coming thick and fast.[56]

Notable among these works was *The Limits to Growth*. A group of scientists in Europe and the United States, commissioned by group of philanthropists calling themselves the Club of Rome, developed a computer model that captured fears about growth, resources, and the environment in frightfully graphic form. By 1972 their model integrated about a thousand different factors, and they published the results of their simulation in the book. They did not aim to predict quantities, magnitudes, or dates, but only to identify dynamics—how would the relationship between humanity and the environment develop over time? They proposed three scenarios based on various assumptions regarding population growth and increases in rates of resource consumption (chart 8.7). The good news was that one of those scenarios suggested that if humans started limiting consumption and population growth soon, they should be able to reach a stable relationship with their environment. The bad news was that in the other two scenarios, population and consumption would overshoot the

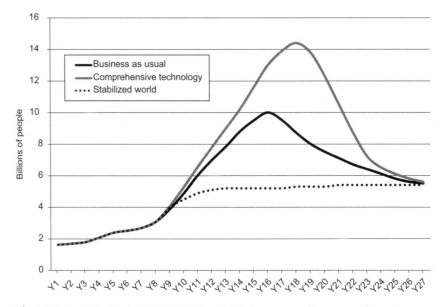

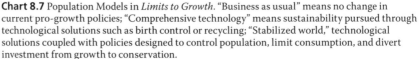

Chart 8.7 Population Models in *Limits to Growth*. "Business as usual" means no change in current pro-growth policies; "Comprehensive technology" means sustainability pursued through technological solutions such as birth control or recycling; "Stabilized world," technological solutions coupled with policies designed to control population, limit consumption, and divert investment from growth to conservation.

carrying capacity of the planet and crash, probably within a century. This message proved extremely interesting: *Limits to Growth* was translated into thirty-seven languages and sold 12 million copies.[57]

One year later, in 1973, the British economist Ernst Friedrich Schumacher published a collection of essays titled *Small Is Beautiful* in which he developed a theoretical foundation for a rational response to this threat. Schumacher was a native of Germany who had emigrated to Britain before World War II and worked as an economist for the state-owned coal industry in Great Britain for twenty years. That experience and his engagement with Buddhist ethics convinced him that the idea (or ideal) of endless growth was irrational, intrinsically violent, and unsustainable for a very simple reason: it treated nonrenewable resources (such as fossil fuels) as income, whereas in fact they are capital. If you spend your capital, eventually you run out of money. The aim of the project of High Modernity, whether in the form of the capitalist welfare state model or the Soviet socialist model, was to achieve ever greater well-being by maximizing production and consumption. In this respect, there was "at present not much to choose between them." Instead, "the aim ought to be to obtain the maximum of well-being with the minimum amount of consumption."[58]

Also in 1973, the Norwegian philosopher Arne Naess developed a term that summed up the core of these ideas: "deep ecology." Drawing on the Gandhian conception of nonviolence (about which he also published), Naess argued that all living things—human and nonhuman—have an intrinsic value and hence the right to live and to thrive independent of their use value for human purposes. The growth of human population and consumption was, clearly, depriving a growing proportion of living things of that right. From an ethical standpoint, it had to stop. The "shallow ecology" of conservation, of resource management, or of setting aside small preserves where a few examples of wild species could survive had to give way to a new, *deep ecology* in which human beings understood themselves to be one part of a larger planetary biological whole, and not more important than any other part. Naess thought that the optimal population of human beings—for humans and for the planet—might be 100 million.[59]

All of these works drew on a long tradition of environmental thinking and environmental ethics reaching back at least to Ludwig Klages and Aldo Leopold. But some also reflected an important connection between this new environmental consciousness and the emergence of the New Left. For some on the political Left, "green" or environmental values seemed a good match with the anti-capitalist, anti-corporate, anti-bureaucratic values that underlay New Left rejections of capitalist and Soviet gigantism in favor of an ethic of human scale and human—not purely economic—values. As one leftist put it, the "deterioration of the natural environment around us is clearly the product of the nature of production and consumption . . . that today holds sway in technological society—American or Soviet."[60] Ecology also converged with the peace movement, as many peace advocates held that humanity had to make peace with the planet as well as between states.

Perhaps the most remarkable institutionalized expression of this connection was the international environmental activist movement Greenpeace, formed in Canada in 1969 to oppose nuclear weapons testing by the United States off the coast of Alaska. It soon evolved into an international organization devoted to using Gandhian nonviolent action and astute manipulation of international media to bring the machinery of war and environmental exploitation to a halt at key high-visibility points. Its first campaigns were devoted to stopping nuclear testing in the Bering Sea and South Pacific between 1971 and 1974. In 1975 it shifted to a campaign to protect whales, then to opposing the harvesting of baby harp seals in the Arctic, clear-cutting of forests, using nuclear power, offshore oil drilling, and the dumping of toxic wastes, among other practices harmful to the environment. By the end of the century Greenpeace had 6 million members worldwide and offices in thirty nations.[61] But Greenpeace was just one of a rapidly growing constellation of environmental organizations around the world in the 1970s and 1980s, with growing total membership. In the United States, for example, three leading environmental organizations had, collectively, 287,000 members in 1970, 615,000 in 1980, and 1.6 million in 1991.[62]

Where particular forms of environmental damage could be identified and addressed, environmentalism achieved some remarkable successes. National and urban governments put in place regulations that drastically improved air quality in many cities; London, for example, reduced the amount of soot and smoke in its air by 98 percent between the 1920s and 2005. Global restrictions on the use of pesticides, such as DDT, led to the recovery of many bird populations. The global whaling ban brought some species of cetaceans back from the brink of extinction.[63] Beyond these pragmatic and issue-specific gains, however, environmental philosophy did not really capture the global imagination. Particularly in more radical forms, such as deep ecology, it remained a fringe phenomenon; but even moderate and pragmatic attempts at more systematic formulations often met with indifference or skepticism. Critics of the Club of Rome—including a study at the University of Sussex in Britain in 1973, and one by the US government's National Commission on Supplies and Shortages in 1976—argued that the authors had made a simple mistake: their model allowed population, consumption, and pollution to rise at an accelerating rate, but didn't allow for an accelerating development of the technological response to those problems. More efficient processes, pollution abatement, cleaner technologies, recycling, materials substitution (for example, plastics for metals), and similar initiatives could reduce the human environmental impact even as population and consumption continued to rise.[64] Again, that is precisely what a raft of practical new laws and regulations accomplished in a number of important cases, such as sewage treatment, air pollution, and garbage disposal, starting in the late 1950s. Critics of Schumacher, too, argued that his theory did not take into account the fact that production could expand by becoming more efficient, thus achieving exactly what he wanted done: producing more while using less. Taken together, the message of these criticisms was simple: we can innovate and grow our way out of the problems of High Modernity.

In a number of crucial instances in the late 1960s and 1970s, that is exactly what appeared to happen. Chapter 9 looks at that development.

Transformative Modernity

REAL DEVELOPMENT, 1975–2000

> On the threshold of the twentieth century we see . . . the monopolist position of a few very rich countries, in which the accumulation of capital has reached gigantic proportions. An enormous "surplus of capital" has arisen in the advanced countries. It goes without saying that if capitalism could develop agriculture, which today is everywhere lagging terribly behind industry, if it could raise the living standards of the masses, who in spite of the amazing technical progress are everywhere still half-starved and poverty-stricken, there could be no question of a surplus of capital.[1]

> V. I. Lenin, 1917

By the early 1970s it seemed to many critics that despite the high hopes generated by the Great Acceleration of the 1950s and 1960s, only some, rather small parts of the world were getting wealthy. Worse, they were doing so by exploiting the rest of the world, where necessary by fostering dictatorships and wars. And worst of all, even in the wealthy pockets of the world the model for continuous growth and ever greater prosperity was stumbling economically at the same time that it was proving ecologically unsustainable in the long term. But from about 1970 onward, just as this critique achieved popularity, something quite remarkable happened. A development strategy emerged that restored the hopes and expectations of many engineers of development and the welfare state. That strategy was founded in large part on the so-called Green Revolution.

The term *Green Revolution* refers to the introduction of modern intensive farming techniques in poor countries, particularly in Asia, in the late 1960s and early 1970s. These included many of the same techniques that had revolutionized per-acre crop yields in much of the North Atlantic and Japan in the 1950s and 1960s: heavy use of fertilizers and pesticides, mechanization, irrigation, and the introduction of improved seed varieties that responded well to those farming techniques. This "revolution" was based on research initiatives heavily subsidized by aid agencies in the North Atlantic—notably the Ford and Rockefeller Foundations in the United States—and later by a number of governments. It was also supported by grants and loans from international aid agencies and wealthier states to governments and farmers in poorer countries in order to support purchases of fertilizer and machinery, and by price supports to create incentives for farmers. It was, therefore, very much a transnational, global project.

A crucial step in this direction was the creation in 1943, with support from the Rockefeller Foundation, of the International Wheat and Maize Improvement Center in Mexico City. By the 1950s this institute (in part by working with a dwarf wheat variety first bred in Hokkaido in the mid-1930s, then transferred to the United States during the American occupation of Japan) had developed improved wheat and corn varieties and dry-plains and grassland farming techniques that helped to raise productivity especially in the North Atlantic region. This was one reason the United States and Canada became massive exporters of wheat and beef in the 1960s, but the new varieties and practices also helped Mexico quadruple agricultural production between 1940 and 1965 and move from being a net importer to being a net exporter of food. By 1985 Mexico produced nearly ten times as much corn and wheat as it had in 1940 and used six times as many tractors and 350 times as much fertilizer.[2]

By the early 1960s, the model was transferred to Asia. By then, India in particular appeared to be in imminent danger of widespread starvation, as population skyrocketed but agricultural productivity did not. In response, a number of foundations, UN agencies, and national governments began to invest in agricultural research to figure out how to raise productivity in Asian wheat and rice farming. The most important instance was the International Rice Research Institute (IRRI), established in Manila with money from the Ford and Rockefeller Foundations.[3] By the late 1960s, the IRRI had developed varieties of rice that could potentially raise productivity quite significantly.

This potential became the core of development strategies for Asia in the 1960s and 1970s. According to the underlying idea, raising agricultural productivity would, not only prevent widespread hunger but also free up labor to move into industry, build capital to fund industrial development, and achieve self-sustaining economic growth. In addition to or even instead of building large industrial installations or infrastructure projects, development aid would start with agriculture. The IRRI was, as a recent study put it, a "Manhattan Project for food." One development expert wrote in 1961 that the idea was to bring about an "industrial revolution in agriculture, whereby agricultural personnel are taken off the land and put to work in factories."[4] Rather than being pulled forward by big industrial projects, Asian economies would be pushed forward by building agricultural surpluses.

This approach should sound familiar: it was in effect a new solution to the very same "problem of the peasant" that many countries had tried to attack in the 1920s and 1930s. Indeed, one historian has called the Green Revolution part of the "War on the Peasant" waged by development advocates throughout the middle decades of the twentieth century.[5] The idea was to turn impoverished, economically and politically isolated subsistence farmers into small-time entrepreneurial capitalist farmers, producing for export (either to domestic urban populations being absorbed into the industrial economy or to industrial centers in other countries) and integrated into their nation's political life. This was a technological strategy for extracting value from the farming sector in order to build industrial power and political integration. In much of the world, capitalist regimes and experts pursued this program, but socialists often followed the same basic script. In Tanzania, to cite one extraordinary example, the post-independence "African socialist" regime of Julius Nyerere used both incentives and compulsion to move some 5 million peasants from more isolated villages into larger, government-sponsored settlements in hopes of generating a more productive agricultural economy.[6]

Oil and natural gas played a critical role in this technological strategy. Natural gas is the raw material for most nitrogen fertilizer, perhaps the most critical element in the Green Revolution. Petroleum-derived fuels drove the tractors critical to industrial farming. Oil-fueled transportation was crucial for the development of the global food market that moved food from centers of production to centers of consumption. The Green Revolution, in other words, was "about" peasants and oil; it was a peaceful alternative to the cataclysmic strategies adopted by many countries in the 1930s.

Obviously, the Green Revolution had close connections to the Cold War. Hungry people are angry people, and angry people might turn to communism. If the Green Revolution could be made to work, it would demonstrate the superiority of the capitalist economic system and, it was hoped, win over the masses of Asia. The Green Revolution, then, would end both the economic problems that sparked World War II and the ideological conflict of the Cold War.

From the outset the Green Revolution met with serious criticism. The form of farming it relied on was capital-intensive—fertilizer, pesticides, pumps, and tractors cost money. It therefore favored larger over smaller farms. As a logical consequence, many smaller farmers—peasants—would be driven out of business. This was essentially the aim; but it did create the problem of what those people would do once they left the countryside. In practice they poured into cities, creating the late-twentieth-century phenomenon of the Third World megalopolis and forming a cheap semi-employed labor force that could be taken advantage of by employers. Even many advocates of the Green Revolution were horrified by the Pandora's box of problems this process created: insurgencies among poorer peasants who were losing their farms to better-off neighbors or to urban investors, and grinding poverty, violence, and radicalization in massive slums in cities such as Mexico, Saigon, Tehran, and Mumbai (Bombay). The burgeoning megacities also generated ever direr pollution problems. And the Green Revolution made agriculture in the developing world dependent not only on the purchase of chemical inputs sold by (no surprise) large chemicals firms in the North Atlantic world, but also ultimately on oil and gas prices—which promptly went through the roof during the first oil crisis of the early 1970s. In a number of cases this constellation of developments and events contributed to the failure of democratic government—for example, in Pakistan in 1969 and the Philippines in 1971.

In addition to its capital-intensive character, critics of the Green Revolution held that it was fundamentally unsustainable. "High yield" varieties, they argued, did not yield more food than traditional crops when measured against inputs of fertilizer, water, pesticides, insecticides, and fuel. Because these crops yielded less straw and fodder that could be used as natural fertilizer, over time they exhausted essential soil nutrients. Green Revolution crops relied heavily on irrigation, raising the threat of the eventual exhaustion of underground aquifers. Monocultures of "improved" varieties, replacing more diverse crops in traditional agriculture, were more vulnerable to insect pests and diseases—thus requiring more and newer pesticides to be continually developed and deployed. The Green Revolution, one critic claimed, had turned peasants into "efficient bandits" pillaging the soil and aquifers for short-term gain. In some cases grim experience seemed to justify such fears. As early as the end of the 1970s, rapid population growth, deforestation and erosion, and the diversion of land from production of food to commercial crops for export meant that Mexico had once again to import food. In Iran, Green Revolution techniques applied to an arid environment and poor, thin soils yielded meager results, and the flood of dispossessed peasants into Tehran was a critical factor that led to the Iranian Revolution of 1979.[7]

At least over the short term, however, this form of development did work, in more than one sense. The new seed varieties and new farming techniques spread rapidly, they raised productivity in agriculture substantially, and they solved the hunger problem. In 1970 one-quarter of farmland in Asia was irrigated; by 1995, one-third was. In 1970, on average Asian farmers used fifty pounds of fertilizer per hectare; by 1995, they used almost four hundred pounds per hectare.[8]

As a result, average yields of the world's major grain crops, in tons of grain per hectare, rose dramatically and steadily over the following three decades (chart 9.1). In the space of forty years, the amount of food produced per acre (or hectare) of land planted to the major grain crops doubled in Thailand, India, Indonesia, Brazil, Mexico, Argentina, Bangladesh, Burma (now Myanmar),

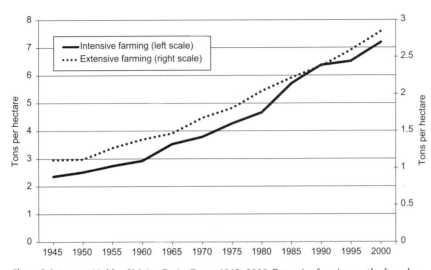

Chart 9.1 Average Yields of Major Grain Crops, 1945–2000. Extensive farming methods make less use of fertilizer, labor, and capital and higher use of mechanization and land.

Germany, France, and the United States. Rice yields in China tripled, and corn or maize yields in Egypt more than tripled.

Not only did the rapid rise of food productivity allow South and East Asia to avoid the famine that those fearful of the "population bomb" had expected, but the average number of calories their populations ate each day rose—in India by almost 15 percent, in China and Southeast Asia by 33.5 percent.[9] By the end of the 1970s, India became a rice-exporting country again—for the first time since the early 1940s. At the end of the 1980s, Thailand exported four times as much rice as it had in the mid-1960s. These countries did not become grain-exporting powerhouses, as the United States, Canada, and Australia did; but given that they had expected to starve, this was an astonishing turnaround. In 1968 Paul Ehrlich had warned that "the battle to feed all of humanity is over. In the 1970s hundreds of millions of people will starve to death in spite of any crash programs embarked upon now. At this late date nothing can prevent a substantial increase in the world death rate."[10] Within a few years it was clear he had been wrong.

By 1971 the Green Revolution strategy had gained sufficient momentum to be translated into official policy, with a consortium of national governments, NGOs, and the United Nations, OECD, and World Bank assuming supervision of multiple research institutes around the world.[11] This shift helped reorient development policy as a whole toward building entrepreneurial opportunity and the "human capital" needed to seize it. By the late 1970s a large proportion of the "underdeveloped" world began to experience rapid growth not only of crop yields but also of the economy's industrial and commercial sectors.

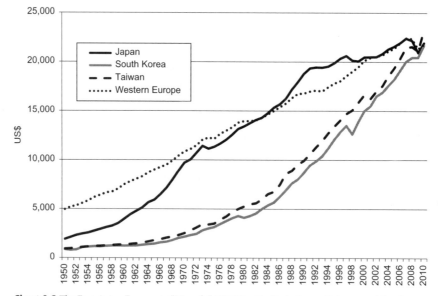

Chart 9.2 The East Asian Economic "Miracle": GDP Per Capita in Japan, Taiwan, and South Korea, 1950–2010.

This was not at all a universal phenomenon. By the year 2000 many Latin American countries still had not completely dug out from the disaster of the debt crisis of 1982. As a proportion of US GDP per capita, GDP per capita in Mexico and Brazil peaked at just under 31 percent in 1980, and then slowly slid down to 22 percent by 2000—just about where those countries had been in 1957. Nigeria and Senegal, in West Africa, started at about 10 percent in 1950 and slowly declined to just 4.5 percent by 2000. And by the early 2000s Eastern Europe had only just recovered from the economic crisis of communism's collapse.

But in much of Asia in particular, the story was different. Taiwan and South Korea were the exceptional cases, becoming major industrial producers and starting, by 2000, to catch up in GDP per capita with Japan, Western Europe, and the United States (chart 9.2). Few other economies performed so well, and most of Asia remains today less than half as wealthy. But growth in per capita incomes in Thailand, India, Indonesia, and China consistently exceeded growth in the North Atlantic from the 1970s onward. The same was true in Turkey and Egypt. By 1990, per capita incomes in the Philippines, Nigeria, Brazil, Chile (but not yet Latin America as a whole), and most of Eastern Europe began to grow faster than in the United States, Western Europe, and now Japan. This occurred in part because growth was slowing in the richer economies, but in most cases these historically poor and sluggish economies were beginning to generate growth in per capita incomes at historically healthy rates, well above 2 percent per year.

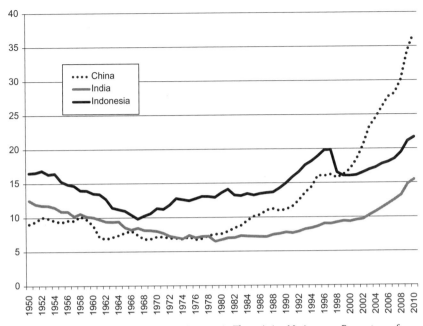

Chart 9.3 Real Development: Per Capita Income in Three Asian Nations as a Percentage of West European Per Capita Income, 1950–2010.

In fact, perhaps more striking even than Taiwan's and South Korea's performance was that of three of the largest, poorest nations on earth: India, Indonesia, and China (chart 9.3). From the 1950s to the late 1970s, per capita income in these societies lost ground relative to that in Western Europe (with the partial exception of Indonesia, where an oil boom raised average income but did not do much to alleviate poverty). But by the 1980s each of them was gaining ground rapidly. The Asian financial crisis at the end of the 1990s proved largely a hiccup in China and India, and was overcome in Indonesia by about 2005. These were still poor societies in 2010, with average incomes between a sixth and a third that of Western Europe. But their economies were growing at an extraordinary rate: between 2000 and 2010, per capita incomes rose at just under 4 percent per year in Indonesia, 6 percent in India, and almost 9 percent in China. These rates of economic growth were comparable to those of the "Economic Miracle" in Western Europe in the 1950s and 1960s; and China's economic growth between 1990 and 2010 almost matched that of Japan between 1950 and 1970.

The overall pattern was striking: while the industrial economies had forged ahead in GDP per capita during the decades of the "Economic Miracle" or Great Acceleration, by 1990 numerous societies around the world were making up that lost ground again. Again, this was particularly true in East Asia; but between the 1960s and the 1970s Turkey, Thailand, and Egypt, too, began to gain on Western Europe in per capita income.

Some notable disasters occurred. A poignant case is that of Iran and Iraq. Both countries experienced rapidly rising per capita incomes in the 1960s and 1970s; but both spent massively on arms, helping to fuel a boom in arms exports from the United States, the Soviet Union, and France in particular.[12] The two countries engaged in a brutal eight-year war with each other starting in 1980, featuring human-wave attacks and widespread missile bombardment of cities. By 1988 per capita income had fallen by over half the 1977 level—and in Iraq it virtually evaporated after the country stumbled into war with the United States by invading neighboring Kuwait in 1990. By 1995 the average Iraqi earned one-seventh as much as in 1980. Algeria sank into a horrific civil war in the late 1980s, and by 1995 Algerians were, on average, not much wealthier than they had been two decades earlier. In Rwanda and the Congo genocide and war in the 1990s obliterated any economic progress, and impoverished and killed millions.

War was not the only stumbling block. As discussed earlier, the major Latin American economies, savaged by the debt crisis at the beginning of the 1980s, were stagnant for two decades thereafter in terms of per capita income. It took almost as long for the former communist economies of Eastern Europe to recover (chart 9.4).[13] Because most economies elsewhere in the world were growing, the net impact on the *relative* wealth of these regions was devastating. All of Eastern Europe and the former Soviet Union was poorer in 2010 relative to Western Europe than in the 1950s. Per capita income in the largest eight Latin American economies was 42 percent that of Western Europe in 1980, then bottomed out at 30 percent in 2003, two decades after the debt crisis began. Iran had reached 53 percent of the West European average in 1976, but bottomed out at 20 percent in 1989.

By the 2000s, however, most of these countries had begun to recover economically and to catch up to the European standard of living. One reason was that outside the Middle East the end of the Cold War brought a substantial decline in Third World arms imports. By 2001 the total value of Third World arms imports, adjusted for inflation, was below where it had been a quarter-century earlier. It then started to rise again, because some Asian nations and many of the neighbors of Iran and Iraq began to spend heavily on high-technology weaponry. But for most of the Third World, the end of the Cold War meant that a substantial "peace dividend" could be diverted to productive investment.[14]

The shrinking of the global arms trade, moreover, was part of a much broader demilitarization of the world in the 1990s and 2000s. In sub-Saharan Africa, to consider a particularly striking case, military expenditures as a proportion of GDP shrank by almost two-thirds between 1989 and 2012. Other

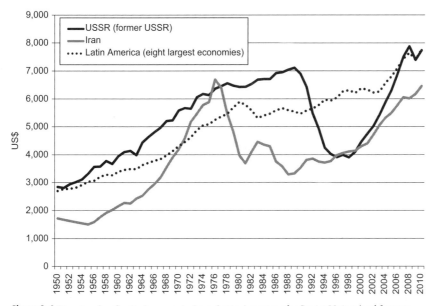

Chart 9.4 Disaster: Per Capita Incomes in Iran, Latin America, the Soviet Union (and former Soviet Union), 1950–2010.

countries made cuts, albeit less drastic. Latin America as a whole reduced its military spending by almost a third in proportion to GDP; Eastern Europe cut its military spending by between a quarter (Poland) and almost three-quarters (Romania); Western Europe by 40 percent; the United States by a third. Russian military spending collapsed; by the 2010s the Russian Federation spent one-sixth as much of its GDP on the military as the Soviet Union had in its last years. As a proportion of world GDP, military expenditures fell more than 40 percent in the 1990s, then rose somewhat in the 2000s; by 2013 military expenditure as a proportion of world GDP was still down by a third compared to 1988, the last year of the Cold War.[15]

In short, not only were people in most areas of the world earning more, but less of what they earned was being spent on things that blow things up. Instead, more of it was spent on things that make life more convenient, such as consumer durables.

Automobiles are a revealing case. Although the North Atlantic and Japan remained far ahead of the rest of the world in rates of automobile ownership, by the 1990s and 2000s the poorer nations of the world were acquiring cars at a furious pace. By 2000 one in nine Brazilians, Turks, and Thais owned an automobile, and one in six Mexicans. In the poorest countries car ownership was still exceptional: only 1.4 percent of Indians and 1.2 percent of Chinese owned one. Still, there were almost nine times as many automobiles in each of those

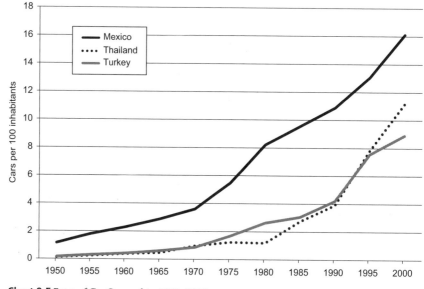

Chart 9.5 Rates of Car Ownership, 1950–2000.

countries as there had been in 1980—a rate of expansion not seen anywhere else since World War II, except in Japan between 1960 and 1980. And some poorer countries were becoming major producers, as well. By 2009, for example, China produced more automobiles than the United States. Telephone ownership showed a similar pattern—Europe, the United States, and Japan were far ahead, but the developing countries were catching up fast. In 1980 one in sixteen Brazilians had a telephone, while by 2000 one in five did; in 1980 one in five hundred Chinese had a telephone, but by 2000 one in nine did. In Turkey it was one in twenty-five versus one in four, in Egypt one in eighty versus one in nine. Other consumer durables—radios, refrigerators, washing machines—followed similar patterns.[16]

These rates of ownership were still far below those in Western Europe and Japan, where the ratio of cars or telephones to people exceeded 1:2. Given that average household size in Brazil or Egypt was probably half again as high as in Western Europe, however, the gap in the number of households with access to these consumer durables was significantly smaller than these figures suggest.

The rising tide of consumer goods, moreover, was increasingly being produced locally, rather than imported. By the 1980s and 1990s industrialization in parts of the "underdeveloped" world was growing rapidly. A good indicator of this change is iron and steel production (chart 9.6). In the 1950s, Western Europe and the United States had produced three-quarters of the world's iron and steel. By the 1990s, the fraction had fallen to one-third. The Soviet Union

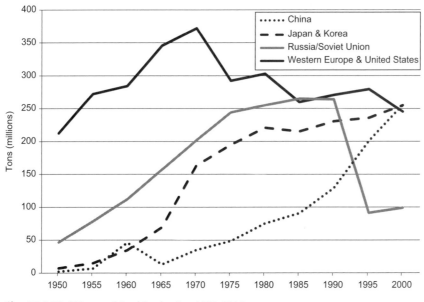

Chart 9.6 World Iron and Steel Production, 1950–2000.

almost reached that level, but production collapsed after 1989. By 2000 there were three steel-producing centers in the global economy, each producing about equal amounts—China; Japan and South Korea; and the United States and Western Europe. But many individual countries that did not become major players in the world steel market also began to produce significant amounts for domestic use, starting in the 1980s. By 2000 Turkey produced only 7 percent as much steel as China, but its steel production had grown faster than China's over the previous twenty years. India and Brazil, too, were becoming major steel producers by 2000; the latter produced more steel than any single European country, and one-third as much as the United States.

In aggregate, such changes generated a significant shift in the composition of exports from the developing world—from commodities to manufactured goods and, by the 1990s in many cases, even high-technology goods like computers and precision machinery (chart 9.7). Overall, manufactures accounted for about one-third of world trade in 1937, two-fifths in 1950, three-fifths in 1973, and three-fourths by 2000.[17]

The distribution of world trade also shifted after about 1980 as developing countries increasingly built trading networks with other developing countries. In 1980 such "South-South" trade exchanges accounted for only 8 percent of world trade; by 2011 the proportion had risen to 26 percent. Developing nations accounted for 33 percent of world output and 25 percent of world trade in 1980, but 45 percent of world output and 47 percent of world trade by 2010. As the

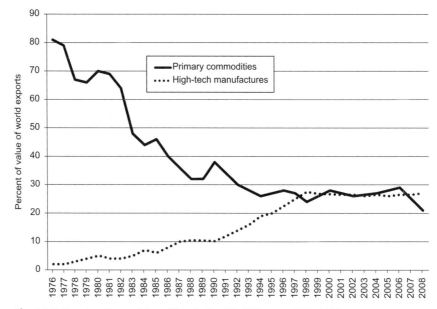

Chart 9.7 Changing Composition of Developing-World Exports, 1976–2008.

United Nations Development Program's (UNDP's) report for 2013 put it, the three decades after 1980 saw "a dramatic rebalancing of global economic power."[18]

An important feature of the period after the late 1970s, however, was that the global economy became increasingly integrated, not only through trade but also through a "transnationalization" of industrial production. Increasingly, different steps in the production of particular goods were accomplished in different parts of the world, depending on comparative advantage. Research, product design, and product management might be done in one country (for example, a wealthy country with a high educational level), the production of basic parts in another (with low labor costs and abundant raw materials), and final assembly in a third (with skilled labor, a high degree of automation, and wealthy consumers). The consumer electronics industry provides one well-known case. The personal computer was born in California in the early 1980s, but by the 1990s the core of the global personal computer industry was built upon a transpacific relationship in which research, design, management, production, assembly, and marketing were divided between California, Japan, Taiwan, South Korea, the Philippines, and (a little later) China.[19] The automobile industry was an even more extreme case. By the 1990s Ford Motor Company produced or assembled parts for one of its popular car models in fifteen countries on three continents, and in the early 2000s the German automotive giant

Volkswagen produced parts and cars in a dozen countries. Falling tariffs and transport costs, the building out of infrastructure around the world, automation of many industrial processes (reducing skill requirements), and the growing efficiency and density of communications all enabled this kind of distributed manufacturing to expand from the mid-1970s onward.[20]

Critical foundations for this transformation had been laid in the quarter century after World War II through the transformation of the global energy industry. Prior to World War II, large corporations in the industrial core regions drove and controlled the electric power industry around the world. Thus electric power generation in Mexico was controlled primarily by Canadian, British, and later US firms; in Russia by French, Belgian, German, and Swiss firms; and in Chile and Argentina by British and German firms. Focused on profitability, these firms often concentrated on serving particular industrial enterprises that were frequently also controlled by companies in the core, or on serving the port cities through which raw-material exports flowed. The result was what one recent study called "enclave electrification." From the late 1940s through the 1960s, a wave of nationalizations transferred control of power generation and distribution from multinational companies to national governments—for example, in South Africa (1948), China (1949), Spain (1949), Argentina (1958), Cuba (1960), Egypt (1961), Mexico (1962), and Chile (1965).[21] As public utilities, national electric generation and distribution systems were less sensitive to cost and efficiency concerns, and more responsive to consumer demand and domestic planning priorities. Providing electric power to national economies and citizenries became a major function of new nation-states, inaugurating what one historian has called the "era of gigantic dams." An emblematic case is the Aswan High Dam in Egypt. Completed in 1970, in 1974 it supplied 53 percent of all power used in the country and was the centerpiece of Egypt's entire national development plan. By the end of the twentieth century there were some 40,000 large concrete dams in the world, and the giant hydroelectric projects of the 1960s and 1970s formed a crucial part of the energy infrastructure, particularly in the less developed world. In the United States, Japan, the Soviet Union, and Northwestern Europe, hydroelectric power constituted only between 10 and 13 percent of all electricity generation in 1985; but in China and Mexico it was about a quarter, in India almost a third, in South America three-quarters, in Zaire (Congo) nearly all.[22]

Nuclear power was less important in transforming world economic patterns, because it was concentrated in Europe and the United States. But by the end of the century there were almost 450 active nuclear reactors in the world in thirty countries, and more nuclear reactors in Asia (concentrated in Japan, China, South Korea, and India) than in North America.[23]

Although the pace slowed after 1975, power generation continued to expand. India produced eight times as much electricity in 1975 as in 1955, and five times as much in 1995 as in 1975; Brazil raised electricity production by a factor of ten between 1950 and 1975, and then by a factor of five between 1975 and 2000; China produced fourteen times as much electricity in 1965 as in 1945, and fourteen times as much again in 1995. In 1975 Europe and North America produced roughly similar amounts of electricity, about two and a half times as much as the Asia-Pacific region. By 2000 the historically poorer large nations of the Asia-Pacific region alone (excluding Japan, South Korea, Taiwan, and Australia) produced 85 percent as much electricity as Western Europe.

The most striking case of this broad pattern of economic change comes from sub-Saharan Africa, the poorest large region on earth and the most economically stagnant between 1945 and the mid-1990s. By the early 2010s, Africa seemed, as one study put it, "a continent on the move." Rising trade volumes, a quadrupling of foreign direct investment since 2000, the collapse of arms expenditures, and an intensifying trade and investment relationship—a "happy synergy"—with China were yielding remarkable economic results. Per capita incomes, which had stagnated or fallen for three decades, rose almost 6.5 percent per year between 2000 and 2010. One critical reason was that expanding demand from newly industrializing nations—China, India, and Brazil—drove up the prices of commodities that Africa supplied, such as oil, uranium, metals, and timber. By 2012 about a million Chinese citizens worked in Africa, in mining, construction, agriculture, and banking—an extreme instance of expanding "South-South" economic relationships.[24]

The economic "transformation of the South"—as the UNDP's 2013 report called it—from about 1990 onward was so unexpected and so rapid that it took some time for observers to catch up. The contrast between the UNDP's 1999 report and its 2013 report reveals this lag graphically. The earlier report was almost unrelievedly gloomy. It focused on radical inequalities in income between countries (with the wealthiest fifth of humanity receiving 86 percent of world GDP); the emergence and power of multinational megacorporations; the uneven global distribution of innovation; the volatility of the global financial sector; the apparent crisis of the welfare state; the growth of economic insecurity generated by corporate restructuring and mergers and acquisitions; the spread of HIV/AIDS (a "poor person's disease" from which some 33 million people, primarily in the least developed countries, were dying, with 6 million more infected each year); the "cultural insecurity" generated by the global media and entertainment industry (waging "onslaughts of foreign culture"); the global reach of organized crime ("criminals are reaping the benefits of globalization" and illegal drugs were 8 percent of world trade); environmental degradation; and the erosion of both public and private care for others by competitive pressures that led states to cut taxes and forced women into the paid labor force. The report did take note of some progress in the 1990s, including a substantial rise in life expectancy even in many poorer countries, the near doubling of the proportion of world population that had access to clean water, and a 25 percent gain in global food production per capita. But in almost every case it pointed to failures, inequalities, and exceptions.[25]

The 2013 report, by comparison, bubbled with optimism. The global distribution of incomes was unequal but becoming slightly less so as per capita income in less developed nations rose faster than those in developed industrial nations. Between 2000 and 2012 sub-Saharan Africa raised per capita income by one-third. Income inequality within many societies was increasing, but rising overall wealth meant that the average standard of health care and education was also rising. Inequality as measured by the Human Development Index (which takes total wealth, health care, and education into account) was therefore falling slightly. The proportion of the world's population that lived in extreme poverty had fallen from 43.1 percent in 1990 to 22.4 percent in 2008. Global educational attainment was becoming more equal at all levels (primary, secondary, and tertiary/university); differentials in the proportion of the population with Internet access were shrinking; and less developed countries were beginning to generate more technological innovation. All of this change amounted to an "unprecedented reduction in deprivation and expansion of human capabilities" globally.[26]

It is tempting to think that the glass was half empty in 1999, whereas it was half full in 2013. Inequality is falling *between* societies, but rising *within* most. Demand for basic raw materials is pulling some poor nations out of economic stagnation, but when the Chinese economy slows down, the structural vulnerability of those raw material–exporting economies (and societies) will be exposed again. Global arms expenditures are still enormous, though falling as a proportion of GDP. And yet, from a more optimistic perspective, over the past three decades, the less developed world recovered gradually from the debt crisis of the early 1980s, then experienced an acceleration of economic growth from the late 1990s on. In fact, total interest owed on debt in the less developed world fell by over half between 2000 and 2010. South Asia's interest costs fell by half, Latin America's by two-thirds, and sub-Saharan Africa paid 4.1 percent of GDP in interest in 2000 but only 1.2 percent in 2009.[27]

Two other broad factors help explain the relative success of "real development" after the mid-1970s. First, by about 1975 the center of commercial innovation in the world economy was decisively shifting to Asia (chart 9.8). By 2010 China, Korea, and Japan together filed more than twice as many patent applications as the United States and Western Europe. One important reason for that difference was that these Asian countries made a gigantic investment in higher education (chart 9.9). Even before World War II some Asian nations had invested heavily in higher education; after the war, they quickly overtook rates of higher education in most of the rest of the world (outside the United States, always exceptional in this respect). By 2000 Thailand and Turkey had as many students per capita as Western Europe; Mexico and Brazil were catching up; Japan, Korea, and Taiwan collectively had about twice as many. China was far

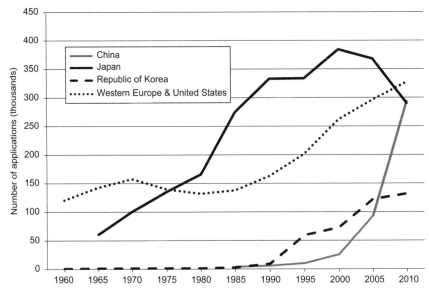

Chart 9.8 Resident Patent Applications, 1960–2010.

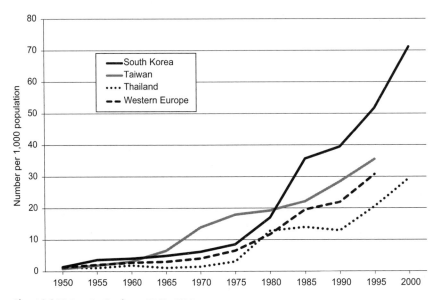

Chart 9.9 University Students, 1960–2012.

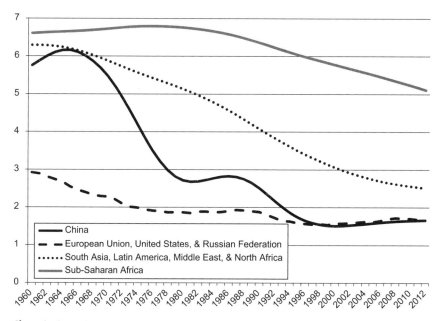

Chart 9.10 Fertility Convergence: Number of Children per Adult Woman, 1960–2012.

behind, with about one-fifth as many students per capita as Western Europe, but the country's population was so large that it already had more university students than the United Kingdom, France, Italy, and Germany combined. The result was a massive surge in the number of people with technical education and skills. In 1952 Egypt, for example, had 1,392 working scientists; by 1973, it had 10,655.[28]

A second factor promoting "real development" was that fertility rates in the nonindustrialized world started to plummet (chart 9.10) in the 1970s at the same time that the rise in life expectancy accelerated (chart 1.7). By 2010 most of the world was converging on zero population growth and a life expectancy of close to seventy years. Sub-Saharan Africa was the only exception. As a result, the world rate of population growth topped out in 1965–70 and has since been cut almost in half.[29] Whereas in earlier decades rapid population growth and high mortality often stifled growth in per capita income, in the past thirty years falling fertility and improving health have helped to ensure that gains in productivity have been translated in more countries into a rising standard of living. In South Korea, for good example, between 1950 and 1967 per capita income was more or less stable relative to that in Western Europe, at about 17 percent. Thereafter it rose steadily, until in 2010 per capita incomes in the two regions were quite close. Contributing to this change was the rise in the proportion of the South Korean population that were working adults, from

32.7 percent in 1973 to almost 43 percent in 1998, about the same as in Western Europe throughout this period.[30]

The net effect of these two factors, again, was that by 2010 Asia in particular had well launched the process of eliminating the advantages that early technological and industrial development had given the societies of the North Atlantic between the mid-nineteenth and mid-twentieth centuries. By 2040, it may appear that those advantages grew greater and greater until the 1960s and then gradually faded over the following three generations. As of 2015 that process is about halfway to completion.

THE NEW RIGHT, 1968–2000

> The fundamental difference between Islamic government, on the one hand, and constitutional monarchies and republics, on the other, is this: whereas the representatives of the people or the monarch under such regimes engage in legislation, in Islam the legislative power and competence to establish laws belongs exclusively to God Almighty.[31]

Ayatollah Ruhollah Khomeini, 1970

> Freedom prospers only where the blessings of God are avidly sought and humbly accepted. The American experiment in democracy rests on this insight. Its discovery was the great triumph of our Founding Fathers, voiced by William Penn when he said: "If we will not be governed by God, we must be governed by tyrants."

Ronald Reagan, 1983

Many people in both the developed and the "developing" nations in the 1970s and 1980s were profoundly disturbed by the political, economic, and cultural implications of "real development" elsewhere, including their own societies' fading economic and political dominance. Many were equally disturbed by the emergence of counterglobalization, the New Left, and the ecological movement. By the middle of the 1970s, these concerns had become the focus for the emergence of a major new factor in the political life of both industrialized and "developing" nations: the New Right.

The global political New Right emerged first in the 1960s and 1970s as a response to the emergence of the New Left, "Third Worldism," and the counterglobalization movements. The movement was a bewildering complex of interacting elements, some of which were mutually contradictory, others mutually reinforcing. Different elements had different degrees of importance in different places around the world, and complex and varied coalitions and negotiations between them arose in different places. To give but one example, a fundamentalist religious revival was central to Ronald Reagan's brand of the New Right in the United States, but Margaret Thatcher, who played a comparable role as political leader and emblematic figurehead of the New Right in Britain, rarely mentioned religion, and indeed religious revival played little role in the British New Right.

Looking at this complex of movements in global perspective, one can discern essentially four elements. The first was anti-communism and an aggressive assertion in political life of the superiority of political democracy, human rights, and the defense of freedom. The second was neoliberalism—a vehement commitment to free-market economics, which the New Right understood to be integrally tied to democracy. Essentially, for the New Right the free market was to economics what political and civil rights are to politics. In this respect the New Right stood the thinking of those who had built the welfare state on its head. Champions of the welfare state believed that freedom sometimes had to be secured through state intervention to ensure that everyone benefited in concrete and practical ways from rising productivity and affluence. The New Right insisted instead that freedom resulted when the state removed itself from economic and social life. The third element was a powerful resurgence of conservative cultural commitments. In some cases this took the form of more aggressive celebration and cultivation of national traditions, an "integral" nationalism that stressed national unity and uniformity; in other cases it took the form of a conservative religious revival; in many cases both went together. Fourth, and closely related to the religious element, was a broad commitment to what we might call sexual conservatism—a conception of sexual life centered on a particular understanding of the family as the foundation of social order, and of distinct gender roles as the foundation of family.

The New Right's aggressive anti-communism was a response both to the Soviet strategic offensive of the 1970s and to a growing awareness of the communist economies' weakness and underperformance, which the New Right saw as a great opportunity. Ronald Reagan, in an important programmatic speech to the National Association of Evangelicals in March 1983, summed up this sense of opportunity by remarking that communism was a "sad, bizarre chapter in human history whose last pages even now are being written."[32] Reagan engaged in a massive military buildup in the 1980s, partly to appeal to American integral nationalists and partly as a way of forcing the Soviets to devote ever more resources to their military budget and thus of ultimately breaking the communist economies completely.[33] Clearly, though, the economic success of a number of the United States' Asian allies also formed a telling contrast to the stagnation of the Soviet-style economies, one that encouraged the crusade against communism. Japan, Taiwan, South Korea, Turkey, and Thailand were great success stories for capitalist development.

The New Right's campaign against the welfare state and development policy grew largely out of the economic difficulties induced by the oil shock of the 1970s—rising unemployment, rising debt, and rising inflation. Some commentators in the early and mid-1970s had worried about "ungovernability," the condition in which any known solution to one of these problems would make the others worse. Countercyclical deficit spending, for example, would make the debt and inflation problems worse; imposing more fiscal discipline to control inflation and debt would make unemployment worse. The New Right, in contrast, argued that these problems shouldn't be governed at all—the state should just let the free market solve them organically. That meant privatizing state-owned industries and companies in order to limit the state's budgetary exposure to economic instability; deregulating labor and financial markets so that greater flexibility in the allocation of labor and investment could create new solutions to the problems of unemployment and inflation; and pursuing further liberalization of trade so that the global economy could solve its problems through a more efficient international division of labor.

Many in the New Right argued that this would yield not only economic benefits but also greater freedom. Margaret Thatcher, for example, had argued as early as 1968 that erecting the welfare state had created a creeping "authoritarianism" of experts and bureaucrats who made more and more decisions for more and more people on the basis of the bureaucrats' alleged expertise rather than of democratic consultation. Therefore, she argued, "the way to get personal involvement and participation is not for people to take part in more and more government decisions but to make the government reduce the area of decision over which it presides and consequently leave the private citizen to 'participate,' if that be the fashionable word, by making more of his own decisions."[34] When she became British prime minister in 1979, she embarked on an ambitious program of deregulation and privatization. Ronald Reagan, elected president of the United States a year later, initiated a similar program in that country. "Thatcherism" and "Reaganism," in turn, served as models for other countries during the 1980s and 1990s.

In its campaign against the welfare state, the New Right benefited substantially from some of the broader trends reshaping the world economy in the 1970s and 1980s. Most important, the rapid growth of world trade and the maturation of the transportation, communications, financial, and even electrical infrastructure in much of the "developing" world, along with the rise of manufacturing in South Korea, Taiwan, Brazil, and the Philippines, seriously weakened organized labor in North Atlantic and Japanese industrial societies. Labor unions had long actively supported the policies of redistributive equity and equal opportunity at the core of the welfare state agenda; under the new economic conditions, they rapidly lost leverage, and then membership, because corporations increasingly could save significant amounts of money, without sacrificing quality or reliable delivery of product to market, by moving production to lower-wage economies. In Great Britain, for example, the state owned the coal-mining industry. Margaret Thatcher broke the power of miners' unions in an epic strike in 1984–85, then privatized most of the coal-mining industry and shut down almost all of Britain's coal mines over the following ten years. In the United States, Ronald Reagan fought an equally emblematic battle against the union of air traffic controllers, who were, like Britain's coal miners, employees of the government. In both cases, economic and technological change played a crucial role: in Britain oil was replacing coal as the dominant fuel in the British economy, and in the United States computers made it possible to safely control as many flights as before the strike with far fewer controllers.[35]

The cultural element in the New Right reflected at least two, quite different developments in the 1970s. One was demographic. Already by the early 1970s, fertility rates in most of the wealthy, industrialized world dropped below the replacement rate of two children per adult woman. In the rest of the world, fertility rates remained much higher until the 1980s and 1990s, while mortality plummeted. For twenty or thirty years, therefore, populations in North Africa, the Middle East, Latin America, and most of Asia were experiencing explosive growth while the developed world was facing an incipient labor shortage. In the late nineteenth and early twentieth century, European immigrants had flooded the Western Hemisphere, Australia, and a few other regions. By the 1960s, in contrast, immigration increasingly flowed back toward Europe, and from Latin America to North America. In the short term, millions of ethnic Europeans fled the newly independent former colonies and "returned" to Europe—the largest groups being some 1.8 million ethnic French or part-French from Algeria and Indochina in the early 1960s, and some 800,000 ethnic Portuguese or part-Portuguese from Africa in the 1970s.[36] But the reversal of direction soon turned out to be permanent. In the United States, for example, between 1950 and 1970 Latin Americans and Asians replaced Europeans and Canadians as the largest immigrant groups (chart 9.11). In 1950, people of European ethnicity made up more than 67 percent of all immigration into the United States; by 1990, Asians and Latin Americans, with a few Africans, made up almost 90 percent. An important secondary reason for this change was the abandonment in 1965 of the old quota system imposed in the 1920s, which had limited immigration from particular countries and regions to historic levels and frozen in place the old nineteenth-century pattern. Australia (1967) and Canada (1973) also abandoned restrictions on Asian immigration.[37] In the United States the New Right's appeal derived in great part from the gradual dismantling of the legal structure of racial discrimination during the Civil Rights Movement of the 1950s and 1960s—a development that, as we have seen, was closely and self-consciously tied to the broader collapse of racist policies and of colonial empires around the world. Internal migration of African Americans to the North and West in the 1940s and 1950s played an important role in broadening the New Right's appeal outside the South.

In Europe, meanwhile, immigration increased in the form of laborers mostly from the former colonies of the European imperial powers in North Africa, the Middle East, and the Caribbean. Between 1950 and 1980, 1.5 million Africans, almost 2 million Turks, 600,000 Indians and Pakistanis, and 650,000 Caribbean islanders emigrated to Europe. In 1950 just over one in one hundred

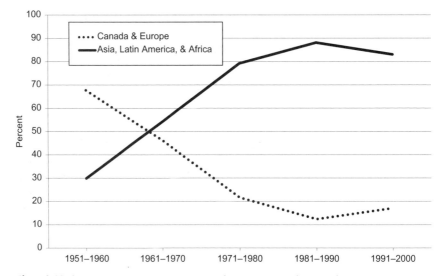

Chart 9.11 The New Immigration Age: Origin of Immigrants to the United States, 1950–2000.

Western Europeans were immigrants; by 2000 the proportion reached one in twenty Europeans. And other centers of economic development also began to attract large numbers of migrants in this period. A million and a half people migrated from southeastern Africa to South Africa; 2 million West Africans went to Nigeria, drawn by the boom in oil production there; and over 1.5 million moved from the Philippines, Pakistan, Indonesia, and the Middle East to the oil-rich Gulf States. A remarkable instance was the recruitment in the 1990s of some 350,000 Brazilians and Peruvians of Japanese descent to work in industry in Japan.[38]

To some people this extraordinary reversal in the pattern of global migrations posed a threat. In the United States many cultural conservatives saw Latinos as ethnically different, not "white." Some American Protestants did not welcome the idea of millions of new Catholic fellow citizens, and the growing presence of Asian religious traditions disturbed those who thought of their country as a Christian nation. The simultaneous emergence of Third Worldism seemed to threaten to turn immigrants from Latin America and many parts of Asia into internal enemies—people committed based on their origins to an anti-capitalist, anti-"Western" program. For people who subscribed to this view, a telling moment was the so-called Third World Strike at San Francisco State University in 1968, followed by a similar strike at the University of California at Berkeley in 1969—the two longest student strikes in American history. In each case, a coalition of African American, Asian American, Latino, and Native American student organizations established a "Third World

Liberation Front" and forced university administrations to establish a new School of Ethnic Studies. Cultural conservatives regarded this as politicization of higher education by radicals.[39] And since many people in ethnic studies programs were highly critical of racial discrimination in US history, integral nationalists also regarded such academic programs as an attack on the dignity and legitimacy of national traditions. Then–California governor Ronald Reagan's bitter rejection of the strikers' agenda made him a national figure.

Europe, too, particularly after the oil shock pushed unemployment up, experienced a growing wave of anti-immigrant sentiment—expressed first in anti-immigrant violence, and then in the formation of single-issue anti-immigration parties. Here many cultural conservatives regarded Muslim immigrants from Turkey and North Africa as culturally different and alien—not Christian, not from countries with a strong democratic tradition, and not loyal to the national traditions of the their adopted countries. In precisely these years, moreover, the shared political and economic institutions that eventually became the European Union were being built as well. Integral nationalists saw their national traditions as under attack both from pro-immigration policies and from the expanding authority of bureaucrats in Brussels, the EU capital.

In both the United States and Western Europe religious prejudices stirred resentment and distrust of the new immigrant groups. But quite independent of the immigration issue, a highly politicized conservative religious revival was also an important part of the New Right phenomenon. The political engagement of American evangelical Protestants was particularly striking given the United States' long tradition of the separation of church and state. This phenomenon took organizational form as early as 1942 with the formation of the National Association of Evangelicals, and the evangelical pastor Billy Graham provided a prominent voice for social conservatism and anti-communism in the 1950s. It became much more important in national political life, however, with the formation of Focus on the Family in 1977 and the Moral Majority in 1979.

Outside the North Atlantic a number of important political movements, though distinct from the New Right in the industrial world, nevertheless shared important parts of its agenda. In most of them, religion played a central role. A powerful conservative Muslim revival arose in the 1960s and 1970s. The Ayatollah Ruhollah Khomeini, who assumed leadership of the Iranian Revolution in 1979, was the most emblematic example. More recently, radical Islamist terrorist organizations have tried to reshape the political order in the Muslim world (not least through confrontation with the West), with the ultimate aim of establishing a theocratic alternative to secular nationalism. In India the Bharatiya Janata Party (BJP) formed in 1980 (albeit with roots in the nationalist movement as far back as the 1920s, and in the conflict over the formation of Pakistan after World War II) and rejected what it saw as the secularist materialism central to both capitalism and communism in favor of a politicized Hindu religiosity. Both the Iranian revolutionary regime and the BJP espouse a form of integral nationalism: they argue that their religion is the foundation of the national political tradition and is what made theirs a great and free nation. The BJP also combined this religious radicalism with a healthy dose of neoliberal economic policy favoring privatization, deregulation, free markets, fiscal conservatism, and entrepreneurship.[40]

The reasons for this upsurge in political religion are complex. For one thing, the 1960s and 1970s saw a quite sudden wave of secularization in some parts of the world—not so much the abandonment of religious belief (though that too grew) as the decline of formal religious practice. Particularly in the developed world attendance at religious services declined precipitously. In Christian countries rates of baptism and of church marriages fell. By 1981, 59 percent of Frenchmen and 48 percent of British people said they never went to church at all. Many sociologists argue that as societies become more affluent and more complex, a process of functional differentiation takes place whereby particular social and cultural functions increasingly become the exclusive responsibility of dedicated institutions and professions. Education, for example, becomes the job of schools and universities; professional concerns become the job of professional associations; mental health becomes the job of psychologists; social assistance becomes the job of social workers; economic life becomes the job of accountants, bankers, and trade union officials. This tends to undermine the authority of religion, which historically in most societies has played a role in all aspects of community life—addressing people's material needs through charities, taking care of their minds through counseling, teaching them in religious schools, and organizing them in peer groups (for example, youth, women's, and professional organizations). And of course in modernizing societies, scientific inquiry and scientists—not the religions and their churches—become responsible for developing an explanation for why the world is the way it is. For deeply religious people, both developments were a profound threat and a call to action. So too was the increasing individualization or "privatization" of religion—the tendency toward a spirituality focused on the individual's experience rather than on the collective practice of faith.[41]

A second, related factor was competition from the state, which everywhere has asserted its authority in the modern world—over education, for example, which it undertakes in public schools in order to foster nationalism, good citizenship, and a uniform national language. Similarly, the welfare state came to compete with religious charities during the first half of the twentieth century. With decolonization and the growth of more effective nationalist bureaucratic governments in the former colonial world, this competition between state and religion became an increasingly important feature of life globally.

In the case of the Muslim world, for example, governments aggressively pursued secularism as a public policy in the 1950s and 1960s. We have seen the early stages of this conflict in the battles between religious conservatives in Iran and Turkey and secularizing nationalist elites who saw the Muslim clergy as representatives of a pre- or nonnational political order and a backward rural society, and tried to reduce their social and political influence. Regimes elsewhere in the Middle East took the same approach. In particular, the Ba'ath Party in Syria and Iraq was strongly influenced by Soviet socialism, which had campaigned against Islam's public functions and against the traditional social order of Soviet Central Asia since 1917—as it had against all religions, which Marxist tradition saw as a reactionary force. Gamal Nasser, in Egypt, was also influenced by socialist secularism, and saw Egypt's Islamic institutions as competing with the state for power. But even the shah of Iran, who was anti-Soviet and allied with the West, continued some of his father's aggressive secularizing policies, including, among others, expanding the rights of women within marriage and giving them the vote in 1963.[42]

Yet we should not interpret the rise of the religious New Right as a purely defensive reaction. As was the case even before World War I, technological, economic, and social change also presented religious activists with energizing new opportunities. Communications technologies such as the radio, the television, print media, cassette tapes, and eventually compact discs and the Internet have enabled religious movements and churches to intensify their relationships with their followers, establishing themselves more firmly in the daily lives of the faithful. Such innovations have also given them more global reach. Even more so than was the case in the nineteenth century, the postwar world has seen an extraordinary global mixing of religious beliefs. This has been true of at least some religious movements of almost every sort—whether fundamentalist or New Age, theologically liberal or conventionally conservative.

Some faiths have in fact achieved remarkable global expansion in the past half century. In 1950 Mormonism had about 1.1 million members, about 3 million in 1970, and over 11 million in 2000. By the early twenty-first century, only half of Mormons in the world lived in the United States, with over 4.5 million in Latin America and the Caribbean and almost 2 million in Europe, Africa, and the Pacific.[43] Charismatic and Pentecostal Christianity have spread rapidly worldwide as well, particularly in Latin America and Africa; by the early twenty-first century there were an estimated quarter billion Pentecostal Christians worldwide. A whole series of religious movements with their origins in the Indian subcontinent have gained followers around the globe, without becoming mass religions but reaching well beyond ethnic Indian diasporas. Examples would include the International Society for Krishna Consciousness (the "Hare Krishnas," formed in 1965); various schools of Buddhism (Theravada, Zen, Tibetan), with some 800,000 converts in the United States by 2005; various forms of yogic practice (starting with Paramahamsa Yogananda, who arrived in the United States in 1920); or Maharishi Mahesh Yogi's Transcendental Meditation.[44]

Globalization has thus created new opportunities for religions to spread worldwide and to deepen and intensify their relationships with their followers.

But that expansion has constituted an enormous threat to the coherence of regional religious communities. These two faces of religious globalization are closely related, as they were at the beginning of the twentieth century. Some religious activists and innovators have been energized and inspired by the emergence of what one scholar has called "a global marketplace full of religious consumers who are looking for a wide variety of options out of which they can create their personal path to salvation."[45] But that same development has also sparked aggressive "fundamentalist" responses, often in the name of greater doctrinal "purity" and rigor. Some of those responses have been closely aligned with New Right integral nationalist agendas.[46]

Religious conservatives found an additional but quite different threat in the growing influence not of religious heterodoxy, but of organized atheist or agnostic secular humanism. Most secular humanists denied the existence of the supernatural and spiritual; saw humans as merely a part of nature, a product of evolution; argued that the pursuit of truth is the province of critical reason and science, not of revealed religion; and held that the highest purpose of mankind is self-realization and the improvement of life here and now, not salvation after death. This doctrine grew directly out of the period of religious innovation before World War I led by such organizations as the Society for Ethical Culture. But it took new and more effective organizational form with the creation of the International Humanist and Ethical Union (IHEU), founded in Holland in 1952, and it was given greater doctrinal clarity with the First Humanist Manifesto of 1933, the second in 1973, and the Secular Humanist Declaration of 1980.[47]

Internationally these ideas had some prominent and influential champions. To give just one example, the first head of the IHEU was Sir Julian Huxley, an influential British evolutionary biologist. Huxley had collaborated with H. G. Wells and his son to publish a three-volume popular science masterpiece titled *The Science of Life* in 1929, a book that helped to popularize the term *ecology*. In 1931 he cofounded Political and Economic Planning, a British think tank that would later play a role in building the British welfare state. In 1946 he became the first head of the United Nations Educational, Scientific, and Cultural Organization (UNESCO), the mission of which was to support human development, international scientific collaboration, human rights, and intellectual freedom and to combat racism and religious intolerance. As head of UNESCO Huxley advocated strongly for the use of contraception throughout the underdeveloped world as a way of preventing the "Population Bomb" from going off. In 1961 he helped found the World Wildlife Federation, which became an important part of the global environmental movement.[48] For cultural conservatives, Huxley was, simply put, a nightmare. A religious skeptic and popularizer of Darwinist evolutionary biology, he made key contributions to the United Nations, the global development project, the creation of the welfare state, and the environmental movement. He seemed to embody a kind of conspiracy—or at least a complex—of converging anti-religious ideas and organizations.

Perhaps most troubling of all for religious conservatives and fundamental-
ists, however, was the fear that by the middle of the 1970s this conspiracy, or
complex, was recruiting perhaps the largest group of people ever to the cause of
undermining traditional religious culture and traditional social structures.
That group was women.

THE GENDER REVOLUTION, 1950–2000

> Miss America represents what women are supposed to be: inoffensive, bland,
> apolitical. If you are tall, short, over or under what weight The Man prescribes
> you should be, forget it. Personality, articulateness, intelligence, and commit-
> ment—unwise. Conformity is the key to the crown—and, by extension, to suc-
> cess in our Society. In this reputedly democratic society, where every little boy
> supposedly can grow up to be President, what can every little girl hope to grow to
> be? Miss America.[49]
>
> New York Radical Women, 1968

The family, gender roles, and sexuality were of intense concern to the New
Right in those regions where religious conservatives formed a critical part of
the New Right coalition. This was not the case in large parts of the world. In
Britain, New Zealand and Australia, and much of Latin America, the New
Right was more purely a neoliberal movement, born out of the conviction that
free markets are economically superior to the welfare state. But in many other
societies the New Right was an alliance—in varying proportions—of neoliberal economic thought and fundamentalist religion. There, sex was a central,
even dominant concern.

The Catholic Church between the 1960s and 1980s offers an illuminating
example. Catholic social teaching had been an important part of the intellectual foundations of the welfare state in Europe in the 1950s and 1960s, and of
the project of worldwide development as well. The influence of John XXIII,
pope from 1958 to 1963, was vital in both respects. His encyclical "*Mater et
Magistra*" (1961) well articulated the central ideas of the welfare state and of
development, and "*Pacem in Terris*" (1963) urged peace, respect for human
rights, and international cooperation to overcome poverty, tyranny, and injustice globally.[50] John XXIII also undertook a historic overhaul of the Church
itself by calling the Second Vatican Council, which met from 1962 to 1965 and
streamlined and modernized the Church's government, loosened the rules
concerning public debate of theological points, opened up dialogue with other
Christian denominations and with Jews and Muslims, and replaced Latin with
local languages in religious ceremonies. As John put it, this was an effort to
"look to the present, to the new conditions and new forms of life introduced
into the modern world," to "update" Catholic practice and at the same time
"bring the modern world into contact with the vivifying and perennial energies
of the Gospel" and prove wrong the "prophets of doom" who saw nothing but

disaster in modernity.[51] He also sought reconciliation with the Jewish world (for example, by revising the traditional Good Friday prayer for the Jews—instead of "Let us pray for the faithless Jews," the faithful intoned, "Let us pray . . . for the Jews to whom God our Lord first spoke"), denounced imperialism, and welcomed women's expanding role in politics and society.[52]

His successor Paul VI at first followed in John's footsteps. He carried on the project of modernizing the Church, by, among other measures, imposing a mandatory retirement age of seventy-five for bishops and eighty for cardinals. He sought dialogue with other world religious leaders and created a Pontifical Council for Interreligious Dialogue in 1964; and he visited all six continents. He also played a role in pushing the Catholic Church in Spain toward a break with the authoritarian regime of Francisco Franco, which helped to bring down that regime in 1975. In 1967 he issued an encyclical that, echoing *"Mater et Magistra,"* encouraged wealthy nations to help poorer nations achieve economic growth and development; in 1968 he sanctioned a major conference of the Latin American bishops that put them on the side of the poor and of social justice. By the late 1960s, however, Paul VI began to take a number of aggressively conservative stances especially on issues related to sexuality. His 1968 encyclical "On Human Life" upheld the Church's opposition to birth control. More liberal Catholics were scandalized, but there was in fact a growing conservative reaction within the Church against what were seen as revolutionary, rather than liberal or progressive, tendencies in the Church and society.[53]

In 1978 the College of Cardinals elected John Paul II, who immediately became a pivotal figure for the global New Right. The new pope was from Poland, and his experiences in his native country had made him a vehement anti-communist. As pope he joined the global offensive against the tottering communist regimes in the 1980s—among other measures by signaling his sympathy with Solidarity, the independent, noncommunist Polish trade union that eventually broke the communist regime in Poland. John Paul II was anything but a mere reactionary, however. He criticized apartheid in South Africa, economic exploitation of the poor in the Third World, and consumerism and materialism in the world's wealthy societies. On a visit to the United States in 1987 he reminded his audience of American society's institutionalized racism and openly supported the Sanctuary Movement, which welcomed refugees from the oppressive and murderous Central American regimes supported by the US government. On a visit to Japan he implored, "Never again Hiroshima! Never again Auschwitz!"—implying moral equivalency between the two. He opposed dictatorships of the Right as well as of the Left, warned that free-market capitalism could be just as imperialistic as communism, and helped to internationalize the Church by appointing thirty new cardinals from twenty-four countries, thirteen of which were outside Europe. He advocated debt forgiveness—the idea of simply canceling the debts of nations that had been burned by the 1982 debt crisis.[54]

Arguably John Paul II's most important utterances as pope came in the form of a book of essays, *The Theology of the Body*, published in 1984, and the encyclical "Religion of Life" of 1995. In these texts he condemned abortion, extramarital sex, contraception, and homosexuality, as well as euthanasia, capital punishment, and war. He also called for what he called a "new feminism . . . which rejects the temptation of imitating models of 'male dominance' in order to acknowledge and affirm the true genius of women in every aspect of the life of society, and overcome all discrimination, violence and exploitation. You [women] are called to bear witness to the meaning of genuine love, of that gift of self and of that acceptance of others" that is central to marriage and should be central to all human relationships. "Motherhood involves a special communion with the mystery of life," and this communion "profoundly marks the woman's personality" and should be the foundation of her participation in society. In other writings—for example, an encyclical on labor in 1981—John Paul II argued in favor of the family wage (that is, an income paid to a male worker sufficient to support a family with the woman staying at home to care for the children). This was a comprehensively conservative vision of what family, gender roles, and sexuality should look like. It was also, from the viewpoint of sexual liberals, rather paranoid—associating, for example, contraception, abortion, war, and the death penalty as interconnected parts of what the pope labeled the modern "culture of death."[55]

But this was a vision widely shared among religious conservatives everywhere. Among the most notable was Phyllis Schlafly, one of the leaders of the Protestant evangelical women's movement in the United States. In 1978 a conservative Christian magazine interviewed Schlafly regarding her opposition to the Equal Rights Amendment (ERA), which would have anchored gender equality in the US Constitution. Schlafly explained that the ERA would "drive the wife out of the home, . . . convert us into a unisex society," eliminate husbands' obligations to support their wives, end women's exemption from military service, and would make women bitter, angry, and "anti-family." The women's liberation movement and ideal, she believed, was "a major cause of divorce. What it does to a woman is much like a disease." She deplored that fact that although the women's movement represented "basically a negative approach toward life," feminists were "making our laws. They are taking over our educational system and the media and they are going to get all the male jobs." They were "in league with pornographers" and sought to make it "impossible to have laws against homosexuals" and to "make homosexuals entitled to the same dignity and respect husbands and wives have." The "National Organization for Women (NOW)," she said, "has always been for the lesbian."[56]

Few New Right activists anywhere could match Schlafly's almost hallucinatory vision of feminist corruption. But in some places they gained greater influence over policy. In Iran, for example, the revolutionary regime of the early

1980s rescinded important women's rights introduced under the shah in the 1960s and 1970s, particularly in family law.[57]

Why was the religious New Right so intensely concerned about gender roles and sexuality? One important reason was the emergence of the so-called Second Wave of feminism in the developed world in the early 1970s—a powerful movement which argued that the promises of democracy, the welfare state, and the free world could not be realized until women had equal opportunities for self-development and self-realization. That meant access to education and careers, equal pay for equal work, protection against discrimination and violence, and equal rights and authority within marriage. That movement grew directly out of the concern of the welfare state to recognize the dignity and realize the potential of every citizen. It also had close ties to 1960s New Left politics that identified women as the largest among many groups whose most fundamental human rights were yet to be recognized and secured. The feminist movement was particularly powerful in Western Europe and North America, where significant advances in women's rights were made in the 1970s in family law, educational opportunities, employment law, anti-discrimination law, and the treatment of rape and domestic violence. Women played a growing role on the world political stage as well, taking office as prime ministers and presidents in sixteen nations between 1960 and 1990.[58]

The women's movements around the world also influenced the development policies of these years. Recall that a major shift occurred in development strategy in the 1970s, away from large industrial and infrastructure projects and toward human development. At the same time, development experts focused on limiting fertility. Out of those two concerns there grew a crucial new focus for development policy: on women's health and welfare, and on women's right to control their own fertility. In 1972 the United Nations (at the urging of its Commission on the Status of Women, established in 1946) declared that 1975 would be International Women's Year and that the decade 1976–85 would be the United Nations Decade of the Woman. At the First World Conference on Women in June 1975 in Mexico City, representatives from 133 nations met to discuss women's rights, and established the UN Development Fund for Women. At the second conference, in Copenhagen in 1980, sixty nations signed the Convention on the Elimination of All Forms of Discrimination Against Women. At the third conference, in Nairobi in 1985, member-state schedules were set for the removal of all legal discrimination against women by 2000.[59] In all of these endeavors, activists were guided in part by the language of human rights; in fact, an important development in the human rights discourse of the later 1970s and 1980s was its extension to include what had once been defined primarily as "social" rights—including women's rights to equal participation in politics and society, as well as the rights of children, the right of the poor to have basic needs met, and the rights of indigenous peoples.

At all these conferences, and at the International Conference on Population and Development in Cairo in 1994, many women advocated explicitly for family planning. The fourth conference, in Beijing in 1995, formalized this commitment, declaring: "The human rights of women include their right to have control over and decide freely and responsibly on matters related to their sexuality, including sexual and reproductive health, free of coercion, discrimination, and violence." That conference even invited governments to consider legalization of abortion, though it did not formally adopt that demand. But already at the first conference, in 1975, the rhetoric had been quite radical. That conference adopted a resolution stating, among other things, that "women of the entire world, whatever differences exist between them, share the painful experience of having received unequal treatment, and . . . as their awareness of this phenomenon increases they will become natural allies in the struggle against any form of oppression, such as is practiced under colonialism, neo-colonialism, Zionism, racial discrimination and apartheid, thereby constituting an enormous revolutionary potential for economic and social change in the world today."[60] Not surprisingly, all of these developments served only as further proof to the New Right that the United Nations was explicitly backing a radical, Third-World revolutionary, secular-humanist, sexually permissive agenda on an international scale.

Two broad structural developments in this period underlay and underlined these political initiatives by and for women—and drove cultural conservatives up the wall. One was the worldwide decline in fertility rates. That change was the product of economic development and opportunity, and of the spreading use of contraceptives of all kinds as part of the broader development of an affluent consumer society in which all kinds of goods are more readily available. Access to contraceptives had a profound effect on popular sexual practices and sexual values in much of the world, since it effectively eliminated one of the most important complicating consequences of promiscuity, unwanted pregnancy. The widening global deployment of antibiotics effectively eliminated the other consequence, venereal disease (until the rise of HIV/AIDS in the 1980s). By the 1970s many cultural conservatives around the world believed and feared that a global tidal wave of promiscuity was sweeping the world, a "sexual revolution."

A second and related structural development was an extraordinary transformation of the global labor force from the 1970s through the 1990s; in these three decades almost everywhere around the world, hundreds of millions of women flooded into paid employment (chart 9.12). Here too the timing differed from place to place, and there were exceptions, particularly where industries with a traditionally female labor force declined or where a large number of families migrated to follow men's job opportunities in new industries. But by the end of the 1990s, most of the world was converging toward a 40 or 45 percent female labor force.

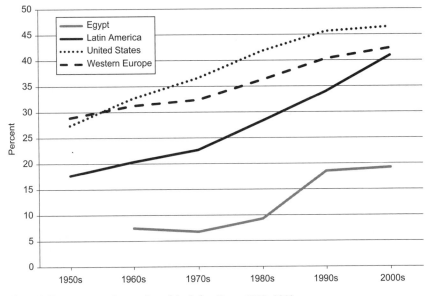

Chart 9.12 Women as a Proportion of the Labor Force, 1950–2009.

What is more, at least in the OECD countries for which we have reliable data, by the 1980s the gap between men's and women's average wages was falling nearly everywhere in the world (chart 9.13). This approach toward parity was partly due to the anti-discrimination laws that women's movements secured in a number of places. But it was also achieved because women were increasingly getting educations that better qualified them for managerial and technical positions—the kinds of well-paid work that had been almost exclusively reserved for men. In the United States, for example, whereas in the late 1960s only one in twenty law school students was female, by the early 2000s half were. The pattern in medical and business schools was similar.[61] This was the concrete background to Phyllis Schlafly's belief that feminists were going to take all the men's jobs. For many in the New Right, committed to a "traditional" model of the family (headed by one, male breadwinner), this extraordinary global trend posed a terrible challenge.

One reason for women's relative success in the global labor market was that they found employment particularly in the service sector—not in agriculture or industry, but in transport, communications, finance, and other services. A second reason stemmed from an extraordinary structural shift in the world economy: by the 1980s, service industries formed the most dynamic and most rapidly growing sector of the world economy (chart 9.14). In Western Europe and Latin America, by the year 2000 three-quarters of women and only half of men worked in the service sector; in the United States, it was 67 percent of men

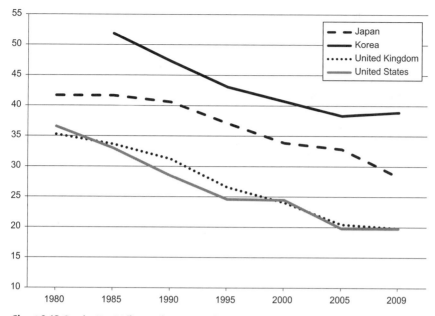

Chart 9.13 Gender Pay Differential since 1980 (percentage difference between women's and men's median wage).

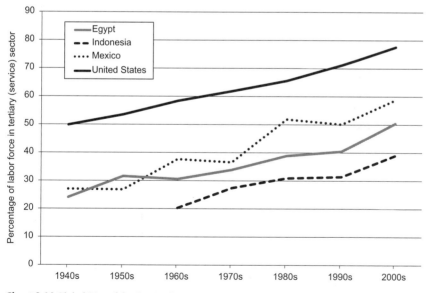

Chart 9.14 Global Rise of the Service Sector, 1940–2009.

and 89 percent of women. In much of the developing world the difference was less pronounced—only 37 and 41 percent in Indonesia, for example—in part because employment in industry in many developing countries was still growing faster than employment in services. But again, in most of the world women were getting paid jobs much faster than men, partly because they were seizing new opportunities in the service sector.

Almost everywhere, then, women were entering the labor force in large numbers. Almost everywhere, they were limiting their fertility drastically in order to have the time to obtain the requisite education for those jobs. The secular humanists in the United Nations, supported by feminists across the globe, were advocating for women's right to do that. The model of the family wage and stay-at-home mother, along with the notion of the stable family as the foundation for a civilized society, was eroding rapidly. Given the opportunity, people sought to maximize family income in order to enjoy greater material security and comfort. Pope John Paul II, in "The Religion of Life" in 1995, called this "economism"; the problem, he believed, was that people increasingly thought that things are more important than people. That kind of complaint was a common theme coming from the New Right around the world—that values, not things, should be the focus of human life.

This development helped to reveal tensions within the New Right in much of the world. Globally half of the New Right was neoliberal, convinced that free markets and democracy go hand in hand and are superior to anything else. The other half was conservative and religious, convinced that certain values had to be defended even against the market. The expansion of women's employment around the globe in the 1970s and 1980s was evidence that the free market was winning out over the commitment of cultural conservatives to the "traditional," single-earner family as the core of social life. In that context, one might expect that these two commitments would come to be understood as mutually contradictory and that neoliberals and religious conservatives would go their separate ways.

In fact, nothing is more indicative of the "schizophrenia" of the New Right than the crucial role played in it by . . . women. The most emblematic case is Margaret Thatcher. Raised in a strict Methodist family, Thatcher earned a university degree in chemistry, entered British politics in the early 1950s (then in her mid-twenties), was elected to Parliament in 1959, became a cabinet minister in 1970, and served as prime minister from 1979 to 1990—Britain's longest-serving prime minister in the twentieth century, and the archetypal neoliberal New Right leader for most of the world.[62] Another example is Violeta Chamorro, who was elected president of Nicaragua in 1990 after a long, bitter struggle, first against the US-backed Somoza dictatorship (which jailed and then assassinated her husband, an opposition newspaper editor) and then against the Marxist revolutionary Sandinista movement that toppled Somoza. Assisted by US funding, Chamorro rapidly moved to adopt neoliberal economic policies after her election.[63] A third case in point is Ayn Rand, a Russian immigrant to the United States and a vehement critic of both socialism and the welfare state who was a highly influential ideological leader for the New Right worldwide.

The roles each of these three women played suggest one critical reason that the New Right did not split. It was welded together by an overridingly important shared project: anti-communism and the fear that the welfare state would undermine the importance of families and churches—and thereby pave the way for godless communism. For many neoliberals and religious conservatives alike, communism was worse than anything else, and the welfare state was as good as communist. Ayn Rand, for example, denounced the Medicare program (government-supported medical insurance for the elderly) in her adopted country as an example of the "appalling recklessness with which men propose, discuss and accept 'humanitarian' projects which are to be imposed by political means, that is, *by force*, on an unlimited number of human beings." Medicare was, she argued, evidence both of a "criminal" mentality identical to that of bank robbers ("There is no moral difference between these two examples") and of the communist mentality, which she characterized as the "savage, blind, ghastly, bloody unreality" that motivates the "collectivized soul."[64]

In the late 1980s and early 1990s, however, the Cold War suddenly came unraveled. Most of the communist single-party states—with important exceptions—disintegrated at the end of the 1980s. This was perhaps the most important political upheaval of the long twentieth century. And for the New Right it was a tremendous triumph and vindication. Not coincidentally, however, between about 1985 and 2000 a large number of dictatorships of all kinds, not just communist ones, also fell apart. This was, in other words, a massive and triumphal wave of democratic revolution, one that eroded and then broke authoritarian regimes of both the Right and the Left.

Chapter 10 turns to that development.

Democracy and Capitalism Triumphant?

THE GLOBAL TRIUMPH OF DEMOCRACY AFTER 1980

> In trying to paralyze life . . . the authorities paralyze themselves and, in the long run, incapacitate themselves for paralyzing life. . . . The machine that worked so well for years, to apparent perfection, faultlessly, without a hitch, falls apart overnight. The system that seemed likely to reign unchanged, world without end, since nothing could call its power into question amid all those unanimous votes and elections, is shattered without warning.[1]
>
> Vaclav Havel, 1975

Chapter 9 discusses a complex of sweeping changes in the world economy and in global society, to which the New Right was largely a response—functional differentiation and secularization, the growing power of the state, the sexual revolution, the surge in women's employment. These were massive, tectonic shifts that no imaginable public policy could really do more than slightly modify or slow. In that sense, the agenda of the conservative religious "branch" or "version" of the New Right faced a monumental challenge. The New Right's integral nationalist branch faced the same problem. Differential fertility patterns meant that the movement of tens of millions of people from parts of the globe rich in people to parts of the globe rich in opportunity was simply irresistible, because economically necessary. In some respects, therefore, ultimately the New Right was doomed to fail from the outset.

Yet in one crucial respect, the New Right was a triumphal success: communism collapsed. In 1989 and 1990, all the communist regimes of Eastern Europe, including the Soviet Union, simply disintegrated, replaced by more or less democratic political systems and more or less free-market economies. It turned out that the New Right was correct about communism: it was, as Ronald Reagan said, a sad and bizarre story, the last chapters of which were being written already in 1980. But that development in Eastern Europe was only one part of the extraordinary global triumph of democratic politics and free-market economics, which had roots reaching back to the middle of the 1970s.[2]

The scope of this wave of democratization was astonishing. Until the mid-1970s most of the world was governed by dictatorships of one kind or another. By one count, in 1975 there were 35 liberal democracies in the world, 101 authoritarian governments, and 11 that fell somewhere in between. Twenty years later there were 78 liberal democracies, 43 authoritarian governments, and 43 that fell somewhere in between.[3] From the mid-1970s a wave of revolutions toppled dictatorial regimes, beginning with the late-fascist regimes in Portugal and Spain (1974 and 1975), the military dictatorship in Greece (1974), and the shah of Iran (1979). In the early and mid-1980s, Latin American dictatorships began to stumble under the impact of the debt crisis and "austerity" programs, which cost them what popular legitimacy they had left. After being defeated in a short war with Great Britain (over the Islas Malvinas [Falkland Islands]) in 1982, the Argentine military dictatorship disintegrated in 1983; by 1990 seventeen of twenty nations in Latin America had democratic governments—an exact reversal of the situation in 1980.[4] By the late 1980s, this trend spread to Asia as well, starting with the Philippines in 1986. At the end of the 1980s, it was the communist regimes' turn in Eastern Europe, and in the 1990s, dictatorships all over Africa stumbled and fell.

The "People Power" revolution in the Philippines helped set the pattern of these revolutions. The quasi-military, quasi-plebiscitary, oligarchical regime of Ferdinand Marcos was overthrown in 1986 by a nonviolent mass mobilization that brought 2 million protesters into the streets of Manila. Until that time, Marcos had dominated the country for twenty-one years, holding mostly rigged elections, declaring martial law when necessary, and receiving financial and military support from the United States (because he was fighting a Marxist peasant insurgency). The key leader of the opposition, Benigno Aquino, was assassinated at the Manila airport when he returned from exile in 1983; that murder sparked an expanding civil resistance movement, and when Marcos stole the presidential election of 1986, the country blew up in a gigantic wave of popular protest. The military divided, the Catholic Church turned publicly against Marcos, Ronald Reagan withdrew US support for the government, and Marcos fled the country (for exile in Hawai'i), while Benigno Aquino's widow, Corazon, was declared president.[5]

Over the following decade and beyond, that scenario was repeated over and over again, with local variations, in every part of the world. There were some terrible failures. In Zimbabwe the Marxist one-party regime that emerged after the end of white rule in 1980 clung to power despite having wrecked the country's economy completely. In Zaire, civil war and genocide in Rwanda in the early 1990s gave rise to a multisided civil and regional war that by 2004 had killed probably 3.8 million people (not counting up to a million killed in genocidal violence in Rwanda).[6] In the former Yugoslavia the birth of six different independent nations out of the collapse of that state cost some 200,000 lives. In China a confused and chaotic attempt to open the political system controlled by the Communist Party oligarchy was defeated by military force in 1989. In other countries peaceful democratic revolutions gave rise to quasi-oligarchic regimes, widespread corruption, and fragile governments. And by the middle of the 2010s the results of a series of popular uprisings in the Middle East and North Africa starting in 2011—the "Arab Spring"—suggested that for much of this region the only viable political alternatives were military dictatorship or theocracy. Nevertheless, this was ultimately the biggest wave of regime change in history, and it was far more successful than the wave of regime change during the "global revolutionary moment" of the early twentieth century. It was also mostly bloodless. The results have been devastating for the Congo, Bosnia, and more recently Syria, but these disasters pale in comparison to the wreckage left by the early-twentieth-century revolutions in Mexico, Russia, Turkey, and China.

The democratization wave also toppled every sort of autocratic regime. In Eastern Europe it overthrew bureaucratic communist regimes in 1989–90; in Mexico, three-quarters of a century of nominally socialist one-party rule gradually wound down through multiple elections in the dozen years after 1988, with a new political party forming the government for the first time in 2000. In East Africa a raft of so-called African socialist one-party dictatorships collapsed in the 1990s. Tanzania held its first free elections since independence (in the early 1960s) in 1995, Zambia in 1991, Kenya in 1992. A number of similar regimes were dismantled in West Africa—for example, in Senegal in 1999. But in South Africa, democratization overthrew the apartheid regime, which had been a democracy for white people only and a capitalist economic powerhouse. In 1990 the leader of the African National Congress (ANC), Nelson Mandela, was released after more than two decades in prison, and in 1994 the country had its first democratic elections ever (which Mandela won). Nigeria suffered five successful and two failed military coups between 1966 and 1999, and was ruled by military dictators for twenty-nine of those thirty-three years; but in May 1999 it held the first elections in sixteen years, establishing a democratic regime that might actually survive.[7]

In fact, while "1989" is usually thought of as the revolution that destroyed communism, in most of the rest of the world the late 1980s and 1990s saw the collapse of anti-communist military regimes. In Indonesia a mass nonviolent uprising in 1998 finally overthrew the military-oligarchic regime installed in 1965; a complicated three-year transition resulted, by 2002, in the election of Megawati Sukarnoputri as prime minister, the daughter of the Republic's first president.[8] In Taiwan, martial law was in effect from 1949 until 1987, but fully open elections were then allowed in 1992, and by 2000 the country had its first non-KMT government. In South Korea, in June 1987 1 million people poured into the streets of Seoul, and five years later, the country had its first civilian president in thirty years. In South America, oligarchic-military dictatorship, which had been the usual form of government since the Great Depression, collapsed in the course of the 1980s. Argentina was an extraordinary case: the country had suffered military coups in 1930, 1943, 1955, 1966, and 1976; in the late 1970s and early 1980s more than 30,000 people were "disappeared" by a military government threatened by New Left radicals. But from 1983 onward democracy gradually prevailed, and by 2003 Argentina even ended the amnesty for the military officers who had murdered all those people. Brazil ended twenty-one years of military dictatorship in 1985, then held free elections in 1989.

Nor is it mere coincidence that in some countries political parties that had consistently won free elections for decades finally lost power in the early 1990s. In Italy, for example, in 1994 the Christian Democratic-Socialist alliance that had kept Europe's largest communist party out of government for a half century imploded in a wave of corruption trials that ultimately destroyed all of Italy's major political parties. In Japan in 1993 a similar set of scandals split the ruling Liberal Democratic Party and yielded a non-LDP government for the first time since World War II.

Different immediate causes brought about the collapse of authoritarian (or oligarchic) rule in different places. The debt crisis was critical in Latin America. In a few cases military defeats played a key role (for Argentina in the Falklands in 1982, for the Soviet Union in Afghanistan by 1987, for South Africa in Angola in 1988). In South Korea, Taiwan, Thailand, and South Africa the removal of the United States' motivation to support "front line" states in the Cold War was important. At bottom, though, there was one fundamental, underlying cause: it turned out that dictatorship was simply incompatible with the ongoing and accelerating global economic revolution.

The communist dictatorships in Eastern Europe present the clearest case of this incongruity. It had become evident as early as the late 1960s that the centrally controlled, centrally planned command economies established by communist regimes simply were not terribly adept at sustaining economic growth past an early stage of intensive development of heavy industry and basic infrastructure—building railroads, steel mills, and power plants, digging coal mines and drilling oil wells. Economic growth in Eastern Europe slowed steadily after the mid-1960s, until ultimately it lagged far behind that in Western Europe (see chart 8.6). In fact, three leading scientists in the Soviet Union submitted an open letter to the Soviet leadership in 1970 that diagnosed quite precisely all the problems that would eventually lead to the Soviet Union's collapse. The Soviet system, they warned, did not foster technological innovation, and "new means of developing production potential are not being discovered or properly put to use, and technical progress has slowed down abruptly"; the leading modern industries, chemicals and computers, were lagging drastically behind their counterparts' development in the West; "our total expenditures for education in all forms are three times below what they are in the United States and are rising at a slower rate"; crime, corruption, bureaucracy, and lack of initiative were spreading; shortages were deepening. Why? Technological innovation and scientific advance require free and open inquiry and discussion, but under the Soviet system "we encounter certain insurmountable obstacles on the road to the free exchange of ideas and information, . . . an obvious lack of confidence in creatively thinking, critical, and energetic individuals, . . . the advancement up the rungs of the official ladder not of those who distinguish themselves by their professional qualities and commitment to principles but of those who verbally proclaim their devotion to the Party." A "scientific approach demands full information, impartial thinking, and creative freedom," yet the Soviet regime favored instead politicization and toadyism; "dynamism and creativity" were being stifled by the "bureaucratic, ritualistic, dogmatic, openly hypocritical, and mediocre style that reigns . . . today."[9]

Two decades later, the Soviet system collapsed as a result of these very problems. The Soviet regime's survival was underpinned from 1970 to 1989 in large part by high oil prices. The Soviet Union became a major exporter of oil and gas from Siberia to Western Europe, earning hard currency that propped the regime up even as the rest of the economy faltered. When oil prices collapsed in the mid-1980s, the regime stumbled and fell. In any case, though, by then, the economic, social, and environmental performance of the East European communist regimes was so completely outclassed by the democratic capitalist West that there was effectively no argument to be made for trying to salvage them. In fact, as the older generation of communists who had created these regimes thirty or forty years earlier began to die, in a number of countries younger communists actually reformed their own systems out of existence—driven forward, in most cases, by tens and hundreds of thousands of protesters in the streets.

The Soviet Union's collapse meant that the West's incentive to support military dictatorships as a bulwark against communist subversion suddenly evaporated. Ironically, the implosion of communism dealt a fatal blow to right-wing dictatorships. The apartheid regime in South Africa, for example, gave up its resistance to democracy in 1990. Although the regime had been undermined by mounting internal subversion, external boycotts and sanctions, and military defeat in Angola in 1988, the actual transition to democracy was eased by the USSR's collapse. The head of the ANC's military branch was also the chairman of the South African Communist Party, but the end of the USSR effectively eliminated the fear that a post-apartheid regime, influenced by Moscow, would drift toward communism. Something similar happened in Central America. The United States waged a bitter proxy war in Nicaragua against the Marxist

Sandinista government there, and supported the government of El Salvador against a Marxist insurgency. Both those countries made the transition to peace and democracy in the early 1990s. Without the backing of cold warriors in the United States and Soviet Union, neither side could make civil war pay; so they reached a settlement.

While Eastern European communist regimes collapsed because they were unable to keep pace with the ongoing economic revolution, in much of the underdeveloped world, economic success actually helped undermine dictatorship. In South Korea and Taiwan, oligarchic-military governments carefully fostered industrial growth from the late 1940s through the early 1980s, creating what some called guided capitalism or the planned free economy. The policy instruments they used included tariff protection for key industries; closely controlled prices, wages, profits, and interest and exchange rates; limitations on foreign ownership and the expatriation of profits by foreign investors; subsidies, cheap credit, and tax incentives; state ownership of key industries and infrastructure; government-promoted formation of major integrated industrial conglomerates; and long-term economic planning. Most of these techniques were copied from Japan, whose oligarchical but democratic government had pioneered them. The whole system was in part bankrolled by massive American military and economic aid, which supplied 80 percent of South Korean investment capital between 1953 and 1961. Some American businessmen and members of Congress complained that in effect "our assistance programs were actually subsidizing state socialism," as one put it. But the United States tolerated and encouraged these policies because all three states were seen as critical to the containment of communism.[10] Singapore, Malaysia, Thailand, Indonesia, and some Latin American countries—particularly Brazil—adopted less thoroughgoing versions of a similar economic strategy. Many of these regimes also made a massive investment in education. Brazil, for example, cut its illiteracy rate in half between 1950 and 1980 (from 50.6 percent to 25.5 percent), and Mexico cut illiteracy by almost two-thirds (43.2 to 16 percent).[11]

But affluent and educated people tend to be critical of the world around them, accustomed as they are to thinking for themselves, seeking out information, analyzing problems, and proposing solutions. Educated people read newspapers and books, they listen to radio and watch television, and they form views on subjects of public importance. Where they are denied opportunities for meaningful political participation, they often join nongovernmental organizations and thereby create a civil society in which they and others can discuss ideas, problems, and policies. In the 1970s and 1980s, rising levels of per capita income had an important psychological and cultural impact. In many countries around the world by the 1980s, the question of mere survival was effectively resolved. A new generation had come to adulthood who were increasingly ready to focus not on just keeping their heads down and getting by, but on being active citizens. Social psychologists and political scientists refer to this as the transition from "survival values" to "self-expression" values.[12] All these patterns of behavior and thought help to erode the systems of patronage and deference on which authoritarian regimes rely. As one study of South Africa in the 1970s puts it, "In the wider public domain created by literacy and urbani[zation], there was room for a different kind of politics in which ideology and camaraderie would . . . replace deferential personalized loyalties" to leaders—and eventually bring down the racist apartheid regime there.[13]

Beyond values and behaviors, "real development" also gave people the practical wherewithal to organize in order to express their political aspirations. In Leipzig in 1989, Manila in 1986, Santiago in 1988, Jakarta in 1998, Seoul in 1987—over and over again the ability to mobilize hundreds of thousands of people to gather in the street and demand political change played a critical part in transitions to democracy. Such mobilization was made possible in part by urbanization. It was difficult early in the twentieth century to marshal rural populations for this kind of political purpose. Not only were they mostly illiterate, with little access to any means of communication, but they also resided far from the centers of government and were scattered. In the 1970s and 1980s many societies around the world crossed a critical threshold: they now had populations that were 20, 30, or 35 percent urban—in Latin America 50 to 60 percent. Simply in geographical terms, these populations were more able to take part in political mobilization.

Urban people also increasingly had access to new, critical communications technologies, one of which was the portable transistor radio. In Manila in 1986 the radio station of the Catholic Church, Radio Veritas, helped keep people informed of events. Its message could reach people because they had handheld radios. By the late 1980s there was a radio for every ten people in the Philippines, one for every seven Indonesians, and enough radios in South Korea for every man, woman, and child to have one. Telephone ownership, too, rose rapidly in most of the world in the 1980s and 1990s (chart 10.1).[14] Civic organizations around the world in the 1980s used the "telephone tree," whereby each participant was assigned other people to call, who in turn called others, to get the word out. A handheld telephone or radio is a powerful political tool. By the late 1980s many people living under various forms of dictatorships had them.

Thus in many of countries democracy triumphed not because dictatorship had been an economic failure, as in Eastern Europe, but because it had succeeded. Again, in that sense the New Right seemed by the turn of the millennium to have been correct: capitalism and democracy did go hand in hand.

Yet, by the end of this cycle of revolutions, particularly after the year 2000, there were also reasons to doubt that belief. Three telling cases can sum up the arguments in concrete form. One is that of New Zealand. Historically, despite the white settler regime's expropriation and exploitation of the indigenous Maori inhabitants, New Zealand was in some respects one of the more democratic countries on earth. It was the first nation, for example, to grant women

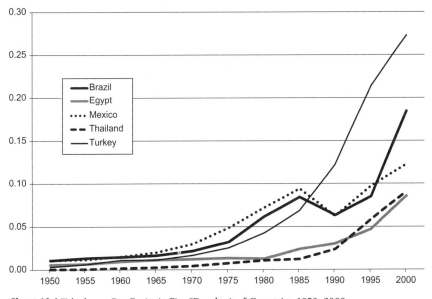

Chart 10.1 Telephones Per Capita in Five "Developing" Countries, 1950–2000.

the right to vote, in 1893. By the 1970s New Zealand was one of the wealthiest societies on earth, and was also a model of social-democratic policy in health care, accident compensation, labor law, and housing. It was even beginning to redress the historical injustice of the settlement process, by establishing an institutional mechanism for transferring some public assets in land and resources (and some cash) to the descendants of those whom the settler state had dispossessed. By the end of the 1980s, however, this welfare regime was groaning under the weight of debt and changing patterns of world trade. In the course of the 1990s it was partially dismantled in a neoliberal quasi-revolution. Capitalism, in other words, could triumph even where democracy was healthy.

The case of India tells a similar story. With the exception of brief periods of instability in the 1970s and 1980s, involving, among other episodes, the assassination of two prime ministers, in 1984 and 1991, India had maintained a successful and stable political democracy for a half century by 2000. It had also leaned, in its economic policy, toward socialism—complete with five-year plans, a fixed exchange rate, extensive public ownership of industrial and financial enterprises, intense regulation of the economy, protective tariffs as part of an "import substitution" strategy, and even an important economic relationship with the Soviet Union. The results were respectable but not impressive—a growth rate in real per capita income averaging just under 2 percent per year from independence through the 1980s. But India faced a debt crisis in 1991, and the government launched a program of substantial economic liberalization. The economy was opened to international investment (by 1998, twenty times as high as in 1991) and trade, business and industry underwent extensive privatization and deregulation, the average tariff rate dropped from 79 percent to 20 percent by 2004, top income and corporate tax rates were lowered by 40 percent, and average annual growth in real per capita income accelerated from nearly 4 percent in the 1990s to 6 percent in the 2000s.[15]

China offers the opposite lesson: that capitalism can triumph in the absence of democracy. The imposition of collectivized agriculture and decentralized industrial production in the so-called Great Leap Forward at the end of the 1950s had devastated the Chinese economy, and millions starved. Between 1966 and 1968 the bizarre political upheaval of the "Cultural Revolution"—the outpouring of popular discontent and utopianism in which Mao Zedong attempted to mobilize young people, in particular, against entrenched bureaucratic interests, corruption, and "bourgeois" consciousness—generated further disruption and dislocation. Casualties may have been as high as a million, and the army was called in to end the chaos. Overall, per capita income in China grew at just under 3 percent from the formation of the People's Republic in 1949 to 1980—a healthy rate, but less than half that of its capitalist neighbors Japan and Taiwan (after 1949 the Republic of China, under KMT rule).

In the early 1970s, however, China drastically revised its position with respect to the rest of the world. After falling out with the Soviet Union in the 1960s, China's leadership established a de facto alliance with the United States and Japan in 1971 and 1972. Diplomatic relations were more or less normalized; the mainland People's Republic took the seat on the UN Security Council until then held by the Republic of China on Taiwan; and over the next five years reformers led by Deng Xiaoping gained control of the one-party regime. After the death of Mao in 1976, the Chinese government launched a massive economic reform program. During the 1970s Chinese agriculture made substantial progress, with use of fertilizers almost tripling and that of tractors more than quintupling. In 1983 the regime almost completely abandoned the system of collective farms. By 1986 use of fertilizers and tractors had doubled again, and rural use of electric power was six times what it had been in 1970. From the early 1980s forward, the regime introduced wage and bonus incentives in industry, shifted from production-based to profit-based management goals, decentralized banking, lowered tariffs and other barriers to trade, reduced restrictions on foreign direct investment, loosened government control of prices, and opened "special economic zones" to foreign investors (focused at first on Chinese living in Hong Kong, Taiwan, and Singapore, and later on investors from South Korea, Japan, the United States, and Europe).[16] It also adopted many of the industrialization policies that Japan, Taiwan, and South Korea had employed successfully—including tax incentives, subsidies, cheap credit, price controls, and encouragement or public ownership of massive industrial conglomerates. The new constitution in 1999 referred to China's "socialist market economy." In the context of extremely low wages and severe labor discipline, these policies generated a massive influx of capital from abroad. The central government shed half its workforce and privatized a major proportion of industry. To make sure productivity gains were not frittered away by high population growth, in 1979 the regime also introduced a draconian one-child system, creating severe financial disincentives to reproduction—a policy that echoed, in a more authoritarian key, an earlier policy in Japan, the government-supported "New Life Movement," which had encouraged small families on a voluntary basis.[17]

The results were spectacular: average annual growth in per capita income of just under 6 percent from 1980 to 2000, rising to over 9 percent in 2000–2010. Along the way China built a private-sector economy larger than its public sector by around 2000.[18] By the early twenty-first century, China was the world's greatest exporting nation. In 1980 it accounted for less than 1 percent of world exports; by 2010 its proportion had risen to 10 percent. Of the major economic regions in the world, only Europe still exported more.[19] The social rewards of this economic success were enormous: per capita incomes in China doubled from 1975 to 1987, doubled again from 1987 to 2000, and then doubled again from 2000 to 2008.[20] These figures are approximate; estimates of Chinese per capita income are highly unreliable and vary widely depending on assumptions regarding real purchasing power—from one-eleventh to one-quarter of the US average. What is more, the process of economic change within China has been accompanied by enormous social strain and hardship; in some cases the organization of labor migration within China has generated forms of employment similar to debt peonage. But the direction of change, here as in much of the rest of Asia, is clear: rapid growth and a gradual narrowing of the gap with the world's wealthier societies.[21]

By 2010 the contrast between India and China suggested an irony. The former case appeared to show that democracy is an environment in which capitalism flourishes; the latter case suggested that (political) communism is an even better one. In both cases rising inequality and corruption has generated intense dissent, but at this writing, unless economic catastrophe strikes the triumph of capitalism appears clearly irreversible in both countries. It is difficult to know at this point, however, what deeper message this irony might hold. The New Right might predict that democracy will inevitably come to China as economic development proceeds, as knowledge of the outside world spreads, as the means of communication and information dissemination penetrate ever deeper into the social fabric, and as a middle class of business and expertise grows. Pessimists might suggest instead that the growth of inequality in both countries indicates that the political form most likely to succeed in the present century is plebiscitary oligarchy—rule by billionaires, underwritten by elections in which control of the media is an important advantage.

Recent developments in electoral politics in Europe and North America, where billionaire businessmen increasingly dominate elections, may underline this latter message. A particularly sorry example is the Italian media mogul Silvio Berlusconi, who was the decisive figure in Italian politics for two decades despite presiding over a government that consistently and comprehensively deepened the country's problems rather than solving them. But elections in the United States, too, have increasingly attracted various more or less eccentric billionaires. At least partially oligarchical structures of business and politics seem typical of many large developing countries as well, including Russia and Indonesia.[22]

The economic results have been mixed: not so good in Italy, where per capita income is declining relative to the rest of Europe; but excellent in China, where the raging pace of economic growth allowed the Communist government to shift toward policies designed to equalize educational opportunity, increase job security and workplace safety, and accelerate technological innovation.[23] And economics aside, intense debate currently prevails over what all this means for the future of politics and policy. In 1999 the American political scientist Francis Fukuyama reiterated the liberal faith of the nineteenth century with undiminished verve: "Nothing causes me to doubt my conclusion: liberal democracy and the market economy are the sole viable possibilities for modern society."[24] A more skeptical observer might conclude that the trend is toward central economic direction by a ruling oligarchy of the superwealthy.

"FINANCIALIZATION"

> When I first stepped out on to the trading floor, I could smell and see the money ... instant money—it was hanging in the air right in front of me, invisible but highly charged, just waiting to be earthed. . . . [A]ll I had to do was give the right signals and it would charge through me as if I were a copper conductor.[25]
>
> Nick Leeson, 1996

In fact—ironically enough—there is one further factor that played a key role in driving democratization in the 1980s and 1990s: financial crisis. Some dictatorships in this period were fairly effective in fostering economic growth, but many were relatively bad at maintaining fiscal discipline. They tended to build up debt. One important reason was the extreme corruption of many. Another was their political fragility, stemming from their lack of legitimacy, so that it was difficult for them to raise and collect taxes. A third reason was that they were often dependent on their military establishments, which they kept happy by buying expensive modern arms and hiring lots of officers. In the 1980s and 1990s these weaknesses came to have important implications. In Latin America the debt crisis of 1982 played a key role in cracking authoritarian regimes, for example, in Argentina, Brazil, and Chile. A second financial crisis in the late 1990s did the same for Mexico and Indonesia. Dictatorships turned out to be poor at managing financial volatility. And the international financial market was increasingly volatile in the last quarter of the twentieth century.

The governments of most of the new democracies that emerged between 1980 and 2000 adopted many of the elements of neoliberal economic policy—the so-called Washington Consensus on what generates economic growth. The list included privatizing state-owned businesses and resources; deregulating industries and the financial sector (by, for example, reducing limitations on how many different kinds of business that banks could engage in, or how much capital they had to have on hand to back loans); loosening regulations on incoming foreign investment; lowering barriers to international trade; lowering tax rates; and granting tax concessions to foreign investors, including internal free-trade or free-enterprise zones.[26] But again, it was not only the new democracies that adopted such policies. India (an "old" democracy) and China (not a democracy) did the same.[27] As a result, the average world tariff rate fell from the late 1980s onward (see chart 7.11). Average tariff rates in the developing world fell from 34.4 percent in the early 1980s to 12.6 percent in 2000, and nontariff barriers, such as import quotas, fell in most of the developing world as well.[28] In fact, through the 1990s, a number of international agreements created several enormous free-trade zones, including Mercosur, a customs union created in 1991 between Argentina, Brazil, Paraguay, and Uruguay, with Bolivia and Venezuela joining later; the European Union and the adoption of a single European currency in 1992; and the North American Free Trade Agreement (NAFTA) between the United States, Canada, and Mexico in 1995. The results could be extraordinary: the value of trade between the Mercosur nations quadrupled in the first five years after that agreement was signed.[29] Those multilateral agreements were complemented by the negotiation in the 1990s of a sudden avalanche of bilateral investment treaties, which reduced regulations on foreign investment, and of double-taxation agreements, which encouraged the movement of capital from one country to another by ensuring that people were not taxed twice (chart 10.2). The Green Revolution, which generated expanding global wheat and rice exports, further stoked international trade (chart 10.3). And the shift in the composition of world trade—the rising level of industrial exports from the developing world—did the same (see chart 9.7). For all these reasons the percentage of global GDP accounted for by trade rose from 10.5 in 1973 to 17.2 percent in 1998—more than three times what it had been in 1950, and more than twice what it had been in 1913.[30]

Real development and the creation of a more open environment for trade in the new democracies around the world also generated enormous opportunities for investment. In particular, foreign direct investment (FDI) in the developing world expanded at a meteoric pace—twice as fast as world GDP between 1970 and 2010. More than thirty times as much foreign investment (adjusted for inflation) flowed into India, Indonesia, China, and Thailand in the 2000s as in

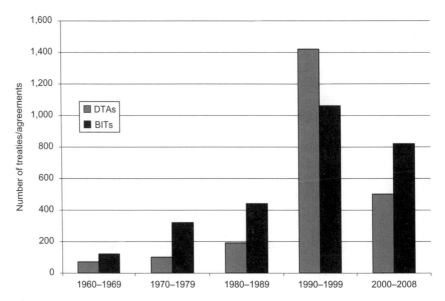

Chart 10.2 Bilateral Investment Treaties (BITs) and Double-Taxation Agreements (DTAs) Signed, 1960–2008.

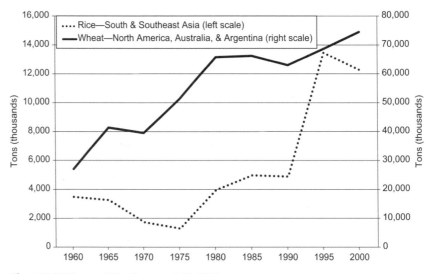

Chart 10.3 Wheat and Rice Exports, 1960–2000.

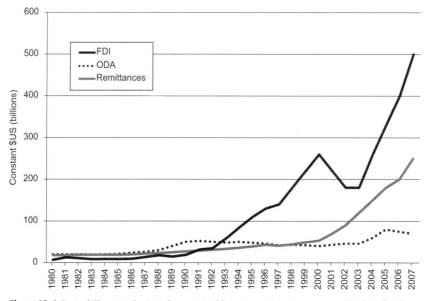

Chart 10.4 Capital Flows to the Developing World: Foreign Direct Investment (FDI), Official Development Aid (ODA), and Remittances, 1980–2007.

the 1980s. Foreigners invested eight times as much in Nigeria and Senegal in the 2000s as in the 1970s, and eight times as much in Mexico, Chile, Argentina, and Brazil in the 2000s as in the 1980s.[31] The United States lagged behind, at "only" three times as much; Europe was only just behind at seven times as much. In inflation-adjusted terms, world GDP in 2010 was four times what it had been in 1970; world exports were eight and a half times; outward foreign direct investment almost eighteen and a half times.[32]

An increasingly important further source of capital for the developing world was remittances. Many of the millions of workers who moved from Africa or the Middle East to Europe, or from South and Southeast Asia to the Persian Gulf states, or from Latin America to the United States sent some of their earnings "home" to their countries of origin—to buy real estate, support families, or start businesses. And official development aid (ODA), while it did not grow at anything like the rate the other capital flows did, was still not insignificant. Taken altogether, a veritable avalanche of money was flowing into the developing world by the first years of the twenty-first century (chart 10.4).

Because the European economies were increasingly integrated, most foreign direct investment in the world continued to go to developed economies. But the gap narrowed radically. In the 1970s and 1980s Western Europe, the United States, Japan, Canada, Australia, and New Zealand received 75 percent of world foreign investments; by the 2000s their proportion fell to just under 55 percent;

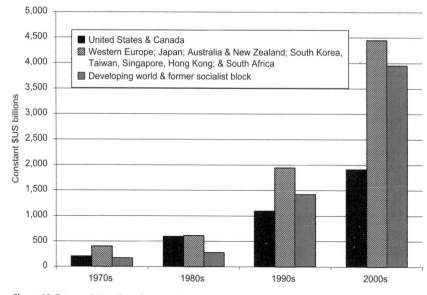

Chart 10.5 Inward FDI Flows by Decade, 1970–2009.

and by the early 2010s, the developing world received the majority of foreign direct investment flows. If South Africa, South Korea, Taiwan, Singapore, and Hong Kong were counted as "developing" nations, the figure would be 61.5 percent (chart 10.5). What is more, in the more developed economies by the year 2000, almost 90 percent of FDI actually took the form of spending on mergers and acquisitions—not expanding economic activity, but merely shifting ownership. In contrast, only a third of FDI in the developed world was accounted for by mergers and acquisitions.[33]

A significant feature of this period, furthermore, is that foreign direct investment from outside the old centers of financial power grew much faster than investment from inside those old centers. US investors put more than six times as much money (adjusted for inflation) into foreign investments in the 2000s as in the 1980s; and West Europeans, just under six times as much. But investors in Taiwan, South Korea, Singapore, Hong Kong, the Middle East, and North Africa committed about fifteen times as much, and investors in China, Thailand, and Latin America about thirty times as much (chart 10.6). In 1970 the developed world had accounted for almost all outward FDI; by 2010 that had fallen to 60.8 percent. If we count South Africa, Taiwan, South Korea, Singapore, and Hong Kong as still-"developing" nations, by 2010 the majority of outward FDI came from the developing world.[34]

One further factor driving the growth of investment was that the cost of communications and financial transactions plummeted after the 1970s. From

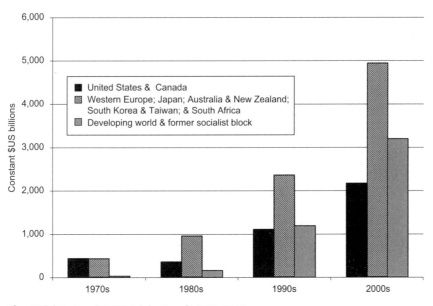

Chart 10.6 Outward FDI Totals by Decade, 1970–2009.

the early 1970s the pace of technological change in communications accelerated, creating a communications network of qualitatively different capacity. Through the early 1980s both multinational or transnational business management and global financial transactions had to rely on telegraph or telephone systems, which could not carry large data volumes. The first telephone cable laid across the Atlantic Ocean, in 1956, could carry only thirty-six simultaneous conversations. The telecommunications satellite Intelsat I, launched in 1965, could carry 240; Intelsat IV, put into orbit in 1971, could carry 2,000; ten years later Intelsat VI could carry 33,000 conversations at the same time, and there were twenty communications satellites in orbit around the earth (nineteen run by a consortium of Western powers plus Japan, and the remaining one by the Soviet Union). The development of fiber-optic cables, first laid in the early 1980s, further expanded capacity. The first transatlantic fiber-optic cable, laid in 1988, could carry 40,000 simultaneous connections. By 2000, both transpacific and transatlantic lines could carry up to 2 million simultaneous conversations.[35] Costs collapsed as a result. A three-minute telephone conversation between New York and London cost twenty dollars in 1970; by 2007, it cost three cents (adjusted for inflation).[36]

The culmination of this development was the emergence of the Internet in 1983 and the World Wide Web in 1989, which grew out of electronics research by the US military and American universities between the late 1960s and the mid-1980s. By 1992 a million computers worldwide had Internet access; six years later, 130 million had it. And although in 1998 half of those computers were in the United States, and probably nine-tenths in the old industrial societies, Internet access soon expanded throughout much of the developing world as well. In 2000, only 3 percent of Brazilians, 5 percent of Mexicans, and 7 percent of Argentines used the Internet; twelve years later, it was half of Brazilians and Argentines and almost 40 percent of Mexicans. Over 40 percent of Chinese and Egyptians had Internet access, as did more than a quarter of Thais and Iranians and between one in seven and one in eight Indians, Indonesians, and Algerians. By 2010, there may have been one billion computers in the world.[37]

The cultural significance of this extraordinary revolution in communications technology lay in its creation of a worldwide forum for the exchange of information, ideas, and commercial entertainments. In a particularly bizarre twist, in the 1990s, "reality" shows became a global television phenomenon, with popular shows copied in multiple markets: *Who Wants to Be a Millionaire?* spread worldwide from its origin in Britain, *Survivor* from Sweden, and *Big Brother* from Holland. Some soap operas, too, achieved global popularity—Britain's *Inspector Morse* was watched in two hundred countries, and Mexican and Brazilian soap operas were screened in China, Russia, Poland, the United States, and Italy, as well as at home. South Korean television programs—and pop music—achieved great popularity in China and Southeast Asia in the late 1990s.[38]

The rapid expansion of mass tourism was important for this kind of cultural globalization, as well. In 1950, there were only 25 million international tourist arrivals globally; the number rose to 222 million by 1975 and 687 million by 2000. Most of these travelers were from Western Europe or the United States; but by the early twenty-first century Asia had the fastest-growing tourism industry in the world, and the second- and third-busiest airports in the world were in Beijing and Tokyo.[39]

Growing cultural cosmopolitanism was powered in part by an extraordinary consolidation in the global culture industry. By the early 2000s, Australia's globe-spanning News Corporation owned fourteen television networks and thirty-three stations, five television production studios, seven movie studios, and seven daily newspapers (in New York, London, and Sydney). The French company Vivendi Universal owned thirty-four television channels in fifteen countries, ten music labels, six movie studios, and cable television operations in eleven nations.[40] Such corporate structures made the financial barriers to the global circulation of cultural products extremely low.

The economic impact of the communications revolution, however, was also tremendous. Fiber-optic cable and the Internet revolutionized management structures by reducing the cost and increasing, by orders of magnitude, the volume of communications and data exchange within and between corporations and other organizations. It transformed many retail businesses. And perhaps most important in the initial stages, it radically changed financial transactions. By the early 2000s, use of the Internet had reduced the cost of financial

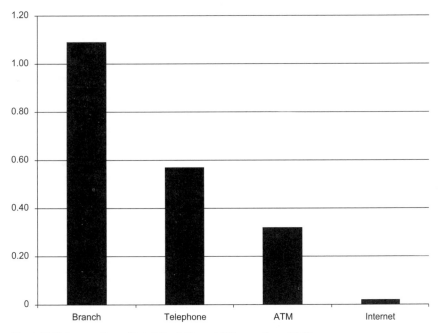

Chart 10.7 Average Cost of Retail Bank Financial Transactions, 2000.

transactions worldwide to less than one-fiftieth of what it had been in the 1950s, and about one-tenth what it had been in the 1960s (chart 10.7).

All of this change was of course wonderful in a sense. Lots of people around the globe were making lots of money because of it. There has been one rather unexpected negative consequence, however. As mentioned earlier, in most societies, inequality was rising. Because of the number of variables involved (household size, taxes and transfers, the informal economy, and the variety of categories of income, to name just four), it is extremely difficult to compare income inequality in different countries. But long-term measurements by various institutions, using various methods, reveal a consistent pattern. Incomes in most societies in the world started to become more unequal sometime in the 1970s or 1980s, and have continued to do so ever since (chart 10.8). Despite some important exceptions, the general pattern has been a more or less steady rise in income inequality within most societies.[41]

At least three factors appear to contribute to rising inequality. The financial benefits of education have risen, so that those with more education have forged ahead of those with less. Less-skilled industrial work has been shifted from higher-wage industrial economies to lower-wage industrializing economies, putting downward pressure on the wages of working people in the former. And investment has grown faster than either production or trade as a proportion of

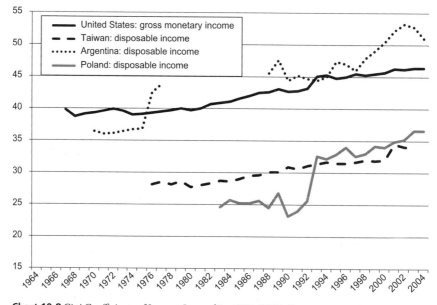

Chart 10.8 Gini Coefficients of Income Inequality, 1964–2004. Gross monetary income is income before taxes and expenditures.

the world economy, so that incomes from investment (and hence incomes of those with money to invest) have come to represent a larger share of total earnings in most societies. In many countries a fourth element has been important: neoliberal policies have reduced taxes and income transfers (through social programs, subsidies for education, public investment in housing, and so forth), so that the state has played a declining role in moderating inequalities generated by purely market forces. As seen in the previous chapter, an important reason for that reduced state role has been the rise of manufacturing in developing nations, which gave the New Right the opportunity to erode the power of labor unions and the effectiveness of the welfare state in reducing or containing inequality.[42] The extreme case was Eastern Europe, where the collapse of communism led to a sudden spike in inequality.

In most societies for which we have data, the historical pattern in the share of all incomes going to the top 1 percent of income earners is similar: high in the early twentieth century; a sharp drop during World War II, when larger incomes were heavily taxed to fund the war; a steady decline from then until the mid-1970s or early 1980s, when the welfare states were aggressively taxing and redistributing incomes; and since then a steady rise in inequality (chart 10.9). The United States was an extreme case: by 2008 only three countries in the OECD, out of twenty-three reporting, had a higher Gini coefficient (a statistical measure of inequality) than the United States: Israel, Mexico, and Turkey.

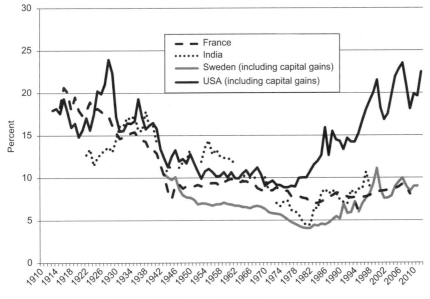

Chart 10.9 Top 1 Percent's Share of All Income, 1910–2012.

By the late 1980s this growing inequality in developed economies was having some serious negative economic implications. For one thing, in a consumer
economy, greater inequality means greater debt. Larger incomes can drive
market prices because buyers with large amounts of disposable income can bid
up prices. This mechanism is especially potent in the case of expensive items
such as houses, automobiles, and university educations. To keep pace with the
market for these items, the average buyer has to borrow more. In the United
States, between 1980 and 2007 household debt in relation to gross domestic
product roughly doubled. Ultimately, of course, there is a limit to this pattern,
because interest on household debt erodes disposable income, and eventually
households cannot afford to take on any more debt—unless they can raise their
income. This was one important reason for the rapid expansion of women's
paid employment, expanding the number of two-income households. But once
all the adults in a household (including any adult children living at home) are
working, household income cannot be expanded in that way. Ultimately, a
downward relative adjustment of the standard of living for those people on the
bottom end of growing income disparity seems inevitable: the incomes of less
skilled workers in developed economies will have to fall to the level of incomes
of people who can do the same work in lower-wage, lower-cost economies.

A second, even more serious problem, however, is that by the early 1990s a
growing number of institutions and individuals had made so much money in

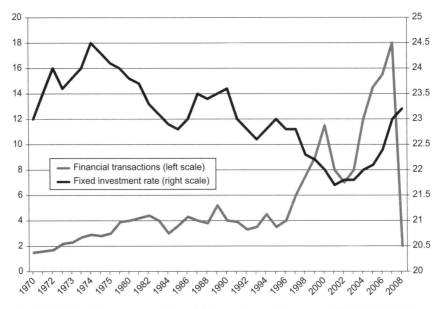

Chart 10.10 Fixed Investment and Financial Transactions as Percentage of World GDP, 1970–2008. Fixed investments are productive machinery, buildings, infrastructure assets, and the like, as distinguished from purchases of financial instruments such as stocks.

the expansion of trade and the financial sector that it was increasingly difficult to find a productive, profitable place to put all those funds. What was more, the integration of world financial markets through the use of computers and the Internet meant that money could be moved very quickly and cheaply from one part of the global economy to another. As a result, a growing mass of money was moving around the world at an accelerating pace in search of profitable investment opportunities. This was one reason, of course, for the rapid growth of FDI. But it also created an enormous temptation for investors to speculate in financial assets and instruments. As more and more yielded to that temptation, the rate of actual productive investment in the global economy (as a proportion of global GDP) declined slightly over the long term, while the speed and volume of world financial activity—much of it speculative—ramped up, particularly in the 1990s (chart 10.10).

In fact, the advance of communications technologies led to some bizarre outcomes in the financial industry. By the 1990s, for example, it became possible for large financial institutions to buy assets (stocks, bonds, futures, commodities, and the like) on one stock market exchange, only to sell them seconds later on another, thousands of miles away, in order to take advantage of miniscule price fluctuations. Given enough transactions in a day, of sufficient volume, the resulting profits could justify the cost of highly sophisticated automated trading programs. Whereas global currency trading, for example, totaled US$17.5 trillion in 1970, by 1995 it had reached almost US$300 trillion.[43] Sudden movement in currency markets could play havoc with national and regional economies—as they did in Asia and to a lesser extent in Latin America in 1998. Opportunities for fraud also multiplied as the speed and complexity of transactions increased, and as computer software came to play a larger and larger role in financial management. In the early 1990s one trader in financial instruments for the British bank Barings used the complexity of his company's computer record-keeping system to hide mounting losses from speculative transactions on the Singapore stock market (by placing them in an account effectively hidden from the firm's computerized monitoring system back in London). By the time his deception was discovered in early 1995, he had piled up US$1.4 billion in losses, and destroyed the bank. There have been multiple similar cases since—as, for example, when a trader at the American firm Goldman Sachs lost clients US$1 billion in investments, and his bank $550 million in fines, in 2010; or when a trader at the London affiliate of American superbank J. P. Morgan Chase lost US$5.8 billion in 2012.[44]

Far more significant was the fact that mushrooming speculation in a succession of different kinds of assets created an escalating series of broader crises in the world financial sector. These were caused by the rapid inflation and then precipitous deflation of asset bubbles, in which investors with money to burn push up prices of one kind of asset after another—for example, real estate, technology stocks, foreign currencies, or most recently, complex financial instruments derived from mounting private debt that amount to shares in mortgages bundled together to form a new kind of "asset" out of private financial liabilities. When the market collectively figures out that a particular kind of asset is overvalued, prices crash. Serious crises struck in 1981, 1987, 1989, 1998, 2001, and 2007. This process was centered on the United States because that nation is home to the world's largest financial sector. But the largest asset bubble in world history was created in Japan in the 1970s and 1980s, and burst in 1989, and the financial crisis of 1998 primarily affected East and Southeast Asia. The crisis of 2007, which created the worst worldwide recession since the 1930s, focused on the North Atlantic, but by no means affected exclusively the United States. In short, the process of "financialization" generated growing volatility and instability in the global economy.

It is worth pausing for a moment to consider just how extraordinary this development was by 2010. For more than a hundred years, the growth of the world economy had been driven by money—by the investments that integrated more and more areas into the world economy, expanded access to more and more resources, promoted employment and generated innovation. But by 2010, money was becoming perhaps the worst enemy of wealth. In short, at the moment of its triumph, it appeared possible that the global capitalist economy would choke on its own success. Unfortunately that was true not only of the money economy but also of the productive economy and indeed of humanity as a species inhabiting its planetary environment.

THE END OF THE WORLD?

> [W]e have now used up all slack in the schedule for actions needed to defuse the global warming time bomb. The next president and Congress must define a course next year. . . . Otherwise it will become impractical to constrain atmospheric carbon dioxide . . . to a level that prevents the climate system from passing tipping points that lead to disastrous climate changes that spiral dynamically out of humanity's control.[45]
>
> James Hansen, 2008

> Thus far no one has seriously demonstrated any scientific proof that increased global temperatures would lead to the catastrophes predicted by the alarmists. In fact, it appears just the opposite is true: that increases in global temperatures may have a beneficial effect on how we live our lives. . . . [A]larmists are attempting to enact an agenda of energy suppression that is inconsistent with American values of freedom, prosperity, and environmental progress, . . . handicapping the American economy through carbon taxes and more regulations.[46]
>
> Senator James N. Inhofe, 2003

As the introduction to this book points out, one development that makes the history of the past two hundred years so profoundly different from any previous period in human history is the extraordinary growth in the number of human beings alive at any one time. As of 2010, there were about six and one half times as many people on earth as there were in 1800. Another crucial difference is that the per capita wealth of those six billion–plus people was higher than it ever had been before—and about eight and a half times what it was in 1820. Critical to this rise in overall wealth and population has been a skyrocketing consumption of energy (chart 10.11). In the broadest terms, life uses energy to fight entropy; and by 2010 there was an enormous amount of life in the human species. The benefits for individual humans were extraordinary. People in India in 2010 could expect to live three times as long as their ancestors in 1820; people in Mexico and Brazil two and a half times as long; people in Japan, North America, Africa, and Western Europe twice as long. The year 2010 was a fantastic time to be a human being.

There was a problem, though. Most of the energy humanity consumed in 2010 was obtained by burning fossil fuels, and that combustion releases carbon dioxide into the atmosphere. As a result, the concentration of that gas in the atmosphere steadily rose. It was about 280 parts per million in the 1900s; by 2010 it was about 360 parts per million.[47] And carbon dioxide (as well as some other gases, such as methane and some sulfur oxides, all of which are also released by modern industrial and agricultural activities) has an interesting property. Energy in the form of light from the sun passes through these gases

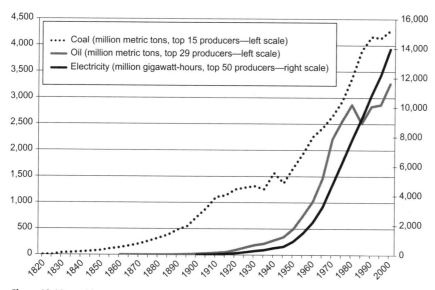

Chart 10.11 World Energy Production, 1820–2000.

without much absorption; but much lower-wavelength energy in the form of heat from the earth warmed by that sunlight is absorbed by them, and they warm up. So the atmosphere gets warmer. This is commonly called the "greenhouse effect," and these gases are often called "greenhouse gases."

In 1938 G. S. Callendar, a researcher for an industrial association in Britain, pointed out that as a result of the greenhouse effect, the earth would gradually grow warmer. This, he thought, was a wonderful thing. Agriculture could be extended farther north, feeding more people. Plants all over the world would grow better, because they require carbon dioxide for growth. And over the long term, the return of ice ages, a terrible scourge for life on earth for millions of years (the last one only 10,000 years ago) would be prevented. As he put it, "The return of the deadly glaciers should be delayed indefinitely."[48] By 1957, two researchers at the Scripps Oceanographic Institute in La Jolla, California, pointed out that this process was clearly accelerating. That was scientifically exciting, they thought, because it would soon tell us what happens to the weather when the planet is warmed up.[49]

Within in a few years, however, alarm bells began to go off. In 1970 U Thant, secretary general of the United Nations, warned of the possibility of "a catastrophic warming effect, melting the polar ice, changing the marine environment, and creating flooding on a global scale."[50] By the 1980s a whole complex of scientific advances allowed scientists to reconstruct the record of the planet's atmospheric temperature over eons. They discovered that temperature tracked with carbon dioxide levels, which fluctuated fairly regularly in a band between about 180 parts per million and 300 parts per million. But the concentration of atmospheric CO_2 was now headed above 350 parts per million.[51] That suggested the potential for warming to average global temperatures not seen for millions of years.

Climate change on that scale might target those very food-producing regions that, over the past two centuries, have permitted the human population to expand in such an unprecedented manner. Desertification of the world's grasslands under cultivation—for example, in the midwestern United States or northern India—could compromise wheat production. Rising sea levels, flooding the world's rice-producing river deltas, might compromise rice production.

The United Nations established the Intergovernmental Panel on Climate Change in 1988, and in 1992 it called a conference to develop a common strategy for dealing with the problem. Meeting in Rio de Janeiro, this conference resulted in the UN Framework Convention on Climate Change, under which the signatory countries agreed to meet regularly to negotiate a phased reduction of greenhouse gas emissions.

This agreement was modeled on the highly successful Vienna Convention for the Protection of the Ozone Layer, signed in 1985. In the late 1970s, it had been discovered that the concentration of ozone in the atmosphere was declining. That was a bad thing, because ozone in the stratosphere absorbs the sun's ultraviolet rays, which even at relatively low intensity cause skin cancers and, at higher intensities, compromise plant growth. Certain chemicals then used in refrigeration systems destroy atmospheric ozone, and the Vienna Convention aimed to phase out the production of those chemicals, replacing them with ones that avoided the harmful side-effect. In 1987 representatives of the nations that were major producers of those chemicals met in Montreal, Canada, and signed the "Montreal Protocol" to the earlier agreement, adopting an accelerated time frame. By 1996, these chemicals were no longer being produced in any great quantities. And by 2005 the level of ozone in the stratosphere appeared to have stabilized. This was an extremely encouraging precedent. World leaders had seen a problem; they had developed a solution; and they had successfully implemented that solution.[52]

Unfortunately, fossil fuels are the foundation of the modern economy, rather than a convenient minor feature of it, and there are as yet no easy ways to replace that foundation. When the world turned to address the greenhouse effect, it proved extremely difficult to generate the kind of collective action that had solved the ozone problem. It took five years to create the "Kyoto Protocol" to the Rio Framework Convention, in 1997. That agreement set targets for the progressive reduction of emissions of greenhouse gases by the developed nations, but it set no such targets for developing nations, which, after all, needed much higher energy consumption to raise their standards of living. And the biggest emitter of greenhouse gases on the planet, the United States, signed the agreement, but then could not get it ratified by Congress.

This meant that other nations in the world effectively had agreed to accept the cost of cutting emissions, while the United States gained competitive economic advantage by not doing so. After that mixed result, little was accomplished for over a decade. Some nations, particularly in Europe, did make progress in slowing the growth of emissions; but growing carbon contributions from developing economies meant that overall emissions continued to rise. By 2010, at yet another climate conference meeting in Cancun, Mexico, the negotiating parties began to focus less on "mitigation" (how to stop the rise in greenhouse gases and global temperatures) than on "adaptation" (how to live with it)—for example, by helping victims of floods and developing varieties of rice that can deal with saltier water so that sea-level rises do not compromise food production.

Meanwhile, both carbon dioxide emissions and average global temperatures continued to rise. By 2009, many scientists concluded that without effective action, average global temperatures might rise 4 or even 6 degrees Celsius by the year 2100. And no one really had any idea what that might mean. Many in the scientific community became increasingly frightened and frustrated by this situation. By late 2012, even the World Bank—hardly a radical environmental organization—published a study warning that the world was on track for a rise of at least 4 degrees by 2100 even if the Kyoto targets were met, and by as early as 2060 if they were not. The result would be "unprecedented heat waves, severe drought, and major floods in many areas, with serious impacts on human systems" and ecosystems.[53]

Beyond that prediction, though, the World Bank warned of the potential for "non-linear responses" that were completely unpredictable. It is not yet known what happens to ocean food production when tropical reefs dissolve as the ocean becomes more acidic—which is one consequence of rising carbon dioxide levels in the atmosphere. It is not known how crops respond to such high average temperatures—some models suggest yields lowered by between 63 and 82 percent at 4 degrees' warming.[54] It is not yet clear how fast the ice caps at the earth's poles might melt; but substantial melting would result in a catastrophic rise in global sea level. It is unknown how much carbon and methane might be released, how fast, by the melting of permafrost and other permanent ice deposits in the Arctic and Antarctic, further accelerating warming. It is not clear whether ecosystems can adapt to change that occurs so fast—or whether populations of insects, trees, birds, amphibians, reptiles, and small mammals might at some point collapse, with unpredictable consequences. Climate scientists refer to this kind of scenario as a "tipping point"—after which natural systems change in a precipitous "cascade" of effects. Whether those tipping points exist, or where they are, or what cumulative effects they might have are all unknowns.

Concern about both the long-term trend and such unpredictable shorter-term fluctuations finally yielded a comprehensive agreement, at a conference in Paris in 2015, to hold the average temperature rise at 2 degrees Celsius. Signed by 195 nations, this agreement was welcomed by some as a triumph since it committed almost the entire world to reducing emissions drastically. But skeptics were quick to point out that the agreement would not go into effect for another half decade, that the emissions targets it established seemed unlikely to actually control rising global temperatures, and that it included no enforcement mechanism. A number of climate scientists and activists immediately denounced the agreement, calling it "naïve," "hollow," an example of "wishful thinking and blind optimism," and characterized by "deadly flaws"—not least of which was the false assurance it gave the world that something radical was actually being done about the problem. James Hansen, an early and prominent activist, even called it "a fraud, really, a fake. . . . There is no action, just promises."[55] Time will tell which perspective is correct; but until 2020, in fact, the agreement requires no one to do much at all.

Aside from widespread fears of climate apocalypse, two features of the discussion of climate change stood out as odd and unsettling. One was that there had been a "pause" or slowing in global warming between the 1940s and the 1970s, and another slowing after 2000. No one could explain these slowdowns. Even odder and more unsettling, however, was that by 2010 solutions to the problem of climate change were already quite clear. Alternative energy sources were available—nuclear, photovoltaic solar, solar-thermal, wind, hydroelectric, and tidal power. Technologies were in development that could capture carbon dioxide from the free air, concentrate it, and store or use it. For example, genetically engineered bacteria or algae could be used to turn CO_2 into complex hydrocarbons that could be burned for fuel, creating a hydrocarbon energy source with zero net carbon dioxide output. Combining these extant and nascent technologies with aggressive energy efficiency and conservation efforts would yield a solution to global warming. That solution would require an economic and social effort probably on the scale of World War II, but no one would get killed in the process.[56]

So why not do it? One reason is that it is not yet clear how fast global warming will proceed or what its consequences will be. It is therefore difficult to go to "war" on the scale suggested above to stop it. People want to spend their money on other things, at least for now. A second is that the growing instability in the world financial system has made governments struggling to retain their popularity and legitimacy in the face of repeated financial crises reluctant to demand major financial sacrifices of their citizens. One 2010 study by two authors on the political Left put it this way: in the view of the people whose job it is to try to manage the global capitalist system, "in order to keep the treadmill of accumulation going, the world needs to risk environmental Armageddon."[57] The following year an introduction to the theory of complex social systems observed that the "key question is whether a system has braking mechanisms at its disposal, or whether only catastrophic developments will finally block the positive feedback that was introduced at an earlier point."[58]

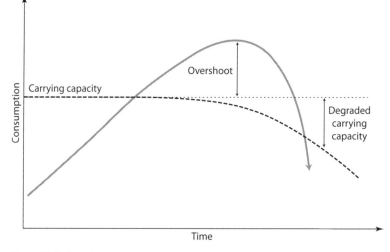

Chart 10.12 Overshoot.

Regarding this particular "system"—the relationship between politics, the economy, and the earth's climate—the answer seems a clear negative, at least for now.

A third reason, however, is that a genuine difference of opinion exists about how to solve the problem effectively. Alongside the World War II model, there is a competing strategy that is much more attractive; and its supporters argue that it is also much more effective. That strategy was summed up by a representative of the political Right in Britain in 2010: "Surely it is reasonable to argue that if one wants to help future generations deal with climate change, the best policies would be those that encourage economic growth. This would endow future generations with the wealth and superior technologies that could be used to handle whatever comes at them, including climate change."[59] In other words, the best way of addressing the negative consequences of growth is more growth. This is the exact opposite of the argument put forward in 1972 in *The Limits to Growth*, or in 1973 in *Small Is Beautiful.*

Such an approach has important historical precedents. The theory of the Club of Rome and of the environmental movement generally is called the theory of "overshoot." It argues that natural populations rise to the point where they exceed the environment's carrying capacity; they then begin to degrade their habitat by eating up the base stock of resources, reducing its original carrying capacity; and then population collapses to a level below that original carrying capacity. The bet of those arguing for adaptation, rather than mitigation, is that we can avoid such a collapse by applying technology to resolving resource shortages—effectively by raising the environment's carrying capacity.

Historical examples abound. The theory of the Green Revolution was that improved agricultural technology would create the economic foundation for rising standards of living, which would cause fertility to fall and ultimately, in turn, resolve the population problem. The recent rapid decline of the rate of human population growth suggests that this may in fact happen. Indeed, since many more affluent societies are actually reproducing at below replacement level, the planetary population may begin to shrink in a few decades.

A second example is oil. By 1956 some petroleum geologists were pointing out that there was not an infinite amount of oil underground and that production would eventually start to fall. In fact, global production of easily accessible (or "conventional") oil appears to have peaked in about 2006. In the early years of the twenty-first century, however, the petroleum industry used a sophisticated technology called hydrochemical fracturing ("fracking") of deep oil-bearing shale rock to solve that problem. US oil production, for example, peaked in the 1960s, but was rising again by 2013. The amount of oil available in oil shales is gigantic, enough for centuries of use.

Of course, from the point of view of those alarmed by climate change, the oil locked in shale rock is not a good thing at all. But rising fuel efficiency may help address that problem. In just twenty years, between 1990 and 2010, much of the world reduced the energy intensity of economic production (the amount of energy burned to generate one dollar of GDP per capita) by amounts varying from 6 percent (Japan) to 60 percent (China). Overall, the trend is toward convergence upon a common average efficiency far greater than in earlier stages of industrial growth (chart 10.13). In short, some historical precedent suggests that the best approach to climate change would be, in effect, to do nothing more than make strategic investments in potential technological solutions.

THE END OF THE "NATURAL" WORLD

> The final goal . . . understood in the broad sense, is a profound rearrangement of the entire living world. . . . All living nature will live, thrive and die at none other than the will of humans and according to their designs.[60]
>
> Nikolai Kashchenko, 1929

At the end of two centuries of unprecedented economic and demographic growth, then, the future of mankind's relationship with the planetary environment appears uncertain. The revolutionary transformations of the past two hundred years appear to have brought us increasingly close to the limit of our planet's carrying capacity. But experience suggests that the same technological revolution may be capable of producing solutions to at least the currently looming crises.

One extraordinary fact underlies both these perspectives, however: human civilization has become so gigantic and so energy-intensive that it has begun to

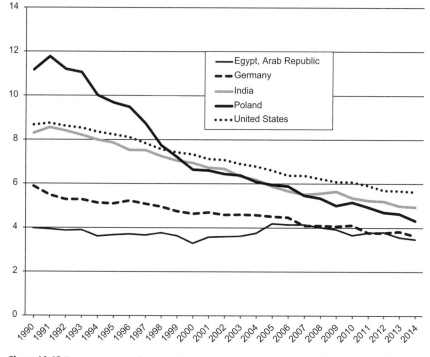

Chart 10.13 Energy Intensity (megajoules of energy used to produce each US dollar of GDP), 1990–2014.

be a geophysical force in its own right. The most obvious recent cases have been ozone and carbon dioxide. But there are others. The massive thirst of modern industry and agriculture for groundwater has begun to draw down ancient stores of water in underground aquifers in many arid regions of the planet. The enormous application of fertilizers in modern agriculture is having a major impact on the natural cycles that regulate concentrations of nitrogen in the environment, leading to the creation of vast zones of eutrophication—in which superabundant nitrogen and phosphorous stimulates overproliferation of simple micro-organisms, choking out all other forms of life. Just as there are finite supplies of oil in easily accessible oil fields, so there are finite supplies of phosphate rock, the main source of phosphate fertilizers.[61] Some observers have begun to refer to the present as a new geologic age, the Anthropocene, in which the conditions for life on earth are determined increasingly by human activity. It is a bit strange to give a period that has so far lasted two centuries a status equivalent to that of geologic epochs that last millions of years, but that is another measure of the enormous scale of the human impact on the planet. By the 2010s, for example, industrial processes fixed more nitrogen from the atmosphere than all natural processes combined.[62]

Perhaps a metaphor can best capture the situation of humanity on Planet Earth today. Human history over the past century and more is the history of the building of an enormously powerful scientific, productive, and social machinery that has made the human species rich, healthy, happy and smart beyond the wildest imaginings of people just two hundred years ago. This machinery is already so powerful that it has begun to have a significant impact on the fundamental conditions of life on this planet—and in most respects it is still accelerating. It is very likely that if we carry on as we are now, we will eventually—though we do not know when—get to 4 degrees' climate warming, and then to 6, and then to 8; and at some point, hypothetically, we will wreck the entire planetary ecosystem. Perhaps we will solve that problem. But our steadily rising energy use will doubtless at some point generate some other problem similar to that of global warming or of ozone depletion—and then another, and another.

To continue to thrive, therefore, humanity will have to work out effective methods for managing its impact on the planetary environment as a whole: it will be forced not only to rely on the earth's natural systems and cycles, but also increasingly to manage those systems directly, to create artificial systems and cycles on a planetary scale. This may be a frightening prospect, because planetary systems are both inconceivably vast and inconceivably complicated. As Ludwig Klages remarked as early as 1913, it appears likely that "in no conceivable case will human beings ever meet with success in their attempt to 'correct' nature." We are not gods; we therefore seem likely to fail at playing God. On the other hand, perhaps H. G. Wells was right in thinking, at the start of the twentieth century, that we will evolve into godlike creatures, masters of the natural world and our own fate. If we do, it may turn out—ironically—that the development and application of an ethic of love, respect, and responsibility toward the earth will be the key to that evolution. Perhaps humanity can become godlike by thinking of itself as not godlike at all—by shifting, as Aldo Leopold put in 1948, "from conqueror of the land-community to plain member and citizen of it."[63]

In any case, the problem of global warming suggests that the governments of nation-states may not be equal to the job of managing the planet. And the great philanthropic organizations that were built on the wealth generated by the natural resource bonanza of nineteenth-century North America and that funded earlier efforts like the Green Revolution have not done better. So someone else has to. But who?

One possible candidate would be universities, many of which have in the modern era become scientific and technological powerhouses capable of bringing together researchers in the multiple fields—genetics, engineering, finance, materials science, organizational psychology, computer science, economics—that will have to contribute to a solution to our emerging planetary predicament. Universities are devoted to the common good; what better way to pursue that mission than by saving our planet?

On the other hand, perhaps major multinational corporations should pay attention as well. The long-term process of business consolidation accelerated from about 1970 onward, as companies moved to take advantage of global transportation, communications, and trade. The total number and value of mergers and acquisitions globally almost quadrupled between 1995 and 2005.[64] That concentration has by now generated corporations of gargantuan scale. In fact by 2011 one study of 43,060 transnational companies found that just less than 300 very tightly connected firms (with 75 percent of ownership concentrated within the group itself) accounted for almost 20 percent of total world business operating revenues. This closely interconnected core of global business exerted substantial ownership influence over a wide network of companies accounting for almost 60 percent of operating revenues.[65] These corporations and networks of corporations wield enormous economic power and the potential to mobilize incomparable scientific, technical, organizational, and financial resources—perhaps even enough to address the problems of the Anthropocene.

Even if global business as a whole does not achieve a high degree of coherence, corporate consolidation may still generate aggregates powerful enough to address the world's looming problems. Of the largest fifty of the companies (measured by assets) in that 2011 study, forty-eight were in the financial sector; and banks and insurance companies have as much reason as anyone to want to solve environmental problems (for example, in order to prevent expensive natural disasters such as fires and floods).[66] Oil companies have a clear long-term interest in solving the problem of carbon dioxide emissions from fossil fuel use. Seven of the ten largest companies in the world (measured by sales) in 2012 were oil companies. The top thirteen had aggregate sales larger than the GDP of all but four nations in the world, and larger than the tax revenues of any nation but the United States. The top one hundred largest corporations in the world have aggregate profits greater than the tax revenues of all but one country (the United States).[67] And profits are in effect disposable income, whereas most tax revenues are already committed to mandated spending.

It may be a good sign, then, that over the past generation the world's multinational corporations have been talking to one another more and more, about ever broader issues of global concern. One example is the Trilateral Commission, formed in New York in 1973 as a forum for the discussion of contemporary problems by leading figures in finance and industry in North America, Europe, and Japan and the Asia-Pacific region. Another is the World Economic Forum (WEF), a similar group formed in 1971 in Switzerland. The WEF's annual meetings in Davos bring together some two thousand representatives of business, government, the media, and universities—about three-quarters of them from the developed world, and three-quarters from the business sector. In recent years it has launched a growing number of study and action initiatives—its Global Health Initiative (2002), Global Education Initiative (2003),

Partnering Against Corruption initiative (2004), and Environmental Initiative (2005, producing a report on global warming in 2008).[68]

A final candidate might be the superwealthy individual beneficiaries of economic globalization. The aggregate wealth of the richest fifty individuals on earth is now greater than the GDP of all but twelve nations. Those richest fifty persons together have a net worth equal to one-eleventh of the GDP of the United States or the European Union; half the total GDP of the entire Arab world; and almost the entire GDP of all of sub-Saharan Africa. There are only ten nations with annual tax revenues greater than the aggregate wealth of the richest five—repeat, five—individuals on earth, and only two with tax revenues greater than the aggregate wealth of the richest fifty.[69] Many observers are disturbed by this development, but if they decided to do so these people could devote as much money to solving the world's problems as entire continents full of their fellow human beings. And why wouldn't they? They live here too.

Of course, none of these three options—and no combination of them—is entirely appealing. Management of the planetary environment by a superwealthy oligarchy, controlling an interlocking web of megacorporations, and buying the services of experts in universities around the world sounds more like a dystopia than a utopia to most. But it increasingly looks like one possible outcome of the past two centuries of social, economic, and technological development; and it might not be the worst possible outcome.

THE END OF THE TWENTIETH CENTURY

> Between the vast, macroscopic systems for which universal laws hold sway and the simple systems that can be analyzed using the fundamental laws of nature, there is a substantial middle ground of systems that are too complex for fundamental analysis but too simple to be universal.[70]
>
> Terence Tao, 2012

By the year 2010 there was increasingly, however, an even deeper reason to be ambivalent about the planetary future—to imagine both utopian and dystopian futures. For by the 1980s at the latest, a whole series of fundamental advances in the sciences began to make it seem that the new century would open with a technological "big bang" similar to that of the late nineteenth century—a complex of basic innovations that have the potential to create an entirely new economic, social, and cultural world. Like the earlier ones, these scientific and technological breakthroughs are rooted in much older conceptual advances, going back to the period between 1900 and 1930. But they appear to have the potential to generate what one economist has called a new "technoeconomic paradigm"—a new energy regime, a new cascade of innovations, a new complex of technologies.[71]

In fact, in field after field in the sciences, a common pattern was emerging around 2000. The most important advances of this period appear to penetrate to the very principles of being—not the hidden structures of being, below the level of the visible, but rather the blueprint on which those structures are built.

Many of these advances had their early origins during World War II, when governments were willing to invest gigantic sums of money and devote enormous numbers of personnel to scientific and technological projects that might yield new weapons with which to defeat their enemies. Subatomic physics, for example, has penetrated beyond the regularities of the periodic table and the physics of protons, electrons, and neutrons to discover some two dozen fundamental particles. In 2012 scientists working with a monstrous experimental apparatus and gargantuan amounts of energy, computing power, and money supplied by multiple national governments detected the last particle posited by this "standard model," the Higgs boson. These are discoveries on the same order of magnitude as the basic discoveries in electricity and magnetism and in thermodynamics that underlay the scientific revolution of the long twentieth century. Genetics has advanced beyond the basic laws of inheritance worked out by Gregor Mendel in 1865 (and rediscovered in the 1890s) to discover the molecular structure of the genetic code. Beginning in the 1970s, techniques were developed that allow scientists to manipulate individual genes—not just through selective breeding but directly at the molecular level.[72] By 2013 there was discussion of the possibility of genetically engineering algae to metabolize atmospheric carbon dioxide and produce complex hydrocarbons as waste—which would allow humanity to continue to consume ever more energy without contributing to global warming. Crops are being genetically engineered in order to enhance, for example, resistance to drought, pests, and soil salination. And new medical therapies based on stem cells may eliminate such problems as cancer, brain and nerve damage, and inherited genetic disorders. It even begins to seem possible that, in perhaps another fifty years, people will no longer die of old age—quite wealthy people, perhaps, sooner than that.

Whether all of these technological breakthroughs are necessarily a good thing is of course open to debate. If the problem is too many people using too much energy, technological advances that allow more people to be fed and to burn more energy are not likely to help, and the end of death by aging is potentially the worst idea imaginable. Fewer people, using less energy, might make more sense. As one historian of technology remarked in 2007, "Calling for innovation is . . . a common way of avoiding change" of a more fundamental nature.[73] A more optimistic perspective would be that it is a good thing if we can figure out how to use more energy without paying one of its key environmental costs; that genetically modified crops may give us time to get our population down through falling fertility; and that not getting old and dying will solve the looming problem of a world with too many old retired people and not enough young working people.

Beyond that, advances in the field of ecology have increased our understanding of the astonishing complexity of biological communities—well beyond the simple model of population dynamics that underlies the theory of overshoot. From the 1970s onward, scientists were developing a growing catalogue of practical ecological principles. One is the idea that predator species are not noxious pests to be eradicated, but useful elements in the broader web of life; for example, rattlesnakes are not there to be killed by ranchers, but to eat the rodents that compete with their livestock for feed on the open range. A more general such principle is the idea that more diverse biological systems are more adaptable and therefore more resistant to environmental or biological challenges (such as new pests or diseases, or changing climatic conditions); for example, diversified food production systems are more resilient and therefore ultimately more stable than those built around one or a small number of crops ("monoculture") and driven by external inputs (such as fertilizer).[74] Already in 1974 James Lovelock and Lynn Margulis formulated the Gaia Hypothesis, which holds that life on earth is in self-regulating equilibrium with the inorganic environment, acting through complex feedback mechanisms to sustain conditions optimal for life—as by influencing atmospheric chemistry.[75] Effectively, the project of creating a managed planetary environment is the project of becoming the mind of a newly self-conscious Gaia.

Every one of these advances—and of course countless others—was built on experiment, observation, and data processing made possible by what is arguably the most astonishing engineering achievement in all of human history: the microelectronic computer.[76] The first electronic computers were developed by the late 1930s, and then refined in the 1940s and 1950s—once again with enormous government funding—in response to the challenges of World War II and the Cold War. With the development of microcomputers in the 1970s and 1980s and the emergence of networked computing and the Internet since the 1990s, the volume, organization, and accessibility of information on a global scale is passing through a qualitative transition.[77]

An optimist might hope that this transition will give humanity the tools it needs to understand and manage its impact on the planetary environment, as well as to build a new and more participatory and democratic blueprint for human social and political organization. Pessimists point to the ubiquity of state surveillance over the emergent forms of Internet-enabled communication (such as email and social networks) as a potential blueprint for totalitarianism in a new and more insidious key.

Will the twenty-first century defined by these new technologies be a miracle or a nightmare? The world revealed by contemporary science is incredibly complex—the "standard model" with its many particles and forces, the almost implausible complexity of factors and conditions that regulate or influence gene expression, the astonishingly sensitive dynamics of ecological systems. This complexity appears to be mirrored in the human world in our time—a mass of diverse, variegated, contrasting social, cultural, economic and political systems, which nevertheless appear increasingly to add up to a dynamically interacting whole. Perhaps the human world will turn out to have some of the resilience and varied potentials of the natural one. If so, it seems likely that neither optimistic nor pessimistic views of the next stage in human history will turn out to be correct. The twenty-first century may be worse than we hope, but better than we fear.

Notes

INTRODUCTION

1. On the question of technological determination in history, see Merritt Roe Smith and Leo Marx, eds., *Does Technology Drive History?* (Cambridge, MA: MIT Pres, 1994).
2. Vaclav Smil, *Creating the Twentieth Century* (Oxford: Oxford University Press, 2005), 8, 9, 13.
3. See, for example, Charles H. Parker, *Global Interactions in the Early Modern Age, 1400–1800* (Cambridge: Cambridge University Press, 2010); Kenneth Pomeranz, *The Great Divergence: China, Europe, and the Making of the Modern World Economy* (Princeton: Princeton University Press, 2000); Immanuel Wallerstein, *The Modern World System,* vols. 1–3 (New York: Academic Press; Berkeley: University of California Press, 1974, 1989, 2011); and Kenneth Pomeranz and J. R. McNeill, "Production, Destruction, and Connection, 1750–Present: Introduction," in *The Cambridge World History,* Vol. 7: *Production, Destruction, and Connection, 1750–Present, Part I: Structures, Spaces, and Boundary-Making,* eds. Pomeranz and McNeill (Cambridge: Cambridge University Press, 2015), 1–47 (esp. 8, 13).
4. *International Historical Statistics,* ed. Palgrave Macmillan Ltd., http://www.palgraveconnect.com/pc/doifinder/10.1057/9781137305688.0737; Database, Maddison Project, http://www.ggdc.net/maddison/maddison-project/data.htm.

CHAPTER 1. THE BIOLOGICAL TRANSFORMATION OF MODERN TIMES

1. Massimo Livi-Bacci, *A Concise History of World Population,* 3d ed. (Malden, MA: Blackwell, 2001), 27.
2. Thomas Whitmore et al., "Long-Term Population Change," in B. L. Turner et al., eds., *The Earth as Transformed by Human Action* (New York: Cambridge University Press, 1990), 31.
3. Ibid., 33.
4. Paul Bairoch, "Agriculture and the Industrial Revolution, 1700–1914," in *The Fontana Economic History of Europe: The Industrial Revolution,* ed. Carlo M. Cipolla (New York: Collins/Fontana, 1973), 453, 460; Dwight H. Perkins, *Agricultural Development in China, 1368–1968* (Chicago: Aldine, 1969); Sam White, "From Globalized Pig Breeds to Capitalist Pigs," *Environmental History* 16 (2011): 94–120; Francesca Bray, *Science and Civilization in China,* Vol. 6: *Biology and Biological Technology, Part II: Agriculture,* ed. Joseph Needham (Cambridge: Cambridge University Press, 1984), 582.
5. See, in particular, Roy Porter, *The Greatest Benefit to Mankind: A Medical History of Humanity from Antiquity to the Present* (New York: HarperCollins, 1997), 370–73.
6. J. R. McNeill, *Something New Under the Sun: An Environmental History of the Twentieth-Century World* (New York: W. W. Norton, 2000), 127–28.

7. Richard A. Easterlin, *Growth Triumphant: The Twenty-First Century in Historical Perspective* (Ann Arbor: University of Michigan Press, 1996), 161; Porter, *Greatest Benefit to Mankind,* 467–75; J. R. McNeill, *Mosquito Empires: Ecology and Wars in the Greater Caribbean, 1620–1914* (Cambridge: Cambridge University Press, 2010), esp. 309–10.
8. Porter, *Greatest Benefit to Mankind,* 453–61; Roy Porter, ed., *The Cambridge Illustrated History of Medicine* (Cambridge: Cambridge University Press, 1996), 231, 269–72; Daniel Headrick, "Botany, Chemistry, and Tropical Development," *Journal of World History* 7 (1996): 4–5; Bouda Etamad, *Possessing the World* (New York: Berghahn, 2000), 26–34; McNeill, *Something New Under the Sun,* 199; Miguel A. Centeno and Joseph N. Cohen, *Global Capitalism: A Sociological Perspective* (New York: Polity, 2010), 101.
9. Oded Galor offers a good discussion in "The Demographic Transition and the Emergence of Sustained Economic Growth," *Journal of the European Economic Association* 3 (2005): 494–504.
10. Jean-Claude Chesnais, *The Demographic Transition,* trans. Elizabeth and Philip Kreager (Oxford: Clarendon, 1992), 441 (quotation), 433, 489.
11. John C. Caldwell and Pat Caldwell, "What Do We Now Know about Fertility Transition?" in *The Continuing Demographic Transition,* ed. G. W. Jones, R. M. Douglas, J. C. Caldwell, and R. M. D'Souza (Oxford: Clarendon, 1997), 21.
12. Quoted in Chesnais, *Demographic Transition,* 4.
13. "'I Was Born a Lakota': Red Cloud's Abdication Speech, July 4, 1903," in James R. Walker, *Lakota Belief and Ritual,* ed. Raymond J. DeMallie and Elaine A. Jahner (Lincoln: University of Nebraska Press, 1980), 137–39.
14. Roy Hora, *The Landowners of the Argentine Pampas* (Oxford: Oxford University Press, 2001); Willard Sunderland, *Taming the Wild Field: Colonization and Empire on the Russian Steppe* (Ithaca, NY: Cornell University Press, 2004).
15. Jeremy Adelman, *Frontier Development: Land, Labour, and Capital on the Wheatlands of Argentina and Canada, 1890–1914* (Oxford: Oxford University Press, 1994), 23.
16. Alexis Dudden, "Japanese Colonial Control in International Terms," *Japanese Studies* 25 (2005): 1–20; Dirk Hoerder, *Cultures in Contact* (Durham, NC: Duke University Press, 2002), 375.
17. McNeill, *Something New Under the Sun,* 161.
18. A. G. Kenwood and A. L. Lougheed, *The Growth of the International Economy* (New York: Routledge, 1999), 51–53; Ulbe Bosma, "European Colonial Soldiers in the Nineteenth Century," *Journal of Global History* 4 (2009): 328; Jeffrey Lesser, *Immigration, Ethnicity, and National Identity in Brazil, 1808 to the Present* (Cambridge: Cambridge University Press, 2013), 72.
19. Basil Davidson, *Africa in History* (New York: Macmillan, 1991), 268.

20. Jeffrey Ostler, *The Plains Sioux and U.S. Colonialism from Lewis and Clark to Wounded Knee* (Cambridge: Cambridge University Press, 2004); Benjamin Madley, "Patterns of Frontier Genocide, 1803–1910: The Aboriginal Tasmanians, the Yuki of California, and the Herero of Namibia," *Journal of Genocide Research* 6 (2004): 167–92; Madley, "Tactics of Nineteenth-Century Colonial Massacre," in *Theaters of Violence*, ed. Philip G. Dwyer and Lyndall Ryan (New York: Berghahn, 2012), 110–25; Mohamed Adhikari, ed., *Genocide on Settler Frontiers* (New York: Berghahn, 2015); Spencer C. Tucker, ed., *Encyclopedia of North American Indian Wars* (Santa Barbara, CA: ABC-CLIO, 2011); Bill Yenne, *Indian Wars: The Campaign for the American West* (Yardley, PA: Westholme, 2006); Hora, *Landowners of the Argentine Pampas*, 41–42; David Moon, "Peasant Migration and the Settlement of Russia's Frontiers, 1550–1897," *Historical Journal* 40 (1997): 884–85; Katsuya Hirano, "Thanatopolitics in the Making of Japan's Hokkaido," *Critical Historical Studies* 2 (2015): 204.

21. Madley, "Patterns of Frontier Genocide," 169 (quotation), 177–78, 181; Madley, "Reexamining the American Genocide Debate: Meaning, Historiography, and New Methods," *American Historical Review* 120 (2015): 98–139.

22. Brett L. Walker, "Meiji Modernization, Scientific Agriculture, and the Extermination of Japan's Hokkaido Wolf," *Environmental History* 9 (2004): 248–74; Lance van Sittert, "'Keeping the Enemy at Bay': The Extermination of Wild Carnivora in Cape Colony, 1889–1910," *Environmental History* 3 (1998): 343.

23. Donald Worster, *Nature's Economy: A History of Ecological Ideas* (Cambridge: Cambridge University Press, 1994), 262–77.

24. Andrew C. Isenberg, *The Destruction of the Bison: An Environmental History, 1750–1920* (Cambridge: Cambridge University Press, 2000), 137, 140, 162 (quotation).

25. Stephen Mosley, *The Environment in World History* (New York: Routledge, 2010), 17, 21, 25, 27; Clive Ponting, *A New Green History of the World* (London: Penguin, 2007), 145, 152–53; Gregory T. Cushman, *Guano and the Opening of the Pacific World* (New York: Cambridge University Press, 2013), 302; Arthur F. McEvoy, "Toward an Interactive Theory of Nature and Culture," in *The Ends of the Earth: Perspectives on Modern Environmental History*, ed. Donald Worster (New York: Cambridge University Press, 1988), 220–23.

26. See Andrew C. Isenberg, "Seas of Grass: Grasslands in World Environmental History," in *The Oxford Handbook of Environmental History*, ed. Isenberg (Oxford: Oxford University Press, 2014), 144–45; David Arnold, *The Problem of Nature: Environment, Culture, and European Expansion* (Oxford: Blackwell, 1996), esp. 123.

27. Michael Brander, *The Perfect Victorian Hero: Samuel White Baker* (Edinburgh: Mainstream, 1982), 173.

28. Ludwig Klages, "Man and Earth (1913)," in *The Biocentric Worldview: Selected Essays and Poems of Ludwig Klages*, trans Joseph D. Pryce (London: Arktos, 2013), 26, 27, 31, 34, 42.

29. Peter J. Bowler, *The Earth Encompassed A History of the Environmental Sciences* (New York: W. W. Norton, 2000), 321, 322.

30. McEvoy, "Toward an Interactive Theory," 217; Clayton R. Koppes, "Efficiency, Equity, Esthetics: Shifting Themes in American Conservation," in Worster, *The Ends of the Earth*, 230–51. On parks, see *Civilizing Nature: National Parks in Global Historical Perspective*, ed. Bernhard Gissibl, Sabine Höhler, and Patrick Kupper (New York: Berghahn, 2012). The classic text is Samuel P. Hays, *Conservation and the Gospel of Efficiency* (Cambridge, MA: Harvard University Press, 1959).

31. Patrick Brantlinger, *Dark Vanishings: Discourse on the Extinction of Primitive Races, 1800–1930* (Ithaca, NY: Cornell University Press, 2003).

32. Figures vary substantially; for a contrasting picture, see McNeill, *Something New Under the Sun*, 213.

33. Calculated from figures from the Center for Sustainability and the Global Environment, Nelson Institute for Environmental Studies, University of Wisconsin–Madison, www.sage.wisc .edu.

34. McNeill, *Something New Under the Sun*, 151–54.

35. Ibid., 217.

36. Hora, *Landowners of the Argentine Pampas*, 47.

37. Max E. Fletcher, "The Suez Canal and World Shipping, 1869–1914," *Journal of Economic History* 18 (1958): 557, 559; Alexander Nützenadel, "A Green International," in *Food and Globalization*, ed. Nützenadel and Frank Trentmann (New York: Berg, 2008), 157, 153; I. L. Buxton, "The Development of the Merchant Ship, 1880–1990," *Mariner's Mirror* 79 (1993): 71–82.

38. David Edgerton, *The Shock of the Old: Technology and Global History since 1900* (New York: Oxford University Press, 2007), 172.

39. Paul H. Kratoska, "Commercial Rice Cultivation and the Regional Economy of Southeast Asia, 1850–1950," in Nützenadel and Trentmann, *Food and Globalization*, 75–90; Michael Adas, "Continuity and Transformation: Colonial Rice Frontiers and Their Environmental Impact on the Great River Deltas of Mainland Southeast Asia," in *The Environment and World History*, ed. Edmund Burke III and Kenneth Pomeranz (Berkeley: University of California Press, 2009), 191–207; Walter Nugent, *Into the West: The Story of Its People* (New York: Knopf, 1999), 111.

40. Etamad, *Possessing the World*, 28–30.

41. McNeill, *Something New Under the Sun*, 307; Paul S. Sutter, "The Tropics: A Brief History of an Environmental Imaginary," in Isenberg, *Oxford Handbook of Environmental History*, 178–204.

42. Sergei Mikhailovich Solov'ev, *Istoriia Rossii*, quoted in Mark Bassin, "Turner, Solov'ev, and the 'Frontier Hypothesis': The National Significance of Open Spaces," *Journal of Modern History* 65 (1993): 498. Solov'ev's work was published in twenty-nine volumes from 1851 to 1876; this quotation is from the second volume.

43. Adam McKeown, "Global Migration, 1846–1940," *Journal of World History* 15 (2004): 156; Jochen Oltmer, "Migration im Kontext von Globalisierung, Kolonialismus und Weltkriegen," in *WBG Welt-Geschichte, Band VI: Globalisierung 1880 bis heute*, ed. Hans-Ulrich Thamer (Darmstadt, Germany: Wissenschaftliche Buchgesellschaft, 2010), 193; Jose C. Moya and Adam McKeown, *World Migration in the Twentieth Century* (Washington, DC: American Historical Association, 2011), 8–9; P. C. Emmer and M. Mörner, introduction to *European Expansion and Migration*, ed. Emmer and Mörner (New York: Berg, 1992), 3; Timothy J. Hatton and Jeffrey G. Williamson, *Global Migration and the World Economy* (New York: Oxford University Press, 1988), 8.

44. McKeown, "Global Migration," 167.

45. Timothy J. Hatton and Jeffrey G. Williamson, *The Age of Mass Migration: Causes and Economic Impact* (New York: Oxford University Press, 1998), 101.

46. Hoerder, *Cultures in Contact*, 319; Emmer and Mörner, introduction to *European Expansion and Migration*, 3.

47. McKeown, "Global Migration," 157–58; Hoerder, *Cultures in Contact*, 387; Jose C. Moya and Adam McKeown, "World Migration in the Long Twentieth Century," in *Essays on Twentieth-Century History*, ed. Michael C. Adas (Philadelphia: Temple University Press, 2010), 16–17.

48. Kenwood and Lougheed, *Growth of the International Economy*, 59.
49. Hatton and Williamson, *Age of Mass Migration*, 9; Walter Nugent, *Crossings: The Great Transatlantic Migrations, 1870–1914* (Bloomington: Indiana University Press, 1992), 35; McKeown, "Chinese Emigration," 108; Hoerder, *Cultures in Contact*, 366; Giovanni Gozzini, "The Global System of International Migration, 1900 and 2000," *Journal of Global History* 1 (2006): 323.
50. Hoerder, *Cultures in Contact*, 377, 379; McKeown, "Chinese Emigration," 112, 113, 117.
51. Oltmer, "Migration im Kontext," 187, 189; Hoerder, *Cultures in Contact*, 387.
52. Philip A. Kuhn, *Chinese among Others: Emigration in Modern Times* (Lanham, MD: Rowman and Littlefield, 2008), 205–36; Freda Hawkins, *Critical Years in Immigration: Canada and Australia Compared* (Montreal: McGill-Queen's University Press, 1991), 8–19.
53. McKeown, "Chinese Emigration," 111.
54. See James Belich, *Replenishing the Earth: The Settler Revolution and the Rise of the Anglo World, 1783–1939* (New York: Oxford University Press, 2009).
55. Hoerder, *Cultures in Contact*, 312.
56. David Moon, "In the Russians' Steppes," *Journal of Global History* 3 (2008): 222.
57. Timothy J. Kloberdanz, "Plainsmen of Three Continents," in *Ethnicity on the Great Plains*, ed. Frederick Luebcke (Lincoln: University of Nebraska Press, 1980), 67.
58. Vitorino Magalhàes Godinho, "Portuguese Emigration," in Emmer and Mörner, *European Expansion and Migration*, 28.
59. Kuhn, *Chinese among Others*, 217, 229.
60. Lesser, *Immigration, Ethnicity, and National Identity in Brazil*, 164; Stefan Berger, Andy Croll, and Norman Laporte, eds., *Towards a Comparative History of Coalfield Societies* (Aldershot, UK: Ashgate, 2005).

CHAPTER 2. FOUNDATIONS OF THE MODERN GLOBAL ECONOMY

1. Hora, *Landowners of the Argentine Pampas*, 8, 9, 11, 46, 49.
2. Moon, "In the Russians' Steppes," 204, 208.
3. Dudden, "Japanese Colonial Control," 8–10; Emily S. Rosenberg, "Transnational Currents in a Shrinking World," in *A World Connecting, 1870–1945*, ed. Rosenberg (Cambridge, MA: Harvard University Press, 2012), 920; Hirano, "Thanatopolitics in the Making of Japan's Hokkaido."
4. Nützenadel, "A Green International?" 161, 164.
5. Data for figures 4.1 to 4.3, in David Held, Anthony McGrew, David Goldblatt, and Jonathan Perraton, *Global Transformations* (Stanford: Stanford University Press, 1999), 193, 194; Mira Wilkins, *The History of Foreign Investment in the United States to 1914* (Cambridge, MA: Harvard University Press, 1989), 454.
6. Held et al., *Global Transformations*, 32.
7. Kenwood and Lougheed, *The Growth of the International Economy*, 30, 32; Held et al., *Global Transformations*, 194, 275.
8. Wilkins, *History of Foreign Investment*, 145, 159, 164–65; James Kirby Martin et al., *A Concise History of America and Its People*, Vol. 2: *Since 1865* (New York: HarperCollins, 1995), 429.
9. Daniel Headrick, *The Invisible Weapon: Telecommunications and International Politics, 1851–1945* (New York: Oxford University Press, 1991), 199.
10. Held et al., *Global Transformations*, 193.
11. George H. Nash, *The Life of Herbert Hoover*, Vol. 1: *The Engineer* (New York: W. W. Norton, 1983), 227, 51, 61, 181, 63, 72–73, 82–83, 424; quotations from William E. Leuchtenburg, *Herbert Hoover* (New York: Times Books, Henry Holt, 2009), 11, 13, 21, 8.
12. William D. Haywood, *Bill Haywood's Book* (New York: International Publishers, 1929), 48–49, 62, 81, 26–29; Ronald L. Lewis, *Welsh Americans: A History of Assimilation in the Coalfields* (Chapel Hill: University of North Carolina Press, 2008), 212–20, 228–38; Thomas G. Andrews, *Killing for Coal: America's Deadliest Labor War* (Cambridge, MA: Harvard University Press, 2008), 14.
13. For a good overview, see Warren Lerner, *A History of Socialism in Modern Times: Theorists, Activists, and Humanists* (Englewood Cliffs, NJ: Prentice-Hall, 1982).
14. Martin et al., *A Concise History of America and Its People*, 2:461, 462, 464, 446; Porter, *Greatest Benefit to Mankind*, 468; McNeill, *Mosquito Empires*, 309.
15. Edward W. Byrn, "The Progress of Invention during the Past Fifty Years," *Scientific American* 75 (July 25, 1896): 82.
16. This section of the chapter derives primarily from Smil, *Creating the Twentieth Century*, and from Christopher Freeman, "Technology and Innovation," in *The Columbia History of the Twentieth Century*, ed. Richard W. Bulliet (New York: Columbia University Press, 1998), 314–44.
17. Quoted in Smil, *Creating the Twentieth Century*, 13.
18. Easterlin, *Growth Triumphant*, 25.
19. Freeman, "Technology and Innovation," 315–16; W. Bernard Carlson, "Innovation and the Modern Corporation: From Heroic Invention to Industrial Science," in *Companion to Science in the Twentieth Century*, ed. John Krige and Dominique Pestre (New York: Routledge, 2003), 203–12, 217, 219.
20. Leuchtenburg, *Herbert Hoover*, 19.
21. Smil, *Creating the Twentieth Century*, 22, 24, 39, 46, 56, 91, 93–95, 181, 207, 217, 222, 226, 273, 276, 277, 308.
22. Freeman, "Technology and Innovation," 324–25.
23. Smil, *Creating the Twentieth Century*, 204–7.
24. Ibid., 158, 162.
25. Ibid., 90–91. For an influential reflection on innovation and technological systems, see Thomas P. Hughes, "The Evolution of Large Technological Systems," in *The Science Studies Reader*, ed. Mario Biagioli (New York: Routledge, 1999), 202–23.
26. Paul Josephson, "The History of World Technology, 1750–Present," in *The Cambridge World History*, Vol. 7: *Production, Destruction, and Connection, 1750–Present, Part 1: Structures, Spaces and Boundary-Making*, ed. J.R. McNeill and Kenneth Pomeranz (Cambridge: Cambridge University Press, 2015), 142.
27. Calculated from B.R. Mitchell, ed., *International Historical Statistics, 1750–2005* (Basingstoke, UK: Palgrave MacMillan, 2007); Kenneth Pomeranz and J.R. McNeill, "Production, Destruction, and Connection, 1750–Present: Introduction," in Pomeranz and McNeill, *The Cambridge World History*, vol. 7, part 1, p. 10.
28. Smil, *Creating the Twentieth Century*, 63–65.
29. Ibid. 301.
30. Mira Wilkins, "Multinational Enterprise to 1930," in *Leviathans: Multinational Corporations and the New Global History*, ed. Alfred D. Chandler and Bruce Mazlish (Cambridge: Cambridge University Press, 2005), 58, 59, 61–62, 66, 70, 75, 77. Michel Beaud, *A History of Capitalism, 1500–2000* (New York: Monthly Review, 2001), 159, gives the figure five thousand British bank branches overseas by 1910.
31. Daniel Yergin, *The Prize: The Epic Quest for Oil, Money, and Power* (New York: Simon and Schuster, 1991), 40, 58–61, 64–66, 73, 82, 93–94.

32. H. G. Wells, *The Discovery of the Future* (New York: B. W. Huebsch, 1913), 57, 59, 60–61.
33. Smil, *Creating the Twentieth Century*, 94, 141, 294.
34. Byrn, "The Progress of Invention during the Past 50 Years," 82–83.
35. Joel A. Tarr, "The Metabolism of the Industrial City: The Case of Pittsburgh," *Journal of Urban History* 28 (2002): 518.
36. Smil, *Creating the Twentieth Century*, 141, 293, 158, 162, 172, 294.
37. Ibid., 93, 278–79.
38. Ibid., 132; Beaud, *History of Capitalism*, 181, 182, 183.

CHAPTER 3. REORGANIZING THE GLOBAL ECONOMY

1. V. I. Lenin, *Imperialism, the Highest Stage of Capitalism*, in *V. I. Lenin: Selected Works in Three Volumes*, vol. 1 (New York: International, 1939), 741.
2. Hora, *Landowners of the Argentine Pampas*, 64; Mirta Zaida Lobato and Juan Suriano, *Atlas Historico de la Argentina* (Buenos Aires: Editorial Sudamericana, 1998), 300, 302.
3. Alexander Nützenadel, "A Green International?" in Nützenadel and Trentmann, *Food and Globalization*, 155.
4. Oltmer, "Migration im Kontext," 185.
5. Kratoska, "Commercial Rice Cultivation," 78.
6. Wolfram Fischer, *Expansion—Integration—Globalisierung: Studien zur Geschichte der Weltwirtschaft* (Göttingen, Germany: Vandenhoeck and Ruprecht, 1998), 129.
7. Miriam Silverberg, "Constructing a New Cultural History of Prewar Japan," in *Japan in the World*, ed. Masao Miyoshi and H. D. Harootunian (Durham, NC: Duke University Press, 1993), 123; Stephen Kotkin, "Modern Times: The Soviet Union and the Interwar Conjuncture," in *The Cultural Gradient: The Transmission of Ideas in Europe, 1789–1991*, ed. Catherine Evtuhov and Stephen Kotkin (New York: Rowman and Littlefield, 2003), 191.
8. Fischer, *Expansion—Integration—Globalisierung*, 134.
9. Thomas E. Skidmore and Peter H. Smith, *Modern Latin America* (New York: Oxford University Press, 1989), 149, 152; Bill Albert, *South America and the World Economy from Independence to 1930* (Hong Kong: Macmillan Press, 1983), 45.
10. John R. Hanson II, "Diversification and Concentration of LDC Exports: Victorian Trends," *Explorations in Economic History* 14 (1977): 65; Oltmer, "Migration im Kontext," 186 (81% of Manchurian soy products in 1889, 60% in 1929); Ines Prodöhl, "Versatile and Cheap: A Global History of Soy in the First Half of the Twentieth Century," *Journal of Global History* 8 (2013): 461–82; Kenwood and Lougheed, *Growth of the International Economy*, 136; Albert, *South America and the World Economy*, 32.
11. Ulrich Pfister, "Globalisierung und Weltwirtschaft," in Thamer, *WBG Weltgeschichte*, VI:295.
12. Victor Bulmer-Thomas, "The Latin American Economies, 1929–1939," in *Latin American Economy and Society since 1930*, ed. Leslie Bethell (Cambridge: Cambridge University Press, 1998), 75.
13. Kenwood and Lougheed, *The Growth of the International Economy*, 138–39.
14. Nützenadel, "A Green International?" 153.
15. Ronald Findlay and Kevin H. O'Rourke, "Commodity Market Integration, 1500–2000," in *Globalization in Historical Perspective*, ed. Michael D. Bordo, Alan M. Taylor, and Jeffrey G. Williamson (Chicago: University of Chicago Press, 2003), 65; Christopher Chase-Dunn, Yukio Kawano, and Benjamin D. Brewer, "Trade Globalization since 1795: Waves of Integration in the World-System," *American Sociological Review* 65 (2000): 77–95.
16. Kenwood and Lougheed, *Growth of the International Economy*, 78.
17. Ibid., 83.
18. Wilkins, "Multinational Enterprise to 1930," 66; Toyin Falola and Matthew M. Heaton, *A History of Nigeria* (New York: Cambridge University Press, 2008), 121.
19. Skidmore and Smith, *Modern Latin America*, 112, 205, 252.
20. Ibid., 82; Geoffrey Jones, "Multinationals from the 1930s to the 1980s," in Chandler and Mazlish, *Leviathans*, 82.
21. Fletcher, "The Suez Canal and World Shipping," 572.
22. Skidmore and Smith, *Modern Latin America*, 88, 131.
23. Ibid., 44, 73, 223.
24. Peter Hugill, *Global Communications since 1844* (Baltimore: Johns Hopkins University Press, 1999), 30, 33, 69–70.
25. "Instructions of the Charge d'Affaires of Great Britain to Chile, September 23, 1853," quoted in Andre Gunder Frank, *Capitalism and Underdevelopment in Latin America* (New York: Monthly Review Press, 1967), 67.
26. *El Mercurio*, May 4, 1868, quoted in ibid., 68–69.
27. J. R. McNeill and William H. McNeill, *The Human Web: A Bird's Eye View of World History* (New York: W. W. Norton, 2003), 252–58.
28. Timothy R. Furnish, *Holiest Wars: Islamic Mahdis, Their Jihads, and Osama bin Laden* (Westport, CT: Praeger, 2005), 46.
29. Alessandro Stanziani, "Abolitions," in *The Cambridge World History*, Vol. 7: *Production, Destruction, and Connection, 1750–Present, Part 2: Shared Transformations*," ed. J. R. McNeill and Kenneth Pomeranz (Cambridge: Cambridge University Press, 2015), 112; Rebecca J. Scott, "Gradual Abolition and the Dynamics of Slave Emancipation in Cuba, 1868–1886," *Hispanic American Historical Journal* 63:3 (1983): 449–77; Peter Kolchin, *Unfree Labor: American Slavery and Russian Serfdom* (Cambridge: Cambridge University Press, 1987), 356, 363.
30. Steeve Coupeau, *The History of Haiti* (Westport, CT: Greenwood Press, 2008), 21–34; Robin Blackburn, "The Role of Slave Resistance in Slave Emancipation," in *Who Abolished Slavery? Slave Revolts and Abolitionism*, ed. Seymour Drescher and Pieter C. Emmer (New York: Berghahn, 2010), 169–78; Celia Maria Marinho de Azevedo, *Onda Negra, Medo Branco: O negro no imaginário das elites—Século XIX* (Rio de Janeiro: Paz e Terra, 1987), 40, 70.
31. Kolchin, *Unfree Labor*, 364.
32. Colin M. McLachlan, *A History of Modern Brazil* (Wilmington, DE: Scholarly Resources, 2003), 39–40, 42.
33. Stanziani, "Abolitions," 115; Kolchin, *Unfree Labor*, 366; Burke and Pomeranz, *The Environment in World History*, 281; J. N. Westwood, *Endurance and Endeavour: Russian History, 1812–2001* (Oxford: Oxford University Press, 2002), 69–73.
34. For a summary of the debate on this point, see John C. Clegg, "Capitalism and Slavery," *Critical Historical Studies* 2 (2015): 281–304, esp. 289–93.
35. Brian Holden Reid, *The Origins of the American Civil War* (New York: Longman, 1996); Paul Bairoch, *Economics and World History: Myths and Paradoxes* (Chicago: University of Chicago Press, 1993), 33–36.
36. Hora, *Landowners of the Argentine Pampas*, 10–11 and passim.
37. Philip D. Curtin, *The Rise and Fall of the Plantation Complex* (Cambridge: Cambridge University Press, 1990), 191–94.
38. Oltmer, "Migration im Kontext," 179.

39. Eric Foner, *Free Soil, Free Labor, Free Men* (New York: Oxford University Press, 1970).

40. See, for example, Thomas E. Skidmore, *Black into White: Race and Nationality in Brazilian Thought* (Durham, NC: Duke University Press, 1993), 18–19, 22–26.

41. See Stanziani, "Abolitions," 127–28; Sven Beckert, "Emancipation and Empire: Reconstructing the Worldwide Web of Cotton Production in the Age of the American Civil War," *American Historical Review* 109 (2004): 1405–38; Norbert Finzsch, "The End of Slavery, the Role of the Freedmen's Bureau, and the Introduction of Peonage," in *The End of Slavery in Africa and the Americas*, ed. Ulrike Schmieder, Katja Füllberg-Stolberg, and Michael Zeuske (Berlin: Lit, 2011), 141–64 (quotation, 146).

42. Kuhn, *Chinese among Others*, 112 (quotation), 114–34, 140–49; C. Vann Woodward, "Emancipations and Reconstructions: A Comparative Study," in Woodward, *The Future of the Past* (New York: Oxford University Press, 1989), 155–61.

43. Gungwu Wang, "Migration History: Some Patterns Revisited," in *Global History of Migrations*, ed. Gungwu (Boulder, CO: Westview Press, 1997), 10; Kuhn, *Chinese among Others*, 182; McKeown, "Global Migration," 157.

44. Basil Davidson, *Africa in History* (New York: Macmillan, 1991), 302–3.

45. Stefan-Ludwig Hoffmann, "Genealogies of Human Rights," in *Human Rights in the Twentieth Century*, ed. Hoffmann (Cambridge: Cambridge University Press, 2011), 8; Alice Conklin, "Colonialism and Human Rights: A Contradiction in Terms?" *American Historical Review* 103 (1998): 419–22; Daniel Laqua, "The Tensions of Internationalism: Trans-national Antislavery in the 1880s and 1890s," *International History Review* 33 (2011): 705–26; Pomeranz and McNeill, "Production, Destruction, and Connection," 27.

46. 33 Cong. Rec. 704–12 (56th Cong., 1st sess.).

47. Wilfred Scawen Blunt, "Britain's Imperial Destiny," in the Internet Modern History Sourcebook, www.fordham.edu/Halsall/mod/1899blunt.asp.

48. George A. Codding Jr., *The Universal Postal Union* (New York: New York University Press, 1964), 26, 35, 37, 48; Francis Lyall, *International Communications: The International Telecommunications Union and the Universal Postal Union* (London: Ashgate, 2011).

49. Pfister, "Globalisierung und Weltwirtschaft," 285.

50. Peter N. Stearns, *The Industrial Revolution in World History* (Boulder, CO: Westview Press, 1998), 82–83; Kenwood and Lougheed, *Growth of the International Economy*, 62–77; Bairoch, *Economics and World History*, 22–42; Michael A. Clemens and Jeffrey G. Williamson, "Why Did the Tariff-Growth Correlation Reverse after 1950?" National Bureau of Economic Research, NBER Working Paper No. 9181, doi:10.3386/w9181, figure 1; Ronald Findlay and Kevin H. O'Rourke, *Power and Plenty: Trade, War, and the World Economy in the Second Millennium* (Princeton: Princeton University Press, 2007), 402.

51. Pfister, "Globalisierung und Weltwirtschaft," 286.

52. Bairoch, *Economics and World History*, 41–42.

53. Jeff Sahadeo, "Progress or Peril: Migrants and Locals in Russian Tashkent, 1906–14," in *Peopling the Russian Periphery*, ed. Nicholas Breyfogle, Abby Schrader, and Willard Sunderland (New York: Routledge, 2007), 157; Philip D. Curtin, "Africa and Global Patterns of Migration," in Gungwu, *Global History of Migrations*, 83; Hoerder, *Cultures in Contact*, 390; Kratoska, "Commercial Rice Cultivation," 78; Kuhn, *Chinese among Others*, 183; Claude Markovits, *The Global World of Indian Merchants, 1750–1947* (Cambridge: Cambridge University Press, 2000).

54. Bairoch, *Economics and World History*, 41, 90–91.

55. Findlay and O'Rourke, *Power and Plenty*, 406, 410; Sugata Bose and Ayesha Jalal, *Modern South Asia* (New York: Routledge, 2004), 80–82.

56. Christopher Clark, *The Sleepwalkers: How Europe Went to War in 1914* (New York: HarperCollins, 2013), 342; Albert Hourani, *A History of the Arab Peoples* (Cambridge, MA: Harvard University Press, 1991), 282; Bairoch, *Economics and World History*, 32; David B. Abernethy, *The Dynamics of Global Dominance* (New Haven: Yale University Press, 2000), 111; William L. Cleveland, *A History of the Modern Middle East* (Boulder, CO: Westview Press, 2004), 86.

57. Findlay and O'Rourke, *Power and Plenty*, 401.

58. Albert, *South America and the World Economy*, 43.

59. Pfister, "Globalisierung und Weltwirtschaft," 295.

60. Jack Beeching, *The Chinese Opium Wars* (New York: Harcourt Brace Jovanovich, 1975).

61. Bairoch, *Economics and World History*, 42; Abernethy, *Dynamics of Global Dominance*, 111.

62. Mike Davis, *Late Victorian Holocausts* (London: Verso, 2001), 295.

63. P. J. Vatikiotis, *The History of Modern Egypt* (Baltimore: Johns Hopkins University Press, 1991), 154–70; Cleveland, *History of the Modern Middle East*, 94–95, 99.

64. Ronald Robinson, "The Excentric Idea of Imperialism, with or without Empire," in *Imperialism and After*, ed. Wolfgang J. Mommsen and Jürgen Osterhammel (London: Allen and Unwin, 1986), 277.

65. Martin et al., *A Concise History of America and Its People*, 2:570–71.

66. Davidson, *Africa in History*, 304–5.

67. See G. N. Sanderson, "The European Partition of Africa: Origins and Dynamics," in *The Cambridge History of Africa*, Vol. 6: *From 1870 to 1905*, ed. Roland Oliver and G. N. Sanderson (New York: Cambridge University Press, 1985), esp. 100–117.

68. K. W. Taylor, *A History of the Vietnamese* (Cambridge: Cambridge University Press, 2013), 447.

69. See Sanderson, "European Partition of Africa," 100–105.

70. Cushman, *Guano and the Opening of the Pacific World*; Bairoch, *Economics and World History*, 65, 67, 72–73.

71. Etamad, *Possessing the World*, 77–78, 70; Adrian Vickers, *A History of Modern Indonesia* (New York: Cambridge University Press, 2005), 10–13; Daniel R. Headrick, *The Tools of Empire* (New York: Oxford University Press, 1981), 121–22, 117, 118, 120.

72. Quoted in C. M. Andrew and A. S. Kanya-Forstner, "Centre and Periphery in the Making of the Second French Colonial Empire, 1815–1920," *Journal of Imperial and Commonwealth History* 16 (1988): 20.

73. Beaud, *History of Capitalism*, 160.

74. Etamad, *Possessing the World*, 39, 47, 52.

75. Bose and Jalal, *Modern South Asia*, 79; H. L. Wesseling, *European Colonial Empires, 1815–1919* (Harlow, UK: Pearson-Longman, 2004), 235.

76. Vickers, *History of Modern Indonesia*, 15, 20; John W. Cell, "Colonial Rule," in *The Oxford History of the British Empire*, Vol. 4: *The Twentieth Century*, ed. Judith M. Brown and William Roger Louis (Oxford: Oxford University Press, 1999), 232, 235.

77. Kevin Shillington, *History of Africa* (New York: Palgrave Macmillan, 2005), 355–58, 332–36; quotation in Davidson, *Africa in History*, 292.

78. Shillington, *History of Africa*, 377, 421; Davidson, *Africa in History*, 292–93, 319, 339.

79. Tucker, *Encyclopedia of North American Indian Wars*; Yenne, *Indian Wars*; William B. Kessel and Robert Wooster, eds., *Encyclopedia of Native American Wars and Warfare* (New York: Facts On File, 2005).

80. Davis, *Late Victorian Holocausts*; Mark B. Tauger, *Agriculture in World History* (London: Routledge, 2010), 83, 94, 98.

CHAPTER 4. LOCALIZATION AND GLOBALIZATION

1. Cecil Rhodes, "Confession of Faith (1877)," in *Sources of World History*, Mark A. Kishlansky (New York: HarperCollins, 1995), 225, 226.

2. Quoted in Pankaj Mishra, *From the Ruins of Empire* (London: Allen Lane, Penguin, 2012), 240.

3. For an informative discussion, see Chris Lorenz, "Representations of Identity: Ethnicity, Race, Class, Gender, and Religion," in *The Contested Nation: Ethnicity, Class, Religion, and Gender in National Histories*, ed. Chris Lorenz and Stefan Berger (New York: Palgrave Macmillan, 2008), esp. 24–31.

4. Pomeranz and McNeill, "Production, Destruction, and Connection," 31.

5. Friedrich Neumann, "Grimm, Wilhelm Carl," in *Neue Deutsche Biographie* 7 (Berlin: Duncker and Humblot, 1966), 77–79.

6. Ranbir Vohra, *The Making of India* (London: M. E. Sharpe, 1997), 76–81.

7. W. G. Beasley, *The Rise of Modern Japan* (London: Weidenfeld and Nicolson, 2000), 54–70, 102–8; R. Bin Wong, "Self-Strengthening and Other Political Responses to the Expansion of European Economic and Political Power," in Pomeranz and McNeill, *The Cambridge World History*, Vol. 7, Part 1, pp. 366–94; Carter Vaughn Findley, "The Tanzimat," in *The Cambridge History of Turkey*, Vol. 4: *Turkey in the Modern World*, ed. Resat Kasaba (Cambridge: Cambridge University Press, 2008), 11–37.

8. Findley, "The Tanzimat."

9. Afaf Lutfi al-Sayyid Marsot, *A History of Egypt* (Cambridge: Cambridge University Press, 2007), 64–77.

10. Skidmore and Smith, *Modern Latin America*, 63; Kevin Passmore, "Politics," in *Europe, 1900–1945*, ed. Julian Jackson (Oxford: Oxford University Press, 2002), 79, 83.

11. George Mosse, *Toward the Final Solution* (New York: Fertig, 1978); Ivan Hannaford, *Race: The History of an Idea in the West* (Baltimore: Johns Hopkins University Press, 1996); George M. Frederickson, *Racism: A Short History* (Princeton, NJ: Princeton University Press, 2003).

12. Marinho de Azevedo, *Onda Negra, Medo Branco*, esp. 64–69, 97; Skidmore, *Black into White*, 23–27, 136–39.

13. See, in particular, Michael Dummett, "The Nature of Racism," in *Racism in Mind*, ed. Michael P. Levine and Tamas Pataki (Ithaca, NY: Cornell University Press, 2004), 27–34; Manfred Berg and Simon Wendt, eds., *Racism in the Modern World* (New York: Berghahn, 2011).

14. Sidney H. Chang and Leonard H. D. Gordon, *All Under Heaven . . . : Sun Yat Sen and His Revolutionary Thought* (Stanford: Hoover Institution Press, 1991), 6–26; Lee Khoon Choy, *Pioneers of Modern China* (Singapore: World Scientific, 2005), 26–33.

15. Jesús Chavarría, *José Carlos Mariátegui and the Rise of Modern Peru, 1890–1930* (Albuquerque: University of New Mexico Press, 1979), 66.

16. John Charles Chasteen, *Born in Blood and Fire: A Concise History of Latin America* (New York: W. W. Norton, 2006), 207.

17. Matthew Arnold, quoted in Norman Davies, *God's Playground: A History of Poland*, Vol. 2: *1795 to the Present* (London: Oxford University Press, 2005), 96.

18. Louis L. Snyder, *Macro-nationalisms: A History of the Pan-movements* (Westport, CT: Greenwood Press, 1989).

19. Ahron Bregman, *A History of Israel* (New York: Palgrave Macmillan, 2003).

20. Matthew Frye Jacobson, *Whiteness of a Different Color* (Cambridge, MA: Harvard University Press, 1998).

21. Martin et al., *A Concise History of America and Its People*, 2:457.

22. Luis A. Marentes, *José Vasconcelos and the Writing of the Mexican Revolution* (New York: Twayne, 2000), 15–17, 20, 30.

23. Chavarría, *José Carlos Mariátegui*, 91.

24. Frank Dikötter, "The Racialization of the Globe," in Berg and Wendt, *Racism in the Modern World*, esp. 30–32; Urs Matthias Zimmermann, "Race without Supremacy," ibid., esp. 264–72; John H. Miller, *Modern East Asia* (Armonk, NY: M. E. Sharpe, 2008), 116, 118.

25. Cleveland, *A History of the Modern Middle East*, 129.

26. Quoted in Louis Hymans, *Leopold Sédar Senghor: An Intellectual Biography* (Edinburgh: University of Edinburgh Press, 1971), 99, 103–4. See Colin Grant, *Negro with a Hat: The Rise and Fall of Marcus Garvey* (Oxford: Oxford University Press, 2008).

27. Luther Standing Bear, *Land of the Spotted Eagle* (1933; reprint, Lincoln: University of Nebraska Press, 1960), ix, 248–50, 255.

28. Tracie Matysik, "Internationalist Activism and Global Civil Society at the High Point of Nationalism: The Challenge of the Universal Races Congress, 1911," in *Global History: Interactions between the Universal and the Local*, ed. A. G. Hopkins (Houndsmills, Basingstoke, UK: Palgrave Macmillan, 2006), esp. 145.

29. First Humanist Manifesto, American Humanist Association, https://americanhumanist.org/what-is-humanism/manifesto1/.

30. Moon, "Peasant Migration and the Settlement of Russia's Frontiers," 884–85.

31. Richard L. Rubenstein, "Jihad and Genocide: The Case of the Armenians," in *Confronting Genocide: Judaism, Christianity, and Islam*, ed. Steven Leonard Jacobs and Marc I. Sherman (New York: Lexington Books, 2009), 133–35.

32. J. A. G. Roberts, *A History of China* (New York: Palgrave Macmillan, 2006), 156.

33. Hermann Roeren, *Zur Polenfrage* (Hamm, Germany: Brer and Thiemann, 1902), 2.

34. Julius Versen, "Negerseele und Kolonialmoral," *Allgemeine Rundschau* 4 (1907): 198–99.

35. Roberts, *A History of China*, 172–78; Amy H. Sturgis, *Tecumseh: A Biography* (Westport, CT: Greenwood Press, 2008); Michael Clodfelter, *Warfare and Armed Conflicts: A Statistical Reference to Casualty and Other Figures, 1618–1991*, Vol. 1 (London: McFarland, 1991), 392; Nelson A. Reed, *The Caste War of Yucatan* (Stanford: Stanford University Press, 2001); James O. Gump, "A Spirit of Resistance: Sioux, Xhosa, and Maori Responses to Western Dominance, 1840–1920," *Pacific Historical Review* 66 (1997): 21–52.

36. Chris Bayly, *The Birth of the Modern World* (Oxford: Blackwell, 2004), 354–55; Daniel Brower, "Russian Roads to Mecca," *Slavic Review* 55 (1996): 579.

37. Patrick Marnham, *Lourdes: A Modern Pilgrimage* (New York: Coward McCann and Geoghegan, 1980), 183.

38. "Dr. James Emmanuel Kwegyir Aggrey," in *African Saints*, ed. Frederick Quinn (New York: Crossroads, 2002), 18–20.

39. 'Abdi Sheik-'Abdi, *Divine Madness: Mohammed 'Abdulle Hassan (1856–1920)* (London: Zed, 1992).

40. Bayly, *Birth of the Modern World*, 333.

41. Ibid., 357.

42. Quoted in David McMahan, *The Making of Buddhist Modernism* (Oxford: Oxford University Press, 2008), 96; Peter van der Veer, "Religion after 1750," in Pomeranz and McNeill, *The Cambridge World History*, Vol. 7, Part 2, pp. 172–75.

43. Michael Axworthy, *A History of Iran* (New York: Basic Books, 2008), 197–99; Mark Sedgwick, *Muhammad Abduh* (Oxford: Oneworld, 2010); Furnish, *Holiest Wars*, 45–58; Cleveland, *History of the Modern Middle East*, 124.

44. Narasingha P. Sil, *Swami Vivekananda: A Reassessment* (Selinsgrove, PA: Susquehanna University Press, 1997), 166–67; Amiya P. Sen, *Swami Vivekananda* (Oxford: Oxford University Press, 2000).

45. Bayly, *Birth of the Modern World*, 338.

46. Shamita Basu, *Religious Revivalism as Nationalist Discourse: Swami Vivekananda and New Hinduism in Nineteenth-Century Bengal* (Oxford: Oxford University Press, 2002), 12–17, 134–38; V.C. Joshi, ed., *Rammohun Roy and the Process of Modernization in India* (Delhi: Vikas, 1975).

47. Ferenc M. Szasz and Margaret Connell Szasz, "Religion and Spirituality," in *The Oxford History of the American West*, ed. Clyde A. Milner, II, Carol A. O'Connor, and Martha A. Sandweiss (New York: Oxford University Press, 1994), 381, 384.

48. Tomoko Masuzawa, *The Invention of World Religions* (Chicago: University of Chicago Press, 2005).

49. Leonard J. Arrington and Davis Bitton, *The Mormon Experience* (Urbana: University of Illinois Press, 1992).

50. Vivian Green, *A New History of Christianity* (New York: Continuum, 1996), 317–19; Kevin Ward, "Africa," in *A World History of Christianity*, ed. Adrian Hastings (Grand Rapids, MI: William B. Eerdmans, 1999), esp. 221–23.

51. Howard D. Gregg, *History of the African Methodist Episcopal Church* (Nashville, TN: AMEC Sunday School Union, 1980); Hilary L. Rubinstein et al., *The Jews in the Modern World: A History since 1750* (London: Arnold, 2002), 46–55.

52. Quotation in J. Stillson Judah, *The History and Philosophy of the Metaphysical Movements in America* (Philadelphia: Westminster, 1967), 173; Catherine L Albanese, *A Republic of Mind and Spirit* (New Haven, CT: Yale University Press, 2007), 359.

53. Howard Radest, *Toward Common Ground: The Story of the Ethical Societies in the United States* (New York: Ungar, 1969), 17, 28 (quotations), 87–89.

54. Inayat Khan, *Biography of Pir-o-Murshid Inayat Khan* (London: East-West, 1979).

55. Quoted in Judah, *History and Philosophy*, 93.

56. Sylvia Cranston, *HPB* (New York: Putnam, 1993); Mary Lutyens, *The Life and Death of Krishnamurti* (London: John Murray, 1990).

57. J.W. Hanson, ed., *The World's Congress of Religions* (Chicago: W.B. Conkey, 1894).

58. Mohandas Gandhi, "Economic vs. Moral Progress," in *Mahatma Gandhi: His Life, Writings, and Speeches*, ed. Sarojini Naidu (Madras, India: Ganesh, 1921), 183, 187, 188, 190.

59. James D. Hunt, *Gandhi in London* (New Delhi: Promilla, 1978), 20–37. For Gandhi's biography I have drawn particularly on Martin Green, *Gandhi: Voice of a New Age Revolution* (New York: Continuum, 1993), and Ramachandra Guha, *Gandhi before India* (New York: Knopf, 2014).

60. Thomas Adam, *Intercultural Transfers and the Making of the Modern World* (Houndsmills, Basingstoke, UK: Palgrave Macmillan, 2012), 125–29. For the broader history, see Nico Slate, *Colored Cosmopolitanism: The Shared Struggle for Freedom in the United States and India* (Cambridge, MA: Harvard University Press, 2012), esp. 21–25, 95, 114–16, 207–11, 221.

61. Tom Lodge, "Resistance and Reform," in *The Cambridge History of South Africa*, ed. Robert Ross, Anne Kelk Mager, and Bill Nasson (Cambridge: Cambridge University Press, 2011), 434; Nigel Worden, *The Making of Modern South Africa* (Chichester, UK: Wiley-Blackwell, 2012), 116–17; Jan Vladislav, ed., *Vaclav Havel or Living in Truth* (London: Faber and Faber, 1986); Adam, *Intercultural Transfers*, 130–34.

62. Kerry Segrave, *American Films Abroad* (Jefferson, NC: McFarland, 1997), 3, 4, 13; quotation in Ian Tyrell, *Reforming the World: The Creation of America's Moral Empire* (Princeton, NJ: Princeton University Press, 2010), 224.

63. David Goldblatt, *The Ball Is Round: A Global History of Soccer* (New York: Riverhead, 2008), 233–34, 237–39; Antonio Missiroli, "European Football Cultures and Their Integration," in *Culture, Sport, Society* 5 (2002): 1–20.

64. Ann Daly, *Done into Dance: Isadora Duncan in America* (Bloomington: Indiana University Press, 1995).

65. Suzanne Shelton, *Ruth St. Denis: A Biography of the Divine Dancer* (Austin: University of Texas Press, 1981).

66. Uttara Asha Coorlawala, "Ruth St. Denis and India's Dance Renaissance," *Dance Chronicle* 15 (1992): 142.

67. Ibid., 123–52.

68. Larraine Nicholas, *Dancing in Utopia: Dartington Hall and its Dancers* (Alton, Hampshire, UK: Dance Books, 2007), 123–124.

69. Midori Takeishi, *Japanese Elements in Michio Ito's Early Period (1915–1924)*, ed. David Pacun (Los Angeles: California Institute of the Arts, 2006), 20–36.

70. Lily Litvak, "Latinos y Anglosajones: Una Polemica de la España fin de Siglo," in Litvak, *España 1900: Modernismo, anarquismo y fin de siglo* (Madrid: Anthropos, 1990).

71. Maria Pilar Queralt, *Tórtola Valencia* (Barcelona: Lumen, 2005).

72. Madeleine Herren, *Internationale Organisationen seit 1865* (Darmstadt, Germany: Wissenschaftliche Buchgesellschaft, 2010), 33.

73. Ibid., 24–25; Cornelia Knab, "Infectious Rats and Dangerous Cows: Transnational Perspectives on Animal Diseases in the First Half of the Twentieth Century," *Contemporary European History* 20 (2011): 289.

74. Herren, *Internationale Organisationen*, 38.

75. Ibid., 31–32, 35.

76. Ibid., 28.

77. Evan Schofer, "Science Associations in the International Sphere, 1875–1990," in *Constructing World Culture: International Nongovernmental Organizations since 1875*, ed. John Boli and George M. Thomas (Stanford: Stanford University Press, 1999), 251.

78. Thomas A. Loya and John Boli, "Standardization in the World Polity," in Boli and Thomas, *Constructing World Culture*, 169, 172.

79. Glenda Sluga, *Internationalism in the Age of Nationalism* (Philadelphia: University of Pennsylvania Press, 2013), 13, 16, 121; Frank J. Lechner, *Globalization: The Making of World Society* (Malden, MA: Wiley-Blackwell, 2009), 42; Nitza Berkovitch, "The Emergence and Transformation of the International Women's Movement," in Boli and Thomas, *Constructing World Culture*, 103–5.

80. Herren, *Internationale Organisationen*, 38; John Boli and George M. Thomas, "INGOs and the Organization of World Culture," in Boli and Thomas, *Constructing World Culture*, 13, 21.

CHAPTER 5. THE GREAT EXPLOSION

1. Emiliano Zapata, "The *Plan de Ayala*, 1911," in Alexander Dawson, *Latin America since Independence: A History with Primary Sources* (New York: Routledge, 2011), 127.

2. Eric Wolf, *Peasant Wars of the Twentieth Century* (1969; reprint, Norman: University of Oklahoma Press, 1999), ix.

3. Sheila Fitzpatrick, *The Russian Revolution* (Oxford: Oxford University Press, 2008); Moshe Lewin, *The Soviet Century* (London: Verso, 2005).

4. Feroz Ahmad, *The Making of Modern Turkey* (London: Routledge, 1993), 34–39, 48–49; M. Şükrü Hanioğlu, "The Second Constitutional Period, 1908–1918," in Kasaba, ed., *Cambridge History of Turkey*, 4:62–111; Andrew Mango, "Atatürk," ibid., 147–74; Cleveland, *History of the Modern Middle East*, 180–83; Ben Kiernan, *Blood and Soil: A World History of Genocide and Extermination from Sparta to Darfur* (New Haven: Yale University Press, 2007), 400–410.

5. Ali M. Ansari, *Modern Iran since 1921* (Edinburgh: Pearson, 2003), 24–39, 67–71; Axworthy, *History of Iran*, 200–219; Michael Zirinsky, "Riza Shah's Abrogation of Capitulations, 1927–1928," in *The Making of Modern Iran*, ed. Stephanie Cronin (New York: Routledge, 2003), 86; Shireen Mahdavi, "Reza Shah Pahlavi and Women: A Re-Evaluation," ibid., 185–86; Cleveland, *History of the Modern Middle East*, 187–89.

6. Pablo Escalante Gonzalbo et al., *Nueva Historia Mínima de México* (Mexico: Colegio de México, 2004), 210; Alicia Hernandez Chavez, *Mexico: A Brief History* (Berkeley: University of California Press, 2006), 182; Colegio de México, *Historia General de México, Version 2000* (México, 2000), 664, 679; Michael C. Meyer, William L. Sherman, and Susan M. Deeds, *The Course of Mexican History* (New York: Oxford University Press, 1979), 425, 431; Wolf, *Peasant Wars*, 41.

7. Robert Ryal Miller, *Mexico: A History* (Norman: University of Oklahoma Press, 1985), 272, 266; Chavez, *Mexico*, 181; Colegio de México, *Historia General*, 663; Chasteen, *Born in Blood and Fire*, 184, 196.

8. For an analysis of the complex origins of the Mexican Revolution, see John Tutino, *From Insurrection to Revolution in Mexico* (Princeton, NJ: Princeton University Press, 1986).

9. Skidmore and Thomas, *Modern Latin America*, 224; Enrique Krauze, *Mexico: Biography of Power* (New York: HarperCollins, 1997), 246, 250–51.

10. Rudolph J. Rummel, *Statistics of Democide: Genocide and Mass Murder since 1900* (Münster, Germany: Lit, 1998), 189.

11. Skidmore and Thomas, *Modern Latin America*, 228, 231, 232–33, 236; Adrian Hastings, "Latin America," in Hastings, *World History of Christianity*, esp. 357.

12. Roberts, *History of China*, 204–11; Marie-Claire Bergere, "The Chinese Bourgeoisie, 1911–1937," in *The Cambridge History of China*, Vol. 12: *Republican China, 1912–1949*, Part 1, ed. John K. Fairbank (Cambridge: Cambridge University Press, 1983), 722–825; Ernest P. Young, "Politics in the Aftermath of Revolution: The Era of Yuan Shih-k'ai, 1912–1916," ibid., 209–58; James E. Sheridan, "The Warlord Era: Politics and Militarism under the Peking Government, 1916–1928," ibid., 284–321; Lloyd E. Eastman, "Nationalist China during the Nanking Decade, 1927–1937," in *The Cambridge History of China*, Vol. 13: *Republican China, 1912–1949*, Part 2, ed. John K. Fairbank and Albert Feuerwerker (Cambridge: Cambridge University Press, 1986), 116–67.

13. Wolf, *Peasant Wars*, 276.

14. Karl Marx and Friedrich Engels, *The Communist Manifesto*, ed. John E. Toews (Boston: Bedford/St. Martin's, 1999), 67.

15. The following account is based on William J. Duiker, *Ho Chi Minh* (New York: Hyperion, 2000).

16. Rifleman Amar Singh Rawat (Garhwal Rifles) to a friend (India), March 26, 1915, in David Omissi, ed., *Indian Voices of the Great War* (New York: St. Martin's, 1999), 45–46.

17. Oltmer, "Migration im Kontext," 201.

18. Robin Prior and Trevor Wilson, *The Somme* (New Haven: Yale University Press, 2006), 301.

19. Clodfelter, *Warfare and Armed Conflicts*, 2:781–82. Figures vary substantially. William Kelleher Storey, *The First World War: A Concise Global History* (Lanham, MD: Rowman and Littlefield, 2009), 153, reports 9.45 million killed in battle.

20. Andrew T. Price-Smith, *Contagion and Chaos: Disease, Ecology, and National Security in the Age of Globalization* (Cambridge, MA: MIT Press, 2009), 59–60; John H. Morrow Jr., "The Impact of the Two World Wars in a Century of Violence," in *Essays on Twentieth-Century History*, ed. Michael C. Adas (Philadelphia: Temple University Press, 2010), 184; Mark Harrison, "Disease and World History from 1750," in McNeill and Pomeranz, *The Cambridge World History*, Vol. 7, Part 1, p. 246.

21. Henry L. Stimson, "The Decision to Use the Atomic Bomb," *Harper's Magazine* (February 1947), in *Sources of Global History since 1900*, ed. James H. Overfield (Boston: Wadsworth Cengage Learning, 2013), 242.

22. Quoted in David Fromkin, *A Peace to End All Peace: Creating the Modern Middle East, 1914–1922* (New York: Henry Holt, 1989), 27.

23. Sean McMeekin, *The Russian Origins of the First World War* (Cambridge, MA: Harvard University Press, 2011), 6; Westwood, *Endurance and Endeavour*, 305.

24. Beasley, *The Rise of Modern Japan*, 102–20, 140–58; Peter Duus, "Economic Dimensions of Meiji Imperialism: The Case of Korea, 1895–1910," in *The Japanese Colonial Empire, 1895–1945*, ed. Ramon H. Myers and Mark R. Peattie (Princeton, NJ: Princeton University Press, 1984), 128–71; Robert Tierney, *Tropics of Savagery: The Culture of Japanese Empire in Comparative Frame* (Berkeley: University of California Press, 2010); Jun Uchida, *Brokers of Empire: Japanese Settler Colonialism in Korea, 1876–1945* (Cambridge, MA: Harvard University Press, 2011); Lewis H. Gann, "Western and Japanese Colonialism: Some Preliminary Comparisons," in Myers and Peattie, *The Japanese Colonial Empire*, 497–525.

25. A. S. Kanya-Forstner, "The War, Imperialism, and Decolonization," in *The Great War and the Twentieth Century*, ed. Jay Winter, Geoffrey Parker, and Mary R. Habeck (New Haven: Yale University Press, 2000), 231; Alfred E. Eckes Jr., *The United States and the Global Struggle for Minerals* (Austin: University of Texas Press, 1979), 12.

26. Quoted in Dirk Boenker, *Militarism in a Global Age* (Ithaca, NY: Cornell University Press, 2011), 34.

27. Ibid., 29.

28. Quotations in ibid., 41, 43, 45, 48–57; Paul Johnson, *Modern Times* (New York: Harper and Row, 1983), 215.

29. See Robert Gerwarth and Erez Manela, eds., *Empires at War, 1911–1923* (New York: Oxford University Press, 2014), 2–3.

30. McMeekin, *Russian Origins*, 6–40. Clark, *Sleepwalkers*, 340, gives the figures 37 percent and 75–80 percent.

31. McMeekin, *Russian Origins*, 30, 36–37; Clark, *Sleepwalkers*, 338–39.

32. Rudi Volti, *Technology and Commercial Air Travel* (Washington, DC: American Historical Association, 2015), 16.

33. F. William Engdahl, "Oil and the Origins of the Great War," *History Compass* 5:6 (2007): 2042, 2050.

34. Ibid., 2047, 2054–55; Yergin, *The Prize*, 161, 187–88.

35. Mao Tse Tung, "Report on an Investigation of the Peasant Movement in Hunan, March 1927," in *Selected Writings of Mao Tse Tung* (New York: Pergamon Press, 1965), 25, 29.
36. Warren S. Thompson, *Population Problems* (New York: McGraw-Hill, 1930), 371.
37. Donald J. Raleigh, "The Russian Civil War, 1917–1922," in *The Cambridge History of Russia*, Vol. 3: *The Twentieth Century*, ed. Ronald Grigor Suny (Cambridge: Cambridge University Press, 2006), 140–67 (figures on 166); Johnson, *Modern Times*, 73.
38. Mark Mazower, *Dark Continent* (New York: Vintage, 1998), 42.
39. Panikos Panayi, "Imperial Collapse and the Creation of Refugees in Twentieth-Century Europe," in *Refugees and the End of Empire*, ed. Panikos Panayi and Pippa Virdee (New York: Palgrave Macmillan, 2011), 3; Dawn Chatty, "Integration without Assimilation in an Impermanent Landscape," ibid., 138; Rummel, *Statistics of Democide*, 83–84; Uğur Ümit Üngör, *The Making of Modern Turkey* (Oxford: Oxford University Press, 2011), 55–106; Gerard J. Libaridian, "The Ultimate Repression: The Genocide of the Armenians, 1915–1917," in *Genocide in the Modern Age*, ed. Isidor Walliman and Michael N. Dobkowski (New York: Greenwood Press, 1987), 203–7; Storey, *The First World War*, 138; Donald Bloxham, "Internal Colonization, Inter-imperial Conflict and the Armenian Genocide," in *Empire, Colony, Genocide*, ed. A. Dirk Moses (New York: Berghahn, 2008), 325–42; Kiernan, *Blood and Soil*, 392–415; Bregman, *A History of Israel*, 13–18.
40. On the relationship between geopolitics and ideology, see, for example, Mark Mazower, *Hitler's Empire: How the Nazis Ruled Europe* (New York: Penguin, 2008), 3–10.
41. Kevin Shillington, *History of Africa* (New York: Palgrave Macmillan, 2005), 336–37.
42. James C. Scott, *Seeing like a State: How Certain Schemes to Improve the Human Condition Have Failed* (New Haven: Yale University Press, 1998), esp. 183–91, 262–306.
43. Carlo Levi, *Christ Stopped at Eboli* (New York: Farrar, Strauss, 1947), 4, 250.
44. Sun Yat Sen, *Principles of National Reconstruction* (n.p.: China Cultural Service, 1925), 84, 98, 99.
45. McNeill, *Something New under the Sun*, 217; Mitchell, *International Historical Statistics*; Giovanni Federico, *Feeding the World: An Economic History of Agriculture* (Princeton, NJ: Princeton University Press, 2005), 48.
46. Wolf, *Peasant Wars*, 90–91; Joseph Stalin, "The Tasks of Business Executives," February 4, 1931, Marxists Internet Archive, www.marxists.org/reference/archive/stalin/works/1931/02/04.htm.
47. Götz Aly and Susanne Heim, *Architects of Annihilation* (Princeton, NJ: Princeton University Press, 2002), 66.
48. Peter Kenez, *A History of the Soviet Union from the Beginning to the End* (Cambridge: Cambridge University Press, 2006), 85, 87; Mazower, *Dark Continent*, 119; David R. Shearer, "Stalinism, 1928–1940," in Grigor, *Cambridge History of Russia*, 3:195–97; Johnson, *Modern Times* 268–72; Clodfelter, *Warfare and Armed Conflicts*, 2:841; Lynne A. Viola, V. P. Danilov, N. A. Ivnitskii, and Denis Koslov, eds., *The War against the Peasantry, 1927–1930* (New Haven: Yale University Press, 2005); Scott, *Seeing like a State*, 202.
49. Mortality figures vary wildly. Shearer, "Stalinism," 194; Vladislav M. Zubok, "Soviet Foreign Policy from Détente to Gorbachev, 1975–1985," in *The Cambridge History of the Cold War*, vol. 3, ed. Melvyn P. Leffler and Odd Arne Westad (Cambridge: Cambridge University Press, 2010), 95; Robert Service, *A History of Twentieth-Century Russia* (Cambridge, MA: Harvard University Press, 1998), 181–84, 190–91.
50. Robert Service, *A History of Twentieth-Century Russia* (Cambridge, MA: Harvard University Press, 1998), 181, 182, 184; Kenez, *History of the Soviet Union*, 93; John Gooding, *Rulers and Subjects: Government and People in Russia, 1801–1991* (London: Arnold, 1996), 209.
51. Mazower, *Dark Continent*, 144, 162; Johnson, *Modern Times*, 414, 416; Aly and Heim, *Architects of Annihilation*, 255; Alex J. Kay, *Exploitation, Resettlement, Mass Murder: Political and Economic Planning for German Occupation Policy in the Soviet Union, 1940–1941* (New York: Berghahn, 2006). The Nazis' calculations were not completely idiosyncratic; see Sunil Amrith and Patricia Clavin, "Feeding the World: Connecting Europe and Asia, 1930–1945," *Past and Present* 218: supplement 8 (2013): esp. 37, 42.
52. Stearns, *Industrial Revolution in World History*, 153–54.
53. Richard Maxwell Brown, "Violence," in Milner, O'Connor, and Sandweiss, *The Oxford History of the American West*, 393–421; Martin et al., *Concise History of America and Its People*, 2:439.
54. Federico, *Feeding the World*, 154.
55. Ibid.

CHAPTER 6. NEW WORLD (DIS)ORDER

1. Kita Ikki, "Plan for the Reorganization of Japan," in *Sources of Japanese Tradition*, ed. Ryusaku Tsunoda, William Theodore de Bary, and Donald Keene (New York: Columbia University Press, 1958), 269.
2. Richard Overy, "Economic Origins of the Second World War," in *The Origins of the Second World War*, ed. Frank McDonough (New York: Continuum, 2011), 486–87; Stearns, *The Industrial Revolution in World History*, 155.
3. Haruo Iguchi, "Japanese Foreign Policy and the Outbreak of the Asia-Pacific War," in McDonough, *Origins of the Second World War*, 467; Louise Young, "Japan at War: History-Writing on the Crisis of the 1930s," in *The Origins of the Second World War Reconsidered*, ed. Gordon Martel (New York: Routledge, 1999), 168; P. M. H. Bell, *Twelve Turning Points of the Second World War* (New Haven: Yale University Press, 2011), 132; Overy, "Economic Origins," 491–92; Dietrich Eichholtz, *War for Oil: The Nazi Quest for an Oil Empire* (Washington, DC: Potomac, 2012), 1.
4. Yergin, *The Prize*, 208, 265.
5. Ibid., 204.
6. Ibid., 183; Brian C. Black, *Crude Reality: Petroleum in World History* (Lanham, MD: Rowman and Littlefield, 2012), 131.
7. For what follows, see, above all, Robert Goralski and Russell W. Freeburg, *Oil and War: How the Deadly Struggle for Fuel in WWII Meant Victory or Defeat* (New York: William Morrow, 1987).
8. Yergin, *The Prize*, 320.
9. Young, "Japan at War," 168; Overy, "Economic Origins," 487.
10. Mark R. Peattie, *Ishiwara Kanji and Japan's Confrontation with the West* (Princeton, NJ: Princeton University Press, 1975), 55, 62, 57.
11. Bell, *Twelve Turning Points*, 135–36; Yergin, *The Prize*, 357.
12. Brian R. Sullivan, "More Than Meets the Eye: The Ethiopian War and the Origins of the Second World War," in Martel, *Origins*, 189, 198; Overy, "Economic Origins," 488, 490.
13. Overy, "Economic Origins," 502; Eichholtz, *War for Oil*, 53; Goralski and Freeburg, *Oil and War*, 124–130.
14. Goralski and Freeburg, *War and Oil*, 55, 63, 81, 110, 115, 181–84, 247–49, 279.
15. Bell, *Twelve Turning Points*, 144–46; Mark Harrison, "The USSR and Total War: Why Didn't the Soviet Economy Collapse

in 1942?" in *A World at Total War,* ed. Roger Chickering, Stig Foerster, and Bernd Greiner (Cambridge: Cambridge University Press, 2005), 140–41.

16. For a comprehensive summary discussion, see Richard Overy, *Why the Allies Won* (London: Jonathan Cape, 1995), esp. 18–25, 314–25.

17. Quoted in Adam Tooze, *The Deluge: The Great War, America, and the Remaking of the Global Order, 1916–1931* (New York: Viking, 2014), 4.

18. Findlay and O'Rourke, *Power and Plenty,* 446.

19. Ibid., 449–51.

20. Beaud, *A History of Capitalism,* 191–92; Findlay and O'Rourke, *Power and Plenty,* 451–52.

21. François Bourguignon et al., "Making Sense of Globalization: A Guide to the Economic Issues," Center for Economic Policy Research, Policy Paper No. 8, http://cepr.org/sites/default/files/geneva_reports/GenevaPP8.pdf, 22; Findlay and O'Rourke, "Commodity Market Integration," 41; Overy, "Economic Origins," 494, 500.

22. Adolph Hitler, *Mein Kampf* (1925), http://www.hitler.org/writings/Mein_Kampf.

23. Jawaharlal Nehru, *Glimpses of World History* (1934; reprinted, Bombay: Asia Publishing House, 1962), 852–53.

24. Young, "Japan at War," 161–65; Stephen S. Large, "Oligarchy, Democracy, and Fascism," in *A Companion to Japanese History,* ed. William M. Tsutsui (Oxford: Blackwell, 2007), 156–71; Miller, *Modern East Asia,* 113–19; Kiernan, *Blood and Soil,* 519–29.

25. Eric Hobsbawm, *The Age of Extremes* (New York: Vintage, 1994), 93.

26. Benito Mussolini, *Fascism: Doctrine and Institutions* (Rome: Ardita, 1932), 10.

27. E. M. Forster, "What I Believe" (1939), in *Two Cheers for Democracy* (London: Edward Arnold, 1951), 73.

28. George Kennan, "The Long Telegram" (February 22, 1946), National Security Archive, George Washington University, http://nsarchive.gwu.edu/coldwar/documents/episode-1/kennan.htm.

29. "Telegram from Nikolai Novikov, Soviet Ambassador to the US, to the Soviet Leadership" (September 27, 1946), Digital Archive, Cold War International History Project, Wilson Center, http://digitalarchive.wilsoncenter.org/document/110808.

30. Mark Mazower, *No Enchanted Place: The End of Empire and the Ideological Origins of the United Nations* (Princeton, NJ: Princeton University Press, 2008); Sluga, *Internationalism in the Age of Nationalism,* 122 (membership figures); Sunil Amrith and Glenda Sluga, "New Histories of the United Nations," *Journal of World History* 19 (2008): 251–74.

31. Herren, *Internationale Organisationen,* 93; Sluga, *Internationalism in the Age of Nationalism,* 121.

32. Boli and Thomas, "INGOs and the Organization of World Culture," 14, 42.

33. "List of Nongovernmental Organizations in Consultative Status with the Economic and Social Council as of 1 September 2013," United Nations, Economic and Social Council (October 4, 2013), esango.un.org/civilsociety/documents/E_2013_INF_6.pdf.

34. Gordon Adams and Steven M. Kosiak, "The United States: Trends in Defence Procurement and Research and Development Programmes," in *Arms Industry Limited,* ed. Herbert Wulf (Oxford: Stockholm International Peace Research Institute, Oxford University Press, 1993), 30.

35. Prasenjit Duara, "The Cold War as a Historical Period: An Interpretive Essay," *Journal of Global History* 6 (2011): 457–80;

Eckes, *The United States and the Global Struggle for Minerals,* esp. 150–52, 243.

36. Robert E. Harkavy, *Great Power Competition for Overseas Bases* (New York: Pergamon, 1982); idem, *Bases Abroad* (New York: Oxford University Press, 1989); James R. Blaker, *United States Overseas Basing: An Anatomy of the Dilemma* (New York: Praeger, 1990).

37. Raymond F. Betts, *Uncertain Dimensions: Western Overseas Empires in the Twentieth Century* (Minneapolis: University of Minnesota Press, 1985), 147–210.

38. Wilfried Loth, "States and the Changing Equations of Power," in *Global Interdependence: The World after 1945,* ed. Akira Iriye (Cambridge, MA: Harvard University Press, 2014), 48, 58 (250,000 to 1 million casualties); Akira Iriye, "The Making of a Transnational World," ibid., 702 (3.4 million); Barbara D. Metcalf and Thomas R. Metcalf, *A Concise History of India* (Cambridge: Cambridge University Press, 2002), 218–19 (up to 1 million dead, 12.5 million refugees); Oltmer, "Migration im Kontext," 199; Ian Talbot, "The End of the European Colonial Empires and Forced Migration," in Panayi and Virdee, *Refugees and the End of Empire,* 38; Hobsbawm, *Age of Extremes,* 51; Shillington, *History of Africa,* 425–26, 394–98, 411–13, 455–57.

39. See, for example, Abernethy, *Dynamics of Global Dominance,* 145.

40. United Nations, "Statement on Race, Paris, July 1950," in United Nations Educational, Scientific, and Cultural Organization, *Four Statements on the Race Question* (Paris: UNESCO, 1969), 32.

41. Abernethy, *Dynamics of Global Dominance,* 125.

42. Falola and Heaton, *History of Nigeria,* 119–20, 127, 138.

43. Abernethy, *Dynamics of Global Dominance,* 334, 338.

44. Richard Reid, *A History of Modern Africa, 1800 to the Present* (London: Wiley-Blackwell, 2009), 205–6; Abernethy, *Dynamics of Global Dominance,* 109, 112, 127–28, 146.

45. Vickers, *History of Modern Indonesia,* 73–83; Johnson, *Modern Times,* 149.

46. Metcalf and Metcalf, *Concise History of India,* 191.

47. Quoted in Mishra, *From the Ruins of Empire,* 251.

48. Bose and Jalal, *Modern South Asia,* 130.

49. Falola and Heaton, *History of Nigeria,* 142–43.

50. Shillington, *History of Africa,* 383, 385, 422, 378–80; Abernethy, *Dynamics of Global Dominance,* 157.

51. Reid, *History of Modern Africa,* 279.

52. Vatikiotis, *History of Modern Egypt,* 391–93.

53. Shillington, *History of Africa,* 382–83; Abernethy, *Dynamics of Global Dominance,* 151.

54. David Ryan and Victor Pungong, eds., *The United States and Decolonization* (New York: St. Martin's, 2000).

55. J. A. S. Grenville and Bernard Wasserstein, eds., *The Major International Treaties of the Twentieth Century,* Vol. 1 (London: Routledge, 2001), 333, 357, 365, 379.

56. Black, *Crude Reality,* 145.

57. Eckes, *The United States and the Global Struggle for Minerals,* 152.

58. Ansari, *Modern Iran since 1921,* 111–24; Rashid Khalidi, *Sowing Crisis: The Cold War and American Dominance in the Middle East* (Boston: Beacon Press, 2009), 49–52; Axworthy, *History of Iran,* 239; Cleveland, *History of the Modern Middle East,* 190, 293.

59. Odd Arne Westad, *The Global Cold War* (Cambridge: Cambridge University Press, 2005), 141; Thomas Borstelmann, *Apartheid's Reluctant Uncle: The United States and Southern Africa in the Early Cold War* (Oxford: Oxford University Press,

1993), 43–45, 50, 92, 198; Lise Namikas, *Battleground Africa: Cold War in the Congo, 1960–1965* (Stanford: Stanford University Press, 2013); Georges Nzongola-Ntalja, *The Congo from Leopold to Kabila: A People's History* (London: Zed Books, 2002), 96–11.

60. Vickers, *History of Modern Indonesia*, 144–59; Elaine Brière, "Shadow Play: Political Mass Murder and the 1965 Indonesian Coup," in *Hushed Voices*, ed. Heribert Adam (Highclere, Berkshire, UK: Berkshire Academic Press, 2011), 163–75.

61. Nicholas R. Lardy, "The Chinese Economy under Stress, 1958–1965," in *The Cambridge History of China*, Vol. 14: *The People's Republic of China*, Part 1, ed. Roderick MacFarquhar and John K. Fairbank (Cambridge: Cambridge University Press, 1987), 370; Yang Jisheng, *Tombstone: The Great Chinese Famine, 1958–1962* (New York: Farrar, Strauss and Giroux, 2013), 409–30; Kiernan, *Blood and Soil*, 529–33.

62. Jean van Lierde, *Lumumba Speaks* (Boston: Little, Brown, 1963), 323–25.

63. Zubok, "Soviet Foreign Policy from Détente to Gorbachev," 99.

64. Eckes, *The United States and the Global Struggle for Minerals*, 248.

65. Jeremi Suri, "The Cold War, Decolonization, and Global Social Awakenings," *Cold War History* 6 (2006): 357–58; Westad, *Global Cold War*, esp. 396–99; Khalidi, *Sowing Crisis*, 18.

66. Quoted in David F. Schmitz, *The United States and Right-Wing Dictatorships, 1965–1989* (New York: Cambridge University Press, 2006), 16; Michael E. Latham, *The Right Kind of Revolution: Modernization, Development, and U.S. Foreign Policy from the Cold War to the Present* (Ithaca, NY: Cornell University Press, 2011), 80.

67. Mark Atwood Lawrence, "The Rise and Fall of Nonalignment," in *The Cold War in the Third World*, ed. Robert J. McMahon (Oxford: Oxford University Press, 2013), 145; Nehru, *Glimpses of World History*, 589.

68. A. W. Singham and Shirley Hune, *Non-alignment in an Age of Alignments* (London: Zed Books, 1986); Vatikiotis, *History of Modern Egypt*, 395–97, 421; Latham, *The Right Kind of Revolution*, 79–80.

69. Skidmore and Smith, *Modern Latin America*, 209–14; Taylor, *History of the Vietnamese*; Shillington, *History of Africa*.

70. Skidmore and Smith, *Modern Latin America*, 92–105, 166–77, 130–39.

71. Stockholm International Peace Research Institute, Arms Transfers Database, https://www.sipri.org/databases/armstransfers; Duara, "The Cold War as a Historical Period," 470.

72. Mark Levine, "Genocide," in Pomeranz and McNeill, *The Cambridge World History*, Vol. 7, Part I, pp. 434–35; Helen Fein, ed., *Genocide Watch* (New Haven: Yale University Press, 1992), 33–36; Kiernan, *Blood and Soil*, 546–53.

CHAPTER 7. HIGH MODERNITY

1. Vance Packard, *The Waste Makers* (New York: Penguin, 1960), 18, 19, 21.

2. Clodfelter, *Warfare and Armed Conflicts*, 2:781–82, 841, 955–56, 1150.

3. Panayi, "Imperial Collapse," 5; Oltmer, "Migration im Kontext," 200–203, 209; Hobsbawm, *Age of Extremes*, 51–52.

4. Database, Maddison Project, www.ggdc.net/maddison /maddison-project/data.htm; Branko Milanovic, "Global Income Inequality by the Numbers," World Bank Development Research Group, Policy Research Working Paper No. 6259 (November 2012), esp. 5.

5. Others have used this term for the same period, in various contexts. See, for example, Will Steffen, Paul J. Crutzen, and John R. McNeill, "The Anthropocene: Are Humans Now Overwhelming the Great Forces of Nature?" *Ambio* 36:8 (2007): 617.

6. Clark R. Mollenhof, *George Romney: Mormon in Politics* (New York: Meredith, 1968), 160–62, 117, 97, 88.

7. Black, *Crude Reality*, 169.

8. Thomas W. Zeiler, "Opening Doors in the World Economy," in Iriye, *Global Interdependence*, 235.

9. See Edgerton, *The Shock of the Old*, 103–13.

10. Findlay and O'Rourke, *Power and Plenty*, 501–5; Marc Levinson, *The Box: How the Shipping Container Made the World Smaller and the World Economy Bigger* (Princeton, NJ: Princeton University Press, 2006).

11. Findlay and O'Rourke, *Power and Plenty*, 476–89, 497.

12. Peter N. Stearns, *Globalization in World History* (New York: Routledge, 2010), 143.

13. Hobsbawm, *Age of Extremes*, 279.

14. Mark Casson, "Introduction and Summary," in *Multinationals and World Trade*, ed. Mark Casson (London: Allen and Unwin, 1986), 51; Bruce Mazlish and Elliott R. Morss, "A Global Elite?" in Chandler and Mazlish, *Leviathans*, 174; Jones, "Multinationals from the 1930s to the 1980s," 94, 89.

15. Holly Sklar, ed., *Trilateralism* (Boston: South End Press, 1980), 10–12.

16. Mazlish and Morss, "A Global Elite?" 170–71.

17. Rudolf Stichweh, *Die Weltgesellschaft* (Frankfurt: Suhrkamp, 2000), 153; Stearns, *Globalization in World History*, 135.

18. Yergin, *The Prize*, 500, 546, 540, 480.

19. Bradley R. Simpson, "Southeast Asia in the Cold War," in McMahon, *The Cold War in the Third World*, 56.

20. Tony Judt, *Postwar: A History of Europe since 1945* (New York: Penguin, 2005), 339.

21. Giovanni Federico, "The Economic History of Agriculture since 1800," in McNeill and Pomeranz, *The Cambridge World History*, Vol. 7, Part 1, p. 91.

22. B. F. Stanton, "Agriculture: Crops, Livestock, and Farmers," in *The Columbia History of the Twentieth Century*, ed. Richard W. Bulliet (New York: Columbia University, 1998), 363.

23. See Johan F. M. Swinnen, "The Growth of Agricultural Protection in Europe in the 19th and 20th Centuries," *World Economy* 32 (2009): 1499–1537.

24. See, for example, Chesnais, *The Demographic Transition*, 433, 442–43.

25. Lara V. Marks, *Sexual Chemistry: A History of the Contraceptive Pill* (New Haven: Yale University Pres, 2001); Edgerton, *The Shock of the Old*, 22–25.

26. Grace Davie, "Europe: The Exception?" in *The Desecularization of the World: Resurgent Religion and Politics*, ed. Peter L. Berger (Washington, DC: Ethics and Policy, 1999), 69.

27. Shillington, *History of Africa*, 421, 423.

28. Yutaka Kosai, "The Postwar Japanese Economy, 1945–1973," in *The Cambridge History of Japan*, Vol. 6: *The Twentieth Century*, ed. Peter Duus (Cambridge: Cambridge University Press, 1989), 526.

29. Jones, "Multinationals from the 1930s to the 1980s," 89; Giuliano Garavani, "Completing Decolonization: The 1973 'Oil Shock' and the Struggle for Economic Rights," *International History Review* 33 (2011): 473–87; Yergin, *The Prize*, 446, 436, 567, 584–85, 628, 647–48, 651–52.

30. Jeffrey Robinson, *Yamani: The Inside Story* (New York: Simon and Schuster, 1988), 39–56; Eduardo Mayobre, *Juan Pablo Pérez Alfonzo, 1903–1979* (Caracas: Banco del Caribe, 2005).

31. Michael S. Minor, "The Demise of Expropriations as an Instrument of LDC Policy, 1980–1992," *Journal of International Business History* 25 (1994): 177–88.

32. Zeiler, "Opening Doors in the World Economy," 299.

33. Yergin, *The Prize*, 666. See also Ricardo Ffrench-Davis, Oscar Muñoz, and José Gabriel Palma, "The Latin American Economies, 1950–1990," in *Latin American Economy and Society since 1930*, ed. Leslie Bethell (Cambridge: Cambridge University Press, 1998), 178.

34. Angus Maddison, *Monitoring the World Economy, 1820–1992* (New York: Development Center of the OECD, 1995), 352, 355–56.

35. "*Mater et Magistra*: Encyclical of Pope John XXIII on Christianity and Social Progress" (1961), Holy See, at www.vatican.va /holy_father/john_xxiii/encyclicals/documents/hf_j-xxiii_enc_ 15051961_mater_en.html.

36. See Gosta Esping-Andersen, *The Three Worlds of Welfare Capitalism* (Princeton, NJ: Princeton University Press, 1990).

37. Martin et al., *A Concise History of America and Its People*, 2:709. On the development and aims of the welfare states, see Esping-Anderson, *Three Worlds of Welfare Capitalism*; Robert E. Goodin, Bruce Headey, Ruud Muffels, and Henk-Jan Dirven, *The Real Worlds of Welfare Capitalism* (Cambridge: Cambridge University Press, 1999); Kees van Kersbergen and Barbara Vis, *Comparative Welfare State Politics* (Cambridge: Cambridge University Press, 2014); Irwin Garfinkel, Lee Rainwater, and Timothy Smeeding, *Wealth and Welfare States* (Oxford: Oxford University Press, 2010); and Christopher Pierson and Francis G. Castles, eds., *The Welfare State: A Reader* (Cambridge: Polity, 2000).

38. Lyndon B. Johnson, "Remarks at the University of Michigan, May 22, 1964," American Presidency Project, www.presidency .ucsb.edu/ws/index.php?pid=26262.

39. Lyndon B. Johnson, "To Fulfill These Rights, June 4, 1965," American Presidency Project, www.presidency.ucsb.edu/ws /index.php?pid=27021.

40. Martin et al., *A Concise History of America and Its People*, 2:734, 777, 786–787.

41. Peter Flora et al., *State, Economy, and Society in Western Europe, 1815–1975* (London: Macmillan, 1983).

42. C. A. R. Crosland, "The Future of Socialism" (1956), excerpt in *Socialist Thought: A Documentary History*, ed. Albert Fried and Ronald Sanders (New York: Doubleday), 540, 541, 538.

43. One Nation Group, *The Responsible Society* (London: Conservative Political Centre, 1959), 32.

44. "*Mater et Magistra.*"

45. Crosland, "Future of Socialism," 539, 536.

46. Organization for Economic Cooperation and Development, *The OECD: History, Aims, Structure* (New York: OECD, n.d.).

47. Mark Frey and Sönke Kunkel, "Writing the History of Development: A Review of the Recent Literature," *Contemporary European History* 20 (2011): 215–32.

48. See Latham, *Right Kind of Revolution*, 51–52, 167–68.

49. International Development Association, *Aid Architecture: An Overview of the Main Trends in Official Development Assistance Flows* (n.p.: World Bank, February 2007), 34.

50. Falola and Heaton, *History of Nigeria*, 164, 183.

51. Summary: Nick Cullather, "Research Note: Development? It's History," *Diplomatic History* 24 (2000): 641–53; classic examples: Frank, *Capitalism and Underdevelopment in Latin America*; Walter Rodney, *How Europe Underdeveloped Africa* (1972; reprinted, Washington, DC: Howard University Press, 1982); and Samir Amin, *Unequal Development* (New York: Monthly Review Press, 1976).

CHAPTER 8. REVOLT AND REFUSAL

1. Stokely Carmichael, "Solidarity with Latin America," in *Stokely Speaks: Black Power to Pan-Africanism* (New York: Vintage, 1971), 101, 102, 104, 105.

2. Helmut Führer, *The Story of Official Development Assistance* (New York: Organization for Economic Cooperation and Development, 1996), 42.

3. Quoted in Schmitz, *The United States and Right-Wing Dictatorships*, 15. See also Latham, *The Right Kind of Revolution*, 60.

4. International Development Association, *Aid Architecture*, 3.

5. Lobato and Suriano, *Atlas Historico de la Argentina*, 522, 555; Mazower, *Dark Continent*, 367; Zubok, "Soviet Foreign Policy from Détente to Gorbachev," 98; Stephen Kotkin, "The Kiss of Debt," in *The Shock of the Global: The 1970s in Perspective*, ed. Niall Ferguson, Charles S. Maier, Erez Manela, and Daniel J. Sargent (Cambridge, MA: Harvard University Press, 2010), 85, 89; Ffrench-Davis, Muñoz, and Palma, "The Latin American Economies, 1950–1990," 224–34.

6. John Loxley, "International Capital Markets, the Debt Crisis, and Development," in *Global Development Fifty Years after Bretton Woods*, ed. Roy Culpeper, Albert Berry, and Frances Stewart (New York: St. Martin's, 1997), 138.

7. Robert K. Schaeffer, *Understanding Globalization* (Lanham, MD: Rowman and Littlefield, 2009), 79; Zeiler, "Opening Doors in the World Economy," 303.

8. Eckes, *The United States and the Global Struggle for Minerals*, 247; Schaeffer, *Understanding Globalization*, 83, 86.

9. Loxley, "International Capital Markets," 142.

10. Bairoch, *Economics and World History*, 116–17.

11. Peter Hjertholm and Howard White, *Survey of Foreign Aid: History, Trends, and Allocations*, Discussion Papers, No. 00-04 (University of Copenhagen, Department of Economics), http:// www.econ.ku.dk; International Development Association, *Aid Architecture*, 2; United Nations Department of Economics and Social Affairs, *World Economic and Social Survey 2010* (New York: United Nations, 2010), 49.

12. Davidson, *Africa in History*, 369; Ffrench-Davis, Muñoz, and Palma, "The Latin American Economies," 228; Zeiler, "Opening Doors in the World Economy," 304; Adebayo Oyebade, "Reluctant Democracy: The State, the Opposition, and the Crisis of Political Transition, 1985–1993," in *The Transformation of Nigeria*, ed. Oyebade (Trenton, NJ: Africa World Press, 2002), 144.

13. Maddison, *Monitoring the World Economy*, 80; Loxley, "International Capital Markets," 146, 149, 152.

14. United Nations Department of Economic and Social Affairs, *World Economic and Social Survey 2010*, 49; International Development Association, *Aid Architecture*, 34; Hjertholm and White, "Survey of Foreign Aid," 34.

15. Martin Rudner, "East European Aid to Asian Developing Countries," *Modern Asian Studies* 30 (1996): 1–28; Quentin V. S. Bach, *Soviet Economic Aid to the Less Developed Countries* (New York: Oxford University Press, 1987); Zeiler, "Opening Doors in the World Economy," 247.

16. Westad, *The Global Cold War*, 207–87; R. Craig Nation and Mark V. Kauppi, eds., *The Soviet Impact in Africa* (Lexington, MA: D. C. Heath, 1984).

17. Ernesto "Che" Guevara, "Message to the Tricontinental," in *Che: Selected Works of Ernesto Guevara*, ed. Rolando E. Bonachea and Nelson P. Valdes (Cambridge, MA: MIT Press, 1982), 170–82.

18. Duiker, *Ho Chi Minh*, 99, 100.

19. What follows is based on Nick Caistor, *Che Guevara: A Life* (Northampton, MA: Interlink, 2010).

20. The following account is based on Peniel E. Joseph, *Stokely: A Life* (New York: Basic Books, 2014).

21. Quoted in Andrew Sinclair, *Viva Che!* (Stroud, UK: Sutton, 2006), 67.

22. Miriam Makeba and James Hall, *Makeba: My Story* (New York: New American Library, 1988).

23. Carlos Moore, *Fela: This Bitch of a Life* (Chicago: Lawrence Hill Books, 2009); Michael Veal, "Fela and the Funk," in *Black President: The Art and Legacy of Fela Anikulapo Kuti,* ed. Trevor Schoonmaker (New York: New Museum of Contemporary Art, 2003), 35–40.

24. From Jay Babcock, "Bootsy Collins on Fela Kuti (1999)," *Arthur* (blog), arthurmag.com/2009/02/bootsy-collins/.

25. Falola and Heaton, *History of Nigeria,* 197.

26. Zeiler, "Opening Doors in the World Economy," 261.

27. Jane S. Jaquete, "Losing the Battle/Winning the War: International Politics, Women's Issues, and the 1980 Mid-decade Conference," in *Women, Politics, and the United Nations,* ed. Anne Winslow (Westport, CT: Greenwood Press, 1995), 47.

28. "Universal Declaration of Human Rights," United Nations, www.un.org/en/documents/udhr.

29. Tom Buchanan, "'The Truth Will Set You Free': The Making of Amnesty International," *Journal of Contemporary History* 37 (2002): 575–97; Stearns, *Globalization in World History,* 144; Kenneth Cmiel, "The Recent History of Human Rights," *American Historical Review* 109 (2004): 129–30; Sarah B. Snyder, *Human Rights Activism and the End of the Cold War* (Cambridge: Cambridge University Press, 2011).

30. Chernobyl Forum: 2003–2005, *Chernobyl's Legacy: Health, Environmental, and Socio-economic Impacts,* 2nd rev. version, International Atomic Energy Agency, https://www.iaea.org/sites/default/files/chernobyl.pdf, 16, 10–11, 33, 42.

31. Kathleen Bauk and Alec Cairncross, *"Goodbye, Great Britain": The 1976 IMF Crisis* (New Haven: Yale University Press, 1992); Stanley Fischer, "Applied Economics in Action: IMF Programs," *American Economic Review* 87 (1997): 23.

32. Paul R. Gregory, *The Political Economy of Stalinism* (Cambridge: Cambridge University Press, 2004), 250.

33. Arne Naess and George Sessions, "A Platform of the Deep Ecology Movement," in Arne Naess, *Ecology, Community, and Lifestyle: Outline of an Ecosophy,* trans. and ed. David Rothenberg (Cambridge: Cambridge University Press, 1989), 29.

34. Mosley, *Environment in World History,* 17, 21, 25, 27; Ponting, *New Green History of the World,* 145, 152–53; Cushman, *Guano and the Opening of the Pacific World,* 302; McEvoy, "Toward an Interactive Theory of Nature and Culture," 220–23.

35. Turner et al., *Earth as Transformed by Human Action,* 164; Michael Williams, *Deforesting the Earth: From Prehistory to Global Crisis* (Chicago: University of Chicago Press, 2006), 420.

36. Douglas R. Weiner, "The Predatory Tribute-Taking State: A Framework for Understanding Russian Environmental History," in Burke and Pomeranz, *The Environment and World History,* 295; Ponting, *A New Green History of the World,* 249.

37. Bowler, *The Earth Encompassed,* 519.

38. Ponting, *New Green History of the World,* 360–70.

39. J. R. McNeill and Peter Engelke, "Into the Anthropocene: People and Their Planet," in Iriye, *Global Interdependence,* 385; McNeill, *Something New under the Sun,* 132–33, 146; Ponting, *New Green History of the World,* 371.

40. Jonathan Neaman Lipman, Barbara Molony, and Michael Robinson, *Modern East Asia* (Boston: Pearson, 2012), 377.

41. Joachim Radkau, *Nature and Power: A Global History of the Environment* (Washington, DC: German Historical Institute; Cambridge: Cambridge University Press, 2008), 255.

42. McNeill, *Something New under the Sun,* 66–67, 70–71, 73, 77, 79.

43. Lynn Hollen Lees, "World Urbanization, 1750 to the Present," in McNeill and Pomeranz, *The Cambridge World History,* Vol. 7, Part 2, p. 55.

44. Rachel Carson, *Silent Spring* (Boston: Houghton Mifflin, 1962).

45. Aldo Leopold, *A Sand County Almanac* (New York: Oxford University Press, 1966), 220, 225, 235, 240; Cushman, *Guano and the Opening of the Pacific World,* 261. On the history of ecology, see Bowler, *The Earth Encompassed,* esp. 364–78, 518–53.

46. Teddy Roosevelt, "On American Motherhood," National Center for Public Policy Research, www.nationalcenter.org/TRooseveltMotherhood.html; Lothrop Stoddard, *The Rising Tide of Color against White World Supremacy* (New York: Charles Scribner's Sons, 1920); Sun Yat-Sen, *San Min Chu I: The Three Principles of the People,* trans. Frank W. Price, ed. L. T. Chen (Shanghai: Commercial Press, 1928), 23; Indian speaker quoted in Matthew Connelly, "To Inherit the Earth: Imagining World Population, from the Yellow Peril to the Population Bomb," *Journal of Global History* 1 (2006): 306.

47. Huxley quoted in Alison Bashford, "Population, Geopolitics, and International Organizations in the Mid-twentieth Century," *Journal of World History* 19:3 (2008): 341.

48. Quoted in ibid., 346.

49. Marks, *Sexual Chemistry,* 27–28.

50. Thomas Robertson, *The Malthusian Moment: Global Population Growth and the Birth of American Environmentalism* (New Brunswick, NJ: Rutgers University Press, 2012), 101. Michael E. Latham, in *The Right Kind of Revolution,* 104–5, reports quite different figures, but still a tripling of funding.

51. Latham, *The Right Kind of Revolution,* 108–9.

52. Quoted in ibid., 24–25.

53. Connelly, "To Inherit the Earth," 315; Bashford, "Population, Geopolitics, and International Organizations," 333–34.

54. Quoted in Robertson, *Malthusian Moment,* 173.

55. Quoted in Wade Rowland, *The Plot to Save the Planet* (Toronto: Clarke, Irwin, 1974), 15.

56. David Kuchenbuch, "'Eine Welt': Globales Interdependenzbewusstsein und die Moralisierung des Alltags in den 1970er und 1980er Jahren," *Geschichte und Gesellschaft* 38 (2012): 158–84 (quotation on 176).

57. Radkau, *Nature and Power,* 251; Fernando Elichirigoity, *Planet Management* (Evanston, IL: Northwestern University Press, 1999), 103, 107.

58. E. F. Schumacher, *Small Is Beautiful: Economics As If People Mattered* (New York: HarperCollins, 1973), 13, 54, 228–30; Barbara Wood, *E. F. Schumacher: His Life and Thought* (New York: Harper and Row, 1984).

59. Naess, *Ecology, Community, and Lifestyle,* 29, 141; Arne Naess, "The Shallow and the Deep, Long-Range Ecology Movements: A Summary," *Inquiry* 16 (1973): 95–100; Naess, *Gandhi and Group Conflict* (Oslo: Universitetsforlaget, 1974).

60. Quoted in Mark Hamilton Lytle, *The Gentle Subversive: Rachel Carson, Silent Spring, and the Rise of the Environmental Movement* (New York: Oxford University Press, 2007), 210.

61. Frank Zelko, *Make It a Green Peace! The Rise of Countercultural Environmentalism* (Oxford: Oxford University Press, 2013); Stearns, *Globalization in World History,* 144.

62. Ramachandra Guha, *Environmentalism: A Global History* (New York: Longman, 2000), 81.

63. McNeill and Engelke, "Into the Anthropocene," 388; Jens Ivo Engels, "Modern Environmentalism," in *The Turning Points of Environmental History*, ed. Frank Uekotter (Pittsburgh: University of Pittsburgh Press, 2010), 119–32; Frank Uekotter, "The Knowledge Society," ibid., 133–45.

64. H. S. D. Cole, Christopher Freeman, Marie Jahoda, and K. L. R. Pavitt, eds., *Models of Doom: A Critique of* The Limits to Growth (New York: Universe, 1973); Eckes, *The United States and the Global Struggle for Minerals*, 245.

CHAPTER 9. TRANSFORMATIVE MODERNITY

1. Lenin, *Imperialism, the Highest Stage of Capitalism*, 723–24.

2. Nick Cullather, *The Hungry World: America's Cold War Battle against Poverty in Asia* (Cambridge, MA: Harvard University Press, 2010); David A. Sonnenfeld, "Mexico's 'Green Revolution,' 1940–1980: Towards an Environmental History," *Environmental History Review* 16 (1992): 28, 33; McNeill, *Something New under the Sun*, 220.

3. Robert S. Anderson, "The Origins of the International Rice Research Institute," *Minerva* 29 (1991): 61–89; Latham, *The Right Kind of Revolution*, 112–15.

4. Nick Cullather, "Miracles of Modernization: The Green Revolution and the Apotheosis of Technology," *Diplomatic History* 28:2 (2004): 233, 244, 240.

5. Nick Cullather, "The War on the Peasant: The United States and the Third World," in McMahon, *The Cold War in the Third World*, 192–207.

6. Shillington, *History of Africa*, 428–29; Scott, *Seeing like a State*, 223–61.

7. Vandana Shiva, *The Violence of the Green Revolution: Third World Agriculture, Ecology, and* Politics (London: Zed Books, 1991), 111; Sandra Postel, *Pillar of Sand: Can the Irrigation Miracle Last?* (New York: W. W. Norton, 1999), 93; Sonnenfeld, "Mexico's 'Green Revolution,'" 28, 35–42; Nikki R. Keddie, *Roots of Revolution: An Interpretive History of Modern Iran* (New Haven: Yale University Press, 1981), 163–69, 181.

8. Peter B. R. Hazell, *The Asian Green Revolution* (Washington, DC: International Food Policy Research Institute, 2009), 3, 4.

9. Ibid., 22.

10. Paul Ehrlich, *The Population Bomb* (1968; reprint, Cutchogue, NY: Buccaneer, 1971), xi.

11. Stanton, "Agriculture," 367.

12. Johnson, *Modern Times*, 685.

13. Database, Maddison Project, www.ggdc.net/maddison/maddison-project/data.htm; Andrei Shleifer, *A Normal Country: Russia after Communism* (Cambridge, MA: Harvard University Press, 2005), esp. 118–20; Thomas Remington, *The Politics of Inequality in Russia* (Cambridge: Cambridge University Press, 2011).

14. Schaeffer, *Understanding Globalization*, 171; Stockholm International Peace Research Institute, online database at www.sipri.org/databases/armstransfers/; Database, Maddison Project, www.ggdc.net/maddison/maddison-project/data.htm.

15. United Nations Statistical Department, data.un.org (see "Military Expenditure [% of GDP]"). Figures vary wildly; see David Childs, *Britain since 1945: A Political History* (London: Routledge, 2012), 460.

16. Josephson, "History of World Technology, 149; all figures calculated from Mitchell, *International Historical Statistics: Africa, Asia, and Oceania*, 501–4, 786–805, 843–52; Mitchell, *International Historical Statistics: Europe*, 597–600, 816–24, 849–60; Mitchell, *International Historical Statistics: The Americas*, 412–14, 611–22, 646–52.

17. Patrick Karl O'Brien, "Intercontinental Trade and the Development of the Third World since the Industrial Revolution," *Journal of World History* 8 (1997): 129–30.

18. United Nations Development Program, *Human Development Report 2013: The Rise of the South* (New York: UNDP, 2013), 2, 13 (http://hdr.undp.org).

19. David Reynolds, *One World Divisible: A Global History since 1945* (New York: W. W. Norton, 2000), 513; John Peter Collett, "The History of Electronics," in *Companion to Science in the Twentieth Century*, ed. John Krige and Dominique Pestre (New York: Routledge, 2003), 253–74.

20. Gary Gereffi, Miguel Korzeniewicz, and Roberto P. Korzeniewicz, "Introduction: Global Commodity Chains," in *Commodity Chains and Global Capitalism*, ed. Gary Gereffi and Miguel Korzeniewicz (Westport, CT: Greenwood Press, 1994), 1; Manfred B. Steger, *Globalization: A Very Short Introduction* (Oxford: Oxford University Press, 2003), 50; Arif Dirlik, *The Postcolonial Aura: Third World Criticism in the Age of Global Capitalism* (Boulder, CO: Westview Press, 1997), 195.

21. William J. Hausman, Peter Hertner, and Mira Wilkins, *Global Electrification* (Cambridge: Cambridge University Press, 2008), 89, 244, 253–56.

22. Bouda Etemad and Jean Luciani, *World Energy Production, 1800–1985* (Geneva: Librairei Droz, 1991).

23. Radkau, *Nature and Power*, 217; Gilbert F. White, "The Environmental Effects of the High Dam at Aswan," *Environment* 30 (1988): 11; Mosley, *The Environment in World History*, 69; Nuclear Energy Institute, "World Statistics: Nuclear Energy around the World," https://www.nei.org/Knowledge-Center/Nuclear-Statistics/World-Statistics; International Atomic Energy Agency, "Nuclear Power Reactors in the World" (2017), at http://www-pub.iaea.org/books/IAEABooks/12237/Nuclear-Power-Reactors-in-the-World-2017-Edition; World Nuclear Association, "World Nuclear Power Reactors and Uranium Requirements," www.world-nuclear.org/information-library/facts-and-figures/world-nuclear-power-reactors-and-uranium-requireme.aspx.

24. Punam Chuhan-Pole and Manka Angwafo, eds., *Yes Africa Can* (Washington, DC: World Bank, 2011), 2, 4, 5; Robert I. Rotberg, *Africa Emerges* (Cambridge: Polity Press, 2013), ix, 151 (quotations), 153.

25. United Nations Development Program, *Human Development Report 1999* (New York: UNDP, 1999), 3–7, 22 (http://hdr.undp.org).

26. United Nations Development Program, *Human Development Report 2013*, 26, 14, 12, 13.

27. Ibid., 165; Falola and Heaton, *History of Nigeria*, 236.

28. Felipe Fernandez-Armesto, *The World: A History*, Vol. 2 (London: Prentice Hall, 2010), 923.

29. McNeill and Engelke, "Into the Anthropocene," 403.

30. Angus Maddison, *The World Economy: A Millennial Perspective* (New York: OECD, 2006), 355–56.

31. Hamid Algar, ed., *Islam and Revolution: Writings and Declarations of Imam Khomeini* (Berkeley, CA: Mizan Press, 1981), 55.

32. Ronald Reagan, "Remarks at the Annual Convention of the National Association of Evangelicals in Orlando, Florida, March 8, 1983," *Public Papers of the Presidents of the United States*, 364 (University of Michigan Digital Library), http://quod.lib.umich.edu/p/ppotpus/.

33. Loth, "States and the Changing Equations of Power," 151.

34. Margaret Thatcher, "What's Wrong with Politics?" lecture at the Conservative Political Center, October 11, 1968, Margaret Thatcher Foundation, http://www.margaretthatcher.org/Speeches/displaydocument.asp?docid=101632&doctype=1.

35. Joseph A. McCartin, *Collision Course: Ronald Reagan, the Air Traffic Controllers, and the Strike That Changed America* (New York: Oxford University Press, 2011); Andrew John Richards, *Miners on Strike: Class Solidarity and Division in Britain* (New York: Berg, 1996).

36. Talbot, "End of the European Colonial Empires," 35; Oltmer, "Migration im Kontext," 197.

37. Howard Adelman, Allan Borowski, Meyer Burstein, and Lois Foster, eds., *Immigration and Refugee Policy: Australia and Canada Compared*, vol. 1 (Toronto: University of Toronto Press, 1994), 10–11; Kuhn, *Chinese among Others*, 323–26, 354–57.

38. Pamela Kyle Crossley, Lynn Hollen Lees, and John W. Servos, *Global Society: The World since 1900* (Boston: Wadsworth, CENGAGE Learning, 2013), 331; Lipman, Molony, and Robinson, *Modern East Asia*, 425.

39. For context, see Maurice Isserman and Michael Kazin, *America Divided: The Civil War of the 1960s* (New York: Oxford University Press, 2008), 294–89; Cynthia A. Young, *Soul Power: Culture, Radicalism, and the Making of a U.S. Third World Left* (Durham, NC: Duke University Press, 2006); Ramón A. Gutiérrez, "Internal Colonialism: An American Theory of Race," *DuBois Review* 1 (2004): 281–95.

40. See Jonah Blank, "Democratization and Development," in *South Asia in World Politics*, ed. Devin T. Hagerty (New York: Rowman and Littlefield, 2005), 219–21, 236–38.

41. See Nancy Christie and Michael Gauvreau, eds., *The Sixties and Beyond: Dechristianization in North America and Western Europe, 1945–2000* (Toronto: University of Toronto Press, 2013); José Casanova, "Rethinking Secularization: A Global Comparative Perspective," in *Religion, Globalization, and Culture*, ed. Peter Beyer and Lori Beaman (Leiden, The Netherlands: Brill, 2007), 101–20; Olivier Tschannen, "La revaloración de la teoría de la secularización mediante la perspectiva comparada Europa Latina-América Latina," in *La Modernidad Religiosa: Europea Latina y América Latina en perspectiva comparada*, ed. Jean-Pierre Bastian (México: Fondo de Cultura Económica, 2004), esp. 355–56.

42. Cleveland, *History of the Modern Middle East*, 297; Keddie, *Roots of Revolution*, 180.

43. Rodney Stark, *The Rise of Mormonism*, ed. Reid L. Neilson (New York: Columbia University Press, 2005), 141.

44. Mark Juergensmeyer, "Introduction: Religious Ambivalence to Civil Society," in *Religion in Global Civil* Society, ed. Juergensmeyer (New York: Oxford University Press, 2005), 17, 15; Shandip Saha, "Hinduism, Gurus, and Globalization," in Beyer and Beaman, *Religion, Globalization, and Culture*, 294, 296, 298; George van Pelt Campbell, "Religion and the Phases of Globalization," ibid., 489, 490, 493.

45. Saha, "Hinduism, Gurus, and Globalization," 498.

46. See Gabriel A. Almond, R. Scott Appleby, and Emmanuel Sivan, *Strong Religion: The Rise of Fundamentalisms around the World* (Chicago: University of Chicago Press, 2003).

47. Humanist Manifesto I, II, and III, American Humanist Association, https://americanhumanist.org/what-is-humanism/manifesto3/.

48. Glenda Sluga, "UNESCO and the (One) World of Julian Huxley," *Journal of World History* 21 (2010): 393–418; Kenneth Waters and Albert van Helden, eds., *Julian Huxley: Biologist and Statesman of Science* (College Station: Texas A&M University Press, 2010).

49. New York Radical Women, "No More Miss America!," August 22, 1968, *Redstockings*, http://www.redstockings.org/index.php?option=com_content&view=article&id=65&Itemid=61.

50. Pope John XXIII, "Pacem in Terris," April 11, 1963, Papal Encyclicals Online, www.papalencyclicals.net/John23/j23pacem.htm; "*Mater et Magistra*."

51. Jean Maalouf, ed., *Pope John XXIII: Essential Writings* (Maryknoll, NY: Orbis, 2008), 111, 115.

52. Thomas Cahill, *Pope John XXIII* (New York: Lipper, Viking, 2002), 175, 209.

53. Peter Hebblethwaite, *Paul VI: The First Modern Pope* (New York: Paulist Press, 1993).

54. Edward Stourton, *John Paul II: Man of History* (London: Hodder and Staughton, 2006), 246; Garry O'Connor, *Universal Father: A Life of Pope John Paul II* (New York: Bloomsbury, 2005), 240.

55. John Paul II, "*Evangelium Vitae*" (1995), Holy See, www.vatican.va/holy_father/john_paul_ii/encyclicals/documents/hf_jp-ii_enc_25031995_evangelium-vitae_en.html; John Paul II, "*Laborem Exercens*" (1981), ibid., www.vatican.va/holy_father/john_paul_ii/encyclicals/documents/hf_jp-ii_enc_14091981_laborem-exercens_en.html.

56. "Interview with Phylis Schlafly on the Equal Rights Amendment, November 1978," in Matthew Avery Sutton, *Jerry Falwell and the Rise of the Religious Right* (New York: Bedford/St. Martins, 2013), 115–18.

57. Cleveland, *History of the Modern Middle East*, 437.

58. Eric Hobsbawm, *The Age of Extremes* (New York: Vintage, 1994), 314.

59. Virginia R. Allen, Margaret E. Galey, and Mildred E. Persinger, "World Conference of International Women's Year," in Winslow, *Women, Politics, and the United Nations*; Jaquete, "Losing the Battle/Winning the War"; Arvonne S. Fraser, "Becoming Human: The Origins and Development of Women's Human Rights," *Human Rights Quarterly* 21 (1999): 853–906.

60. Statements available at United Nations, *Report of the World Conference of the International Women's Year* (New York, 1976), 9, http://www.un.org/womenwatch/daw/beijing/otherconferences/Mexico/Mexico%20conference%20report%20optimized.pdf, and "The United Nations Fourth World Conference on Women: Platform for Action," UN Women (September 1995), item 96, http://www.un.org/womenwatch/daw/beijing/platform/health.htm.

61. Claudia Goldin, "The Quiet Revolution That Transformed Women's Employment, Education, and Family," *American Economic Review* 96 (2006): 10–11.

62. Eric Evans, *Thatcher and Thatcherism* (New York: Routledge, 2004).

63. Violeta Barrios de Chamorro, *Dreams of the Heart* (New York: Simon and Schuster, 1996).

64. Ayn Rand, "Collectivized Ethics," in Rand, *The Virtue of Selfishness* (New York: New American Library, 1964), 105, 107, 108.

CHAPTER 10. DEMOCRACY AND CAPITALISM TRIUMPHANT?

1. Vaclav Havel, "Letter to Dr. Gustav Husak, General Secretary of the Czechoslovak Communist Party," in *Vaclav Havel, or Living in Truth*, ed. Jan Vladislav (London: Faber and Faber, 1986), 27, 30.

2. Council on Foreign Relations, *The New Arab Revolt* (New York: Council on Foreign Relations, 2011), describes the complexity of events well.

3. D. Potter, M. Kiloh, and P. Lewis, eds., *Democratization* (Cambridge: Polity Press, 1997), 9.

4. Schaeffer, *Understanding Globalization*, 153.

5. Amado Mendoza Jr., "'People Power' in the Philippines, 1983–1986," in *Civil Resistance and Power Politics*, ed. Adam Roberts and Timothy Garton Ash (Oxford: Oxford University Press, 2009), 179–97.

6. Thomas Turner, *The Congo Wars: Conflict, Myth, and Reality* (London: Zed, 2007), 3; Thomas Turner, *Congo* (Cambridge: Polity Press, 2013), 15–31.

7. Oyebade, "Reluctant Democracy," 137.

8. Vickers, *History of Modern Indonesia*, 199–213.

9. Andrei Sakharov, Roy Medvedev, and Valentin Turchin, "A Reformist Program for Democratization," in *An End to Silence*, ed. Stephen F. Cohen (New York: W. W. Norton), 318–19, 321, 323.

10. Nick Cullather, "Fuel for the Good Dragon: The United States and Industrial Policy in Taiwan, 1950–1965," *Diplomatic History* 20 (1996): 2, 21, 16 (quotation); Alice H. Amsden, *The Rise of "the Rest": Challenges to the West from Late-Industrializing Economies* (London: Oxford University Press, 2001); Lipman, Molony, and Robinson, *Modern East Asia*, 383.

11. Orlinda de Oliviera and Bryan Roberts, "Urban Social Structures in Latin America, 1930–1990," in *Latin American Economy and Society since 1930*, ed. Leslie Bethell (Cambridge: Cambridge University Press, 1998), 289; Miller, *Modern East Asia*, 182.

12. Ronald Inglehart and Christian Welzel, "How Development Leads to Democracy," *Foreign Affairs* 88 (2007): 40.

13. Tom Lodge, "Resistance and Reform," in *The Cambridge History of South Africa*, ed. Robert Ross, Anne Kelk Mager, and Bill Nasson (Cambridge: Cambridge University Press, 2011), 417.

14. Zeiler, "Opening Doors in the World Economy," 279.

15. Database, Maddison Project, www.ggdc.net/maddison/maddison-project/data.htm; Blank, "Democratization and Development," 237; Christophe Jaffrelot, "India," in *Pathways to Power: The Domestic Politics of South Asia*, ed. Arjun Guneratne and Anita M. Weiss (New York: Rowman and Littlefield, 2014), 137.

16. Park Bun Soon, "Riding the Wave: Korea's Economic Growth and Asia in the Modern Development Era," in *Asia Inside Out: Connected Places*, ed. Eric Tagliacozzo, Helen F. Siu, and Peter C. Perdue (Cambridge, MA: Harvard University Press, 2015), 369.

17. Lipman, Molony, and Robinson, *Modern East Asia*, 373–75.

18. Miller, *Modern East Asia*, 170–76; Dwight H. Perkins, "China's Economic Policy and Performance," in *The Cambridge History of China*, Vol. 15, *The People's Republic, Part 2: Revolutions within the Chinese Revolution, 1966–1982*, ed. Roderick MacFarquhar and John K. Fairbank (Cambridge: Cambridge University Press, 1991), 525, 518, 510–11; Richard Madsen, "The Countryside under Communism," ibid., 646; Archie Brown, *The Rise and Fall of Communism* (New York: CCCO, HarperCollins, 2009), 442–43; Yingyi Qian, "The Process of China's Market Transition, 1978–1998," in *China's Deep Reform*, ed. Lowell Dittmer and Guoli Liu (New York: Rowman and Littlefield, 2006), esp. 240, 242; Database, Maddison Project, www.ggdc.net/maddison/maddison-project/data.htm; Zeiler, "Opening Doors in the World Economy," 321.

19. World Trade Organization, stat.wto.org; Miller, *Modern East Asia*, 197.

20. Database, Maddison Project, www.ggdc.net/maddison/maddison-project/data.htm. On the difficulty of developing reliable comparative real income data, see Robert C. Feenstra, Hong Ma, J. Peter Neary, and D. S. Prasada Rao, "Who Shrunk China? Puzzles in the Measurement of Real GDP," *Economic Journal* 123 (2013): 1100–1129; and Robert Feenstra, Hong Ma, and D. S. Prasada Rao, "Consistent Comparisons of Real Incomes across Time and Space," *Macroeconomic Dynamics* 13, Supplement 2 (2009): 169–93.

21. Here I draw on datasets from the Maddison Project, the Penn World Tables project, and the US Department of Agriculture: www.ggdc.net/maddison/maddison-project/data.htm; the Penn World Table version 9.0 is available at the Groningen Growth and Development Center, http://www.rug.nl/ggdc/productivity/pwt/; International Macroeconomic Data Set, USDA Economic Research Service, http://www.ers.usda.gov/data-products/international-macroeconomic-data-set.aspx#26190. On internal migration, see Kuhn, *Chinese among Others*, 332–34.

22. Paul Ginsborg, *Silvio Berlusconi* (London: Verso, 2004); Geoff Andrews, *Not a Normal Country: Italy after Berlusconi* (London: Pluto Press, 2005); Donald Sassoon, *Contemporary Italy: Economy, Society and Politics since 1945* (New York: Longman, 1997), 80–85; Shleifer, *A Normal Country*, 166–79.

23. Barry Naughton, "Economic Growth: From High-Speed to High-Quality," in *China Today, China Tomorrow: Domestic Politics, Economy, and Society*, ed. Joseph Fewsmith (New York: Rowman and Littlefield, 2010), 83–84; Sebastian Heilmann, "Economic Governance: Authoritarian Upgrading and Innovative Potential," ibid., 115.

24. Quoted in Beaud, *A History of Capitalism*, 284.

25. Nick Leeson, *Rogue Trader: How I Brought Down Barings Bank and Shook the Financial World* (Boston: Little, Brown, 1996), 33.

26. John Williamson, "What Should the World Bank Think about the Washington Consensus?" *World Bank Research Observer* 15 (2000): 251–64; Dani Rodrik, "Goodbye Washington Consensus, Hello Washington Confusion?" *Journal of Economic Literature* 44 (2006): 973–87.

27. United Nations Development Program, *Human Development Report 1999*, 29.

28. Findlay and O'Rourke, *Power and Plenty*, 499.

29. Lobato and Suriano, *Atlas Historico de la Argentina*, 559.

30. Bourguignon et al., "Making Sense of Globalization," 22.

31. World Bank Open Data, data.worldbank.org.

32. World Bank Open Data, data.worldbank.org; WTO Statistics Database, World Trade Organization, http://stat.wto.org/Home/WSDBHome.aspx?Language=; United Nations, UN data, data.un.org.

33. Giorgio Barba Navaretti and Anthony J. Venables, *Multinational Firms in the World Economy* (Princeton, NJ: Princeton University Press, 2004), 9–10.

34. Data from the UN Conference on Trade and Development, UNCTADstat, unctadstat.unctad.org.

35. Baldwin and Martin, "Two Waves of Globalization," 12; Hugill, *Global Communications since 1844*, 233, 237.

36. Daniel R. Headrick, *Technology: A World History* (New York: Oxford University Press, 2009), 140.

37. Ibid., 142–43; data from World Bank Open Data, data.worldbank.org; Josephson, "History of World Technology," 155.

38. Lechner, *Globalization*, 56–71; Soon, "Riding the Wave," 365–68.

39. See "International Tourism Arrivals," Osservatorio Nazionale del Turismo, http://www.ontit.it/opencms/export/sites/default/ont/it/documenti/archivio/files/ONT_2006-01-01_01014.pdf; "World Top 30 Airports," World Airport Codes, https://www.world-airport-codes.com/world-top-30-airports.html.

40. Steger, *Globalization*, 79–81.

41. Organization for Economic Cooperation and Development (OECD) *Divided We Stand: Why Inequality Keeps Rising* (New

York: OECD, 2011), 25; G. A. Cornia, "Inequality, Growth, and Poverty," in *Inequality, Growth, and Poverty in an Era of Liberalization and Globalization,* ed. Giovani Andrea Cornia (New York: Oxford University Press, 2010), esp. 6–23; Bob Sutcliffe, "World Inequality and Globalization," *Oxford Review of Economic Policy* 20 (2004): 15–37.

42. OECD, *Divided We Stand,* 34–38; Xavier Sala-i-Martin, "The Disturbing 'Rise' of Global Income Inequality," National Bureau of Economic Research, Working Paper No. 8904 (April 2002), doi:10.3386/w8904; and Sutcliffe, "World Inequality and Globalization," offer highly skeptical assessments.

43. Held et al., *Global Transformations,* 209.

44. Leeson, *Rogue Trader;* John Gapper and Nicholas Denton, *All That Glitters: The Fall of Barings* (London: Hamish Hamilton, 1996); Stephen Fay, *The Collapse of Barings* (London: Richard Cohen, 1996).

45. James Hansen, "Global Warming Twenty Years Later: Tipping Points Near," in *The Global Warming Reader,* ed. Bill McKibben (London: Penguin, 2012), 275–76.

46. James N. Inhofe, "The Science of Climate Change: Senate Floor Statement," in McKibben, *Global Warming Reader,* 169, 185, 191.

47. Schaeffer, *Understanding Globalization,* 281.

48. G. S. Callendar, "The Artificial Production of Carbon Dioxide and Its Influence on Temperature" (1938), in McKibben, *Global Warming Reader,* 37.

49. Ibid., 41–42.

50. Quoted in Rowland, *The Plot to Save the Planet,* 29.

51. John L. Brooke, *Climate Change and the Course of Global History* (New York: Cambridge University Press, 2014), 551.

52. Reiner Grundmann, *Transnational Environmental Policy: Reconstructing Ozone* (New York: Routledge, 2001); Black, *Crude Reality,* 219–21.

53. World Bank, *4°: Turn Down the Heat* (World Bank, Potsdam Institute for Climate Impact Research and Climate Analytics, November 2012), xiv.

54. Ibid., 61.

55. See Tom Bawden, "COP21: Paris Deal Far Too Weak to Prevent Devastating Climate Change, Academics Warn," *Independent,* January 8, 2016, http://www.independent.co.uk; Oliver Milman, "James Hansen, Father of Climate Change Awareness, Calls Paris Talks "a Fraud,'" *The Guardian,* December 12, 2015, http://http://www.theguardian.com.

56. For an early example of such a scheme, proposed in 1978, see Jerome Martin Weingart, "Going Solar," in *Visions of Technology: A Century of Vital Debate about Machines, Systems, and the Human World,* ed. Richard Rhodes (New York: Simon and Schuster, 1999), 323–28.

57. John Bellamy Foster, Brett Clark, and Richard York, *The Ecological Rift: Capitalism's War on the Earth* (New York: Monthly Review, 2010), 156.

58. Niklas Luhmann, *Introduction to Systems Theory,* ed. Dirk Baecker, trans. Peter Gilgen (New York: Polity Press, 2011), 36.

59. Ronald Bailey, "Stern Measures," *Reason Magazine,* November 3, 2006, http://reason.com/archives/2006/11/03/stern-measures/print. For a good discussion of divergent visions of the relationship between environment and technology, see Fredrik Albritton Jonsson, "The Origins of Cornucopianism: A Preliminary Genealogy," *Critical Historical Studies* 1 (2014): 151–68.

60. Quoted in Weiner, "The Predatory Tribute-Taking State," 290.

61. Cushman, *Guano and the Opening of the Pacific World,* 344–46; Postel, *Pillar of Sand.*

62. Steffen, Crutzen, and McNeill, "The Anthropocene" 617; McNeill and Engelke, "Into the Anthropocene'."

63. Klages, "Man and Earth (1913)," 33; Wells, *The Discovery of the Future;* Leopold, *A Sand County Almanac,* 218, 220.

64. Sebastián Royo, *Varieties of Capitalism in Spain* (Houndsmills, Basingstoke, UK: Palgrave Macmillan, 2008), 13.

65. Stefania Vitali, James B. Glattfelder, and Stefano Battiston, "The Network of Global Corporate Control," *PloS ONE* 6:10 (2011): 3, 5, 6.

66. Ibid., 33, 7.

67. GDP from data.un.org; tax revenues from stats.oecd.org; sales and profits from www.forbes.com/global2000/list/.

68. Bruce Mazlish and Elliott R. Morse, "A Global Elite?" in Chandler and Mazlish, *Leviathans,* 167–84; Geoffrey Allen Pigman, *The World Economic Forum: A Multi-stakeholder Approach to Global Governance* (New York: Routledge, 2007); Sklar, *Trilateralism;* Diane Stone, "Knowledge Networks and Policy Expertise in the Global Polity," in *Towards a Global Polity,* ed. Morten Ougaard and Richard Higgott (London: Routledge, 2002), 136–38.

69. "The World's Biggest Companies" (2017 ranking), *Forbes Magazine,* https://www.forbes.com/global2000/list/; Chase Peterson-Withorn, "Forbes Billionaires: Full List of the Richest People in the World 2015" (March 2, 2015), *Forbes Magazine,* https://www.forbes.com/sites/chasewithorn/2015/03/02/forbes-billionaires-full-list-of-the-500-richest-people-in-the-world-2015/#629fcdcd45b9.

70. Terence Tao, "*E pluribus unum:* From Complexity, Universality," *Daedalus* 141 (2012): 34.

71. Carlota Perez, quoted in Freeman, "Technology and Invention," 327.

72. Reynolds, *One World Divisible,* 519–27; Daniel J. Kevles, "From Eugenics to Genetic Manipulation," in Krige and Pestre, *Companion to Science in the Twentieth Century,* 301–17.

73. Edgerton, *Shock of the Old,* 210. See also John M. Staudenmaier, *Technology's Storytellers: Reweaving the Human Fabric* (Cambridge, MA: MIT Press, 1985), 151.

74. See Sharon E. Kingsland, *The Evolution of American Ecology, 1890–2000* (Baltimore: Johns Hopkins University Press, 2005); Worster, *Nature's Economy.* Influential analyses include Scott, *Seeing like a State,* esp. 309–57; and Shiva, *Violence of the Green Revolution.*

75. James E. Lovelock and Lynn Margulis, "Atmospheric Homeostasis by and for the Biosphere: The Gaia Hypothesis," *Tellus* 26 (1974), 2–10. On the development of ecology in the late twentieth century, see Bowler, *Earth Encompassed,* 519–53.

76. See, in particular, Emerson W. Pugh, *Building IBM: Shaping an Industry and Its Technology* (Cambridge, MA: MIT Press, 1995).

77. Collett, "History of Electronics," 253–74.

Select Bibliography

ONLINE STATISTICAL SOURCES

Center for Sustainability and Global Environment, Nelson Institute for Environmental Studies, University of Wisconsin. www.sage.wisc.edu.

EH.net Encyclopedia. Edited by Robert Whaples. Economic History Association. eh.net.encyclopedia/article/khan.patents.

International Historical Statistics. Edited by Palgrave Macmillan Ltd. http://www.palgraveconnect.com/pc/doifinder/10.1057/9781137305688.0737.

Maddison Project, Database. www.ggdc.net/maddison/maddison-project/data.htm.

Natural Resources Defense Council, http://www.nrdc.org/nuclear/nudb/datab19.asp.

Organization for Economic Cooperation and Development, https://www.oecd.org.

Paris School of Economics. World Wealth and Income Database, http://www.parisschoolofeconomics.eu/en/research/data-production-and-diffusion/the-world-wealth-income-database/.

Stockholm International Peace Research Institute. Online database. http://www.sipri.org/databases.

United Nations Conference on Trade and Development. UNCTADstat, unctadstat.unctad.org.

United Nations Department of Economic and Social Affairs. *World Economic and Social Surveys.* New York: United Nations. https://www.un.org/development/desa/dpad/document_gem/wess-report/.

United Nations Development Program. *Human Development Report* (various years). http://hdr.undp.org/.

United Nations Statistics Division, unstats.un.org/unsd/mdg/.

World Bank, data.worldbank.org.

World Trade Organization. stat.wto.org

BOOKS AND ARTICLES

Abernethy, David B. *The Dynamics of Global Dominance.* New Haven: Yale University Press, 2000.

Adam, Heribert, ed. *Hushed Voices: Unacknowledged Atrocities in the Twentieth Century.* Highclere, Berkshire, UK: Berkshire Academic Press, 2011.

Adam, Thomas. *Intercultural Transfers and the Making of the Modern World.* Houndsmills, Basingstoke, UK: Palgrave Macmillan, 2012.

Adelman, Howard, Allan Borowski, Meyer Burstein, and Lois Foster, eds. *Immigration and Refugee Policy: Australia and Canada Compared.* Volume 1. Toronto: University of Toronto Press, 1994.

Adelman, Jeremey. *Frontier Development: Land, Labour, and Capital on the Wheatlands of Argentina and Canada, 1890–1914.* Oxford: Oxford University Press, 1994.

Adhikari, Mohamed, ed. *Genocide on Settler Frontiers.* New York: Berghahn, 2015.

Aghion, Philip, and Jeffrey Williamson. *Growth, Inequality and Globalization.* Cambridge: Cambridge University Press, 1998.

Ahmad, Feroz. *The Making of Modern Turkey.* London: Routledge, 1993.

Albanese, Catherine L. *A Republic of Mind and Spirit.* New Haven: Yale University Press, 2007.

Albert, Bill. *South America and the World Economy from Independence to 1930.* Hong Kong: Macmillan Press, 1983.

Algar, Hamid ed. *Islam and Revolution: Writings and Declarations of Imam Khomeini.* Berkeley, CA: Mizan Press, 1981.

Almond, Gabriel A., R. Scott Appleby, and Emmanuel Sivan. *Strong Religion: The Rise of Fundamentalisms around the World.* Chicago: University of Chicago Press, 2003.

Aly, Götz, and Susanne Heim. *Architects of Annihilation.* Princeton, NJ: Princeton University Press, 2002.

Amin, Samir. *Unequal Development.* New York: Monthly Review Press, 1976.

Amrith, Sunil, and Glenda Sluga. "New Histories of the United Nations." *Journal of World History* 19 (2008): 251–74.

Amrith, Sunil, and Patricia Clavin. "Feeding the World: Connecting Europe and Asia, 1930–1945." *Past and Present* 218: Supplement 8 (2013).

Amsden, Alice H. *The Rise of "the Rest": Challenges to the West from Late-Industrializing Economies.* Oxford: Oxford University Press, 2001.

Anderson, Robert S. "The Origins of the International Rice Research Institute." *Minerva* 29 (1991): 61–89.

Andrew, C. M., and A. S. Kanya-Forstner. "Centre and Periphery in the Making of the Second French Colonial Empire, 1815–1920." *Journal of Imperial and Commonwealth History* 16 (1988): 9–34.

Andrews, Geoff. *Not a Normal Country: Italy after Berlusconi.* London: Pluto Press, 2005.

Andrews, Thomas G. *Killing for Coal: America's Deadliest Labor War.* Cambridge, MA: Harvard University Press, 2008.

Ansari, Ali M. *Modern Iran since 1921.* Edinburgh: Pearson, 2003.

Ansperger, Franz. *The Dissolution of Colonial Empires.* London: Routledge, 1989.

Arnold, David. *The Problem of Nature: Environment, Culture, and European Expansion.* Oxford: Blackwell, 1996.

Arrington, Leonard J., and Davis Bitton. *The Mormon Experience.* Urbana: University of Illinois Press, 1992.

Aulakh, Preet S., and Michael G. Shechter, eds. *Rethinking Globalization(s): From Corporate Transnationalism to Local Interventions.* New York: St. Martin's, 2000.

Axworthy, Michael. *A History of Iran.* New York: Basic Books, 2008.

Babcock, Jay. "Fela: King of the Invisible Art." arthurmag. com/2009/22/bootsy-collins/.

Bach, Quintin V. S. *Soviet Economic Assistance to the Less Developed Countries.* Oxford: Clarendon Press, 1987.

Bairoch, Paul. "Agriculture and the Industrial Revolution, 1700–1914." In *The Fontana Economic History of Europe: The Industrial Revolution.* Edited. by Carlo M. Cipolla. New York: Collins/Fontana, 1973.

———. *Economics and World History: Myths and Paradoxes.* Chicago: University of Chicago Press, 1993.

———. "Les Trois Révolutions agricoles du monde développé." *Annales Economies, Societés, Cultures* 44 (1989): 317–53.

Baldwin, Richard E., and Philippe Martin. "Two Waves of Globalization: Superficial Similarities, Fundamental Differences." National Bureau of Economic Research. Working Paper No. 6904. 1999. doi:10.3386/w6904.

Barbier, Edward B. *Scarcity and Frontiers: How Economies Have Developed through Natural Resource Exploitation.* Cambridge: Cambridge University Press, 2011.

Barnett, Michael, and Liv Coleman. "Designing Police: Interpol and the Study of Change in International Organizations." *International Studies Quarterly* 49 (2005): 593–619.

Bashford, Alison. "Population, Geopolitics, and International Organizations in the Mid-Twentieth Century." *Journal of World History* 19:3 (2008): 327–47.

Bassin, Mark. "Turner, Solov'ev, and the 'Frontier Hypothesis': The National Significance of Open Spaces." *Journal of Modern History* 65 (1993): 473–511.

Bastian, Jean-Pierre, ed. *La Modernidad Religiosa: Europea Latina y América Latina en perspectiva comparada,.* México: Fondo de Cultura Económica, 2004.

Basu, Shamita. *Religious Revivalism as Nationalist Discourse: Swami Vivekananda and New Hinduism in Nineteenth-Century Bengal.* Oxford: Oxford University Press, 2002.

Bateman, Fiona, and Lionel Pilkington. *Studies in Settler Colonialism: Politics, Identity, and Culture.* New York: Palgrave Macmillan, 2011.

Bauk, Kathleen, and Alec Cairncross. *"Goodbye, Great Britain": The 1976 IMF Crisis.* New Haven: Yale University Press, 1992.

Bayly, Chris. *The Birth of the Modern World.* Oxford: Blackwell, 2004.

Beasley, W. G. *The Rise of Modern Japan.* London: Weidenfeld and Nicolson, 2000.

Beaud, Michel. *A History of Capitalism, 1500–2000.* New York: Monthly Review, 2001.

Beckerlegge, Gwylim. *Colonialism, Modernity, and Religious Identities: Religious Reform Movements in South Asia.* Oxford: Oxford University Press, 2008.

Beckert, Sven. "Emancipation and Empire: Reconstructing the Worldwide Web of Cotton Production in the Age of the American Civil War." *American Historical Review* 109 (2004): 1405–38.

Beeching, Jack. *The Chinese Opium Wars.* New York: Harcourt Brace Jovanovich, 1975.

Belich, James. *Replenishing the Earth: The Settler Revolution and the Rise of the Anglo World, 1783–1939.* New York: Oxford University Press, 2009.

Bell, P. M. H. *Twelve Turning Points of the Second World War.* New Haven: Yale University Press, 2011.

Bender, Thomas. *A Nation among Nations: America's Place in World History.* New York: Hill and Wang, 2006.

Bender, Thomas, ed. *Rethinking American History in a Global Age.* Berkeley: University of California Press, 2002.

Berg, Manfred, and Simon Wendt, eds. *Racism in the Modern World.* New York: Berghahn, 2011.

Berger, Peter L., ed. *The Desecularization of the World: Resurgent Religion and Politics.* Washington, DC: Ethics and Policy, 1999.

Betts, Raymond F. *Uncertain Dimensions: Western Overseas Empires in the Twentieth Century.* Minneapolis: University of Minnesota Press, 1985.

Black, Brian C. *Crude Reality: Petroleum in World History.* Lanham, MD: Rowman and Littlefield, 2012.

Blackburn, Robin. "The Role of Slave Resistance in Slave Emancipation." In *Who Abolished Slavery? Slave Revolts and Abolitionism.* Edited by Seymour Drescher and Pieter C. Emmer. New York: Berghahn, 2010.

Blaker, James R. *United States Overseas Basing: An Anatomy of the Dilemma.* New York: Praeger, 1990.

Blank, Jonah. "Democratization and Development." In *South Asia in World Politics.* Edited by Devin T. Hagerty. Lanham, MD: Rowman and Littlefield, 2005.

Bloxham, Donald. *Genocide, the World Wars, and the Unweaving of Europe.* London: Vallentine Mitchell, 2008.

———. "Modernity and Genocide," *European History Quarterly* 38 (2008): 294–311. Reprinted in Eric D. Weitz. *A Century of Genocide: Utopias of Race and Nation.* Princeton, NJ: Princeton University Press, 2003.

Boenker, Dirk. *Militarism in a Global Age.* Ithaca, NY: Cornell University Press, 2011.

Boli, John, and George M. Thomas, eds. *Constructing World Culture: International Nongovernmental Organizations since 1875.* Stanford: Stanford University Press, 1999.

Bourguignon, François, et al. "Making Sense of Globalization: A Guide to the Economic Issues," Center for Economic Policy Research, Policy Paper no. 8 (2002), http://cepr.org/sites /default/files/geneva_reports/GenevaPP8.pdf.

Boyer, Paul S. *The Oxford Companion to United States History.* Oxford: Oxford University Press, 2001.

Breyfogle, Nicholas, Abby Schrader, and Willard Sunderland, eds. *Peopling the Russian Periphery.* London: Routledge, 2008.

Bentley, Jerry H. *The Oxford Handbook of World History.* Oxford: Oxford University Press, 2011.

Berend, Ivan T. *History Derailed: Central and Eastern Europe in the Long Nineteenth Century.* Berkeley: University of California Press, 2003.

———. *An Economic History of Twentieth-Century Europe* Cambridge: Cambridge University Press, 2006.

Berg, Maxine, ed. *Writing the History of the Global: Challenges for the 21st Century.* Oxford: British Academy, Oxford University Press, 2013.

Berger, Stefan, Andy Croll, and Norman LaPorte, eds. *Towards a Comparative History of Coalfield Societies.* Aldershot, UK: Ashgate, 2005.

Berghahn, Volker R. *Modern Germany: Society, Economics, and Politics in the Twentieth Century.* Cambridge: Cambridge University Press, 1987.

Bethell, Leslie, ed. *Latin American Economy and Society since 1930.* Cambridge: Cambridge University Press, 1998.

Beyer, Peter, and Lori Beaman, eds. *Religion, Globalization, and Culture.* Leiden, The Netherlands: Brill, 2007.

Bordo, Michael D., Alan M. Taylor, and Jeffrey G. Williamson. *Globalization in Historical Perspective.* Chicago: University of Chicago Press, 2003.

Borstelmann, Thomas. *Apartheid's Reluctant Uncle: The United States and Southern Africa in the Early Cold War.* Oxford: Oxford University Press, 1993.

Bose, Sugata, and Ayesha Jalal. *Modern South Asia*. New York: Routledge, 2004.

Bosma, Ulbe. "European Colonial Soldiers in the Nineteenth Century." *Journal of Global History* 4 (2009): 317–36.

Bosworth, R. J. B. *Mussolini*. New York: Oxford University Press, 2002.

Bowler, Peter J. *The Earth Encompassed: A History of the Environmental Sciences*. New York: W. W. Norton, 2000.

Brantlinger, Patrick. *Dark Vanishings: Discourse on the Extinction of Primitive Races, 1800–1930*. Ithaca, NY: Cornell University Press, 2003.

Bray, Francesca. *Science and Civilization in China*, Vol. 6: *Biology and Biological Technology, Part II: Agriculture*. Edited by Joseph Needham. Cambridge: Cambridge University Press, 1984.

Bregman, Ahron. *A History of Israel*. New York: Palgrave Macmillan, 2003.

Brière, Elaine. "Shadow Play: Political Mass Murder and the 1965 Indonesian Coup." In *Hushed Voices*. Edited by Heribert Adam. Highclere, Berkshire, UK: Berkshire Academic Press, 2011.

British Petroleum. *BP Statistical Review of World Energy*. June 2012.

Brooke, John L. *Climate Change and the Course of Global History*. New York: Cambridge University Press, 2014.

Brooker, Paul. *Twentieth-Century Dictatorships: The Ideological Origins of One-Party States*. New York: New York University Press, 1995.

Brookings Institution. *Cascade of Arms: Managing Conventional Weapons Proliferation*. Washington, DC: Brookings Institution, 1997.

Brown, Archie. *The Rise and Fall of Communism*. New York: CCCO, HarperCollins, 2009.

Brown, Richard Maxwell. "Violence." In *The Oxford History of the American West*. Edited by Clyde A. Milner II, Carol A. O'Connor, and Martha A. Sandweiss. New York: Oxford University Press, 1994.

Brown, Judith M., and William Roger Louis, eds. *The Oxford History of the British Empire*, Volume 4: *The Twentieth Century*. Oxford: Oxford University Press, 1999.

Buchanan, Tom. "'The Truth Will Set You Free': The Making of Amnesty International." *Journal of Contemporary History* 37 (2002): 575–97.

Bulliet, Richard W., ed. *The Columbia History of the Twentieth Century*. New York: Columbia University Press, 1998.

Bulmer-Thomas, Victor. "The Latin American Economies, 1929–1939." In *Latin American Economy and Society since 1930*. Edited by Leslie Bethell. Cambridge: Cambridge University Press, 1998.

Burke, Edmund, III, and Kenneth Pomeranz, eds. *The Environment and World History*. Berkeley: University of California Press, 2009.

Busse, Matthias. "Tariffs, Transport Costs and the WTO Doha Round: The Case of Developing Countries." *Estey Center Journal of International Law and Trade Policy* 4 (2003): 15–31.

Butrica, Andrew J., ed. *Beyond the Ionosphere: Fifty Years of Satellite Communication*. Washington, DC: NASA, 1997.

Buxton, I. L. "The Development of the Merchant Ship, 1880–1990." *The Mariner's Mirror* 79 (1993): 71–82.

Byrn, Edward W. "The Progress of Invention during the Past 50 Years." *Scientific American* 75 (July 25, 1896): 82–83.

Cahill, Thomas. *Pope John XXIII*. New York: Lipper, Viking, 2002.

Caistor, Nick. *Che Guevara: A Life*. Northampton, MA: Interlink, 2010.

Caldwell, John C., and Pat Caldwell. "What Do We Now Know about Fertility Transition." In *The Continuing Demographic Transition*. Edited by G. W. Jones, R. M. Douglas, J. C. Caldwell, and R. M. D'Souza. Oxford: Clarendon, 1997.

Campbell, George van Pelt. "Religion and the Phases of Globalization." In *Religion, Globalization and Culture*. Edited by Peter Beyer and Lori Beaman. Leiden, The Netherlands: Brill, 2007.

Carlson, W. Bernard. "Innovation and the Modern Corporation: From Heroic Invention to Industrial Science." In *Companion to Science in the Twentieth Century*. Edited by John Krige and Dominique Pestre New York: Routledge, 2003.

Carnevali, Francesca, and Julie-Marie Strange. *Twentieth Century Britain: Economic, Cultural, and Social Change*. Harlow, UK: Pearson-Longman, 2007.

Carson, Rachel. *Silent Spring*. Boston: Houghton Mifflin, 1962.

Carter, Nick. *Modern Italy in Historical Perspective*. London: Bloomsbury Academic, 2010.

Casanova, José. "Rethinking Secularization: A Global Comparative Perspective." In *Religion, Globalization and Culture*. Edited by Peter Beyer and Lori Beaman. Leiden, The Netherlands: Brill, 2007.

Casson, Mark, ed. *Multinationals and World Trade*. London: Allen and Unwin, 1986.

Centeno, Miguel A., and Joseph N. Cohen. *Global Capitalism: A Sociological Perspective*. New York: Polity, 2010.

Chamorro, Violeta Barrios de. *Dreams of the Heart*. New York: Simon and Schuster, 1996.

Chandler, Alfred D., and Bruce Mazlish, eds.. *Leviathans: Multinational Corporations and the New Global History*. Cambridge: Cambridge University Press, 2005.

Chang, Sidney H., and Leonard H. D. Gordon. *All Under Heaven . . . : Sun Yat Sen and His Revolutionary Thought*. Stanford: Hoover Institution Press, 1991.

Chase-Dunn, Christopher, Yukio Kawano, and Benjamin D. Brewer. "Trade Globalization since 1795: Waves of Integration in the World-System." *American Sociological Review* 65 (2000): 77–95.

Chasteen, John Charles. *Born in Blood and Fire: A Concise History of Latin America*. New York: W. W. Norton, 2006.

Chavarría, Jesús. *José Carlos Mariátegui and the Rise of Modern Peru, 1890–1930*. Albuquerque: University of New Mexico Press, 1979.

Chavez, Alicia Hernandez. *Mexico: A Brief History*. Berkeley: University of California Press, 2006.

Chernobyl Forum: 2003–2005. *Chernobyl's Legacy: Health, Environmental and Socio-Economic Impacts*. 2nd revised version. https://www.iaea.org/sites/default/files/chernobyl .pdf.

Chesnais, Jean-Claude. *The Demographic Transition*. Translated by Elizabeth and Philip Kreager. Oxford: Clarendon, 1992.

Chickering, Roger, Stig Foerster, and Bernd Greiner, eds. *A World at Total War*. Cambridge: Cambridge University Press, 2005.

Childs, David. *Britain since 1945: A Political History*. New York: Routledge, 2012.

Choy, Lee Khoon. *Pioneers of Modern China*. Singapore: World Scientific, 2005.

Christie, Nancy, and Michael Gauvreau, eds. *The Sixties and Beyond: Dechristianization in North America and Western Europe, 1945–2000*. Toronto: University of Toronto Press, 2013.

Christopher, Emma, Cassandra Pybus, and Marcus Rediker, eds. *Many Middle Passages: Forced Migration and the Making of the Modern World*. Berkeley: University of California Press, 2007.

Chubarian, A. O., Warren F. Kimball, and David Reynolds, eds. *Allies at War: The Soviet, American, and British Experience, 1939–1945*. New York: St. Martin's, 1994.

Chuhan-Pole, Punam, and Manka Angwafo, eds. *Yes Africa Can.* Washington, DC: World Bank, 2011.

Clark, Christopher. *The Sleepwalkers: How Europe Went to War in 1914.* New York: HarperCollins, 2013.

Clarke, Peter. *Hope and Glory: Britain, 1900–1990.* London: Allen Lane, Penguin, 1996.

Clegg, John C. "Capitalism and Slavery." *Critical Historical Studies* 2 (2015): 281–304.

Clemens, Michael A., and Jeffrey G. Williamson. "Why Did the Tariff-Growth Correlation Reverse after 1950?" National Bureau of Economic Research. NBER Working Paper No. 9181, September 2002. doi:10.3386/w9181.

Cleveland, William L. *A History of the Modern Middle East.* Boulder, CO: Westview Press, 2004.

Cline, William R. *Trade Policy and Global Poverty.* Washington, DC: Institute for International Economics, 2004.

Clodfelter, Michael. *Warfare and Armed Conflicts: A Statistical Reference to Casualty and Other Figures, 1618-1991,* Volume 2. Jefferson, NC: McFarland, 1991.

Cmiel, Kenneth. "The Recent History of Human Rights." *American Historical Review* 109 (2004): 117–35.

Codding, George A., Jr. *The Universal Postal Union.* New York: New York University Press, 1964.

Cole, H. S. D., Christopher Freeman, Marie Jahoda, and K. L. R. Pavitt, eds. *Models of Doom: A Critique of* The Limits to Growth. New York: Universe, 1973.

Colegio de México. *Historia General de México, Version 2000.* México: Colegio de México, 2000.

Collett, John Peter. "The History of Electronics." In *Companion to Science in the Twentieth Century.* Edited by John Krige and Dominique Pestre. New York: Routledge, 2003.

Conklin, Alice. "Colonialism and Human Rights: A Contradiction in Terms?" *American Historical Review* 103 (1998): 419–42.

Connelly, Matthew. "To Inherit the Earth: Imagining World Population, from the Yellow Peril to the Population Bomb." *Journal of Global History* 1 (2006).

Coorlawala, Uttara Asha. "Ruth St. Denis and India's Dance Renaissance." *Dance Chronicle* 15 (1992): 123–52.

Coppa, Frank J. *The Modern Papacy since 1789.* New York: Longman, 1998.

Cornia, Giovanni Andrea, ed.. *Inequality, Growth, and Poverty in an Era of Liberalization and Globalization.* Oxford: Oxford University Press, 2010.

Council on Foreign Relations. *The New Arab Revolt.* New York: Council on Foreign Relations, 2011.

Coupeau, Steeve. *The History of Haiti.* Westport, CT: Greenwood Press, 2008.

Cranston, Sylvia. *HPB: The Extraordinary Life and Influence of Helena Blavatsky.* New York: Putnam, 1993.

Cronin, Stephanie, ed. *The Making of Modern Iran.* New York: Routledge, 2003.

Crossley, Pamela Kyle, Lynn Hollen Lees, and John W. Servos. *Global Society: The World since 1900.* Boston: Wadsworth, CENGAGE Learning, 2013.

Cullather, Nick. "Fuel for the Good Dragon: The United States and Industrial Policy in Taiwan, 1950–1965." *Diplomatic History* 20 (1996): 1–25.

———. *The Hungry World: America's Cold War Battle against Poverty in Asia.* Cambridge, MA: Harvard University Press, 2010.

———. "Miracles of Modernization: The Green Revolution and the Apotheosis of Technology." *Diplomatic History* 28:2 (2004): 227–54.

———. "Research Note: Development? It's History." *Diplomatic History* 24 (2000): 641–53.

———. "The War on the Peasant: The United States and the Third World." In *The Cold War in the Third World.* Edited by Robert J. McMahon. Oxford: Oxford University Press, 2013.

Culpeper, Roy, Albert Berry, and Frances Stewart, eds. *Global Development Fifty Years after Bretton Woods.* New York: St. Martin's, 1997.

Curtin, Philip D. "Africa and Global Patterns of Migration." In *Global History and Migrations.* Edited by Gungwu Wang. Boulder, CO: Westview Press, 1997.

———. *The Rise and Fall of the Plantation Complex.* 1st ed. Cambridge: Cambridge University Press, 1990.

Cushman, Gregory T. *Guano and the Opening of the Pacific World.* New York: Cambridge University Press, 2013.

Daly, Ann. *Done into Dance: Isadora Duncan in America.* Bloomington: Indiana University Press, 1995.

Davidson, Basil. *Africa in History.* New York: Macmillan, 1991.

Davie, Grace. "Europe: The Exception?" In *The Desecularization of the World: Resurgent Religion and Politics.* Edited by Peter L. Berger. Washington, DC: Ethics and Policy, 1999.

Davies, Norman. *God's Playground: A History of Poland.* Volume 2: *1795 to the Present.* Oxford: Oxford University Press, 2005.

Davies, Thomas. *NGOs: A New History of Transnational Civil Society.* New York: Oxford University Press, 2014.

Davis, John. *A History of Britain, 1885–1939.* New York: St. Martin's, 1999.

Davis, Mike. *Late Victorian Holocausts.* London: Verso, 2001.

Dawson, Alexander. *Latin America since Independence: A History with Primary Sources.* New York: Routledge, 2011.

Dikötter, Frank. "The Racialization of the Globe." In *Racism in the Modern World.* Edited by Manfred Berg and Simon Wendt. New York: Berghahn, 2011.

Dirlik, Arif. *The Postcolonial Aura: Third World Criticism in the Age of Global Capitalism.* Boulder, CO: Westview Press, 1997.

Di Scala, Spencer M. *Europe's Long Century: Society, Politics, and Culture, 1900–Present.* Oxford: Oxford University Press, 2013.

Dittmer, Lowell, and Guoli Liu, eds. *China's Deep Reform.* New York: Rowman and Littlefield, 2006.

Drescher, Seymour, and Pieter C. Emmer, eds. *Who Abolished Slavery? Slave Revolts and Abolitionism.* New York: Berghahn, 2010.

Duara, Prasenjit. "The Cold War as Historical Period: An Interpretive Essay." *Journal of Global* History 6 (2011): 457–80.

Dudden, Alexis. "Japanese Colonial Control in International Terms." *Japanese Studies* 25 (2005): 1–20.

Duiker, William J. *Ho Chi Minh.* New York: Hyperion, 2000.

Dummett, Michael. "The Nature of Racism." In *Racism in Mind.* Edited by Michael P. Levine and Tamas Pataki. Ithaca, NY: Cornell University Press, 2004.

Duus, Peter. "Economic Dimensions of Meiji Imperialism: The Case of Korea, 1895–1910." In *The Japanese Colonial Empire, 1895–1945,* 128–71. Edited by Ramon H. Myers and Mark R. Peattie Princeton, NJ: Princeton University Press, 1984.

Dwyer, Philip G., and Lyndall Ryan, eds. *Theatres of Violence: Massacre, Mass Killing, and Atrocity throughout History.* New York: Berghahn, 2012.

Easterlin, Richard A. *Growth Triumphant: The Twenty-First Century in Historical Perspective.* Ann Arbor: University of Michigan Press, 1996.

Eckes, Alfred E., Jr. *The United States and the Global Struggle for Minerals.* Austin: University of Texas Press, 1979.

Edgerton, David. *The Shock of the Old: Technology and Global History since 1900.* New York: Oxford University Press, 2007.

Eichholtz, Dietrich. *War for Oil: The Nazi Quest for an Oil Empire.* Washington, DC: Potomac, 2012.

Elichirigoity, Fernando. *Planet Management.* Evanston, IL: Northwestern University Press, 1999.

Emmer, P. C., and M. Mörner, eds. *European Expansion and Migration.* New York: Berg, 1992.

Engdahl, F. William. "Oil and the Origins of the Great War." *History Compass* 5:6 (2007): 2041–2060.

Ehrlich, Paul. *The Population Bomb.* 1968. Reprint, Cutchogue, NY: Buccaneer, 1971.

Esping-Anderson, Gosta. *Three Worlds of Welfare Capitalism.* Princeton, NJ: Princeton University Press, 1998.

Estevadeordal, Antoni, Brian Frantz, and Alan M. Taylor. "The Rise and Fall of World Trade, 1870–1939." National Bureau of Economic Research, Working Paper No. 9318 (2002). http://www.nber.org/papers/w9318.pdf.

Etamad, Bouda. *Possessing the World.* New York: Berghahn, 2000.

Etemad, Bouda, and Jean Luciani. *World Energy Production, 1800–1985.* Geneva: Librairei Droz, 1991.

Evans, Eric. *Thatcher and Thatcherism.* New York: Routledge, 2004.

Fairbank, John K. ed. *The Cambridge History of China.* Volume 12: *Republican China, 1912–1949,* Part 1. Cambridge: Cambridge University Press, 1983.

Fairbank, John K., and Albert Feuerwerker, eds. *The Cambridge History of China.* Volume 13: *Republican China, 1912–1949,* Part 2. Cambridge: Cambridge University Press, 1986.

Falola, Toyin, and Matthew M. Heaton. *A History of Nigeria.* New York: Cambridge University Press, 2008.

Fay, Stephen. *The Collapse of Barings.* London: Richard Cohen, 1996.

Federico, Giovanni. "The Economic History of Agriculture since 1800." In *The Cambridge World History,* Volume 7: *Production, Destruction, and Connection, 1750–Present, Part 1: Structures, Spaces and Boundary-Making.* Edited by J. R. McNeill and Kenneth Pomeranz. Cambridge: Cambridge University Press, 2015.

———. *Feeding the World: An Economic History of Agriculture.* Princeton, NJ: Princeton University Press, 2005.

Feenstra, Robert C., Hong Ma, and D. S. Prasada Rao. "Consistent Comparisons of Real Incomes across Time and Space." *Macroeconomic Dynamics* 13, Supplement 2 (2009): 169–93.

Feenstra, Robert C., Hong Ma, J. Peter Neary, and D. S. Prasada Rao. "Who Shrunk China? Puzzles in the Measurement of Real GDP." *Economic Journal* 123 (2013): 1100–1129.

Fein, Helen, ed. *Genocide Watch.* New Haven: Yale University Press, 1992.

Ferguson, Niall, Charles S. Maier, Erez Manuela, and Daniel J. Sargent, eds. *The Shock of the Global: The 1970s in Perspective.* Cambridge, MA: Harvard University Press, 2010.

Fernandez-Armesto, Felipe. *The World: A History,* Volume 2. London: Prentice Hall, 2010.

Fewsmith, Joseph, ed. *China Today, China Tomorrow: Domestic Politics, Economy, and Society.* New York: Rowman and Littlefield, 2010.

Ffrench-Davis, Ricardo, Oscar Muñoz, and José Gabriel Palma. "The Latin American Economies, 1950–1990." In *Latin American Economy and Society since 1930.* Edited by Leslie Bethell. Cambridge: Cambridge University Press, 1998.

Findlay, Ronald, and Kevin H. O'Rourke. "Commodity Market Integration, 1500–2000." In *Globalization in Historical Perspective.* Edited by Michael D. Bordo, Alan M. Taylor, and Jeffrey G. Williamson. Chicago: University of Chicago Press, 2003.

———. *Power and Plenty: Trade, War, and the World Economy in the Second Millennium.* Princeton, NJ: Princeton University Press, 2007.

Finzsch, Norbert. "The End of Slavery, the Role of the Freedmen's Bureau, and the Introduction of Peonage." In *The End of Slavery in Africa and the Americas.* Edited by Ulrike Schmieder, Katja Füllberg-Stolberg, and Michael Zeuske. Berlin: Lit, 2011.

Fischer, Conan. *Europe between Democracy and Dictatorship, 1900–1945.* Chichester, UK: Wiley-Blackwell, 2011.

Fischer, Stanley. "Applied Economics in Action: IMF Programs." *American Economic Review* 87 (1997): 23–27.

Fischer, Wolfram. *Expansion—Integration—Globalisierung: Studien zur Geschichte der Weltwirtschaft.* Göttingen, Germany: Vandenhoeck and Ruprecht, 1998.

Fitzpatrick, Sheila. *The Russian Revolution.* Oxford: Oxford University Press, 2008.

Flandreau, Marc, and Frédéric Zumer. *The Making of Global Finance.* New York: Organization for Economic Cooperation and Development, 2004.

Fletcher, Max E. "The Suez Canal and World Shipping, 1869–1914." *Journal of Economic History* 18 (1958).

Flora, Peter, et al. *State, Economy, and Society in Western Europe, 1815–1975.* London: Macmillan, 1983.

Foner, Eric. *Free Soil, Free Labor, Free Men.* New York: Oxford University Press, 1970.

Foster, John Bellamy, Brett Clark, and Richard York. *The Ecological Rift: Capitalism's War on the Earth.* New York: Monthly Review, 2010.

Frank, Andre Gunder. *Capitalism and Underdevelopment in Latin America.* New York: Monthly Review Press, 1967.

Fraser, Arvonne S. "Becoming Human: The Origins and Development of Women's Human Rights." *Human Rights Quarterly* 21 (1999): 853–906.

Frederickson, George M. *Racism: A Short History.* Princeton, NJ: Princeton University Press, 2003.

Freeman, Christopher. "Technology and Innovation." In *The Columbia History of the Twentieth Century.* Edited by Richard W. Bulliet. New York: Columbia University Press, 1998.

Frey, Mark, and Sönke Kunkel. "Writing the History of Development: A Review of the Recent Literature." *Contemporary European History* 20 (2011): 215–32.

Fromkin, David. *A Peace to End All Peace: Creating the Modern Middle East, 1914–1922.* New York: Henry Holt, 1989.

Führer, Helmut. *The Story of Official Development Assistance.* New York: Organization for Economic Cooperation and Development, 1996.

Fulbrook, Mary. *A Concise History of Germany.* Cambridge: Cambridge University Press, 1990.

Fulbrook, Mary, ed. *Europe since 1945.* Oxford: Oxford University Press, 2001.

Furnish, Timothy R. *Holiest Wars: Islamic Mahdis, Their Jihads, and Osama bin Laden.* Westport, CT: Praeger, 2005.

Galor, Oded. "The Demographic Transition and the Emergence of Sustained Economic Growth." *Journal of the European Economic Association* 3 (2005): 494–504.

Gandhi, Mohandas Karamchand. "Economic vs. Moral Progress." In *Mahatma Gandhi: His Life, Writings & Speeches.* Edited by Sarojini Naidu. Madras, India: Ganesh, 1921.

Gann, Lewis H. "Western and Japanese Colonialism: Some Preliminary Comparisons." In *The Japanese Colonial Empire, 1895–1945,* 497–525. Edited by Ramon H. Myers and Mark R. Peattie. Princeton, NJ: Princeton University Press, 1984.

Gapper, John, and Nicholas Denton. *All That Glitters: The Fall of Barings*. London: Hamish Hamilton, 1996.

Garavini, Giuliano. "Completing Decolonization: The 1973 'Oil Shock' and the Struggle for Economic Rights." *International History Review* 33 (2011): 473–87.

Garfinkel, Irwin, Lee Rainwater, and Timothy Smeeding. *Wealth and Welfare States: Is America a Laggard or a Leader?* Oxford: Oxford University Press, 2010.

Gereffi, Gary, and Miguel Korzeniewicz, eds. *Commodity Chains and Global Capitalism*. Westport, CT: Greenwood Press, 1994.

Gerwarth, Robert, and Erez Manela, eds. *Empires at War, 1911–1923*. New York: Oxford University Press, 2014.

Geyer, Michael, and Charles Bright. "World History in a Global Age." *American Historical Review* 100 (1995): 1034–60.

Geyer, Michael, and Sheila Fitzpatrick, eds. *Beyond Totalitarianism*. New York: Cambridge University Press, 2009.

Ginsborg, Paul. *Silvio Berlusconi*. London: Verso, 2004.

Gissibl, Bernhard, Sabine Höhler, and Patrick Kupper, eds. *Civilizing Nature: National Parks in Global Historical Perspective*. New York: Berghahn, 2012.

Goldblatt, David. *The Ball Is Round: A Global History of Soccer*. New York: Riverhead, 2008.

Goldin, Claudia. "The Quiet Revolution That Transformed Women's Employment, Education, and Family." *American Economic Review* 96 (2006): 1–21.

Gonzalbo, Pablo Escalante et al. *Nueva Historia Mínima de México*. Mexico: Colegio de México, 2004.

Goodin, Robert E., Bruce Headey, Ruud Muffels, and Henk-Jan Dirven. *The Real Worlds of Welfare Capitalism*. Cambridge: Cambridge University Press, 1999.

Gooding, John. *Rulers and Subjects: Government and People in Russia, 1801–1991*. London: Arnold, 1996.

Goralski, Robert, and Russell W. Freeburg. *Oil and War: How the Deadly Struggle for Fuel in WWII Meant Victory or Defeat*. New York: William Morrow, 1987.

Goryushkin, Leonid M. "Migration, Settlement, and the Rural Economy of Siberia, 1861–1914." In *The History of Siberia*. Edited by Alan Wood. London: Routledge, 1991.

Gozzini, Giovanni. "The Global System of International Migration, 1900 and 2000." *Journal of Global History* 1 (2006): 321–41.

Grant, Colin. *Negro with a Hat: The Rise and Fall of Marcus Garvey*. Oxford: Oxford University Press, 2008.

Green, Martin. *Gandhi: Voice of a New Age Revolution*. New York: Continuum, 1993.

Green, Vivian. *A New History of Christianity*. New York: Continuum, 1996.

Gregory, Paul R. *The Political Economy of Stalinism*. Cambridge: Cambridge University Press, 2004.

Grenville, J. A. S., and Bernard Wasserstein, eds. *The Major International Treaties of the Twentieth Century*, Volume 1. London: Routledge, 2001.

Greve, Bent. *The Routledge Handbook of the Welfare State*. New York: Routledge, 2013.

Griffiths, Tom, and Libby Robin, eds. *Ecology and Empire: Environmental History of Settler Societies*. Seattle: University of Washington Press, 1997.

Grundmann, Reiner. *Transnational Environmental Policy: Reconstructing Ozone*. New York: Routledge, 2001.

Guha, Ramachandra. *Environmentalism: A Global History*. New York: Longman, 2000.

———. *Gandhi before India*. New York: Knopf, 2014.

Gump, James O. "A Spirit of Resistance: Sioux, Xhosa, and Maori Responses to Western Dominance, 1840–1920." *Pacific Historical Review* 66 (1997): 21–52.

Guneratne, Arjun, and Anita M. Weiss, eds. *Pathways to Power: The Domestic Politics of South Asia*. New York: Rowman and Littlefield, 2014.

Gungwu Wang, ed. *Global History and Migrations*. Boulder, CO: Westview Press, 1997.

Gutiérrez, Ramón A. "Internal Colonialism: An American Theory of Race." *DuBois Review* 1 (2004): 281–95.

Gwynne, Robert N., and Cristóbal Kay, eds. *Latin America Transformed: Globalization and Modernity*. London: Arnold, 1999.

Hagen, William. *Germany in Modern Times*. New York: Cambridge University Press, 2012.

Hagerty, Devin T., ed. *South Asia in World Politics*. New York: Rowman and Littlefield, 2005.

Hannaford, Ivan. *Race: The History of an Idea in the West*. Baltimore: Johns Hopkins University Press, 1996.

Hanson, John R., II. "Diversification and Concentration of LDC Exports: Victorian Trends." *Explorations in Economic History* 14 (1977): 44–68.

Harkavy, Robert E. *Bases Abroad*. New York: Oxford University Press, 1989.

———. *Great Power Competition for Overseas Bases*. New York: Pergamon, 1982.

Harley, C. Knick. *The Integration of the World Economy, 1850–1914*. 2 Vols. Cheltenham, UK: Edward Elgar, 1996.

Harrison, Mark. "Disease and World History from 1750." In *The Cambridge World History*. Volume 7: *Production, Destruction, and Connection, 1750–Present, Part 1: Structures, Spaces and Boundary-Making*. Edited by J. R. McNeill and Kenneth Pomeranz. Cambridge: Cambridge University Press, 2015.

———. "The USSR and Total War: Why Didn't the Soviet Economy Collapse in 1942?" In *A World at Total War*. Edited by Roger Chickering, Stig Foerster, and Bernd Greiner. Cambridge: Cambridge University Press, 2005.

Hastings, Adrian, ed. *A World History of Christianity*. Grand Rapids, MI: William B. Eerdmans, 1999.

Hatton, Timothy J., and Jeffrey G. Williamson. *The Age of Mass Migration: Causes and Economic Impact*. New York: Oxford University Press, 1998.

———. *Global Migration and the World Economy*. New York: Oxford University Press, 1988.

Hausman, William J., Peter Hertner, and Mira Wilkins. *Global Electrification*. Cambridge: Cambridge University Press, 2008.

Hawkins, Freda. *Critical Years in Immigration: Canada and Australia Compared*. Montreal: McGill-Queen's University Press, 1991.

Hays, Samuel P. *Conservation and the Gospel of Efficiency*. Cambridge, MA: Harvard University Press, 1959.

Haywood, William D. *Bill Haywood's Book*. New York: International Publishers, 1929.

Hazell, Peter B. R. *The Asian Green Revolution*. Washington, DC: International Food Policy Research Institute, 2009.

Headrick, Daniel. "Botany, Chemistry, and Tropical Development." *Journal of World History* 7 (1996): 1–20.

———. *The Invisible Weapon: Telecommunications and International Politics, 1851–1945*. New York: Oxford University Press, 1991.

———. *Technology: A World History*. New York: Oxford University Press, 2009.

————. *The Tools of Empire*. New York: Oxford University Press, 1981.

Hebblethwaite, Peter. *Paul VI: The First Modern Pope*. New York: Paulist Press, 1993.

Held, David, Anthony McGrew, David Goldblatt, and Jonathan Perraton. *Global Transformations*. Stanford: Stanford University Press, 1999.

Herren, Madeleine. *Internationale Organisationen seit 1865*. Darmstadt, Germany: Wissenschaftliche Buchgesellschaft, 2010.

Hewa, Soma, and Darwin H. Stapleton. *Globalization, Philanthropy, and Civil Society: Toward a New Political Culture in the Twenty-First Century*. New York: Springer, 2005.

Hirano, Katsuya. "Thanatopolitics in the Making of Japan's Hokkaido." *Critical Historical Studies* 2 (2015): 191–218.

Hjertholm, Peter, and Howard White. *Survey of Foreign Aid: History, Trends, and Allocations*. Discussion Papers, No. 00-04. University of Copenhagen, Department of Economics. http://www.econ.ku.dk.

Hobsbawm, Eric. *The Age of Extremes*. New York: Vintage, 1994.

Hoerder, Dirk. *Cultures in Contact*. Durham, NC: Duke University Press, 2002.

Hoffmann, Stefan-Ludwig, ed. *Human Rights in the Twentieth Century*. Cambridge: Cambridge University Press, 2011.

Hopkins, A. G., ed. *Global History: Interactions between the Universal and the Local*. Houndsmills, Basingstoke, UK: Palgrave Macmillan, 2006.

Hora, Roy. *The Landowners of the Argentine Pampas*. Oxford: Oxford University Press, 2001.

Hourani, Albert. *A History of the Arab Peoples*. Cambridge, MA: Harvard University Press, 1991.

Howard, Michael, and William Roger Lewis, eds. *The Oxford History of the Twentieth Century*. New York: Oxford University Press, 1998.

Hughes, J. Donald. "The Greening of World History." In *Palgrave Advances in World History*. Edited by Marnie Hughes-Warrington. Houndsmills, Basingstoke, UK: Palgrave Macmillan, 2005.

Hughes, Thomas P. "The Evolution of Large Technological Systems." In *The Science Studies Reader*, 202–23. Edited by Mario Biagioli. New York: Routledge, 1999.

Hugill, Peter. *Global Communications since 1844*. Baltimore: Johns Hopkins University Press, 1999.

Hunt, James D. *Gandhi in London*. New Delhi: Promilla, 1978.

Hymans, Louis. *Leopold Sédar Senghor: An Intellectual Biography*. Edinburgh: University of Edinburgh Press, 1971.

Iguchi, Haruo. "Japanese Foreign Policy and the Outbreak of the Asia-Pacific War." In *The Origins of the Second World War*. Edited by Frank McDonough. New York: Continuum, 2011.

Inglehart, Ronald, and Christian Welzel. "How Development Leads to Democracy." *Foreign Affairs* 88 (2007): 33–48.

Ingulstad, Mats. "The Interdependent Hegemon: The United States and the Quest for Strategic Raw Materials during the Early Cold War." *International History Review* 37 (2015): 59–79.

Iriye, Akira. "The Making of a Transnational World." In *Global Interdependence: The World after 1945*. Edited by Akira Iriye. Cambridge, MA: Harvard University Press, 2014.

Iriye, Akira, ed. *Global Interdependence: The World after 1945*. Cambridge, MA: Harvard University Press, 2014.

Isenberg, Andrew C. *The Destruction of the Bison: An Environmental History, 1750–1920*. Cambridge: Cambridge University Press, 2000.

————. "Seas of Grass: Grasslands in World Environmental History." In *The Oxford Handbook of Environmental History*. Edited by Andrew C. Isenberg. Oxford: Oxford University Press, 2014.

Isserman, Maurice, and Michael Kazin. *America Divided: The Civil War of the 1960s*. New York: Oxford University Press, 2008.

Jackson, Julian, ed. *Europe, 1900–1945*. Oxford: Oxford University Press, 2002.

Jacobs, Steven Leonard, and Marc I. Sherman, eds. *Confronting Genocide*. New York: Lexington Books, 2009.

Jacobson, Matthew Frye. *Whiteness of a Different Color*. Cambridge, MA: Harvard University Press, 1998.

James, Harold. *Europe Reborn, 1914–2000*. Harlow, UK: Pearson, 2003.

Jansen, Marius B. *The Cambridge History of Japan*. Volume 5: *The Nineteenth Century*. New York: Cambridge University Press, 1988.

Jaquete, Jane S. "Losing the Battle/Winning the War: International Politics, Women's Issues, and the 1980 Mid-Decade Conference." In *Women, Politics, and the United Nations*. Edited by Anne Winslow. Westport, CT: Greenwood Press, 1995.

Jerven, Morten. *Poor Numbers: How We Are Misled by African Development Statistics and What to Do about It*. Ithaca, NY: Cornell University Press, 2013.

Johnson, Paul. *Modern Times*. New York: Harper and Row, 1983.

Jones, Adam, ed. *New Directions in Genocide Research*. New York: Routledge, 2012.

Jones, G. W., R. M. Douglas, J. C. Caldwell, and R. M. D'Souza, eds. *The Continuing Demographic Transition*. Oxford: Clarendon Press, 1997.

Jones, Geoffrey. "Multinationals from the 1930s to the 1980s." In *Leviathans*. Edited by Alfred Chandler and Bruce Mazlish. Cambridge: Cambridge University Press, 2005.

Jonsson, Fredrik Albritton. "The Origins of Cornucopianism: A Preliminary Genealogy." *Critical Historical Studies* 1 (2014).

Joseph, Peniel E. *Stokely: A Life*. New York: Basic Books, 2014.

Josephson, Paul. "The History of World Technology, 1750–Present." In *The Cambridge World History*, Vol. 7: *Production, Destruction, and Connection, 1750–Present, Part 1: Structures, Spaces, and Boundary-Making?* Edited by J. R. McNeill and Kenneth Pomeranz. Cambridge: Cambridge university Press, 2015.

Joshi, V. C., ed. *Rammohun Roy and the Process of Modernization in India*. Delhi: Vikas, 1975.

Judah, J. Stillson. *The History and Philosophy of the Metaphysical Movements in America*. Philadelphia: Westminster, 1967.

Judt, Tony. *Postwar: A History of Europe since 1945*. New York: Penguin, 2005.

Juergensmeyer, Mark, ed. *Religion in Global Civil Society*. New York: Oxford University Press, 2005.

Kanya-Forstner, A. S. "The War, Imperialism, and Decolonization." In *The Great War and the Twentieth Century*. Edited by Jay Winter, Geoffrey Parker, and Mary R. Habeck. New Haven: Yale University Press, 2000.

Khan, B. Zorina. "An Economic History of Patent Institutions." EH.net Encyclopedia. Edited by Robert Whaples. Economic History Association, 2008. http://eh.net/encyclopedia /an-economic-history-of-patent-institutions/.

Kalu, Ogbu U., and Alaine M. Low, eds. *Interpreting Contemporary Christianity: Global Processes and Local Identities*. Grand Rapids, MI: Eerdmans, 2008.

Kanet, Roger E. "The Superpower Quest for Empire: The Cold War and Soviet Support for 'Wars of Liberation.'" *Cold War History* 6 (2006): 331–52.

Kasaba, Resat, ed. *The Cambridge History of Turkey,* Volume 4: *Turkey in the Modern World.* Cambridge: Cambridge University Press, 2008.

Kay, Alex J. *Exploitation, Resettlement, Mass Murder: Political and Economic Planning for German Occupation Policy in the Soviet Union, 1940–1941.* New York: Berghahn, 2006.

Keddie, Nikki R. *Modern Iran.* New Haven: Yale University Press, 2006.

———. *Roots of Revolution: An Interpretive history of Modern Iran.* New Haven: Yale University Press, 1981.

Keevak, Michael. *Becoming Yellow: A Short History of Racial Thinking.* Princeton, NJ: Princeton University Press, 2011.

Kenez, Peter. *A History of the Soviet Union from the Beginning to the End.* Cambridge: Cambridge University Press, 2006.

Kent, Susan Kingsley. *The Influenza Pandemic of 1918–1919: A Brief History with Documents.* Boston: Bedford/St. Martin's, 2013.

Kenwood, A. G., and A. L. Lougheed. *The Growth of the International Economy.* New York: Routledge, 1999.

Kersbergen, Kees van, and Barbara Vis. *Comparative Welfare State Politics.* Cambridge: Cambridge University Press, 2014.

Kessel, William B., and Robert Wooster, eds. *Encyclopedia of Native American Wars and Warfare.* New York: Facts On File, 2005.

Kevles, Daniel J. "From Eugenics to Genetic Manipulation." In *Companion to Science in the Twentieth Century.* Edited by John Krige and Dominique Pestre. New York: Routledge, 2003.

Khalidi, Rashid. *Sowing Crisis: The Cold War and American Dominance in the Middle East.* Boston: Beacon Press, 2009.

Khan, Inayat. *Biography of Pir-o-Murshid Inayat Khan.* London: East-West, 1979.

Kiernan, Ben. *Blood and Soil: A World History of Genocide and Extermination from Sparta to Darfur.* New Haven: Yale University Press, 2007.

Kindleberger, Charles P. *The World in Depression.* Berkeley: University of California Press, 1986.

Kingsland, Sharon E. *The Evolution of American Ecology, 1890–2000.* Baltimore: Johns Hopkins University Press, 2005.

Kishlansky, Mark A., ed. *Sources of World History.* New York: HarperCollins, 1995.

Kitchen, Martin. *A History of Modern Germany, 1800–2000.* Malden, MA: Blackwell, 2006.

Klages, Ludwig. "Man and Earth (1913)." In *The Biocentric Worldview: Selected Essays and Poems of Ludwig Klages.* Translated by Joseph D. Pryce. London: Arktos, 2013.

Kloberdanz, Timothy J. "Plainsmen of Three Continents." In *Ethnicity on the Great Plains.* Edited by Frederick Luebcke. Lincoln: University of Nebraska Press, 1980.

Knab, Cornelia. "Infectious Rats and Dangerous Cows: Transnational Perspectives on Animal Diseases in the First Half of the Twentieth Century." *Contemporary European History* 20 (2011): 281–306.

Kolchin, Peter. *Unfree Labor: American Slavery and Russian Serfdom.* Cambridge: Cambridge University Press, 1987.

Kosai, Yutaka. "The Postwar Japanese Economy, 1945–1973." In *The Cambridge History of Japan,* Volume 6: *The Twentieth Century.* Edited by Peter Duus. Cambridge: Cambridge University Press, 1989.

Kotkin, Stephen. "Modern Times: The Soviet Union and the Interwar Conjuncture." In *The Cultural Gradient: The Transmission of Ideas in Europe, 1789–1991.* Edited by Catherin Evtuhov and Stephen Kotkin. New York: Rowman and Littlefield, 2003.

Kotkin, Stephen. "The Kiss of Debt." In *The Shock of the Global: The 1970s in Perspective.* Edited by Niall Ferguson, Charles S. Maier, Erez Manela, and Daniel J. Sargent. Cambridge, MA: Harvard University Press, 2010.

Kramer, Paul A. "Power and Connection: Imperial Histories of the United States in the World." *American Historical Review* 115 (2011): 1348–91.

Kratoska, Paul H. "Commercial Rice Cultivation and the Regional Economy of Southeastern Asia, 1850–1950." in *Food and Globalization,* 75–90. Edited by Alexander Nützenadel and Frank Trentmann. New York: Berg, 2008.

Kuchenbuch, David. "'Eine Welt': Globales Interdependenzbewusstsein und die Moralisierung des Alltags in den 1970er und 1980er Jahren." *Geschichte und Gesellschaft* 38 (2012): 158–84.

Kuhn, Philip A. *Chinese among Others: Emigration in Modern Times.* Lanham, MD: Rowman and Littlefield, 2008.

Lal, Vinay. *Empire of Knowledge: Culture and Plurality in the Global Economy.* London: Pluto Press, 2002.

———. "Much Ado about Something: The New Malaise in World History." *Radical History Review* 91 (2005): 124–30.

Laqua, Daniel, ed. *Internationalism Reconfigured: Transnational Ideas and Movements between the World Wars.* London: Tauris, 2011.

Large, Stephen S. "Oligarchy, Democracy, and Fascism." In *A Companion to Japanese History.* Edited by William M. Tsutsui. Oxford: Blackwell, 2007.

Latham, Michael E. *The Right Kind of Revolution: Modernization, Development, and U.S. Foreign Policy from the Cold War to the Present.* Ithaca, NY: Cornell University Press, 2011.

Lawrence, Mark Atwood. "The Rise and Fall of Nonalignment." In *The Cold War in the Third World.* Edited by Robert J. McMahon. Oxford: Oxford University Press, 2013.

Lechner, Frank J. *Globalization: The Making of World Society.* Malden, MA: Wiley-Blackwell, 2009.

Lees, Lynn Hollen. "World Urbanization, 1750 to the Present." In *The Cambridge World History,* Volume 7: *Production, Destruction, and Connection, 1750–Present, Part 2: Shared Transformations.* Edited by J. R. McNeill and Kenneth Pomeranz. Cambridge: Cambridge University Press, 2015.

Leffler, Melvyn P., and Odd Arne Westad, eds. *The Cambridge History of the Cold War.* 3 Volumes Cambridge: Cambridge University Press, 2010.

Leftwich, Adrian. *States of Development: On the Primacy of Politics in Development.* Cambridge: Polity, 2000.

Lenin, Vladimir Ilyich. *Imperialism, the Highest Stage of Capitalism.* In *V. I. Lenin: Selected Works in Three Volumes.* Volume 1. New York: International Publishers, 1939.

Leopold, Aldo. *A Sand County Almanac.* New York: Oxford University Press, 1966.

Lerner, Warren. *A History of Socialism in Modern Times: Theorists, Activists, and Humanists.* Englewood Cliffs, NJ: Prentice-Hall, 1982.

Lesser, Jeffrey. *Immigration, Ethnicity, and National Identity in Brazil, 1808 to the Present.* Cambridge: Cambridge University Press, 2013.

Leuchtenberg, William E. *Herbert Hoover.* New York: TimesBooks, Henry Holt, 2009.

Levene, Mark. *Genocide in the Age of the Nation-State.* London: Tauris, 2008.

Levine, Michael P. and Tamas Pataki, eds. *Racism in Mind.* Ithaca, NY: Cornell University Press, 2004.

Levinson, Marc. *The Box: How the Shipping Container Made the World Smaller and the World Economy Bigger*. Princeton, NJ: Princeton University Press, 2006.

Levy-Livermore, Amnon. *Handbook on the Globalization of the World Economy*. Cheltenham, UK: Edward Elgar, 1998.

Lewin, Moshe. *The Soviet Century*. London: Verso, 2005.

Lewis, Ronald. *Welsh Americans: A History of Assimilation in the Coalfields*. Chapel Hill: University of North Carolina Press, 2008.

Lieven, Dominic. "The Russian Empire and the Soviet Union as Imperial Polities." *Journal of Contemporary History* 30 (1995): 607–36.

———. *Globalisierung Imperial und Sozialistisch: Russland und die Sowjetunion in der Globalgeschichte 1851–1991*. Edited by Martin Aust. Frankfurt: Campus, 2013.

Lipman, Jonathan Neaman, Barbara Molony, and Michael Edson Robinson. *Modern East Asia*. Boston: Pearson, 2012.

Litvak, Lily. "Latinos y Anglosajones: Una Polemica de la España fin de Siglo." In Lily Litvak, *España 1900: Modernismo, anarquismo y fin de siglo*. Madrid: Anthropos, 1990.

Livi-Bacci, Massimo. *A Concise History of World Population*, 3rd ed. Malden, MA: Blackwell, 2001.

Lobato, Mirta Zaida, and Juan Suriano. *Atlas Historico de la Argentina*. Buenos Aires: Editorial Sudamericana, 1998.

Lodge, Tom. "Resistance and Reform." In *The Cambridge History of South Africa*, 409–91. Edited by Robert Ross, Anne Kelk Mager, and Bill Nasson. Cambridge: Cambridge University Press, 2011.

Lorenz, Chris. "Representations of Identity: Ethnicity, Race, Class, Gender and Religion." In *The Contested Nation: Ethnicity, Class, Religion and Gender in National Histories*. Edited by Chris Lorenz and Stefan Berger. New York: Palgrave Macmillan, 2008.

Loth, Wilfried. "States and the Changing Equations of Power." In *Global Interdependence: The World after 1945*. Edited by Akira Iriye. Cambridge, MA: Harvard University Press, 2014.

Loxley, John. "International Capital Markets, the Debt Crisis and Development." In *Global Development Fifty Years after Bretton Woods*. Edited by Roy Culpeper, Albert Berry, and Frances Stewart. New York: St. Martin's, 1997.

Lundestad, Geir. "'Empire by Invitation' in the American Century." *Diplomatic History* 23 (1999): 189–217.

Lyall, Francis. *International Communications: The International Telecommunications Union and the Universal Postal Union*. London: Ashgate, 2011.

Lytle, Mark Hamilton. *The Gentle Subversive: Rachel Carson,* Silent Spring, *and the Rise of the Environmental Movement*. New York: Oxford University Press, 2007.

Maalouf, Jean, ed. *Pope John XXIII: Essential Writings*. Maryknoll, NY: Orbis, 2008.

MacFarquhar, Roderick, and John K. Fairbank, eds. *The Cambridge History of China*. Vol. 14: *The People's Republic of China*, Part 1. Cambridge: Cambridge University Press, 1987.

———, eds. *The Cambridge History of China*. Volume 15: *The People's Republic, Part 2: Revolutions within the Chinese Revolution, 1966–1982*. Cambridge: Cambridge University Press, 1991.

Maddison, Angus. *Monitoring the World Economy, 1820–1992*. New York: Development Center of the OECD, 1995.

———. *The World Economy: A Millennial Perspective*. Volume 2. New York: Organization for Economic Cooperation and Development, 2006 (data updated at The Maddison Project, www.ggdc.net/maddison/maddison-project/data.htm).

Madley, Benjamin. "Patterns of Frontier Genocide, 1803–1910: The Aboriginal Tasmanians, the Yuki of California, and the Herero of Namibia." *Journal of Genocide Research* 6 (2004): 167–92.

———. "Reexamining the American Genocide Debate: Meaning, Historiography, and New Method." *American Historical Review* 120 (2015): 98–139.

Maier, Charles S. "Consigning the Twentieth Century to History: Alternative Narratives for the Modern Era." *American Historical Review* 105 (2000): 807–31.

Makeba, Miriam, and James Hall. *Makeba: My Story*. New York: New American Library, 1988.

Manning, Patrick. *Navigating World History: Historians Create a Global Past*. New York: Palgrave Macmillan, 2003.

Manning, Patrick, ed. *Global Practice in World History: Advances Worldwide*. Princeton, NJ: Markus Wiener, 2008.

Marentes, Luis A. *José Vasconcelos and the Writing of the Mexican Revolution*. New York: Twayne, 2000.

Marinho de Azevedo, Celia Maria. *Onda Negra, Medo Branco: O negro no imaginário das elites—Século XIX*. Rio de Janeiro: Paz e Terra, 1987.

Markovits, Claude. *The Global World of Indian Merchants, 1750–1947*. Cambridge: Cambridge University Press, 2000.

Marks, Lara V. *Sexual Chemistry: A History of the Contraceptive Pill*. New Haven: Yale University Press, 2001.

Marnham, Patrick. *Lourdes: A Modern Pilgrimage*. New York: Coward McCann and Geoghegan, 1980.

Marr, Andrew. *A History of Modern Britain*. New York: Macmillan, 2007.

Marsot, Afaf Lutfi al-Sayyid. *A History of Egypt*. Cambridge: Cambridge University Press, 2007.

Martel, Gordon, ed. *The Origins of the Second World War Reconsidered*. New York: Routledge, 1999.

Martin, Bernd. *Japan and Germany in the Modern World*. Providence, RI: Berghahn, 1995.

Martin, James Kirby, Randy Roberts, Steven Mintz, Linda O. McMurry, James H. Jones, and Sam W. Haynes. *A Concise History of America and Its People*. 2 Vols. New York: HarperCollins, 1995.

Marx, Karl, and Friedrich Engels. *The Communist Manifesto*. Edited by John E. Toews. Boston: Bedford/St. Martin's, 1999.

Masuzawa, Tomoko. *The Invention of World Religions*. Chicago: University of Chicago Press, 2005.

Matysik, Tracie. "Internationalist Activism and Global Civil Society at the High Point of Nationalism: The Challenge of the Universal Races Congress, 1911." In *Global History: Interactions Between the Universal and the Local*. Edited by A. G. Hopkins. Houndsmills, Basingstoke, UK: Palgrave Macmillan, 2006.

Mayobre, Eduardo. *Juan Pablo Pérez Alfonzo*. Caracas: Banco del Caribe, 2005.

Mazlish, Bruce. "Comparing Global History to World History." *Journal of Interdisciplinary History* 28 (1998): 385–95.

Mazower, Mark. *Dark Continent*. New York: Vintage, 1998.

———. *Hitler's Empire: How the Nazis Ruled Europe*. New York: Penguin, 2008.

———. *No Enchanted Place: The End of Empire and the Ideological Origins of the United Nations*. Princeton, NJ: Princeton University Press, 2008.

McCartin, Joseph A. *Collision Course: Ronald Reagan, the Air Traffic Controllers, and the Strike That Changed America*. New York: Oxford University Press, 2011.

McCauley, Martin. *Stalin and Stalinism*. New York: Longman, 1996.

McDonough, Frank, ed. *The Origins of the Second World War*. New York: Continuum, 2011.

McEvedy, Colin, and Richard Jones. *Atlas of World Population History*. Harmondsworth, UK: Penguin; London: Allen Lane, 1978.

McEvoy, Arthur F. "Toward an Interactive Theory of Nature and Culture." In *The Ends of the Earth: Perspectives on Modern Environmental History*. Edited by Donald Worster. New York: Cambridge University Press, 1988.

McKeown, Adam. "Chinese Emigration in Global Context, 1850–1940." *Journal of Global History* 5 (2010): 95–124.

———. "Global Migration, 1846–1940." *Journal of World History* 15 (2004): 155–89.

McKibbin, Bill, ed. *The Global Warming Reader*. London: Penguin, 2012.

McLachlan, Colin M. *A History of Modern Brazil*. Wilmington, DE: Scholarly Resources, 2003.

McMahan, David L. *The Making of Buddhist Modernism*. Oxford: Oxford University Press, 2008.

McMahon, Robert J., ed. *The Cold War in the Third World*. Oxford: Oxford University Press, 2013.

McManners, John. *The Oxford History of Christianity*. Oxford: Oxford University Press, 1993.

McMeekin, Sean. *The Russian Origins of the First World War*. Cambridge, MA: Harvard University Press, 2011.

McMillan, James, and William Doyle. *Modern France, 1880–2002*. Oxford: Oxford University Press, 2003.

McNeill, J. R. *Mosquito Empires: Ecology and Wars in the Greater Caribbean, 1620–1914*. Cambridge: Cambridge University Press, 2010.

McNeill, J. R. *Something New Under the Sun: And Environmental History of the Twentieth-Century World*. New York: W. W. Norton, 2000.

McNeil, J. R., and Kenneth Pomeranz, eds. *The Cambridge World History*, Volume 7: *Production, Destruction, and Connection, 1750–Present, Part 1: Structures, Spaces and Boundary-Making* and *Part 2: Shared Transformations?* Cambridge: Cambridge University Press, 2015.

McNeill, J. R., and Peter Engelke. "Into the Anthropocene: People and Their Planet." In *Global Interdependence: The World after 1945*. Edited by Akira Iriye. Cambridge, MA: Harvard University Press, 2014.

McNeill, J. R., and William H. McNeill. *The Human Web: A Bird's Eye View of World History*. New York: W. W. Norton, 2003.

McNeill, William H. "World History and the Rise and Fall of the West." *Journal of World History* 9 (1998): 215–36.

Mendoza, Amado, Jr. "'People Power' in the Philippines, 1983–1986." In *Civil Resistance and Power Politics*. Edited by Adam Roberts and Timothy Garton Ash. Oxford: Oxford University Press, 2009.

Metcalf, Barbara D., and Thomas R. Metcalf. *A Concise History of India*. Cambridge: Cambridge University Press, 2002.

Meyer, Michael C., William L. Sherman, and Susan M. Deeds. *The Course of Mexican History*. New York: Oxford University Press, 1979.

Meyer, Michael. *Response to Modernity: A History of the Reform Movement in Judaism*. Oxford: Oxford University Press, 1988.

Michie, Jonathan, ed. *The Handbook of Globalization*. Cheltenham, UK: Edward Elgar, 2003.

Milanovic, Branko. "Global Income Inequality by the Numbers." World Bank Development Research Group, Policy Research Working Paper No. 6259. November 2012. http://documents.worldbank.org/curated/en/959251468176687085/pdf/wps6259.pdf.

Miller, John H. *Modern East Asia*. Armonk, NJ: M. E. Sharpe, 2008.

Miller, Robert Ryal. *Mexico: A History*. Norman: University of Oklahoma Press, 1985.

Minor, Michael S. "The Demise of Expropriations as an Instrument of LDC Policy, 1980–1992." *Journal of International Business History* 25 (1994): 177–88.

Mishra, Pankaj. *From the Ruins of Empire: The Revolt against the West and the Remaking of Asia*. London: Allen Lane, Penguin, 2012.

Missiroli, Antonio. "European Football Cultures and Their Integration." In *Culture, Sport, Society* 5 (2002): 1–20.

Mitchell, B. R., ed. *International Historical Statistics, 1750–2005*. 3 Vols. Basingstoke, UK: Palgrave Macmillan, 2007.

Miyoshi, Masao, and Harry D. Harootunian. *Japan in the World*. Durham, NC: Duke University Press, 1993.

Mollenhof, Clark R. *George Romney: Mormon in Politics*. New York: Meredith, 1968.

Mommsen, Wolfgang J., and Jürgen Osterhammel, eds. *Imperialism and After*. London: Allen and Unwin, 1986.

Moon, David. "In the Russians' Steppes: The Introduction of Russian Wheat on the Great Plains of the United States of America." *Journal of Global History* 3 (2008): 203–25.

———. "Peasant Migration and the Settlement of Russia's Frontiers, 1550–1897." *Historical Journal* 40 (1997)

Moore, Carlos. *Fela: This Bitch of a Life*. Chicago: Lawrence Hill Books, 2009.

More, Charles. *Britain in the Twentieth Century*. Harlow, UK: Pearson-Longman, 2007.

Morgan, Kenneth O. *The Oxford History of Britain*. Oxford: Oxford University Press, 1999.

Morrow, John H., Jr. "The Impact of the Two World Wars in a Century of Violence." In *Essays on Twentieth-Century History*. Edited by Michael C. Adas. Philadelphia: Temple University Press, 2010.

Mosley, Stephen. *The Environment in World History*. New York: Routledge, 2010.

Moses, A. Dirk, ed. *Empire, Colony, Genocide*. New York: Berghahn, 2008.

Moss, Walter G. *An Age of Progress? Clashing Twentieth-Century Global Forces*. London: Anthem, 2008.

Mosse, George. *Toward the Final Solution*. New York: Fertig, 1978.

Moya, Jose C., and Adam McKeown. "World Migration in the Long Twentieth Century." In *Essays on Twentieth-Century History*. Edited by Michael Adas. Philadelphia: Temple University Press, 2010.

———. *World Migration in the Twentieth Century*. Washington, D.C.: American Historical Association, 2011.

Moyn, Samuel. *The Last Utopia: Human Rights in History*. Cambridge, MA: Harvard University Press, 2010.

Moyn, Samuel, and Andrew Sartori, eds. *Global Intellectual History*. New York: Columbia University Press, 2013.

Myers, Ramon H., and Mark R. Peattie, eds. *The Japanese Colonial Empire, 1895–1945*. Princeton, NJ: Princeton University Press, 1984.

Naess, Arne. *Ecology, Community and Lifestyle*. Translated and edited by David Rothenberg. Cambridge: Cambridge University Press, 1989.

———. "The Shallow and the Deep, Long-Range Ecology Movements: A Summary." *Inquiry* 16 (1973): 95–100.

Namikas, Lise. *Battleground Africa: Cold War in the Congo, 1960–1965*. Stanford: Stanford University Press, 2013.

Nash, George H. *The Life of Herbert Hoover.* Vol. 1: *The Engineer.* New York: W. W. Norton, 1983.

Nation, R. Craig, and Mark V. Kauppi, eds. *The Soviet Impact in Africa.* Lexington, MA: D. C. Heath, 1984.

Navaretti, Giorgio Barba, and Anthony J. Venables. *Multinational Firms in the World Economy.* Princeton, NJ: Princeton University Press, 2004.

Nehru, Jawaharlal. *Glimpses of World History.* 1934. Reprinted, Bombay: Asia Publishing House, 1962.

Neiberg, Michael. *Fighting the Great War: A Global History.* Cambridge, MA: Harvard University Press, 2005.

Nicholas, Larraine. *Dancing in Utopia: Dartington Hall and its Dancers.* Alton, Hampshire, UK: Dance Books, 2007.

Njolstad, Olav, ed. *The Last Decade of the Cold War.* London: Frank Cass, 2002.

Northrop, Douglas, ed. *A Companion to World History.* Malden, MA: Blackwell, 2012.

Nugent, Walter. *Crossings: The Great Transatlantic Migrations, 1870–1914.* Bloomington, IN: Indiana University Press, 1992.

———. *Into the West: The Story of Its People.* New York: Knopf, 1999.

Nützenadel, Alexander, and Frank Trentmann, eds. *Food and Globalization.* New York: Berg, 2008.

Nzongola-Ntalja, George. *The Congo from Leopold to Kabila: A People's History.* London: Zed Books, 2002.

O'Brien, Patrick Karl. "Colonies in a Globalizing Economy, 1815–1948." In *Globalization and Global History.* Edited by Barry K. Gills and William R. Thompson. London: Routledge, 2006.

———. "Intercontinental Trade and the Development of the Third World since the Industrial Revolution." *Journal of World History* 8 (1997): 75–133.

———. "Metanarratives in Global Histories of Material Progress," *International History Review* 23 (2001): 345–367

O'Connor, Garry. *Universal Father: A Life of Pope John Paul II.* New York: Bloomsbury, 2005.

Oliver, Roland, and G. N. Sanderson. *The Cambridge History of Africa,* Volume 6: *From 1870 to 1905.* New York: Cambridge University Press, 1985.

Oliviera, Orlinda de, and Bryan Roberts. "Urban Social Structures in Latin America, 1930–1990." In *Latin American Economy and Society since 1930.* Edited by Leslie Bethell. Cambridge: Cambridge University Press, 1998.

Olstein, Diego. *Thinking History Globally.* New York: Palgrave Macmillan, 2015.

Oltmer, Jochen. "Migration im Kontext von Globalisierung, Kolonialismus und Weltkriegen." In *WBG Welt-Geschichte,* Band VI: *Globalisierung 1880 bis heute.* Edited by Hans-Ulrich Thamer. Darmstadt, Germany: Wissenschaftliche Buchgesellschaft, 2010.

Organization for Economic Cooperation and Development. *Divided We Stand: Why Inequality Keeps Rising.* New York: OECD, 2011.

Ostler, Jeffrey. *The Plains Sioux and U.S. Colonialism from Lewis and Clark to Wounded Knee.* Cambridge: Cambridge University Press, 2004.

Overfield, James H., ed. *Sources of Global History since 1900.* Boston: Wadsworth Cengage Learning, 2013.

Overy, Richard. "Economic Origins of the Second World War." In *The Origins of the Second World War.* Edited by Frank McDonough. New York: Continuum, 2011.

———. *Why the Allies Won.* London: Jonathan Cape, 1995.

Oyebade, Adebayo, ed. *The Transformation of Nigeria.* Trenton, NJ: Africa World Press, 2002.

Panayi, Panikos, and Pippa Virdee, eds. *Refugees and the End of Empire.* New York: Palgrave Macmillan, 2011.

Parker, Charles H. *Global Interactions in the Early Modern Age, 1400–1800.* New York: Cambridge University Press, 2010.

Paxton, Robert O. *The Anatomy of Fascism.* New York: Knopf, 2004.

Payne, Stanley G. *A History of Fascism.* Madison: University of Wisconsin Press, 1995.

Peattie, Mark R. *Ishiwara Kanji and Japan's Confrontation with the West.* Princeton, NJ: Princeton University Press, 1975.

Pelling, Mark, David Manuel-Navarette, and Michael Redclift. *Climate Change and the Crisis of Capitalism.* New York: Routledge, 2012.

Perkins, Dwight H. *Agricultural Development in China, 1368–1968.* Chicago: Aldine, 1969.

Pfister, Ulrich. "Globalisierung und Weltwirtschaft." *WBG Welt-Geschichte,* Band VI: *Globalisierung 1880 bis heute.* Edited by in Hans-Ulrich Thamer. Darmstadt, Germany: Wissenschaftliche Buchgesellschaft, 2010.

Pierson, Christopher, and Francis G. Castles, eds. *The Welfare State: A Reader.* Cambridge: Polity, 2000.

Pigman, Geoffrey Allen. *The World Economic Forum: A Multi-stakeholder Approach to Global Governance.* New York: Routledge, 2007.

Pomeranz, Kenneth. *The Great Divergence: China, Europe, and the Making of the Modern World Economy.* Princeton, NJ: Princeton University Press, 2000.

Ponting, Clive. *A New Green History of the World.* London: Penguin, 2007.

Porter, Roy. *The Greatest Benefit to Mankind: A Medical History of Humanity from Antiquity to the Present.* New York: HarperCollins, 1997.

Porter, Roy, ed. *The Cambridge Illustrated History of Medicine.* Cambridge: Cambridge University Press, 1996.

Postel, Sandra. *Pillar of Sand: Can the Irrigation Miracle Last?* New York: W. W. Norton, 1999.

Potter, D., M. Kiloh, and P. Lewis, eds. *Democratization.* Cambridge: Polity Press, 1997.

Price-Smith, Andrew T. *Contagion and Chaos: Disease, Ecology, and National Security in the Age of Globalization.* Cambridge, MA: MIT Press, 2009.

Prior, Robin, and Trevor Wilson. *The Somme.* New Haven: Yale University Press, 2006.

Prodöhl, Ines. "Versatile and Cheap: A Global History of Soy in the First Half of the Twentieth Century." *Journal of Global History* 8 (2013): 461–82.

Pugh, Emerson W. *Building IBM: Shaping an Industry and Its Technology.* Cambridge, MA: MIT Press, 1995.

Queralt, Maria Pilar. *Tórtola Valencia.* Barcelona: Lumen, 2005.

Quinn, Frederick, ed. *African Saints.* New York: Crossroads, 2002.

Radest, Howard. *Toward Common Ground: The Story of the Ethical Societies in the United States.* New York: Ungar, 1969.

Radkau, Joachim. *Nature and Power.* Washington, DC: German Historical Institute; Cambridge: Cambridge University Press, 2008.

Raleigh, Donald J. "The Russian Civil War, 1917–1922." In *The Cambridge History of Russia.* Volume 3, *The Twentieth Century,* 140–67. Edited by Ronald Grigor Suny. Cambridge: Cambridge University Press, 2006)

Read, Christopher. *The Making and Breaking of the Soviet System.* Basingstoke, UK: Palgrave, 2001.

Red Cloud. "'I Was Born a Lakota': Red Cloud's Abdication Speech, July 4, 1903." In James R. Walker, *Lakota Belief and Ritual,* 137–39. Edited by Raymond J. DeMallie and Elaine A. Jahner. Lincoln: University of Nebraska Press, 1980.

Reed, Nelson A. *The Caste War of Yucatan*. Stanford: Stanford University Press, 2001.

Reid, Brian Holden. *The Origins of the American Civil War*. New York: Longman, 1996.

Reid, Richard. *A History of Modern Africa, 1800 to the Present*. London: Wiley-Blackwell, 2009.

Remington, Thomas. *The Politics of Inequality in Russia*. Cambridge: Cambridge University Press, 2011.

Reynolds, David. *One World Divisible: A Global History since 1945*. New York: W. W. Norton, 2000.

Rhodes, Richard, ed. *Visions of Technology: A Century of Vital Debate about Machines, Systems, and the Human World*. New York: Simon and Schuster, 1999.

Richards, Andrew John. *Miners on Strike: Class Solidarity and Division in Britain*. New York: Berg, 1996.

Riley, James C. *Rising Life Expectancy: A Global History*. Cambridge: Cambridge University Press, 2001.

Robbins, Keith. *The British Isles, 1901–1951*. New York: Oxford University Press, 2002.

Robert, Karen. "Teaching the Global Twentieth Century through the History of the Automobile." *World History Connected* 12:2 (2016).

Roberts, Adam, and Timothy Garton Ash, eds. *Civil Resistance and Power Politics*. Oxford: Oxford University Press, 2009.

Roberts, J. A. G. *A History of China*. New York: Palgrave Macmillan, 2006.

Robertson, Thomas. *The Malthusian Moment: Global Population Growth and the Birth of American Environmentalism*. New Brunswick, NJ: Rutgers University Press, 2012.

Robinson, Jeffrey. *Yamani: The Inside Story*. New York: Simon and Schuster, 1988.

Robinson, Ronald. "The Excentric Idea of Imperialism, with or without Empire." In *Imperialism and After*, 267–89. Edited by Wolfgang J. Mommsen and Jürgen Osterhammel London: Allen and Unwin, 1986).

Rodney, Walter. *How Europe Underdeveloped Africa*. 1972. Reprinted, Washington, DC: Howard University Press, 1982.

Rodrik, Dani. "Goodbye Washington Consensus, Hello Washington Confusion?" *Journal of Economic Literature* 44 (2006): 973–87.

Ropp, Paul S. *China in World History*. Oxford: Oxford University Press, 2010.

Rosen, Andrew. *The Transformation of British Life, 1950–2000: A Social History*. Manchester: Manchester University Press, 2003.

Rosenberg, Emily S. "Transnational Currents in a Shrinking World." *A World Connecting, 1870–1945*. Edited by Emily S. Rosenberg Cambridge, MA: Harvard University Press, 2012.

Ross, Robert, Anne Kelk Mager, and Bill Nasson, eds. *The Cambridge History of South Africa*. Cambridge: Cambridge University Press, 2011.

Rotberg, Robert I. *Africa Emerges*. Cambridge: Polity Press, 2013.

Rowland, Wade. *The Plot to Save the Planet*. Toronto: Clarke, Irwin, 1974.

Rubenstein, Richard L. "Jihad and Genocide: The Case of the Armenians." In *Confronting Genocide: Judaism, Christianity, and Islam*. Edited by Steven Leonard Jacobs and Marc I. Sherman. New York: Lexington Books, 2009.

Rubinstein, Hilary L., et al. *The Jews in the Modern World: A History since 1750*. London: Arnold, 2002.

Rudner, Martin. "East European Aid to Asian Developing Countries." *Modern Asian Studies* 1 (1996): 1–28.

Rummel, Rudolph J. *Statistics of Democide: Genocide and Mass Murder since 1900*. Münster, Germany: Lit, 1998.

Ryan, David, and Victor Pungong, eds. *The United States and Decolonization*. New York: St. Martin's, 2000.

Sagall, Sabby. *Capitalism, Human Nature, and Genocide*. London: Pluto Press, 2013.

Saha, Shandip. "Hinduism, Gurus, and Globalization." In *Religion, Globalization and Culture*. Edited by Peter Beyer and Lori Beaman. Leiden, The Netherlands: Brill, 2007.

Sahadeo, Jeff. "Progress or Peril: Migrants and Locals in Russian Tashkent, 1906–14." In *Peopling the Russian Periphery*. Edited by Nicholas Breyfogle, Abby Schrader, and Willard Sunderland. New York: Routledge, 2007.

Sala-i-Martin, Xavier. "The Disturbing 'Rise' of Global Income Inequality." National Bureau of Economic Research. Working Paper No. 8904 (April 2002). doi:10.3386/w8904.

Sanderson, G. N. "The European Partition of Africa: Origins and Dynamics." In *The Cambridge History of Africa*, Volume 6: *From 1870 to 1905*. Edited by Roland Oliver and G. N. Sanderson. New York: Cambridge University Press, 1985.

Sassoon, Donald. *Contemporary Italy: Economy, Society and Politics since 1945*. London: Longman, 1997.

Schaeffer, Robert K. *Understanding Globalization*. Lanham, MD: Rowman and Littlefield, 2009.

Schmitz, David F. *The United States and Right-Wing Dictatorships, 1965–1989*. New York: Cambridge University Press, 2006.

Schofer, Evan. "Science Associations in the International Sphere, 1875–1990." In *Constructing World Culture: International Nongovernmental Organizations since 1875*. Edited by John Boli and George M. Thomas. Stanford: Stanford University Press, 1999.

Schumacher, E. F. *Small Is Beautiful: Economics As If People Mattered*. New York: HarperCollins, 1973.

Scott, James C. *Seeing like a State: How Certain Schemes to Improve the Human Condition Have Failed*. New Haven: Yale University Press, 1998.

Scott, Rebecca J. "Gradual Abolition and the Dynamics of Slave Emancipation in Cuba, 1868–1886." *Hispanic American Historical Journal* 63:3 (1983): 449–77.

Sedgwick, Mark. *Muhammad Abduh*. Oxford: Oneworld, 2010.

Segrave, Kerry. *American Films Abroad: Hollywood's Domination of the World's Movie Screens from the 1890s to the Present*. Jefferson, NC: McFarland, 1997.

Sen, Amiya P. *Swami Vivekananda*. Oxford: Oxford University Press, 2000.

Service, Robert. *A History of Twentieth-Century Russia*. Cambridge, MA: Harvard University Press, 1998.

Shapin, Steven, and Simon Schaffer, *Leviathan and the Air-Pump: Hobbes, Hoyle, and the Experimental Life*. Princeton, NJ: Princeton University Press, 1985.

Sheik-'Abdi, 'Abdi. *Divine Madness: Mohammed 'Abdulle Hassan (1856–1920)*. London: Zed, 1992.

Shelton, Suzanne. *Ruth St. Denis: A Biography of the Divine Dancer*. Austin: University of Texas Press, 1981.

Shepard, Todd. "Algeria, France, Mexico, UNESCO: A Transnational History of Anti-racism and Decolonization, 1932–1962." *Journal of Global History* 6 (2011): 273–97.

Shillington, Kevin. *History of Africa*. New York: Palgrave Macmillan, 2005.

Shiva, Vandana. *The Violence of the Green Revolution: Third World Agriculture, Ecology, and Politics*. London: Zed Books, 1991.

Shleifer, Andrei. *A Normal Country: Russia after Communism*. Cambridge, MA: Harvard University Press, 2005.

Silverberg, Miriam. "Constructing a New Cultural History of Prewar Japan." In *Japan in the World*. Edited by Masao Miyoshi and

H. D. Harootunian. Durham, NC: Duke University Press, 1993.

Sil, Narasingha P. *Swami Vivekananda: A Reassessment*. Selinsgrove, PA: Susquehanna University Press, 1997.

Simpson, Bradley R. "Southeast Asia in the Cold War." In *The Cold War in the Third World*. Edited by Robert J. McMahon. Oxford: Oxford University Press, 2013.

Sinclair, Andrew. *Viva Che!* Stroud, UK: Sutton, 2006.

Singham, A. W., and Shirley Hune. *Non-alignment in an Age of Alignments*. London: Zed Books, 1986.

Sittert, Lance van. "'Keeping the Enemy at Bay': The Extermination of Wild Carnivora in Cape Colony, 1889–1910." *Environmental History* 3 (1998): 333–56.

Skidmore, Thomas E. *Black into White: Race and Nationality in Brazilian Thought*. Durham, NC: Duke University Press, 1993.

Skidmore, Thomas E., and Peter H. Smith. *Modern Latin America*. New York: Oxford University Press, 2005.

Sklar, Holly, ed. *Trilateralism*. Boston: South End Press, 1980.

Sklair, Leslie. "Discourses of Globalization: A Transnational Capitalist Class Analysis." In *The Postcolonial and the Global*. Edited by Revathi Krishnaswamy and John C. Hawley. Minneapolis: University of Minnesota Press, 2008.

Slate, Nico. *Colored Cosmopolitanism: The Shared Struggle for Freedom in the United States and India*. Cambridge, MA: Harvard University Press, 2012.

Sloterdijk, Peter. *Was Geschah im 20. Jahrhundert?* Frankfurt: Suhrkamp, 2016.

Sluga, Glenda. *Internationalism in the Age of Nationalism*. Philadelphia: University of Pennsylvania Press, 2013.

———. "UNESCO and the (One) World of Julian Huxley." *Journal of World History* 21 (2010): 393–418.

Smil, Vaclav. *Creating the Twentieth Century*. Oxford: Oxford University Press, 2005.

Smith, Bonnie G. *Europe in the Contemporary World, 1900 to the Present*. Boston: Bedford/St. Martin's, 2007.

Smith, Denis Mack. *Modern Italy: A Political History*. Ann Arbor: University of Michigan Press, 1997.

Smith, Merritt Roe, and Leo Marx, eds. *Does Technology Drive History?* Cambridge, MA: MIT Press, 1994.

Snyder, Louis L. *Macro-nationalisms: A History of the Pan-movements*. Westport, CT: Greenwood Press, 1989.

Snyder, Sarah B. *Human Rights Activism and the End of the Cold War*. Cambridge: Cambridge University Press, 2011.

Sonnenfeld, David A. "Mexico's 'Green Revolution,' 1940–1980: Towards an Environmental History." *Environmental History Review* 16 (1992): 28–52.

Soon, Park Bun. "Riding the Wave: Korea's Economic Growth and Asia in the Modern Development Era." In *Asia Inside Out: Connected Places*. Edited by Eric Tagliacozzo, Helen F. Siu, and Peter C. Perdue. Cambridge, MA: Harvard University Press, 2015.

Standing Bear, Luther. *Land of the Spotted Eagle*. 1933. Reprint, Lincoln: University of Nebraska Press, 1960.

Stanton, B. F. "Agriculture: Crops, Livestock, and Farmers." In *The Columbia History of the Twentieth Century*. Edited by Richard W. Bulliet. New York: Columbia University Press, 1998.

Stanziani, Alessandro. "Abolitions." In *The Cambridge World History*, Volume 7: *Production, Destruction, and Connection, 1750–Present, Part 2: Shared Transformations?* Edited by J. R. McNeill and Kenneth Pomeranz. Cambridge: Cambridge University Press, 2015.

———. "Serfs, Slaves, or Wage Earners? The Legal Status of Labour in Russia from a Comparative Perspective, from the Sixteenth to the Nineteenth Century." *Journal of Global History* 3 (2008): 183–202.

Staples, Amy L. *The Birth of Development*. Kent, OH: Kent State University Press, 2006.

Stark, Rodney. *The Rise of Mormonism*. Edited by Reid L. Neilson. New York: Columbia University Press, 2005.

Staudenmaier, John M. *Technology's Storytellers: Reweaving the Human Fabric*. Cambridge, MA: MIT Press, 1985.

Stearns, Peter N. *Globalization in World History*. New York: Routledge, 2010.

———. *The Industrial Revolution in World History*. Boulder, CO: Westview Press, 1998.

Steffen, Will, Paul J. Crutzen, and John R. McNeill. "The Anthropocene: Are Humans Now Overwhelming the Great Forces of Nature?" *Ambio* 36:8 (2007): 614–21.

Steger, Manfred B. *Globalization and Culture*. Cheltenham: Edward Elgar, 2012.

———. *Globalization: A Very Short Introduction*. Oxford: Oxford University Press, 2003.

Stichweh, Rudolf. *Die Weltgesellschaft: Soziologische Analysen*. Frankfurt: Suhrkamp, 2000.

Stone, Diane. "Knowledge Networks and Policy Expertise in the Global Polity." In *Towards a Global Polity*. Edited by Morten Ougaard and Richard Higgott. London: Routledge, 2002.

Storey, William Kelleher. *The First World War: A Concise Global History*. Lanham, MD: Rowman and Littlefield, 2009.

Stourton, Edward. *John Paul II: Man of History*. London: Hodder and Staughton, 2006.

Stuchtey, Benedikt, and Eckhardt Fuchs, eds. *Writing World History, 1800–2000*. Oxford: Oxford University Press, 2003.

Sun Yat-Sen. *San Min Chu I: The Three Principles of the People*. Translated by Frank W. Price. Edited by L. T. Chen. Shanghai: Commercial Press, 1928.

Sunderland, Willard. *Taming the Wild Field: Colonization and Empire on the Russian Steppe*. Ithaca, NY: Cornell University Press, 2004.

Suny, Ronald Grigor, ed. *The Cambridge History of Russia*. Volume 3: *The Twentieth Century*. Cambridge: Cambridge University Press, 2006.

Suri, Jeremi. "The Cold War, Decolonization, and Global Social Awakenings." *Cold War History* 6 (2006): 353–63.

Sutcliffe, Bob. "World Inequality and Globalization." *Oxford Review of Economic Policy* 20 (2004): 15–37.

Sutter, Paul S. "The Tropics: A Brief History of an Environmental Imaginary." In *The Oxford Handbook of Environmental History*. Edited by Andrew C. Isenberg. Oxford: Oxford University Press, 2014.

Sutton, Matthew Avery. *Jerry Falwell and the Rise of the Religious Right: A Brief History with Documents*. New York: Bedford/St. Martins, 2013.

Swinnen, Johan F. M. "The Growth of Agricultural Protection in Europe in the 19th and 20th Centuries." *World Economy* 32 (2009): 1499–1537.

Szasz, Ferenc M., and Margaret Connell Szasz, "Religion and Spirituality." In Clyde A. Milner, II, Carol A. O'Connor, and Martha A. Sandweiss, eds., *The Oxford History of the American West*. New York: Oxford University Press, 1994.

Talbot, Ian. "The End of the European Colonial Empires and Forced Migration." In *Refugees and the End of Empire*. Edited by Panikos Panayi and Pippa Virdee. New York: Palgrave Macmillan, 2011.

Tao, Terence. "*E pluribus unum:* From Complexity, Universality." *Daedalus* 141 (2012).

Tarr, Joel A. "The Metabolism of the Industrial City: The Case of Pittsburg." *Journal of Urban History* 28 (2002): 511–45.

Tauger, Mark B. *Agriculture in World History*. London: Routledge, 2010.

Taylor, K. W. *A History of the Vietnamese*. Cambridge: Cambridge University Press, 2013.

Thamer, Hans-Ulrich, ed. *WBG Welt-Geschichte*, Band VI: *Globalisierung 1880 bis heute*. Darmstadt, Germany: Wissenschaftliche Buchgesellschaft, 2010.

Thomas, Martin, and Andres Thompson. "Empire and Globalization: From 'High Imperialism' to Decolonization." *International History Review* 36:1 (2014): 142–70.

Tierney, Robert. *Tropics of Savagery: The Culture of Japanese Empire in Comparative Frame*. Berkeley: University of California Press, 2010.

Tooze, Adam. *The Deluge: The Great War, America, and the Remaking of the Global Order, 1916–1931*. New York: Viking, 2014.

Tschannen, Olivier. "La revaloración de la teoría de la secularización mediante la perspectiva comparada Europa Latina-América Latina." In *La Modernidad Religiosa: Europea Latina y América Latina en perspectiva comparada*. Edited by Jean-Pierre Bastian. México: Fondo de Cultura Económica, 2004.

Tsunoda, Ryusaku, William Theodore de Bary, and Donald Keene, eds. *Sources of Japanese Tradition*. New York: Columbia University Press, 1958.

Tsutsui, William M., ed. *A Companion to Japanese History*. Oxford: Blackwell, 2007.

Tucker, Robert P., and J. F. Richards, eds. *Global Deforestation and the Nineteenth-Century World Economy*. Durham, NC: Duke University Press, 1983.

Tucker, Spencer C., ed. *Encyclopedia of North American Indian Wars*. Santa Barbara, CA: ABC-CLIO, 2011.

Turner, B. L., et. al, eds. *The Earth as Transformed by Human Action*. New York: Cambridge University Press, 1990.

Turner, Graham. "A Comparison of The Limits to Growth with Thirty Years of Reality." CSIRO Working Papers Series 2008–2009. Canberra, Australia: CSIRO, 2007.

Turner, Thomas. *Congo*. Cambridge: Polity Press, 2013.

———. *The Congo Wars: Conflict, Myth and Reality*. London: Zed Books, 2007.

Tutino, John. *From Insurrection to Revolution in Mexico*. Princeton, NJ: Princeton University Press, 1986.

Tyrell, Ian. *Reforming the World: The Creation of America's Moral Empire*. Princeton, NJ: Princeton University Press, 2010.

Uchida, Jun. *Brokers of Empire: Japanese Settler Colonialism in Korea, 1876–1945*. Cambridge, MA: Harvard University Press, 2011.

Uekotter, Frank, ed. *The Turning Points of Environmental History*. Pittsburgh: University of Pittsburgh Press, 2010.

Üngör, Uğur Ümit. *The Making of Modern Turkey*. Oxford: Oxford University Press, 2011.

Van der Veer, Peter. "Religion after 1750." In *The Cambridge World History*. Volume 7: *Production, Destruction, and Connection, 1750–Present, Part 2: Shared Transformations?* Edited by J. R. McNeill and Kenneth Pomeranz. Cambridge: Cambridge university Press, 2015.

Vatikiotis, P. J. *The History of Modern Egypt*. Baltimore: Johns Hopkins University Press, 1991.

Veal, Michael. "Fela and the Funk." In *Black President: The Art and Legacy of Fela Anikulapo Kuti*. Edited by Trevor Schoonmaker. New York: New Museum of Contemporary Art, 2003.

Vickers, Adrian. *A History of Modern Indonesia*. New York: Cambridge University Press, 2005.

Viola, Lynne, V. P. Danilov, N. A. Ivniitski, and Denis Kozlov, eds. *The War against the Peasantry, 1927–1930*. New Haven: Yale University Press, 2005.

Vitali, Stefania, James B. Glattfelder, and Stefano Battiston. "The Network of Global Corporate Control." *PloS ONE* 6:10 (2011). http://journals.plos.org/plosone/article?id=10.1371/journal.pone.0025995.

Vohra, Ranbir. *The Making of India*. London: M. E. Sharpe, 1997.

Volti, Rudi. *Technology and Commercial Air Travel*. Washington, DC: American Historical Association, 2015.

Walker, Brett L. "Meiji Modernization, Scientific Agriculture, and the Extermination of Japan's Hokkaido Wolf." *Environmental History* 9 (2004): 248–74.

Wallerstein, Immanuel. *The Modern World System* 3 Vols. New York: Academic Press; Berkeley: University of California Press, 1974, 1989, 2011.

Wallimann, Isidor, and Michael N. Dobkowski, eds. *Genocide in the Modern Age*. New York: Greenwood Press, 1987.

Ward, Kevin. "Africa." In *A World History of Christianity*. Edited by Adrian Hastings. Grand Rapids, MI: William B. Eerdmans, 1999.

Waters, Kenneth, and Albert van Helden, eds. *Julian Huxley: Biologist and Statesman of Science*. College Station: Texas A&M University Press, 2010.

Weiner, Douglas R. "The Predatory Tribute-Taking State: A Framework for Understanding Russian Environmental History." In *The Environment and World History*. Edited by Edmund Burke III and Kenneth Pomeranz. Berkeley: University of California Press, 2009.

Wells, H. G. *The Discovery of the Future*. New York: B. W. Huebsch, 1913.

Wesseling, Henk L. *The European Colonial Empires, 1815–1919*. New York: Pearson-Longman, 2004.

———. *Imperialism and Colonialism: Essays on the History of European Expansion*. Westport, CT: Greenwood Press, 1997.

Westad, Odd Arne. *The Global Cold War*. Cambridge: Cambridge University Press, 2005.

Westwood, J. N. *Endurance and Endeavor: Russian History, 1812–2001*. Oxford: Oxford University Press, 2002.

White, Gilbert F. "The Environmental Effects of the High Dam at Aswan." *Environment* 30:7 (1988): 4–40.

Whitmore, Thomas, et al., "Long-Term Population Change." in *The Earth as Transformed by Human Action*. Edited by B. L. Turner et al. New York: Cambridge University Press, 1990.

Wilkins, Mira. *The History of Foreign Investment in the United States to 1914*. Cambridge, MA: Harvard University Press, 1989.

Wilkinson, James, and H. Stuart Hughes. *Contemporary Europe: A History*. Upper Saddle River, NJ: Pearson, 2004.

Williams, Michael. *Deforesting the Earth: From Prehistory to Global Crisis*. Chicago: University of Chicago Press, 2003.

Williams, Trevor I. *A Short History of Twentieth-Century Technology, c. 1900–c. 1950*. Oxford: Oxford University Press, 1982.

Williamson, John. "What Should the World Bank Think about the Washington Consensus?" *World Bank Research Observer* 15 (2000): 251–64.

Winslow, Anne, ed. *Women, Politics, and the United Nations*. Westport, CT: Greenwood Press, 1995.

Winter, Jay, Geoffrey Parker, and Mary R. Habeck, eds. *The Great War and the Twentieth Century*. New Haven: Yale University Press, 2000.

Wood, Barbara. *E. F. Schumacher: His Life and Thought*. New York: Harper and Row, 1984.

Woodward, C. Vann. "Emancipations and Reconstructions: A Comparative Study." In Woodward, *The Future of the Past*. New York: Oxford University Press, 1989.

Wolf, Eric. *Peasant Wars of the Twentieth Century*. 1969. Reprint, Norman: University of Oklahoma Press, 1999.

Wong, R. Bin. "Self-Strengthening and Other Political Responses to the Expansion of European Economic and Political Power." In *The Cambridge World History*, Volume 7: *Production, Destruction, and Connection, 1750–Present, Part I: Structures, Spaces, and Boundary-Making*. Edited by Kenneth Pomeranz and J. R. McNeill. Cambridge: Cambridge University Press, 2015.

Worden, Nigel. *The Making of Modern South Africa*. Chichester, UK: Wiley-Blackwell, 2012.

World Bank. *4°: Turn Down the Heat*. World Bank, Potsdam Institute for Climate Impact Research and Climate Analytics, November 2012.

Worster, Donald, ed. *The Ends of the Earth: Perspectives on Modern Environmental History*. New York: Cambridge University Press, 1988.

———. *Nature's Economy: A History of Ecological Ideas*. Cambridge: Cambridge University Press, 1994.

Wright, Gordon. *France in Modern Times*. New York: W. W. Norton, 1995.

Wulf, Herbert, ed.. *Arms Industry Limited*. Oxford: SIPRI, Oxford University Press, 1993.

Yang Jisheng, *Tombstone: The Great Chinese Famine, 1958–1962*. New York: Farrar, Strauss and Giroux, 2013.

Yenne, Bill. *Indian Wars: The Campaign for the American West*. Yardley, PA: Westholme, 2006.

Yergin, Daniel. *The Prize: The Epic Quest for Oil, Money, and Power*. New York: Simon and Schuster, 1991.

Young, Cynthia A. *Soul Power: Culture, Radicalism, and the Making of a U.S. Third World Left*. Durham, NC: Duke University Press, 2006.

Young, Louise. "Japan at War: History-Writing on the Crisis of the 1930s." In *The Origins of the Second World War Reconsidered*. Edited by Gordon Martel. New York: Routledge, 1999.

Zeiler, Thomas W. "Opening Doors in the World Economy." In *Global Interdependence: The World after 1945*. Edited by Akira Iriye. Cambridge, MA: Harvard University Press, 2014.

Zelko, Frank. *Make It a Green Peace! The Rise of Countercultural Environmentalism*. Oxford: Oxford University Press, 2013.

Zimmermann, Urs Matthias. "Race without Supremacy." In *Racism in the Modern World*. Edited by Manfred Berg and Simon Wendt. New York: Berghahn, 2011.

Zubok, Vladislav M. "Soviet Foreign Policy from Détente to Gorbachev, 1975–1985." In *The Cambridge History of the Cold War*. Edited by Melvyn P. Leffler and Odd Arne Westad. Cambridge: Cambridge University Press, 2010.

Illustration Credits

CHARTS

1.1. Massimo Livi-Bacci, *A Concise History of World Population*, 3rd ed. (Malden, MA: Blackwell, 2001), 27.

1.2. Livi-Bacci, *Concise History of World Population*, 27.

1.3. Derived from Livi-Bacci, *Concise History of World Population*, 27.

1.4. Livi-Bacci, *Concise History of World Population*, 27, 137.

1.5. B. R. Mitchell, *International Historical Statistics: Africa, Asia, and Oceania, 1750–2005* (Basingstoke, UK: Palgrave Macmillan, 2007), 86–89; Mitchell, *International Historical Statistics: Europe, 1750–2005* (Basingstoke, UK: Palgrave Macmillan, 2007), 122, 124, 126.

1.6. Mitchell, *International Historical Statistics: Africa, Asia, and Oceania,* 74–75; Mitchell, *International Historical Statistics: Europe,* 99, 106, 113; Mitchell, *International Historical Statistics: The Americas, 1750–2005* (Basingstoke, UK: Palgrave Macmillan, 2007), 72, 77.

1.7. Angus Maddison, *The World Economy: A Millennial Perspective* (n.p.: Organization for Economic Cooperation and Development, 2006), 2:32.

1.8. Mitchell, *International Historical Statistics: Africa, Asia, and Oceania,* 74–75, 77–78, 80; Mitchell, *International Historical Statistics: Europe,* 99, 106, 113; Mitchell, *International Historical Statistics: The Americas,* 72, 77.

1.9. B. R. Mitchell, *International Historical Statistics: Africa, Asia, and Oceania,* 74–75; Mitchell, *International Historical Statistics: Europe,* 97, 103, 110, 117; Mitchell, *International Historical Statistics: The Americas,* 72, 77.

1.10. Center for Sustainability and the Global Environment (SAGE), Nelson Institute for Environmental Studies, University of Wisconsin–Madison, www.sage.wisc.edu.

1.11. J. R. McNeill, *Something New Under the Sun: An Environmental History of the Twentieth-Century World* (New York: W. W. Norton, 2000), 180.

1.12. McNeill, *Something New Under the Sun,* 217.

1.13. Mitchell, *International Historical Statistics: Africa, Asia, and Oceania,* 723, 726, 728; Mitchell, *International Historical Statistics: Europe,* 738–46; Mitchell, *International Historical Statistics: The Americas,* 561–63, 565–68, 570.

1.14. Derived from Colin McEvedy and Richard Jones, *Atlas of World Population History* (Harmondsworth, UK: Penguin; London: Allen Lane, 1978).

1.15. Timothy J. Hatton and Jeffrey G. Williamson, *The Age of Mass Migration* (New York: Oxford University Press, 1988), 156.

2.1. David Held, Anthony McGrew, David Goldblatt, and Jonathan Perraton, *Global Transformations* (Stanford: Stanford University Press, 1999), 193.

2.2. Held et al., *Global Transformations,* 194.

2.3. Held et al., *Global Transformations,* 193.

2.4. Maddison, *The World Economy,* 2:264.

2.5. Maddison, *The World Economy,* 2:241, 264.

2.6. Mitchell, *International Historical Statistics: Europe,* 546–550; Mitchell, *International Historical Statistics: The Americas,* 391–92.

2.7. B. Zorina Khan, "An Economic History of Patent Institutions," *EH.net Encyclopedia,* ed. Robert Whaples (Economic History Association, 2008), http://eh.net /encyclopedia/an-economic-history-of-patent-institutions/.

2.8. Derived from Mitchell, *International Historical Statistics: Europe,* 81–83, 86–87, 90, 998, 1000, 1002; Mitchell, *International Historical Statistics: The Americas,* 59, 61, 64–65, 793, 795–96.

2.9. Mitchell, *International Historical Statistics: Africa, Asia, and Oceania,* 373–87, 513–24; Mitchell, *International Historical Statistics: Europe,* 464–76, 611–14; Mitchell, *International Historical Statistics: The Americas,* 327–36, 423–28.

3.1. Mitchell, *International Historical Statistics: Europe,* 226–33, 291–99; Mitchell, *International Historical Statistics: The Americas,* 154–59, 165, 181, 185, 189.

3.2. Mitchell, *International Historical Statistics: Africa, Asia, and Oceania,* 354–55; B. R. Mitchell, *International Historical Statistics: Europe,* 445–48; Mitchell, *International Historical Statistics: The Americas,* 303–6.

3.3. Mitchell, *International Historical Statistics: Africa, Asia, and Oceania,* 355–56, 359; Mitchell, *International Historical Statistics: The Americas,* 294–95.

3.4. Ken Swindell, "African Food Imports and Agricultural Development: Peanut Basins and Rice Bowls in the Gambia, 1843–1933," in *Agricultural Change, Environment and Economy,* ed. Keith Hoggart (London: Mansell, 1992), 167.

3.5. Mitchell, *International Historical Statistics: Africa, Asia, and Oceania,* 428–33; Mitchell, *International Historical Statistics: The Americas,* 352–59.

3.6. Mitchell, *International Historical Statistics: Africa, Asia, and Oceania,* 228–37; Mitchell, *International Historical Statistics: The Americas,* 202–9.

3.7. Mitchell, *International Historical Statistics: Africa, Asia, and Oceania,* 382–87; Mitchell, *International Historical Statistics: The Americas,* 333–36; Mitchell, *International Historical Statistics: Europe,* 475–76.

3.8. Mitchell, *International Historical Statistics: The Americas,* 408–10; Mitchell, *International Historical Statistics: Europe,* 593–95.

3.9. John R. Hanson II, "Diversification and Concentration of LDC Exports: Victorian Trends," *Explorations in Economic History* 14 (1977): 65, reprinted in C. Knick Harley, ed., *The Integration of the World Economy, 1850–1914,* vol. 2 (Cheltenham: Elgar Reference, 1996), p. 569.

3.10. A. G. Kenwood and A. L. Lougheed, *The Growth of the International Economy* (New York: Routledge, 1999), 80.

3.11. Kenwood and Lougheed, *Growth of the International Economy*, 84.

3.12. Mitchell, *International Historical Statistics: Europe*, 738–46; Mitchell, *International Historical Statistics: Africa, Asia, and Oceania*, 723, 726, 728.

3.13. Ulrich Pfister, "Globalisierung und Weltwirtschaft," in *WBG Weltgeschichte*, Band VI: *Globalisierung 1880 bis Heute* (Darmstadt, Germany: Wissenschaftliches Buchgesellschaft, 2010), 285.

3.14. Mitchell, *International Historical Statistics: Africa, Asia, and Oceania*, 723–28; Mitchell, *International Historical Statistics: The Americas*, 561–70; Mitchell, *International Historical Statistics: Europe*, 738–46.

3.15. Mitchell, *International Historical Statistics: Africa, Asia, and Oceania*, 277–79; Mitchell, *International Historical Statistics: The Americas*, 315, 317.

5.1. Maddison, *The World Economy*, 101.

5.2. Maddison, *The World Economy*, 101.

5.3. Mitchell, *International Historical Statistics: Africa, Asia, and Oceania*, 382–85; Mitchell, *International Historical Statistics: Europe*, 475–76; Mitchell, *International Historical Statistics: The Americas*, 333–36.

5.4. Mitchell, *International Historical Statistics: Europe*, 816–24, 827–31; Mitchell, *International Historical Statistics: The Americas*, 610, 614, 618, 624, 628.

5.5. Mitchell, *International Historical Statistics: Europe*, 103–4, 154; Mitchell, *International Historical Statistics: The Americas*, 114, 116.

6.1. Mitchell, *International Historical Statistics: Africa, Asia, and Oceania*, 175–77, 181, 183–84, 210, 212, 217–19.

6.2. Mark Harrison, "The USSR and Total War: Why Didn't the Soviet Economy Collapse in 1942?" in *A World at Total War*, ed. Roger Chickering, Stig Forster, and Bernd Greiner (Cambridge: Cambridge university Press, 2005), 140–42.

6.3. Harrison, "The USSR and Total War," 140–41.

6.4. Mitchell, *International Historical Statistics: Africa, Asia, and Oceania*, 441–42, 446–47; Mitchell, *International Historical Statistics: Europe*, 496–503; Mitchell, *International Historical Statistics: The Americas*, 375–78.

6.5. Antoni Estevadeordal, Brian Frantz, and Alan M. Taylor, "The Rise and Fall of World Trade, 1870–1939," National Bureau of Economic Research, Working Paper No. 9318 (November 2002), http://www.nber.org/papers/w9318.pdf, p. 36.

6.6. Estevadeordal, Frantz, and Taylor, "The Rise and Fall of World Trade, 1870–1939," 38.

6.7. Natural Resources Defense Council, "Global Nuclear Stockpiles, 1945–2006," in *Bulletin of the Atomic Scientists* 62:4 (2006): 66, archived at Wm. Robert Johnston, "Nuclear Stockpiles: World Summary" (2007), http://www.johnstonsarchive.net/nuclear/nucstock-0.html.

6.8. James R. Blaker, *United States Overseas Basing* (New York: Praeger, 1990), 33.

6.9. Stockholm International Peace Research Institute, SIPRI Arms Transfers Database, http://www.sipri.org/databases /armstransfers/.

7.1. Database, Maddison Project, www.ggdc.net/maddison /maddison-project/data.htm.

7.2. Database, Maddison Project, www.ggdc.net/maddison /maddison-project/data.htm.

7.3. Database, Maddison Project, www.ggdc.net/maddison /maddison-project/data.htm.

7.4. Database, Maddison Project, www.ggdc.net/maddison /maddison-project/data.htm.

7.5. Mitchell, *International Historical Statistics: Africa, Asia, and Oceania*, 373–88, 440–48; Mitchell, *International Historical Statistics: Europe*, 468–76, 496–512; Mitchell, *International Historical Statistics: The Americas*, 327–36, 375–79.

7.6. Mitchell, *International Historical Statistics: Africa, Asia, and Oceania*, 786–805; Mitchell, *International Historical Statistics: Europe*, 816–24; Mitchell, *International Historical Statistics: The Americas*, 610–22.

7.7. World Intellectually Property Organization, IP Statistics Data Center, http://www.wipo.int/ipstats/en/#resources.

7.8. Mitchell, *International Historical Statistics: Africa, Asia, and Oceania*, 1053–54, 1056–57; Mitchell, *International Historical Statistics: Europe*, 998–1003; Mitchell, *International Historical Statistics: The Americas*, 793, 795–99.

7.9. Mitchell, *International Historical Statistics: Africa, Asia, and Oceania*, 1053–57; Mitchell, *International Historical Statistics: Europe*, 998–1003; Mitchell, *International Historical Statistics: The Americas*, 193–99.

7.10. Matthias Busse, "Tariffs, Transport Costs and the WTO Doha Round: The Case of Developing Countries," *Estey Center Journal of International Law and Trade Policy* 4 (2003): 24.

7.11. Michael A. Clemens and Jeffrey G. Williamson, "Why Did the Tariff-Growth Correlation Reverse after 1950?" National Bureau of Economic Research, Working Paper No. 9181, September 2002, doi:10.3386/w9181, figure 1.

7.12. Kenwood and Lougheed, *Growth of the International Economy*, 302.

7.13. Richard E. Baldwin and Philippe Martin, "Two Waves of Globalization," National Bureau of Economic Research, Working Paper No. 6904 (January 1999), 17, doi:10.3386/ w6904.

7.14. Mitchell, *International Historical Statistics: Europe*, 230–33, 295–99; Mitchell, *International Historical Statistics: The Americas*, 154, 159, 165–67, 172, 181, 185, 189–90, 195.

7.15. Mitchell, *International Historical Statistics: Africa, Asia, and Oceania*, 175–76, 178, 181–83, 187, 210–13, 217–18, 221.

7.16. Giovanni Federico, *Feeding the World: An Economic History of Agriculture* (Princeton, NJ: Princeton University Press, 2005), 99.

7.17. Federico, *Feeding the World*, 48.

7.18. Mitchell, *International Historical Statistics: Africa, Asia, and Oceania*, 354–55; Mitchell, *International Historical Statistics: Europe*, 445–47; Mitchell, *International Historical Statistics: The Americas*, 303–6.

7.19. Mitchell, *International Historical Statistics: Africa, Asia, and Oceania*, 355–56, 359; Mitchell, *International Historical Statistics: The Americas*, 294–95.

7.20. Mitchell, *International Historical Statistics: Africa, Asia, and Oceania*, 195–99, 209–17, 221–25; Mitchell, *International Historical Statistics: Europe*, 291–99, 310–12, 322–24; Mitchell, *International Historical Statistics: The Americas*, 181–82, 185–86, 190, 195.

7.21. Maddison, *The World Economy,*, 183, 185, 193, 195, 213, 215, 222, 224.

7.22. Mitchell, *International Historical Statistics: Africa, Asia, and Oceania*, 59, 61–62, 65–67; Mitchell, *International Historical Statistics: Europe*, 82–91.

7.23. Helmut Führer, *The Story of Official Development Assistance* (n.p.: Organization for Economic Cooperation and Development, 1996), 42; Quintin V. S. Bach, *Soviet Economic Assistance to the Less Developed Countries* (Oxford: Clarendon Press, 1987), 7.

7.24. Database, Maddison Project, www.ggdc.net/maddison/maddison-project/data.htm.

7.25. Database, Maddison Project, www.ggdc.net/maddison/maddison-project/data.htm; Mitchell, *International Historical Statistics: Africa, Asia, and Oceania*, 382–83.

8.1. Database, Maddison Project, www.ggdc.net/maddison/maddison-project/data.htm.

8.2. Mitchell, *International Historical Statistics: Africa, Asia, and Oceania*, 382–85; Mitchell, *International Historical Statistics: Europe*, 475–76; Mitchell, *International Historical Statistics: The Americas*, 333–36.

8.3. *BP Statistical Review of World Energy* (British Petroleum Global, 2017), 20, http://www.bp.com/content/dam/bp/en/corporate/pdf/energy-economics/statistical-review-2017/bp-statistical-review-of-world-energy-2017-full-report.pdf.

8.4. Mitchell, *International Historical Statistics: The Americas*, 123–25; Mitchell, *International Historical Statistics: Europe*, 171–77.

8.5. Paul E. Gregory, *The Political Economy of Stalinism* (Cambridge: Cambridge University Press), 250.

8.6. Maddison, *The World Economy*, 614.

8.7. Graham Turner, "A Comparison of *The Limits to Growth* with Thirty Years of Reality," CSIRO Working Papers Series 2008–9 (Canberra, Australia: Commonwealth Scientific and Industrial Research Organisation, 2008), 43.

9.1. Mitchell, *International Historical Statistics: Europe*, 226–33, 291–99; Mitchell, *International Historical Statistics: Africa, Asia, and Oceania*, 154, 157, 164, 173–74, 176, 180, 183, 196, 200, 209, 212, 216, 218; Mitchell, *International Historical Statistics: The Americas*, 154, 159, 165, 167, 172, 181, 185, 189–90, 195.

9.2. Database, Maddison Project, www.ggdc.net/maddison/maddison-project/data.htm.

9.3. Database, Maddison Project, www.ggdc.net/maddison/maddison-project/data.htm.

9.4. Database, Maddison Project, www.ggdc.net/maddison/maddison-project/data.htm.

9.5. Mitchell, *International Historical Statistics: The Americas*, 61, 64–65, 647, 649; Mitchell, *International Historical Statistics: Africa, Asia and Oceania*, 64, 68, 851.

9.6. Mitchell, *International Historical Statistics: Europe*, 507–12; Mitchell, *International Historical Statistics: Africa, Asia and Oceania*, 446–47; Mitchell, *International Historical Statistics: The Americas*, 378.

9.7. United Nations Department of Economic and Social Affairs, *World Economic and Social Survey 2010: Retooling Global Development* (New York: United Nations, 2010), 75.

9.8. World Intellectual Property Organization, "IP Statistics Data Center," http://www.wipo.int/ipstats/en/#resources.

9.9. Mitchell, *International Historical Statistics: Europe*, 87–91, 1000–1003; Mitchell, *International Historical Statistics: Africa, Asia, and Oceania*, 62–63, 66, 68, 1054, 1056–57.

9.10. World Bank, Data, "Fertility Rate, Total (births per woman)," http://data.worldbank.org/indicator/SP.DYN.TFRT.IN.

9.11. Timothy J. Hatton and Jeffrey G. Williamson, *Global Migration and the World Economy* (New York: Oxford University Press, 1998), 208.

9.12. Mitchell, *International Historical Statistics: Europe*, 147–68; Mitchell, *International Historical Statistics: The Americas*, 114–21; Mitchell, *International Historical Statistics: Africa, Asia, and Oceania*, 97, 105.

9.13. OECD Data, "Gender Wage Gap," https://data.oecd.org/earnwage/gender-wage-gap.htm.

9.14. Mitchell, *International Historical Statistics: The Americas*, 114, 116, 118; Mitchell, *International Historical Statistics: Africa, Asia, and Oceania*, 97, 105.

10.1. Mitchell, *International Historical Statistics: The Americas*, 64–65, 68–69, 649, 651–52; Mitchell, *International Historical Statistics: Africa, Asia, and Oceania*, 55, 64, 68, 844, 851.

10.2. UN Department of Economic and Social Affairs, *World Economic and Social Survey 2010*, 95.

10.3. Mitchell, *International Historical Statistics: The Americas*, 295; Mitchell, *International Historical Statistics: Africa, Asia, and Oceania*, 701, 704–5, 708.

10.4. UN Department of Economic and Social Affairs, *World Economic and Social Survey 2010*, xiv.

10.5. United Nations Conference on Trade and Development, UNCTADstat, unctadstat.unctad.org.

10.6. United Nations Conference on Trade and Development, UNCTADstat, unctadstat.unctad.org.

10.7. Michael Mussa, "Factors Driving Global Economic Integration," in *Global Economic Integration: Opportunities and Challenges*, ed. Federal Reserve Bank of Kansas City (New York: Books for Business, 2001), p. 42, chart 7.

10.8. United Nations University, UNU-WIDER, "World Income Inequality Database—WIID3.4," https://www.wider.unu.edu/database/world-income-inequality-database-wiid34.

10.9. World Wealth and Income Database, http://wid.world/data/.

10.10. UN Department of Economic and Social Affairs, *World Economic and Social Survey 2010*, xxi.

10.11. World Energy Production, from Mitchell, *International Historical Statistics: Europe*, 464–76, 611–14; Mitchell, *International Historical Statistics: The Americas*, 327–37, 422–28; Mitchell, *International Historical Statistics: Africa, Asia, and Oceania*, 373–87, 513–24.

10.12. Paul Chefurka, "Population: The Elephant in the Room" (May 2007), graph under subheading "Overshoot," http://www.paulchefurka.ca/Population.html.

10.13. World Bank data portal, http://data.worldbank.org/indicator/EG.EGY.PRIM.PP.KD?year_low_desc=false.

FIGURES

4.1. Hans F. K. Günther, *The Racial Elements of European History*, trans. G. C. Wheeler (New York: Dutton, 1927), 205.

4.2. Günther, *Racial Elements of European History*, 118.

4.3. George Grantham Bain Collection, Library of Congress Prints and Photographs Division, Washington, DC (LC-B2- 1160-11).

4.4. George Grantham Bain Collection, Library of Congress Prints and Photographs Division, Washington, DC (LC-B2- 1150-11).

4.5. George Grantham Bain Collection, Library of Congress Prints and Photographs Division, Washington, DC (LC-B2- 915-11).

5.1. George Grantham Bain Collection, Library of Congress Prints and Photographs Division, Washington, DC (LC-B2- 4157-10).

5.2. George Grantham Bain Collection, Library of Congress Prints and Photographs Division, Washington, DC (LC-B2- 2899-7).

5.3. George Grantham Bain Collection, Library of Congress Prints and Photographs Division, Washington, DC (LC-B2- 171-8).

5.4. George Grantham Bain Collection, Library of Congress Prints and Photographs Division, Washington, DC (LC-USZ62-55902).

6.1. Photograph by Böhmer. Bundesarchiv, Bild 101I-269-0240-11A / Böhmer / CC-BY-SA 3.0. Courtesy Wikimedia Commons.

6.2. Photograph by Jerry J. Joswick. National Museum. Courtesy Wikimedia Commons.

6.3. Photograph by 米;軍撮影. Courtesy of Wikimedia Commons.

8.1. Wikimedia Commons, https://upload.wikimedia.org /wikipedia/commons/3/3e/Vietnam_War_protestors_at_ the_March_on_the_Pentagon.jpg (supplied by Lyndon B. Johnson Library).

8.2. August Siren, courtesy of Donora Historical Society, Donora, Pa.

8.3. *Lloyd Rich*/British Library via Flickr.

MAPS

2.1. Redrawn from map in H. Hearder, *Europe in the Nineteenth Century* (New York: Longman, 1966), 76. Reproduced by permission of Taylor & Francis Books UK.

3.1. Redrawn, by permission, from map in Walter Nugent, *Crossings: The Great Transatlantic Migrations, 1870–1914* (Bloomington: Indiana University Press, 1992), 115.

6.1. Redrawn, by permission, from map in Eric Dorn Brose, *A History of Europe in the Twentieth Century* (New York: Oxford University Press, 2005), 228.

6.2. Based on a map from *Fasttrack to America's Past*, Fasttrack Teaching Materials, Springfield, VA, 2015, by David Burns, at www.fasttrackteaching.com.

Index

Abduh, Muhammad, 112
Adler, Felix, 109, 115, 119
affirmative action, 227
African Methodist Episcopal Zion Church, 112, 114
African National Congress, 119, 244, 300
African socialism, 194, 265, 300
Aggrey, James Emmanuel Kwegyir, 111
Ahmad, Muhhammad, 94, 112
al-Azhar mosque, Egypt, 111
Alfonzo, Juan Pablo Perez, 222
Ali, Muhammad, 89, 244
All-Indian Muslim Conference, 119
American Civil Liberties Union, 115, 119
American Civil War, 79–83, 90, 100, 161
Americanization, 102
Amnesty International, 247
Anglo-Iranian Oil Company. *See* British Petroluem Co.
Anglo-Persian Oil. *See* British Petroleum Co.
Anglo-Saxonism, 98, 104, 105
Anthropocene, 327, 328
apartheid, 117, 120, 244, 247, 290, 293, 300, 302, 304
Aquino, Benigno, 299
Aquino, Corazon, 299
Arab Socialism, 189
Arab Spring, 300
arms trade, 196, 197, 270
Arnold, Matthew, 104
Aryan "race," 102, 106, 160, 175, 177
Aswan High Dam, 193, 231, 275
Atatürk, Kemal, 133, 137, 177
Atkinson, William Walker, 115
Atlantic Revolutions, 17, 78, 82
automobiles, 52, 54, 61, 92, 120, 144–45, 148–49, 152, 203–5, 212, 271–72, 274–75, 317
Axis, in World War II, 170–73, 175, 189

Ba'ath Party, 287
Baha'ism, 114
Baker, Samuel White, 23–24
bananas, 62, 211
Bandung Conference, 190, 193
barbed wire, 26
Belafonte, Harry, 244
Belasco, David, 121
Belgian Congo, 145, 187, 190
Bell, Alexander Graham, 51

Berlin to Baghdad railway, 147, 149
Berlusconi, Silvio, 308
Bessemer process, 53, 60
Beveridge, Albert, 85
Bharatiya Janata Party (BJP), 285–86
Bhopal disaster, 254
bicycle, 53, 61, 92, 120
bison, 23, 252
Black Act, 118
Black Panther Party, 243–45
Black Power, 243, 245
Black Sea Germans, 36
Black, Joseph, 48
Blavatsky, Helena, 116
Blitzkrieg, 169
Blunt, Winfred Scawen, 85
Boer War, Second (1899–1902), 67, 93–94, 118
Boers, Boer republics, 21–22, 117; Great Trek, 21–22
Bolshevism, 132, 136, 151, 158
Bosporus, 147
Boxer Rebellion, 43, 135
Brahmo Samaj, 113
Brazil, 19, 21, 24, 33, 34, 36–7, 43, 58, 70–72, 78–83, 89, 93, 96, 101, 102, 177, 194, 196, 206, 210, 224, 253, 267, 269, 271–73, 275–77, 282, 301, 303, 308, 309, 314, 320
Bretton Woods Agreement, 188, 206
British Petroleum Co., 58, 149, 189
Brown, James, 245
Buffalo Bill, 109
Burbank, Luther, 51

California, 20, 22, 24, 26, 28, 29, 32, 34, 36–38, 42, 43, 51, 67, 69, 81, 113, 116, 123, 135, 160, 245, 254, 256, 274, 284, 285, 321
Campaign for Nuclear Disarmament, 247
Canada, 15, 20–21, 32, 34, 36, 41, 46, 65, 69, 70, 74, 80, 121, 141, 144, 146, 216, 227, 241, 254, 262, 264, 267, 283, 309, 311–13, 322
Caporetto, Battle of, 141
Capron, Horace, 39
carbon dioxide, 320–30
Cargill Co., 211
Carmichael, Stokely, 236, 243–45
carrying capacity, 257, 261, 325

Carson, Rachel, 256
cash register, 61
Caste War in the Yucatan, 110
Castro, Fidel, 196, 242–43
Central Intelligence Agency, CIA, 189, 190
Césaire, Aimé, 108
chainsaw, 29
Chamberlain, Houston Stuart, 102
Chamorro, Violetta, 296
chemistry, 48, 55, 120, 141, 144, 296
Chernobyl, 248
Chiang Kai Shek. *See* Jiang Jieshi
China, 4, 12, 15, 29, 31–34, 42, 48, 58–59, 62, 71–72, 84–90, 96, 100, 102, 108, 110, 139, 144, 146, 150, 163–66, 175–77, 180, 183–84, 189, 210, 219, 257, 267–70, 272–77, 300, 305, 308, 312, 314, 326; economic reforms, 306–7; one-child policy, 258, 307; Revolution (1911), 135–37, 157; Revolution (1949), 191
Chinese Communist Party, 136, 139, 176
Chinese Exclusion Act, 34, 102
Christ Stopped at Eboli, 155
Christian Democracy, 225, 228, 301
Christian fundamentalism, 113
Christian missions, 4, 22, 103, 110, 113, 114
Christian Science Journal, 112
CIA, 318. *See* Central Intelligence Agency
Civil Rights Act (1964), 227, 228
Civil Rights Movement in USA, 119, 205, 243, 283
Civil War, Russia, 131–32, 158
Clark, William Smith, 39
climate change, 320–26
Club of Rome, 260, 262, 325
CMEA, Council for Mutual Economic Assistance, 188, 208
coal, 36–37, 44, 48, 51, 54–55, 57, 59, 62, 72, 145, 148, 160, 164, 203, 212, 222, 261, 282–83
Cobden-Chevalier Treaty, 87
Coca Cola, 61
coffee, 62, 65, 70–71, 82, 89, 92, 96, 173
collectivization of agriculture; China, 191, 306; Soviet Union, 159, 162, 199
colonialism, colonial rule, 4–6, 29, 39, 65, 72, 76, 78, 79, 83–84, 88, 91–97, 103–4, 106, 122, 142, 144–47, 161, 163, 175, 179–94, 218, 241

Comintern, 139, 151
Committee of Union and Progress, 133
commodity extraction, 63–77, 80–81, 131, 134, 191–92, 195, 210, 233, 237
communism, 45, 132, 152, 175, 178–79, 225–30, 248, 258, 266, 297, 298–302; fall of, 268, 281, 290, 298–302, 307, 316
Conference on the Human Environment, United Nations (1972), 260
Conferences on Population, United Nations, 258
Congo, 96, 184, 187, 270, 300
Congo Free State, 84, 85, 126, 246
Congo Reform Association, 126
Congress of Racial Equality, 119, 243
conservationism, 24–25, 261, 324
Constitutional Democratic Party, Russia, 131
consumer economy, consumer society, 7, 52–54, 61–62, 82, 120, 181, 203, 205–6, 230, 259, 271–75, 290, 293, 317
contraception, 16–17, 19, 220–21, 258, 283, 288, 291, 293
Convention for the Protection of the Ozone Layer (1985), 322
Convention on the Elimination of All Forms of Discrimination Against Women, 292
copper, 62, 72, 93, 190, 206, 237
Cosmic Race. *See* Vasconcelos
Cossacks, 22
cotton, 48–51, 59, 62, 71, 80–82, 89–90, 93, 96, 134, 161, 185, 212
Council for Mutual Economic Assistance, see CMEA
Crosland, C. A. R., 229–30
Cuba, 71–73, 78, 91, 93, 129, 194; abolition of slavery, 78; Revolution (1959), 196, 24–44, 275
Cultural Revolution, China, 306
Curzon, George Lord, 144, 165

Dan Fodio, Usman, 112
Dartington Hall, 123
debt crisis (1980s), 237–39, 268, 270, 277, 290, 301, 305, 308
decolonization, 179, 194, 241
democracy, 176–79, 187, 193
democracy, liberal, 152, 176–79
Deng Xiaoping, 306
development, development policy, 29, 38–47, 63, 70, 80, 87, 88, 95–96, 100, 126, 134, 137, 143–47, 153, 158–59, 184, 189, 193, 204, 229–36; human development, 199; and women, 292–93
Development Assistance Committee, of OECD, 231
Dharmapala, Anagarika, 112, 116, 119
Díaz, Porfirio, 100, 134–45, 204
dictatorship; in 1930s, 175–77; in Cold War, 188–97; fragility of, 298–304
disease, 12–14, 19, 60, 80, 125, 141, 254; and antibiotics, 14; HIV/AIDS, 276, 293; influenza, 141; malaria, 13, 29, 45; typhus, 12, 60
Dominion Lands Act (1872), 21, 38

Dreyfus Affair, 105
Duncan, Isadora, 121, 141
Dutschke, Rudi, 243

East India Company, 100
ecology, environmental movement, 252–63, 288, 332
Eddy, Mary Baker, 114
Edison, Thomas, 51
education, schooling, 15, 51, 99, 101, 113, 133–35, 138, 226–27, 239, 277, 279, 286, 292, 303, 315; and decolonization, 183, 222; and innovation, 223, 265; women's, 294, 296; in colonial regions, 96; and democracy, 303–4
Egypt, 9, 14–15, 18, 24, 40, 51, 71, 81, 85, 89, 90–92, 94, 101–2, 104, 111–13, 122, 127, 143, 146, 152, 168, 187, 190, 193, 231, 241, 267–70, 272, 275, 279, 287, 314
Ehrlich, Paul, 258, 267
electricity, electrification, 54–55, 57, 59, 148, 160, 275–76, 321
electronics, computers, 210, 259, 273–74, 283, 302, 313–14, 318–19, 328, 332
Emirate of Sokoto, 94, 112
energy, 5, 6, 48, 54–55, 57–59, 164, 189, 212, 222, 238, 248, 275, 320–23, 324, 326, 331; hydroelectric, 53–54, 227, 231, 275, 314; nuclear, 55, 247–48, 262, 275
Equal Rights Amendment, 291
Estado Novo, Brazil, 177
ethnicity, 99–111, 117, 130, 151–52, 175
European Economic Community, EEC, 209, 223, 229, 231, 283
European Union, 209, 285, 319, 330

Falkland Islands. *See* Malvinas Islands
famine, 9, 12, 31, 80, 96–97, 105, 160, 186, 191, 258, 268
Fanon, Frantz, 243
fascism, 152, 177–79, 225, 226
fertility, 2, 10, 15–19, 219–24, 239, 256–57, 279–80, 283, 292–93, 296, 298, 326, 331
fertilizer, 7, 10, 29, 48, 62, 71, 93, 161, 212, 215, 264–67, 306, 327
FIFA, 121, 127
First Universal Races Congress, 109
Fitzgerald, F. Scott, 146
Five Year Plans, 159, 193, 305
Focus on the Family, 285
food, 4, 5–6, 8, 27, 60, 62–67, 73, 74, 85, 96–97, 129, 131, 137, 155, 158–60, 212–13, 216, 238, 257, 264–66
Food and Agriculture Organization, FAO, United Nations, 180, 257
football (soccer), 120–21
Ford Foundation, 264
Ford Motor Co., 58, 61, 274
Forster, E. M., 178
fossil fuels, 7, 8, 164, 212, 320–29
Framework Convention on Climate Change, 322

France, 12, 13, 17, 20, 39, 62, 72, 78, 87, 92, 101, 102, 115, 132, 141, 145, 151–53, 175, 179, 180, 186–88, 211, 221, 236, 241, 267, 270, 279
Franco, Francisco, 177, 290
Free Officers Movement, Egypt, 187
Friends of the Earth, 247
Fukuyama, Francis, 308

Gaia Hypothesis, 332
Gandhi, Mohandas Karamchand, 117–20, 125, 243, 261, 262
Garvey, Marcus, 108
GATT, General Agreement on Tariffs and Trade, 188, 206, 208
Gaulle, Charles de, 186
General Federation of Women's Clubs, 127
General Motors Co., 211
Geneva Convention, 126
genocide, mass murder, 6, 22, 33, 96, 97; Armenian, 1151–52; in Cold War, 197; and decolonization, 183–84; and National Socialism, 163; Rwanda, 270, 300
Germany, 14, 17–19, 21, 24, 35–37, 39, 51–53, 58, 62, 72, 82, 87, 92, 97, 94–100, 102, 104, 105, 110, 114–15, 120, 125, 133, 139, 141, 144–51, 153, 158, 160–61, 163–73, 175, 188–89, 200, 206, 210–12, 216, 243, 247, 254, 267
Germanization, 102, 110
global warming. *See* climate change
Gobineau, Arthur de, 102
gold, 36, 37, 42–43, 62, 67, 91, 93
gold standard, 87, 96–97
Goulart, João, 196
Government of India Act (1935), 185
Graham, Billy, 285
Grant, Madison, 106
grasslands, 20–23, 25–28, 35–39, 42, 62, 96, 161, 322
Great Britain, 14, 24, 27, 32, 34–35, 53, 59, 62, 76, 101–2, 115, 120, 125, 132, 151, 211, 226, 236, 247, 250, 256, 262, 299, 314; abolitionism, 78–80; Cold War, 179–80, 187; decolonization, 185–88; foreign investment, 40–42, ; and the New Imperialism, 50, 90–95, 119, 132, 143–47; New Right, 280, 282–83, 289, 296, 325; trade and trade policy, 64–65, 72–73, 74, 87–89, 90; and origins of World War I, 146–47, 149; in World War I, 146, 152–3; and origins of World War II, 163, 165, 173, 175; in World War II, 169–72
Great Plains, 20–22, 35, 38–39, 81
Great Depression, 142, 153; and origins of World War II, 173–74
Great Leap Forward, China, 306
Great Mutiny, India, 100
Great Northern Telegraph Co., 74
Great Sioux War, 20, 22, 109
Great Society, 226–27, 241
Green Revolution, 264–68, 325–26

Greenpeace, 262
Grimm, Jakob, 100
Group of 77, 245–46
guano, 48, 93
Guevara, Ernesto "Che," 241–44
gunboat diplomacy, 77, 90, 192
Günther, Hans F. K., 105–6
Guomindang, KMT, 136–37, 184, 301

Hansen, James, 320, 324
Hassan, Mohammed 'Abdulle, 112
Hauhau movement, 110
Havel, Vaclav, 298
Hawai'i, 32–33, 36, 37, 93, 103, 299
Haywood , William "Big Bill," 44
Helsinki Accords (1975), 247
Hertz, Heinrich, 60
Herzl, Theodor, 105
Hitler, Adolf, 160, 169, 172–73, 175, 177
Hitler-Stalin Pact, 169
Ho Chi Minh, 139, 241
Hokkaido, 20–23, 39
Holocaust, 105
Homestead Act (1862), 21, 38, 161
Hong Kong, 90, 103, 139, 306, 312
Hong Xiuquan, 110
Hoover, Herbert, 42–43
Human Development Index, 277
human rights, 49, 180, 246–47, 288–89,
    292–93; International Covenant on
    Civil and Political Rights (1966), 246
Humanist Manifesto, 109, 288
Huxley, Julian, 258, 288

IHEU. *See* International Humanist and
    Ethical Union
IMF. *See* International Monetary Fund
imperialism, 34, 42, 77–78, 84–97, 100, 101,
    103–4, 110, 114, 121, 126, 132, 136,
    137; and racism, 103, 118; and World
    War I, 130–31, 143–47
import substitution, 19, 305
India, 4, 13, 15, 20–21, 24, 27, 29, 31–34,
    48, 50–51, 62, 71, 73, 76–77, 81, 83, 85,
    88, 89, 94–96, 100, 104, 111, 113, 116–
    19, 122–23, 140, 144, 149, 158, 163,
    174, 182–83, 185–86, 193, 200, 216,
    219, 254, 257–58, 264, 266–69, 271,
    273, 277, 285, 287, 305, 309, 320, 322
Indian National Congress, 104, 117–19,
    123, 193
indigenism, indígenismo, 108, 125, 135, 184
Indonesia, 29, 32, 50, 58, 65, 69–72, 76–77,
    88, 95, 104, 111, 149, 163, 165, 168,
    18–83, 285–87, 190, 194, 197, 266, 268–
    69, 284, 296, 300, 303, 304, 3008–9, 314
Industrial Revolution, 5, 48, 49
Industrial Workers of the World, IWW, 44
inequality, 277, 307, 315–17
infant mortality, 12–14
International Non-Governmental Organi-
    zations, INGOs, 125–27, 180
Inter-Allied Petroleum Conference, 165
Inter-American Development Bank, 231

Intergovernmental Panel on Climate
    Change, United Nations, 322
internal combustion engine, 27, 29, 52,
    53–55, 141, 144, 148, 165
International Agricultural Institute, 39, 126
International Congress of Agriculture. *See*
    International Agricultural Institute
International Humanist and Ethical Union,
    IHEU, 288
International Labor Organization, 180
International Monetary Fund, 188, 238, 250
International Office of Public Hygiene, 125,
    180
International Olympic Committee, 127
International Rice Research Institute, 264
International Telegraph Union, 85, 126
International Telephone and Telegraph Co.,
    58, 74
International Wheat and Maize Improve-
    ment Center, 264
International Women's Year, 292
International Workingmen's Association, 138
Internet, 277, 287, 313–15, 318, 332
investment, 40–42, 67, 69–76, 87–88, 95,
    129, 183–85, 225–27, 232–33, 248, 270,
    276–77, 303, 306–12, 318; from Great
    Britain, 40–42; by overseas Chinese,
    306; and World War I, 141–42
Iran, Persia, 40, 72, 89, 133, 140, 148–49,
    164–65, 173, 189, 194, 210, 257, 271,
    28–87, 291–92; Revolution (1906),
    132–34, 146; Revolution (1979), 137,
    248, 286
IRRI. *See* International Rice Research
    Institute
irrigation, 21, 26, 48, 96, 154, 161, 193, 264,
    266
Ishiwara Kanji, 166–67
Israel, 184, 187, 246, 248, 316
Italy, 34, 82, 86–87, 90, 97, 101, 115, 146,
    150, 151, 158, 164–65, 170, 175, 212,
    250, 301, 308

Japan, 4, 17–21, 23, 31, 33, 36–37, 39, 40,
    43, 46, 62, 69, 72–73, 77, 85, 90, 93–94,
    97, 100–1, 108, 110, 127, 131, 135–36,
    141, 144, 146, 151, 163–73, 175–76,
    187, 200–202, 206, 212, 215–16, 220–
    25, 227, 250, 255, 264, 273–77, 281,
    284, 301, 311, 313, 319
Jews, Judaism, anti-Semitism, 105–10, 114,
    152, 160–61, 175–78, 289–90
Jiang Jieshi, Chiang Kai Shek, 136, 176
Jim Crow, 243
John Paul II, Pope, 290–91, 296
John XXIII, Pope, 225, 230
Johnson, Lyndon B., 226–28

Kennecott Co., 72
Khan, Inayat, 115, 125
Khomeini, Ruhollah, 280, 285
Khrushchev, Nikita, 181
King Jr, Martin Luther, 119
Kita Ikki, 163

Klages, Ludwig, 24, 25, 261, 328
KMT. *See* Guomindang
Krishnamurti, Jiddu, 116
Ku Klux Klan, 83, 106
kulaks, 159
Kuti, Fela Ransome/Anikulapo, 244–45

Lambeth Palace conferences, 113
Lattimer Massacre, 44
Lee Kuan Yew, 186
Lenin, Vladimir Ilyich, 45, 63, 132, 136
Leninism, 177
Leopold, Aldo, 256, 361, 328
Levi, Carlo, 154–55
Limits to Growth (1972), 259–60, 325
Little Bighorn, battle, 22
Lomé Convention (1975), 223
Lourdes, 111
Lovelock, James, 332
Lumumba, Patrice, 190–91, 242

Madero, Francisco, 135
Makeba, Miriam, 244
Malvinas Islands, 299
Manchuria, 20–21, 31, 32, 71, 131, 136, 144,
    163, 165
Mandela, Nelson, 244, 300
Mao Tse Tung. *See* Mao Zedong
Mao Zedong, 136, 150, 176, 306
Marconi, Guglielmo, 60
Marcos, Ferdinand, 120, 194, 299
Margulis, Lynne, 332
Mariátegui, José Carlos, 103–4, 108
Marshall Plan, 187, 188, 230
Martí, José, 104
Marx, Karl, 138, 152
Mata Hari, 122
Mater et Magistra (1961), 228, 230, 289
Medicare, 297
Meiji Restoration, 100
Mendel, Gregor, 331
Mendele'ev, Dmitri, 48
Mercosur, 309
Mexico, 137, 157, 158, 164, 177, 203, 206,
    210, 211, 224, 238, 255, 264, 266, 268,
    275, 300, 303, 309, 311, 320; Revolution
    (1910), 134–35, 143–44
migration, 4, 20–21, 30–37, 64, 80; assisted
    or subsidized, 21; and emancipation,
    83; and remittances, 311; and unfree
    labor, 83
military bases, Cold War, 182, 240–41
Minamata disaster, 256
Mitteleuropa, 145
Mobutu Sese Seko, 190
Molly Maguires, 44
Moral Majority, 285
Mormonism, 114, 203, 204, 287
Morrill Acts (1862, 1890), 51
Mossadeq, Mohammed, 189
Mothers of the Plaza de Mayo, 247
movies, film industry, 58, 120
Mugabe, Robert, 196
Muhammad Ahmad, the Mahdi, 94, 112

Muhammad Ali, 89
multinational corporations, 58, 73, 76, 97, 209–11, 222, 275–76, 313, 329; Alcoa, 204; Anaconda Co., 72; Barings Bank, 319; Bertelsmann, 211; British Petroleum Co., 49, 58, 189; Citibank, 73; Exxon, 211; General Electric, 51; Goldman Sachs, 319; Gulf Oil Co., 58; International Telephone and Telegraph, 58; J. P. Morgan Chase, 319; McDonald's Co., 210; McKinsey & Co., 211; News Corporation, 314; Pathé, 58, 120; Siemens, 51, 53, 59–60, 211; Vivendi Universal, 314; Volkswagen, 275
Muslim Brotherhood, 186, 193
Mussolini, Benito, 169, 178
mutual assured destruction, 181

Naess, Arne, 252, 261
Napoleon Bonaparte, 79
Nasser, Gamal, 187, 190, 193, 287
National Association for the Advancement of Colored People, 119
National Association of Evangelicals, 281, 285
National Organization for Women, 291
National Socialism, Nazi Party, 150, 152, 160, 175
National Urban League, 115, 119
nationalism, 98, 112, 113, 116–18, 144, 151, 176, 185–86, 193, 197; integral, 281, 285–86, 288, 298
nationalization, 187, 196, 210, 222, 223, 275
Native Baptist Church, Nigeria, 114
négritude, 108, 184
Nehru, Jawaharlal, 176, 193
neo-colonialism, 234, 237, 245
neo-liberalism, 281, 286, 289, 296, 297, 305, 309; Washington Consensus, 309
New International Economic Order, 223
New Left, 241, 243, 261, 281, 292, 301
New Right, 280–89, 304, 307, 316
New Thought, 114–15
Nigeria, 29, 71–72, 92, 94, 99, 112, 114, 184–86, 233, 238, 244–45, 268, 284, 300, 311
Nixon, Richard, 205
Non-Aligned Movement, 190, 193, 245
North American Free Trade Agreement, 309
North Atlantic Treaty Organizatiom, 181
Nyerere, Julius, 265

Organization for Economic Cooperation and Development, OECD, 231, 267, 294, 316
oil, 5, 8, 54–55, 57–59, 62, 69, 93, 132, 140, 144–45, 148–50, 152, 162, 164, 168–70, 172, 188–91, 196, 203, 210–12, 221–24, 231, 233, 237, 240, 248–50, 255, 265–66, 269, 276, 283–84, 302, 328, 329; and the Cold War, 188–90; "crisis" 1970s, 221–24, 237–40, 248–50, 281, 285, 302; in the Green Revolution, 266–67; in Nigeria, 233; and origins of World War I, 140,

148–50; and origins of World War II, 152, 162, 164–65; unconventional sources, 326
Omdurman, battle of, 94
One Nation Group, Tory Party, 229
one-child policy, China, 258, 307
OPEC, Organization of Oil Exporting Nations, 221–22
Opium Wars, 89–90, 97
Organization of American States, 188
Osservatore Romano, 112
Ottoman Empire, 4, 13, 78, 85, 89, 90, 100–101, 104, 108, 110, 119, 125, 140, 145, 146–47, 151–52, 164, 165, 199, 246; revolution, 131–32; Tanzimat reforms, 100, 146

Pacem in Terris (1963), 289
Pahlavi, Mohammad Reza, 133, 189
Palestine, 105, 152, 184, 194
pan-Africanism, 104, 108
Panama Canal, 27, 45, 85, 91
pan-Germanism, 104
pan-Islamism, 104, 112
pan-Slavism, 104
Parliament of the World's Religions, 116, 121
parliamentary government, 101, 127, 131–33, 144, 176, 193
Partial Test Ban Treaty, 247
partition, in Cold War, 183–84, 194
Party of Institutional Revolution, Mexico, 135
passenger pigeon, 23
Patagonia, 22, 93, 96
patents, 26, 49–50, 52, 144, 206–7, 277
Paul VI, Pope, 290
peanuts, peanut oil, 65, 67, 154, 185
Pearl Harbor, 165
Pearl River Delta, 37
peasants, 5, 22, 50, 80, 83, 129, 131–37, 150–62, 176, 177, 191, 265–66, 299
Pentecostalism, 113, 287
People Power, 299
People's Liberation Army, 136, 184
Permanent Court of International Justice, 126
Peron, Juan, 196
Persia, *see* Iran
phosphate, 62, 93, 327
pilgrimage, 111, 125
Pilsudski, Jozef, 177
plantations, plantation agriculture, 29, 33, 44, 65, 72, 81, 83–84, 92, 95, 134, 155, 216, 223, 253
plastics, 26, 54, 206, 212, 238, 263
Political and Economic Planning, 288
pollution, 253–55, 258, 261, 266
population, 29–30, 162–63, ; demographic transition, 9–20; and economic growth, 216–19, 223–24, 233, 257–58, 279–80; life expectancy, 2, 15–16, 218, 276, 279; mortality, 2, 10, 12–18, 31, 254, 279, 283
Population Bomb (1968), 258, 267

quinine, 13, 29

racism, racial thought, 34–35, 85, 102–10, 114, 117–19, 123, 124, 133, 134, 144, 152, 160, 168, 172–73, 175, 179, 184, 187–88, 193, 257, 284, 290
radio, transistor, 203, 272, 287, 303, 304
railroads, 23, 27–29, 36, 42, 45, 48, 53, 74, 76, 84, 86, 101, 120, 145, 147, 149, 165, 227, 301
Rand, Ayn, 297
Reagan, Ronald, 280–82, 285, 299
Red Cloud, Lakota Sioux chief, 20, 22
Red Cross, 126
refrigeration, 28, 61, 65, 74, 203, 204, 212, 272, 322
religion, 5, 99, 109–16 ; and colonialism, 110; and nationalism, 105–6
Rerum Novarum (1891), 228
Rockefeller Foundation, 40, 264
Romney, George W., 203–5
Roosevelt, Theodore, 257
Roy, Ram Mohan, 113
Royal Society for the Protection of Birds, 24
rubber, 62, 65, 71, 82, 84, 88, 92, 93, 96, 165, 175, 220
Russia, 4, 6, 20–22, 31–32, 35–36, 39, 43, 45, 58, 62, 64–5, 69, 72–4, 78–83, 89–90, 101, 104–5, 111, 136–37, 141, 144–51, 153, 158–60, 165, 175, 211, 236, 271, 275, 308; Revolution (1905), 131–32; Revolution (1917), 131, 151–52, 158,
Russification, 102, 109–10

Sada Yacco, 122
Salter, William Mackinder, 118, 119
Sanders, Liman von, 147
Sandinista movement/government, 296, 303
Satyagraha, 118–20
Schlafly, Phylis, 291, 294
Schumacher, Ernst Friedrich, 261
Science of Life (1929), 288
Scramble for Africa, 91
Second Great Awakening, 79, 114
secular humanism, 288, 293, 296
secularization, 220–21, 286
Senghor, Leopold, 108
serfdom, 78–83, 131
sharecropping, 83–84, 154
Shridharani, Krishnalal, 119
Silent Spring (1962), 256
Sino-Japanese War (1894–1895), 135
slavery, forced labor, 31, 33, 78–84
Small is Beautiful (1973), 261, 325
Smoot-Hawley Tariff, 173
Social Democracy, 45, 152, 225, 228, 230, 234, 252, 257, 260, 265, 287, 300, 305
socialism, 44–45, 103, 126–27, 131–32, 137–40, 152, 177, 210, 231; and anti-colonialism, 137; and decolonization, 119, 130, 191–93
Society for Ethical Culture, 109, 115, 118, 288

Somme, Battle of the, 141
South Africa, 20–23, 32–35, 37, 46, 67, 83, 92, 94, 110, 117, 120, 127, 143, 192, 206, 232, 275, 284, 312; apartheid, 103, 184, 244, 247, 290, 293, 300, 302, 304
Soviet Union, USSR, 21, 137, 151, 159, 169–73, 175, 177–82, 187–93, 199, 206, 208, 211, 226, 230–32, 236, 241, 243, 246, 248, 250, 261, 270–73, 281, 287, 298, 301–3, 306, 313
soy, 71, 131
Spiritualism, 114, 135
St. Denis, Ruth, 121–25
Stalin, Joseph, 132, 158–59
Standing Bear, Luther, 109
steamships, 27, 48, 54, 81, 82, 85
steel, 26, 52, 53, 55, 59, 60, 70, 144, 160, 172, 203, 206, 272, 273
Stimson, Henry, 142
Stoddard, Lothrop, 257
Strategic Arms Limitations Talks (1972, 1979), 247
Student Non-Violent Coordinating Committee, SNCC, 243
Suez Canal, 27, 85, 91, 140, 169, 187
suffrage, voting rights, 101, 102, 127, 133, 287
Sufism, 112, 115, 125, 133
sugar, 4, 37, 50, 62, 67, 69, 71, 73, 80, 82, 89, 93, 134, 254
Suharto, 190, 194
Sukarno, 190
Sukarnoputri, Megawati, 300
Sun Yat Sen/Sun Zhongshan, 103, 136, 157, 176, 257

Tagore, Rabindranath, 98, 123
Taiping Rebellion, 97, 100, 110, 114
Tanzimat, 100, 146
tariffs, tariff levels, 81, 87–90, 173–75, 188, 206, 208–10, 275
Tata Co., 185
technology, 3–5, 8, 10, 18–19, 26, 43, 47–62, 120, 169, 206–8, 210–11, 218–19, 223, 225–28, 250, 277–78, 302, 313–14, 318, 325–26, 330–32; agriculture, 10, 26, 36, 39, 80, 153, 161, 216, 264; communications, 76, 103, 112, 120, 126, 140, 210, 287, 304, 313–14, 318; medical, 13, 18–20, 29, 45, 331; military, 12, 80, 149, 269; military, 93–94, 130, 141, 167, 181, 270; transportation, 27, 29, 53, 82, 85, 115, 126
telegraph, 42, 58, 60, 74, 76, 85, 101
telephones, 58, 74, 76, 203, 208–20, 272, 304–5, 313
television, 7, 203, 287, 303, 314
Thatcher, Margaret, 280, 282, 296

Theosophy, Theosophical Society, 116, 117, 123, 185
Third World Strikes (1968), 284
Tolstoy, Leo, 118
Torrey Canyon disaster (1967), 256
totalitarianism, 161, 175, 178–79, 190, 226, 229, 246
tourism, 180, 314
tractors, 26–27, 60, 149, 158, 159, 161, 162, 215–16
trade, 2, 6, 9, 62, 67, 72–74, 77–90, 99, 103, 122, 126, 129, 134, 145, 147, 173–75, 188, 208–9, 211–13, 216, 272–73, 276, 282, 305–6, 309, 315, 318; slave trade, 31, 113; South-South, 273; treaties, 87, 97, 179, 195
Transcendental Meditation, 287
transnational organizations, 39, 125–28, 247–48
Trans-Siberian railway, 145
Treaty of Rome (1957), 209, 229
Treaty Ports, China, 90, 136
Tri-Continental, 234
Trilateral Commission, 329
Truman, Harry, 226
Tudeh Party, 189
Tunisia, 91, 92, 186
Turkey, 28, 58, 89, 121, 127, 131, 152, 173, 177, 194, 206, 232, 268, 270, 272–73, 277, 281, 285, 286, 300, 316

U Thant, 259, 321
Unilever Co., 72, 211
Union of International Associations, 127
United Auto Workers, UAW, 205
United Kingdom, *see* Great Britain
United Nations, 179–80, 184, 223, 244, 246, 259, 267, 292, 296, 322; and climate change, 322; General Assembly, 181, 246; Security Council, 180, 306; statement on race (1950), 184
United Nations Decade of the Woman, 292
United Nations Development Program, 274
United Nations Economic and Social Council, ECOSOC, 180
United Nations Educational Scientific and Cultural Office, UNESCO, 180, 257, 288
United States of America, 6, 15, 17, 23–24, 28, 33–35, 39, 42–46, 51, 53, 59–62, 64–66, 69–73, 76, 78–85, 87–88, 91, 102, 105–6, 114–15, 119, 121, 132, 134, 141–42, 151, 153, 187–89, 200, 205–6, 211–12, 215, 221–23, 231, 236, 238, 241–43, 246–48, 250, 264, 268, 272–73, 277, 294, 299, 301–3, 306–7, 309, 311, 314, 316, 319, 322, 323; advanced agriculture, 158, 162, 215–16, 264, 267; Cold War, 179–92, 301, 303; ecological momen, 254, 256, 259, 262; Great

Depression, 153, 174–75; and the New Imperialism, 93–96; New Right, 280–85, 291, 297; and origins of World War I, 144–50; and origins of World War II, 163–69; slavery and abolition, 78–83; welfare state, 226–30
United States Agency for International Development, USAID, 231
Universal Postal Union, 85, 126
Urabi, Ahmed, 90, 104
urbanization, 64, 120, 304

Valencia, Tórtola, 124–25
Vargas, Getulio, 177
Vasconcelos, José, 106
Vatican Council, First (1869–1870), 113
Vatican Council, Second (1962–1965), 289
Vedanta, 113
Verdun, Battle of, 141
Viet Nam war, 29, 43, 65, 88, 92, 96, 129, 139, 145, 165, 181–83, 186, 192, 194, 197, 216
Villa, Francisco "Pancho," 135
Vivekananda, 113, 116, 119
Vladivostock, 90, 144
Volga Germans, 35, 102, 104
Voting Rights Act (1965), 227

Warsaw Pact, 181, 188
welfare state, 225–30, 241, 260, 263, 276, 281–82, 286, 288–89, 292, 297, 316
welfare-state, 441
Wells, H. G., 59, 140, 259, 288, 328
Wilson, Woodrow, 151
Women's Christian Temperance Union, 127
World Bank, 188, 231, 238, 267, 323; and climate change, 323
World Conference on Women (1975, 1980, 1985, 1995), 292
World Cup (soccer), 121
World Economic Forum, 329
World Health Organization, 180, 256
World War I, 140–50
World War II, 164–78
World Wildlife Federation, 288
Wretched of the Earth (1961), 243

Yamani, Ahmed Zaki, 222
Yellow Peril, 168, 257
Yellow River, 97
yoga, 115, 287
Yogananda, Paramahamsa, 287
Young Turks. *See* Committee of Union and Progress
Yuan Shikai, 136

Zapata, Emiliano, 129, 135
Zionism, 105, 293
Zollverein, 87